M000199422

CAMPAIGN CROSSROADS

PRESIDENTIAL POLITICS IN INDIANA
from LINCOLN *to* OBAMA

Campaign Crossroads was made possible through
the generous support of the Care Institute Group, Inc., and the
O'Bannon Foundation, a fund of the Indianapolis Foundation

CAMPAIGN CROSSROADS

PRESIDENTIAL POLITICS IN INDIANA
from **LINCOLN** *to* **OBAMA**

ANDREW E. STONER

Indiana Historical Society Press 2017

© 2017 Indiana Historical Society Press

This book is a publication of the
Indiana Historical Society Press

Eugene and Marilyn Glick Indiana History Center
450 West Ohio Street
Indianapolis, Indiana 45202-3269 USA
www.indianahistory.org

Telephone orders 1-800-447-1830

Fax orders 1-317-234-0562

Online orders @ http://shop.indianahistory.org

Library of Congress Cataloging-in-Publication Data

Names: Stoner, Andrew E., author
Title: Campaign crossroads : presidential politics in Indiana from Lincoln to
   Obama / Andrew E. Stoner.
Description: Indianapolis, Indiana : Indiana Historical Society Press, 2017.
   | Includes bibliographical references and index.
Identifiers: LCCN 2016022409 (print) | LCCN 2016040896 (ebook) | ISBN
   9780871954022 (cloth : alk. paper) | ISBN 9780871954039 (epub)
Subjects: LCSH: Indiana—Politics and government. | Presidents—United
   States—Election—History.
Classification: LCC F526 .S86 2016 (print) | LCC F526 (ebook) | DDC
   320.09772—dc23
LC record available at https://lccn.loc.gov/2016022409

♾ No part of this publication may be reproduced, stored in or introduced into a retrieval
system, or transmitted, in any form or by any means (electronic, photocopying, recording,
or otherwise) without the prior written permission of the copyright owner.

The paper in this publication meets the minimum requirements of American National
Standard for Information Sciences—Permanence of Paper for Printed Library Materials,
ANSI Z39. 48–1984

For my mother, Sandra Joy (Palmer) Stoner

Contents

Acknowledgments

My thanks to: Alabama Department of Archives and History, Montgomery, Alabama; American Presidency Project, Gerhard Peters and John T. Wooley, University of California at Santa Barbara; Ball State University Archives and Special Collections, Muncie, Indiana; Benjamin Harrison Presidential Site, Indianapolis, Indiana; William Bridges, professor emeritus, Franklin College, Franklin, Indiana; Butler University Library and Archives, Indianapolis, Indiana; California State University-Sacramento Library and Archives, Sacramento, California; Calumet Regional Archives, Indiana University-Northwest, Gary, Indiana; Center for Politics, University of Virginia, Charlottesville, Virginia; David L. Shank, Indianapolis, Indiana; DePauw University Library and Archives, Greencastle, Indiana; Dwight D. Eisenhower Presidential Library and Museum, Abilene, Kansas; Edmund S. Muskie Archive, Bates College of Maine, Lewiston, Maine; Eugene V. Debs Papers, Indiana State University Library, Terre Haute, Indiana; Gerald R. Ford Library and Museum, Grand Rapids, Michigan; Harry S Truman Library and Museum, Independence, Missouri; Henry A. Wallace Papers, University of Iowa Libraries, Iowa City, Iowa; Hubert H. Humphrey Papers, Minnesota Historical Society, Minneapolis, Minnesota; Ray E. Boomhower, Kathy Breen, Ethan R. Chitty, Paula Corpuz, and Andrew Halter, Indiana Historical Society, Indianapolis, Indiana; Indiana State Library, Indiana Division, Indianapolis, Indiana;Indiana University Southeast Library, New Albany, Indiana; John F. Kennedy Presidential Library and Museum, Boston, Massachusetts; Lyndon Baines Johnson Library and Museum, University of Texas at Austin; Manchester College Library, North Manchester, Indiana; Miller Center of Public Affairs, University of Virginia, Charlottesville, Virginia; Roger D. Branigin Papers, B. F. Hamilton Library, Franklin College, Franklin, Indiana; Rutherford B. Hayes Presidential Center, Fremont, Ohio; University of Notre Dame Library and Archives, South Bend, Indiana; University of Wisconsin-Stevens Point Library & Archives, Stevens Point, Wisconsin; U.S. Census Bureau; Wayne County Historical Society, Richmond, Indiana; Walter F. Mondale Papers, Minnesota Historical Society, Minneapolis, Minnesota; Wheaton College of Illinois Archival Collection, Wheaton, Illinois.

Introduction

Strike up the band, unfurl the bunting and festoon Main Street with red, white, and blue as Indiana readies for the arrival of the president of the United States. Whether by happenstance or political necessity, Indiana stands at the crossroads on the road to the White House. Playing host to the nation's chief executive on dozens of occasions, the state has also welcomed the cadre of men (and one woman) who sought the nation's highest office, but failed.

Indiana presidential visits have been both politically necessary and routine. Consistently, the communities of Indiana have been a welcome spot for presidents throughout the decades to try out political messages or to align support behind ideas and candidacies. Hoosiers, like all Americans, have sought to see their president and presidential hopefuls up close and in person. It is, apparently, a bipartisan need—both as Democrat Grover Cleveland found during his 1892 foray into the "western state" of Indiana acknowledging his audience's desire to satisfy its curiosity of the office and the man,[1] and as Republican Alf Landon told Hoosiers in 1936, "I know all you folks came to town to look me over. Well, it works both ways. I am glad to see you, too."[2]

Presidential visits to Indiana have brought moments of mishaps and memorable words that soothed a nation, such as:

- Abraham Lincoln stopping briefly to address the people of Indiana as he traveled to his inauguration as president in 1861—a stop that would be repeated in 1865 as Lincoln's body lay in repose at the Indiana Statehouse en route to his final resting place in Springfield, Illinois.
- William Jennings Bryan articulating his "anti-imperialism" views as he launched his campaign from Military Park in Indianapolis.
- Robert F. Kennedy disclosing to a mostly African American audience news about the assassination of Doctor Martin Luther King Jr., and his successful pleas for peace in the streets of Indianapolis.
- A young Madison boy fatally wounded while helping fire a twenty-one-gun salute to Herbert Hoover, along with a Michigan City woman seriously injured when an elevated speaker fell on her at a Bill Clinton rally, and stage and grandstand collapses at numerous campaign events over the years.
- Franklin D. Roosevelt visiting the Indiana State Fair during the Great Depression and dedicating the George Rogers Clark Memorial at Vincennes.
- Benjamin Harrison's 1888 campaign—conducted entirely from the front porch of his Delaware Street home in Indianapolis—drawing thousands of voters who in those days went *to* the candidate, not the other way around.
- Estes Kefauver confusing the people of Franklin by telling them how happy he was to be in Alexandria.
- A rare moment of annoyance for Ronald Reagan as he lists concerns about germs in declining to kiss a baby, or shake hands with Hoosiers during a campaign stop in Fort Wayne.
- A hoarse John F. Kennedy unable to speak after a day of campaigning has a local resident read his remarks to a Richmond audience.

- Antiwar protestors shouting down Vice President Spiro Agnew in Fort Wayne as he campaigns for President Richard Nixon.
- Lyndon Johnson playing "Comforter in Chief" for victims of the Palm Sunday tornado that claimed 137 Indiana lives and injured 1,200 more, and later Johnson's obsession with events in Vietnam that keep seeping into his remarks as he leads the celebration of Indiana's sesquicentennial.
- George Wallace taking on "pointy-headed liberals" in trying to explain his opposition to integration to sometimes unfriendly audiences around Indiana.
- Harry Truman's unrelenting whistle-stop campaign of Indiana while his erstwhile opponent Thomas E. Dewey skipped the Hoosier State.
- Eugene McCarthy barnstorming Indiana with actor Paul Newman at his side.
- Richard Nixon pausing amidst his Watergate troubles to comfort his ailing daughter at an Indianapolis hospital.
- Bob Dole in fast retreat at Terre Haute after suggesting all major U.S. wars were started by Democratic presidents.
- Barack Obama playing three-on-three basketball at a Kokomo High School during a person-to-person quest for Hoosier votes.
- Hillary Clinton slamming Boilermakers (a shot of whiskey, followed by a beer) on a Saturday night at a Crown Point bar.

Campaign Crossroads is a look back over the varied, sometimes important, sometimes irrelevant, but always interesting presidential campaign cycles in the history of Indiana. By taking in the influences of technology, transportation, and communication itself, we see an evolution in the political process that is not only altogether Hoosier, but also altogether American in its qual-

ity and importance. While Indiana enjoyed the position of being a battleground state for the better part of a century from the 1870s until the 1960s, it has also been ignored, dismissed, and occasionally provided the backdrop for some of the most unexpected political drama America has to offer.

Of particular importance and review in this work is the role of Indiana newspapers—the state is flush with hometown papers of all political persuasions in communities big and small. The reporting demonstrated throughout the nearly two centuries of campaigns reflects an evolution in journalism, from open partisanship to at least some semblance of objectivity (though campaigns and candidates would likely disagree). The text here attempts to take those limitations into account, pointing them out where they exist, but also recognizing the value of the accounts contained in the "paper of record" reports on speeches and events. The Associated Press wire dispatches are of interest particularly given that they most often originated with local, hometown reporting that was prepared for consumption by a larger statewide, and even national, audience.

The role of railroads and other transportation, as well as technology, is also on display and has played a major role in shaping how campaigns occur. From Lincoln's Spencer County visits on horseback for the 1844 campaign, to the ubiquitous use of rear-train platforms, candidates have slogged literally millions of miles across the state of Indiana in search of votes and support. Interestingly, despite the advances in transportation and technology, even recent examples exist, as in the 2008 Democratic primary, in which no technological advance replaced the value of one-to-one retail politics of candidates out directly asking Hoosiers for their vote.

In the end, there's nothing like a visit from a president or a presidential candidate, from the mighty preparations that modern visits by a chief executive require, to the traditions of placing the Great Seal of the President of the United States, or the playing of "Hail to Chief" as the president enters an event. In moments big and small, it is an awe-inspiring Indiana story.

1

Era of Expansion and Political Reform, 1816–59

Indiana's role on the national election stage got off to a rocky start. Just as Indiana was about to become a state in 1816, its role in the presidential election contest between Secretary of State James Monroe (who had served retiring President James Madison) and U.S. Senator Rufus King of New York was at the center of an Election Day dispute about whether Indiana was legally entitled to cast votes in the Electoral College vote. One of King's supporters objected to the inclusion of the three electoral votes from Indiana (the state having been admitted by Congress to the Union on December 11, 1816). But the long debate about whether Indiana had actually been a state after it adopted its constitution but before Congress took it into the Union by a formal act in December was finally settled, and Congress voted to count Indiana's electoral votes, all of them going to the eventual victor, Monroe.[1]

Subsequent elections in the decades that followed did not truly engage candidates to Indiana, but historian Thomas W. Howard found that Hoosiers were eager to participate. Howard reported that 37.5 percent of the state's eligible voters participated in the bifurcated 1824 election, well above the national average of 26.5 percent.[2] Fellow historian Logan Esarey noted, "This political interest is even more striking when viewed against the frontier conditions of

Indiana in the 1820s. Roads were few, and the isolated, self-sufficient farmer seldom traveled from his homestead or had visitors from distant parts of the state."[3] Settlements popped up in the southern and northern portions of the state, but access remained remote until the arrival of canals and railroads. Later, telegraphs and newspapers delivered via the railroad carried news of presidential politics "from the east" in a growing number of Indiana newspapers. Almost every Indiana community, regardless of size, had rival Whig and Democratic and later Republican and Democratic weekly and daily newspapers. The papers relied heavily on their counterparts in the East and on local political activities for news as the state continued to grow. As a result, presidential campaigns were virtually nonexistent in the state beyond what state and local party organizations could muster. By 1820 Indiana had just under 150,000 residents, but grew rapidly with the state's population surging to 685,000 by 1840 and topping 1.3 million in 1860 as the threat of the Civil War loomed.[4] In highly sectional voting in subsequent presidential elections, Indiana voters chose General Andrew Jackson over Secretary of State John Quincy Adams (the winner) in the 1824 election. Jackson carried Indiana in 1828 and again in 1832, becoming the seventh U.S. president. Vice President Martin Van Buren won the 1836 election (with Jackson's backing), but without the votes of Indiana, as Hoosiers preferred William Henry Harrison by a wide margin of more than 8,000 votes (in a statewide election where only 73,759 votes were cast).

In each of the elections until 1880, Indiana was one of a small number of "October states." Election Day came weeks earlier than the traditional first Tuesday after the first Monday in November. As writer Paul Tincher Smith reported, the phrase "the way Indiana and New York go, so goes the nation" gained support from the fact that Indiana voted early, and because with the exception of 1836, 1848, and 1876, Hoosiers correctly picked the eventual winner in the presidential contest. "The two facts, namely that Indiana usually selected the right man and that it was an 'October' state, meant much of importance as to the handling of the state campaign," Smith wrote. "Neither party could afford to let one stone remain unturned in the effort to carry the state over the line in the right direction."[5]

Henry Clay

Among the first politicians to ever travel to Indiana to seek the Hoosier vote was a Virginia native, Henry Clay, who was born to a wealthy slaveholding family. Clay married well and relocated to Lexington, Kentucky, in 1797. By the age of twenty-eight he was elected to the Kentucky legislature, the first in a long list of elected offices, including multiple terms in the U.S. House of Representatives and the U.S. Senate. Rising quickly in the ranks of the Democratic Party, Clay was chosen as Speaker of the House on his very first day in Congress—a feat never before achieved and never repeated in congressional history.

In 1824 Clay launched his first campaign for president amidst a highly divided Democratic-Republican Party and won only three states (Kentucky, Missouri, and Ohio) and thirty-seven electoral votes in a controversial election eventually won by John Quincy Adams. After Jackson's election to the presidency in 1828 (as a Democrat), Clay joined with National Republicans who had formed a new Whig Party and was its presidential nominee in 1832 against Jackson, who easily won a second term over Clay (who carried only six states, an interesting mix of Kentucky, Connecticut, Massachusetts, Delaware, Rhode Island, and Vermont). In losing the 1832 election, however, the Whigs emerged as the primary challenger to the Democratic Party, and Clay remained active in Kentucky politics (winning a U.S. Senate seat from Kentucky in 1831, more than twenty years after his first tenure in the upper chamber). In 1840 Clay lost the Whig Party nomination to former Indiana territorial governor Harrison.

By 1844 Clay's path to regain the Whig Party nomination was clear—though it was a tentative hold, given the rise of antislavery feelings in northern states (key parts of the Whig coalition) and conflicting views in the South. Clay, a slaveholder, was viewed, however, as an effective candidate and one who could lead the party to victory as Harrison had done four years earlier. To keep the Whig Party together, Clay articulated the party's opposition to the annexation of Texas (amidst unsettled questions of whether Texas was a territory of Mexico, and whether new states would be allowed to be slaveholding states). Clay muddied the party's position with a separate "Alabama letter" in which he suggested slaveholding, under certain circumstances, might be acceptable in Texas as a new state.

In preparation for the 1844 election, Clay made one of the very first campaign forays by any candidate ever to Indiana, including a memorable exchange on October 1, 1842, in Richmond on the state's east-central border with Ohio. A procession of more than eight hundred carriages and a crowd of at least five thousand gathered as Clay was conveyed from the train depot to a special stand constructed downtown to make his speech.[6] One local report indicated, "Mr. Clay was greeted by his fellow citizens . . . received not with the loud roar of artillery, but with the deafening and spontaneous shouts of the yeomanry of the country. It was a reception worthy of the unbought devotion of Patriots in welcoming to their midst, a great statesman—the undaunted 'Harry of the West.' The procession passed through several portions of the city, and everywhere that venerable man, with his loft form

LIBRARY OF CONGRES

An 1850s portrait of Henry Clay

and noble bearing, was greeted by enthusiastic cheers, and the waving of white handkerchiefs by the ladies from the open windows on each side of the streets."[7]

Few remember Clay's speech that day because of what followed his remarks. After he finished speaking, it was announced, as expected in advance, that the "Committee of Abolitionists" (known as the Indiana Anti-Slavery Society) wished to present a petition to Clay regarding his own slaves. The abolitionists had declined an earlier invitation to present the petition privately to Clay the following day at his Richmond hotel and were more than willing to participate in the senator's second option to have the petition presented to him publicly at a pro-Clay rally. The petition was not welcome; many in the crowd jeered and heckled the abolitionist representative, Hiram Mendenhall of Randolph County, who had situated himself close enough to the stand to be able to reach Clay and present the petition—a rolled piece of paper. As historian Charles W. Osborn recalled, "Mendenhall was a fit person to work his way through a hooting, jeering, threatening crowd, for he was a tall, muscular man, weighing two hundred pounds, then in the prime of manhood, being forty-one years old. He arrived at the speaker's stand with his coat badly cut by the mob, and doubtless would have received personal injury had not Clay stepped to the front of the platform and begged the crowd for his sake and for God's sake to not insult nor do violence to the committee. Mendenhall stepped upon the platform, handed Clay the petition, and when he saw they were not going to give him a chair, he sat down on the floor, a little to one side of the speaker."[8]

The petition presented by Mendenhall was crafted by activist Indiana Quakers a month before Clay's arrival in Richmond based on news reports he would speak there. The abolitionist petition was straightforward:

> To Henry Clay: We, the undersigned citizens of Indiana, in view of the declarations of rights contained in the charter of American Independence, in view of that justice that is due from man to his fellow-man; in view of all those noble principles which should characterize the patriot, the philanthropist and the Christian, ask you most respectfully to "unloose the heavy burdens," and that you let the oppressed under your control who call you master go free. By doing so you would give liberty to whom liberty is due, and do no more than justice to those under your charge, who have long been deprived by you of the sacred boon of freedom; and set an example that would result in much good to suffering and debased humanity, and do an act altogether worthy a great and good man.
>
> Resolved, That should Henry Clay refuse to emancipate his slaves, the committee to present the petition be instructed to request him to give his reasons for so refusing.[9]

Various accounts exist as to Clay's response to the petition, but he essentially told Mendenhall and the Indiana abolitionists to mind their own business, a reply that received rowdy applause from the audience. But his bluntness gained significant interest and highlighted dramatically the tenuous position of the Whig Party on the slavery issue—one that promised to split the party in two between northern and southern interests. The local media reported that Clay received the petition in a "severe, yet courteous, gentlemanly and even mild manner" and that he had been insulted by the abolitionists. "He was a private citizen and an invited guest of the people," the *Centerville-Wayne County Record* reported. "He had responded to their urgent solicitation to receive the hospitalities of the citizens of Indiana, and he thought that

a decent respect for his feelings, for the feelings of his friends and for their own characters as citizens of the state to which he had been invited, should have induced them to have withheld the presentation of the petition at the time."[10] The *Centerville-Wayne County Record* account added that "the petition was doubtless got up by the Abolitionists . . . for the purpose of insulting Mr. Clay, and placing him, as they conceived they would do, in an embarrassing situation before the people."[11]

Questions were quickly raised about the validity of the petition, some claims focusing on the fact that fictitious names may have been included, and other claims that "Negro signers" had been recruited at a "Negro meeting in Henry County" to sign their names, and still further questions about the signatures of women (who held no right to vote at the time). Clay's response to the petition presented that day at Richmond figures prominently in a published history of his famous Senate and campaign speeches. His "Reply to Mr. Mendenhall" is featured in the Clay speech text, reporting that Clay said in reply to the Indiana abolitionists, "I hope that Mr. Mendenhall may be treated with the greatest forbearance and respect. I assure my fellow-citizens here collected, that the presentation of the petition has not occasioned the slightest pain, nor excited one solitary disagreeable emotion. . . . I entreat and beseech my fellow-citizens, for their sake, for my country's sake, for my sake, to offer no disrespect, no indignity, no violence, in word or deed, to Mr. Mendenhall."[12]

Clay said he questioned the presenting of the petition of him given that he viewed himself as a fellow and equal citizen to Mendenhall and the abolitionists he represented. "I am a total stranger, passing through your State, on my way to its capital, in consequence of an invitation with which I have been honored to visit it, to exchange friendly salutations with such as my fellow-citizens of Indiana think as proper to meet me," Clay said, somewhat understating his earned position in the minds of most Americans (having sought the Whig Party nomination for president and being its national nominee in 1832). Clay, reminding his audience that he was a man "advanced in years," resented the public presentation of the petition that "you might at any time within these last twenty-five or thirty years, have presented your petition to me at Ashland [Kentucky]. If you had gone there for that purpose, you should have been received and treated with perfect respect and liberal hospitality."[13]

In spite of his stated desire for a respectful exchange, Clay's remarks often turned pointed. He turned to Mendenhall and asked, "Let us reverse conditions, and suppose that you had been invited to Kentucky to partake of its hospitality; and that, previous to your arrival, I had employed such means as I understand have been used to get up this petition, to obtain the signatures of citizens of that State to a petition to present to you to relinquish your farm or other property, what would you have thought of such a proceeding? Would you have deemed it courteous and according to the rites of hospitality?"[14] Among Clay's remarks were also questions about the validity of the petition signers themselves (despite his earlier remarks about presenting himself as an equal citizen to the people of Indiana), ridiculing the fact that rumors indicated some of the signers were "free blacks, men, women, and children, who have been artfully deceived and imposed upon."[15] He also suggested that Indiana Democrats, who favored slavery, had actually affixed their signatures to the document as a means of embarrassing a leader of the opposition Whigs.

He continued, "I know well, that you and

LIBRARY OF CONGRESS

A formal campaign portrait of Whig presidential candidate Clay, after the painting by John Neagle done at Ashland, Clay's estate in Kentucky.

those who think with you, controvert the legitimacy of slavery, and deny the right of property in slaves. But the law of my state and other States has otherwise ordained. The law may be wrong in your opinion, and ought to be repealed; but then you and your associates are not the law-makers for us, and unless you can show some authority to nullify our laws, we must continue to respect them."[16]

Regarding slavery, Clay's next remarks provided a curious juxtaposition as in the same text in which he argued strongly for his own legal right to hold about fifty slaves—"property" he said were valued at $15,000—he also said, "I desire no concealment of my opinions in regard to the institution of slavery. I look upon it as a great evil, and deeply lament that we have derived it from the parental government, and from our ancestors. I wish every slave in the United States was in the country of his ancestors. But here they are, and the question is, how they can be best dealt with?"[17] Clay said the evil of slavery was nothing, however, compared to the "greater evils which would inevitably flow from a sudden, general, and indiscriminate emancipation," noting that in several states the slave population equaled or exceeded the white population. "What would be the condition of the two races in those States, upon the supposition of an immediate emancipation?" Clay asked. "Does any man suppose that they would become blended into one homogeneous mass? . . . What then would certainly happen? A struggle for political ascendancy; the blacks [seeking] to acquire, and the whites seeking to maintain, possession of the government." Clay said he was certain that "a contest would inevitably ensue between the two races—civil war, carnage, pillage, conflagration, devastation, and the ultimate extermination of the blacks."[18]

To the issue of his own slaves, Clay said several of them were infirm by reasons of age or mental incapacity, and that "sending them forth into the world with the boon of liberty" would find their lives ended in a "wretched existence in starvation." Turning to Mendenhall, Clay asked, "Do you believe as a Christian, that I should perform my duty toward them by abandoning them to their fate?"[19]

With that, Clay took the unusual turn of introducing one of his personal slaves traveling with him, known only as Charles. Pointing to Charles, Clay said the man had been free to go about his life for many years, but had never sought to leave Clay's Kentucky farm. "Excuse me, Mr. Mendenhall, for saying that my slaves are as well fed and clad, look as sleek and hearty, and are quite as civil and respectful in their demeanor, and as little disposed to wound the feelings of any one, as you are," Clay said.[20]

Ending on a dismissive note, Clay played to the crowd and addressed Mendenhall directly, saying, "Go home, and mind your own business, and leave other people to take care of theirs. Limit your benevolent exertions to your own neighborhood. . . . Dry up the tears of the afflicted widows around you, console and comfort the helpless orphan, clothe the naked, and feed and help the poor, black and white, who need succor; and you will be a better and wiser man than you have this day shown yourself."[21]

Clay's soliloquy may have served the purpose of "giving hell" to the Indiana abolitionists who dared to confront him directly, and it also served to reveal Clay's true feelings about the nature of slavery and the severely conflicted position in which he resided—a stated hatred of slavery while crafting effective arguments against emancipation.

After the rally, Clay remained in Richmond overnight and attended Sunday services at a local Friends (Quaker) meetinghouse, drawing a large, curious crowd of onlookers. He left later that day and made quick stops at Cambridge City before arriving at Indianapolis.[22] The welcome in the capital was triumphant, a twenty-six-gun salute offered by Captain Mead's Company from Lafayette. The *Indianapolis Journal* reported, "After considerable time and difficulty . . . the military, carriages, wagons and horsemen, were formed into a procession. The thousands upon thousands who were on foot, lined the fence tops, the house tops, and sidewalks, eager to catch only a glimpse of Mr. Clay, through the thick clouds of dust that filled and hung over the town."[23] Following the procession through downtown, a rally and barbeque were held at a grove of trees at the site of the current Indiana Statehouse, located near the corner of West Market and Tennessee (now Capitol Avenue) Streets, where a speaker's stand had been constructed. Former governor Noah Noble, also a Whig, offered the official welcome for Clay. The *Indianapolis Journal* noted that Clay "descanted with great plainness, but with thrilling interest, upon the important questions of public policy which now agitate the public mind. . . . He contrasted the creeds of the two great parties in the United States, and called upon the people, by all they hold dear and sacred, to ponder carefully the great questions which divide the two parties, and to think and act for themselves in view of their own welfare and happiness."[24]

Clay was the undisputed nominee of the Whig Party in 1844 and did better than his earlier presidential run in 1832, but he still lost to former Tennessee governor James K. Polk, who had won the Democratic nomination in a hot convention battle against former president Martin Van Buren. The Democrats made extensive headway in presenting the conflicting nature of Clay, casting him as an abolitionist in the South and as a slaveholder in the North. Polk, who did no campaigning in Indiana, won a narrow popular-vote victory, 49.5 percent to 48 percent (with incumbent President John Tyler having abandoned his third-party bid before Election Day). Clay carried eleven states—an interesting amalgam of Kentucky and several northeastern states. Indiana went to Polk by a narrow margin, marking the second time Clay had failed to carry his neighboring state.

Clay remained politically active and served multiple, nonconsecutive terms in the U.S. Senate until his death on June 29, 1852, at the age of seventy-five.

Martin Van Buren

Indiana remained off the political map for the most part, partially because of the rugged terrain of the still-developing state. The difficulty of travel in the new state was perhaps best evidenced by a June 1842 visit from former president Martin Van Buren, who had lost the 1840 election to Harrison. Van Buren made stops at Richmond, Indianapolis, Plainfield, and Terre Haute along the National Road (later US 40), although only Richmond, Indianapolis, and Terre Haute were scheduled stops. Van Buren's trip to Indiana, part of a "western tour" of Ohio, Indiana, and Illinois, was widely viewed by opposition Whig leaders as preparatory to a Van Buren attempt to regain the presidency in 1844. Van Buren had angered many voters because of his opposition to federal funding for improvements to the trail that ran west from Washington, D.C., through Cumberland, Wheeling, Columbus, Indianapolis, and on to Saint Louis. It was a decision the ex-president would come to regret.

Van Buren entered Indiana at Richmond on Friday, June 10, 1842, where several thousand curious Hoosiers (and some Ohio residents) awaited their first glimpse of an American president. On Saturday, June 11, 1842, Van Buren reached Indianapolis at noon and was given a grand welcome at the junction of the National Road (later Washington Street) and Meridian Street in downtown Indianapolis. A welcoming committee had conveyed Van Buren to Indianapolis from Greenfield in a horse-drawn carriage (after he had traveled from Richmond to Greenfield via a mail stagecoach), and once in the city was escorted in an "open barouche" to the Palmer House Hotel by a military escort and band.[25]

An 1860s portrait of President Martin Van Buren.

LIBRARY OF CONGRESS

At the Palmer House, Van Buren was formally welcomed and responded that he was grateful to the citizens of Indianapolis for their welcome. The *Indiana State Sentinel* paraphrased Van Buren's remarks, noting:

> The opportunity which was this day afforded him, to meet and have familiar intercourse with so many thousands of his western fellow citizens, he esteemed a great privilege, as he was sure it would be to him a source of much enjoyment. It was one of a series of introductions to the people of the West, which he had long wished for, and which had, perhaps, been too long delayed. The repeated expressions of regret that he had not come among them sooner rendered it proper for him to say that the delay had not been in any degree occasioned by any indisposition on his part. His wish had always been to make his first visit to the West under circumstances which would effectually preclude a misinterpretation of his motives, and satisfy all, as was not the fact, that he came to see the country and the people on their account, and not for any purposes of his own.[26]

The *Sentinel* reported that Van Buren said he came to Indiana with "high anticipations in respect to the moral, physical and intellectual condition of this great state," and added, "I am happy to say that so far as I have had opportunities for judging and am capable of doing so, I have found my expectations, great as they were, more than realized. That [Indiana] was suffering from the adverse results of past improvidence, and from those misfortunes to which every people and every state are more or less exposed, and that such patience and some sacrifices would be necessary, to secure permanent relief, was undoubtedly true. But with such lands, such hands to work, with such minds to direct and such experience as they have passed through to guide them—their final success was only a question of time."[27] He

declared that Indiana was now prepared to "take rank among her sister states, not only as one of the most powerful, but the most prosperous of the members which constituted this glorious . . . perpetual confederacy."[28]

After a short rest and lengthy reception at the hotel, Van Buren visited guests at the Union Hotel and then called on Governor Samuel Bigger and toured the Indiana Statehouse. During the evening at social events at the Palmer House, the *Sentinel* reported that "there was a perfect jam; the parlors were filled with beautiful women who were severally received by the ex-President with that peculiar suavity for which he has ever been noted. The entertainment was worthy of the occasion and reflected great upon the committee of arrangements, upon Mr. Parker of the Palmer House and his co-laborers. Unalloyed pleasures seemed to prevail throughout."[29] As the *Indianapolis Journal* reported, "the reception and entertainment of the ex-President on his visit to this place was announced by his friends as being without distinction of party," and citizens were urged to turn and greet him in his "capacity altogether as a private citizen."[30] The *Washington (DC) Globe* reported that Van Buren had received a "hearty welcome" in Indianapolis and that the local Whig Party opponents of Van Buren "broke through the selfish, churlish and contracted orders of their [newspaper] editors, who are behind the age they live in, and vied with the Democrats in doing honor to one so richly deserving their regard, and Mr. Van Buren did not fail to express his pleasure at this courteous behavior of his former opponents."[31]

Van Buren's "hearty welcome" apparently did not extend to all parts of the state. The *Indiana Statesman*, a Democratic newspaper published at Evansville, reprinted an account from the *Cincinnati Post* that noted: "Everybody is disappointed

LIBRARY OF CONGRESS

Van Buren's inability to bridge the distance between the "Conscience," or abolitionist, Whigs and conservative Democrats is portrayed as his downfall in the 1848 presidential race in this Nathaniel Currier lithograph.

when they see Mr. Van Buren. All expected to see a dandified looking personage, but, instead of being gratified in that way, they find him to be a gray-haired man, thick set, larger than expected, and looks more like a dandy than we do."[32]

On Sunday, June 12, 1842, Van Buren attended morning services at the Methodist Episcopal Church (now Roberts Park United Methodist Church) and afternoon services led by Henry Ward Beecher at Second Presbyterian Church. On Monday morning he departed Indianapolis on a mail stagecoach to continue his trip westward. The *Journal* reported: "The ex-President has traveled on the National Road through the whole extent of Indiana. As the road is now in rather bad condition, he must have had a fair opportunity of seeing and judging, from his own personal observations, how much this road—which has never been regarded as national in its character—needs the fostering aid of the government

for its improvement."[33] From here a great legend grew, as reports emerged from Plainfield, about fifteen miles west of Indianapolis, "that the stage coach in which Mr. Van Buren traveled from this place upset near Plainfield" and that "particulars of the disaster" had not been disclosed but that no serious injury was sustained by the former president or anyone else.[34] The *Sentinel* carried a slightly varied report, indicating that Van Buren had suffered a shoulder injury when the coach tipped.

After reports of the accident reached Washington, D.C., by telegraph, the *Globe* noted, "We are pained at this indeed. We hope the injury is slight. Knowing something of the nature of the road west of Indianapolis, we endeavored to prevail on Mr. Van Buren to go to Madison [Indiana] and take steamboat to St. Louis."[35] The Democratic *Journal* took a less favorable tact in reporting on Van Buren's accident, noting that "it is well remembered of him that he did not even condescend to recommend an appropriation on [the National Road] during his whole administration."[36] Regarding the accident, "mortifying as it was to his friends and injurious to all, forbids sympathy for any inconvenience which he may have experienced in encountering its numerous mud-holes and deep ruts." The accident, the *Journal* added, "for the superstitious, if there are any such, would be willing almost to regard this [accident] as a judgment on the ex-President! To say the least of it, it is a pretty severe chastisement for the perverseness of President Van Buren in this matter at least. If he should ever again reach the Presidential chair . . . he will hardly forget the condition of the road when he traveled it on his tour to see the good people of the West, whether he should deem it proper to favor its improvement by national means or not."[37]

Van Buren's party eventually reached Terre Haute and was met east of the city by a welcoming committee and escorted into town to the Prairie House Hotel for a reception at a speaker's stand there. After formal welcoming remarks, Van Buren said he offered "sincere thanks for the friendly and even flattering terms in which you have alluded to me and my public acts. You have done but justice to my feelings and this testimonial of the respect and kind feelings of my fellow citizens if far from being the less grateful to me because it is not dictated by political preference."[38] Van Buren said he was disappointed that "misunderstandings" had prevented some who had hoped to visit him from being present, and "I am sorry that from my traveling arrangements, my stay will necessarily be so short among you as to prevent me, in great measure, from partaking of those hospitalities which have been so liberally tendered to me through you. Permit me, in conclusion, to thank you heartily for the friendly and becoming manner in which you have made known to me the expressions of friendship and respect of your fellow citizens."[39] After visiting with local and state dignitaries present, Van Buren continued west to Springfield, Illinois.

Van Buren failed in subsequent efforts to be nominated for president, most notably in 1848, and retired from public life. He died where he was born, Kinderhook, New York, with death coming on July 24, 1862, at the age of seventy-nine after a short bout of pneumonia.

William Henry Harrison

In 1840 Harrison easily won Indiana during his quest for the presidency, just as he had done in 1836, but this time he also won the nation's highest office. A familiar and popular name from his tenure as the territorial governor of Indiana from 1801 to 1812, there is scant evidence of a

LIBRARY OF CONGRESS

An early 1840s portrait of William Henry Harrison, ninth president of the United States.

Harrison campaign in Indiana, although his 1840 effort is noted among many historians as breaking with past tradition and resembling more of the active campaigning that modern campaigns undertake for the presidency.

Prior to Harrison's first try for the Whig Party nomination in 1836, he made speeches in many states, including Indiana, where he was well known, to keep his name before voters. Part of his speechmaking reflected his struggle to find a place in politics and public life after his Indiana Territory governorship ended.[40] In a May 1835 speech at Vincennes, following his elected terms to the U.S. House and U.S. Senate and service as U.S. Minister to Colombia for the administration of President John Quincy Adams, Harrison defined his reputation as one who favored allowing slaveholding southern states to keep their policies in place. He offered his caution against the growing number of societies and councils focused on the abolition of slavery. He said they offered "weak, presumptuous and unconstitutional" ideas that could end "in the utter extirpation [extinction] of those whose cause they advocate [the slaves]."[41] He ridiculed abolitionists who said they simply sought an amendment to the nation's Constitution: "Now can an amendment of the constitution be effected without the consent of the southern States? What then is the proposition to be submitted to them? It is this—'The present provisions of the constitution secure to you the right . . . to manage your domestic concerns in your own way; but as we are convinced that you do not manage them properly, we want you to put in the hands of the general government, in the councils of which we have the majority, the control over these matters, the effect of which will be virtually to transfer the power from yours into our hands.'"[42]

Articulating states' rights arguments that would prevail for decades to follow, Harrison noted that in some slaveholding states blacks outnumbered controlling whites and asked, "Is there any man of common sense who does not believe that the emancipated blacks, being a majority, will not insist upon a full participation of political rights with the whites; and when possessed of these, they will not contend for a full share of social rights also? . . . Further; the emancipators generally declare that it is their intention to effect their object . . . by no other means than by convincing the slave-holders that the emancipation of the slaves is called for, both by moral obligation and sound policy."[43] Harrison said abolitionists were within their rights to engage the dialogue about ending slavery, but noted that the constructors of the Constitution "took care to have the right secured to them" to hold slaves and "to follow and reclaim such of them as were fugitives to other states." This was

Poster championing Harrison's 1840 election.

INDIANA HISTORICAL SOCIETY, BASS PHOTO COMPANY COLLECTION, P.130

LIBRARY OF CONGRESS

Whig broadside recounting Harrison's career exploits.

INDIANA HISTORICAL BUREAU, GOVERNORS' PORTRAIT COLLECTION

Hoosier Group artist T. C. Steele painted this official governor's portrait of Harrison in 1916.

a clear indication, Harrison said, that abolition of slavery was never intended and that those who encourage slaves "to leave their masters, but to cut their throats before they do so" are advocating a violation of law. He said allowing abolitionists to outlaw slavery for all states would "defeat one of the great objects of its [the Constitution's] formation, which was that of securing the peace and harmony of the states which were parties to it" and that "it could have never been expected that it [the Constitution] would be used by the citizens of one portion of the states for the purpose of depriving those of another portion, of the rights which they had reserved at the adoption of the constitution."[44]

Harrison issued a warning to his fellow Hoosiers:

> Every movement which is made by the abolitionists in the non-slaveholding states, is viewed by our southern brethren as an attack upon their rights, and which, if persisted in, must in the end eradicate those feelings of attachment and affection between the citizens of all the states, which was produced by a community of interests and dangers in the war of the revolution, which was the foundation of our happy union, and by a continuance of which, it can alone be preserved.[45]

By 1836 the Whig Party, a highly fractured and sectionalized coalition of members, mostly drawn together by their desire to defeat the Democrats, emerged as the only serious challenger to the Democratic Party. The Whig coalition of northern and southern states—all the time avoiding significant engagement on the slavery issue and other questions—was a difficult one to hold together. As a result, in 1836 the party officially put forth at one time as many as four presidential candidates: Harrison, U.S. Senator Daniel Webster of Massachusetts, U.S. Senator Hugh Lawson White of Tennessee, and U.S. Sena-

tor Willie Person of North Carolina. Eventually the party settled on the candidacies of Harrison in the northern states making up the Whig Party and White in the South. Insiders calculated by running two candidates, the Whig Party could successfully throw the presidential election into the House of Representatives, where it might stand a better chance of winning. Harrison won Indiana over the Democratic nominee, Vice President Van Buren, despite a horseback campaign waged in the state by Van Buren's running mate, former U.S. senator Richard Mentor Johnson of Kentucky. Johnson visited each of these Indiana cities: Carlisle, Connersville, Crawfordsville, Evansville, Indianapolis, Lafayette, New Harmony, Roachdale, Rockport, Terre Haute, and Vincennes. Historian Adam Leonard noted, "At Vincennes [Johnson] was met ten miles north of the city by three hundred horsemen. At the edge of the city he was met by a crowd on foot and horseback and the entire gathering paraded the streets led by the Vincennes band."[46] While Harrison carried Indiana, Van Buren won an easy national victory, capturing 51 percent of the vote in a three-way race (Harrison won 37 percent and White 10 percent). Regardless, Harrison proved an effective campaigner, setting him up for fuller party consideration in 1840.

The 1840 campaign for the Whig Party nomination was an altogether more organized effort than four years before, with the party holding its first national convention in Baltimore (although a party platform was still not adopted). Traditional nominee balloting took place with Clay taking a narrow lead on the first four ballots. Winner-take-all rules concerning state delegate votes, however, locked Clay's support into a string of southern states and kept him from gathering at least a minority portion of delegate votes from some northern states, including Indiana. As a result, compromise was at hand, and on the fifth ballot delegates chose Harrison as their nominee. They also named former U.S. senator John Tyler of Virginia as the vice presidential nominee. Historian Leonard suggests that Harrison's popularity among northern Whigs was not at all surprising: "The mere fact that Harrison was a candidate at all made him the choice of the Indiana Whigs. No one could poll so large a Whig vote in Indiana as her first territorial governor and the hero of Tippecanoe."[47]

Harrison's campaign emphasized his simple roots (with countless loyal Whig newspaper editors happy to help), even providing drawings of his log cabin home and his role in the Battle of Tippecanoe. Once Harrison was nominated, Whig-run newspapers across Indiana and the nation kicked into a massive public-relations campaign about the candidate. "Whig editorial efforts were supplemented by stump oratory," said historian Robert G. Gunderson. "For the first time, a presidential candidate abandoned the traditional Olympia of seclusion for the fervid clamor of the arena. In what his opponents damned as an unseemly exhibition, Harrison delivered twenty-three speeches in Ohio in support of his own candidacy."[48]

As was typical with Whig Party nominees, Harrison avoided deep penetration into certain issues and, combined with his military pedigree, was able to avoid the normal attacks waged by opponents.[49] One historian, Reginald Horsman, suggested that as the Whig nominee in 1840, Harrison's so-called Log-Cabin and Hard-Cider Campaign "began a new era in election image-making. At the age of sixty-seven Harrison showed great enthusiasm in playing his role. The Whig strategy was remarkably successful in creating the kind of candidate they wished to place before the people. Although southern Whig

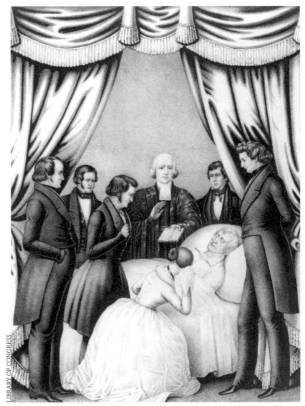

LIBRARY OF CONGRESS

An 1846 lithograph depicting mourners huddling around Harrison's deathbed.

supporters were wooed by reference to Harrison's long record of noninterference with the rights of slaveowners, the primary image was of a simple, noble character."[50] Horsman further described Harrison as "a tireless campaigner, and for the first time a presidential candidate actually took to the hustings. He talked in generalities and avoided issues, except for opposing the excessive use of presidential power. He argued for serving a single term and the limited use of the presidential veto. Harrison stressed his military service to the country and his life as a practical farmer. He was vague on issues such as the bank, the tariff, and slavery. His opponents attacked his military career, stressed that he was no simple farmer, and accused him of being a Federalist because he had served under John Adams."[51]

In the final tally of the rematch, Harrison defeated Van Buren, carrying nineteen states (including Indiana) while winning 53 percent of the popular vote. In Indiana Harrison's total was impressive, as he bested his opponent by a margin of 56 percent to 44 percent. Following his victory, president-elect Harrison planned a visit to Louisville and Frankfort, Kentucky, the home turf of longtime Whig leader Clay, to help salve any remaining wounds Clay felt for having been passed over for the nomination and to buttress the party's first serious crack at national power. Arriving in Kentucky on November 17, 1840, "the citizens of Louisville were joined by people from Jeffersonville and New Albany, Indiana, in a spectacular celebration. Thousands paraded the streets past lighted windows decorated with transparencies, mottos, and wreaths of flowers, while other thousands gazed in amazement at the spectacle," with one local Whig newspaper comparing the excitement of the people "with that of the poor cripple in the Scriptures who leaped for joy when restored by the Savior."[52]

Little historical record was ever compiled by the Harrison administration. The president died from pneumonia and pleurisy on April 4, 1841, just thirty days after having taken the oath of office. He was sixty-seven years old and the first sitting president to die in office. As Horsman noted, "Once in office, Harrison had very little time to enjoy his triumph. . . . He showed signs in his brief tenure that he would have shaped his own course. His inaugural was extremely long. It emphasized a limited role for the presidency, with little use of the veto and service for a single term."[53] While historians have little with which to make a comprehensive assessment of the Harrison presidency, his impact on the campaigning for the office is widely accepted as noteworthy. As author Robert Friedenberg

noted, Harrison's campaign "not only broke with tradition by aggressively speaking on his own behalf, but he won. His victory seemed to legitimatize presidential campaign addresses. From 1840 forward, presidential candidates would much more actively and openly campaign for the office. Today, we cannot even imagine a campaign in which the candidates do not travel throughout the country speaking about the issues of the day. But in 1840, William Henry Harrison dramatically broke with tradition to become the first presidential candidate to speak aggressively on his own behalf. In doing so, he overturned the precedent set by another general [George Washington] and helped set the stage for contemporary campaigns."[54]

Contemporary news accounts of Harrison's untimely death seemed to struggle with the reality that a president could expire so quickly after having taken office, and with so few Americans even knowing very much about him beyond what the campaign had revealed. Even the announcement of Harrison's death had to be handled in an unusual manner, as Vice President Tyler was not in Washington the day the president died. Five members of the president's new cabinet, including Secretary of State Daniel Webster, Secretary of the Treasury Thomas Ewing, and Attorney General J. J. Crittenden—announced:

> An all-wise Providence having suddenly removed from this life, William Henry Harrison, late President of the United States, we have thought it our duty, in the recess of Congress, and in the absence of the Vice President from the seat of government, to make this afflicting bereavement known to the country, by this declaration, under our hands. He died at the President's House, in this city, this fourth day of April 1841, at 30 minutes before one o'clock in the morning. The people of the United States, overwhelmed like ourselves, by an event so

unexpected and so melancholy, will derive consolation from knowing that his death was calm and resigned, as his life has been patriotic, useful and distinguished; and that the last utterance of his lips expressed a fervent desire for the perpetuity of the Constitution, and the preservation of its true principles. In death, as in life, the happiness of his country was uppermost in his thoughts.[55]

In Indianapolis the *Sentinel* reported, "Our town, the Union is mourning. A giant man has fallen in Israel. Gen. William Henry Harrison has gone to that bourne whence no traveler returns. Let a nation weep and be clothed in the habiliments of woe, for it is much afflicted. The melancholy intelligence reached town last Saturday morning. It cast a deep gloom over our citizens, and many shed tears, but none murmured because of the saddening disposition of an all-wise Providence."[56]

In the days following Harrison's death, Indiana leaders organized a memorial for him at Indianapolis, conducted on April 10, 1841. Fellow Whig Party leader, Governor Bigger, led the Indiana observance at the Marion County Courthouse. "This event has occurred at a time when least expected and when calculated to produce the greatest shock," said Bigger. "Had a thunderbolt dropped among us in the clear sunshine, it would not have been more astounding. President Harrison had just closed a year of the most intense interest, growing out of his intimate connection with the great contest for the first office within the gift of the American people."[57] The governor lamented that Harrison's many friends and supporters were just beginning to bask in the celebration of his inauguration and to await his first moves as president, "when Heaven, for purposes no doubt wise in themselves, but to us are inscrutable, has seen proper to remove him from life."[58]

Bigger also noted that the entire nation mourned the passing of the president, "but in the west, and in Indiana especially, so long under his fostering care and always the object of his most affectionate regard, will this event awaken feelings of the most poignant grief. President Harrison was a western man in the full sense of that expression. Nearly fifty years ago, young, undistinguished, he came to the west, then a wilderness. He has witnessed its rapid and continually advancing changes, has participated in its dangers and privations, has periled his life in its defense, and has identified his own so closely with its history that the one cannot be written without the other. . . . Such is the man whose loss we mourn; but in giving vent to our grief, let us turn to the counseling reflection that though dead, he has gone where the wicked cease from troubling, and the weary are at rest."[59]

The official state funeral for Harrison was conducted on April 7, 1841, in Cincinnati, and Harrison was laid to rest in the Congressional Cemetery in Washington, D.C. Later, his remains were moved to be closer to his home at North Bend, Ohio, where a national monument was erected in his honor. Harrison's death highlighted the lack of specificity in the Constitution about presidential succession. Article II, Section 1 of the constitution simply stated, "In case of the removal of the President from office, or of his death, resignation, or inability to discharge the powers and duties of the said office, the same shall devolve on the Vice President."[60] Vice President Tyler, who reached Washington, D.C., two days after Harrison's death, removed any doubt about succession, having himself sworn into office and taking over the reins of the federal government.

Lewis Cass

Lewis Cass of Michigan was quite familiar with Indiana, particularly the northern part of the state, as his travels often took him there during separate terms as governor of the Michigan Territory (1813–31), U.S. Ambassador to France (1836–42), and U.S. Senator from Michigan (1849–57). In 1848 Cass won the Democratic nomination for president, denying Van Buren another shot at the nation's highest office. Van Buren later accepted the nomination of a third party, the Free-Soil Party, effectively denying Cass a victory as Whig nominee Zachary Taylor of Louisiana won the election. While Taylor won overall by a comfortable margin, it was Cass who carried Indiana, 49 percent to 46 percent for Taylor (Van Buren received 5 percent of the Indiana vote).

There is little evidence of an active Cass (or Taylor or Van Buren) campaign in Indiana in 1848, but Cass did offer a well-remembered address on July 4, 1843, at Fort Wayne upon the completion of the Wabash and Erie Canal between Toledo, Ohio, and Lafayette, Indiana. Fort Wayne made sense for the celebration, as it was about halfway through the 460-mile canal route and a central port for the waterway. The canal represented an incredible engineering and industrial feat, promising the opening of trade from the Great Lakes west to the Ohio and Mississippi Rivers (via the canal stretching across Ohio and Indiana to the Wabash River at Lafayette). The

LIBRARY OF CONGRESS

A campaign banner for Democratic candidates Lewis Cass (left) and William O. Butler produced for the 1848 presidential election.

An 1833 James B. Longacre portrait of Cass.

LIBRARY OF CONGRESS

canal operated for about a decade before failing financially, in part due to corruption, construction problems, and the growth of railroads.

The Fort Wayne event was staged on a farm that later became Swinney Park and included the reading of the Declaration of Independence. News reports indicated that Cass's speech was punctuated by the firing of a cannon at various points, "which excited the cheers of the multitude without the range of his voice."[61] In comments well designed for the pride Fort Wayne's citizens were feeling, Cass said, "We have come here to rejoice together. Memorable deeds make memorable days. There is a power of association given to man, which binds together the past and the present, and connects both with the future. Great events hallow the sites where they pass. Their returning anniversaries, so long as these are remembered, are kept with sorrow or joy as they are prosperous or adverse. Today a new work is born, a work of peace, not of war. We are celebrating a triumph of art and not of arms."[62]

Cass also said it was his hope that "centuries hence, we may hope the river you have made will flow both east and west, bearing upon its bosom the riches of a prosperous people, and that our descendants will come to keep the day which we have come to mark; and that as it returns they will remember the exertions of their ancestors while they gather the harvest."[63]

A large portion of Cass's earlier remarks concerned the Oregon Territory and other western areas of the growing nation that were at risk of being claimed by England. Cass warned the audience that England "is planting her standard wherever there is a people to be subdued, or the fruits of their industry to be secured. With professions of philanthropy, she pursues the designs of ambition. And she is encircling the globe with her stations wherever she can best accomplish

LIBRARY OF CONGRESS

Campaign banner for Democratic presidential candidate Cass.

her schemes of aggrandizement." Cass said the United States' claims to western portions of the continent were as undeniable as the nation's rights gained in battles at Bunker Hill and New Orleans, "and who will call in question our right to those blood-stained fields?" Cass noted he was not favorable to war, but noted that "war is a great evil, but not so great as national dishonor." He said the nation should "draw no red lines upon the map of Oregon. Let us hold to the integrity of just claim. And if war comes, be it so."[64]

1852 and 1856 Elections

For the elections of 1852 and 1856, Indiana remained a competitive state but failed to attract campaigning by the nominees themselves. In 1852 Democratic nominee and eventual winner Franklin Pierce of New Hampshire carried Indiana over General Winfield Scott of New Jersey, despite no campaigning in the state. By 1856 the Whig Party had disintegrated altogether, leaving Indiana open to an easy win by James C. Buchanan of Pennsylvania over Republican John C. Fremont of California, and former president Millard Fillmore, who had accepted the nomination of the American Party, unofficially known as the Know Nothing Party.

2

Civil War and Reconstruction, 1860–79

Abraham Lincoln

The 1860 election presented the nation with unprecedented circumstances—the National Democratic Party (or northern Democrats) eventually nominated U.S. Senator Stephen A. Douglas of Illinois, while the Republican Party nominated an Illinois counterpart, former congressman Abraham Lincoln. Douglas was only selected, however, after 110 southern delegates walked out after an incredible fifty-seven separate ballots had failed to settle the matter, mostly in part to Douglas's positions on slavery. The break-off southern Democrats formed the Constitutional Democratic Party and nominated Vice President John C. Breckinridge of Kentucky (a pro-slavery candidate) as its nominee. Breckinridge's selection was hardly unanimous, with serious acrimony remaining among proslavery Democrats, but he emerged a strong vote getter among southern Democrats. Former U.S. senator John Bell of Tennessee became the nominee of the short-lived Constitutional Union Party, representing the discontent former Whigs and so-called Know Nothing Democrats.

In considering Lincoln's presence in Indiana, the story starts with his childhood days spent in Spencer County between 1816 and 1830. While Lincoln grew from a boy to a six-foot, four-inch young man on Hoosier soil, his time as a resident of Indiana is deeply treasured by the state's residents, but it is his political accomplishments in Illinois and Washington, D.C., that catapulted him into the hearts of millions of Americans. While Lincoln's brief remarks in Indiana while en route to his March 1861 inauguration are commemorated in Indiana history, they were not Lincoln's first political speeches in the state.

In 1844 a thirty-five-year-old Lincoln accepted the invitation of the Whig Party to return to Rockport, Indiana, just over a dozen years after his family had moved west to Illinois. Lincoln, who had served multiple terms in the Illinois House of Representatives between 1834 and 1842, visited Indiana before he was elected to the U.S. House of Representatives from Illinois in 1846. Historian David Vanderstel wrote of the visit, "On the evening of 30 October, Lincoln spoke to a large audience at the courthouse, expressing his support for protective tariffs. *The Rockport Herald* noted that Lincoln 'handled that subject in a manner that done honor to himself and the Whig cause. Other subjects were investigated in a like manner. His speech was plain, argumentative and of an hour's duration.'"[1] Vanderstel said Lincoln's appearance at Rockport was "clear indication that Lincoln was gaining recognition as a political leader in the West." During his visit to his old Indiana home, Lincoln visited "the neighborhood . . . in which [he] was raised, where [his] mother and only sister were buried," the *Rockport Herald* account noted.[2] It is believed Lincoln, who rode to Indiana on horseback, stayed in the state from October 24 until Election Day. Other speeches were reportedly made, although only the Rockport speech was reported in the press.[3]

There is no record of Lincoln speaking again in Indiana until September 19, 1859. Just a year removed from the famous Lincoln-Douglas senatorial debates of 1858, Lincoln spoke at the Masonic Hall in downtown Indianapolis in support of Republican Party principles and candidates. Lincoln had spoken previously in Columbus and Cincinnati, Ohio, and was en route to his home in Springfield, Illinois, when he accepted the invitation to speak in Indianapolis. News accounts of Lincoln's appearance referred to him as "the champion Republican of Illinois" and said his rhetoric did not disappoint. The *Williamsport-Warren Republican* reported that Lincoln provided "one of the most thorough dissections of the misrepresentations of his own and of the Republican views ever witnessed anywhere," and he devoted a large portion of his speech to correcting the "perversion which Mr. Douglas has made a Democratic tenet" about the Republican positions regarding slavery. Lincoln had successfully indicted the Democratic Party for "degrading the Negro to the level of a brute" and for "repudiating the Golden Rule of Christianity."[4]

Lincoln opened his lengthy remarks by addressing the audience as "fellow citizens of Indiana" and provided a third-person account of his own life history intertwined with that of the Hoosier State. He recalled his trip through the state en route to Indianapolis earlier in the

day and noted, "These scenes he passed through to-day are wonderfully different from the first scenes he witnessed in the State of Indiana, where he was raised, in Spencer County, on the Ohio river. There was an unbroken wilderness there then, and an axe was put in his hand; and with the trees and logs and grubs he fought until he reached his twentieth year."[5] Lincoln acknowledged in his remarks that as a Republican he was becoming well known as someone who "could not speak of anything but the Negro" and reminded the audience of his quickly becoming well-known turn of a phrase that "this government of ours cannot 'endure permanently, half slave and half free; that a house divided against itself cannot stand.'"[6] Lincoln said answering the question of a half-slave, half-free nation was the centerpiece of his planned remarks in Indianapolis. He noted:

> It was true that our fathers made this government, and that when it was made it was part slave and part free. But the assumption of the interrogatory is, that our fathers made the government part free and part slave from choice—that they had chosen to make it so because they thought a government thus made, was the best that could be made. Of choice they made it part free and part slave. . . . It was not the judgment of the framers of the Constitution, that it was best that the States should be part free and part slave. There was no provision made for peopling one portion of the States with slaves. There was no place spoken of where slaves could be got. There was no provision made in the Constitution, that the African slave trade should ever be suppressed—that it should be repealed. There was a total silence on that question. There is a misunderstanding with some people on this subject.[7]

Lincoln said he believed the constitutional fathers had intended for slavery to end after twenty years: "All the States of the South had a considerable amount of slavery in them. The trade of importing slaves was carried on by the commerce of those States where the small amount of slavery existed. It was so carried on that the whole government had an interest invested in some way or other. The Southern people were cultivating their soil with slaves, and it was in deference to that state of things that the framers of the Constitution put in the provision, that Congress should not prohibit that trade until after the expiration of twenty years."[8] He buttressed his argument by noting the Ordinance of 1787 was adopted prohibiting slavery into the Northwest Territory and that Ohio (in 1803), Indiana (in 1816), Illinois (in 1818), Michigan (in 1837), and Wisconsin (in 1848) had each sought statehood without any provision for slavery included. "Thus, down through a period of sixty years, until the last inch of that Territory came into the Union, the prohibition of slavery was religiously adhered to," he said.[9]

The Constitution bears no mention of slavery, Lincoln said, because it was never the plan that the nation should be half slave and half free. "It was not done by accident but by design—as every one could see the framers of the Constitution expected that the institution [of slavery] would die," he said. Lincoln expanded his theme by continually disassembling the states' rights ideas proffered by Douglas and others, declaring his views on "popular sovereignty" to be "the debauching of public sentiment. The maxims [Douglas] taught in regard to the institution of slavery, and by relative operation upon the principle of liberty itself, were more pernicious than anything else. The Judge [Douglas] said he did not care whether slavery was voted up or voted down. That was as much as to say, that he does not believe it to be wrong. This was not the opinion held by the good men of the Revolution of it." Lincoln said the nation allowed Douglas "to debauch public sentiment among you" and

that Douglas and the Democrats had "taken the [N]egro out of the catalogue of man" and that blacks had no share in the Declaration of Independence and that "the Negro was thus being debased from the condition of a man of some sort to that of a brute."[10]

Lincoln's 1860 campaign for the presidency was spent entirely in Springfield (his positions on slavery made him an unwelcome guest in southern states). Douglas, however, campaigned in twenty-three northern and southern states. The campaigns of Breckinridge and Bell were entirely regional in appeal. Lincoln captured the troubled election of 1860 and became the nation's sixteenth (and first Republican) president, but it was clear, due to the highly divided nature of the nation, acceptance of his presidency in many parts of the South would remain in doubt. While Lincoln's support among northern Republicans provided him a solid block in the Electoral College vote, and although the Democrats were highly splintered, the final results indicated that even if the Democratic votes had been combined, Lincoln would have won.[11]

Due for his inauguration in Washington, D.C., on March 4, 1861, Lincoln set out from Illinois with the knowledge that he was to take office at a highly divisive time in the country's history. In fact, secession was declared in South Carolina in December 1860, just one month after Lincoln's election and before he could take office. Eventually, ten more southern states would follow South Carolina's lead and secede from the Union, in order: Mississippi, Florida, Alabama, Georgia, Louisiana, Texas, Arkansas, North Carolina, Virginia, and Tennessee. In May 1861, just two months into Lincoln's term, the southerners made it official with the formation of the Confederate States of America. The Civil War was at hand. Indiana historian George S. Cottman wrote that with Lincoln's election to the presidency, "his position in the maelstrom suddenly became that of supreme leader for weal or woe. Nothing was to be expected of his predecessor [James Buchanan], who still held the helm, but who was simply swamped by the magnitude of affairs, and so the eyes of the country were turned on the president-elect, noting his every act and word."[12]

It was in this troubled time that Lincoln passed through Indiana by train on his way to take on his new duties. His first stop was on February 11, 1861, in State Line City in Warren County (a small hamlet about ten miles northeast of Danville, Illinois). There, an account in the *Lafayette Courier* said, he told the gathering of supportive Hoosiers, "Gentlemen of Indiana: I am happy to meet you on this occasion, and enter again the state of my early life, and almost of maturity. I am under many obligations to you for your kind reception, and to Indiana for the aid she rendered our cause which, I think, a just one. Gentlemen, I shall address you at greater length at Indianapolis, but not much greater. Again, gentlemen, I thank you for your warm-hearted reception."[13] The inaugural special then made its way through Tippecanoe County for a stop in Lafayette. Lincoln offered more remarks, beginning with expressing his amazement at the speed at which he was able to travel via the rails, noting that it had taken only six hours to travel the approximately 185 miles from his home in Springfield to Lafayette. "I find myself far from home surrounded by the thousands I now see before me, who are strangers to me," Lincoln said. "Still we are bound together, I trust in Christianity, civilization and patriotism, and are attached to our country and our whole country. While some of us may differ in political opinions, still we are all united in one feeling for the Union. We all believe in the maintenance of the Union, of every star and every stripe of the glorious flag, and

permit me to express the sentiment that upon the union of the States, there shall be between us no difference. My friends, I meet many friends at every place on my journey, and I should weary myself should I talk at length, therefore permit me to bid you an affectionate farewell."[14]

In Boone County, the train made brief stops at both Thorntown and Lebanon. In Thorntown, Lincoln miscalculated the time he had to speak and was halfway through an anecdote about a man who ran for office while riding horseback, but was not able to complete the story before the train began to pull away. Lincoln finished the story once he reached Lebanon, leaving those in Thorntown puzzling about the story's ending.[15]

Once in Indianapolis, Lincoln spoke to a large crowd gathered near Washington and Missouri Streets, just west of the Indiana Statehouse (near the site of the Indiana Government Center today). "Here, as the time of arrival approached, was a crowd that jammed the streets and filled all available windows, house-tops and even telegraph poles," noted Cottman. "Governor Oliver P. Morton, in a barouche to which was attached a matched team of four beautiful white horses decorated with plumes and flags, was stationed at the crossing ready to receive the president-elect with a speech of welcome."[16] Lincoln's remarks reflected the grave and worrisome tasks ahead of him as the Union appeared to be splintering down the Mason-Dixon Line. Responding to the unexpectedly long and political welcome offered by Morton, Lincoln told his Hoosier friends, "I appeal to you to constantly bear in mind that not with politicians, not with presidents, not with office-seekers, but with you is the question: Shall the Union and shall the liberties of this country be preserved to the latest generations? It is your business if the Union of these states and the liberties of this people shall be lost. It is your business to rise up and preserve the Union." He added, "The salvation of the Union needs but one single thing—the hearts of people like yours. When the people rise in masses on behalf of the Union and the liberties of their country, truly may it be said, 'the gates of hell shall not prevail against them.'"[17]

Lincoln added regarding his new duties, "In all trying positions in which I shall be placed—and doubtless I shall be placed in many such—my reliance will be placed upon you and the people of the United States; and I wish you to remember, now and forever, that it is your business and not mine; that if the Union of these states and the liberties of this people shall be lost it is but little to any one man of fifty-two years of age, but a great deal to the thirty millions of people who inhabit these United States, and to their posterity in all coming time."[18]

To emphasize his true election as president of all of the United States, local Indianapolis officials arranged for a thirty-four-gun artillery salute in recognition of the number of states that were members of the Union at the time of the 1860 election. Lincoln rode from the train stop at Washington Street in a carriage led by the four white horses, although carriages provided for the rest of his party were scooped up by "ill-mannered local politicians" for the short ride to the hotel. One of those left behind at the train was the president-elect's son, Robert, who was carrying "a certain black bag" that contained personal items of his father, including a draft of the inaugural address.

Lincoln wanted a short rest at the Bates House Hotel, but the large crowd in the streets continued to demand remarks from him. Lincoln appeared on a balcony of the hotel above Illinois Street and offered additional remarks focused entirely on troubling secession reports emerging

from South Carolina and elsewhere in the South. Later disagreement arose from accounts of the day about whether Lincoln had given his remarks to members of the Indiana General Assembly inside the hotel's lobby or the general public gathered in the street. Newspaper accounts indicated the latter version was correct. In his speech Lincoln addressed his "fellow citizens of the State of Indiana" and said, "I am here to thank you for this magnificent welcome and still more for the generous support given by your state to that political cause which I think is the true and just cause of the whole country and the whole world." Lincoln offered a Solomon quote that advised there "is a time to keep silence," and noted that "when men wrangle by the mouth with no certainty that they mean the same thing while using the same word, it perhaps were as well if they would keep silent. The words 'coercion' and 'invasion' are much used in these days, and often with some temper and hot blood. Let us make sure, if we can, that we do not misunderstand the meaning of those who use them. Let us get exact definitions of these words, not from dictionaries, but from the men themselves, who certainly depreciate the things they would represent by the use of the words. What then is coercion? What is invasion? Would the marching of an army into South Carolina, without the consent of her people and with hostile intent toward them, be invasion? I certainly think it would; and it would be coercion also, if the South Carolinians were to submit. But if the United States should merely take and hold its own forts and other property, and collect the duties on foreign importations, or even withhold the mails from the places where they were habitually violated, would any or all of these things be invasion or coercion?"[19]

Lincoln asked whether "professed lovers of the Union, but who spitefully resolve that they will resist coercion and invasion, understand that such things as these, on the part of the United States, would be coercion or invasion of a state? If so, their idea of means to present the object of their affection would seem exceedingly thin and airy. . . . In their view, the Union as a family relation would seem to be no regular marriage, but a sort of free-love arrangement to be maintained only on passional attraction."[20] The president-elect noted that each state had a position assigned to it in the U.S. Constitution and that it cannot presume to "carry out" of the Union. "On what rightful principle may a state, being not more than one-fiftieth part of the nation in soil and population, break up the nation, and then coerce a proportionally larger subdivision of itself in the most arbitrary way?" Lincoln asked.

"What mysterious right to play tyrant is conferred on a district of country, with its people, by merely calling it a state?"[21] Lincoln concluded by saying, "Fellow citizens, I am not asserting anything. I am merely asking questions for you to consider," the loaded nature of the questions notwithstanding.[22]

Following his remarks, Lincoln attended an invitation-only dinner inside the hotel and retired for the night. The following morning, Lincoln's fifty-second birthday, he had breakfast with Morton at the governor's home on West Market Street and traveled to and from the meal without making any public comments. "The Lincoln party had some difficulty getting to the [Union] station by reason of the demonstrative crowd," Cottman reported. "At 11:00 a.m. the

ABRAHAM LINCOLN,
OF ILLINOIS.

ANDREW JOHNSON,
OF TENNESSEE.

An 1864 campaign banner for the Republican ticket, Abraham Lincoln (left) and Andrew Johnson.

LIBRARY OF CONGRESS

special train pulled out amid the shouting of the multitude, many persons even running down the track after the receding cars. The train was decorated elaborately with flags and red, white and blue bunting, with an image of the American eagle amid flag draperies over the platform of the rear car. The smokestack of the locomotive was encircled with thirty-four white stars on a blue field, and on its front the engine bore pictures of all the presidents, with George Washington conspicuous. Flags, ribbons and evergreens gaily ornamented boiler, framework and tender."[23]

As his train made its way east, Lincoln made one more Indiana stop for short remarks at Lawrenceburg along the Ohio River. There he said, "My fellow-countrymen, you call upon me for a speech; I have none to give to you, and have not sufficient time to devote to it if I had. I suppose you are all Union men here, and I suppose that you are in favor of doing full justice to all, whether on that side of the river [pointing to the Kentucky shore], or on your own. If the politicians and leaders of parties were as true as the people, there would be little fear that the peace of the country would be disturbed. I have been selected to fill an important office for a brief period, and am now, in your eyes, invested with an influence which will soon pass away; but should my administration prove to be a very wicked one, or what is more probable, a very foolish one, if you, the people, are but true to yourselves and to the Constitution, there is but little harm I can do, thank God!"[24]

Lincoln never again visited Indiana during the remaining days of his life, including the 1864 election conducted amidst the Civil War. Shot by Confederate sympathizer John Wilkes Booth on April 14, 1865, while attending a play at Ford's Theatre in Washington, D.C., the president died nine hours later on April 15, 1865. Vice President

Andrew Johnson was sworn into office about three hours later. Plunged into grief, the Union grappled to understand the circumstances of Lincoln's assassination. His body lay in state in both the East Room of the White House and later in the Rotunda of the U.S. Capitol from April 19–21. Thirteen northern cities of any size between Washington, D.C., and Lincoln's home in Springfield, Illinois, planned elaborate events to memorialize the slain president, including Indianapolis. At 7:00 a.m. on a rainy Sunday, April 30, 1865, fifteen days after the president's death, the funeral train arrived in Indianapolis. Cottman wrote that every aspect of the day seemed to conspire "to deepen the sense of gloom which spread like a pall over the nation. For days before the coming of the funeral train the solemnity was fed by preparations for the sad event."[25]

Downtown Indianapolis buildings were appropriately draped in black crepe for the event, though the decorations suffered under relentless heavy rain. According to Cottman, the Indiana Statehouse "presented the most impressive decorations of all. The fence about the grounds, a canopy spanning the south approach, and the eight great pillars of the Capitol portico were festooned and wrapped with black and white. The building within was converted into a mausoleum. The entrances were hung with long, heavy black curtains that swept to the floor, shutting out the exterior world. The walls of the open halls and rotunda were hung with black and with garlands of laurel, myrtle and evergreen, and the darkened interior was dimly lighted by the flames of the gas chandeliers. All this, be it repeated, represented days of preparation, the effect of which was to key the public mind to the culminating gloom of the funeral day."[26]

Morton had traveled east to Richmond, where the nine-car funeral train arrived at 2:00

a.m. Sunday morning and traveled slowly under a floral arch erected over the tracks, to accompany the slain president's body to Indianapolis. The governor stayed with the cortege carrying Lincoln's remains until they were in place inside the rotunda of the Indiana capitol. The cortege carrying Lincoln's body was drawn by the same four white horses that had delivered him to the Bates House Hotel in February 1861 during his last visit to the city. At the rotunda, Lincoln's casket was opened and placed on "a raised dais, shrouded in black, with a canopy above falling in sable folds, the whole making a catafalque. At the head of the coffin stood a bust of the dead man, crowned with a chaplet of laurel," noted Cottman.[27] Soon the doors were opened and a steady stream of Hoosiers numbering in the thousands walked by the casket for hours "for a last brief view of America's greatest son," Cottman said, adding that the "solemn silence within, as the throngs passed between the statue-like guards, was broken only by the tramp of countless feet muffled by new matting that had been spread upon the floor for this occasion."[28] The building remained open until 11:00 p.m. to accommodate the estimated one hundred thousand mourners who came to pay their respects.

Outside, the "dull booming" of a cannon signaled each half hour throughout the day as more than 5,000 of the visitors to the capitol were Sunday School children brought downtown for the solemn and historic occasion. Downtown streetcars were festooned with banners expressing the city's grief, with phrases such as "Rest in peace, thou Gentle Spirit; souls like thine with God inherit Life and Love," "He has gone from Works to his Reward," "Thou art gone, and Friend and Foe alike appreciate thee now," and "Fear not, Abraham, I am thy Shield; thy Reward shall be exceedingly great."[29]

Just before midnight, Lincoln's remains were returned to the funeral train, and it began its final leg toward Illinois, going to Springfield by way of Chicago (adding more than four hundred miles to the trip). While Indianapolis was supposed to be the only official stop of the Lincoln train in the state, a stop at Michigan City to allow Chicago and Illinois officials to join the train resulted in an "impromptu funeral" and public viewing in La Porte County. The funeral train had taken eight hours to travel the 150 miles from Indianapolis and passed under another elaborate floral arch constructed over the rail line to honor the slain leader. "Officials in charge of the funeral train decided on the spot to open the coffin to display the remains, breaking the rule which had stated that the coffin would be opened only in the cities holding official funerals," historian Geoff Elliott wrote. "Then townspeople were permitted to board the funeral car to file past the coffin while the people who had been riding the train were breakfasting inside the depot. Quick prayers were said and hymns were sung as the smallest funeral for Lincoln began inside the funeral car. It was later said that the grief shown by the Michigan City townspeople was as palpable that day inside the car as it was in the other cities where the official funerals had been held. The entire ceremony that day was also the shortest as the unexpected stop lasted barely an hour. The service was over in just thirty-five minutes."[30]

Stephen A. Douglas

Senator Douglas of Illinois had aspirations to be the nominee of the Democratic Party for president for at least eight years before he finally won the nomination in the troubled election of 1860. An accomplished man with strong leadership skills, Douglas's place in history remains highly debated primarily because of the shadow of slavery that hung over his public life. While disagreement still persists about whether Douglas was a proslavery Democrat, or rather a pro-states' and territorial rights Democrat, there is no question he was a forceful and important figure in the life of the Republic.

By 1860 Douglas was a well-known politician. He first won election to the U.S. House of Representatives from Illinois in 1843 and three years later took a seat in the U.S. Senate. As a senator, he was responsible for the Compromise of 1850 that sought to address growing tension between slaveholding states and free states. Senator Henry Clay, a Whig from Kentucky, drafted the

An 1860 portrait of the "Little Giant," Stephen A. Douglas.

LIBRARY OF CONGRESS

compromise with Douglas that was given credit for holding off increasingly violent interstate conflicts for at least four years. In 1854, as the Kansas and Nebraska territories prepared to become states, the issue of whether they would be allowed to determine for themselves whether or not to allow slavery erupted. Douglas drafted the Kansas-Nebraska Act of 1854 that essentially repealed the Missouri Compromise of 1820, thus allowing the white settlers of Kansas and Nebraska to decide the slave issue. Douglas's act gave birth to a concept he often referenced—popular sovereignty—representing his view that each state or territory should decide its own slavery/free position. Douglas attempted to keep the Union together by offering his compromise as a centerpiece of his 1860 campaign.

In the free state of Indiana, where opinions were hardly unanimous on the slavery issue, Douglas likely saw an opportunity possibly to win a northern state and help deliver him to the White House. In many parts of Indiana, particularly southern Indiana, views on slavery resembled those of their Kentucky neighbors, and Democrats in those parts of the state were referred to as "Copperhead Democrats" or "Butternut Democrats" (the latter reflecting their lack of outright opposition to Confederate ideals of states' rights). Douglas's approach to the 1860 campaign also meant that speeches and appearances in Indiana made sense. While his Republican opponent, Lincoln, remained home in Illinois speaking to groups who came to him, Douglas broke new ground with an aggressive campaign that took him to twenty-three of the thirty-two states over a 160-day period, including many stops in Indiana.[31] Douglas also freely ventured into Breckinridge's home state of Kentucky (giving him exposure to southern Indiana Democrats), something Lincoln could not do because of the fear of possible violence against Republicans and abolitionists in slave-holding states.[32]

Douglas made three major swings through Indiana, visiting four cities in mid-September, Indianapolis at the end of September, and four more stops in the state in early October. While en route to Indianapolis for a September 28, 1860, appearance, Douglas spoke from the rear platform of a train at Lawrenceburg, Greensburg, and Shelbyville, and was in a fighting mood by the time he reached the state capital. While in Indianapolis, he abruptly challenged the positions of Breckinridge (his biggest challenger for Butternut Democrat votes in Indiana) and quickly dismissed questions posed by the Whig newspaper in Indianapolis. A large parade that included "the most imposing feature" of "a young lady attired as the Goddess of Liberty" led Douglas from the Bates Hotel in downtown Indianapolis to Military Park. Crowd estimates varied widely from 35,000 to 100,000. Indianapolis Republican newspapers attributed the large turnout mostly to curiosity, rather than as support for Douglas's campaign.

Indiana lieutenant governor Abraham A. Hammond (later elected governor) introduced Douglas to the throng. "Such a demonstration as this I have never before witnessed upon the American continent," Douglas declared in his opening remarks. "What means this vast concourse of citizens? There must be some cause which calls together so large a number at this central point. In a time of profound peace, when the country abounds with plenty and prosperity, it is remarkable to find discord and irritation prevailing in the land."[33] Douglas said "one would support that a grateful people would be content with the blessings which we enjoy, and yet we find this country distracted by sectional hate and

sectional strife, alienating one portion of the American people from another."[34]

Douglas said to rousing applause that the source of this discontent was "the attempt on the part of the federal government to control the domestic institutions of the people of the territories." The Illinois senator said that congressional "interference" in the issue of slavery in the states and territories had "aroused the fiercest passions of the American people, and arraying North from the South" and that Congress must reconcile this "interference" with a commitment to "restoring peace to a distracted country."[35]

"Then I ask you," Douglas declared, "is it not our duty as patriots to pursue that line of policy which will restore peace and a fraternal feeling

Campaign banner for Stephen A. Douglas's 1860 presidential effort.

LIBRARY OF CONGRESS

to all portions of the American people and make us a vast body of brethren under a common Constitution?"[36]

Keeping the Union intact was at the center of Douglas's positions, he said; although that meant some states would likely remain slaveholding while others, such as Indiana, would remain free states. This contrasted dramatically with Republican positions articulated by Lincoln that a nation so divided could not stand and the declaration that slavery was immoral (a position often advanced by Lincoln's fellow Republican William Seward). Douglas said little had changed since the Compromise of 1850 and called out "Union-loving men" who had supported that effort who now were dug in on the idea that slavery could not stand in any state of the Union. "After the compromise measures of 1850 had been adopted, both of the great political parties in this country agreed to carry out the principles of those measures as the future policy of this country," Douglas reminded his opposition Republicans.[37]

Perhaps attempting to draw away Whig votes in Indiana, Douglas recalled that it was a Democratic-Whig coalition that had come together on many issues of the day, including tariffs. "While you Whigs and we Democrats then agreed on the slavery question, we differed on other questions. We quarreled about the bank, the tariff distribution," said Douglas. "Differing on these we pledged our faith one to the other and to the country that we would stand together by the principle of non-intervention on the slavery questions in order to preserve the peace of the Union."[38] Noting that the disagreements between the two parties had been "assigned to history," he declared, "The only plank now left of the Whig and Democratic platforms is the principle of non-intervention by Congress with slavery in the territories. I wish to inquire whether the old Whigs

who were pledged to the doctrine of non-intervention are now going to abandon it." Douglas proclaimed to loud applause, "I say to you today, as I have said on so many previous occasions, I shall not abandon that principle if every Whig and every Democrat in America abandons it! I believe the perpetuity of this Union is dependent upon its maintenance!"[39]

Douglas's remarks, as usual, avoided discussion about the morality of slavery and instead attempted to reset the discussion as one of states' rights—an issue that held strong appeal among many pioneering Hoosiers who had settled and built a strong, prosperous, and populous state in a remarkably short period of time.

During this same campaign swing, Douglas made a lengthy speech on October 1, 1860, in Lafayette, where he expressed amazement at the level of partisan and sectional divide he found among Americans. "Our country has never been more bountifully blessed than during the present season," he said. "In the midst of this abundance, and surrounded by prosperity which ought to make any people grateful and happy for such blessings, we are amazed to find sectional strife and discord disturbing the different portions of the country. It cannot be denied that there are causes in operation which are steadily alienating the people of the south from those of the north. . . . My object is to inquire of you what are the causes of this irritation and what the proper remedies to restore harmony."[40]

Douglas said he took it for granted that his audience, like him, sought the preservation of the Union "to transmit our liberties unimpaired to our posterity." That said, he quickly moved to what he believed was the cause of the "divide" and "irritation" to be found among Americans: "I affirm, without fear of contradiction from any intelligent and impartial man that the causes of this sectional strife are to be found in the attempt on the part of Congress to control the domestic institutions of the people."[41] He declared, "Congress has never touched the slavery question without producing discord and ill-feeling. Such discord has continued just so long as Congress has interfered with that vexed question. Whenever Congress has abandoned all interference and banished the slavery question from its halls and remanded it to the people, peace and harmony have been restored."[42]

Noting that Indiana had decided the "slavery question" for itself by not allowing the owning of slaves, he wondered aloud, "Why should Congress interfere with the question of slavery?" He drew applause with his summation that in Indiana, "having determined that question for yourselves, you have performed your whole duty and ought to be content to allow everybody else to decide it for themselves, and mind your own business and let your neighbors alone."[43] He derided Republican claims that newly added territories to the United States should not be allowed to allow slavery and that such questions should be answered by the people in the territories themselves.

"What good has been done to the white man by this agitation? What good has been done to the Negro?" Douglas asked. "I know the evils resulting [from such agitation] and I desire to know what good there is to compensate for those evils? Among the evils you find is this alienation of feeling between the different sections of the country. You find that this slavery agitation, this hostile feeling has entered into the family circle and separated brother from brother—it has entered the legislative counsels and produced strife and discord. . . . It has entered the house of God and separated brethren of a common faith. . . . These are the evils that have resulted

from this agitation. How long can this agitation continue and yet the Union be preserved? You are frittering away one tie after another which binds our people together, until almost the last vestige is gone."[44]

The more he spoke, however, the more Douglas revealed that a major issue undergirding the "slavery question" was not just confined to states' rights or to tamping down discord among Americans. Drawing loud applause and cheers from his audience, he asserted that "a Negro descended from a slave parent is not a citizen, and cannot be. I do not think a Negro is a citizen. I do not think a Negro ought to be a citizen. I believe this to be a white man's government, made by white men, for the benefit of white men, and should be administered by white men and nobody else."[45]

Addressing the rising rebellion in South Carolina, Douglas drew continued cheers when he said Indiana residents should not seek to impose their views and laws on that state, especially since there were few blacks in Indiana (by his estimation). Rights for blacks could not be granted safely in South Carolina "where slaves outnumber the whites two to one. Hence, you people in Indiana take care of your own Negroes, give them such rights as you choose, and then mind your own business and let South Carolina alone. Let the people of South Carolina take care of their own Negroes, make their own laws, mind their own business, and let you alone. Do that, and there will be peace between South Carolina and Indiana!"[46]

Lest Douglas think his presence in Indiana was altogether welcome, news dispatches from some of the state's Republican newspapers indicated otherwise. The *Williamsport-Warren Republican* reported on Douglas's visit to Lafayette in particularly unflattering terms, repeatedly refer-

LIBRARY OF CONGRESS

Bust of Douglas over Northern Democratic Party's presidential campaign shield, 1860.

ring to him as the "Little Giant" with "the swaggering manners of a pot-house politician" and his audience as "an ignorant mob."[47] The report also indicated that a good portion of Douglas's audience consisted of curious Republicans who wanted to witness firsthand "the man who broke up the Democratic Party" and that his appearance in Lafayette was accompanied by a band playing a song similar to a funeral dirge, along with "feeble cheers" from the audience. Noting an audience of "not more than 4,000" gathered at the Tippecanoe County Courthouse to hear Douglas, the Republican dispatch reported, "Douglas mounted the stand and remained in an upright position in order to afford the multitude an opportunity of seeing him. His face wore a troubled expression,

as though disappointed in the crowd and the enthusiasm of his reception. . . . Judge Douglas after clearing his voice with a lemon, commenced a rehearsal of his clam-bake speech in defense of 'my great principle.' We shall not insult the intelligence of our readers with even an abstract of his speech."[48]

Not surprisingly, a Democrat-controlled newspaper, the *Logansport Democratic Pharos*, provided a more positive review of Douglas's appearance in the region. The newspaper noted that a friendly crowd greeted Douglas despite a problem he was having with his speaking voice, aggravated by speaking in a light rain at Lafayette. Similarly, it reported "a large crowd greeted him at the depot at Logansport, on the arrival of the train, along with the Logan Brass Band, which volunteered for the occasion. Judge Douglas in a few words expressed his deep regret that the state of his health would not permit him to address the democracy of Cass County, as he greatly desired to do, [and] the train moved off amid strains of music and the enthusiastic cheers of the people."[49]

Andrew Johnson

Though elected to the U.S. House and as governor of Tennessee, it was during Johnson's tenure as a U.S. Senator from Tennessee, and the rising tumult about the issue of slavery, that cast the beginning of the end of Johnson's political career in his home state. By 1859 secession of the southern states continued to loom, and Johnson gained note among northern political leaders for his remarks in the U.S. Senate that stood in contrast to most of his fellow southerners: "I will not give up this government. . . . No; I intend to stand by it . . . and I invite every man who is a patriot to . . . rally around the altar of our common country . . . and swear by our God, and all

Andrew Johnson portrait, circa 1860s.

LIBRARY OF CONGRESS

that is sacred and holy, that the Constitution shall be saved, and the Union preserved."[50] When he failed in his efforts to block a popular vote in Tennessee on secession, he campaigned unsuccessfully for his state to remain in the Union. In June 1861 Tennessee left the Union to join the Confederacy. Eventually Johnson's home (and his personal slaves) were seized by Confederate loyalists, and he accepted appointment as the military governor of Tennessee, while spending most of his time in exile in Ohio and Kentucky.

Lincoln's 1860 running mate, U.S. Senator Hannibal Hamlin, had served admirably as vice president and was willing to run again. However, Lincoln sought a War Democrat as a running mate as a symbolic gesture toward unity in what remained of the Union in 1864. While Lincoln had expressed his trust in Johnson, a pro-Union Democrat, he remained "suspect" among many Northern supporters of the president, and particularly so among Radical Republicans. As the 1864 campaign began, Johnson made numerous appearances in Indiana on behalf of the Lincoln-Johnson ticket heading the coalition National Union Party. In October 1864 Johnson made brief appearances in Indianapolis, Logansport, Mitchell, Seymour, Tipton, and Vincennes. At Logansport and Indianapolis, Johnson appeared along with U.S. House Speaker Schuyler Colfax of Indiana with "Andy Johnson speaking from one stand and Schuyler Colfax speaking from the other, the crowd being well divided. Johnson spoke about three hours, making a powerful argument in favor of the Union ticket and an earnest appeal to the patriotism of honest Democrats who have been divided," the *Indianapolis Journal* reported.[51] During his visit to Indianapolis, Johnson visited the "Sanitary Fair" display at the Indiana State Fairgrounds and spoke even though his voice was failing him because of so many open-air speeches in the cold autumn air. Johnson told his audience that America could not let stand the Southern rebellion, saying he could "not entertain the thought that the graves of Washington and Jackson should be left in the keeping of traitors, through any degrading and dishonorable settlement of the difficulty forced upon the country" and that "he did not believe our blood could ever grow so thin, our hearts so timid and our arms so feeble as to permit the triumph of the rebellion."[52]

Johnson thanked Lincoln and the people of Indiana for their support of his position on the Union Party's ticket, noting that he had paid a dear price for his positions on the Southern rebellion, having lost his personal belongings in his home state of Tennessee. "If the present Administration should be overthrown and the opposite party prevails in the coming election," said Johnson, "it would be, in effect, the triumph of Jeff Davis. The only hopes of that party [the Democrats] are based on the misfortunes of the government. They can only rise upon the sufferings and blood of your brothers and sons."[53]

Later, at the Cadle Tabernacle downtown, Johnson regained his voice and delivered a fiery address in which he declared that "no armistice and compromise" could be reached with the South, and that despite Democratic claims that the war had been a failure. Johnson said, "The war for the Union has not been a failure, [but] had reclaimed territory [to the Union]."[54] The cheers offered for Johnson that night signaled what was to come—Lincoln and Johnson were easily elected to lead the nation in the November 1864 balloting, carrying Indiana by a wide margin. The Democratic nominee, General George B. McClellan of New Jersey, did little active campaigning (none in Indiana) and carried only three states in the final tally.

Upon Lincoln's assassination and Johnson's elevation to president, Johnson initially gained significant support for his efforts to reunify the Union as quickly as possible following the war's conclusion. Although at odds with Radical Republicans who sought to enact sweeping civil rights for blacks in the North and the South, including voting rights everywhere, Johnson pushed forward with initial Reconstruction efforts. A little more than a year into his presidency, however, Johnson was in trouble with congressional Republicans and looked instead to northern Democrats for some solace. With support waning for his moderate approach to Reconstruction among powerful northern Republicans, Johnson embarked on the "Swing Around the Circle" in August and September 1866 that brought him to several northern communities, including Indianapolis. His Indiana visit prompted an interesting and surprisingly violent and unpleasant "welcome," despite the fact that he traveled the Hoosier state accompanied by prominent Civil War leaders for the Union and Lincoln loyalists: Secretary of State Seward (who survived the assassination attempt made on him the day Lincoln was stricken), General Ulysses S. Grant (popular among moderate Republicans despite being a political novice), Admiral David G. Farragut (the admiral famed for his phrase, "Damn the torpedoes, full speed ahead!"), and General Solomon Meredith (commander of the Iron Brigade of the Army of the Potomac, who had won distinction for his actions at the Battle of Gettysburg).

Johnson's train first entered Indiana across the northern third of the state en route to Chicago and other points in the West, including a brief stop at Michigan City. Although he traveled through Saint Joseph County, the home of Colfax, the Speaker of the House joined other prominent Indiana Republicans in ignoring the president's presence in the state. Days later, following appearances in Saint Louis, Johnson reentered Indiana from the west as he moved east rolling across Illinois, reaching Terre Haute just after 4:00 p.m. on September 9, 1866. The *New York Times* reported that Johnson's train halted at Terre Haute "for a few minutes" and that "thousands of people had congregated, notwithstanding the rain was falling at the time. Many were on horseback."[55] The president spoke briefly from the back of the train, making note that the welcome at Terre Haute was not just for him, but evidence of the importance of the questions facing the nation regarding Reconstruction. "We have just passed through a perilous and fiery ordeal," Johnson said. "We have just come out of a rebellion and the new duty devolves upon you and the government to restore peace and the Constitution to a people recently divided. The cry comes up, 'What shall be done?' The great object in suppressing the rebellion was to recover peace and to uphold the doctrine that no states have a right to secede, they all being states of this Union; and now, that the rebellion in the South is suppressed, there is a cry at the other end of the line that the Union is dissolved and shall not be resumed." Johnson added to the cheers of the crowd, "I come in the name of the Constitution. I come with the flag of the country, not with twenty-five, but thirty-six states. Who in this vast assembly would stretch forth his impious arm and strike the flag from one or all the states?"[56]

He added, "My fellow countrymen, I stand here today as I did in the midst of the rebellion; and I call upon you to rally to the support of the country, for the time has come—the rebellion having been suppressed which threatened the dissolution of the Union—when we must decide whether the Constitution shall be obliterated or rubbed out, and a consolidated government established in its place. This is the issue before the American people. The time has come when we must say whether or not we will continue to be governed by the Constitution of our fathers. . . . We say to all of you, let the Constitution be preserved as our fathers made and handed it down to us."[57]

Moving east, the president's train stopped briefly at Brazil in Clay County, with the *Indianapolis Gazette* reporting that the crowd gathered was repeatedly reminded by Farragut that they were greeting "The President of the United States" and "This is Andrew Johnson, gentlemen!" Few cheers emerged and "with blushes, [Johnson] retired chop fallen into the car."[58] At 6:00 p.m. Johnson's train reached Greencastle, where a crowd estimated at more than 4,000 gathered near the train depot to see the president, who promptly introduced Seward, Grant,

and Farragut. Although the crowd expected that Johnson might make a few remarks, the train began slowly pulling away after only a few moments, with Johnson bowing and waving his hat, acknowledging the cheers.[59]

By nightfall Johnson and party reached Indianapolis. The downtown streets near Union Station and the Bates Hotel were crowded with supporters and the curious. Once at the hotel, Meredith introduced Johnson from the same balcony where Lincoln had delivered his last remarks in Indiana en route to the presidency in February 1861. Reporters noted that audience members continued to call for the introduction of Grant and noted that the applause for the general greatly exceeded that offered for Johnson, Seward, Farragut, or Meredith. In his introductory remarks, Meredith declared, "It affords me pleasure, Mr. President, to assure you that the

LIBRARY OF CONGRESS

Johnson takes the oath of office as president in the small parlor of the Kirkwood House hotel, Washington, D.C., April 15, 1865, following Lincoln's assassination.

great body of the people of Indiana approve your plan for the restoration of the Union. It is plain, simple and just."[60]

Despite Meredith's warm remarks welcoming Johnson to Indiana, reporters noted that "a few groans, huzzas . . . cries for General Grant and some rude remarks" were heard as the president stepped forward. Speaking over the continued cries for the general, Johnson started to speak: "It is not my intention to make a long speech. If you give me your attention for five minutes," but he was interrupted by the continued cries for Grant and others making rude remarks calling him a "traitor" and demanding that he "shut up." Understanding the audience could not be quieted in order that he could speak, "the President paused a few moments, and then retired from the balcony." Johnson had had enough and went back inside the hotel and took his dinner while loud

After leaving the White House, Johnson returned to Tennessee. In 1875 the state's legislature elected him to a seat in the U.S. Senate.

activities continued in Illinois Street outside, the New York Times reported.[61] "Some disturbances occurred with lamented results. Pistol shots were fired, by which one man was wounded in the eye and another in the knee. According to the best information obtainable, a Marshal on horseback was seen riding along the line of march and evidently giving directions, as the men soon thereafter stretched out their ranks," the Times noted.[62] The crowd (that at its maximum topped more than 10,000) finally broke up around 10:00 p.m., although additional media reports surfaced that Grant at one point reappeared on the hotel portico to demand the demonstrators not only comport their behavior, but also disband.

An account in the Indianapolis Gazette reported that Johnson's efforts to speak were "a good joke" and that "he was hooted, groaned and hissed down, and compelled again to retire into the room. The blinds of the parlor windows were then drawn, and the fiasco of the 'Presidential reception' closed. The excitement was intense; never has Indianapolis seen such a terrific scene of tumult and confusion."[63] The Gazette described the events that followed as "what may be fairly termed a riot," with multiple persons reported having suffered gunshot wounds, "and the firing of the pistols having the effect to stampede the crowd . . . the street cars bore their loads rapidly away from the vortex of the seething tumult, and the riot was stopped in a few minutes."[64]

Troubling headlines began emerging in the East from Johnson's tour, designed to rally support for his Reconstruction ideas. The New York Times called it "The Disgraceful Scenes at Indianapolis" and noted, "This is the first unpleasant day the party has had since it left Washington."[65] The Associated Press dispatch indicated, "All the journals of this morning deeply regret the disturbance of last night in connection with the reception of the President and his suite." The *Indianapolis Journal* reported, "Had such a scene been anticipated, the most strenuous efforts would have been made by Union citizens to prevent it; but in such a mass and jam there was no possibility of doing anything with the excited people after the uproar commenced." The *Indiana Herald* offered, "It is evident the whole thing was preconcerted, rumors of a disturbance having been rife throughout the day."[66]

At 7:30 a.m. the next morning, September 11, 1866, Johnson was rested and ready to try again and offered departing remarks at the hotel, but before a much smaller audience of only 1,500. An AP dispatch said, "Better order could not anywhere have prevailed among so large a number." The beginning portion of Johnson's speech that morning was the one he had planned for the night before. The president said he sought to "see as many of my fellow citizens as I could, and ascertain the public sentiment with reference to the questions now agitating and distracting the public mind. I have been toiling since the difficulty commenced to preserve the Union of these States and see that the Constitution was enforced. So far we have succeeded. But on the crushing of the rebellion we find the revolutionary spirit manifesting itself on the other end of the line. . . . I stand here today where I stood two years ago; I stand precisely where I did then, on the Constitution and the Union of these States. There I intend to stand."[67]

Although he did not address the disturbance from the night before, the president did remark, "I had hoped the time had arrived when all people had become patriots, and would stand up for the country regardless of party shackles and party consideration. . . . I had hoped the time had come when we all could rally around the Constitution, and lift ourselves above party to preserve our country, one and united. Fellow citizens, as I did two years ago, I do now proclaim that none of the states have the right to go out of the Union. Though they may revolt or rebel, they have no constitutional right to go out of the Union. Whether this doctrine is assailed South or North, I plant my feet firmly against it."[68]

Concluding his remarks, and likely feeling less than welcome in the Republican territory of Indianapolis, Johnson said, "Let me say in parting that I have always placed my hopes and confidence in the integrity, virtue and intelligence of the great mass of the American people, who through my public life of a quarter of a century— where is the man who can say with truth that Andrew Johnson ever betrayed or proved false to a friend? I leave you here today, believing you will never desert me."[69]

Before departing, the president called on Seward to make some remarks, his first speech ever to the people of Indiana. Calling on Seward made sense—Grant was departing the train at Indianapolis to go on a separate train to Ohio— and some effort to overcome the ugliness of the night before had to be made. Seward did not waste the occasion, offering lengthy remarks of more than fifteen minutes that dwarfed the brief remarks the president had just offered. "I am very sorry that the circumstances under which I appear before you are unpropitious to speaking now," Seward said. "But there is time enough left before passing from this platform . . . to call your attention to a single proposition, which, if it shall gain the suitable reflection of the American people, may guide us safely through the subsiding excitements of a great and desolating war to the calm and happy shores of a blessed peace. It is this: In all other states and nations since the beginning of time, governments have been called into being without popular consent by reason of the want of education, intelligence and equality among the people. . . . We have been blessed with a measure of intelligence and equality and with a form of government in which all needful progress and reform can be carried on through the instruments of peace and peaceful measures."[70]

Seward also addressed the "curse of slavery" in the nation that he had hoped could be removed by peaceful means; however, "the party upholding slavery thought it right to resist by revolutionary means. The consequences we have just passed through, with the blessings of God and the valor of the people of the United States. . . . We have passed through a reform through the agency of free speech and the ballot box, putting down and suppressing a revolution which sought to overthrow the Government." He added, "If the attempted revolution at the South had succeeded it would have been said that we in the North had not bravery, virtue and intelligence enough to prosecute any reforms through the constitutional agency of free speech and free suffrage. Give us free speech and a free ballot and there is no measure of social amelioration and progress which the American Government cannot accomplish."[71]

Seward identified a specific task for the people of Indiana, noting that it had "become a border State" and "the result of the war is that the Southern States are to be henceforth loyal to the Union, while prejudices and passions still reviving the contest seem to make the Northern States unfraternal and jealous." Indiana residents "have it in your power to mediate between the extremes" and help the nation avoid falling into another Civil War, he said. Seward, declaring Johnson to be "the Cato of our nation," said that God and goodness had prevailed, rather than "Jeff Davis and other ambitious revolutionary leaders" and called on Hoosiers to sustain

the president. "By sustaining him by your free suffrage—that all of you can do—let him be sustained and then the world will marvel to see how quietly and noble our ship of State will glide through the streams of the revolutionary sea, and attach herself to the ancient wharves, where she may be expected to rest henceforth in safety and unchangeable tranquility," Seward declared.[72] The *Indianapolis Gazette* said "the aged Secretary was listened to with profound silence, and retired with the good will, at least, of all who heard him."[73]

With that, the "Swing Around the Circle" continued south from Indianapolis, with a succession of quick stops at Franklin, Edinburgh, Columbus, Seymour, and tiny Vienna in Scott County. Cannon fire and a large crowd of about 5,000 residents greeted Johnson's party as it arrived in Jeffersonville. Johnson left the train and mounted a specially constructed stand and offered similar remarks to what he had given in Terre Haute and Indianapolis about his belief in the "sacredness" of the nation's constitution. Johnson told his audience that "now that the war is over, and those [Southern] states have accepted the conditions recommended," he believed it was important to veto the "Freedmen's Bureau Bill" that he said would have set four million slaves free, only to further enslave them in crippling legislation. After about a ninety-minute visit to Jeffersonville, the president's party mounted a wharf along the riverfront and made their way to Louisville, Kentucky, for events there. After leaving Louisville later that evening, Johnson boarded the steamer *States* (which made a half-hour stop at Madison, Indiana) en route to Cincinnati. One dispatch from Madison indicated that Johnson's reception there resembled what he had received in Indianapolis and overshadowed an overwhelming welcome he had enjoyed in Louisville. Referring to the president as "his Accidency," Johnson was again greeted at Madison by shouts for Grant and Farragut and "during the confusion, an excited returning veteran, well known in this place, stepped up to Mr. Johnson and assured him that 'he was not desired to speak, and he should not.'"[74]

The rest of Johnson's tour did little to garner support, and multiple impeachment efforts were undertaken by Republicans in the House of Representatives (in 1867) and the U.S. Senate (in 1868) due to vitriolic disagreements with Johnson about Reconstruction issues. None of those efforts resulted in removing Johnson from office, as was the goal. For the November 1868 election, Johnson wanted to revive the National Union Party that had nominated Lincoln and Johnson in 1864, but most Republicans had returned to the Republican Party and stood in contrast to the Democratic Party. Southern votes were not to be included in the 1868 election, and so Johnson had calculated that the coalition party previously successful would be his best choice. His attempts to occupy a space between the Radical Republicans and the Democrats, however, were unsuccessful, and he failed not only to gain the nomination of any coalition party, but also his original Democratic Party. His final months in the presidency continued to be controversial, including pardons offered to many Confederate figures (former Rebel president Jefferson Davis, for one). Johnson left office on March 4, 1869, declining to attend the inauguration of his Republican successor, Grant. Returning to Tennessee, Johnson, in 1874, was elected again to the U.S. Senate, the only former president ever elected to the Senate. He served only from March to July 1875, however, dying after an unexpected stroke at his daughter's home in Elizabethtown, Tennessee, on July 30, 1875. He was sixty-six years old.

Ulysses S. Grant

As one of the most popular and honored Union generals in the Civil War, Grant was a likely candidate for president, although one who had a surprisingly tough fight gaining the office. A native of Ohio and raised to adulthood in Galena, Illinois, Grant was politically inactive and somewhat inclined to the Democratic Party in the years prior to the Civil War. Recruited by Illinois leaders to help answer Lincoln's call for a Union force to defend the nation against the secessionist states after the events at Fort Sumter, Grant proved to be an effective, brave, and powerful military leader, rising quickly through the ranks. At the time of Lincoln's murder in April 1865, Grant had been serving as commander of all Union forces for a year. Grant accepted the surrender of the Confederate States from General Robert E. Lee at Appomattox Courthouse,

LIBRARY OF CONGRESS

Circa 1880 portrait of Ulysses S. Grant.

Virginia, on April 9, 1865, preserving forever his prominence in American history. Grant traveled with President Johnson in the Reconstruction years following the Civil War as the nation sought to bind its wounds, but did so mostly to appear loyal to the Union rather than loyal to Johnson.

For the 1868 election, Johnson was crippled politically and summarily unwanted by either his own party or the Republicans, opening the door for a unanimous selection of Grant by the Republicans as the party's presidential nominee. Grant's nomination solidified the Republican Party with Radical Reconstruction, supporting voting rights for freed slaves in southern states (while leaving the issue open for northern states to resolve). Nominated to run with Grant as vice president was House Speaker Colfax of Indiana. Grant did not engage an active campaign, con-

sistent with tradition at the time, and still swept to victory in twenty-three states. His stated support of black suffrage made a difference as Grant received a huge plurality among the nearly 700,000 blacks who voted in a presidential election for the first time and made Grant the first president elected while carrying a minority of the white vote, defeating former New York governor Horatio Seymour, the nominee of the "reunited" postwar Democratic Party.

While en route from Illinois to Washington, D.C., just after securing victory in the November 1868 general election, the president-elect was greeted with large, enthusiastic crowds, including one at Fort Wayne, where Grant's special train stopped briefly. "He is traveling in a quiet manner, it being his request that no notice should be given of his coming," the AP reported. "Despite the efforts of the railroad officials to carry out his

Wood engraving showing Grant and Schuyler Colfax taking the oath of office administered by Chief Justice Salmon P. Chase on the east portico of the U.S. Capitol in Washington, D.C., March 4, 1869.

LIBRARY OF CONGRESS

wishes, there was gathered at the different towns along the route thousands of admiring friends of the President-elect, who greeted him with the booming of cannon, the music of bands, and tremendous cheering."[75] News reports indicated Grant did not speak during the train stop at Fort Wayne (or subsequent ones in Ohio), instead he tipped his hat and waved to the crowd.

In April 1871 Grant paid an unexpected visit to Indianapolis for an event at the Academy of Music in support of U.S. Senator Oliver P. Morton, a fellow Republican. During the event, the two Indiana politicians, Morton and Governor Conrad Baker, spoke longer than the president. Grant, known as a man of few words when it came to public speaking, limited his remarks to essentially explaining how he had ended up in Indianapolis: "I thank you heartily for this cordial greeting, for I assure you it is unexpected. When I left Washington it was with the view of going to St. Louis without stopping by the way, but on meeting your distinguished Senator, Governor Morton at Pittsburgh, he requested me to remain here during this day. That I consented to do, expecting to see you and the people of Indianapolis turn out to greet your Senator, and not expecting a greeting to me. I therefore leave him to thank you in more appropriate terms than I could do if I were to try."[76]

In his remarks Morton expanded upon how the president's visit had been made possible and noted that "the vast assemblage tonight to meet him is evidence, stronger than any words that can be uttered, of the distinguished esteem and regard in which he is held by the people of Indiana, and such evidence as I believe greets him wherever he goes."[77] Earlier in the day Grant also stopped briefly at the Indianapolis Board of Trade to shake hands. Following his speech on behalf of Morton, the president boarded his train

LIBRARY OF CONGRESS

An 1872 campaign woodcut touting Grant for president and showing vignette portraits of U.S. presidents from George Washington to Andrew Johnson and statistical data for past presidential elections.

at 10:30 p.m. for an overnight trip to Saint Louis.

Five months later Grant traveled through Indiana twice, once en route to a dedication ceremony for the Chicago and Southwestern Railroad at Leavenworth, Kansas. Following that, he conducted a brief stay at his home in Galena, Illinois, and political receptions in Chicago. Grant again moved across Indiana en route to Dayton, Ohio, to greet disabled Civil War veterans at a hospital there. Grant's absence from Washington, D.C., for long periods of time (reflecting his disinterest in the mundane rigors of government service) did not go unnoticed and provided fuel to his critics. As the *Indianapolis People* noted,

Although often criticized for his time in the White House, Grant noted that "the most confident critics are generally those who know the least about the matter criticized."

LIBRARY OF CONGRESS

"President Grant was drifting through the greater part of last week. . . . Ours might very properly be called a drifting administration."[78]

On its way to Kansas, Grant's train moved through Richmond and New Castle, but none of his Indiana appearances included speeches, another aspect of the office he disliked. "President Grant and family passed through New Castle on their way to Chicago last Monday morning," the *New Castle Courier* reported. "The news was pretty well generally circulated a few hours before train time, and the whole town was at the depot, hoping to catch a glimpse of the great man, or perhaps shake his hand. The President's palace car was attached to the rear of the train and the rear platform was so arranged that he could show himself to the crowd without being overwhelmed by the rabble." Grant "submitted to a course of hand-shaking from the crowd," the *Courier* reported, and "even the ladies pressed forward and thought themselves happy if they got a squeeze at his little finger. Mrs. Grant, being unwell, did not make her appearance."

The news account added, "The President has grown old rapidly under the pressure of his official duties, as everyone remarked who was familiar with his face in war times, but there is nerve enough left in the man to fight a good fight against the enemy yet."[79] Commentary about Grant's appearance was not limited to his age. The *Brownstown Banner* (declaring itself an "Independent Democratic" newspaper) openly declared that many in Washington, including members of Congress, were disturbed by Grant's drinking of alcohol.[80]

The *Fort Wayne Daily Sentinel*, a Democratic vehicle, offered negative accounts about Grant's visit to New Castle and Anderson, making the claim that in heavily Democratic Anderson the local postmaster "and other government officials"

ran through the city's downtown district calling out, "Grant is coming! He will be at the depot in 20 minutes!—failing to raise a crowd in that way, they got out a brass band and then only succeeded in getting out about two hundred curiosity hunters."[81] The *Sentinel* also reported that "one little incident occurred worthy of notice. An enthusiastic radical holding a government office . . . rushed up to the President with his little girl in his arms to shake hands with the President. The President stepped down to kiss the little darling 'for her mother.' But the little girl could not see it in that light. Clasping her hand over her mouth she hallooed out, 'No you don't!' and he didn't."[82]

Despite reservations among some Republicans about Grant's ability to be a charismatic leader for the party and the nation, he easily won nomination to a second term in 1872 and sailed to an easy re-election. For his 1872 campaign in Indiana, Grant relied heavily on surrogates to do his bidding, including Morton, one of the most popular Civil War figures in the state. An event attracting about 10,000 supporters in New Albany was typical as Morton recalled the successes of Grant's first term, noting, "The people have confidence in each other. Individually they are prosperous. Trade is on a firm basis flourishing as never before. The currency is sound, the best ever devised. The taxes have been reduced and yet the fidelity and frugality of the administration have enabled it to pay off a vast sum of the national debt." Morton also referred to a "righteous and firmly-pursued Indian" policy under Grant that "has brought us nearer to quiet on our Indian frontier than ever before, and done much to give honor to the national name."[83]

Addressing the array of allegations of graft and corruption Democrats continued to raise about Grant and his administration, Morton declared, "General Grant is a safe, stable, considerate man of strong common sense [who] gives confidence to all classes. Against all this no policy, no principle nor new proposition is offered. . . . The attack is carried by a general system of slander and detraction. It is a campaign of calumny; General Grant's personal character is traduced in a hundred ways."[84] Expanding on his theme by saying his fellow Hoosier, Thomas A. Hendricks, was perpetuating a lie that Grant had accepted bribes even as he was being sworn in as president, Morton said that Grant was "a man of deep, calm intellect, of strong practical sense, of immense knowledge, endowed with an excellent memory and wide experience and though not a talker, with a faculty of making the greatest and most difficult subjects simple and plain. He is a man of exemplary life as a son, husband and father."[85]

Grant never visited Indiana officially during his second term. As he left office in 1877, he undertook an ambitious two-year world tour that included stops in England, Ireland, Belgium, Germany, France, Italy, Switzerland, India, Burma, Siam, Vietnam, Hong Kong (China), and Japan. At the end of his tour in 1879, Grant returned to his hometown of Galena, but, encouraged by supporters, entertained the idea of a run for a third term as president. In December 1879 Grant presided over a massive celebration in Chicago and then departed for Indianapolis, with his train making water stops and slowing to greet crowds gathered along the rail line to get a glimpse of the former president at Schererville and Crown Point in Lake County, North Judson in Starke County, and Winamac in Pulaski County. His first official stop was at Logansport, a visit proclaimed by locals as "a complete success" despite a cold, heavy rain. The ex-president left the train for a luncheon in his honor at the Hotel Murdock in Logansport and was welcomed by crowds lining

Print of a Republican campaign banner for the Ulysses S. Grant-Schuyler Colfax ticket. Printed at the bottom are the words of Grant's famous dispatch to Washington, D.C., during the Spotsylvania campaign, "We Will Fight It Out on This Line."

the parade route estimated at 10,000.

At the hotel, Grant was welcomed to the city by the mayor of Logansport, but as he was speaking the platform on which the men were standing collapsed. "Mayor [Samuel] Jacobs was well through with his address of welcome when, just as he was in the act of introducing General Grant to the audience, there was an ominous crack, succeeded by a crash, and the structure with its distinguished burden fell, and great was the fall thereof. The occupants of the stand rolled and tumbled over one another and the crowd yelled and laughed at the ridiculous spectacle presented," an account in the *Logansport Journal* reported. "The Mayor, who stood in the corner, wrapped his arm around one of the uprights and was the only one who did not participate in the general tumble. In an amazing short time, General Grant had regained his feet and was introduced to the people. With an ill-concealed grin at the ludicrousness of his position, General Grant commenced one of his characteristic addresses and was getting well under way when the remaining timber under him gave way again, causing another fall."[86]

Grant was polite but brief in his remarks (making no reference to the accident), referring to his just-completed world tour. "Mr. Mayor and gentlemen of Logansport, my return to America has afforded me great gratification and the reception I have received at every point since my first landing upon the shores of my own country, up to my arrival at Logansport, has been a greeting which has been very grateful to me," Grant said. "I assure you that in all my travels, and in all that I have seen, I have seen nothing to diminish my life, my admiration, for my own country, and for my own countrymen. We have in this grand country of ours a great deal to be proud of, and something that makes us prouder and prouder as we see more and more of the other nations of the earth, and are able to contrast our great resources with those of others. Gentlemen, I thank you. Mr. Mayor, I thank you."[87]

After leaving Logansport, Grant's train continued on to Indianapolis and once there the ex-president stayed true to form, commenting only, "I feel most grateful to the citizens of Indiana and the citizens of Indianapolis, and the old soldiers whom I met here, for the hearty welcome which I receive. The two and a half years that I have spent abroad have been, as you say, among all the nations of the globe. In every one of them, I have received the welcome which you have described, but it has been a welcome to my country, when is becoming appreciated abroad as it has not been heretofore, and I am afraid some of your own people do not appreciate it. If they could have a little experience in seeing countries abroad and seeing the difficulties with which a living is procured in many of them, they would be prepared, at least to appreciate ours—the grandest of all countries. . . . I thank the citizens of

Indianapolis, the citizens of Indiana, and the ex-soldiers here assembled for the welcome which I have received."[88]

The guest of honor at a dinner in the Indianapolis home of U.S. Treasurer John C. New, Grant later attended a reception at the Marion County Courthouse, where hundreds of Civil War veterans passed through, shaking hands with their former commander. Grant remained at the courthouse for three and a half hours, shaking hands and talking before briefly attending a choral concert at Roberts Park United Methodist Church on North Delaware Street. He then retired for the night.

Grant, as expected, entered the 1880 Republican National Convention at Chicago as a candidate for the presidential nomination. In a record-setting convention for the GOP, Grant led a large field of candidates on the first thirty-five ballots—the most ballots the Republicans had ever required to settle on a nominee. By the thirty-sixth ballot, Grant's opponents (primarily U.S. Senators James G. Blaine of Maine and John Sherman of Ohio) combined their forces behind Congressman James A. Garfield of Ohio to deny Grant the victory. In the years that followed, Grant turned to penning columns and other writings in order to earn money, having forfeited his military pension when elected president. With no presidential pension provided, he worked for years to recover from the swindles of his personal savings and bad investments. As a means of raising money, Grant undertook writing a personal memoir, which was well received and provided a comfortable sum to his wife and heirs following his death from throat cancer on July 23, 1885, at the age of sixty-three. Grant had just completed the memoir and never lived to see what a literary and financial success it became.

Horatio Seymour

For the 1868 Democratic National Convention, a seemingly reunited party gathered in New York City, including delegates from the former Confederate states of Arkansas, Alabama, Florida, North Carolina, South Carolina, Georgia, and Louisiana, which had all been readmitted to the Union. The Confederate states of Mississippi, Texas and Virginia had not been readmitted to the Union and did not participate in the convention. A crowded field of contenders lined up for the nomination, including Senator Hendricks of Indiana, former congressman George H. Pendleton of Ohio, General Winfield Scott Hancock of Pennsylvania, and U.S. Supreme Court Chief Justice Salmon P. Chase of Ohio. It took twenty-two ballots until the Democrats settled on a compromise choice, former Governor Horatio Seymour of New York. As a twice-elected governor of New York, a pivotal state for winning the general election, Seymour was a common-sense choice.

For his campaign, Seymour undertook more public appearances and speeches than did Grant, partially out of necessity. While Grant had gained acclaim throughout the nation (particularly in the North) as a hero of the Civil War, Seymour was little known outside of New York. On October 20, 1868, Seymour traveled through Indiana from Chicago with a variety of quick stops along the rail line, including one at Lafayette. A highly partisan dispatch from a "special correspondent" for the New York Times referred to Seymour's Lafayette stop as "a great humiliation" and focused on the small size of the crowd. Clearly written by a Republican sympathizer, the Times report from Lafayette indicated an "extremely frigid reception" greeting Seymour and that he "looked rather vexed and disappointed when he reached Lafayette. . . . To the great surprise of every-body, however, less than a thousand persons, a majority of whom were Republicans, gathered around the stand to which Governor Seymour was escorted by a beggarly-looking squad of 40 or 50 White Boys in Blue, a local veterens group. There was a faint cheer when he alighted from his carriage and ascended the stand, and some anxiety on the part of the crowd to see him." The derogatory report continued, indicating "feeble" applause to Seymour's remarks that "left the audience exceedingly cold."[89] Following Seymour's remarks, a delegation of prominent Democrats joined him to make the trip south to Indianapolis. Once in the city, Seymour was carried in a torchlight parade from Union Station to the Palmer House Hotel, where he ate dinner with the White Boys in Blue.

LIBRARY OF CONGRESS

Horatio Seymour photograph from a group of images titled "Seymour at Home."

"My fellow citizens, I left my state in no self-seeking spirit, but with a disposition to discuss before the people of the country the great issues of this campaign," Seymour told his Indianapolis audience. "I left my home, I trust, a patriotic man filled with the love of my country and animated by a wish to serve this people, but my patriotism has been quickened and my love of country has grown upon me as, in the course of my journey, its magnificence and its vast extent has burst upon my mind."[90]

Seymour added, "When this day I was borne across your broad prairies, when I saw the magnificence of your natural advantages, when I felt how much Almighty God had done for the people in your great territory, its rich soil, its magnificent lakes, its wonderful rivers, I felt that human passions and human infirmities should not in any degree impair the blessings which we, as a people should enjoy." Seymour also said his remarks were intended to express unity and to address what he viewed as "party passions that are today to such a degree arraying one portion of the American people against the other and producing those animosities, those wicked charges, those unkind aspersions, and those cruel imputations," and called upon his fellow citizens to seek "the spirit which animated our soldiers when they went forth to battle for our Union, and the spirit which animated them as they lay bleeding on the battle field looking upon and loving the nation as they were suffering and dying."[91]

Specifically addressing his comments to any Republicans in the audience, he said, "My Republican friends, you may be mistaken in your sentiments of us. We may be wrong in argument and views, but we were not untrue to our country. If the vast organization known as the Democratic Party was not loyal, did not love our country, what would become of this glorious Union? On

LIBRARY OF CONGRESS

Horatio Seymour.

the other hand, I am ready to say, if I did not know and feel that the great Republican Party was made of truly honest men, acting upon their convictions, harsh as they have been towards me; if I did not feel they sought the good of their country, I too, should despair of this republic."[92]

Despite the presence of Indiana's Colfax on the Republican ticket, the general election race in

LIBRARY OF CONGRESS

An illustrated cover for an 1868 campaign song written for Democratic candidates Seymour and Francis P. Blair Jr.

Indiana was incredibly close; Grant garnered 51 percent to Seymour's 49 percent. Grant, however, easily swept to victory elsewhere (including in Seymour's home state of New York). Seymour quickly faded from prominence nationally, but remained active in the Democratic Party in New York and campaigned briefly for Grover Cleveland in 1884. Following a long illness, he died on February 12, 1886, at the age of seventy-five.

Schuyler Colfax

Born and raised in the first decade of his life in New York City, Colfax and his family moved to tiny New Carlisle in western Saint Joseph County in 1836 when he was a teenager. The young Colfax showed an early interest in journalism,

and by age nineteen he was named editor of the *South Bend Free Press*, a Whig Party newspaper (later renamed the *Saint Joseph Valley Register*). His writing caught the attention of many, including Horace Greeley, editor of the *New York Tribune*, who published some of Colfax's stories about politics in the "western" state of Indiana.

By age twenty-six Colfax had gained enough notice to be named a delegate to the state constitutional convention in 1849 and by 1855 had made the transition from the dissipating Whig Party to the Republican Party and was elected to his first term in the U.S. House of Representatives. A strong abolitionist, Colfax's writing continued to gain him notice among party faithful across the nation, and in 1862 he was elected Speaker of the House. His role as Speaker was forever immortalized in history—in 1865 it fell to him to announce proudly the passage of the Thirteenth Amendment that abolished slavery.

During the 1868 Republican National Convention, the party's choice of Grant as its presidential nominee was a foregone conclusion, but the vice presidential nomination was more in doubt. Colfax, however, prevailed on the sixth ballot to run with Grant, with the congressman's roots in the battleground state of Indiana aiding his chances considerably. On July 30, 1868, Colfax arrived in South Bend for a grand welcome from his fellow Hoosiers. The throng exceeding 10,000 residents overwhelmed Colfax, a man known for being good with words, who said, "I confess I scarcely know how to speak to you this afternoon in response to this most enthusiastic welcome you have given me. There is one word in the English language, brief but impressive; it thrills every heart that is not calloused and hardened; it makes the life-blood course through our veins more rapidly—it is the word 'home.' If there is any man in this broad land, from the

Atlantic to the Pacific, who has cause to love his home, it is he who now addresses you, ever kind, ever considerate, ever devoted, ever affection-ate." He noted that as the train carrying him sped west from Washington, D.C., through the Allegheny Mountains and into the Ohio valley, "there was one thought that filled me full—it was the thought of my own beloved home on the banks of the beautiful St. Joe. I have been absent from you much in the past few years, but your friendship has not been measured by my presence with you. Abroad, as well as at home, it has upheld me."[93]

Colfax made extended references to the heroism and leadership of Grant in the just-completed Civil War, saying, "You know how my faith has been in the times of national and party reverses, never flagging, never quailing, never abating. I have faith today. I think I can see in all the signs of the times the triumphant victory that awaits the great leader of our Union hosts, rivaling in its brilliancy and its beneficent effects upon our country the brilliant victories won by him against the armies of the rebellion. I believe an over-guiding Providence holds the destinies of our Union in His Hands. He has preserved as a Union when treason seemed to threaten our existence; He strengthened our hearts for every sacrifice at our hands; He lifted us to a noble plane of patriotism because He had determined, as I believe, that treason should never rule in this fair land of ours."[94] Colfax reiterated his "Radical Republican" views, distinguishing his commitment to the Union from those only interested in a shortened path of "genial hand-shaking and conciliation" instead of strict requirement that the former Confederate states restate their commitment to the Constitution. "We have built our steadily-increasing majority in this country by unity and harmony," he said. "I am for reconciliation,

nationally, on the only safe obedience, obedience to the Constitution, the laws and the guaranty of liberty to all, justice to all, and protection to all. For this reason I voted while in the House as your representative for every bill relieving from political disability all in the South who asked it and professed their obedience."[95]

Colfax spoke at length and said he wanted cheers raised for Grant, rather than himself. Drawing laughter from the crowd, Colfax said, "I have nothing to say about myself as a candidate, for I suppose to tell the truth that if General Grant should be elected, I should probably also be so. They say [Grant] can't make speeches. . . . He has made one speech—when the Committee on the Chicago Convention announced his nomination. . . . It was a speech of only eight lines, but there were two lines in it that were as weighty, that were as valuable as if they had filled the many volumes . . . they were these: 'If elected, I shall have no policy to enforce against the will of the people.' That is a declaration worthy of the cause."[96]

Before arriving in his home in South Bend, there was a demonstration of support for Colfax as he made his way northwest through Indiana via Fort Wayne. There he made brief remarks from the train saying, "I am very glad to meet your smiling faces this afternoon. When I arrived, a few moments ago, I could not have spoken for I was too hungry. Now I cannot speak for I am too full! But I am glad you have allowed me to eat my dinner before giving me this reception. I do not intend making much of a speech, and I think the engineer of our train is favorable to short speeches!"[97] Crowds continued to greet Colfax's train along the route from Fort Wayne to Chicago, and then the next day from Chicago east to South Bend.

By October the fall campaign was under way

in earnest, and Colfax traveled widely across the nation on behalf of the Republican ticket, as Grant did not actively campaign. In Indiana Colfax visited familiar territory and new haunts. In Logansport, once a part of his congressional district, he was greeted by a large, friendly crowd estimated at more than 15,000. The *New York Times* reported that his remarks there "were full of patriotism, devoid of bitterness and truly eulogistic of the glorious record made during the past seven years by the Republican Party. . . . Mr. Colfax is the idol of his old constituents. They are proud of him. He is grateful. They feel that, as he says, they took him up when young and tried and trusted him, giving him a chance."[98] In an over-dinner interview with the *Times*'s correspondent in Indiana, Colfax wavered from his previously stated commitment to not ridicule or name-call the Democratic, or Copperhead, Party. "It has always been my belief that we should beat them, but I never felt before as I now do, that in this Presidential election we will effectually bury this Democratic Party forever beyond the hope of resurrection They have this campaign openly allied themselves with treason, and must go down with all its odium," Colfax told the reporter.[99]

Given Indiana's role as a battleground state in the 1868 election, Colfax's strategy to reach beyond his base in northern Indiana made sense and found him speaking in Indianapolis and locales south of the capital, where he had not previously traveled as a congressman. As a result, a massive rally for Colfax staged at Cambridge City in Wayne County caused writers for the *Indianapolis Journal* to declare that it was "the most enthusiastic greeting ever given to any man on Indiana soil." They further reported that speaking stands were erected in the town for the "acres of people" gathered and "the anxiety to see and hear Mr. Colfax was so intense that an hour before

the time for the speaking to commence, twice as many people as could be reached by any man's voice were collected about the stand from which he was to speak. It was with the utmost difficulty that a way was made for him to the stand. The audience would not wait for him to mount the platform, but got upon the seats in spite of the efforts of the marshals to keep order, and stretched their necks to get a glimpse of the distinguished and much loved Indianian." The *Journal* reporter also noted that "there is something peculiar in the affection which the people of Indiana feel for Schuyler Colfax. It is not the kind of mingled curiosity and admiration with which men generally greet those who have become celebrated, but partakes of the character of that affection which people feel for kinsmen and tried friends."[100]

For his speech at Cambridge City, Colfax did not miss an opportunity to thank the citizens of Wayne County for their support of the Union during the war. He said that "the patriotic heroism of your sons, who left happy homes to crush the power of the rebellion and treason in this land, is known in the South and in the North, and in the East and in the West. A nation's gratitude is due to you, who so freely gave your bravest and best to go forth to the field of battle and die that this Republic might live."[101]

Turning to the coming election, Colfax told his fellow Hoosiers, "This is the time, and this is the place, and this is the eventful campaign that must tie fidelity to principal. The eyes of the nation are turned to Indiana as the battlefield of this contest. Ohio and Pennsylvania are safe in this election, and if in this contest we win the victory that your devotion to our country deserves . . . it will be as it was in the days of the rebellion, when the hosts of treason were vanquished and beaten back, and the champions of liberty and patriotism were in pursuit." Colfax said he gave thanks to God for the Republican Party and said "had it not been for that party, your country itself would have been blotted out from the map of the world. Your country lives today because when traitors threw down the gauntlet of defiance and attempted to sunder the golden chain which held the Union together, the Republican Party said, 'the last man and the last dollar shall be given but this rebellion shall be crushed, and the nation saved.'"[102]

Later in October, Colfax went deep into the heart of Democratic turf in Indiana for a rally and speech at New Albany along the Ohio River. While in the city, Colfax had a room at the Israel Hotel and met with a long line of local dignitaries (of both parties) and Republican faithful. He later went on a tour of all of the manufacturing facilities in the community and ended his tour with a downtown rally that drew an estimated ten thousand residents and guests from nearby Jeffersonville and Louisville, Kentucky. The *New Albany Daily Commercial* reported that while crowds were large for Colfax's visit, "we have not attended a Republican meeting during the canvas [campaign] at which so few Democrats were present. The Democracy seemed to be afraid to hear the eloquent words of truth that they knew would fall from the lips of the distinguished speaker."[103]

For the first half of his speech, Colfax took the unusual step of reading aloud a report from the *Louisville Courier* that suggested his antislavery views were perhaps not as strongly held as believed, and that he had ignored attempts by the paper in the past to clarify his positions. Colfax denied both allegations and took on an account in the *New Albany Tribune* that referred to him as "smiling Colfax." He replied, "I do not deny the soft impeachment. I have lived a happy life and I thank God he has given me that happiness. . . . When I lay my head upon my pillow at night, I

LIBRARY OF CONGRESS

Writing about his time in Congress, Schuyler Colfax noted that he had never been "brought so palpably and tryingly into collision with the embodied scroundrelism of the nation as while in Congress."

am happy in the approval of conscience, and can rejoice to reflect that no man that lives on God's footstool is trod down in the scale of humanity by the influence of the Republican Party. The endeavor of that party has been to lift up, instead of trample down, to give all an equal start with us in the race of life, and this done, God judge between us."[104]

"The glory of a free government," Colfax added, "is that it is the bulwark of the humble and poor, because it can go down to the cabin of the poorest and most friendless, and it will protect these with the same power that it will defend the richest man in New Albany. This is what gives us hope in the future, because we know that under the administration of our hero of the century, Ulysses S. Grant, who next March will be sworn in as President of the United States, which under the providence of God he saved, we will have that just and equal protection."[105]

Hitting on familiar themes, Colfax asked his audience to recall that "when the storm cloud of war broke over our land and the degenerate sons of the Republic lit up the torch of civil war, when they tried to ruin the country they could no longer rule; when this country was rocked to its very center by the shock of contending armies; when men proved themselves unworthy of their birth and sought to trample in the dust the banner of beauty and glory; when they turned themselves into homicides filled with hate against the land that protected them from their childhood . . . forgetful of their allegiances to the country, forgetful of their oaths, they dared to lift their fratricidal hands against their country; and when

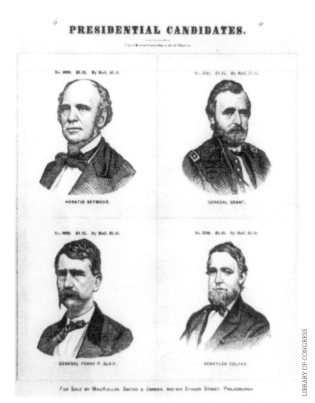

Head-and-shoulders portraits of the candidates in the 1868 presidential election: Horatio Seymour, Ulysses Grant, Frank P. Blair, and Schuyler Colfax.

they did so, from the Atlantic to the Pacific came the best and the bravest of the land to protect their country and protect the flag."[106]

Grant and Colfax were successful on Election Day and became the youngest duo ever elected to the nation's highest offices at ages forty-six and forty-five, respectively, a record not broken until the election of Bill Clinton and Al Gore in 1992.[107] As vice president, Colfax played an unremarkable role in the Grant administration and made more news for how his tenure ended than anything he had done while in office. On July 4, 1871, Colfax was the honored guest of the citizens of Valparaiso, in part because the Porter County community was en route between Colfax's home in Saint Joseph County and Chicago. From a speaker's stand on the courthouse lawn, Colfax said, "No one of you who have come up here from your homes can be more grateful than myself for the opportunity and the occasion which brings us together." He disclosed that his physician had told him to remain at home rather than to make a speech, but the significance of Independence Day was too great to resist, he said.[108]

As the 1872 campaign approached, rumors continued to grow about Colfax's alleged interest in running for president rather than vice president. Part of Colfax's ambition was driven by the fact that Grant, though a beloved war hero, was an uninspiring and lacking public speaker, while Colfax was brimming with the skills of a journalist and orator. The Colfax speculation was fueled by a resolution from the State Republican Convention in Indianapolis in 1872 that urged the nomination of Colfax for president. Colfax's ambition, then, served as part of his downfall as he narrowly lost the race for renomination for vice president at the Republican National Convention in June 1872 to U.S. Senator Henry Wilson of

LIBRARY OF CONGRESS

Massachusetts. Further hurting Colfax's effort was a lack of active, open support from Grant, who publicly appeared neutral on the choice of his running mate, and the continued linkage of Colfax's name to the growing Credit Mobilier scandal (a controversy about railroad stocks made available to various members of Congress, including Colfax, in exchange for their support of rail construction projects).

Humiliated by his defeat to Wilson, Colfax eventually returned to South Bend in June 1872 and was welcomed home once again as a local hero. The *South Bend Tribune* reported that thousands surrounded the train carrying the now lame-duck vice president home to Indiana. As was characteristic of Colfax, his remarks that day reflected his affection for the people of Indiana and for the welcome he had received. He said he spoke in order "to thank you for this renewed evidence of the regard in which you have held me for so many years, and to tender gratitude for a lifetime of unwavering confidence and affectionate esteem. . . . I very much preferred to come to my home quietly, and to retire to that private life which stretches before me now; but, found on my arrival, that in spite of that protest, you had determined to convince me that here I had not only a home in your midst, but, far better, a home in your hearts."[109]

Reflecting the melancholy nature of the event, Colfax remarked, "It is easy to greet the rising sun, but it requires more disinterested attachment to pay the same respect and the same regards for the setting sun, politically." He added, "All of you have read the Proceedings of the (Republican) Convention . . . and you are aware that another than myself was selected as the Republican candidate for Vice-President of the United States. With the action of that Convention I have no fault to find. Ups and downs are the fate of all in political life. . . . After a good many 'ups' in my life, it was fitting that I, too, should have my 'down'; but I feel more for those who nobly supported me, and for my friends here, than for myself."[110] Colfax pledged his full support for Grant and Wilson as the nominees of the Republican Party and backed his statement up by agreeing to be a principal speaker for the GOP campaign. He declared to his fellow party members, "Let not the work of the past be endangered by the disbandment of the workmen; but let us work as we have so often heretofore worked for our principles, and vote cordially and unitedly for those faithful standard-bearers, Grant and Wilson."[111]

As a former vice president, Colfax was a popular lecturer and campaigner for the Republican Party and died on January 13, 1885, in Nebraska while preparing to return to South Bend from a speaking engagement. His death, attributed to a heart attack, felled Colfax at the age of sixty-one.

Horace Greeley

A still crippled Democratic Party met in convention in July 1872 to determine a nominee to challenge Grant's re-election and took an unusual path. The party nominated one of its most outspoken critics, newspaper publisher Horace Greeley of New York, in a convention that lasted just six hours. Officially the nominee of the newly formed Liberal Republican Party, the Democrats seemed to accede the election altogether with the selection of Greeley. The quick and odd move to place Greeley at the top of the ticket did signal, however, the first of many slow and painful steps of the Democratic Party away from its anti-Reconstruction positions that dominated the party in the years after the Civil War. Greeley's selection, over three other northern candidates, was also noteworthy for the lack of any significant southern influence about the party's choice.

A prominent advocate of the Whig Party, and later the Republican Party, Greeley was the powerful publisher of the *New York Tribune* and a strong advocate for the abolition of slavery. Greeley's interest in the 1872 presidential election seemed driven in part by his disgust with what he viewed as ongoing graft and corruption among members of Grant's administration. In late September 1872 Greeley brought his aspiring campaign across the Ohio River from Louisville, Kentucky, to Jeffersonville. Newspaper reports were unfavorable, with one indicating that fewer than fifty people gathered outside the Galt House Hotel in Louisville to bid Greeley best wishes on his journey north. At Jeffersonville, a small crowd of five hundred gathered outside the Burnet House Hotel for a formal reception and to hear remarks by Greeley.

Emphasizing his roots as a farmer, a mechanic's shop assistant, and later as a printer, Greeley said the sympathies of his lifetime had been with workingmen and those who "are required to subsist by their own manual industry. I have meant to be in my politics as in my business the friend of labor." Greeley said he had spent most of his public life opposing slavery "because I thought slavery inconsistent with the rights, the dignity, the highest well-being of free labor. That might have been a mistake, but it was at any rate an earnest conviction. So when our great trouble came upon us, I was anxious first of all for labor, that the laboring class should be everywhere, free men. I was anxious next that our country's unity might be preserved without bloodshed, if that were possible, [but] by means of bloodshed, if that dire alternative should be forced upon us."[112]

Declaring that his life had been an open book by means of his published writings, Greeley defended his views about Reconstruction and the fracture that had developed between him

LIBRARY OF CONGRESS

Horace Greeley, 1871

and Radical Republicans. "No one who heard my utterances or listened to them in any way directly after the close of the war," Greeley said, "when I pleaded for mercy, for magnanimity, for forbearance, for the speediest possible effacement of all sores and sorrows from the public mind, no one heard me then can doubt where I should stand today, no one." Greeley said he stood against all lawlessness and violence and against the Ku Klux Klan, saying they needed to be driven "down with a strong hand, for mercy to them is quite different from mercy to the quiet, peaceable men of the country."[113]

Following the Civil War, Greeley said he argued for "universal amnesty" and said that doing so did not mean he was against punishing those who had committed crimes, such as murder, during the Civil War, "or committed acts contrary to the laws of humane war," but said of Confederate foes, "I have no feeling of vengeful wrath after they laid down their arms and complied with all reasonable requirements of the government and of public safety. For security and peace, anything; for vengeance and wrath, nothing, nothing." Greeley concluded his remarks by asserting the following:

> The time has come when we should proclaim that amnesty. Having secured the rights of every black man in the country, so that he is just as good as you or I, we should give the white man a chance too. Let us say to those who were mistaken, who were on the wrong side: "Fellow countrymen, you were on the wrong side; you undertook to divide a country that ought not be divided. You were mistaken, but that is all over; the country is reunited, all are free now; let us make you free also. Let us all together, every one of us, be citizens of this country, with equal liberties and privileges so far as men can give them. If God has imposed disabilities, we can't remedy that. We can only say the law is just as good for the colored people as for me or you. Their standing in courts is the same as yours; their oath is the same; let everyone tell his story and let the jury, giving each story due weight, determine which is correct, and let not color entitle to favor or respect."[114]

After leaving Jeffersonville, Greeley met a similarly meager but receptive audience at Columbus, where he addressed the widespread belief that Republican bribes were being used to solicit votes in southern Indiana: "Everything I have seen and heard since I crossed the mountains cheers and encourages me. I have faith in the good people of Indiana. I do not believe they can be bribed out of their convictions and

I am quite certain they cannot be bought. So I feel certain that your verdict will be given in the coming election for equal rights for all men, including those for our fellow citizens now disenfranchised."[115]

From Columbus, Greeley spoke next at Franklin, where he emphasized he was not in favor of a change in the nation's financial policies despite reports being raised that indicated otherwise. "It is hard to understand how many considerable number of people could have been led, as they undoubtedly have been, to believe that the election of one President more than the election of another could have a disastrous effect on the finances [of the nation]," Greeley said.[116]

At Indianapolis, Greeley greeted both an audience at Union Station as well as visited the Board of Trade, where he addressed agriculture and the gold standard. Later that evening, a torchlight parade was held for Greeley that ended at the statehouse with a speech focused on graft in the Grant administration or an issue that he described as "purification." Describing the "deadly peril" of the corruption in the government as a "cancer eating into her vitals," Greeley explained at length the scandal emerging from the Credit Mobiler of America issue related to the construction of the Union Pacific Railway. "I would fix your attention on this as a sample of the means whereby scheming, selfish, avaricious men contrive to glut their own greed," he said, "while they talk of public interest and public beneficence."[117]

Greeley said the scandal represented an effort by business leaders and members of the federal government "to pay themselves twice the fair cost of entirely building and equipping the [rail] road, and building the road with proceeds of the bonds loaned by the government, they proceeded to divide among themselves the other bonds, equal to amount for which Congress had made a mortgage on the entire road, and by these means, 20 or 30 million dollars were divided among the parties, and all that money so divided, we are called to pay. . . . So on this day, the people of this country are paying some millions per anum out of their hard savings for interest on these bonds loaned to the Pacific Road; paying this money as interest to meet the vast sums divided among these greedy men, among themselves as dividends of the Credit Mobiler of America."[118]

Greeley's Indiana speeches were part of some two hundred he made that fall, all while wearing a white overcoat meant to emphasize his views on the need for "purification" of the federal government.[119] His appearances in Indiana were not his first. In his autobiography Greeley wrote about a taxing trip he made across northern Indiana in October 1853 after attending and speaking at an agricultural fair at Indianapolis and trying to make a second speaking engagement on the topic of temperance at La Porte. He wrote about his adventures, including traveling sixty-four miles via a hand-driven rail car while trying to get from Lafayette to La Porte, in a colorful essay titled "A Night Ride Across the Prairies" and admitted he was not made for the manual labor of moving a hand-rail car.[120]

On Election Day, November 5, 1872, it was clear Greeley's campaign had moved few voters—he captured only 43 percent of the vote, doing only slightly better in Indiana, gathering 47 percent to Grant's 53 percent. It was just part of a

Greeley relaxes with his family. Although Greeley is often credited for coining the phrase, "Go West, young man, and grow up with the country," it was first stated by John Babsone Lane Soule in an 1851 editorial in the Terre Haute Express.

LIBRARY OF CONGRESS

troubling period in Greeley's life—his wife, Mary Young Cheney, dying unexpectedly on October 30, 1872, while her husband campaigned for president. A month later, on November 29, the grieving Greeley died at Pleasantville, New York. His death came before the Electoral College met and formally certified Grant had been reelected.

Rutherford B. Hayes

Twice elected governor of Ohio, Hayes went into the 1876 Republican National Convention perhaps thinking as everyone else did that Speaker of the House James G. Blaine would be the party's nominee. In fact, after the first ballot, Blaine led among all candidates, including Indiana's Morton, who was placed second. Morton's fortunes faded fast on subsequent ballots as Republicans debated the electability of Blaine against the likely Democratic nominee, New York Governor Samuel J. Tilden. By the sixth ballot, a compromise candidate had emerged—Hayes—who bested Blaine and the only other remaining candidate, Treasury Secretary Benjamin Ristow. The 1876 campaign is noteworthy for its close finish and is also remembered as one where both candidates did little active campaigning.

Although Indiana was again a key swing state in the race, neither Hayes nor his opponent Tilden spent time in the state. Instead, Hayes stayed home in Fremont, Ohio, and relied on surrogates, including Morton in Indiana and U.S. Senator Roscoe Conkling in New York. One of Hayes's Indiana surrogates was noteworthy—former slave and abolitionist leader Frederick A. Douglass, who spoke at Crawfordsville on behalf of Hayes on October 2, 1876. An account in the *Crawfordsville Saturday Evening Journal* mentioned Douglass's "beautiful diction, his cogent reasons and his magnetic eloquence" as he made "an earnest appeal for his race" and urged his au-

dience to support Hayes for president and General Benjamin Harrison for Indiana governor.[121]

On Election Day, Tilden and his Indiana running mate, Thomas A. Hendricks, won a plurality of the popular vote, including carrying Indiana by a narrow margin of only 5,515 votes. Hayes appeared to have come up short until the votes from Florida, Louisiana, and South Carolina were finally decided, surprising many by favoring the Republican nominee. Hayes lost the popular vote, 51 to 48 percent, but with the three southern states locked up he won the Electoral College vote by a margin of one, 185 to 184. The Great Compromise of 1877 also helped—Republicans agreed to withdraw federal troops from former Confederate states and the Democrats pledged to support Hayes as the winner.

Once elected, Hayes paid his first visit as president to Indiana at Richmond in September 1877, after learning Morton was bedfast and seriously ill recovering from a debilitating stroke at the home of his brother-in-law, John A. Burbank, the governor of the Dakota Territory. Hayes's special train arrived in Richmond from Dayton, Ohio, and local residents were excited to see the president, but were subdued with their welcome, quietly lining the streets from the depot to 115 North Twelfth Street, where Morton was convalescing. Hayes visited with the senator for only ten minutes and "as he entered his carriage, President Hayes briefly thanked the citizens of Richmond for the cordiality of their reception and the evident good will expressed by it," the *New York Times* reported.[122]

The *Cincinnati Enquirer* provided a more detailed report, picked up nationally by many newspapers, that indicated Hayes met privately with Morton and that the "President became at once deeply affected, and advancing to the bedside took the Senator's hand in his, and addressing him in affectionate terms stooped over and kissed him on the forehead. Mr. Morton addressed the President by name and spoke of his gratification at seeing him there."[123] Morton's doctor called the meeting between the two men to a conclusion, and "then the President's emotion again overpowered him. Great choking sobs swelled up in his throat, the tears chased one another down his cheeks, he vainly tried to express his feeling in words, and seizing the Senator's hand he pressed it long between his own, impressed another kiss upon his forehead, and with choking utterances, bade him an earnest, agonizing farewell and hurried from the room sobbing aloud."[124] Although Morton had pledged to the president he was eager to return to his work in Washington, D.C., it was not to be. Although well enough to be transferred to his own Indianapolis home in October, Morton died there on November 1, 1877.

Less than a month later, Hayes paid another visit to Indiana, this time via the river ferry *Sherley*, which departed Louisville, Kentucky, and arrived a short distance away at Jeffersonville on September 18. Although Tilden had carried Indiana in the election less than a year earlier, "Whatever might have been our individual opinions as to the settlement of the great and important contest which waged so warmly from November until March; whatever we may have believed ought to have been the result of that contest, we now, one and all, recognize in you the President of the United States. And now, in behalf of the citizens of Jeffersonville, Indiana, and for myself individually, I bid you a cordial welcome to our city," Jeffersonville Mayor L. F. Warder intoned.[125]

Hayes responded graciously: "In the very few short, off-handed addresses which I have been required to make since I left Washington, I have endeavored always to give utterance simply to two ideas—to give encouragement to two sentiments. I have supposed it was true, as the Mayor has said, that men of all classes, of all political opinions, would be satisfied with the general government, whose course generally throughout shall favor these sentiments: First—That the general government shall alike equally regard the welfare and happiness of all sections of the country. Secondly—That the general government shall, by its influence, by its example and its power, regard alike the equality of all men of all races. If so, I believe that all sections, all races, may come together again in the fraternal harmony of the days of Washington, Franklin, Jefferson, and Adams. I thank you for this reception."[126]

Following his remarks, Hayes and the rest of his party moved along Front Street, where about one thousand Jeffersonville students stood alongside the street and sang in unison, "My Country, 'Tis of Thee." Colorful banners adorned several of the downtown buildings, including one on the Laun Store that read, "Hurrah for Hayes, our noble President; conquer we must, because it is just; this is our motto, in God we trust; hurrah for R.B. Hayes." At the *Jeffersonville National Democrat*, a decidedly Democratic enterprise, the banner read, "Democratic to the core, but a firm, ardent supporter of Hayes' policy."[127] Local reports indicated as many as ten thousand residents and visitors turned out to see Hayes. While in the city Hayes visited boatyards along the Ohio River and a local glass manufacturing facility, where he witnessed casting of plate-glass windows.

In October 1879 during a "western swing," Hayes visited Indianapolis as the guest of honor for an "industrial parade" through the downtown district. Hayes rode in the parade briefly, bowing and tipping his hat from his carriage, and then

LIBRARY OF CONGRESS

Rutherford B. Hayes

joined his wife, Lucy Webb, to view the parade from a stand along Meridian Street amidst a crowd estimated at 40,000. Following the parade, a luncheon reception was hosted by Benjamin Harrison and his wife, Caroline Scott, at their Delaware Street home. Later, Hayes spoke at the Indiana State Fairgrounds, where he commented on his departed friend, Morton: "And when we come to speak of Indiana among the old friends and neighbors of Oliver P. Morton, we cannot pass without pausing for a moment to pay tribute to his memory. Morton as a Senator and as a debater absolutely matches Morton as a leader of a political party, and as to this my friends of the Democratic Party will agree with my friends of the Republican Party. There was not a living man in his time who was above him . . . his power before an audience like this was wonderful. Crippled as he was, from necessity sitting in a chair, he was want to hold spell-bound thousands of his countrymen by the hour. No other man under like circumstances could accomplish what he did in this respect, and yet it is not because of that I mention his name . . . but to make this simple and truthful statement, that no other Governor in any other state under such difficulties as he encountered bore up the flag of the Union as it was borne up by Oliver P. Morton."[128] The president's remarks indicating the "crippled" nature of Morton referred to the stroke the senator suffered in 1876 that left him partially paralyzed for the last year of his life. The day's events in Indianapolis concluded with a spectacular fireworks display at dusk to honor the president and his wife.[129]

In 1880 Hayes kept his pledge not to seek a second term and backed the winning candidate, James A. Garfield, as his successor. Hayes attended the December 1885 funeral for Vice President Hendricks in Indianapolis, and the *New York Times* commented on his appearance noting, "Ex-President Hayes has become somewhat stouter and his beard is whiter than when he was last in Indianapolis, five years ago. He talked with various gentlemen in the lobby of the Denison Hotel, and attracted much attention. He was dressed very plainly, and had the appearance of a well-to-do farmer, rather than a statesman. He said that he was well-acquainted with Mr. Hendricks, and was inexpressibly shocked to hear of his sudden death."[130]

In August 1888 Hayes was the honored guest of the Maumee Valley Monumental and Historical Association, a group interested in preserving the rich military and pioneer history of Fort Wayne and Allen County. After praising the wide array of local and state dignitaries present, Hayes said, "My friends, one of the objects of this association is to call attention to what has here been done in the past, and to the great names and early history and the actions and deeds of those that had not great names—for the great work at last is done by the plain men and the plain women that endure the hardships and encounter the dangers required to settle, to rescue, to bring up to civilization, a country like this. Let us see to it as one of the lessons of this occasion that we shall know all about Anthony Wayne—there is not a greater character in Grecian or Roman or Jewish history, or one that surpasses him in all that ennobles and graces heroic character." Hayes noted that Americans had widely embraced the idea of monuments and remembrances for those who had fought in the Civil War, calling it "wise" and "patriotic work that has been done by our country to mark the graves of the men who fell in the war for liberty and union" in more than sixty cemeteries across the nation. "It is right that they should be remembered; but, my friends, we who are connected in one way or another with the men who settled this valley can but recall with more or less sadness the face that the men who fought at Fort Wayne or near it, at Fort Meigs, at Standing Rock or at the battle of Fallen Timber[s], have not been treated as the men who fought in '61 and '65 have been treated," Hayes suggested. "Let a just government remember that when a man comes up and signs the roll and takes the oath he gives his life if necessary to save his country. Let it be understood that that country and its government are always ready to care for him and his, while he lives and to mark suitably the place that contains his remains when he dies."[131]

"Ex-President Hayes was the picture of health," the *Fort Wayne Sentinel* reported about Hayes, who had been out of office for almost a decade. "His hair grows whiter, but otherwise time seems to deal lightly with the former chief executive. He had a pleasant word for nearly every caller and chatted with characteristic modesty with his friends."[132]

Hayes paid his final visit to Indiana in November 1892 for the funeral of Caroline Harrison in Indianapolis (just three months before his own death). Following his single term as president, Hayes remained active in public life for several years, including leading discussions about "the Negro question" as Americans continued to reconcile the great divisions that had erupted during the Civil War. He died of a heart attack at his Ohio home on January 17, 1893, at the age of seventy.

Samuel J. Tilden

Tilden had to fight hard for everything he won in 1876, including the Democratic nomination for the presidency; he defeated Hendricks on a second ballot at a hotly contested convention, and the Indiana governor was nominated to be

Tilden's vice presidential candidate. The strategy was clear—use Tilden and Hendricks and their presumed popularity and political strength in both of their home states (New York and Indiana), added to a strong southern vote, to win the White House. Tilden did no active campaigning, as was the tradition, but Hendricks was dispatched frequently throughout Indiana and elsewhere to rustle up votes. Hendricks's position on the ticket excited a lot of Indiana Democrats. In his hometown of Shelbyville the locals set about erecting the "tallest pole" in the state's history to commemorate the Tilden-Hendricks ticket. The pole, measuring 229 feet tall and 26 inches in diameter at its base, bested a 120-foot pole constructed by Shelbyville Republicans for the same election. After the election, local Democrats continued to show some enterprise by cutting up the hickory pole and offering the pieces for sale as Democratic walking canes.[133]

Thomas A. Hendricks

Hendricks, born in Ohio but who settled in Shelbyville, was a lawyer and former member of the Indiana General Assembly (1848–50), a former member of the House of Representatives (1851–55), and a senator from Indiana for one term between 1863 and 1869. Proving the old maxim that "the third time is the charm," his third attempt to be elected governor of Indiana succeeded in 1872, and Hendricks became the first Democrat to be elected governor of a Union state since the close of the Civil War. His rise to the governorship made him an attractive running mate for Tilden in 1876. In his July 24, 1876, acceptance letter for the vice presidential nomination, Hendricks stated his agreement with not only the party's adopted platform, but its selection of Tilden. "Permit me . . . to express my satisfaction at being associated with a candidate for the presidency who is first among his equals as a representative of the spirit and of the achievements of reform. . . . The people know [Tilden] to be thoroughly in earnest; he has shown himself to be possessed of powers and qualities which fit him in an eminent degree for the great work of reformation which this country now needs; and if he shall be chosen by the people to the high office of President of the United States, I believe that the day of his inauguration will be the beginning of a new era of peace, purity, and prosperity."[134]

As Tilden did no active campaigning, Hendricks's work in Indiana was particularly important. A September 1876 speech in Fort Wayne was typical of the approach he employed. Hendricks opened his remarks by asking his audience, "What is your opinion on the subject of reform? What are your ideas on the subject of purity in the government? What think you as to the number of public officers necessary? What do you say about the expenditures of the government?"[135] These were themes that allowed him to highlight Tilden's reform efforts in New York. Hendricks accused the Republicans of wishing to go back in time—referring to their complaint that the United States had a "Confederate Congress" because "there were soldiers of the old rebel army among its members. This is as it should be. We cannot and would not seek to alter the voice of the constituencies that sent those men to Washington. The people there had elected them. . . . We hear it frequently charged that while all Democrats were not rebels, all rebels were Democrats. . . . This is not true, but is a little unfortunate for the Republican Party the voices of these same men, as far as they can be heard from behind the cross bars of their prisons, are shouting lustily for Hayes."[136] Hendricks added, "This country is like a man suffering from a wasteful and consuming hemorrhage, and these

LIBRARY OF CONGRESS

FOR PRESIDENT.
GROVER CLEVELAND
OF NEW YORK.

FOR VICE PRESIDENT.
THOS A HENDRICKS
OF INDIANA.

Campaign lithograph for Grover Cleveland and Thomas Hendricks.

millions of public plunder well represent the vital blood of the nation. Let it not be sapped and the country die from its loss, but let hope and enterprise move among American industries. Labor seeks employment everywhere, and the people demand a change that it may meet with sufficient reward."[137]

Noted for his ability to turn a phrase, Hendricks's voice rose as he declared, "Our country is more blessed by God than any in the world. In richness of soil, in our salubrious climate, in the wealth of our mines, we stand without a rival, yet poverty is abroad and our laborers throng our streets and demand at our doors the reform we need. Do you want better times? Will you vote for change? Do you want honest men alone to hold office? . . . I believe Governor Tilden to be the right man. He is a stern reformer and a rigid economist. Under his leadership, the evils of the day may be made to disappear."[138]

Despite his best efforts (Indiana did go for Tilden in 1876), Hendricks was not elected vice president that year. He may have questioned whether his national political career was at an end, but good politicians often have many lives. Hendricks remained active in Democratic Party politics and in 1884, still a popular Democrat in an important state needed to win the presidency, Hendricks was tapped again for vice president, this time as Grover Cleveland's running mate. A large delegation of Democrats brought the news to Indianapolis on July 12, 1884, and Hendricks seemed excited about the upcoming campaign. He told his fellow Hoosiers that the Democratic Convention had "selected two men to carry the banner; and leaving that Convention and going out before the people, the question is, will you help carry the banner?"[139] Hendricks said, "I do not expect—I have no right to expect—that I will escape criticism, and it may be slander, of the opposite party. I have not in my life suffered very much from that; but I come before you, Democrats, Conservatives, Independents, all men who wish to restore the Government to the position it occupied before these corrupt times, and to all such men I make my appeal for your support for the high office for which I have been nominated." Hendricks declared that Cleveland "is a man of established honesty of character" who would lead efforts to open the nation's books and reveal whether those in high office had ever "yielded to temptation."[140]

In rather candid remarks about the coming campaign, Hendricks said, "For myself, I had no expectations. In no sense was I a candidate for any office whatever" and that "not that I want the office to which I was nominated, for you know

that I did not desire that, but somebody must be nominated for Vice President to run on the ticket with the candidate for President; and when a ticket is presented to you, you are called upon to pass judgment upon it in respect to his merits throughout. That is the question—will you support it?"[141] His appeals were successful on the whole, as Cleveland and Hendricks were elected.

Hendricks offered his last address in Indianapolis on September 8, 1885, at the Masonic Hall regarding independence and self-rule for Ireland. Hendricks said he favored self-rule of Ireland by the Irish people: "What shall be the government of Ireland? For many years it has not been a controverted question that Ireland has been dealt hardly by. . . . On the contrary she has been denied the rights of equal citizenship, and has been despoiled of her lands. Every Irishman here to-night, every Irishman in America, is a protest against the bad governing of England toward Ireland. How is it that you are here, having left almost the most beautiful land in the world? Perhaps no part of this globe is more attractive than Ireland, and yet you left Ireland. You are here because you could not get good government in Ireland."[142] Hendricks said the Irish people were correct "to claim the right to make their own laws, simply because they can regulate their own affairs better than any one else can regulate them. So Irishmen on their own soil, for that simple reason, must be the legislators for Ireland."[143]

Fate intervened, however, in the life of Hendricks. During a visit to Indianapolis, he fell ill and died suddenly at his home at the corner of Tennessee (now Capitol) Avenue and West Saint Clair Street on November 25, 1885. He was sixty-six years old. He had served only 266 days in office—one of the shortest tenures for a vice president in American history. Hendricks and his wife, Eliza, had returned to Indianapolis for the Thanksgiving holiday following several official appearances in Chicago. The night before his death, he attended a reception in the Indianapolis home of State Treasurer John J. Cooper and returned to his own home at midnight, complaining of feeling cold and reportedly rested poorly overnight. Hendricks, who suffered from abdominal pain, was attended by a physician throughout the day, but succumbed at about 4:45 p.m. while his wife was out of the room, greeting a caller at their home. As the Associated Press telegraph message reported to the nation, "The end of a long and eventful life had come peacefully and quietly. He lay on the bed outside of the covering, only partially disrobed, with his eyes only half closed, as if he were in a gentle sleep. On his face there were no trace of pain or suffering, but a pallor had come over it that indicated only too plainly that he had passed away. It needed no close examination to tell that he was dead, and Mrs. Hendricks screamed and ran down the stairs." As news spread that Hendricks had expired, "a hundred or more of Mr. Hendricks' close political and personal friends had hurried to the house. Very soon a great crowd collected around the entrance and on the street, and it was found necessary to refuse admission to any and all comers except immediate relatives."[144]

Following Hendricks's death, the vice president's personal physician, Dr. W. C. Thompson, speculated to reporters that Hendricks may have died of "instantaneous paralysis of the brain and heart" but that a postmortem examination would reveal more. "For several years he had not been a robust man and was subject to 'bad spells' as he called them," the doctor told reporters.[145] Other unnamed family friends told reporters that Hendricks was ready to retire from public life and had firmly rebuffed suggestions that he be a presidential candidate in 1888. Hendricks's friend quoted him as saying, "I shall not be a candidate under any circumstances. I was not a candidate for the position I now hold, but it was forced upon me, and now my political ambition is fully satisfied. I want to retire and rest for the remainder of my life."[146]

News of Hendricks's demise reached Cleveland just as he sat down for dinner at the White House. He quickly fired off a telegram to Eliza that read, "The sudden and lamentable death of your husband excites my profound sympathy for you in this hour of your great bereavement, and I sincerely mourn the loss of one so lately associated with me in the execution of the people's highest laws, while the nation mourns the loss of an honored citizen and a faithful public servant."[147] After a hastily called meeting of his cabinet, Cleveland issued a public statement that officially announced Hendricks's death to the nation and noted, "In respect to the memory and the eminent and varied services of this high official and patriotic public servant, whose long career was so full of usefulness and honor to his state and to the United States, it is ordered that the national flag be displayed at half-mast upon all public buildings of the United States . . . and the usual emblems of mourning be adopted for 30 days."[148]

Official state funeral services were conducted at Saint Paul Episcopal Cathedral in Indianapolis on December 1, 1885, although Cleveland did not attend despite his earlier statements that he would go to Indianapolis. He told White House reporters, "In the first moment of the shock of Mr. Hendricks's death, I yielded to my inclination and declared my intention to be present at the funeral. Of course, in reaching that conclusion, I did not put out of view a peremptory press of public business, or what I deemed a sufficient consideration of my duty to the people. The public business I thought I could dispose of by additional application and more hours of work, and I considered it to be my duty to the people to answer a tender sentiment of respect and affection to the dead Vice President, which does them great honor."[149]

News reports offered intricate details of the funeral plans for Hendricks. The Associated Press noted the following:

> On the outside [of Hendricks's home], the crowd increased until it reached a block away from the house in each direction. All the streets downtown were filled with people who hurried about searching for eligible locations from which to see the procession. The side streets were filled with carriages and the usual religious observances of the day were for the greater part not attended. All morning the weather had been threatening but about 10 o'clock the sun came out brightly and continued to shine throughout the day. From the family residence to the Courthouse, where the body now lies in state, is a distance of about six squares and the announcement that the line of the march would be along Washington Street, the main thoroughfare of the city, was sufficient to cause it to be crowded long before the procession formed. The street cars and other vehicles were unable to get through the crowd, and finally by order of the police, they were kept off the street altogether. . . . The hearse drawn by four black horses was covered with silk flags, festooned with crape. Promptly at 11 o'clock the burial casket was placed in the hearse, and the procession slowly moved towards the Courthouse.[150]

Reporters estimated that as many as 25,000 citizens, including thousands of schoolchildren, walked through the courthouse to view Hendricks's open casket placed upon an elaborate bier. For his official funeral to follow, members of the U.S. Supreme Court, cabinet members, leaders of Congress, and former president Hayes were in attendance. The *New York Times* reported, "The interior of St. Paul's Cathedral was draped and decorated with insignia of mourning in a very appropriate manner. At each side of the altar were elaborate and beautiful floral designs, one representing a broken column, with a ladder leaning against it, surmounted by a dove, and the other a very large floral shield, over which were the words, 'The Nation's Loss.'"[151]

Following the Episcopal Mass for Hendricks, the funeral procession made its way north up Meridian Street to Crown Hill Cemetery. The *Times* report indicated, "All along the march, both sides of the street a dense crowd was witnessed. Every available space on the broad sidewalks and in the streets was occupied by the thousands of admirers of the dead statesman. From every window in every story of all the business houses along the line appeared the anxious faces of women and children, who wisely avoided the crowd below them. The roofs were crowded with men and boys who desired to see the magnificent display and add their mite of respect to the memory of Indiana's idol."[152]

With no provision in the Constitution for replacing a deceased vice president, Cleveland served the remainder of his first term without one. Cleveland later backed the Presidential Succession Act, which addressed presidential succession, and placed in line after the vice president the heads of each executive department of the federal government in the order in which the department was created—a system that remained in effect until 1947.

3

The Gilded Age, 1880–99

James A. Garfield

As the 1880 presidential election approached, Congressman James A. Garfield of Ohio already had a new job on his agenda. Members of the Ohio legislature had confirmed Garfield as their choice as the new U.S. senator, with the key backing of former U.S. Senator John Sherman, secretary of the treasury under both President Abraham Lincoln and President Rutherford B. Hayes, and who had visions of being the Republican nominee for president in 1880. Sherman's visions were buttressed by Hayes's stated commitment to serve only one term in the White House. Sherman's support of Garfield for his former Senate seat, however, came with the proviso that Garfield back Sherman for the Republican presidential nomination. Garfield placed Sherman's name in nomination at the GOP Convention in Chicago in June 1880, although the early favorites, James G. Blaine and Ulysses S. Grant, all gathered more votes on early convention ballots, with Sherman placing a distant third. After twenty-eight ballots, neither Blaine, Grant, nor Sherman had enough votes to win the nomination, and none of the three men was willing to budge. Ultimately, party leaders, seeking an alternate candidate, selected Garfield as a compromise candidate to break the deadlock; on the thirty-sixth ballot Garfield won the nomination.

Once Garfield won the presidency in the November election, Sherman won the consolation prize by being selected by Ohio legislators to replace Garfield as the state's U.S. senator. In the early days of his presidential campaign, however, Garfield had work to do to heal some of the divisions in his party. To placate Grant supporters, known as the Stalwarts and led by U.S. Senator Roscoe Conkling of New York, Garfield selected Chester A. Arthur, a customs collector from New York and a Conkling ally, as his running mate. In the election, Garfield and Arthur faced off against the Democratic ticket of Winfield Scott Hancock, a hero of the Battle of Gettysburg in the Civil War, and his running mate, William H. English, a former Indiana congressman and a wealthy businessman in Indianapolis.

Geography placed Indiana in the beginning days of Garfield's campaign. He traveled from the convention in Chicago via train on the Lake Shore Line to his home near Cleveland, Ohio. As the telegraph forwarded the news that Garfield's travels home would take him across northern Indiana, crowds gathered along the rail line, including at Otis, a tiny hamlet in western La Porte County, and an even larger crowd at La Porte, the county seat, where the train stopped. Although the crowd continually called for Garfield to make a speech, he left the public remarks to Ohio governor Charles Foster and General L. A. Sheldon, both personal friends of Garfield. The GOP presidential nominee was introduced to the crowd, but simply waved, removed his hat, and bowed, declining repeated calls to make remarks. A short time later the train arrived at South Bend, where a large cannon was sounded in salute to Garfield, but again he did not speak. At Elkhart, farther east, the train stopped to allow passengers to take their dinner at a hotel while several thousand onlookers surrounded the train at the depot. As the *New York Herald* reported, "There was a band of music on the depot ground, and several thousand people gathered in the vicinity of the depot. General Garfield descended from the car and walked arm-in-arm with Governor Foster to the dining hall. The Indiana crowd did not recognize Garfield, and it was not until after he had arrived in the dining room and commenced eating that his presence was positively known to the mass of people assembled. The throng crowded up to the doors and when Garfield made his exit they gave vent to their hereto pent-up enthusiasm, having at last found the object. 'We are very glad to see you nominated, General,' an ex-soldier said, stepping up to Garfield and shaking his hand."[1]

Garfield was introduced to the crowd by Judge William A. Woods of Goshen, who eventually rose from an Elkhart County bench to the Indiana Supreme Court, and later the U.S. District Court of Indiana. Woods, who had gained position as one of Garfield's top advisers at the convention and traveled with him from Chicago as far east as Goshen, told the throng, "This is your next President, gentlemen!" Despite the introduction, however, Garfield again did not speak, leaving those duties to Foster and reserving any remarks until he reached his home state.

At Goshen, Woods again presided and excited local Republicans had mounted a cannon on a log and "the first discharge dismounted the piece, but the crowd made up in enthusiasm for this mishap."[2] Similar stops were conducted at Ligonier, Kendallville, Waterloo, and Butler as the Ohio line drew nearer. "At Butler, the last station in Indiana, General Garfield suffered the first ordeal in baby kissing," the *New York Tribune* reported.[3]

Garfield's postconvention trip through Indiana was his only personal foray into the battleground state. The importance of the Hoosier vote was emphasized later in July when the Republicans dispatched Interior Secretary Carl C. Schurz of Missouri to Indianapolis to deliver an address considered the launching of the successful fall campaign for Garfield and Arthur. Conkling was also a popular draw in Indiana on behalf of Garfield. An October rally in Indianapolis brought thousands to the city to view the Republican parade (although the advertised appearances of Grant and fellow Civil War hero William Tecumseh Sherman did not materialize).[4]

Another popular speaker for Garfield was Indiana's Benjamin Harrison, a decorated Civil War general. Harrison was beloved across Indiana, so much so that the Republicans counted on him to help dip into Democratic voters in Shelby County, a county always seemingly equally divided between Democrats and Republicans. Harrison was speaking at the Shelby County Courthouse in Shelbyville on October 9, 1880, before a large crowd when a tragic and ugly testament to the strong feelings invoked in the election arose. As Harrison completed his remarks before a massive audience estimated at about five thousand, "Democratic ruffians" in Shelbyville gathered at a tavern near Harrison and Broadway Streets. The *Indianapolis Journal* reported that

LIBRARY OF CONGRESS

President James Garfield

some Shelbyville residents asserted that "General Harrison made an inflammatory speech" to Democrats, although it was given several blocks away from the subsequent riot "and none of the speech was heard by any of the rioters. The riots were taking place on and near the public square during the progress of the Republican meeting at the courthouse."[5]

Soon drinking and political arguing proved a volatile combination, and a fight broke out, requiring Shelby County sheriff Albert McCorkle to be summoned to break it up. Witnesses later reported that McCorkle had gone into the tavern and dragged out eighteen-year-old Edwin Kennedy, a Republican and a local resident known to the police, who was in the bar arguing

Campaign poster showing head-and-shoulders portraits of James Garfield and Chester A. Arthur, with text and patriotic images including an American eagle and men gathered around flag.

LIBRARY OF CONGRESS

with Democrats gathered there. Witnesses said the sheriff appeared to be arresting Kennedy, while the young man begged with McCorkle for his release, promising that he would "go home and make no more trouble" when a large crowd of almost three hundred Democrats surrounded the scene.

While the incident might have actually been a rather typical police action dealing with an unruly drunk, the political environment and the presence of Harrison and the Republican rally nearby inflamed the situation. The *New York Times* reported that "a party of Democratic ruffians assaulted the Garfield Guards [at the Harrison speech], causing a bloody riot, in which five or six persons were badly hurt. In the melee, Sheriff McCorkle of the county was fatally shot through the lungs, and the Deputy Sheriff was severely wounded." Without explanation, the *Times* declared that McCorkle "has been the leader of the riots which have disgraced that Yazoo of Democracy during the past year" and that "he was a Democratic bully of the worst type."[6] Ultimately, McCorkle's death would be viewed locally as a tragedy, prompting a telegram of support from English, who noted, "I mourn with you at loss of your dear McCorkle. You have lost a valuable friend and the Democratic Party a noble worker. You have my sympathy."[7]

The *Indianapolis Journal*'s take on the events of the day in Shelbyville said that "everything would have passed off orderly had not about 300 Democrats made their appearance in town. Embraced in this number was the worst element of the county, a portion of whom, it seemed, had come for no other purpose than to create a disturbance. They commenced shouting for Winfield Scott Hancock and appeared bent on provoking and insulting the Republicans. This continued until the afternoon when they became more boisterous, from freely partaking of liquor, and a collision occurred between a small party of Republicans and Democrats."[8] Kennedy fled the scene of the shooting and was at large for three years until surrendering in October 1883. He was later convicted of a lesser offense upon claims of self-defense against the sheriff and served two years in the penitentiary.[9]

In-state media reports indicated that the fracas at Shelbyville was just the latest in a crude effort by Democrats, the GOP claimed, to steal the election in the state. Another report from Rockport in Spencer County in the final days of the campaign claimed that black citizens attending a Garfield rally at the courthouse were chased, beaten, and shot. The report from Rockport indicated "a mob of two or three-hundred Democrats" set upon black men who had listened to speeches promoting Garfield's campaign, "and another Negro was badly cut at the same time." The black man shot was identified as Uriah Webb, and "as he lay in the street was surrounded by Democrats in uniform swinging their bats and cheering for Hancock."[10]

The emotional outbreaks in the state were reflected in the vote on Election Day, with Garfield scoring a narrow victory by a margin of 50 percent to 47 percent over Hancock. The race was even closer nationally, with Garfield and Hancock both carrying nineteen states, and Garfield winning with a miniscule plurality of approximately 9,000 votes out of almost ten million cast nationwide.

As president, Garfield had few opportunities to visit the states, as he died during his first year in office, on September 19, 1881, about ten weeks after he was shot at the Baltimore and Potomac Railroad Depot in Washington, D.C., on July 2, 1881. The president was leaving Washington on vacation when he was shot by Charles J.

Guiteau of Illinois, a man who had hoped for but was denied a federal job after Garfield was elected. When he was shot, Garfield was accompanied by his two young sons and Secretary of War Robert Todd Lincoln (President Lincoln's oldest son) and Secretary of State James G. Blaine.

Winfield S. Hancock

Hancock of Pennsylvania was a political novice in 1880, but in every right an American hero in the hearts of Union backers as a wounded veteran of the famed battle of Gettysburg—fame that Democrats hoped would help his chances as their presidential candidate in 1880. Like Garfield, Hancock did no personal campaigning in Indiana, relying instead on surrogates to solicit the vote (with the state's early Election Day on October 12 the campaign got an earlier start than elsewhere). The Democrats not only calculated that a "War Democrat" and war hero such as Hancock might attract more northern voters to the party, heretofore lost in bulk to the Republicans, but they also calculated that his running mate, English, was a good choice to attract votes in the battleground Hoosier State.

A score of Democratic newspaper editors across the state were convinced that victory was in sight, as evidenced by emotional appeals to voters appearing in Democratic papers in every city and town. The *Boonville Weekly Enquirer* in Warrick County, in a treatise titled "Stand by Your Colors," declared:

> It is perfectly plain that the leaders of the Republican Party intend to use all means, fair or foul, by the use of corruption, money, supervisors and deputy marshals, to intimidate and bulldoze the people of Indiana into support of the Republican Party. They are desperately earnest in the effort to save their party from the ignominious defeat that awaits it if Democrats maintain the vantage

ground they now occupy. . . . We say to our Democratic friends, let come what may, stand by your colors, support the ticket from Governor on down. . . .vote the Democratic ticket, that is the only hope of liberty and equality, and the man who wavers in the fight, or doubts as to his duty, will have cause to regret his timidity and want of faith in the action of the majority of his party. Let every Democrat do his duty on Election Day.[11]

In support of its claims of potential Republican fraud, the Hancock campaign pushed the Indiana Democratic Executive Committee to forward and publish letters from out-of-state sources alleging the importation of African-American voters to Indiana to tip things in favor of the GOP. The letters included vivid physical descriptions of black men allegedly recruited to leave their homes in Illinois and Kentucky to vote in Indiana. They further predicted widespread intimidation and fraud in the tabulating of votes from Democratic areas. The Boonville editors declared, "It is about time, indeed, for all self-respecting colored men to realize the estimate in which their race is held by the Republican leaders, when Republican agents are sent into the South to purchase outright ignorant Negroes to be shipped northward, like so many cattle, for Republican campaign purposes. The opportunity to protest against this sort of thing is now come. The Republican Party is fond of whispering into the ear of the Negro all sorts of melancholy fate that is to be found for him outside the Republican Party fold, but when it may be readily seen that the Republican Party in Indiana today has no use for the Negro save to vote him."[12]

Charges were equally troubling on the Republican side, with widespread suggestions being made that English, as a founder of the First National Bank of Indianapolis, was selected only for his ability to spread out two-dollar

bills as bribes for votes in central and southern Indiana counties. The Republicans opened their campaign inside a Democratic stronghold, Terre Haute, with Secretary of the Navy Richard W. Thompson, a Kentucky native who eventually settled in Bedford, recruited to sing the praises of Garfield and Arthur. In a speech of more than two hours, Thompson said the Republicans were devoted to an honest election and suggested that even the U.S. military could be engaged to ensure such. "If General Hancock is elected fairly and honestly, of course he will take his seat; but, if he is not elected fairly and honestly, he will not take his seat, and that is all there is about it, and the people of the United States will not be scared or bull-dozed by all this personal bluster as to what the Democrats are going to do," Thompson said. He added that "the right and privilege of every citizen to vote as he pleased in the coming contest would be secured, if necessary, by the exercise of all the power of the Administration, and if need be, by the Army and Navy."[13]

The Republican Party also enlisted a former president, Grant, in its effort to defame Hancock

Banner touting the campaign of Winfield Scott Hancock and William H. English.

LIBRARY OF CONGRESS

and reduce his military record among voters. Though vanquished in his effort to win the Republican nomination, Grant joined in the effort to stop Hancock. "General Grant denounced General Hancock, the Democratic standard-bearer, as media-hungry and a mere puppet of the Democratic elites who would do anything for the spotlight, despite his valiant and extremely able service during the Civil War," noted electoral historian Larry J. Sabato. "It was the first time a former president had actively campaigned for another candidate for president."[14] Regarding the threat of election fraud in Indiana that may be employed to help Hancock, Grant said that leading Republicans were prepared to fight to prevent such fraud and declared, "We must elect Garfield; he is a great man; he has but few intellectual peers in his life. He is every way worthy." Grant said he was hopeful about Garfield's chances, "but I expect to witness the most gigantic frauds in Indiana and New York City."[15]

William H. English

A Scott County native, English enjoyed a brief, varied, but powerful political career in Indiana and Washington, D.C., with his biggest success in the private sector (at one point becoming one of the wealthiest men in the state of Indiana). Although a conservative Democrat, English supported defending the Union against Confederate forces in the 1860s. His position on the slavery, issue, however, was more complicated. English had drafted key legislation regarding the admission of Kansas into the Union, while questions of whether the proposed new state would or would not be a slave-holding state (and/or who would decide that). This legislation resulted in the Kansas-Nebraska Act, which replaced the Missouri Compromise. An early supporter of the Martin Van Buren and James Polk ticket in

Indiana, English served in the U.S. House of Representatives from 1853 to 1861. As the threat of Civil War loomed, English explained that he was in Congress "as one of the representatives of a western State. It is a conservative State. . . . I know that it is the feeling of the people of Indiana that the interests and rights of the South should never be trodden under foot. We do not intend to surrender any of our rights, and we do not believe that the people of the South desire to trespass upon our rights; if they did, we should rise up as one man to resist it, and we would resist it to the last. While we shall be careful to protect our rights, we shall be equally careful not to trespass upon the rights of our brethren in other States. Upon such broad, national grounds as this we can all stand; and if we do, this confederacy will continue increasing in prosperity and glory."[16]

English retired from political life at the outset of the Civil War, but returned to politics in 1880 as the Democratic nominee for vice president on a ticket led by Hancock. English was notified of his nomination while a guest of Hancock at Governor's Island, New York, on July 13, 1880, following a unanimous vote for his nomination at the Democratic National Convention in Cincinnati. In a brief reply, English said, "I will say plainly, and in a very few words, that I accept the high trust you have tendered me. . . . In doing this I fully recognize the great responsibility of this position, the great turmoil and anxiety, the misrepresentation and abuse which are certain to follow. I understand that the resources and power of our political foes of the whole country are to be centered upon us in Indiana, my native State, in one of the earliest and probably the great battles of the campaign."[17]

Once back in Indiana, English issued a longer, more formal acceptance letter from

Indianapolis on July 30, 1880 (the same day Hancock also formally accepted his nomination). In the letter, English referred to two decades of Republican rule of the White House: "Twenty years of continuous power is long enough, and has already led to irregularities and corruptions which are not likely to be properly exposed under the same party that perpetuated them; besides, it should not be forgotten that the four last years of power held by that [the Republican] party were procured by discreditable means, and held in defiance of the wishes of a majority of the people."[18] English accused members of the Hayes administration of open graft and said the nation was prosperous not because of, but in spite of, Republican policies, and that "even the members of the Cabinet are strolling about the country making partisan speeches instead of being in their departments at Washington discharging the public duties for which they are paid by the people." English proffered the idea that it was the Democratic Party, with its ability to attract support from southerners, that could once and for all "restore harmony and good feeling between all the sections [of the nation], and make us in fact, as well as in name, one people."[19]

Republicans made repeated allegations that English's presence on the ticket was meant not only to offset Hancock's short political resume, but also because of his role as an Indiana banker. Historian Kenneth D. Ackerman reported that Republican "scouts" in the final weeks of the Indiana campaign were alleging that "William English . . . was the chief spear-carrier for the payoffs. English is said to be receiving large amounts of money, and those who know him best say that he counts on buying all the votes in the market." Other Garfield campaign officials estimated as many as 30,000 Indiana voters were willing to "sell" their vote and concluded, "Democrats are

IHS, WILLIAM ENGLISH PAPERS, M 98

William H. English

raising heaven and earth to carry the state at the October election, and are relying solely on the lavish use of money in the last two or three days before the election."[20]

Republican newspaper editors did their part. In August they published a number of reports about "judgments and foreclosures" and the tactics used to enforce them by English's bank on various Indiana families and farmers. Under the headline "The 'Poor Man's Friend' in Indiana," the articles attacked English and made for an interesting juxtaposition—business friendly Republicans attacking a Democratic banker for what they suggested were immoral and unkind banking practices that left many Hoosiers owing money for property they had forfeited. The Republicans counted on the socially conscious Christian Church (Disciples of Christ) and its 22,000 members in Indiana to identify with fellow Disciple Garfield and to be off-put by the reports generated about English's business practices.[21]

The Hancock-English ticket's defeat in 1880 ended English's political career. Many Democrats blamed him for failing to deliver Indiana, with the *New York Times* declaring the Indiana vote "the Democrat's Waterloo."[22]

In spite of his national political defeat, English enjoyed continued business success at home, opening the famed English Opera House on Monument Circle in Indianapolis; it was one of the nation's finest facilities, seating two thousand patrons. In the years to come, the opera house served as the backdrop for successive generations of political activity in the state, primarily for Democratic candidates. English died at Indianapolis on February 7, 1896, at the age of seventy-three.

Chester A. Arthur

The nation's twenty-first president spent considerable time overcoming the title of "the accidental President," as he was elevated to the nation's highest office just six months after being sworn in as vice president. A product of the New York political machine and selected by Garfield for the post simply on the basis of political needs, rather than any noteworthy achievements, Arthur was either distrusted or unknown—a combination that ensured he was locked into a single term as president.

Arthur's only known visit to Indiana came due to a happenstance of geography, as the president set out for a "western tour" to visit Yellowstone Park in the summer of 1883. Arthur's party left Washington, D.C., on July 30 and arrived at Louisville, Kentucky, a day later. In Louisville, a delegation of Indiana leaders joined the group, including Lieutenant Governor Thomas Hanna,

as the train moved north across the Ohio River into Indiana. The *New Albany Daily Ledger* took note of Arthur's scheduled trip across Indiana en route to Chicago, planned to maximize opportunities to greet voters along the way. The trip was giving Hoosiers "an opportunity to see and hear and become acquainted with [Arthur], and it may be said that the impression left by him upon the mind of the people thus favored was most favorable," said the newspaper. "It was that the President is a thorough American and an accomplished, genial gentleman. . . . It was apparent, however, to those well versed in political matters that President Arthur is a candidate for the Republican nomination in 1884."[23] Doubts, remained, however, about Arthur's viability as a candidate—many party faithful favored Secretary of War Robert Todd Lincoln or Postmaster General Walter Q. Gresham, a Harrison County native who had also served as a judge on the U.S. Court of Appeals and as Secretary of the Treasury, and Secretary of State under President Grover Cleveland. Both Lincoln and Gresham (along with Treasury Secretary Charles J. Folger) were along for Arthur's trek from southern to northern Indiana in 1883.

Arthur's first stop in Indiana was at the Vincennes Street crossing in downtown New Albany on August 2, 1883. Several thousand residents showed up for an early morning appearance. A twenty-one-gun salute boomed through the morning sky announcing the president's arrival. Interestingly, a lot of attention was focused on the train carrying the president's party. "The train is the finest one ever run over a western railroad," the *New Albany Daily Ledger* declared. "The cars are Pullmans—perfect palaces of luxury, comfort and beauty. The dining car has all the appliances for cooking and is the finest of its kind in the United States. The engine was magnificently decorated with flags and natural flowers."[24] Although Gresham introduced the president, his remarks were scarcely reported beyond a telegraphic message farther north on the line at Orleans in Orange County that "President Arthur was much gratified by his reception at New Albany" and "The President speaks highly of Indiana and pays the state some deserved compliments."[25]

After departing New Albany, Arthur's train made stops at Salem, Orleans, Mitchell, Bedford, Bloomington, and Gosport. If Arthur noticed the overwhelming response his travel companions, mostly Gresham, received at every stop, he did not mention it. At Gosport in Owen County, the president said, "Ladies and gentlemen— I thank you for this kind greeting. This is my first visit to Indiana and I am greatly pleased with the appearance of the State and the people, and I only regret that I have not the opportunity now to become better acquainted with you."[26]

At Greencastle another large crowd gathered and gave three cheers to the president at Hanna's urging. "In a rash moment, [Arthur] began shaking hands with the people, and it was soon evident that he had entered upon a greater undertaking than he had anticipated. The crowd became so great about the car that the platform broke down with a loud crash, and for a time much confusion prevailed, but fortunately no person was hurt and order was soon restored," one news dispatch reported.[27]

At Crawfordsville Arthur said, "I am glad to see you, citizens of Crawfordsville, for I have often heard of your city, and have had the pleasure of personally knowing some of your people. Your reception to us to-day is most gratifying." Lincoln was introduced at this stop as "one of the boys," which drew a big smile to his face, and an enthusiastic audience member rushed to the front of

the crowd shouting, "Hurrah for Gresham! He's the man for President of these United States," ignoring Arthur's own ambitions and apparently with little concern he may insult the president.[28]

At Lafayette, Lincoln addressed the throng, saying, "This is not the first time I have been at Lafayette, and neither is it the first time I have met with a kindly reception here." The *Lafayette Daily Courier* reported that Lincoln "is a rather portly gentleman, with full brown beard and ruddy complexion" and noted that "Mr. Lincoln shows his youthfulness in his manner. He is a gentleman, yet with a tinge of what is known as freshness in his composition. . . . He will with years outgrow what one can now easily overlook."[29]

The same report indicated that the "President's personal appearance is very much in his favor, and the current pictures of him do not do him justice. He is a magnificent specimen of physical manhood, and his manners and conversation are those of a polished and dignified gentleman."[30] Arthur's remarks were notably short as well, saying "I thank you cordially for your kindly welcome, and heartily regret that our stay is so short. I only wish that I could grasp you all by the hand."[31]

A floral arrangement was presented to the president, "a gift of the colored people of the city, and presented by a little colored boy." W. S. Lingle, editor of a local African American newspaper, was allowed to speak and told Arthur that "the colored citizens of Indiana cannot permit you to pass through our beautiful state from south to north without an unobtrusive expression of our deep sense of gratitude to a manly man, a statesman and a patriot. We recall a time when under the old barbarism we made bricks without straw, and as we remember how later on as the irrepressible conflict was precipitated,

LIBRARY OF CONGRESS

An 1881 print of Chester A. Arthur

could observe the ground that had made famous the life of William Henry Harrison. The *Lafayette Courier* reported, "The Indiana delegation pointed out the place where the Indians had come up, the place where the fight took place, the site of Harrison's headquarters, and detailed history like a thread run from a reel. An iron fence surrounds [the site], but no monument has ever been erected." As the train remained in place, "three barefooted urchins came up to the train as it stood on the site of this Indian battle spot," the *Courier* report continued, "and asked to see the president. One of the windows in the car was raised, and the president shook hands with each of them. The urchins grinned and gave one hurrah each."[34]

At Monona in White County, a crowd of three thousand assembled, although the stop was extremely brief. The president was eager to stay on schedule for his planned 7:00 p.m. arrival in Chicago. Arthur's last stop in Indiana, at Cedar Lake in Lake County, featured "a good-natured, half tipsy crowd who offered to treat the President to champagne," but General Gresham was the only one to partake.[35]

Grover Cleveland, 1884

For his 1884 presidential campaign, Cleveland, the governor of New York, gave only two formal speeches in his race against James G. Blaine, neither of them in Indiana. As expected, the Republican nominee Blaine emphasized the need for strict tariffs to support the American worker and farmer, while Democrat Cleveland emphasized efficiency and honesty in government—a tactic that highlighted his successful battles against Tammany Hall corruption in New York. Cleveland and his campaign brain trust were counting on his ability to carry New York along with most, if not all, of the southern states,

you were for the underdog in the fight. You stood for justice for an oppressed people. It was not a popular side. Quite the contrary. . . . You stood by us, stood for justice, citizenship, and the right of life, liberty and the pursuit of happiness. . . . God bless you and keep you, Mr. President, in the hollow of His hand."[32]

As the presidential train prepared to depart, a mother in the crowd also cried out, "I want the President to kiss my baby," and the president obliged as the baby was handed over the heads of the crowd to the rear platform of the train.[33]

Moments later, as the train reached the Tippecanoe Battlefield outside of Lafayette, Arthur asked that the train be stopped so he as a winning strategy. The strategy also allowed Cleveland to duck growing questions about whether he had fathered a child out of wedlock to a New York woman who was later committed to a mental asylum. Cleveland's denials were not absolute (some of them even suggesting he had given in to one, singular, momentary lapse in his life), while his surrogates quickly turned attention to what they viewed as support of institutional graft and corruption by the Republican forces backing Blaine. Amidst an ugly campaign crafted by the GOP that included a widely spread cartoon featuring a child resembling Cleveland calling out, "Ma, Ma, Where's My Pa?," Cleveland's campaign was damaged but not derailed in 1884. Cleveland defeated Blaine by a narrow margin.

During the campaign, Cleveland relied on surrogates in Indiana and elsewhere to make his case. Cleveland's Indiana campaign was aided in no small manner by the presence of former Indiana governor Thomas A. Hendricks as his running mate. A fine speaker and well-liked leader in Indiana, Hendricks helped Cleveland carry Indiana (a swing state again in the 1884 balloting) by a razor-thin margin of 6,515 votes in a contest that drew 500,000 votes statewide. Cleveland-Hendricks won Indiana by a margin of 1.78 percent—one of thirteen states decided by margins of less than 5 percent. Cleveland's nationwide vote percentage was 48.85 percent, compared to Blaine's 48.28 percent. Because of "winner takes all" rules in the states, including Indiana, Cleveland's Electoral College victory was more impressive, 219 to 182.

As president, Cleveland visited Indiana only once during what was dubbed a "goodwill tour" in October 1887 prior to his 1888 re-election campaign. At the time of his visit, he could not have known he was visiting the home territory of his upcoming opponent—Benjamin Harrison. At the time of Cleveland's visit, Harrison was listed on no one's short list of contenders and emerged only later as a dark-horse Republican challenger to the incumbent president.

Cleveland's first stop in Indiana was at Richmond, where "a large, but orderly crowd greeted the President who shook hands with as many as he could during the five-minute stop." The crowd at Richmond reportedly asked the president to present his wife, Frances, who remained inside the traveling car of the train. Cleveland declined, saying she was resting. A second stop came moments later at Cambridge City, located fifteen miles west. Once in Indianapolis Cleveland "was escorted to the State House by an immense throng of people. First came a squad of mounted police, behind came the moving mass, with flying flags and the flashing of military accoutrements . . . the President's carriage was followed at either side by ranges [of people] in rows of two abreast. The open carriage, hidden almost by a drapery of flags, was drawn by eight powerful gray horses gaily caparisoned."[36] Elaborate descriptions continued in news dispatches: "Hats were waved and handkerchiefs fluttered from every window. But manifestly the carriage was the chief object of the eyes. . . . The President in his customary suit of black, with hat to match, manifested a presence that met all that high expectation had looked for. Curiosity and criticism were alike satisfied, and as the carriage moved slowly up the street, there was a distinctly felt social atmosphere and greeting which was a tribute altogether fitting."[37]

As Cleveland's parade made its way through downtown, near the corner of Alabama and Washington Streets, across from the Marion County Courthouse, hundreds of schoolchildren stood, each equipped with a small American

LIBRARY OF CONGRESS

Grover Cleveland

flag. "When the Presidential carriage arrived at the corner of Alabama Street, this resplendent spectacle immediately attracted the eyes of the occupants," news reporters wrote. "Mrs. Cleveland particularly was quick to take it in. She burst forth in an exclamation of delight, and immediately rose to her feet and stood until the carriage had crossed Alabama Street. It was a graceful act the children saw and appreciated. Mrs. Cleveland's face was wreathed in smiles." A portion of the group of children were from the state's "deaf and dumb institute," and "although they could not talk, they made their hands and eyes fly in their mute expressions of delight."[38]

To a crowd estimated at more than 25,000, Governor Isaac P. Gray introduced the president in a lengthy speech (perhaps forgetting the crowd had gathered to see and hear Cleveland, not their governor). Gray was an interesting Indiana political figure. Elected as a Republican, he switched to the Democratic Party after growing angry about alleged corruption in the Ulysses S. Grant administration. Cleveland was complimentary of the welcome he had received and said, "The citizens of the State of Indiana have abundant cause for congratulation in the volume and variety of their products, their public educational advantages, their charitable institutions, and all that contributes to the greatness of a state. But it seems to me that not the least cause for such Indianan's pride should be his state capital. Forty years growth has given [Indianapolis] a population of at least 100,000 and all the business activity that characterizes a prosperous American city."[39]

Cleveland, a former governor, made a special point of highlighting the just-completed Indiana Statehouse as evidence of the progressive nature of the city and state. It also allowed him to remind voters of his frugal ways, as he focused on eliminating government waste and graft.

"I am told that your spacious and handsome State House, just completed, was actually built within the limits of the expense originally fixed," Cleveland said. "In these days of waste, extravagance and miscalculation in regarding to public buildings, it is a thing so unusual that you may be well proud of it."[40]

Part of the appeal and excitement of Cleveland's visit was that it came just two years after the death of his vice president, Indiana's own Hendricks. While Cleveland had not attended Hendricks's December 1885 funeral, he quickly turned the bulk of his remarks into a tribute to his former running mate and political partner. Cleveland had endured some criticism after his last-minute decision to forego Hendricks's funeral and saw the Indianapolis visit as an attempt to mend some fences in an important state for his re-election. Cleveland said:

> I am at this moment much impressed with another thought connected with this place. Its suggestion cannot fail to awaken in your minds an affectionate sentiment, and the subject directs the interested attention of the nation to this spot. Here lived and died a man—your neighbor and your friend— whose name was a household word throughout the land, trusted and respected by his fellow men and by them invested with the highest civic trusts. A loyal and true son of your state, amid his honors, he never forgot the people of Indiana and his fellow townsmen of Indianapolis. And while he loved you, he brought honor to you by his faithful discharge of functions of public office and by a firm devotion and adherence to patriotic principles. All will join you in the respect you cherish for his memory, and the kindly, tender thought of the people of the land will always turn to your city as the place where your distinguished citizen lived and died, and where rests his remains among the surroundings he so much enjoyed.[41]

Cleveland said remembering Hendricks gave him happiness to be in Indianapolis, "to greet you as the friends and neighbors of a man honored by the nation and connected with me by ties of friendship, by the fortunes of political life, and in the discharge of duties."[42] Following his remarks, the president and his wife greeted several hundred guests who filed through the statehouse rotunda for more than ninety minutes (several hundred others were left waiting as the president departed), and he then traveled a few blocks north to call on Hendricks's widow, Eliza. The president's party then moved farther north, along Meridian Street, to the home of former U.S. senator Joseph E. McDonald, a Democrat.

Although the weather did not cooperate (cold and overcast, but no rain), Cleveland's party boarded the special train at Union Station and traveled west to Terre Haute. Before arriving at Terre Haute, the presidential train passed through both Greencastle and Brazil, and although several thousand had gathered along the rail line, the train did not stop. A crowd estimated at 20,000 waited for Cleveland's arrival in Terre Haute and crowded the platform built for the occasion in front of the Normal School (now Indiana State University). As the Associated Press printed from local reports, "The populace seemed on fire with enthusiasm, accompanying the carriages on their way and maintaining one unceasing din of cheers. Thousands of national flags were flying from the windows along the way and many buildings were elaborately decorated with bunting. It was dark before the procession reached its stand and the time for the departure of the train was already past. The great square contained as nearly as could be estimated by the glare of the electric light, more than 20,000 persons."[43]

While in Terre Haute, Cleveland was accompanied by Indiana's legendary Senator Daniel W. Voorhees, a Copperhead Democrat and outspoken opponent of the Civil War. Known as "the tall sycamore of the Wabash," Voorhees was directly referred to by Cleveland in his remarks as one of the great exports from western Indiana: "But of all your products, perhaps the most widely known is the tall sycamore of the Wabash, for this place has been pretty well advertised as the home of that particular lofty tree. During the last two and a half years, I have become somewhat acquainted with this sycamore, and have made up my mind that it has height enough and size enough for any purpose."[44]

Enthusiasm in Terre Haute seemed a little over the top at certain moments. Reporters indicated that Frances Cleveland had to ask one man to "please let it go" because he was clutching her hand so fervently. As the presidential train began to pull out of the station, others jumped on the running boards near the back to get one last chance to shake Cleveland's hand. News reports quoted the president calling out, "I cannot shake your hands while the train is in motion. Some of you will get hurt, and I want to avoid that."[45] After his successful visit to Indiana, Cleveland continued his "western tour" to Illinois, Missouri, Wisconsin, Minnesota, and Nebraska.

Never noted for his oratory skills, Cleveland skipped Indiana for the 1888 campaign, while his Republican opponent, Harrison, made more than eighty speeches, almost all of them in Indiana. Cleveland skipped visiting Indiana altogether during his second term in office, from 1893 to 1897.

Grover Cleveland, 1888–1892

The differences in campaign styles between Harrison and Cleveland remain, historically, quite contrasted, as Harrison conducted the most successful "front porch campaign" in the history of the presidency in 1888 and delivered dozens of speeches in Indiana and elsewhere as a candidate and incumbent president seeking re-election. Those contrasts continued in their rematch in 1892, with Harrison staying primarily in the White House during the fall campaign months (especially given his wife's failing health). In contrast, Cleveland (who holds the distinction of being the only person in American history to have been elected to two, nonconsecutive terms as president) in 1892 relied heavily on the powerful Democratic machines in New York, parts of the northeast, and the South still reeling from the aftermath of the Civil War, whose former Confederate voters remained highly skeptical of any candidate associated with the party of Abraham Lincoln.

The contest in Indiana was characteristically close in 1892, although it relied almost entirely upon district meetings of Republican and Democratic clubs with guest speakers or surrogates for Cleveland and Harrison. One estimate indicated that more than four thousand such meetings were held in the state by both parties in the last weeks of the campaign, with Cleveland's campaign calling on vice presidential nominee Adlai E. Stevenson I and Congressman William Bourke Cockran of New York, and the Republicans calling on vice presidential nominee Whitelaw Reid, New York railroad executive (and eventual Senator) Chauncey M. Depew, and Governor William McKinley of Ohio. As one analyst wrote, "The issue most discussed on the Indiana stump was the tariff. The state had become an important manufacturing area, and in the industrial centers the tariff was a lively topic." A *New York Herald* survey of Indiana just before the election correctly predicted the state would go to the Democrats by a close margin.[46]

James G. Blaine

Although a Republican incumbent resided in the White House in 1884 (Arthur who became president on September 19, 1881, upon the death of Garfield), it was clear Arthur was not a force for his party's nomination for a term of his own right. Arthur's name was placed in nomination by Republican delegates at the convention in Chicago, but it was former house speaker James G. Blaine of Maine who was the favorite candidate. It took only four ballots for Blaine to dispatch Arthur and U.S. Senator John A. Logan of Illinois for the nomination. Logan was eventually named to the ticket as the vice presidential nominee, and Arthur remained in Washington, his lame-duck status unquestionably confirmed.

Blaine, a classic Republican power broker in the post–Civil War years in America, had been a serious contender for the GOP nomination in 1880 that went to Garfield and was a determined candidate four years later. Blaine's long record in Washington, however, had also won him enemies and critics who believed he was part and parcel of a corrupt political bureaucracy. His candidacy gave rise to a Republican sect known as Mugwumps, who wanted government and political reform. The Mugwump movement eventually proved troublesome for Blaine, as it eroded Republican support for his candidacy, with those votes going instead to the Democratic nominee, Cleveland, who had a reputation as a reformer.

In October 1884 Blaine campaigned in several Indiana cities in an attempt to counteract the presence of Hoosier, Hendricks, on the Democratic ticket. At a stop in South Bend, Blaine spoke from a speaker's stand erected at the Saint Joseph County Courthouse and emphasized that maintenance of strict tariffs was key to protecting the American economy and the livelihoods of

LIBRARY OF CONGRESS

James G. Blaine

workers. He also warned against the increasing role of labor unions in the nation's manufacturing interests. Blaine's remarks were received favorably by one of the city's most prominent leaders, Clement L. Studebaker, who hosted Blaine and his party for dinner at his South Bend home at 620 West Washington Street (now known as Tippecanoe Place). Studebaker, with his brother, Henry, started a successful wagon company that eventually became a twentieth-century automotive manufacturer, the Studebaker Corporation.[47] During the next week Blaine visited more than twenty Hoosier communities, primarily speaking from the rear platform of his train at stops in Auburn, Brazil, Crawfordsville, Elkhart, Evansville, Fort Wayne, Goshen, Greencastle, Huntington, Indianapolis, Kendallville, Kokomo, Lafayette, Ligonier, Logansport, Martinsville, Noblesville, Peru, Princeton, Spencer, Sullivan, Terre Haute, Tipton, Vincennes, Wabash, Waterloo, and Worthington.[48]

Large crowds greeted Blaine at Elkhart, Goshen, and particularly Auburn, where one estimate placed the crowd at 25,000. In Ligonier, a small Noble County community not accustomed to attention from political candidates, 8,000 people turned out to see and hear Blaine. The editors of the *Ligonier Leader* seemed quite taken with Blaine's appearance and commented:

> Mr. Blaine appeared on the platform, carrying his silk hat in his hand, which he held as he made his gestures. He spoke with precision and great emphasis. . . . Mr. Blaine was dressed in a double-breasted, black diagonal cloth coat, closely buttoned; dark pants and gaiters to match, and wore heavy, thick-soled shoes, standing collar and black silk tie. His black plug hat looked rather worse for the campaign. He was dressed for comfort and not for style. . . . Standing straight as an arrow and waiting for the cheers which greeted him to subside, Mr. Blaine showed

> a man fully six feet tall, broad breasted and broad shouldered, muscular and with every evidence of good health and the ability to endure a great amount of fatigue, as he has done. He seemed to be in a pleasant mood, and one could not look at him without admiring the man, for a nobler looking specimen of manhood it would be difficult to find than Mr. Blaine, standing erect in the full prime of a glorious and useful life, his full beard, mustache and hair silvered almost to snowy whiteness.[49]

In his remarks, Blaine said, "You have it in your power to say whether you want your industries protected or whether you want your products to come in competition with those made by the pauper labor of Europe. Are you ready to vote the Democratic ticket and thus signify your willingness to leave the government to its former enemies?"[50] He said the Democrats were counting on moving Indiana into their column for the first time since before the war, but said he doubted Hoosiers truly wanted such an outcome. "You are free men and can express your opinions by your ballots," he said. "I leave the question with you and bid you a good morning."[51]

At Fort Wayne the audience was rowdy and a rival Democratic event happening at the same time helped build the crowd size to more than 40,000, but also sparked some fireworks. As the *Fort Wayne Weekly Gazette* reported, "Cheer after cheer was given and just as the crowd was getting quiet, an Ohio Democratic clown, a very able grimacer, cut an antic upon some old lumber in the south entrance to the court house and a gang of hoodlums yelled discordantly. . . . The fact is there were so many questions and they were so noisy that Mr. Blaine did not attempt to speak, and on a suggestion . . . the speakers and crowd en masse adjourned to Library Hall, leaving the clown to tumble his flip-flaps on the courthouse steps, and a few unhappy Democrats still fighting among themselves as to what Cleveland really was the father of."[52]

When he was finally able to speak, Blaine warned, "There is not a line of administration upon which the government is conducted today to which the Democrats of the South are not recorded as hostile and to give them control would mean a change the like of which has not been known in modern times. Such a triumph would be a fearful misfortune to the South itself. It would organize an administration of resentment, reprisals and revenge."[53]

"I am not speaking for myself," Blaine added. "I am pleading no personal cause. I am pleading the cause of the American people. I am pleading the cause of the American farmer, and the American mechanic, the American manufacturer, and the American laborer against the world. I am reproached by some excellent people for appearing before these multitudes of my countrymen upon the ground that it is inconsistent with the dignity of the office for which I am named. I do not feel it to be so. There is not a courtier in Europe so proud but that he is led to uncover his head in the presence of the sovereign. So I uncover in the presence of the only earthly sovereignty I acknowledge, and bow with pride to the free people of America."[54]

The *Fort Wayne Weekly Gazette* reported that "Mr. Blaine was manifestly affected by this magnificent tribute [received in Fort Wayne], and with a graceful gesture commanded silence. He has a very peculiar way of starting his speech. He makes a gesture at every portion of the crowd with his right hand index finger and then gravely bows, and after a moment of silence so proud that you could hear a pin drop, he commented very abruptly."[55] Two days later, at Indianapolis, Blaine delivered a major address at Military Park,

accompanied by Benjamin Harrison, then a U.S. senator, and Governor Albert G. Porter. Largely overstated crowd estimates said as many as 100,000 Hoosiers gathered to hear Blaine proclaim, "We stand on the eve of an important election; an election on whose decision Indiana will produce her potential vote. She is looked to by our opponents, as she has been in former years, as an ally to the solid South and as against her sister states of the North . . . but may I be permitted to press the opinion that no more unpatriotic thing can be done than for northern men to urge the southern states to a continued solidification of the memories of the rebellion."[56]

"It has been the aim and desire of the Republican Party not only to develop the material interests of the South and to make them forget and

An 1884 lithograph touting the campaign of Blaine of Maine and John A. Logan of Illinois.

LIBRARY OF CONGRESS

the nation forget that we had ever been foes," Blaine noted, "but also to make them feel that we are common citizens living under a common union and government. But our opponents meet us with an entirely different course of action and they evoke, instead, the memories of the union, the prejudices of the rebellion in their aid, and they ask that New York and Indiana shall join the unholy alliance and turn the government over to the South. I do not believe it can be done. I don't believe that Indiana will do under its present leadership any more than it would have done under the leadership of Oliver P. Morton."[57]

Blaine said Indiana had "grown into a great commonwealth, great in her population and great in her enterprises. As a manufacturing state, since the Republican Party came into power in 1861, she now turns out in a single year $150 million worth of manufacturing products, and therefore with these increased dependencies as it has been heretofore a protective tariff is now of the highest interest to every citizen."[58]

To further drive a wedge between any wayward Indiana voters and the resurgent Democratic Party, and its powerful support among southerners, Blaine noted that Hoosiers were free "but in the South we have half a million of our friends who have not a free ballot. The South today has 37 electors based on the vote of the colored man, and yet the colored men in the South, half a million in number, cannot elect a single Presidential elector, and deprived of that power, the power of the white man in the South politically is greatly increased over the powers of the white man in Maine or Indiana."[59]

Blaine noted that "now, for the time, we will not argue the question of Negro suffrage, but I will submit as a fair proposition to every man in the land that if the South gets 37 electors by reason of her colored vote, the Negro himself

ought to be allowed to cast a ballot. The issue is in your hands." He said he knew that among Indiana's residents he was standing with patriots and "upon the ground of enlightened self-interest" and that "Indiana may be relied upon to maintain a protective tariff and as an instrumentality thereto, a Republican ballot."[60]

Despite Blaine's ambitious effort in Indiana, Cleveland carried the state by a razor-thin margin of less than 1 percent en route to the first presidential victory by a Democrat since 1856. Blaine remained a popular figure among Republicans, however, and left the country to finally quell efforts to draft him as the party's nominee in 1888. Instead, the party nominated Indiana's Harrison, a candidacy Blaine embraced and campaigned for in Indiana and other battleground states. In mid-October Blaine campaigned across Indiana from north to south, one of his largest stops coming at Goshen with a generous crowd estimate of 45,000 (which would have incredibly dwarfed the population of Goshen, which had a population of approximately 6,000 citizens in 1888).

The next day in Indianapolis, Blaine called on Harrison at his home, and the two men led a grand parade from the New-Denison Hotel on Pennsylvania Street to Fort Wayne Avenue, then to Delaware Street and on to the Indiana State Fairgrounds. Once there, Blaine and Harrison greeted thousands of Republican faithful, and Blaine spoke briefly saying he was certain that Harrison could carry Indiana into the victory column for the Republicans by a margin of 15,000 votes (a victory he had been unable to accomplish himself four years earlier). Later that evening a large throng gathered at Tomlinson Hall for a joint appearance by Harrison and Blaine. In his remarks Blaine warned Hoosiers that the Democrats were actively attempting to scare them into supporting lower tariffs on American goods and noted, "I maintain—and in the few minutes I shall occupy your attention—I shall endeavor to prove by figures and by facts that the West, the great, growing, teeming prosperous West has gained more out of the protective tariff than any section of the whole Union."[61]

Blaine laid out a detailed account of statistics about how the tariff had benefited the nation and noted, "When you drive the free traders from every other ground, they will tell you that the protective tariff has stifled the export trade of the United States; that it has built up a lot of factories and railways, but that the foreign commerce of the country has all gone to pieces." He concluded, "Remember, gentlemen, it is the home market of the United States that every day is affording more and more to the agriculturalists of this country their best market, and the home market of the United States is the result, logically and indisputably, of the protective tariff."[62]

After Indianapolis, Blaine made his way to Terre Haute, Vincennes, Princeton, and Evansville. At Terre Haute, speaking from the train, Blaine said, "I am compelled to be so careful with my voice that I cannot speak between my regular appointments," the next one being Evansville, but added, "but at the same time I cannot refrain from acknowledging the compliment of your call and of giving you my sincere thanks for your warm greeting."[63] All of his speeches were devoted to the need for a strong tariff and advocating Harrison's election. His efforts paid off—Harrison won Indiana in 1888 by a narrow margin of less than ½ of 1 percent and named Blaine to his cabinet as secretary of state, a post Blaine held until June 1892. During his time as secretary of state, three of Blaine's seven children died unexpectedly, and he was ready to retire from public life when Harrison ran for re-election. Despite

Harrison's suspicions, Blaine had no interest in challenging him for the party's nomination, but also offered scant help in Harrison's rematch with Cleveland, a contest Harrison lost. In retirement, Blaine's health declined rapidly, and he died at his Washington, D.C., home on January 27, 1893, at the age of sixty-two.

Benjamin Harrison

Always first in the hearts of his fellow Hoosiers, Harrison was not first among Republican contenders for the GOP nomination in 1888. In fact, party regulars were hoping to prevail upon their 1884 nominee, Blaine, to make a second run for the White House. Blaine declined the offer, but his behind-the-scenes support of Harrison was influential in making Harrison the Republican nominee on the eighth ballot cast at the convention in Chicago. Harrison bested a crowded field of hopefuls, including Senator Sherman of Ohio, former Michigan governor Russell Alger, and a fellow Hoosier, former treasury secretary Gresham. Governor Levi P. Morton of New York was easily confirmed as Harrison's running mate. The selection of Harrison appeared to be one welcomed by many. An Iowa newspaper described him as "calm, cool, deliberate, polished, candid, dignified and strong," but Harrison was better at speech making than he was in one-to-one contact, with a reputation for possessing a cold personality.[64] One anecdote that grew around Harrison's public appearances purported that his campaign aides and supporters made sure that as soon as he finished speaking, he departed, whether on foot or by train, so as to not undo the positive feelings his speech may have inspired.

As the Republican convention closed, traffic to and from Harrison's home at 674 North Delaware Street in Indianapolis, just north of the downtown business district, began to increase. Indiana Republicans were practically giddy at the prospect of a Hoosier leading their national ticket, confirming the importance of the state in the era's political arena. Timing being everything in politics, the Republicans waited until Independence Day to go to Indianapolis and officially deliver the notice to Harrison of his nomination. While only a formality, it provided the pageantry and interest the party was hoping for as Harrison planned and carried out the most successful front-porch campaign in the nation's history. Before the official Republican delegation arrived on July 4, 1888, Harrison received a delegation from the Harrison League of Indiana African American veterans of the Civil War. The three hundred men gathered outside of Harrison's home and were greeted with remarks that reflected the ability of Harrison to articulate not only the basic prin-

ciples of the Republican Party, but also of abolitionist forces that had prevailed in the war in which Harrison had served as a general. He said: "I assure you that I have a sincere respect for, and a very deep interest in, the colored people of the United States. My memory, as a boy, goes back to the time when slavery existed in the Southern States. I was born upon the Ohio River, which was the boundary between the free State of Ohio and the slave State of Kentucky. Some of my earliest recollections relate to the stirring and dramatic interest which was now and then excited by the pursuit of an escaping slave for the hope of offered rewards."[65] Harrison related that as a boy he saw in a thicket near the family's orchard "a colored man with the frightened look of a fugitive in his eye, and attempting to satisfy his hunger with some walnuts he had gathered. He noticed my approach with a fierce, startled

Benjamin Harrison of Indiana and his vice presidential running mate, Levi P. Morton of New York

IHS, BENJAMIN HARRISON PICTURES, P. 482

look, to see whether I was likely to betray him; I was frightened myself and left him in some trepidation, but I kept his secret," with his latter remark drawing applause from the men.[66] He also recalled scenes from his Civil War service, witnessing what he estimated to be a nearly one hundred-year-old slave woman dancing with an "exultation of spirit" as Union forces marched through her tiny village in North Carolina.

Harrison praised the progress "in the legislation relating to your race, and the progress that the race itself has made since that day" and recalled his earliest days in Indiana when "an unfriendly black code was in force" that included prohibitions upon black men appearing in court in matters related to a white plaintiff or defendant. He added that Indiana's laws even "prevented your coming here. In every way you were at a disadvantage, even in the free States. I have lived to see this unfriendly legislation removed from our statute-books and the unfriendly section of our State Constitution repealed. I have lived not only to see that, but to see the race emancipated and slavery extinct."[67] Harrison spoke proudly of the fact that nothing gave him "more pleasure among the results of the war than this. History will give a prominent place in the story of this great war to the fact that it resulted in making all men free, and gave to you equal civil rights. The imagination and art of the poet, the tongue of the orator, the skill of the artist will be brought under contribution to tell this story of the emancipation of the souls of men. Nothing gives me so much gratification as a Republican as to feel that in all the steps that led to this great result the Republican party sympathized with you, pioneered for you in legislation, and was the architect of those great measures of relief which have so much ameliorated your condition."[68]

Harrison invoked the memory of President

Abraham Lincoln and the Emancipation Proclamation, which he compared in importance to the nation's Declaration of Independence, and praised the veterans for their service on behalf of the Union: "I remember your faithfulness during the time of the war. I remember your faithful service to the army as we were advancing through an unknown country. We could always depend upon the faithfulness of the black man. He might be mistaken, but he was never false."[69]

Harrison concluded by telling a story from his war service recalling "an aged man, a fugitive from slavery, had found freedom in our camp," staying up late working to learn the words in a spelling book given to him by a chaplain. "I have seen him . . . lying prone upon the ground taxing his old eyes, and pointing with his hardened finger to the letters of the alphabet, as he endeavored to open to his clouded brain the avenues of information and light. I am glad to know that that same desire to increase and enlarge your information possesses the race to-day. It is the open way for the race to that perfect emancipation which will remove the remaining prejudices and secure to you in all parts of the land an equal and just participation in the government of this country. It cannot much longer be withholden from you." Tenderly, then, Harrison offered his gratitude for the visit of the old men, and said he would "be glad to take by the hand any of you who desire to see me."[70]

The official declaration party of the GOP arrived at Harrison's home at noon on July 4 and brought with it an overflow crowd of more than 5,000, crowding every space on the house's lawn and flowing out into the street for several blocks in each direction, north and south. Humbled, Harrison said the Republican Party and its leaders had "concluded that the great principles enunciated in the platform adopted by the convention could be in some measure safely confided to my care is an honor of which I am deeply sensible and for which I am very grateful. I do not assume or believe that this choice implies that the convention found in me any pre-eminent fitness or exceptional fidelity to the principles of government to which we are mutually pledged."[71]

"I accept the nomination with so deep a sense of the dignity of the office and of the gravity of its duties and the responsibilities as altogether to exclude any feeling of exultation or pride," Harrison said. "Relying wholly upon the considerate judgment of our fellow-citizens and the gracious favor of God, we will confidently submit our cause to the arbitrament of a free ballot."[72]

For the next month Harrison refrained from public appearances and speeches, as he and party leaders, along with congressional leaders of the Republican Party, conferred on how to proceed with the campaign set to open in August, and be under way in earnest in September and October. Harrison and the Republicans faced an uphill battle in unseating the incumbent president, Cleveland, but the Cleveland administration had won an assortment of new enemies for his policy of lowering tariffs, and for opposition to pension reform for Civil War veterans. Key to Harrison's success would be a strong showing in northern and then "Western" states, such as Indiana. Just two decades removed from the close of the Civil War, Harrison and the Republicans knew better than to expend any energy in trying to capture votes south of the Ohio River in former Confederate territory.

Harrison broke his private planning on August 8 when he went to Tomlinson Hall in downtown Indianapolis to briefly address delegates at the Indiana Republican State Convention as they prepared for the fall campaign. Days later, Harrison left for two weeks of vacation at Lake Erie as the guest of Ohio governor Joseph B. Foraker. Harrison's vacation was not all play—he met with many visitors who advised him about how to conduct the forthcoming campaign before returning to Indiana just after Labor Day. The trip back to Indianapolis, however, was no simple undertaking—nothing would be simple for the Harrisons for a long time. As the Republican nominee, word of his travels spread fast, and as his train approached Fort Wayne from the east it was clear that the thousands assembled there at the station were excited to see the nominee. Harrison spoke to the crowd, thanking them for their "cordial demonstration," adding remarks that reflected he was ready to go as a campaigner: "I thank you not so much for myself as for the party to which most of us have given the consent of our minds. I am glad to know that the people are moved to a thoughtful consideration of those questions which are this year presented for their determination."[73] Harrison said Republicans and Democrats alike could agree that "the questions involved in this campaign do have a very direct bearing upon the national prosperity, and upon the prosperity and welfare of the individual citizen. I think it is conceded that the result of this election will affect beneficently or injuriously our great manufacturing interests, and will affect for weal or for woe the workingmen and working women who fill these busy hives of industry."[74]

Harrison asked his audience to compare the tariff positions of the Republican and Democratic parties and made it local: "Here in this city of Fort Wayne, so important and so prosperous, we have a fine illustration of the accruing advantages of a large factory and shop population. It has made your city prosperous as well as populous, and it has made these outlying Allen County farms vastly more valuable than they otherwise would have been. These interests harmonize . . .

your interests and those of your families and of this community, and of every other like community in this country, are to be affected, favorably or unfavorably. . . . I do not doubt that the working people of this country will this November forever settle the question that American customs duties shall by intention, by forethought, have regard to the wages of our working people."[75]

Harrison's train moved on and made another stop at nearby Huntington, where more than 2,000 supporters gathered around the depot. Harrison refrained from any significant policy remarks at Huntington, instead noting that he had been away from the state on vacation, but nothing had occurred "to win away my interests and affection from the great State of Indiana. It is great in the capabilities, both of its soil and its citizenship; great in its achievements during the war. When our country was imperilled, no State more nobly or magnificently responded to the demands which were made by the general Government for men to fight and to die for the flag."[76] Large crowds continued along the way, with Harrison stopping to make remarks at Peru, Kokomo, Tipton, and Noblesville before finally reaching home in Indianapolis. At Peru, Harrison thanked his fellow Hoosiers for the "utmost consideration" they had always given him, but noted, "I have not time to-day to discuss the issues of this campaign. . . . I can only ask you to think of them, and not to mistake the issue. It is very plain. It is the question of whether our tariff laws shall be a protection to American workingmen and a protection to American manufacturing establishments." Before departing he added that he trusted leaving the question of the nation's future "in the kind hands of these intelligent citizens of Indiana and of the United States."[77]

The Harrison party reached Kokomo at twilight, finding the city "aglow" in natural-gas

lights and a rowdy crowd of 3,000 supporters. Harrison offered lengthier remarks, opening by noting, "Kokomo has been for many years a very prosperous place. It has been the happy home of a very intelligent and thrifty people. You are now, however, realizing a development more rapid and much greater than the most sanguine among you could have anticipated three years ago." He noted that creative, entrepreneurial business leaders from across the country had been attracted to Kokomo and the promise its manufacturing base provided. "There is not a resident of Kokomo, there is not a resident of Howard County," Harrison said, "who does not rejoice in this great prosperity. I am sure there is not a man or woman in this city who does not realize that this new condition of things gives to your boys, who are growing up, new avenues of useful thrift. It opens to those who might otherwise have pursued common labor access to skilled trades and higher compensation. There is not a merchant in Kokomo who does not appreciate the added trade which comes to his store. There is not a farmer in Howard County who has not realized the benefits of a home market for his crops."[78] Wrapping up his remarks on tariff and trade policies, he said, "I would leave this thought with you: Will the prosperity that is now realized by you, and that greater prosperity which you anticipate, be better advanced by the continuance of the protective policy or by its destruction?"[79]

At Tipton only a few hundred folks gathered near the depot to greet Harrison, and he made his remarks exceedingly brief, noting, "There is no time this evening for me to say more than that I thank you very sincerely for this cordial evidence of your kindly feeling. I will not have time to discuss any public questions." Instead, his train departed for Noblesville.[80] In the Hamilton County seat, Harrison's train was met by a special train carrying supporters and members from Indianapolis's Columbia Club; they were there to escort him home. He again begged off making any lengthy remarks, but noted Noblesville and Hamilton County's place in the "gas belt" of Indiana and the enterprise local citizens had shown by "opening the way for the coming of new industrial enterprises. You have felt it worthwhile not only to invite them, but to offer pecuniary inducements for them to come. If it has been worthwhile to do so much in the hope of developing your town and to add value to your farms by making a home market for your farm product, is it not also worth your while so to vote this fall as to save and enlarge these new industrial enterprises?"[81]

Finally reaching Indianapolis well after dark, Harrison addressed yet another large throng outside his home, where he said, "Two weeks ago to-day I left Indianapolis quietly for a brief season of rest. We met in Ohio very considerate and hospitable friends. . . . But, notwithstanding all the attractions of that island home in Lake Erie, we are to-night very happy to be again at home. . . . I think I may conclude that nothing has happened since I have been gone that has disturbed your confidence or diminished your respect. At the outset of this campaign I said I would confidently commit all that was personal to myself to the keeping of the intelligent and fair-minded citizens of Indiana. We will go on our way in this campaign upon that high and dignified plane upon which it has been pitched, so far as it lay in our power, commending the principles of our party to the intelligent interest of our fellow-citizens, and trusting to truth and right for the victory."[82]

Taking a day to rest from the long trip home returning from his vacation rest, Harrison went to the Denison Hotel on Pennsylvania Street in downtown Indianapolis on September 6, 1888, to view a parade featuring 10,000 Republican Party members and clubs from across the state and the Midwest. Almost daily, then, Republican groups large and small made their way to Harrison's Delaware Street home, where he greeted almost every group with a speech from his front porch. One of the more interesting groups to make its way to Harrison's home arrived on September 8, 1888, a delegation of one hundred girls between the ages of seven and fifteen who followed a six-year-old boy, Charles Pettijohn, who sat atop a pony and led a drum corps of eight boys. The girls, bedecked in matching red, white, and blue uniforms, carried Japanese lanterns and serenaded the general and Caroline (Scott) Harrison. Harrison told them, "When some one asked this afternoon, over the telephone, if I would receive some children who wanted to pay me a visit, I gave a very cheerful consent, because I thought I saw a chance to have a good time. That you little ones would demand a speech from me never entered my mind, nor did I expect to see a company so prettily uniformed and so well drilled, both in marching and in song."[83]

"Children have always been attractive to me," he said in kind, grandfatherly tones. "I have found not only entertainment but instruction in their companionship. Little ones often say wise things. In the presence of such a company as this, one who has any aspirations for the things that are good and pure cannot fail to have them strengthened. The kind words you have addressed to me in song come, I am sure, from sincere and loving hearts, and I am very grateful for them and for your visit. Some of the best friends I have are under ten years of age, and after to-night I am sure I shall have many more, for all your names will be added."[84]

With that, the Harrisons broke with their

tradition and invited all their little guests inside their home in order that "we can see you and show you whatever there is in our home to interest you. I would like you all to feel that we will be glad if you will come to see us often."[85]

On September 13, 1888, the Harrisons traveled west to the Hendricks County village of Clayton — just west of Plainfield — to attend the fourteenth annual reunion of the Seventieth Indiana Regimental Association. The Seventieth, which included Civil War soldiers recruited from Hendricks, Johnson, and Marion Counties, had achieved a distinguished record during the war and was the first of 159 such regiments sent from Indiana following President Lincoln's call for Union service. Attending the reunion was a priority for Harrison—not only because he enjoyed times with former soldiers, but also because it was the first regiment recruited by a then Second Lieutenant Harrison in 1862. The regiment served 34 months in action and lost 189 men during 11 separate battles. An added bonus in attending benefited his campaign by reminding voters once again of his Civil War record—plus the event drew 5,000 Hoosiers and guests from many other states to honor the veterans. In his remarks Harrison thanked the people of Clayton for making the veterans feel welcome and noted, "I am sure we have never assembled under circumstances more attractive than those that now surround us. The mellow sunshine of this autumn-time that falls upon us, the balmy air which moves the leaves of those shadowing trees, the sweet calm and spell of nature that is over everything, makes the day one of those that may be described in the language of the old poet as 'A bridal of the earth and sky.'"[86]

Harrison's remarks soared with patriotism: "The autumn-time is a fit time for our gathering, for our spring-time is gone. It was in the spring-time of our lives that we heard our country's call. Full of vigor and youth and patriotism, we responded to it. The exhaustion of march and camp and battle, and the civil strife of the years that have passed since the close of the war, have left their marks upon us, and, as we gather from year to year, we notice that signs of advancing age, and the roster of our dead is lengthened."[87]

After recalling some of the departed members of the Seventieth since their last meeting, Harrison said, "As I look into those familiar faces I notice a deep sense of satisfaction, but I have not failed to observe that there are tears in many eyes. We are not moved to tears by any sense of regret that we gave some service to our country and to its flag, but only by the sense that we are not all here to-day, and that all who are here will never gather again in a meeting like this. We rejoice that we were permitted to make some contribution to the glory and credit and perpetuity of the Nation we love."[88] Harrison made special mention of "comrades who served under other regimental flags" who were also present and said, "we do not boast of higher motives or greater service than yours. We welcome you to a participation in our reunion" and noted collectively that "we are veterans and yet citizens, pledged, each according to his own conscience and thought, to do that which will best promote the glory of our country and best conserve and set in our measures those patriotic thoughts and purposes that took us into the war."[89]

Following this event, Harrison returned to a more "normal" routine of receiving almost daily throngs of visitors to his home, including a colorful group of six hundred Chicago "drummers" accompanied by a regiment band that entertained both at Harrison's home and throughout the streets of downtown Indianapolis on September 22. Days later, on October 6, Harrison appeared again at Tomlinson Hall to address a crowd of 10,000 Republicans that included hundreds of supporters from Chicago and several other states, including Michigan, Ohio, Kentucky, Wisconsin, and Pennsylvania. Harrison's remarks to this group were regarded by some observers as some of the most significant of his campaign in laying out the Republican position of maintaining strict tariffs as part of the nation's trade policy. Harrison summarized his argument in a singular statement: "I believe we should look after and protect our American workingmen; therefore I am a Republican."[90] A week later, on October 11, Harrison shared the stage with the party's 1884 nominee, former Governor Blaine of Maine, attracting crowds estimated at more than 30,000 to Indianapolis. Harrison and Blaine addressed a large GOP gathering at the fairgrounds and later reviewed a lengthy Republican parade from a balcony at the Denison Hotel, and later both addressed an audience at Tomlinson Hall. Later in the month, Senators John C. Spooner of Wisconsin and Henry W. Blair of New Hampshire joined with an up-and-coming Protectionist congressman from Ohio, William McKinley Jr., to lead a large delegation of eastern state guests to Indianapolis to meet Harrison. McKinley's presence was important. Harrison had successfully captured the support of both the McKinley and Foraker wings of the fractured Republican Party of Ohio. At Tomlinson Hall, Harrison noted that he had "listened to many addresses full of the kindest expressions toward me personally; but, among them all, none have been more grateful to me, none have more deeply touched me than this great assemblage."[91] Harrison addressed himself to "false and scandalous stories" being circulated by the Democrats regarding his views toward workingmen and organized labor organizations. "The purpose of all these stories was to poison the minds of the workingmen against the candidate of the party that stands in this campaign for the principle of protection to American labor," Harrison said. "The story that I ever said that one dollar a day was enough for a workingman, with all its accompaniments and appendages, is not a perversion of anything I ever said—it is a false creation."[92] Harrison said the "catalog of campaign slanders" produced by the Democrats against him had grown large, and he was unable to address each and every one of them, but felt compelled to add that "it is equally false that anywhere or at any time I ever spoke disparagingly of my fellow-citizens of Irish nativity or descent" and said it reflected the inroads the Republicans were making with Irish-descent voters.

"Those who will encamp their army in the swamp will abandon the victory to the army that is on the heights," Harrison declared. "The Republican Party stands to-day as the bulwark and defence of the wage-earners of this country against a competition which may reduce American wages even below the standard they falsely impute to my suggestion."[93]

As the campaign entered its final days, the parade of visitors to Indianapolis continued with Harrison personally reviewing a parade of more than 7,000 "railroad men" who marched past the Denison Hotel on October 27. The same day, Caroline welcomed a delegation of eighty young women from Oxford College of Ohio, her alma mater. Even on Election Day, November 6, 1888, visitors continued to come, including the Commercial Club of Cincinnati. Harrison gave one final front-porch speech, telling them, "The time for speech-making is over. The debate is closed, and I believe the polls are closed. I will only thank you for your call to-night and for that friendly spirit which you have shown to me during the campaign."[94]

The final vote was close, with Harrison and Cleveland splitting the four "swing states" of Indiana, New York, Connecticut, and New Jersey (Harrison winning the former two with a margin of 1 percent or less). In his home state of Indiana, Harrison won an amazingly close vote by a margin of 2,348 votes in a contest where more than half a million votes were recorded. Harrison's national victory became only the third time in U.S. history in which the winning candidate received a smaller popular vote than the losing candidate, but won the presidency in the Electoral College. Similar results were recorded in 1824, 1876, and more than a century later in 2000.

In the weeks that followed, President-elect Harrison made few, if any, public appearances, breaking his solitude for a brief visit to a January 1, 1889, ceremony for the Indianapolis chapter of the Grand Army of the Republic and its annual officer installation. There, Harrison offered only brief remarks noting that, "It affords me pleasure to meet with you again on this occasion. When I left the army so many years ago I little expected to enter it again, as I soon will. Among the many honors which may be placed on me in the future there will be none, I can assure you, that will esteem more highly than my membership in this order. . . . I wish to say before parting with you, if I may never look upon your faces collectively again, that the parting request I would make of you would be that each of you, without regard to party . . . stand shoulder to shoulder, as we did during the war, to preserve a free and honest ballot."[95]

On February 25, 1889, President-elect and Mrs. Harrison prepared to depart Indianapolis for the inauguration scheduled for March 4 in Washington, D.C. As expected, a huge throng of well-wishers showed up at Union Station in downtown Indianapolis to provide the Harrisons

a warm send-off. Reporters noted the emotion in Harrison's voice as he spoke fondly of his Indiana home: "My Good Friends and Neighbors—I cannot trust myself to put in words what I feel at this time. Every kind thought that is in your minds and every good wish that is in your hearts for me finds its responsive wish and thought in my mind and heart for each of you. I love this city. It has been my own cherished home. Twice before I have left it to discharge public duties and returned to it with gladness, as I hope to do again. It is a city on whose streets the pompous displays of wealth are not seen. It is full of pleasant homes, and in these homes there is an unusual store of contentment. The memory of your favor and kindness will abide with me, and my strong desire to hold your respect and confidence will strengthen me in the discharge of my new and responsible duties. Let me say farewell to all my Indiana friends. . . . My family unite with me

LIBRARY OF CONGRESS

President Harrison, 1888

in grateful thanks for this cordial good-bye, and with me wish that these years of separation may be full of peace and happiness for each of you."[96]

While Harrison saved his most personal remarks for his Indianapolis departure, the inaugural special could not escape Indiana without multiple stops to greet large crowds of excited Hoosiers. Stops included Knightstown in Henry County, where the president-elect told those assembled that "I can detain the train but a moment, and I only stopped at the request of the Superintendent of the Soldiers' Orphans' Home, so that the children might have an opportunity to see me and that I might wish them the bright and prosperous future which the sacrifices of their fathers won for them."[97] The other stop was at Richmond on the Indiana-Ohio state line and Harrison noted, "I have so long had my home among you that I cannot but feel a sense of regret in leaving the soil of Indiana. I go with a deep sense of inadequacy, but I am sure you will be patient with my mistakes, and that you will all give me your help as citizens in my efforts to promote the best interests of our people and the honor of the Nation we love."[98]

The demands of the presidency soon set upon Harrison and his family, but they did not keep him from a memorable return to Indiana for the August 22, 1889, dedication of the Soldiers and Sailors Monument in downtown Indianapolis. Indiana governor Alvin P. Hovey joined the president's train at College Corner, just inside the eastern border of the state at Union County. Ever the gentleman, Harrison offered brief remarks for the locals gathered, thanking Hovey for the welcome on behalf of the entire state, and added, "You have well said that the people of Indiana have been kind to me, and if, when my public career is ended, I can return to you the happy possessor of your respect and good-will, I shall not leave public office with regret."[99] Upon reaching Indianapolis, the president was again greeted by a large and loud local crowd. He noted, "It was not my expectation when I left Indianapolis a few months ago, under so serious a sense of my responsibilities, that I would return again so soon to my home. But this occasion was one which I could not well be absent from. It is one that should enlist to a degree that nothing else can do our patriotic interests and State pride. . . . I am glad, therefore, to be present and see this monument started. I reverently rejoice with you on this occasion."[100]

The next day, Harrison spoke before a crowd estimated at more than 20,000 to dedicate the monument in the heart of downtown Indianapolis. As historian Charles Hedges wrote, "When Governor Hovey introduced the Chief Executive of the Nation the vast audience swayed with enthusiasm. In a voice low, and with a slight tremble in it, President Harrison began his fine tribute to the men who responded to the country's call. As he proceeded his voice rose higher until it rang out clear as a bugle and drew from the multiple repeated and vociferous cheers."[101] Harrison declared that "there have been few occasions in the history of our State so full of interest, so magnificent, so inspiring, as that which we now witness. The suggestion that a monument should be builded to commemorate the valor and heroism of those soldiers of Indiana who gave their lives for the flag attracted my interest from the beginning."[102] Harrison said he loved the idea of the monument because it was "not to any man, not to bear on any of its majestic faces the name of a man, but a monument about which the sons of veterans, the mothers of our dead, the widows that are yet with us, might gather, and, pointing to the stately shaft, say, 'There is his monument.'"[103]

Following the ceremonies at Monument Circle, the presidential party moved east along Market Street to Tomlinson Hall, where another 5,000 veterans and residents gathered to commemorate the day. "I am sure . . . that those who survive you may point to this shaft, which is being reared yonder, as a worthy tribute of your services in defense of your country."[104] The president and Mrs. Harrison then retired to their own home on Delaware Street, but returned to Tomlinson Hall the next day for the fifteenth reunion of the Seventieth Regiment, an event Harrison referred to as "a family affair." He lamented that perhaps his presence as president made having the annual reunion in a smaller, more rural setting impossible. Regardless, Harrison pledged to shake hands with each member of the Seventieth Regiment and the First Brigade present inside Tomlinson Hall.

Harrison's work as president kept him away from the state until he departed on a "western tour" of the nation beginning on October 6, 1890. While en route west, Harrison's train stopped at the Harrison family homestead in North Bend, Ohio, where he made no public comments, and stopped by Lawrenceburg in Dearborn County. From the rear platform of his train, Harrison said, "All the scenes about here are very familiar to me. This town of Lawrenceburg is the first village of my childish recollections, and as I approached it this morning, past the earliest home of my recollections, the home in which my childhood and early manhood were spent, memories crowded in upon me that were very full of interest, very full of pleasure, and yet full of sadness. They bring back to me those who once made the old home very dear, the most precious spot on earth."[105]

As he moved west across the state, Harrison's train stopped at North Vernon in Jennings Coun-

ty, and he told the locals that "it is always a pleasure to see my old Indiana friends" and that "we have had this morning a delightful ride across the southern part of the State, one that has given me a great deal of refreshment and pleasure."[106] As he did in Lawrenceburg, the president introduced General Benjamin F. Tracy, secretary of the navy, who was accompanying him on his travels west. At Seymour in Jackson County, a large crowd of more than 2,000 gathered to see the president, and Harrison said he was heeding a request "that I speak a few minutes to the school children here assembled. I scarcely know what to say to them, except that I have a great interest in them, and the country has a great interest in them. Those who, like myself, have passed the meridian of life realize more than younger men that the places we now hold and the responsibilities we now carry in society and in all social and business relations must devolve upon those who are now in the school. Our State has magnificently provided for their education, so that none of them need be ignorant, and I am sure that in these happy homes the fathers and mothers are not neglecting their duties, but are instilling into these young minds morality and respect for the law which must crown intelligence in order to make them."[107]

The president's train also stopped briefly at Shoals in Martin County, where he offered only two sentences of greeting, and in Sullivan where he also spoke quite briefly. Later at Terre Haute, a crowd of more than 10,000 gathered near a special speakers' stand near the depot, and steam whistles and church bells in the city were rung simultaneously to announce Harrison's arrival. "I have known this pretty city for more than thirty years, and have watched its progress and growth," he told local Terre Haute residents. "It has always been the home of some of my most cherished personal friends, and I am glad to know that your city is in an increasing degree prosperous, and your people contented and happy. . . . I was told as we approached your city that there was not an idle wheel in Terre Haute."[108] Acknowledging the city's long history as being a "Democrat Town," Harrison said, "We differ widely in our views of public politics, but I trust every one of us is devoted to the flag which represents the unity and power of our country and to the best interests of the people, as we are given to see and understand those interests."[109] From there, Harrison's trip continued on west through Illinois, Missouri, Kansas, Colorado, Wyoming, and California. Harrison later backed the development of U.S. national forest preserves as part of the Land Revision Act of 1891.

As he made his way back east more than a week later, the president's train stopped in Indianapolis on October 12, 1890, where he spent a quiet day in his own home before setting off again for Washington, D.C., the next morning. As usual, his travels were not simple. As he left the state, his train made stops at Pendleton and Anderson, the latter reached at 7:10 a.m. on a Monday morning. He told the early morning audience, "I am here to-day, returning to my duties at Washington from a trip taken to meet some of my old comrades during the war. There are some here this morning. I bid them Godspeed" and again recalled his love of Indiana.[110] A short time later, an even larger crowd of more than 10,000 gathered near the depot in Muncie to get a glimpse of the Hoosier president. In his remarks Harrison recalled an earlier visit to Muncie at the time the vast natural gas reserves in this part of the state were being discovered and declared, "How rapidly events have crowded each other since! You have delved into the earth and have found the supply of this most adaptable and extraordinary fuel inexhaustible; and what

has it done for you? No longer are you transporting coal from the distant mines to feed your furnaces. No longer are you sending the choppers into the woods to cut your trees and haul them in, that they may bring you winter heat and fuel. The factories have been coming to you. This convenient heat and serviceable fuel is found in the humblest home in Muncie. How it has added to your comfort . . . how much it has added to your prosperity and development of manufactures here you have only begun to know."[111] The early hour and good weather seemed to invigorate the president as Harrison happily offered lengthy greetings for two more stops at both Winchester and Union City (the latter an Indiana town that straddles the Indiana-Ohio state line).

In the spring of 1891 the president and Mrs. Harrison set out on an historic tour of southern and western states that were not use to presidential visits in earlier times. Particularly noteworthy were Harrison's travels to the "unfriendly South" with stops in Virginia, Tennessee, Georgia, Alabama, Mississippi, Arkansas, and Texas. Continuing west, the party made first-ever presidential visits to New Mexico, Oregon, and Washington and paid extended visits to several parts of both California and Colorado. In May the president made his way back east, stopping off in Springfield, Illinois, to pay tribute to the martyred President Lincoln. On May 14, 1891, his train reached Montezuma, a tiny western Indiana town on the Wabash River border with Illinois. Governor Hovey joined the president's party, and he offered brief remarks: "We have had a long journey, and one that has been attended by a great many pleasant incidents. We have had cheers of welcome reaching from our first stop, at Roanoke, Virginia, stretching across the mountains of Tennessee and Northern Georgia and Alabama, down through Arkansas and Texas, and along the Pacific coast. Everywhere we have had the most cordial and kindly greeting; but as I cross to-day the border line of Indiana and meet again these old friends I find in your welcome a sweetness that exceeds it all."[112] Reporters at the scene noted that Harrison's eyes then welled with tears, and his voice became choked and he did not continue. By the time Harrison's train reached Indianapolis just before 5 p.m., a crowd of more than 50,000 had gathered in Jackson Place outside Union Station to greet their hometown president. Harrison told them, "I do not think I can speak much to-day. The strain of this long journey, the frequent calls that have been made upon me to speak to my fellow citizens from Washington to the Golden Gate . . . has left me somewhat exhausted in body and in mind, and has made my heart so open to these impressions, as I greet my old home friends, that I cannot, I fear, command myself sufficiently to speak to you at any length."[113]

Harrison told his audience of the vast orchards he had visited in California and the mountain vistas in Colorado and other states. His comments quickly turned, however, to his hometown saying, "My manhood has known no other home but this. It was the scene of my early struggles; it has been the scene, and you have been the instruments and supporters in every success I have achieved in life. . . . I left you a little more than two years ago to take up the work of the most responsible office in the world. I went to these untried duties sustained by your helpful friendliness. I come to you again after these two years of public office to confess many errors, but to say to you that I have had but one thought in my mind. It was to use whatever influence had been confided to me for the general good of all our people."[114] After leaving Indianapolis, Harrison's train stopped at Richmond, where

he again offered familiar greetings and reported on his western trip: "We have seen regions that were new to me, people that were strangers, and yet, throughout the whole of this journey we have been pervaded, surrounded, inspired by the magnificent spirit of American patriotism."[115]

In the next year Harrison's travel schedule was severely curtailed as multiple health issues began to encroach further upon the life of his often fragile wife. Some reports indicated Caroline had caught a cold during the extensive trip into the western states in 1891 and that it eventually settled into pneumonia, and then tuberculosis. By the summer of 1892 the president delivered his wife to a retreat in the Adirondack Mountain region of New York in hopes that her health would improve. Her most serious complication was TB that required clear, clean air and orders to get rest, but it is also likely she suffered from undiagnosed and untreated depression. In September 1892 Caroline returned to the White House, her struggle a major distraction to the president who was officially a candidate for re-election in the November balloting. Her struggle came to an end in the Lincoln Bedroom at the White House early on the morning of October 25, 1892, when she succumbed at the age of sixty. At her side, along with the president, were her children and her niece, Mary Scott Lord (who would later become the second Mrs. Harrison). The heartbroken president and his family made plans to return Caroline to Indianapolis for her final rest in Crown Hill Cemetery, and the presidential campaign for both parties essentially came to an end out of respect for the departed First Lady.

"To the President, (Mrs. Harrison's) death is an unspeakable loss," the *Indianapolis Journal* reported. "The bride of his youth, the wife of his mature years, the companion of a lifetime, the sharer of his joys and sorrows, his triumphs and defeats, her death leaves him alone in his high place, alone in the performance of weighty duties, alone at morning, noon and at night, alone though surrounded by the pomp and circumstance of office."[116] The *Journal* added, "Those who know (President Harrison) best know his heart will be torn and shattered by this blow, and how silently and bravely he will bear the grief that cannot be told nor shared. The President will have the sincere sympathy of all Americans."[117] Caroline's Indianapolis funeral on October 28, 1892, drew a wide array of political insiders from both parties, including former president Rutherford B. Hayes, members of Harrison's cabinet and congressional leaders, although former president Cleveland did not attend.

As expected, the president made no public statements during his return to Indianapolis to lay his wife to rest. Surrounded by his children throughout the proceedings, the grieving president was emotional and was observed openly weeping as he followed the pallbearers carrying Caroline's casket into the First Presbyterian Church for simple, but heartfelt services. The First Lady was buried at Crown Hill Cemetery, following a funeral procession that drew thousands of citizens who stood silently as the president's party passed. Harrison and his family boarded a special train to return to Washington shortly after services were completed. Harrison's press secretary released a statement to the people of Indiana, "My dear old friends and neighbors, I cannot leave you without saying that the tender and gracious sympathy which you have today shown for me and my children, and much more the touching evidence you have given of your love for the dear wife and mother, have deeply moved our hearts. We yearn to tarry with you and to rest near the hallowed spot where your loving hands have laid our dead, but the

little grandchildren watch in wondering silence for our return and need our care, and some public business will no longer wait upon my sorrow. May a gracious God keep and bless you all. Most gratefully yours, Benjamin Harrison."[118]

Harrison's political struggles in 1892 prior to Caroline's decline were as distracting, no doubt, as were his personal ones. A "draft" effort was begun among some disaffected Republicans to convince Secretary of State Blaine to again accept the party's nomination. Blaine provided mixed messages both publicly and privately, and Harrison ultimately delivered an ultimatum that Blaine either openly reject the draft effort meant to usurp his own candidacy, or resign as a cabinet member. Blaine resigned his cabinet post, but the "draft" effort floundered, and Harrison was successfully renominated at the GOP convention in Minneapolis in June. Vice President Levi Morton did not accept nomination for a second term and was replaced by New York editor, Ambassador Whitelaw Reid, as Harrison's running mate. For the Democrats, former president Cleveland successfully turned back token opposition and easily won his party's nomination for the rematch with Harrison. An alliance of farm and labor formed a new People's Party as well and nominated former congressman James B. Weaver of Iowa (who successfully drew off votes from some of Harrison's Republican base in the West). The fall campaign between Harrison and Cleveland resembled closely the 1888 race, with Harrison again favoring strict tariff laws and Cleveland arguing for more open trade as a means of economic advancement.

On November 8, 1892, Cleveland won an impressive victory, returning him to a nonconsecutive second term as president (despite having virtually suspended his campaigning for the last sixteen days of the contest). Besting Harrison

MRS. BENJAMIN HARRISON.

THE BURIAL-GROUND AT CROWN HILL CEMETERY, INDIANAPOLIS.
From a Photograph by Clark, Indianapolis.

MRS. HARRISON'S SITTING-ROOM AT THE WHITE HOUSE.

IHS, BENJAMIN HARRISON PICTURES, P-482

AT THE RAILROAD DEPOT, WASHINGTON.—From a Photograph by Bell, Washington.

THE FUNERAL AT ALBANY.—From a Photograph by Bell, Washington.

THE FUNERAL OF MRS. HARRISON.—[SEE PAGE 1062.]

Harper's Weekly *illustrations regarding the death of Caroline Scott Harrison.*

by a margin of 46 to 43 percent (with Weaver drawing almost 9 percent of the vote), Cleveland's coattails also successfully delivered a Democratic majority to both the House and Senate for the first time since the Civil War. Harrison won in only sixteen states, but his most painful loss was in his home state of Indiana, where Cleveland won a victory with a 1.29 percent margin, or a difference of just 7,125 votes over Harrison, in a race where more than half a million votes were cast. Further hurting Harrison's chances, despite his entreaties to the western states as president, were surprise wins by Weaver's third-party candidacy in Colorado, Idaho, Kansas, Nevada, and North Dakota, enough for twenty-two Electoral College votes.

The election over, many observers openly speculated that Harrison was actually pleased to be able to go home and give up the duties of public office. Following Cleveland's inauguration on March 4, 1893, Harrison set for home and arrived at Indianapolis on March 6, where a large crowd gathered at Union Station to welcome him. As the Associated Press reported, "The welcome home of General Harrison was as warm as was his Godspeed to Washington enthusiastic four years ago. As (General Harrison's) carriage proceeded slowly up Illinois Street to Washington, thence east to Pennsylvania Street, the ex-president was kept busy bowing and lifting his hat to the cheers of people along the way. The procession disbanded at the New-Denison Hotel, and later in the afternoon General Harrison was driven to his old home, 674 North Delaware Street."[119] Later, Harrison and his children and grandchildren were reported to have traveled to Crown Hill Cemetery to visit the grave of his departed wife and an evening reception at the "new" Indiana Statehouse, "so great was the crush that the capacity of the great structure was tested."[120]

Harrison addressed the statehouse reception, "Four years ago, if the calendar is consulted, I left you to assume high responsibilities. If I should consult heart and mind, I should say 10 years had elapsed since I bade goodbye to my Indianapolis friends. Not the rising and the setting of the sun, but our experiences, give the true sense of duration. I come back to Indianapolis, for since I came to manhood I have had no other home."[121] The former president said, "suggestions of an attractive sort" had been made to him to make his home elsewhere, "but it seemed to me that the only home for me was Indianapolis. I am too old to make a new home; not too old, I hope, to renew those old associations that made this so dear a home, and to take within the circle of my affectionate regard the multitude of new faces that I see here tonight." Briefly alluding to Caroline's passing just five months earlier, Harrison said, "I come to you again accompanied by a great sorrow," but said he trusted the welcome he had received reflected he was still held in esteem and care in the heart of his fellow Hoosiers. He concluded, "I shall be glad to take as many of you as I may by the hand, and in those days and weeks that are to come, to meet you in my home and in your homes as opportunity may offer. May God bless you all." As Harrison's party left the statehouse and the downtown region, an Indianapolis regiment band played "Auld Lang Syne" as he passed.[122]

As a former president, Harrison remained active in Republican politics in the years after he left office. In April 1894 he accepted an invitation to appear before the State Republican Convention at Tomlinson Hall and offered greetings to the assemblage and offered, "I will not stand between you and the important work which you have assembled to do, and which you are eager to be about. At some time during the campaign which so auspiciously opens today—if it will be the pleasure of my fellow citizens—I shall hold myself at their service for a fuller discussion."[123] He enthusiastically lent his support to the McKinley campaign in 1896, in part as a return favor to the Ohioan who had campaigned vigorously for Harrison's unsuccessful 1892 re-election bid. Indiana remained a swing state for the 1896 election, and while Harrison had heartily lost the national campaign four years prior, he remained a popular and beloved figure among his fellow Hoosiers. In the closing days of the 1896 campaign, Harrison made his way across the state for two campaign swings in late October and again in early November for McKinley, making speeches in Alexandria, Anderson, Auburn, Decatur, Fort Wayne, Geneva, Goshen, Greenfield, Kendallville, Knightstown, Ligonier, Marion, Muncie, North Manchester, Portland, Summitville, Wabash, Warsaw, Waterloo, and Winchester. The editors of the *Goshen Daily News* expressed their excitement at Harrison's visit, noting, "The air was somewhat raw, but the love of Old Glory was so warm that the mercury had little or nothing to do with the ceremony which was the grandest, best arranged and most thoroughly disciplined demonstration this section of the state ever beheld. It was of magnificent proportions, cosmopolite as to industries, gorgeously attired and presenting a spectacle never before seen in this nor any other city in Northern Indiana, the city has such private residences, public buildings, trades rooms and buildings, all one sea of wealth in bunting and ornateness otherwise. The day may well go on record as an epoch."[124] A crowd of more than 10,000 awaited the former president on the lawn of the Elkhart County Courthouse in Goshen as Harrison was escorted from the train, accompanied by a band playing "Yankee Doodle Dandy." During his

remarks, he countered claims by the Democratic nominee, William Jennings Bryan, that the Republicans were campaigning in a disguise or mask and addressed GOP policy on the nation's monetary measure.

At Decatur, the county seat of Adams County and considered friendly territory for the Democrats, Harrison spoke before about 4,000 citizens, including some who cheered whenever Bryan's name was uttered. Harrison attempted to cut into the Democratic vote by urging local residents to resist voting a straight party ticket. "For whom shall you vote?" he asked. "For Bryan and (Arthur) Sewall? You cannot do it if you should carry Indiana five of your electoral votes would go for Thomas Watson of Georgia, who is not a Democrat, and does not claim to be a Democrat. They have put five populists upon your electoral ticket and if you vote it, two-thirds of your vote goes to Bryan and Sewall, your ticket, and one-third of it goes to Bryan and Watson, the populist nominee. And if Thomas Watson should hold the balance of power in the Electoral College, you would have Thomas Watson for vice president or nobody. You, who have been taking the straight thing for these years, cannot get the straight thing this year by voting the Democratic ticket. But you can vote a straight Republican ticket and thereby uphold many of the principles for which Jackson and Jefferson stood, principles that are now attacked by Mr. Bryan and the Chicago platform."[125] Harrison drew large crowds everywhere—an estimated 30,000 at Fort Wayne and a likely—overstated estimate of 20,000 at tiny Winchester in Randolph County.

During the same year that Harrison actively barnstormed Indiana for the McKinley effort, at the age of sixty-two he remarried, taking the niece of his deceased wife, Mary Scott Lord Dimmick (a woman twenty-five years his junior), as his bride. As the last Civil War general to serve as president of the United States, his perspectives on that era grew in importance and interest for many, and he accepted the invitation of Stanford University of California to deliver a series of lectures on his military and political experiences. He also accepted a legal assignment as chief counsel for the government of Venezuela during a boundary dispute with British Guiana and joined the Board of Trustees of Purdue University (a position he held for fifteen years). In February 1901 he developed influenza and grew increasingly ill and died March 13, 1901, at his Delaware Street home in Indianapolis. He was sixty-seven years old. He was buried at Crown Hill Cemetery next to his first wife, following an elaborate funeral as tens of thousands of Hoosiers lined the streets of Indianapolis to offer their final respects to the only president from Indiana.

Adlai E. Stevenson I

The Cleveland campaign in 1892 relied heavily upon surrogates for the nominee, including the vice presidential nominee, former Representative and General Adlai E. Stevenson I from neighboring Illinois. Stevenson was a compromise choice for Democrats, with the party's nominee, Cleveland, preferring Governor Isaac P. Gray of Indiana. Stevenson began his campaign efforts in Indiana in early September with speeches in Vincennes, Bloomington, Indianapolis, Marion, Alexandria, Summitville, Anderson, Clay City, and Brazil. For his Vincennes appearance, Stevenson accepted callers at the Grand Hotel and shook hands with hundreds of them before addressing an outdoor meeting of more than 5,000 surrounding the Knox County Courthouse. Focusing primarily on the tariff issue and praise for the first Cleveland term that had been "economical, honest and devoid of scandal," he ex-

pressed particular concern about a projected $54 million federal deficit. He also briefly advocated for market supports for corn farmers, similar to those proposed for sugar plantation owners in southern states.

"The points I have discussed are the issues of this campaign," Stevenson said, "and I fully believe that your interests and the interests of all the people of this country are bound up in the success of the Democratic Party under Grover Cleveland, the man who gave you an honest administration of government and with whom the principle in action was 'a public office is a public trust.'"[126]

Stevenson appeared in Indianapolis at Tomlinson Hall for a special ceremony honoring former vice president Thomas Hendricks's birthday. Hendricks died in office during Cleveland's first term in 1885. Stevenson spoke, though media reports focused on a statement sent by Cleveland about his former running mate in which he noted, "Your organization does a fitting thing when it thus recalls to his fellow citizens the honor which Mr. Hendricks shed upon his state and the usefulness in every relation which characterized his career. Not only the city of Indianapolis but the state of Indiana is to be congratulated that their people have such an inspiration to disinterested public service as is afforded by the contemplation of the memory of the lamented statesman."[127]

For his part, Stevenson said "When I would speak of Thomas A. Hendricks, I am reminded of the words of the great French orator Bossnet [Jacques-Bénigne Bossuet]. When he pronounced his matchless eulogy upon the Prince of Conde said he, 'At the moment I open my lips to celebrate the immortal glory of the Prince of Conde, I find myself equally overwhelmed by the greatness of the theme and the needlessness of

LIBRARY OF CONGRESS

Adlai E. Stevenson I

the task. What part of the habitable globe has not heard of his victories and the wonders of his life!'"[128]

Stevenson recalled Hendricks's strong opposition to the Reconstruction plans advanced by radical forces within the Republican Party and predicted that history would treat his views favorably, and that he was pleased to know that Hendricks had lived long enough to see the Democratic Party restored "to power under an administration which would have reminded him of the early days of the republic."[129]

The next day at Marion, a large crowd and brass band greeted Stevenson upon his arrival. In his speech Stevenson said, "It has taken a long time for the people of this country to learn that a tariff is a tax, but I think now they understand that fact. The tariff is of no benefit to the farmer or to the laboring man. The farmer sells his produce in the open markets of the world. He should be permitted to go into the markets of the world to buy what his necessities and the necessities of his family demand without paying a high tribute to the protected classes of this country."[130]

"As to the laboring man, tariff has no effect upon his wages except to diminish the purchasing power of the wages he receives," Stevenson said. "If it were true that high tariff makes high wages to the laborer, then why is it that during the 30 years that we have had a high tariff, the wages of the workingmen have not increased? . . . We wage no war upon manufacturers. We wage no war on any business industry. We favor a reduction of the tariff upon the necessities of life so that substantial blessings will come to the people of this country who earn their bread by toil. That is the doctrine of the Democratic Party."[131]

As vice president, Stevenson was an infrequent but welcome guest to Indiana, and his fall 1896 visit to Goshen was typical as he campaigned for fellow Democrats (having been summarily passed over by delegates at the Democratic National Convention to be its presidential nominee in lieu of an up-and-coming William Jennings Bryan of Nebraska). Though in his last months of office, Stevenson's visit was cause for celebration in Goshen, the *Goshen Daily News* reporting that "today was a typical day for the Silver Democrats in granting ovation to the Vice President of the United States, and it may be said the whole city of all parties felt honored by his presence and for the time lost sight wholly of any political preference and did honor to the distinguished individual, for seldom do these exalted officials give audience to the lesser cities. The day was all that could be wished, the people apparently being inoculated with the beauty of the weather, were out in force and their best attire and for which the Democratic Party is entitled to thanks, since it has accorded to us what possibly will not happen again in a generation."[132] While in Goshen, Stevenson rode at the front of a lengthy parade and then reviewed it from a stand, and later spoke on the lawn of the Elkhart County Courthouse where "he reviewed the position of the various parties and their present attitude to that important issue. He is slow and deliberate in his manner of delivery, but a very earnest speaker, and made a strong plea for the free silver cause."[133]

Whitelaw Reid

With Vice President Levi P. Morton indicating he was not interested in a second term, Republicans turned to former U.S. ambassador to France and *New York Tribune* editor Whitelaw Reid to replace him as President Harrison's running mate. Reid carried most of the campaign workload for the Harrison ticket in 1892, as the president's wife Caroline continued her rapid decline in health. In fact, as Reid was traveling to Indiana stumping for votes in late October, sad reports emerged that Caroline was in the last hours of her life and finally succumbed on October 25, 1892.

During his Indiana swing, Reid made campaign stops in Logansport, Kokomo, Sharpsville (in Tipton County), Tipton, Noblesville, and Indianapolis. By the time Reid's party reached Indianapolis, the news was confirmed, however, that Caroline had died, greatly changing the tenor of the scheduled events. Reid was accompanied on his speaking tour by Chauncey M. Depew, president of the New York Central Railroad Company. In Indianapolis, Reid spoke briefly from the balcony of the Denison Hotel on Pennsylvania Street for excited local Republicans, and later at two separate speeches at the English Opera House on Monument Circle and Tomlinson Hall on Market Street.[134]

Reid's appearances drew direct comparisons with those of U.S. Representative William Bourke Cockran of New York, a noted orator for the Democratic Party, who was in Indianapolis at the same time speaking on behalf of Cleveland's campaign. Local media reports indicated competing parades for Reid and Cockran passed one another on Washington Street during the evening's events, without incident. "Fears were expressed of a riot, should the two parades meet, but this was averted by the opposing marshals who amicably agreed upon lines of march that should not trespass upon each other," an Associated Press report indicated.[135]

During Reid's remarks at the English Opera House, special tribute was offered to Caroline with Reid commenting on Harrison's loss: "And now the light of the house is going out, into the holy circle of that grief none of us may venture. We can give no aid. We can only say, as the whole

LIBRARY OF CONGRESS

An 1892 Thomas Nast tribute to Harrison and his running mate, Whitelaw Reid.

land does today, 'May the God of their fathers and of our fathers be with them both.' You will not blame me, men and women of Indianapolis, if at this time, in this city, and in the presence of this universal sympathy, you find me little inclined to partisan vehemence in discussing merely partisan disagreements."[136]

Regardless of his stated reticence to engage in open partisan remarks, Reid did take a few moments to outline the benefits of the Harrison administration and noted that "even our enemy" endorsed most of the progress Republicans had brought to the nation and commemorated Harrison's administration as "the first national administration Indiana ever had" that was "a clean and honorable one with a record as dis-

Whitelaw Reid

LIBRARY OF CONGRESS

tinguished as any in the country's history." He added, "I call you to witness that the trivialities are the sum and substance of the few and scattering complaints against your Indiana President. No man questions his ability or his integrity, or the character of the administration, or its great success. Every man here knows that whether as a lawyer, or soldier, or senator, or President, (Benjamin Harrison's) life is a model; that he is laboriously devoted to his work; that he is a good citizen, a good friend, a good neighbor, with a heart as tender as a woman's to the call of sorrow or distress and with a sense of duty that absolutely dominates his life."[137]

Earlier in the day, before arriving at Indianapolis, Reid and Depew drew a crowd of about 3,000 in Logansport for companion speeches in a city park. Reid's remarks were praiseworthy of the city of Logansport and the entire Wabash valley, with the sights he had seen from the train ride from Chicago convincing him that Democratic claims of "calamity" in the nation were false. "I am grateful, gentlemen," he said, "that I do not belong to the party which finds it necessary to its own success to calumniate the country. Whether there is, or is not, there is a party in this country which seeks its triumph only in national disasters. I beg to assure you that the Republican Party is not hunting for that. We are not anxious that you should have bad crops; we are not anxious that you should be overtaken by calamities; we are not anxious to belie and calumniate the country in order to convince you that it is necessary to have a change."[138]

Arguing for Harrison's re-election, Reid said, "You have tried your statesman and you have seen the results of his administration. They say that sometimes a prophet has no honor in his own land, but the (Indiana) which I knew in my boyhood is greatly changed if there is not

always, and especially now, a very warm spot in every gallant and chivalrous Indianian's heart for Benjamin Harrison, the tried and incorruptible President, the honored private citizen."[139]

As was often the case in this era, news accounts of the Reid and Depew rallies and speeches varied widely, depending upon who was reporting them. The *Logansport Journal*, a Republican vehicle, for example, proclaimed all of the related events a grand success. The competing *Logansport Daily Pharos*, a decidedly Democratic publication, offered a widely speckled account that was openly insulting of Reid and the Republicans. The Democratic report referred to Reid and Depew as "mouthpieces of monopoly" and "cold-blooded politicians" and asserted their speeches drew as many curious Democrats as supportive Republicans, the "Democrats who were attracted there through the same kind of curiosity that would attract them to a side-show to see Jojo, the dog-faced boy." The scathing account continued, "Not a word of argument was uttered by either of these well-fed, well-clothed gushers in support of the Republican rubber tariff; instead that took turns heaping abuse upon Grover Cleveland and the Democratic Party."[140]

William McKinley

For the 1892 election, Harrison called upon a variety of Republican surrogates to plead his case for a second term, among them Ohio governor William McKinley, a former powerful member of the U.S. House of Representatives and a major figure among Republicans. On one of his many trips on behalf of Harrison, McKinley visited Elwood for the opening of a new tinplate factory, a Memorial Day appearance at Indianapolis in May 1892, and again in late October for a speech in Peru under a large circus tent erected for the occasion. "A stand had been built in the center of the tent, and for over an hour (Governor McKinley) discussed the tariff and currency issues," the *New York Times* reported. McKinley offered strong endorsements for the Republican candidates for Congress and governor in Indiana.[141]

The circus tent erected for McKinley's speech at Peru was provided by Colonel Ben Wallace of Miami County, who founded Wallace and Company's Great World Menagerie, Grand International Mardi Gras, Highway Holiday Hidalgo, and Alliance of Novelties in 1882.[142] As expected, McKinley spent the bulk of his remarks arguing for stronger tariffs as a means of promoting the nation's economy and his opposition to abolishing the 10 percent tax on state banks. McKinley said the tax had protected the safety and security of the nation's banks and monetary systems. "If there is anything in the country the people should insist upon letting alone, that thing is the present money system," McKinley said.[143]

Prior to his Peru stop in October, however, McKinley made headlines for a speech at Elwood on September 14, 1892, where he led locals in celebrating the opening of the American Tinplate Company that employed three hundred men in six mills and produced about six train carloads of tinplates, caps, pans, and "nearly everything else that could be hammered out of tin," the *Warsaw Daily Times* reported.[144] Excited local residents crowded the streets of Elwood, despite a consistent rain, adorned with tin-made souvenirs pinned to their clothes. The rain forced McKinley to move his speech inside the opera house, but another 2,000 supporters remained outside, waiting to get a glimpse of the governor. McKinley did not disappoint, addressing those outside the theater from a balcony, essentially repeating the themes offered in his speech inside the opera house about Republican positions on tariffs. McKinley said tariffs on foreign imports to the

U.S. "did nothing for the needs of the people" and "raised tariffs on foreign goods simply and purely raised revenue for the public treasury." One news account noted, McKinley "seized a pitcher from the desk, tapped it with his fingers and said with an air of pride, 'There is a tariff on this pitcher of 60 percent; that is the result of the Republican protective tariff. It was put there to build up the pottery industry of this country, which, I am glad to say, has been successful. I put that there myself.'"[145]

McKinley said, "The Democratic tariff puts a tariff on foreign products that do not compete with our home products. We put a tariff on products that compete with us. The things we can't produce go free to the American people."[146] He added, "There is not a man in Indiana who knows

William McKinley at his desk, June 7, 1898.

from actual suffering that there is such a thing as a protective tariff. On the contrary, there is not a man or woman in the state who doesn't know that he or she is enjoying its blessings." The numerous glassworks in Elwood and nearby Muncie were also noted by McKinley and that all of their products are "of the protected class."[147]

By 1894 McKinley was a widely sought GOP speaker on behalf of congressional and state candidates across the nation, based largely on his well-received speeches in 1892 on behalf of Harrison's losing re-election effort. As historian Charles Morris noted, McKinley journeyed more than 10,000 miles in 1894 and delivered more than 371 speeches during an eight-week period, sometimes as many as seven speeches in one day. Estimates were that McKinley spoke before as many as two million Americans in the 1894 election cycle. "Wherever he went he was received with an ovation, people gathering in the thousands and clamoring to hear him at all the railroad stations on his line of travel," Morris wrote. "Everywhere his fame spread in advance, and the people flocked in numbers, coming hundreds of miles to see him at the larger cities where he was engaged to speak. On September 26, he faced at Indianapolis the largest audience ever gathered in the Hoosier state."[148] His Indianapolis visit, at Tomlinson Hall for a meeting of Indiana Republicans, included an appearance by former president Harrison. News reports indicated Harrison offered brief introductory remarks for McKinley (viewed as a strong endorsement by many Republicans), and McKinley spoke for an hour and twenty minutes "without manuscript and from scant notes."[149] His remarks focused mostly on tariffs, including those on sugar cane.

His term as governor of Ohio ended in January 1896, and McKinley immediately set upon a quest for the Republican presidential nomina-

tion, particularly given that other major players such as Senator John Sherman of Ohio also had presidential designs. His years of work on behalf of Republican candidates across the nation served him well, as did his support of the gold standard, the latter point gaining him the financial backing of the nation's banking and business interests. He easily won the GOP nomination and became the last Civil War veteran to be nominated by either major party for the presidency. McKinley chose New Jersey state legislator Garret A. Hobart as his running mate. McKinley's campaign reverted to a successful GOP formula that had worked before, a "front porch campaign" with more than 500,000 voters making their way to McKinley's home in Canton, Ohio. The campaign tactic worked. McKinley won the November election, drawing just more than 51 percent of the vote nationally, and likewise in Indiana, McKinley scored a narrow 51-48 percent victory, one of eight states where the governor edged out victory with a margin of 5 percent of vote or less.

Once in office, McKinley made his first visits to Indiana in October 1898 to lobby Americans in support of a peace treaty in the Philippines. On October 15, 1898, at Terre Haute, McKinley made an 8 a.m. speech in which he briefly fooled his audience by saying he was glad to be in the hometown of "my friend, your neighbor, a veteran statesman and patriot," and then referred to former Secretary of the Navy and Congressman Richard W. Thompson (a Republican). He added, "I do not forget that this is also the home of that other distinguished Indianian, whose eloquence moved Senates and swayed great audiences, and whose friendship I enjoyed, the Hon. Daniel W. Voorhees."[150] Voorhees, a Democrat, had lost re-election to the Senate in 1896 to McKinley's friend and adviser, Republican Charles Warren Fairbanks. McKinley remarked that his seven-day trip across "the west" had resulted in "great assemblages," but that he understood that represented American patriotism rather than any personal indulgence of his own. "It means that all the people of all the sections are once more united under one flag, united in purpose and patriotism."[151]

On October 21, 1898, as the president's train made its way back east to Washington, D.C., he stopped in nine Indiana communities, including Logansport, Kokomo, Tipton, Atlanta, Noblesville, Indianapolis, Rushville, Connersville, and College Corner. For his first stop at Logansport for a 7 a.m. speech, he noted, "About a week ago I entered your state at eight o'clock in the morning and was greeted by tens of thousands of people in the city of Terre Haute. An hour earlier in the day I meet this great throng of my fellow countrymen."[152]

The president said that no hour of the day was too early for Americans to meet "since Dewey entered Manila Bay on that early morning in May" and won the Philippine conflict. "The flag never seemed so dear to us as it does now," McKinley said. "And it never floated over so many places as it does now. As I have journeyed the country, I have rejoiced at the patriotism of the people. The flag of our country is in every man's hands and patriotism is in every man's heart. That is a good omen for our country. Our army and our navy have done brilliant service, have added new honors to the American name, have given a new meaning to American valor; and it only remains for us, the people, who in a country like ours are masterful when they speak, to do the rest, and to embody in honorable treaty the fruitage of this war."[153]

The presidential train stopped next at Kokomo, and he offered similar remarks before an audience of 10,000 and said he believed America presents "a spectacle of seventy-five millions of people, representing every race and nationality and section, united in one faith and under one flag, and that is the glorious old Stars and Stripes we love so much. And we must continue to stand together. So long as we have any differences abroad we must have none at home. Whenever we get through with our differences with another nation, then it will be time for us to resume our old disputes at home. Until that time we must stand for a common purpose, until the settlements of war shall be embodied in the permanent form of a public treaty [in the Philippines]."[154] McKinley declared that "we commenced the war, not for the gain or greed of new possessions. We commenced it for freedom and to relieve our neighbors of oppression." He offered praise to Indiana for fulfilling its quota for soldiers to fight the conflict: "I thank you all, in the name of the nation, for your patriotic devotion to the country."[155] The Kokomo throng was disappointed, however, as the Associated Press reported, "The President had hardly finished speaking when the train pulled out, thus depriving all of the privilege of shaking hands with him."[156]

A short time later at Tipton, McKinley's train stopped again, and he hit on similar themes, including noting that the war had brought the nation together and held the promise of better lives for the Filipino people. "As I look into your earnest faces," he said, "I know that you would have this nation help the oppressed people who have by the war been brought within the sphere of our influence."[157] Moving his remarks away from military conflict, the president added, "Here in this great gas belt, I am reminded of what nature has done for your great manufactories. I congratulate you again upon the prospect for better business in the United States. It is a great thing for the farmer to have men employed in shop and factory. It is a great thing for men to be employed; and I have discovered that when the employer seeks labor, labor gets better pay than when the laborer seeks employment."[158]

At tiny Atlanta in Hamilton County, the president acknowledged his friend, U.S. Representative Charles Beary Landis of Logansport (who was running for re-election) and praised local tinplate manufacturers. He concluded his brief remarks by adding a friendly touch, "I wish you all prosperity in your workshops and love and contentment in your homes."[159] In the Hamilton County seat of Noblesville, McKinley said, "This is a most inspiring spectacle. Present here this morning are all of your civic bodies, the old soldiers and the new soldiers, and all the people. Such a sight as this could scarcely be witnessed anywhere else. You are here because you are interested in your country. You are here because you love your country. You are here because you rejoice in the victories of our army and navy, and

LIBRARY OF CONGRESS

McKinley and his vice presidential running mate, Theodore Roosevelt.

you're here because you rejoice in the suspension of hostilities, the return of many of your boys to their homes, and the hope and belief that you will soon have a lasting and triumphant peace, resting in justice, righteousness, and humanity."[160] McKinley attempted to remove any idea that he was simply present for political purposes, declaring, "Here none are for a party, but all are for the State. Here Democrats and Republicans and men of all parties have assembled to show their appreciation of the services rendered to the government by the army and navy of the United States."[161]

At Indianapolis, McKinley thanked Hoosiers for sending Fairbanks to Washington, D.C., but added, "We meet in no party name. We meet in the name of the country, of patriotism, and of peace." He wisely added in the name of another beloved Hoosier and Republican, former president Harrison, whom he called "an illustrious statesman." To verify his desire for promoting bipartisanship, he also raised the name of former Vice President Thomas A. Hendricks, an Indiana Democrat. He said these Indiana men "are remembered by all of you, and [both Harrison and Hendricks] have been distinguished in the service of their country."[162] He implored his Indianapolis listeners, "The war has been successful. It ended in a little over 100 days. Matchless victories on land and sea! Our Army and our Navy are entitled to every honor their generous nation can bestow. Peerless army and navy! They have done their part; the rest remains with us. The war was inaugurated for humanity; its settlements must not overlook humanity. It was not commenced in bitterness. It was not commenced in malice. It was commenced in a spirit of humanity, of freedom, to stop oppression in a neighboring island. We cannot shirk the obligations of the victory if we would, and we would not if we could."[163]

For his remarks at Rushville, McKinley seemed to articulate better the purpose of his campaign and his hopes for a treaty settlement for the Philippines: "Providence has been very kind to us. We've been through a war which lasted only a little more than one hundred days, a war happily not on our own, but on distant shores. And in that short time, we sent our boys—and your contribution was among them—7,000 miles by sea. And yet in that short time, we have achieved a victory which will be memorable in history. There has been nothing like it recorded in military annals. Now, having triumphed in war, we must be sure that in the settlements of the war we shall see that justice and righteousness and humanity shall prevail. The work is now with you; for in a government like ours the people constitute the power of the government. It rests and resides with you, and your will is the command of the Congress and to the Executive, and it is at last formed into public law and public policy."[164]

Showing the strain of the day and the repeated speeches, McKinley gave particularly brief remarks at both Connersville and College Corner. In the latter community, a tiny hamlet west of Richmond in Union County, he remarked, "If I had ever been uncertain about the size of Indiana, that uncertainty has been dispelled to-day. I have been speaking since seven o'clock this morning to vast audiences at every station from Logansport to your town. And now the time is come when I must say farewell to Indiana and give hail to my native state."[165]

McKinley was back in Indiana about a year later for three southwest Indiana stops in Evansville, Vincennes, and Terre Haute. At the Vanderburgh County Fairgrounds in Evansville on October 11, 1899, McKinley addressed a reunion of both Union and Confederate soldiers.

"It gives me great pleasure to participate with you, men of the North and men of the South, in this glad reunion," he said. "We are unified. The peace which Grant and Lee made at Appomattox has been kept, not by law or restraint, but by love and for fraternal regard; and the Union to-day rests, not in force, which might fail, but in the hearts of the people, which cannot fail." McKinley affirmed that "we have been more than reconciled—cemented in faith and affection; and are reuniting as men baptized in the best blood of both sections of our beloved country" and "it rests upon us to put the past behind us, except as a sacred and glorious memory and to look to the future."[166] Before departing Evansville by train, McKinley lamented to the cries of a large crowd at the railroad depot and offered greetings from the rear platform of his train and again praised the North-South reunion he had just attended.

Later at Vincennes in Knox County, McKinley's remarks grew somewhat more political when he noted, "We have been blessed with good crops and fair prices. Wages and employment have waited upon labor, and, differing from what it was a few years ago, labor is not waiting on the outside for wages. Our financial condition was never better than now. We have good money and plenty of it circulating as our medium of exchange. National banks may fail, fluctuation in prices come and go, but the money of the country remains always good; and when you have a dollar of it you know that dollar is worth one hundred cents. Not only have we prosperity, but we have patriotism; and what more do we want?" He quickly added, "We are at peace with all the nations of the world, and were never on better terms and closer relations with each of them than we are today. We have yet some trouble in the Philippines, but the gallantry of the brave boys who have gone there will, I trust, soon put down that rebellion against the sovereignty of the United States."[167] During a quick stop in Terre Haute, McKinley said he was "greatly pleased, as I have journeyed your State, with what I have seen and heard—the evidences of good feeling and cheerfulness on the part of the people, and of prosperity in your fields and your workshops."[168]

Six days later on October 17, 1899, McKinley's train made an unexpected but welcomed stop at Michigan City, where he made remarks of less than five minutes, including phrases perhaps now familiar to Hoosier audiences: "This is an unexpected, but, I assure you, most appreciated greeting from my fellow-citizens of Indiana. I'm glad to see the school-children here, waving the flag of their country, the flag they love so much, the flag that means so much to all of us."[169]

The audience gathered that day at Michigan City did not know it, but they were among the last ever to hear McKinley speak on Hoosier soil. A popular and respected figure, the last Civil War veteran elected president, McKinley died on September 14, 1901, as a result of an assassin's wounds just six months after being sworn into a second term. McKinley was shot on September 6, 1901, by Leon Czolgosz, an Alpena, Michigan, man of Polish descent and a troubled anarchist. Czolgosz shot McKinley twice in the abdomen as the president greeted visitors inside the Hall of Music at the Pan-American Exposition in Buffalo, New York. McKinley's wounds had caused a serious infection in his stomach and bowels, and he succumbed after showing initial signs of improvement.

4

Industrial Revolution, 1900–11

Theodore Roosevelt

The close of the nineteenth century and the beginning of the twentieth century was the era of Theodore Roosevelt, the once obscure New York politician rising quickly, not only to the nation's highest offices, but also in affection in the hearts of Americans.

For the 1900 election, Roosevelt took on the traditional role for vice presidential nominees— the low road—and kept up the pressure on the Democrat's nominee, William Jennings Bryan. In early September he embarked on twenty-one separate speeches in Michigan and Indiana, including speaking before a large audience at South Bend on September 9, 1900. Under a tent erected on the lawn of the Saint Joseph County Courthouse, Roosevelt took up the gold vs. silver standard issue, as well as Democratic charges of American imperialism in the Philippines. "We have the same right and title to the Philippines that we have to Hawaii and Alaska," Roosevelt said. "If we are morally and legally bound to leave the one, we are morally and legally count to leave the others, and incidentally, to surrender New Mexico and Idaho and pretty much every other Western state to the aboriginal inhabitants. The cry that 'the Constitution follows the flag,' of course means nothing. If Judge Taft and his associates and General MacArthur and his fellow-officers in the Philippines are representatives of the imperial idea, then so is every officer and every Indian agent on a Sioux or Ute or Comanche reservation. It is difficult to discuss patiently such an assumption!"[1]

Roosevelt declared in his typical clenched-fist manner that America could not "surrender" the Philippines because "of our duty to ourselves and . . . our duty to the people of the islands. If we stay there, peace and order and a far greater measure of freedom and self-government than the Filipinos have ever known, will be theirs as soon as their present insurrection ceases. . . . To treat the Filipinos on the 'consent of the governed' in the way in which Mr. Bryan proposes, would be, without their consent, to put them under a military oligarchy, and nothing would be so certain to involve us in a perpetual career of militarism."[2]

Roosevelt was back in Indiana a month later for an ambitious two-day agenda of speeches scheduled for early October, including stops at Frankfort, Logansport, Peru, Wabash, Huntington, Fort Wayne, Marion, Fairmount, Alexandria, Anderson, Muncie, Winchester, Richmond, Indianapolis, Plainfield, Greencastle, Brazil, Terre Haute, Linton, Vincennes, Princeton, and Evansville. For his Fort Wayne speech, the New York governor took up comments attributed to Bryan

IHS, BASS PHOTO COMPANY COLLECTION, P 130

Roosevelt and his second wife, Edith, who served as First Lady from 1901 to 1909.

the day before an audience at Macomb, Illinois. He challenged reports that Bryan had asserted that "the real object for permanently increasing the army is to intimidate the labor element when it presents just complaints" and that the federal government was interested in erecting forts near major cities "to meet all the demands of labor."[3]

"I earnestly hope that the *Indianapolis Sentinel* has misquoted Mr. Bryan," Roosevelt retorted. "I am not willing to believe that any responsible party leader, and least of all the candidate of any such party for the Presidency, would permit himself to make such statements. There is not one shadow of excuse for them."[4] Roosevelt termed the comments attributed to Bryan as "appealing to the basest and most evil passions of mankind by deliberate misrepresentation of the intention and action of patriotic and law-abiding

citizens."[5] Roosevelt said Bryan should know his remarks were wrong and distorted the purpose of the American military, or if he did not know they were wrong, he was unfit for office. "There is no idea of erecting forts near the large cities, and never has been, save where they are used for defense against a foreign foe," Roosevelt explained. "There is no fort near Indianapolis, for instance, because it cannot be minced by a foreign foe."[6] His comments came before Indianapolis became the home to Fort Benjamin Harrison in 1903. Bryan "either knows or ought to know that our standing army relative to the size of the population is nearly one-half less than it was in Thomas Jefferson's time, and that there is no more thought of using it to coerce the labor element or any other element than there was the thought of using it in the days of Jefferson."[7]

Before leaving Fort Wayne, momentary excitement resulted when a rock was thrown at Roosevelt, missed, and struck another man in the mouth. "After the train left Fort Wayne, the stone throwing incident in the streets of that city was the chief topic of conversation," the Associated Press reported. "It was considered beyond the doubt to have been the work of hoodlums." Roosevelt himself said, "I was not injured at all. There is danger that this matter may be magnified. It amounted to nothing."[8]

Roosevelt moved on to another speech in Hammond, where he was met with "several companies of Rough Riders (who) escorted him to the public square."[9] Roosevelt also spoke at tiny Monon in White County, as well as at Rensselaer, Lafayette, and Frankfort. Except for the Fort Wayne, Lafayette, and Hammond speeches, all of his remarks emanated from the rear platform of his campaign train. While in Lafayette, the *New York Times* reported that "the Governor headed a procession a mile and a half long to the Lincoln Club, in the yard of which a speakers' stand had been erected. When Gov. Roosevelt, passing through the club house, appeared on the platform, a mighty cheer went up from the Rough Riders present and the thousands who thronged the streets. A unique feature of the parade was a citizen mounted on a bull and wearing a coonskin cap."[10]

Roosevelt's October swing also took him through central Indiana, including a stop at Richmond, where a crowd of 10,000 Indiana and Ohio residents showed up to hear him speak at the bottom of a hill, which has subsequently been known as Roosevelt Hill since that October day in 1900. Appearing with him at Richmond again were a contingent of Rough Riders who escorted him to the speaker's stand near the hill in Glen Miller Park.[11]

Once in Indianapolis, Roosevelt was feted to a large "fall festival" parade that allowed Republicans to showcase their candidates. Roosevelt watched the parade from a stand erected outside the Marion County Courthouse at East Washington and Delaware Streets. "The candidate for Vice President was continually bowing to the multitude and shaking hands with men and women who clustered around his carriage," a news dispatch indicated. "The Courthouse square and grounds and streets surrounding it were congested with a throng, which greeted the Governor's arrival with a storm of cheers, and as he alighted at the Courthouse entrance, cannons boomed salutes."[12]

Roosevelt made brief remarks before the two-hour parade and acknowledged his introduction by Captain William E. English, "a Democrat who believes in what were once the old Democratic doctrines of hard money, expansion, and the honor of the flag. That is what Andrew Jackson fought for and lived for, and he would turn in his grave if some of these modern Bryanized Democrats walked over it." Roosevelt challenged his Indianapolis audience to carefully review what Bryan had said during his speeches in the city four years ago. "Our opponents became ashamed of the issues they had raised four years ago," he said. "They champion them still, but they don't dare argue about them, and they sought to make a new issue, and that issue is the dishonor of the American flag. . . . And already they are shifting their issues, already they recognize what a hollow sham it is to talk about imperialism and militarism, and now they are doing that worst of evil deeds in a republic—preaching the doctrine of envy, of class hatred, striving to stir up brother against brother, section against section, class against class."[13]

President William McKinley and Roosevelt were successful in winning the 1900 campaign, including a narrow victory in Indiana by a margin of 18,447 votes (McKinley drawing just above 50 percent of the vote), though their Indiana victory aligned with a clean sweep of northern states to win the presidency. Perhaps it was fate that had delivered Roosevelt from the lowly position of state assemblyman to vice president in the span of just more than a dozen years. Fate never seemed far from the center of Roosevelt's life. As a young man in his twenties, Roosevelt enjoyed success, elected as a New York state assemblyman, but in the same era lost his first wife Alice Hathaway Lee, who died two days after his daughter Alice Lee was born in 1884. Two years later he was a candidate for mayor of New York City, but finished last in a three-way contest. Following his loss, the "nature cowboy" in Roosevelt took over as he explored many parts of the West but eventually returned to public life for the 1888 presidential contest, campaigning for Indiana's Benjamin Harrison.

After a distinguished military career as a colonel in the Spanish-American War, Roosevelt returned to New York and won election as governor in 1898 by a narrow margin. Supporters and detractors alike joined forces to promote Roosevelt for the vice presidential nomination of the Republican Party, and he proved an aggressive and helpful running mate for McKinley, who had served the last year of his first term as president with no vice president when Garret Hobart died in November 1899 following an extended illness. With Roosevelt as his running mate, McKinley won a second term to office in the 1900 election, but most historians agree the vice presidency was probably a poor fit for the outspoken and colorful Roosevelt. He remained a popular figure for the media, who promoted many of his pronouncements, including his repeating of the West African proverb, "Speak softly and carry a

Roosevelt steps from the train on a campaign stop at Terre Haute's Union Station.

big stick, and you will go far." Sworn in as vice president of the United States on March 4, 1901, fate intervened just six months later on September 6, 1901, as McKinley was assassinated. Roosevelt, who had visited the wounded president days after he was shot and was attempting to recuperate, was on a return trip to Buffalo when he learned of McKinley's passing and his installation as the twenty-sixth president of the United States.

President Roosevelt wasted little time embracing his new role, delivering a lengthy speech to a joint session of Congress laying out a progressive agenda of his own. In September 1902 Roosevelt set out on a "western trip" that included a couple of stops in Indiana, including Logansport and Indianapolis. Days before, however, Roosevelt had injured his leg in a fall from a trolley car in Pittsfield, Massachusetts. The president's leg injury began to flare up as he rode his train south across Indiana, and by the time he stopped at Logansport at just after 7:00 a.m., a physician on the train and the president's friend, Senator Albert Beveridge of Indiana, compelled him to be examined by doctors upon his arrival in Indianapolis. This did not stop Roosevelt from

IHS, MARTIN'S PHOTO SHOP COLLECTION, P 129

making lengthy remarks at Logansport while a light rain fell. He left the presidential train and was driven to the high school, where most of the audience members stood under umbrellas, blocking the view of most of the assembled of the president. He told the audience, "I will make a bargain with you; I won't have an umbrella over my head if you won't have one over you," and hundreds of umbrellas were lowered allowing those farther back to see Roosevelt.[14]

In his remarks at Logansport, Roosevelt asked his audience "to take what I say at its exact face value, as I like whatever I say to be taken." Praising the industrial and agricultural strength of Indiana, Roosevelt said, "It is the merest truism to say that in the modern world, industrialism is the great factor in the growth of nations. Material prosperity is the foundation upon which every mighty national structure must be built. Of course, there must be more than this. There must be a high moral purpose, a life of the spirit which finds its expression in many different ways; but unless material prosperity exists also, there is scant room in which to develop the higher life."[15]

"A great and successful commonwealth like ours in the long run works under good laws," Roosevelt said, "because a people endowed with honest and practical common sense ultimately demand good laws. But no law can create industrial well-being, although it may foster and safeguard it, and although a bad law may destroy it. The prime factor in securing industrial well-being is the high average of citizenship found in the community. . . . No scheme of legislation or of social reform will ever work good to the community unless it recognizes as fundamental the fact that each man's own individual qualities must be the prime factors in his success."[16]

The president explained that the best support the federal government could give its citizens

is to "insure its financial stability" and that "an honest currency is the strongest symbol and expression of honest business life." He warned that any tampering with the currency and unchecked debt, regardless of its reason, could have fatal consequences to the nation's economy. Calling for patriotism above partisanship, Roosevelt said, "What we really need in this country is to treat the tariff as a business proposition from the standpoint of the interests of the country as a whole, and not from the standpoint of the temporary needs of any political party."[17]

Roosevelt urged his Hoosier audience to "think for yourselve" and said, "We won in the Civil War because we had the manhood to which to appeal. We are going to win as a nation in the great industrial contest of the present day, because the average American has in him the stuff out of which victors are made–victors in the industrial and victors in the military world. . . . Now, gentlemen, we can win and we will win as citizens of this Republic by showing in the complex, hard, pushing life of this century, the same qualities that were shown by the men of the Civil War in that contest; and above all, by keeping the high average of individual citizenship which made the armies that saw Appomattox the finest which the world has ever seen."[18]

Having kept his commitment in Logansport despite his growing physical pain, the presidential party made its way back to the special train and departed Cass County for quick stops at Kokomo, Tipton, and Noblesville en route to Indianapolis.

A much larger crowd awaited Roosevelt at Kokomo, with local estimates indicating more than 15,000 massed the area around the Howard County Courthouse. Removing his hat as he spoke, Roosevelt made remarks much shorter in length than he had offered at Logansport, although it was unclear whether the irritation of his leg was causing him discomfort. "Here in Indiana you have agencies that can be developed for the food of mankind," he said. "But after all, man is necessary to take advantage of the opportunities and natural resources. Our prosperity is not ephemeral. The waves will go up and down, but prosperity will go on."[19]

Pointing to a Howard County Civil War veteran in the audience, Roosevelt said, "You, my friend and comrade over there, because you believed in the republic, we have big feats to do, of course, but we are big enough to do them. We spread and we preach the gospel of hope which, the men of the west, so signally illustrate in your lives."[20] A short time later Roosevelt's train reached Tipton, and news reports indicated Roosevelt "stepped from the (train) platform and took but a half dozen steps to reach the stand from which he spoke" and noted the president "held his silk hat behind him during the speech" to a crowd about 4,000, including hundreds of schoolchildren at the front of the crowd. Further reports noted that factory whistles blew between Tipton and Noblesville as "several hundred Hoosiers craned their necks to get a view of the President, the train checking its speed to accommodate them."[21]

Although arriving a half hour later than scheduled, a crowd of more than 5,000 greeted the president as he arrived at the depot in Noblesville in Hamilton County. During his remarks, Roosevelt spoke about Spanish-American War veterans and praised the natural gas resources of this portion of Indiana. In brief reference to his remarks earlier at Logansport about the role of corporations in the nation, Roosevelt said, "We do not war on them; we war on any evil in them."[22] Reporters on the scene seemed amused that the two prisoners at the nearby Hamilton

County Jail were afforded prime seats to see the president, peering out from a second-floor window of the jail to catch a glimpse of the downtown spectacle.

At Indianapolis, Roosevelt was met by doctors who "accompanied the party to Tomlinson Hall (in downtown Indianapolis)," and they were assumed by reporters to be part of the Roosevelt welcoming committee. While at Tomlinson Hall, Roosevelt briefly addressed the third annual "encampment" or reunion of veterans of the Spanish-American War. There he said, "In speaking to the men who volunteered for the Spanish War, I wish to lay particular stress on the need of preparedness. Modern war of a serious kind is determined quite as much by what the antagonists have done in advance of the outbreak as by what they do afterward. Modern conditions have brought all parts of the world closer together, and while this nearness tells for good generally, it may at times tell for evil also."[23]

He explained, "As a result of the Spanish War, we took a world position which had never hitherto been ours. We now have before us a destiny which must be one of great failure or success. We cannot play a small part in the world, no matter how much we might wish to. We shall be obliged, willingly or unwillingly, to play a large part; all that we can determine is whether we will play that large part well or ill." The result of the new position America occupied in the world was that a "regular army" was no longer needed, that the nation needed a smaller but smarter and better equipped army coupled with an unmatched navy force. Roosevelt argued that a strong navy was essential to enforce the Monroe Doctrine in the Americas. "The fleet is in a peculiar sense the property of the nation as a whole," he said. "Every American, whether inland or on a seacoast, if he is both far-sighted and patriotic, should be particularly jealous about the efficiency of the navy. . . . The navy must be built up, and it must be continually exercised and trained so that the officers and men may attain the highest degree of excellence in handling the great war engines intrusted to their care."[24]

Following his remarks, an AP dispatch indicated that "the trip to the Columbia Club followed without any feature that would give even a hint that the great western trip of the President was at an end. It was a throng that marched into the club to take luncheon and have a short rest, but instead of going into the dining room, the President was taken to a private room, where, un-

known to the bustling crowd inside and outside (on Monument Circle) of the club, he was made the subject of a serious consultation by the physicians. His leg was bared and swelling examined," and a decision was made that an abscess surgery was necessary to avoid blood poisoning.[25]

As the private medical examinations of Roosevelt continued inside the Columbia Club, rumors began to spread through the large crowd outside as the delay in Roosevelt taking the rostrum erected in front of the club grew noticeably longer. Unknown to those waiting outside, the president made brief remarks inside the Columbia Club and was reported to be in a clear voice.

IHS, LIEBER-BUSHMANN COLLECTION, P 268

Roosevelt addresses an Indianapolis crowd gathered for the dedication of a statue honoring Major General Henry W. Lawton at the Marion County Courthouse, Memorial Day, 1907. Poet James Whitcomb Riley can be seen to Roosevelt's right.

In those remarks he commented on the "sea of people that has as a background the majestic and beautiful monument which you have reared to the sons of Indiana who did well for the Republic in the past. I have come through your state this morning, seeing on every hand the proofs of the marvelous and abounding prosperity which we now as a people enjoy." He concluded by remarking that "this nation is to play a great part in the world, and it moves into the arena where the nations strive for the great opportunity of shaping the destinies of mankind. We feel our veins fill with the evident faith that our children and our children's children will be given days to face dangers and glories; not to shirk them, to do our duty at home and abroad. To dare to be great and make our nation what it shall be, the greatest upon which the sun ever shone. I thank you."[26]

On Monument Circle, rumors continued to swirl as more time elapsed and the president did not appear. "When he did not appear, the rumors began to take on a more serious character. It was said that the President was sick, that he had fainted and finally a rumor was started that he had been shot," the AP reported. "A half hour or more passed and finally it was noticed that a movement of some kind was on. The President's carriage stood in front of the entrance of the club. The soldiers of the National Guard were drawn up just in the rear. The Secret Service men and the police and detectives crowded the sidewalk in front of the club, keeping back the people. The command was given to 'make room,' and a path was cleared from the club entrance to the carriage and, as if in answer to the rumors of his illness, the President accompanied by Senator (Charles Warren) Fairbanks, with a quick and sturdy gait, came down the steps of the club and hastily entered the carriage."[27]

The carriage carrying Roosevelt reached Saint Vincent Hospital just before 4:00 p.m., and the president walked into the hospital on his own strength. Secret Service men quickly stationed themselves at the entrances to the hospital as doctors prepared to relieve the president's discomfort. News reports indicated the nuns of

On August 3, 1904, a committee from the Republican convention arrived in Indianapolis to officially notify Charles W. Fairbanks that he had been selected to serve as the vice presidential running mate with GOP presidential candidate Theodore Roosevelt.

IHS, M 100, CHARLES WARREN FAIRBANKS COLLECTION

Saint Vincent's prepared Room 52, described as "a cozy fourth-floor apartment room fronting on South Street," while "white-capped nurses hurried here and there under the direction of the sisters."[28] Roosevelt's surgery occurred in a fifth-floor surgery suite, where the president had yet another discussion with the surgeons at Saint Vincent about whether he could continue his western speaking tour after the procedure, but they prevailed upon him that he would need rest afterward. The AP reported, "The President walked to the operating table alone and as he lay down remarked with a smile, 'Gentlemen, you are formal. I see you have your gloves on.'"

While the procedure was under way, Governor Winfield T. Durbin and Senator Samuel M. Ralston waited at the hospital with a growing horde of reporters. About an hour later, at 5:00 p.m., "Sister Superior" announced to the reporters that the issue was addressed and Roosevelt had returned to his private room. "The President is in fine humor and is talking and joking," the *Indianapolis Sentinel* quoted Sister Superior as saying.[29] Roosevelt rested briefly, and "at 7:40 p.m., a blanket was thrown around him, and escorted by a company of infantry, was carried on a stretcher to the car a block away by four Negro porters from the train," and by 8:00 p.m. the president's special train moved into position on the tracks near the hospital east of Union Station, and the president was loaded on board for a quick return trip to Washington, D.C.

Doctor John Oliver, a surgeon at Saint Vincent, told reporters that "the operation was performed successfully, but it really was not a serious one. The fear was that if the serum (in his leg) had been allowed to remain, blood poisoning might set in, but I believe there is no further cause for apprehension. The swelling in the President's leg was about as big as an open hand

laid on the leg. The operation only took a short time and in no way affected the physical condition of the President. He is the same today as any other, a well man, outside of the sore place on his leg."[30] Roosevelt's personal secretary, George B. Cortelyou, added, "As a result of the bruise received in the accident at Pittsfield there was found to be a circumscribed collection of perfectly pure serum in the middle of the left anterior tibial region, the sac containing about two ounces, which was removed. The indications are that the President should make a speedy recovery. It is absolutely imperative, however, that he should remain quiet and refrain from using the leg. The trouble is not serious, but temporarily disabling."[31]

Roosevelt's visit to Indiana in November 1904 was considerably less dramatic and came after having won a full term of his own by an impressive margin over Alton B. Parker, including a substantial 54–40 percent victory in Indiana. Roosevelt had scored that win with a Hoosier on the ticket, Fairbanks, who was elected vice president. On November 25, 1904, Roosevelt's train reached Richmond, where he addressed a large gathering, in part to thank Hoosiers for the vote of confidence he had won just weeks earlier. "I want to say what a pleasure it is to be here. It has been some time since I was in Richmond, but I always cherish the warmest memories of my visit to your beautiful city. You must allow me to say that, naturally, I am very pleased to be going through Indiana in view of the way Indiana looked at me a couple of weeks ago. Now, gentlemen, the election is over. I am the President of all the country, of all Americans of whatever party, and so far as strength is given me, I shall try to be a good and decent President the next four years."[32]

Arriving in Indianapolis just after 8:00 p.m. (considerably earlier than the originally scheduled midnight arrival), a large crowd greeted him at

Union Station. "I have always thought a great deal of Indianapolis," he said, "and now I have reason to think more of her than ever. I thank you all for coming out here to see me and I assure you that I appreciate it."[33] The stop lasted for only ten minutes, and no formal remarks were offered, the president instead waving and tipping his hat to the applause offered.

Roosevelt's train brought him through Indiana again in April 1905 as he departed Washington, D.C., for an eight-week trip to the West, principally to join a reunion of a Rough Rider regiment of the Spanish-American War meeting at San Antonio, Texas. En route, Roosevelt's first stop was at Louisville, Kentucky, where a large welcome was staged. After leaving Kentucky, Roosevelt's train crossed the Ohio River north into Indiana and made two unexpected, but well-received stops at both Milltown in Harrison County and Huntingburg in adjacent Dubois County. At Milltown, Roosevelt was introduced by a local official as "the greatest dignitary on Earth" and offered traditional words of greeting, stating briefly:

> I am very glad to have the pleasure of seeing you and saying a word of greeting to you. It cannot but be pleasant to any President to have the chance of going through the country and meeting his fellow countrymen and being greeted as you have greeted me. I am glad to see you all—the men, the women, and the children. I am glad to see here, and wherever I go, the type of man and of woman which I believe makes the future welfare of this country—the man and woman who believe in doing their duty in facing life, knowing that life has in it any amount that is hard, but who are going to do their part to make things right for themselves and for their neighbors. There is not anything very difficult in government. It is simply the applying of certain common-sense principles that we apply among ourselves. The man who is a decent man will be

a decent husband, a decent father, a decent neighbor, and in public life he will do the right thing.[34]

A short time later at Huntingburg, Roosevelt offered similar greetings: "It is a great pleasure to catch this glimpse of you and greet you on my way down to the reunion of my old regiment at San Antonio, Texas. There is one thing I am always impressed with in going through this country, and that is, down at bottom, east or west, north or south, wherever you meet the average American, he is a pretty good American. In greeting all of you, I want to say that while I am particularly glad to see the men and the women, I think I am even more glad to see the children. I think the American stock is a middling good one, and I do not want to see it die out. I see here men who wear the button that shows that they fought in the great war. They have left us a legacy not only of how to do our duty in war, but in peace. Let us of the younger generation try to keep up their standard."[35]

A change of engines required a short stop at East Junction in Gibson County allowing

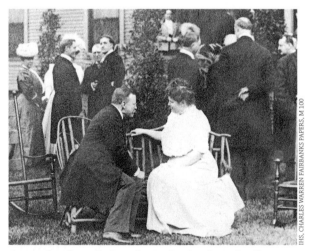

IHS, CHARLES WARREN FAIRBANKS PAPERS, M 100

Roosevelt talks with Cornelia Fairbanks, the wife of his vice presidential running mate Charles Fairbanks, at the Fairbankses' Indianapolis home, Memorial Day, 1907.

Roosevelt to personally meet some lucky southern Indiana Hoosiers. The *Washington Post* reported, "the President jumped down from the rear platform of the train to shake hands with a number of employees of the railroad shops there. The train then ran through Princeton slowly to give the President an opportunity to hastily review several hundred school children who had been assembled near the railroad tracks."[36]

Two years later, for the Memorial Day holiday in 1907, Indianapolis leaders had put together a major celebration in order to dedicate a statute to Major General Henry W. Lawton, which was placed upon the lawn of the Marion County Courthouse. (The Lawton monument was moved to Garfield Park in Indianapolis in 1917.) Roosevelt accepted the invitation to appear at the event, along with Vice President Fairbanks of Indianapolis. Eastern newspaper political reporters took delight in pointing out that the trip would require Roosevelt and Fairbanks to spend considerable time in one another's company, something they normally avoided in Washington, D.C., the relationship between the two men having become noticeably cold and distant. As usual, Roosevelt gave a lengthy speech that paid tribute to Lawton and recognized Fairbanks, but focused mostly on railroad issues in the nation. Roosevelt and Fairbanks led a parade from Union Station east to the courthouse that included thirteen companies of the Grand Army of the Republic and marching bands. During the event, Indianapolis poet James Whitcomb Riley recited a poem composed for the occasion.

In his remarks Roosevelt said:

For more than one reason I am peculiarly glad that this year I speak on Memorial Day in the State of Indiana. There is no other class of our citizens to whom we owe so much as to the veterans of the great war. To them it was given to perform the one feat with which no other feat can be compared, for to them it was given to preserve the Union. Moreover, you men who wore the blue, blessed beyond the victors in any other war of recent times, have left to your countrymen more than the material results of the triumph, more even than the achieving of the triumph itself. You have left a country so genuinely reunited that all of us now, in whatever part of this Union we live, have a right to feel the keenest pride, not only in the valor and self-devotion of you, the gallant men who wore the blue, but also in the valor and self-devotion of your gallant opponents who wore the gray.[37]

Addressing the large crowd of Indiana Union veterans present, Roosevelt drew heavy applause when he noted that "Indiana, in the Civil War, furnished even more than her share of brave soldiers. It also fell to Indiana to furnish the greatest of all the war Governors who upheld the hands of Abraham Lincoln, for when history definitely awards credit for what was done in the Civil War, she will put the services of no other civilian, save alone those of Lincoln, ahead of the services of Governor [Oliver P.] Morton. No other man who rendered such services as he rendered worked under such terrible disadvantages, and no man without his iron power could have achieved what he achieved during the last two years of the war, when he managed the state government of Indiana, solely on money obtained by pledging his own personal honor and personal fortune, and yet never for one moment relaxed in the help he gave to Lincoln and [Salmon] Chase and [William] Seward and [Edwin] Stanton in the Cabinet, to [Ulysses S.] Grant and [William T.] Sherman and [Philip] Sheridan and [George] Thomas in the field. It was work that only the strongest man could have done, and it was work vitally necessary for the sake of the nation to do."[38]

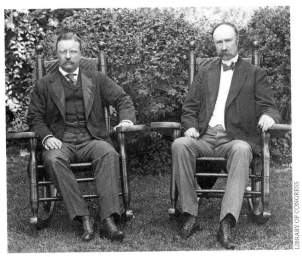

Roosevelt and Fairbanks pose stiffly for the camera at Sagamore Hill, Roosevelt's home in Oyster Bay, New York.

Referring to the Lawton monument, Roosevelt said it recognized that Lawton's life "bore singular testimony to the completeness of the reunion. General Lawton in his youth fought gallantly in the Civil War. Thirty-three years afterward, he again marched to war, this time against a foreign foe, and served with distinguished ability and success as a general officer, both in Cuba and in the Philippines."[39]

Following the ceremonies, the president and vice president visited Crown Hill Cemetery, where Roosevelt placed a wreath on the grave of former president Benjamin Harrison.

Charles Warren Fairbanks

Roosevelt, who had assumed the office of president after McKinley's assassination, had served since 1901 with no vice president. Many who knew Roosevelt's big personality suspected that he was not particularly concerned about not having a political partner. During the 1904 Republican National Convention, party conservatives were restless with the nomination of Roosevelt (but powerless to stop it), and thus accepted a secondary prize with the unopposed

nomination of Senator Fairbanks of Indiana for the vice presidential nomination. All indications were not only that Roosevelt had little interest in having a running mate, but he also had little interest in Fairbanks, a patrician politician who lacked a rugged outdoor manner.

An effective campaigner, Fairbanks understood his role was to help deliver Indiana's critical electoral votes to the Republicans and so campaigned extensively in his home state. For a final swing through Indiana (one reported to be of more than thirteen hundred miles in length), Fairbanks was well received on his home turf with stops at Indianapolis, Tipton, Elwood, Marion, and Huntington, before reaching Fort Wayne for a big rally. "Eight years ago, conditions were different from what they are today," Fairbanks told a crowd of several thousand at Fort Wayne on Halloween day, 1904. "Then we were told if we would adopt the free coinage of silver, manufacturing would increase, and that prosperity among the people would be largely augmented. Our Democratic friends said unless we coined silver freely there would be no prosperity on the farm." He continued, "We refused to accept their advice then. We did not believe it was good then, and we have not changed our minds since. We have not changed our minds, either, as to the wisdom of the Democratic policies or as to the wisdom of Democratic leadership."[40]

Fairbanks spent the night in Fort Wayne and then proceeded north to Elkhart. As the *Elkhart Daily Review* reported, "The meeting at Fort Wayne last night was very large and the trip from Fort Wayne to Goshen was one series of public demonstrations, creditable to the confidence which Indianans feel in their senior senator and evidently a source of gratification and a feeling of their honor on his part."[41] En route to Elkhart, Fairbanks stopped at almost every town along

IHS, BRETZMAN PHOTOGRAPH STUDIO COLLECTION, P 338

Charles Warren Fairbanks, April 23, 1916.

the way—Butler, Auburn, Waterloo, Kendallville, Wolcottville, LaGrange, and Goshen. He momentarily "dipped" into Michigan for a quick stop at Sturgis. After Elkhart, Fairbanks stopped for speeches at South Bend, La Porte, Hammond, and Michigan City.

"The senator is in fine condition," the *Elkhart Daily Review* indicated. "No one, to look at him or hear him talk, would have supposed for a moment that he has been traveling from ocean to ocean and from the gulf to the lakes making speeches many times a day and shaking hands with thousands of people. Those who thought that the senator and vice presidential candidate could not stand the strenuosity of a campaign like this have another thought coming. His strength and endurance is a surprise even to those who know him best."[42]

"I WONDER IF I AM HIS VALENTINE."

A 1907 Puck *cover depicts Fairbanks as an old woman sitting in a rocking chair in front of a fireplace, holding a portrait of the Republican Elephant; he is wearing a pair of shoes labeled "Nomination Sneakers" and there is a basket of knitting labeled "Political Fancy Work" on the floor next to the chair.*

LIBRARY OF CONGRESS

At the Elkhart County Courthouse in Goshen, Fairbanks tarried for nearly thirty minutes before a crowd of more than 2,000 but delivered essentially the same speech as he had in Fort Wayne. He noted, "We have no more prosperity than we want, therefore we cannot afford to entrust the great affairs of government to the hands of Democratic leaders. Would Democratic triumph increase our prosperity in Indiana? If so, then we should as wise and patriotic citizens of the Republic, adopt Democratic policies? If you believe, my friends, that the present prosperity is the fruit of Republican policies and Republican administrations, then it is in the part of wisdom to continue in force and effect Republican policies and a Republican administration."[43] Fairbanks cited the boom in housing in many parts of the nation as evidence of Roosevelt's proper direction for the nation and said, "I wish everyone had a home. . . . We wish to keep open the door of opportunity that those who have not may have a chance, under our institutions and under the inspiration of our policies, to have homes where love and contentment abide."[44]

For the third day of his speaking tour, Fairbanks made more than twenty speeches with stops at Walkerton, Plymouth, Argos, Rochester, Peru, Logansport, Lafayette, Monticello, and Delphi. A fourth and fifth day of campaigning followed, with speeches at Greencastle, Crawfordsville, Newport, Terre Haute, Vincennes, Sullivan, Linton, Odon, Elnora, Washington, Princeton, Poseyville, Mount Vernon, and Evansville among many other cities. In Crawfordsville, Fairbanks seemed pleased to see a large contingent of men from nearby Wabash College in the audience and declared, "We are obliged in a few days to declare our allegiance to some political party. It matters not what we say here, or what we think here upon political questions, but it is all important

LIBRARY OF CONGRESS

In addition to his political career, Fairbanks had a secret, majority partnership in the Indianapolis News, *as well as the* Indianapolis Journal.

what we do at the ballot box next Tuesday. If we are in favor of Republican policies and their continuance, we must so declare our potent judgment at the ballot box."[45]

During his remarks at the Monroe County Courthouse in Bloomington, Fairbanks acknowledged nearly 2,000 Indiana University students who had skipped class and walked downtown to greet him. "We are proud of our state institutions, we are proud of this magnificent university, we are especially proud of the fifteen hundred young men and women who are here," he said. "It never meant more to be an American than it means this year. The United States never stood for more than it stands for now among the nations of the world. Our country has grown in power at home and has grown in admiration of all the nations of the earth. It has grown under

the inspiration of Republican policies and administrations."[46]

Continuing his focus on IU and its students, Fairbanks said, "the state does well to educate; she does well to open the doors of this great institution to the young men and the young women of the state. There are some who raise the question as to whether the appropriation of public funds for the education of the youth of the state is not beyond the functions of the state. There are those who regard that policy as paternalistic, but in a Republican, in a state whose safety and whose future rests upon intelligence, it is indeed the high and appropriate function of the state to educate the young men and the young women upon whose patriotic shoulders in due time the responsibilities of promoting its welfare must rest."[47]

Fairbanks's exhaustive tour ended where it began—in Indianapolis on November 5, 1904. Speaking from a stand outside the Columbia Club on Monument Circle, Fairbanks told his supporters that "we may survey the great campaign which is closing with complete satisfaction. We have put the debate on a high plane, as becomes a discussion which involves the prosperity of the people and the destiny of the Republic. We have not indulged in ungenerous personalities, for they have no rightful place in the discussion of great and vital national issues. Those are indeed the weapons of a discredited and lost cause."[48]

Elected to the vice presidency, a position that generally won him little notice from the president or the world, Fairbanks returned to Indiana in March 1907 to address a joint session of the Indiana General Assembly. Addressing primarily trade and tariff issues, Fairbanks said, "We will keep open the avenues to free and just competition, but we will restrain within appropriate limits those agencies or combinations which may seek to disregard fair laws of trade and competition, and to override the interest of the body of people. Capital which is properly employed will be properly protected, and that which is not so engaged must fall under the sharp condemnation of the law."[49]

Fairbanks's chances for the Republican nomination for president in 1908 were undercut considerably by Roosevelt's support of Secretary of War William Howard Taft. Fairbanks finished fifth in a six-candidate race for the GOP nomination, a race dominated by Taft.

William Jennings Bryan

Fresh from the fame won from his "Cross of Gold" speech in July 1896 declaring his opposition to the gold monetary standard, a speech wrapped in evangelical Christian overtones, Bryan opened his Indiana campaign on October 21, 1896, with a stop at Richmond (after completing his day of campaigning in Ohio at 2:30 a.m. the night before).[50] An audience estimated at 6,000 people gathered on a frosty October morning in Richmond to hear Bryan speak from a balcony at the Hotel Westcott. He invoked the name of Indiana's famed Civil War governor and later U.S. senator Oliver P. Morton (a Republican) to introduce his views on the nation's monetary policies. "Senator Morton was declaring against the policy of contraction," Bryan said, "and we are today declaring against the policy of contraction. (Morton) asserted that an increase in the supply of money would bring prosperity and progress and enterprise, and we assert the same thing today."[51]

Bryan continued, "We assert that an increase in the supply of money will reverse the grinding conditions under which we have suffered for the past few years, and the position which we take must be approved by any person who will study the money question without putting before his eyes enough gold coin to blind himself with the proof."[52]

Reporters noted a large number of "yellow badges" sported by many in the audience, reflecting their support of Bryan's Republican opponent, McKinley. Bryan noticed, commenting, "Any person who has an opinion ought to have a reason to base it on. I want to speak to those who, by wearing yellow badges, indicate their support of Republican ideas, to consider two or three things."

"If the Republican Party believes that the gold standard is a good thing, ask yourselves why the Republican Party always talks about 'sound money' instead of a gold standard," Bryan questioned. "Why do they use two ambiguous phrases

William Jennings Bryan, circa 1907

LIBRARY OF CONGRESS

to conceal their meaning? I assert that if the Republican Party thought the gold standard was good, they would not attempt to deceive people by saying 'sound money,' but they would say 'gold,' and let the world know they mean gold!"[53]

Reaching Cambridge City, a crowd heard Bryan make brief remarks from the rear platform of the train, while an even larger gathering of more than 10,000 waited for him at Rushville. His remarks running long, Bryan left another large audience at New Castle waiting for more than an hour. At Muncie, Bryan addressed the campaigning former president Benjamin Harrison was doing in Indiana on behalf of McKinley, saying Harrison's "policy during the last administration was worse on the money question than during the first administration" but that "a change has come over the Republican leaders" that seeks "to make the American people bend to a foreign yoke and pay tribute to a foreign despotism."[54] By the time Bryan's campaign train reached Marion, several thousand orange badges were distributed to counteract the large number of yellow badges still present, reflecting McKinley supporters in the Bryan crowd.

Though the vanquished Democratic nominee from 1896, as the nineteenth century drew to a close Bryan remained a powerful and popular figure in the party. As 1900 approached, Bryan had distinguished himself for his support of the Spanish-American War and other positions advocated by McKinley. Bryan easily claimed the 1900 Democratic nomination with the backing of "fusion" Populists who had suffered at the hands of southern Democrats since the last election, but still needed the numbers of voters the Democratic Party could deliver. Bryan's only "opponent" for the nomination was Admiral George Dewey of Vermont, who had an inauspicious start in politics when it was revealed he had previously never

voted in a presidential election. Former vice president Adlai E. Stevenson I of Illinois joined the ticket as Bryan's running mate for the 1900 rematch against McKinley and Roosevelt.

Again counting on a strategy of trying to cut into the Republican's stronghold in northern midwestern states, Bryan focused attention on Indiana. A year before the 1900 campaign, in January 1899, Bryan made a quick stop in Indianapolis while en route from Cincinnati to Chicago. He declined to comment on current political affairs, including his own plans for 1900, by saying, "Very often people express views different from my own and then I am asked for an expression on them. I do not care to make any statements or give comparisons between my own views and the views of others. When I have anything to say, I prefer to prepare it, and I always receive an opportunity to express myself if I so desire."[55]

Six months later, in the summer of 1899, Bryan met with Hoosier Democrats to fire up the troops for the coming battle and held closed-door meetings on how they might finally wrestle the state away from the GOP. An AP wire report from the confab reported, "It was learned that Mr. Bryan regarded the outlook for the party (in Indiana) as much better than it was three years ago, and that he had confidence that the questions involved in the acquisition of new territory would bring to the Democratic Party many German voters who left it on account of the money question in 1896."[56]

The National Democratic Party or "Gold Standard Democrats" convened their national convention in Indianapolis in 1896 and opposed the nomination of Bryan while the Democratic National Convention, or "Silver Standard Democrats," met in Chicago and nominated Bryan. The "Gold Standard Democrats" lost the fight over which monetary policy would prevail and held its last convention in 1900, again in Indianapolis, but this time endorsed Bryan. Bryan and his also-nominated running mate Stevenson were in Indianapolis on August 8, 1900, where he was to receive official notification of his nomination for the presidency by the Democratic Party at its convention in Kansas City, Missouri. As the *New York Times* reported, "The notification occurred in the Military Park, a beautifully shaded tract of land in the centre of the city. The park contains probably 30 acres of ground, and it was well covered with people. In the vicinity on the speakers' stand the crowd was very dense, and the entire park was well filled. . . . There was a general gathering of the members of the Democratic National Committee. The occasion was, therefore, regarded of national importance."[57] The ceremonies at Military Park drew a crowd estimated to be 50,000 and were preceded by a parade, and the *Times* reported, "The weather was hot, but toward the close of the ceremonies a slight breeze alleviated to some extent the suffering occasioned by the high temperature. At one time it appeared as if actual suffocation might be the result of the terrible crowding in front of the stand . . . but beyond a few fainting attacks and much personal discomfort, no evil resulted."[58] Mayor Thomas Taggart of Indianapolis and U.S. Representative James D. Richardson of Tennessee attempted to make preliminary speeches, but eventually cut them short amidst cries of discomfort from the overheated and over-stuffed crowd.

Bryan's speech would become one of his most famous, certainly equal to his previously noted "Cross of Gold" speech, and articulated the anti-imperialistic views of many Americans in the aftermath of the Spanish-American War and military battles in the Philippines (both of which appeared to some Americans to be overt grabs for control of lands external to the continental United States). Despite the harsh conditions at Indianapolis that day—a typically sweltering hot and humid August afternoon—the *Times* reported, "Mr. Bryan never appeared to better advantage. His face was slightly flushed, but his eye was clear and calm and his voice was never more completely at his command. He was dressed in a black sack coat, which was loosely buttoned about the waist. A white shirt and white necktie gave an appearance of coolness which comported well with the speaker's personal bearing. His voice was far reaching and that he was heard at a great distance was made evident by the fact that people far out in the crowd listened apparently as intently as did those who sat on the platform."[59]

Bryan opened his remarks by apologizing for reading them from a text in his hand but explained, "I must read what I am going to say. It would be more pleasant to me and more agreeable to you to speak without notes, but I want to address that larger constituency which we reach through the newspapers, for it is a thousand times as numerous as any crowd that could assemble here, and therefore, in order that I may speak to all throughout the land I have committed to writing what I desire to say, and will ask for your indulgence while I read my speech."[60] Bryan declared that the election of 1900 would be "a contest between Democracy on the one hand and plutocracy on the other," asserting that "on the important issues of the day the Republican Party is dominated by those influences which constantly tend to substitute the worship of mammon for the protection of the rights of man." Quoting Thomas Jefferson and Abraham Lincoln, Bryan declared that "the instrumentalities of government are being used to advance the interests of those who are in a position to secure favors from the government. The Democratic

Party is not making war upon the honest acquisition of wealth; it has no desire to discourage industry, economy and thrift. On the contrary, it gives to every citizen the greatest possible stimulus to honest toil when it promises him protection in the enjoyment of the proceeds of his labor. Property rights are most secure when human rights are most respected. Democracy strives for civilization in which every member of society will share according to his merits."[61]

The Republican Party had "abandoned" its previous position related to the gold standard, were giving excuses for allowing national banks control of the nation's paper money, supported a growing national debt, supported powerful trusts, supported a growing standing army, happily enjoined foreign alliances as opposed to American independence, and supported "forcible annexation" of new lands into the nation. He asserted that McKinley had laid before the Senate a plan supporting the independence of Cuba while at the same time "provided for the cession of the Philippine Islands to the United States" and introduced "the menace of imperialism."[62]

"Someone has said that a truth once spoken can never be recalled," Bryan said. "It goes on and on, and no one can set a limit to its ever-widening influence. But if it were possible to obliterate every word written or spoken in defense of the principles set forth in the Declaration of Independence, a war of conquest would still leave its legacy of perpetual hatred, for it was God himself who placed in every human heart the love of liberty. He never made a race of people so low in the scale of civilization or intelligence that it would welcome a foreign master." He added a strong assertion: "Those who would have this nation enter upon a career of empire must consider not only the effect of imperialism on the Filipinos, but they must also calculate its effects upon our own

nation. We cannot repudiate the principle of self-government in the Philippines without weakening that principle here."[63]

Bryan recalled Lincoln's belief that the safety of the nation did not lie in its military, "but in the spirit which prizes liberty as the heritage of all men, in all lands, everywhere, and he warned his countrymen that they could not destroy this spirit without planting the seeds of despotism at their own doors."[64]

"Even now we are beginning to see the paralyzing influence of imperialism," Bryan said. "Heretofore this nation has been prompt to express its sympathy with those who were fighting for liberty. . . . We have felt it due to ourselves and to the world, as well as those who were struggling for the right to govern themselves, to proclaim the interest which our people have, from the date of their own independence, felt in every contest between human rights and arbitrary power."[65]

The Republican Party has confused imperialism with expansion and said "the forcible annexation of territory to be governed by arbitrary power differs as much from the acquisition of territory to be built up into states as monarchy differs from a democracy. The Democratic Party does not oppose expansion when expansion enlarges the area of the republic and incorporates land which can be settled by American citizens, or adds to our population people who are willing to become citizens and are capable of discharging their duties as such." He again added that an imperialistic policy for America would result in the need for a larger and larger military establishment and its possible domination of the people. "A large standing army is not only a pecuniary burden to the people," he said, but "if accompanied by compulsory service, a constant source of irritation," and a "menace to a republican form of government."[66]

As was often the case with Bryan's rhetoric, a certain Christian and evangelical flare was at the center of his anti-imperialism argument. This was apparent in the analogy he made with a young man, who upon "reaching his majority, can do what he pleases. He can disregard the teachings of his parents; he can trample upon all that he has been taught to consider sacred; he can disobey the laws of the state, the laws of the society of God. He can stamp failure upon his life and make his very existence a curse to his fellow man and he can bring father and mother in sorrow to the grave; but he cannot annul the sentence 'The wages of sin is death.' And so it is with this nation. It is of age and it can do what it pleases; it can spurn the traditions of the past; it can repudiate the principles upon which the nation rests; it can employ force instead of reason; it can substitute might for right; it can conquer weaker people; it can exploit their lands, appropriate their property and kill their people; but it cannot repeal the moral law or escape the punishment decreed for the violation of human rights."[67]

Bryan openly challenged the idea that divine Providence "had delivered the Filipinos into our hands for their good and our glory" and the companion idea promoted by some that bullets, cannons, and flags could be used to bring righteousness. "If there is poison in the blood of the hand it will ultimately reach the heart," Bryan warned. "It is equally true that forcible Christianity, if planted under the American flag in the faraway Orient, will sooner or later be transplanted upon American soil. If true Christianity consists of carrying out in our daily lives the teachings of Christ, who will say that we are commanded to civilize with dynamite and proselyte with the sword?" He asked his audience to "compare, if you will, the swaggering, bullying, brutal doctrine of imperialism with the Golden Rule and the commandment 'Thou shalt love thy neighbor as thyself.'"[68]

During the closing days of the 1900 campaign, Bryan was back in Indiana for an October tour by train trying to salvage what he could of the race. Entering the state from the west, Bryan's first stop was at Plainfield. He "discussed trusts and told the people that they had the remedy in their own hands" and compared American involvement in the Philippine Islands to that of a thief.[69] At Brazil in Clay County, he addressed an audience comprised mostly of local mine workers and addressed issues important to labor.

As his train made its way to Greencastle, Bryan "good-naturedly left his breakfast table and went to speak to the people, who had congregated in large numbers."[70] He particularly noted the DePauw University students present in the crowd: "He warned them against trusts, as calculated to materially reduce the opportunities of the rising generation, if not to destroy the chances of many of them." He said, "Any system calculated to curtail opportunities for individual endeavor dooms the build of the aspiring young men of the country to perpetual clerkships and should be universally condemned."[71]

Addressing what he viewed as the dangers of "imperialism" with a large and growing standing army, Bryan said, "You cannot raise people up by sitting down on them."[72] Regarding the Philippine situation, he declared, "The Republicans, your President, has no plan. Your cabinet has no plan; your Congress has no plan. Search your heads, search your hearts, you know you have no plan that you would even dare tell your neighbor. On the contrary, the Democrats have a well-defined plan. They would have the Filipinos treated as the President has promised to treat the Cubans; in other words, we would give them their liberty. Then he would have the United States

LIBRARY OF CONGRESS

Always a popular speaker, Bryan addresses thousands assembled for a Chautauqua meeting in Madison, Indiana, July 6, 1901.

stand by them as an older brother."[73]

In all, Bryan's October swing took him to nine Indiana counties for twelve separate speeches, most of them focused on trust manufacturing issues, labor issues, and the Philippine situation. He made speeches at Indianapolis, Noblesville, Arcadia, Tipton, Elwood, Alexandria, Anderson, Marion, Hartford City, Muncie, Winchester, Richmond, and New Castle. The *New York Times* reported, "The speeches (in Indiana) average half an hour in duration, though the Anderson speech was much longer and most of them were made either from the (train) car platform, or from stands erected in the immediate vicinity of the stopping places. In one or two instances, Mr. Bryan refused to go to distant stands because of the difficulty getting through the crowds and the loss of time." At Elwood, Bryan chided then-Governor McKinley's 1892 visit to the city upon the opening of a new tin factory. "Whenever an institution is opened," Bryan said, "the Republicans make a great day of it and invite distinguished people from abroad to be present at the opening, but when a trust closes a factory, it does not invite a President or anybody else to preside at the closing. . . . The Republican Party is building up an industrial despotism that compels millions of people to get on their knees in the morning and pray to the trust, 'Give us this day our daily bread.'"[74]

Just before Election Day in November 1900, Bryan made one last swing through Indiana following a rail line from Cincinnati to Indianapolis and ending at Chicago. Indiana stops included brief remarks from the rear platform of the campaign train at Crawfordsville, Darlington, Frankfort, Monticello, Monon, Rensselaer, Lowell, and Hammond. At Rensselaer, Indiana Republicans were conducting a party meeting, and a great many McKinley supporters were in town. Bryan noted the large number of McKinley backers in his audience and noted, "I am sorry that it has so happened that my meeting comes on the same day as the Republican gathering, but I am sure that here we can meet together as members of different parties and that there need be no friction between those who think as I do and those who are opposed to the opinions which I advocate. I am sure, too, that it will not do Republicans any harm to listen to a Democratic speech, and I hope the Democrats will return the courtesy shown by these Republicans by listening to the Republican speeches which are to be delivered."[75]

Bryan told reporters upon arrival at Chicago, "From reports which have come to me and from my own observation, I am satisfied that Indiana is as safely Democratic as is Missouri."[76] In the final tally, Bryan was half right. He did win Missouri by a comfortable margin but lost the Indiana vote, with McKinley polling 51 percent of the vote to Bryan's 47 percent (another 2 percent going to the Prohibition Party nominee John Woolley, while native-son Eugene Debs's Socialist Party drew less than 1 percent of the Indiana vote).

Following his second defeat in the 1900 election, Bryan remained a fixture on the speaking circuit, drawing large crowds and continued support among Democrats. One of his forays to keep his prospects alive included a February 1903 visit to Indiana that included stops at Williamsport in Warren County for a party as the guest of Judge James McCabe, and a later stop at Crawfordsville, where he addressed students at both Crawfordsville High School and Wabash College and attended a meal in his honor before delivering an address titled "A Conquering Nation" in the college's Music Hall.[77] As the local media reported, "Students of Wabash were favored this morning by William Jennings Bryan. All classes were dismissed the first hour for that purpose. Mr. Bryan took for his theme the superior advantages of the small college and the value of the molding force of high ideals."[78]

Bryan proved a popular surrogate in Indiana for Alton B. Parker, the 1904 Democratic nominee. The *Indianapolis Star* reported that Bryan's reception for an October 12, 1904, speech at Tomlinson Hall confirmed that "he is still the idol of Indiana Democrats" and that "pandemonium seemed to break loose when Bryan rose to speak—for five minutes it continued unabated."

"I have appeared in this very hall in times past in an entirely different role from what I am tonight," Bryan said. "Many believed then that I would be the Moses to lead my party out of the wilderness. But tonight I come as an Aaron—ready and anxious and willing to speak in behalf of Judge Parker, whom I believe to be the party's Moses." Bryan vowed that he planned to remain active in the Democratic Party and said, "My interest will not cease with this campaign. I intend to be more radical in the future than in the past, especially in my fight against monopolists and plutocrats."[79]

Bryan did feel the need to explain his support for Parker, a Gold-standard Democrat: "Shall I try to defeat Parker because the gold Democrats tried to defeat me? Should silver Democrats try to do it? To the Republican who would suggest such a thing, I would tell him that I would not stoop so low as to do such a thing. We have more important work ahead of us than to follow up and punish those who voted against me. Life is too important, time too precious to carry a load of revenge." He added that if anyone doubted his position they should not "because I believe in the doctrine of independence, in the doctrine of self-government and in the constitution more than I ever believed in either gold or silver or any other thing."[80]

His travels across the nation in the fall of 1904 on behalf of Democratic candidates produced another quick headline as Bryan spent five days in the state giving speeches at Lafayette, Lebanon, Frankfort, Delphi, Logansport, Converse, and Marion. The Associated Press reported that "Bryan has a slight cold, but his voice is strong," and that en route to Lebanon Bryan found himself face-to-face with Republican gubernatorial nominee J. Frank Hanly, who was also out hustling for votes. "The two shook hands cordially and exchanged pleasantries," the AP reported.[81] Hanly was elected governor in November and later was nominated as the Prohibition Party's nominee for president in 1916. A reporter standing nearby quoted Bryan as telling Hanly, "I understand that you have been paying me the compliment of being a sincere man." Hanly reportedly laughed and smiled broadly as he replied, "I have, but I am afraid you have lapsed a little since you have been in Indiana. I think, though, you will recover after you get out of Indiana and into West Virginia."[82]

Earlier in October 1904 in speeches at both Winamac in Pulaski County and Hammond in

Lake County, Bryan was aggressive in his rhetoric against the Republican Party. He railed against claims by Republicans that the American flag had newfound respect and admiration around the world, as never before in history. Bryan asked, "What do you think of 'the old days when the flag stood for nothing'? Washington held that flag in his hands. Did it stand for nothing then? Did it stand for nothing when our Revolutionary fathers followed it from Bunker Hill to Yorktown? Did it stand for nothing in the hand of Jefferson, the author of the Declaration of Independence? . . . Did it stand for nothing in the hands of Lincoln, and in the hands of Grant?"[83]

For the 1910 midterm elections, the *Petersburg-Pike County Democrat* reported, "Colonel Bryan spent a whole week in Indiana, and at every place where he made a speech he was greeted by immense crowds. He made more than 20 speeches in the state, and there can be no doubt that he made thousands of votes for the Democratic ticket."[84] They delighted in reporting that Bryan had "finished the job of skinning the ex-president" and that Roosevelt's "nationalistic language" reflected he was seeking "to fix things so that he could have himself elected president again and then assume the role of a dictator."[85] Bryan had warned Indiana voters that "the new nationalism (favored by Roosevelt) was dangerous; it proposes to put into the hands of the federal government many of the powers now held by the various states to govern themselves. Home rule would vanish, and if Roosevelt had his way, Roosevelt would be the power in the land."[86]

During the same campaign swing in a speech at Crawfordsville on October 20, 1910, Bryan arrived just a week after Roosevelt had been in town touting the GOP nominee for re-election, U.S. Senator Albert Beveridge. Bryan's efforts were focused on the campaign of Democrat John

W. Kern, and he spent about forty-five minutes in the Montgomery County seat making a quick stop for rest at the Crawford Hotel. The *Crawfordsville Daily Journal* reported that both the town band and the town's "Colored Band" played and that "the crowd was so big at the Airdome Theatre that Bryan was forced to speak twice, once to an overflow of people outside and again to people inside." The crowd included several hundred local schoolchildren who were dismissed for the day to go downtown to see the famous visitor.[87]

William Howard Taft

Secretary of War William Howard Taft entered the 1908 election with a big advantage over any other Republican hopefuls—the backing of popular incumbent Roosevelt (who decided to keep his promise not to seek a third term). Taft easily dispatched a small group of challengers and approached the fall campaign in a traditional manner with plans for a front-porch Republican effort, where voters would visit him at his homes in Virginia and Ohio.

A front-porch style would fit Taft, who lacked Roosevelt's political acumen and the same level of appetite for retail politics. As historian Edgar A. Hornig noted, "Because no one issue predominated during the 1908 campaign, the candidates themselves became one of the most important issues."[88] Taft may have understood this better than his opponent, taking his policy positions from both liberal Democrats and Progressive Republicans, essentially nullifying any chance of a real challenge by the Democrats. Taft easily won election in a landslide victory in both the popular and Electoral College vote against third-time Democratic hopeful Bryan, although the Indiana contest was closer than many other parts of the nation. In Indiana Taft won a narrow

48–47 victory over Bryan (Hoosier native Debs, the Socialist Party nominee, polled 2 percent).

Recognizing the importance of winning the Indiana vote, Taft's first foray away from his Ohio home was to the Brook, Indiana, home of famed Hoosier writer George Ade in Newton County. As historian Howard F. McMains wrote, "A dozen aerial bombs shattered the calm around the usually peaceful prairie countryside" surrounding Ade's home, announcing the arrival of Taft for his first campaign speech on September 23, 1908. "A caravan of cars brought Taft to Ade's farm from the railroad, eight miles distant . . . for perhaps the biggest campaign rally northwestern Indiana had ever seen," McMains wrote.[89]

Taft's visit to Indiana reflected his doubts about the efficacy of a front-porch campaign,

LIBRARY OF CONGRESS

A 1925 photograph of Hoosier author George Ade, who once noted that he loved "to put on big parties or celebrations and see a throng of people having a good time."

and this was his first step off the porch into the fray and an effort to address factionalism among Indiana Republicans. Setting off from Cincinnati, Taft's special train made a brief five-minute stop at Union Station in downtown Indianapolis before a small crowd of three hundred supporters (reflecting that Indianapolis had not been announced as a stop and no formal remarks were offered). Taft reportedly waved to the small crowd from the back of the train and remarked, "We have been traveling 60 miles an hour, and could not see anything for the dust. . . . But I hope the voters will not get any dust in their eyes for Election Day."[90] Taft's train stopped again briefly in Lafayette en route to Newton County, where he shook hands with a few folks and moved on. The train stopped at the settlement of Ade, six miles west of Brook and eight miles from Ade's palatial spread. McMains reported that Taft's train was an hour early, again limiting the size of the welcome he received.

Once at the Ade farm, several thousand guests trampled the grounds to get a glimpse of Taft. "The Brook Band, the Purdue (University) Military Band, and the Juvenile Band of Monticello performed. . . . A variety of local politicians addressed the crowd, much of which sat on two long sections of circus bleachers arranged facing the house and underneath the large shade trees," McMains found. "Tents had been set up where refreshments were sold and where campaign literature, badges, and souvenir post cards were given away."[91] Taft enjoyed a private luncheon inside Ade's home, while those outside were provided "full pail lunches" of sandwiches and pickles. Emerging from the house to address the gathered throng, Taft explained he could not resist an opportunity to address Indiana farmers. "I seized the opportunity," Taft said, "to ask you . . . whether your experience as farmers with Mr.

The Honeysuckle and the Bee

The entrance to the farm

Showing the triumph of mind over brute creation

The fifth year "Are these really fruit trees?"

The house, as approached from the south through the old-fashioned flowers

IHS, NEWSPAPER GRAPHICS COLLECTION, P. 100

Looking from the water tower across the rugged and picturesque landscape, typical of the corn belt

The out-door swimming pool, fed by artesian wells. (There are three voluntary and unassisted gushers on the farm with a total flow of more than 5,000 gallons an hour)

THE FARM HOME OF A HUMORIST

SCENES ON GEORGE ADE'S "HAZELDEN FARM" OF FOUR HUNDRED ACRES, ON THE EDGE OF THE CORN BELT, NEAR BROOK, INDIANA

THE TITLES FOR THESE PHOTOGRAPHS WERE WRITTEN BY MR. ADE HIMSELF

A Harper's Weekly *photo display of Ade enjoying himself on his Hazelden Farm near Brook, Indiana.*

Bryan . . . is such as to commend him to you as the person into whose hands you wish to put the executive power over the destinies of this Nation for four years."[92] Challenging Bryan's position on tariffs and the gold standard, Taft played up the value of Republican-backed tariffs in raising prices farmers could gain for their crops. "I submit to you gentlemen that till the soil; I submit to you who through the rural delivery receive the newspapers and magazines with which to follow current events and take the measures of public men, whether the experience of the country in the economic theories of Mr. Bryan is such as to warrant the belief that if he is elected in November he will restore the necessary confidence and bring out the capital, the delay in the coming of which makes our business future hang in the balance."[93] As much as Taft may have been enjoying himself, he did not stick around long, with reporters clamoring behind him as he exited during Senator Thomas E. Watson's speech. Taft was excited about the crowd's reaction, his campaign aides noted, and the Indiana visit solidified in his mind the need to go out and ask for the vote, rather than wait on his front porch back in Ohio.

Taft was back in Indiana late in October for an ambitious railroad tour of nearly every corner of the state as it became clear the state's vote was going to be close. On October 22, 1908, Taft started a three-day tour of Indiana and headlined "the largest political meeting ever held in Indiana" at Evansville and later stops at Terre Haute, Linton, Mitchell, Bedford, North Vernon, and Lawrenceburg. In total, he delivered sixteen speeches in one day to Hoosier audiences, "rejuvenated in voice, energy and enthusiasm by his one-day rest, the candidate handled the campaign with an even greater degree of positiveness than heretofore," the *Philadelphia Record* reported.[94]

At Linton, Taft spoke to an audience that included dozens of local mine workers and their families and defended injunctions he had issued as a judge in previous labor battles, in defense of scathing antilabor attacks Bryan had launched against Taft's record. "An injunction is merely an order with reference to the prevention of the abuse made before the fact occurs which is to injure or not injure the party," Taft explained. He likened it to an order to stop someone from chopping down someone else's tree while the ownership of the tree remained in question. "That kind of remedy has been in force for 400 years and is the most remedial writ that we have," Taft said. "It arose to protect poor men, not to oppress them. . . . (The injunction) grew up to protect the poor against injuries for which they could not have adequate remedy at law."[95] In Terre Haute, the hometown of Debs, Taft broke from his practice of only talking about the Democratic nominee and predicted that the American people were unwilling to accept a Socialist approach to its government.

Press reports focused on the fact that women, although they still could not vote in 1908, turned out in large numbers for Taft's early morning rally at Lawrenceburg. "He was greeted by an enthusiastic crowd of several hundred persons and an enthusiastic band at the railroad station at 7:35 o'clock," the Associated Press reported. "Even the women turned out early, and there were many gathered along the track when the Republican candidate arrived. The women are showing great interest in Judge Taft's tour. There are many women in all the audiences."[96] Crowds were reportedly equally excited at Bedford with crowds gathered on all sides of the Lawrence County Courthouse square—the crowd estimated to be as large at ten thousand. After his successful Bedford, Mitchell, and Terre Haute stops, the AP dispatched that "the largest outdoor gathering Mr. Taft said he had ever addressed was assembled at Terre Haute when the special train arrived there this afternoon. There were many in the carload of politicians which escorted the candidate to the city that said it was the largest gathering the city had ever had."[97]

On October 24, 1908, Taft started off with a 7:00 a.m. rally at Brazil in Clay County and followed a fifty-mile "circuit" around Indianapolis, including rain-soaked stops at Crawfordsville, Lafayette, Frankfort, Kokomo, Muncie, Anderson, and Marion. News reports indicated that Taft's voice was "worse for the wear" after a full day of speechmaking the day before, and a request was sent ahead to local communities reached after dark to dispense with "poisonous red fire" as the smoke was particularly taxing on his voice.[98] At Kokomo, a small platform holding about two hundred spectators collapsed during Taft's remarks, but no injuries were reported.[99] One man in the crowd also thrust a note into Taft's hand that the candidate later shared with reporters. It read, "Mr. Taft, Twelve years ago I drove a mortgaged mule to this city to hear Mr. Bryan speak. Today I came in my own automobile to hear you. Can you guess whom I am going to vote for?"[100] In downtown Lafayette, a line of Civil War veterans stood along the street and saluted Mr. Taft as he passed by, the former war secretary lifting his hat to them in return.[101] At Muncie, slightly exaggerated reports indicated that apologies were offered to Taft for "possible injuries" for "being hauled over the impaired streets in the capital of Delaware County."[102]

At Anderson, Taft remembered Indiana's favorite son, Harrison, saying, "It is to me an intense pleasure to have received from the people of Indiana such a cordial welcome as we have had yesterday and today. Indiana's giving the nation General Benjamin Harrison made me always feel grateful because he, more than any other public man, first gave me the assistance, the sympathy and the support to aspire me to judicial office. General Harrison was a great lawyer and a great man, and Indiana may celebrate, as she is about to do, his memory, by the erection of a monument in Indianapolis."[103] As the rain intensified, Taft said, "My friends, it is raining and I cannot keep you here. Your coming here in such numbers testifies to your interest in the election in November; testifies to the fact that Indiana is Republican; that you appreciate the importance of continuing the prosperity that we have by rejecting Mr. Bryan again and continuing the Republican Party in power."[104] Asking his Anderson audience to recall more than a decade of prosperity enjoyed under Republican leadership, Taft said, "The interests of labor, of the farm and the businessman are identical" and "you must not put in a man who is constantly advocating new experiments and whose experiments heretofore have always failed."[105]

Ending his second day of campaigning in Indianapolis, Taft addressed a massive gathering. The *Indianapolis Star* reported that more than 100,000 Hoosiers had turned out so far to hear him speak in his current tour--crowds that dwarfed those for Bryan a few days earlier.[106] While in the state capital, Taft rode in a parade and made three separate speeches, two before outdoor audiences—one at New York and Meridian Streets, and another at Monument Circle from a stand in front of the Columbia Club. News reports indicated that the outdoor audiences strained to hear him speak amidst his failing voice. A third speech was given inside at an auditorium on Virginia Avenue. Taft sat atop an observation stand at the Marion County Courthouse on East Washington Street for a rain-soaked parade lasting more than two hours.

"Dozens of marching clubs participated in the parade, which was one of the greatest ever seen in this city," the *Indianapolis Star* reported. "Bands were out in great numbers and drum corps were as thick as banners, and a squadron of mounted police led the demonstration followed by the Taft cavalry, out in great numbers."[107]

As Taft worked his way north across the state on a third day of campaigning, the *Elkhart Daily Review* noted that the candidate was making forty-three separate speeches in the state although "for reasons that have been explained—the stress on his voice—few of them will be long." In fact, in Elkhart he was scheduled to speak for less than ten minutes, and comparisons continued to be made between Bryan's outstanding oratorical skills and the lesser speaking skills of Taft. As the *Elkhart Daily Review* indicated, "However, it is the man himself the people desire to see; they have had ample opportunity to read and study his utterances that reflect his stand on the questions now before the people. The nation has on more occasions than the two defeats of William Jennings Bryan showing that in the final analysis (and action), it does not judge a candidate for high office on his abilities as an orator, but upon the people's conception of his individual honesty, constructive statesmanship, steadfast adherence to principle, administrative ability, and predominate administrative ability and predominate integrity."[108]

Along with Elkhart, Taft's train stopped briefly at almost every city and town along the way, including Greenfield, Cambridge City, Richmond, Winchester, Portland, Decatur, Fort Wayne, Columbia City, Warsaw, Goshen, South Bend, La Porte, Michigan City, Hammond, and Gary. Crowd estimates were impressive—more than 20,000 at South Bend, 15,000 at Fort Wayne, 18,000 at Gary, and audiences of more

than 10,000 at Elkhart, Goshen, and Richmond, respectively. Before he was done, the Taft campaign had reached a total audience of more than 420,000 people. As the *New Albany Tribune* gushed, "It was one of the greatest demonstrations ever given a presidential candidate in Indiana and at the close of the tour predictions were made by the Republican leaders that Taft would carry Indiana by a majority of at least 60,000 votes."[109]

A different account of Taft's success was reported by some of the state's Democratic newspapers. The *Goshen Daily Democrat* reported on "an absolute lack of enthusiasm and marked indifference on the part of the common people, particularly so the shop hands and day laborers, were the pronounced features Saturday of Secretary Taft's visit to Goshen."[110] Questioning the crowd estimates of 10,000 at Goshen, the local report added, "Secretary Taft's voice was in such bad condition that he could be heard only a short distance away. . . . The balance of Mr. Taft's speech had to do with an appeal to the people to vote the Republican ticket. It is doubtful any political speaker of national prominence ever evoked as little genuine enthusiasm here as did Secretary Taft. What cheering was indulged in was of the laborious style, palpably forced and not coming from sincere depths. The Republican nominee wore his ever-famous smile and seemed to be in a jolly mood."[111] Even the "automobile parade" that followed Taft's visit did not escape the negative reviews of the *Goshen Daily Democrat,* noting that they were appropriately decorated, but there "were no workingmen among the marchers. The entire Taft meeting seemed to take on an aspect of aristocracy. It appeared to be a silk stocking kind of affair."[112]

Reporters noted the train that carried the Republican nominee to almost every corner of the

William Howard Taft, circa 1916

LIBRARY OF CONGRESS

state was noteworthy for its time, consisting of a dining car, baggage car, two compartment cars, a Pullman car, and a private car for Judge Taft and his party. Included in Taft's party was his own personal physician, Doctor J. J. Richardson of Washington, D.C., "who makes an examination of Mr. Taft's throat at regular intervals." Taft reportedly had "lived" on the train for four weeks of solid campaigning by the time it reached Indiana.[113]

As president, Taft made it known he had scratched Indianapolis off his scheduled visits "to the west" in the spring of 1910 following news from the Indiana Republican State Convention that it had adopted resolutions opposing the administration's tariff policies, reflecting the lack of support given to them in Washington by Senator Beveridge and other more progressive Republicans. "The general talk here at the Capitol is that the President is offended by the action of the Indiana Republican State Convention," the *Boston Evening Transcript* reported.[114] A previously published itinerary for Taft's travels had indicated that he would spend several hours in Indianapolis on May 5 as the guest of former vice president Fairbanks, but those plans were scrubbed at Taft's order. Behind-the-scenes efforts were made to persuade the president to change his mind, but Taft remained firm and traveled through Indiana for his trip, but skipped Indianapolis. With the Taft-led national Republicans incensed at his opposition to the Payne-Aldrich tariff, Beveridge struggled and lost his bid for a third term to Democrat Kern. He later bolted the GOP for the Progressive "Bull Moose" Party movement, but later rejoined the Republicans (he never again held elective office). Taft's internal struggles with the Republican Party, however, were not over, as the 1912 election demonstrated.

In 1911, with Beveridge gone and the 1912 elections approaching along with the likelihood of an internal GOP challenge from former president Roosevelt, Taft got over his row with Indiana Republicans and paid two visits to the state on July 3 and 4, 1911. Arriving at Marion in Grant County from Cleveland, Ohio, just as the merciless sun began to sink—temperatures had soared above one hundred degrees during those July days with more than five hundred deaths reported nationwide as a result—a hot, humid Indiana was not spared the sweatbox. The *Marion Chronicle-Tribune* declared that "in Marion's history no greater throng of people or more enthusiastic one has ever greeted any visitor than the immense crowd gathered to receive President Taft."[115]

Escorted from the train to the veterans' home at Marion, Taft told the veterans that "all foreign wars with this country could have been avoided without bloodshed" and repeated his belief that the United States had successfully held off bloody strife in both Central and South America. Declaring that he was "neither an optimist nor a wild enthusiast" about pending peace treaties between England, France, and Germany, he nonetheless said they were a step in the right direction.[116]

"It was by war this country gained its independence from Great Britain," Taft said. "If England had been better advised, the war likely would not have ensued and we would now be as Canada is, cherishing an attachment to the mother country without exercising complete independence. Certain it is, however, the lesson we taught England she took to heart, and in her colonial policy she has continued to lighten the burdens of the colonists."[117] Continuing his theme, the president said, "The War of 1812 might easily have been avoided by arbitration. War measured on questions is capable by solution of tribunals. Whether the Civil War could have been avoided is a very difficult question to answer. When slavery had become imbedded in the social fabric of the country, it is possible that only the incision of the knife of war could remove the cancer."[118]

He added, "I will not attempt to answer similar questions as to the Spanish War, but I do believe that submission of the issues to a tribunal might have affected Spain's treatment of Cuba so as to have made the war unnecessary."[119]

Taft left Marion later that evening and arrived in Indianapolis just after midnight, greeted by former vice president Fairbanks who was to host the president and his wife overnight. The next morning, Taft kept his commitments in the city despite soaring heat, and appeared before smaller-than-expected crowds at Monument Circle. Taft sat atop a platform constructed outside the Columbia Club to review the "safe and sane" Indianapolis Independence Day Parade— the "safe and sane" campaign promoting ways to celebrate the holiday that did not include dangerous fireworks and other displays. "For an hour, bands, military organizations and floats, both historical and flora, passed before the president and the crowd, which surged about the reviewing stand and cheered. All the flags were dipped, and many of the marching delegations doffed their hats to the chief executive, who returned their salutes with bows and smiles," the Associated Press reported.[120]

The parade was not without incident, however, as Secret Service and Indianapolis Police searched for two men overheard by a woman discussing a "paper bag bomb" to throw at the president's party.[121] Before Taft arrived at Monument Circle, one woman was struck by a .38 caliber bullet, injuring her thigh. The woman, Mrs. Harry D. Tutewiler, described as "the wife of a prominent

citizen," was seated near the president's box and had the wound treated and then later returned to her seat to watch the parade. "Neither the President nor any members of his party were told about the affair," the Associated Press reported. "Detectives were sent to the top of the (Soldiers and Sailors) monument as soon as the matter was reported to police headquarters, but a search of the persons there and a search of the crowd in neighboring buildings failed to bring to light any .38 caliber revolvers, loaded or unloaded."[122]

Following the parade, the president spoke briefly at the Marion County Commercial Club and later took a meal at the Columbia Club. While billed as a nonpolitical trip meant to celebrate America's independence, local Republicans had other ideas. During his introduction at the Marion Club, Taft received rousing applause from the emcee who declared that Indiana Republicans "supported you in 1908, and we will support you again in 1912!"[123] Taft clearly recognized the events in Indianapolis were not altogether nonpolitical—his hosts at the Columbia Club famous for their support of Republican presidential candidates since the days of Benjamin Harrison.

In his remarks before Indiana business leaders, Taft addressed the proposed reciprocity treaty with Canada that would promote free trade between the United States and its northern neighbors with no tariffs imposed. "I find, with respect to reciprocity that there is a disposition by some Republicans to dispute the proposition that Republicans can consistently support the adoption of the present agreement with the Canadian government," Taft said. "It is said that this kind of reciprocity is not Republican reciprocity. It is said that this reciprocity covers competitive products of each country and that the reciprocity of former Republican leaders was intended to include only a lowering or abolition of duties on products of other countries, which did not compete with the products of this country."[124]

Taft countered that "the sound Republican doctrine has become the imposition of duties only where the conditions are naturally unequal and where duties are necessary to enable our manufacturers and other producers to meet on level competition with foreign producers. The Canadian reciprocity agreement squares exactly with this doctrine."[125] Taft said the agreement would "not be made at the expense of farmers" but acknowledged it probably would not significantly lower the cost of living. "It will, however, steady prices by enlarging the reservoir of supplies for those things that are raised in both countries," he said, "and will make more remote the possibility of cornering commodities and extorting expensive prices for them from the public."[126]

"Indiana," Taft said, "is fairly representative of the states of the Middle West in its relation to Canadian reciprocity. Its consumers will benefit by the remission of duties on food products and on fish, and they will share in the advantages of the $1.6 million remission of duties on gypsum, a constituent element in cement, in building stone and other articles. Indiana vegetables and fruits, including watermelons of all kinds, will go to the Canadian market free of duty. The Indiana manufacturing industry will be especially benefitted by the reduction of duties on agricultural implements, motor vehicles and paving brick."[127]

The future of the U.S.-Canadian Reciprocity Treaty would remain dramatic. Taft signed the treaty on the afternoon of July 26, 1911, but hours later the Canadian parliament was adjourned without acting on the matter. The Canadian Conservative Party was swept into power later in the year primarily on the basis of its opposition to the treaty Taft had signed.

Theodore Roosevelt

Taft had a legitimate reason to keep looking over his shoulder as the divide between him and his once-close friend, Roosevelt, continued to grow over policy issues that divided conservative and progressive Republicans. Perhaps further widening the gap, however, was former Roosevelt's continued active role in the Republican Party, including widespread campaigning in Indiana for the 1910 midterm elections. Appearing primarily in support of Beveridge's re-election campaign, Roosevelt continued to draw large crowds wherever he went—crowds larger than those Bryan was able to attract in his efforts to help Beveridge's Democratic opponent, Kern. As the *New York Times* reported in October 1910, "Colonel Roosevelt started today on the first real old-fashioned political campaigning he has done since he was elected to the Vice Presidency 10 years ago. All across Indiana he spoke to great crowds, and everywhere he gave Senator Albert J. Beveridge, one of the seven Republican insurgents who voted against the Payne-Aldrich Tariff bill, the most enthusiastic and unqualified endorsement."[128]

At tiny Covington in Fountain County, a crowd of only one thousand showed to greet the former president, but he remained fired up in his remarks in support of Beveridge. "He is a man who embodies our struggle for popular government and honesty in public life," Roosevelt said. "If Indiana defeats him, you can't explain his defeat on any other grounds than that Indiana declines to keep in the public service a man who refuses to ally himself with the corrupt interests. If you defeat Senator Beveridge, you put a premium on jackpotting in your public life. You are bound to support him because he is an honest man and embodies the cause of honesty in public life." Moments later at another Fountain

County town, Veedersburg, he declared, "I am a game fighter for the right, and that's why I am here to speak for Albert Beveridge. You people of Indiana sent your share of men to the Civil War to preserve the Union. Indiana is now engaged in a struggle that emphatically is a moral struggle. It is a struggle for the immutable principles of righteousness."[129]

Later in Crawfordsville, the crowds improved as Roosevelt made his way from the train station to the football field at Wabash College to speak to an audience of about 8,000. "The college boys gave him a demonstration of their ability to yell," the *Times* reported. Roosevelt was introduced as "the most maligned and most feared, the best known and best beloved man in all of America."[130] Another 8,000 people greeted Roosevelt and Beveridge at Lafayette for a speech at the Lincoln Club. Enthusiasm remained low, the *Times* account indicated, until Roosevelt turned his remarks specifically to the large number of Purdue University students in the audience. "A man who plays football isn't worth his salt," Roosevelt joked, "unless he hits the line hard."[131]

Specifically addressing Beveridge's vote on the tariff bill, Roosevelt noted that he had proposed his own tariff proposal. "Senator Beveridge did not split from his party," he said. "He merely stood by the bulk of it, because the real party consists of the mass of the people who wished to see done just what he did. And before the next Presidential election comes around, the platform will be fairly and squarely the platform for which Senator Beveridge stands."[132]

Before arriving in Indianapolis, Roosevelt's train stopped in Crawfordsville in Montgomery County, tiny Colfax in Clinton County, and Thorntown and Lebanon in Boone County (the latter audience numbering more than 4,000). Roosevelt reminded his Hoosier audiences, "Dur-ing my term as President, Senator Beveridge stood with me in all progressive legislation."[133]

While in Indiana, Roosevelt's train made seven stops across the state. He spoke to crowds ranging in estimates from 1,000 to 50,000 (although national reporters tended to estimate the Indianapolis audience at about half of the 50,000 the Republicans estimated). "At Indianapolis, there was a monster meeting at the great war monument, and fully twenty-five thousand people were crowded around when the Colonel began to talk from the balcony of the English Hotel."[134] Despite such impressive crowd numbers, the *Times* reported that "they did not cheer with such enthusiasm and frequency as have been shown elsewhere" in Indiana. "For the most part, people stood silently watching every movement of (Roosevelt), and apparently listening very closely to what he said, but it was only at rare intervals that they showed their appreciation, and when they did cheer appreciation, the outburst was never of long duration."[135]

Veering from his stump speech for Beveridge, Roosevelt took up issues of "conservation" and said, "In Alaska, our aim is to control the development of the coal fields so that all the profit and uses shall not go to a single group of enormously wealthy men. Now, we want to give them a proper profit, and that is their objection to it. The people who want to develop by exploiting the coal fields purely in their own interests are not Alaskans, they live in New York and Colorado."[136] Reflecting the more progressive nature of his views, Roosevelt said he was "amused" by arguments for states' rights made to him about exercising control over Alaska's resources. "We are for state rights wherever state rights mean popular rights," Roosevelt explained, "and we are for national rights whenever national rights mean the rights of the people."[137]

After returning from his African expedition in 1910, former president Theodore Roosevelt went on a speaking tour through several cities across the country, including this speech at the Big Four Railroad Depot in Lebanon, Indiana, on October 13, 1910.

After Indianapolis, Roosevelt made two more stops at Anderson and Muncie but skipped Richmond because of scheduling conflicts with a return train to New York City. His decision about Richmond left about 4,000 people gathered at the Coliseum there disappointed and sent home without seeing the former president.

Indiana Democrats were certain Roosevelt's efforts were not going to make a difference. The *Petersburg-Pike County Democrat* declared, "The tour which Roosevelt made through the state was a sore disappointment to the Republicans, for it did not arouse the enthusiasm which they expected it would. The crowds which turned out to hear him were not as large as they had expected, and there was no noise to speak of. Roosevelt seems to have lost his hold on the people of Indiana through his effort to straddle the tariff question. Hoosiers like a man who will come out and stand on one side or the other of a question, but they do not take kindly to one who will try to stand on both sides, as Roosevelt has done."[138]

5

World War I and the Great Depression, 1912–31

Woodrow Wilson

For the remarkable 1912 campaign, New Jersey governor Woodrow Wilson made a late campaign stop in October at Indianapolis's Washington Park baseball stadium, where media reports indicated a crowd of 25,000 gathered to get a glimpse of the Democratic nominee. "Two-thousand more in white trousers, carrying red fire torches, danced a serpentine around the (baseball) diamond," the *New York Times* reported. "At their head was a banner carrying legends proclaiming Taft to be 'That Fat Buckeye' and Roosevelt 'A Great Bull Loose.'"[1] Wilson was in the company of Indiana's Democratic boss Thomas Taggart—something that drew the notice of reporters—as Wilson had avoided "political bosses" on stops in other states. The *Boston Evening Transcript* described Wilson's Indianapolis speeches as the first "extended attack on the administration of President William Howard Taft and former President Theodore Roosevelt" and quoted Wilson as saying Roosevelt had been "incompetent" and that Taft had created a favorable environment that trust and monopoly interests could only have dreamed of.[2]

"This constitutes a supreme moment in my life," Wilson told the audience. "I believe there is abroad in this country a very profound interest in the present political situation and that is what

brings you all out. For the issues are issues of life and death, and they stir the people deeply."[3] Wilson said, "What I want to call your attention to is that the new third party (the Progressives) has not drawn to itself the full strength, or even all the principal leaders of the insurgent Republicans, because this circumstance appeals to every man who thinks the present situation over: The very things that we are protesting against, the very conditions that we are trying to alter, are conditions which were created under the two leaders of the two branches of the present Republican Party, because it is true that these conditions were just as much created under Mr. Roosevelt as under Mr. Taft."[4] Wilson said the Republican split between Taft and Roosevelt was "an extraordinary spectacle" and carefully dismantled what he said was the unwillingness or inability of Taft and Roosevelt to deal with the risk of monopolies dominating the economy.

While in Indianapolis for an entire day, Wilson attended a luncheon at the University Club with Taggart and stopped by the home of former vice president Charles Warren Fairbanks, a Republican. He later addressed a meeting of the National Conservation Congress at the Indiana State Fairgrounds. "Governor Wilson came out upon the platform to speak to the conservationists arm-in-arm with former Vice President Fairbanks," the *Times* reported, "and the pair so strangely mated for the march to the platform received a hilarious ovation."[5] Wilson's speech to the Conservation Congress made news for assumptions that the governor had become "an over speedy convert" to the conservationist movement. Wilson addressed that issue directly, noting that "for that is what learning is for," he said. "If a man does not keep his mind open to receive the facts and yield to them, he will sooner or later be very sorry, because the facts are our masters. . . . When I see great bodies of men like this running ahead of the law and beckoning it on to their fair enterprises, I know that I see the rising tide that is going to bring these things about."[6]

Although Wilson had already spent a long day of campaigning in the city, news reports emerged that the governor kept his promise to visit a conservation exhibition created by students from Emmerich Manual Training High School in Indianapolis. With little fanfare, Wilson and his entourage entered an almost vacant Indiana Statehouse after 10:00 p.m. to view the displays and shake hands with the handful of students who remained at that late hour. The displays included a "model house" reconstructed inside the rotunda of the statehouse and Wilson, removing his overcoat, visited every room of the house with a student describing the various aspects of the design. In the dining room of the "model house," Wilson sat down at a table and ate a biscuit made by one of the female "domestic sciences" students from Manual.

"Dr. Wilson was much interested in what she said," the *Indianapolis Star* reported, "and he did not leave the building until he had viewed the exhibit on each of the three floors and had visited the House of Representatives chamber, where he witnessed a demonstration of the appliances

used in mine rescue work. . . . The visit of the Governor at such a late hour came as a surprise and there were scarcely 100 persons in the building when he arrived. He was greeted cordially by those who had waited to see him."[7]

Wilson, though showing that he was tired after a long day of campaigning, listened to a brief presentation about workplace safety and replied, "We are proud of our factory laws (in New Jersey)," he said. "I think we have gone as far as any state in the giving of protection to workers from fire and dust, and I think we are doing some better than Indiana because our factory inspectors are under civil service and are not selected because of politics."[8] Before he departed the statehouse, Wilson stopped and shook hands with an eight-year-old boy, Gordon Harding, of Brownsburg, who "accosted" the governor to get noticed. "You are well fixed," Wilson told the boy, pointing out that he was wearing a Wilson for President campaign button on both lapels of his coat.[9]

Finally able to retire at the Denison Hotel at 11:00 p.m., Wilson was up early the next day and boarded a train for Chicago, but stopped for six short visits throughout northern Indiana along the way. At Kokomo he told his audience that Taft and Roosevelt had "presided over the very processes that got the country into trouble. No man in the United States was ever more trusted than the leader of the third party (Roosevelt) during the seven and a half years he was President. Is it possible that he has just discovered the deep needs of humanity? Is it possible that he now, for the first time, sees that he wasted seven and a half years during which he could have led the American people to any triumph of reform to which he had chosen to lead them?"[10]

In Plymouth, his next stop, Wilson said he had noticed posters in Indiana featuring "a

Woodrow Wilson, November 1912

LIBRARY OF CONGRESS

handsome picture of Mr. Taft in the middle" and information about the high cost of living not only in the U.S., but across the world. Wilson acknowledged that the cost of living had increased everywhere, but "the interesting circumstance is that it has increased much greater in the United States than anywhere else, and that in the most low tariff countries, it has hardly increased at all."[11] While in the Marshall County seat, Wilson also made a pitch to workingmen and reminded them of the support the Democratic Party had provided to labor reform and increased wages for workers.

Arriving at Gary, Wilson told his large audience that "when I was told that I was going to speak at Gary, Indiana, I said I thought the United States Steel Corporation was all for the new (Progressive) party and I was told that made no difference; that the men employed by the United States Steel Corporation were free Americans, 21 years old and knew how to take care of themselves."[12]

"I want to ask the people in Gary if it is in their observation that the employees of the Unit-

President Wilson acknowledges the crowd on Monument Circle in Indianapolis as part of Centennial Highway Day celebration on October 12, 1916. Joining Wilson are (left to right) Indiana governor Samuel Ralston and Indianapolis mayor Joseph Bell, both Democrats.

IHS, BASS PHOTO COMPANY COLLECTION, P 130

ed States Steel Corporation are better paid than the average employees in the United States?" Wilson asked. "The whole country knows that wherever it has business depressed wages sink to the lowest level. Now the American Steel Corporation . . . is one of the chief beneficiaries of the tariff, and you have been told ever since you can remember that the tariff meant high wages to you. I do not have to prove to this audience that this is a piece of buncombe."[13]

Wilson won the three-way contest for president in 1912, and during his dramatic first term faced the prospect of deciding whether to seek re-election in 1916 in opposition to the Democratic national platform adopted in 1912 or to abide by it. On January 8, 1915, invited as the keynote speaker at the annual Jefferson-Jackson Day Dinner hosted by the Indiana Democratic Party in Indianapolis, it was still unclear what Wilson's plans were for the election year to follow. His primary purpose in coming to Tomlinson Hall in downtown Indianapolis was to support U.S. Senator John W. Kern's campaign, but his remarks stood out as some of his most political to date. As one historian noted, "He gave an address to the party faithful in Indianapolis. . . . He spoke again with the tone of irritating self-assurance that got under the skin of his opponents"[14] before an approving audience of about 14,000. His remarks came as World War I raged into its first year, but Wilson and America continued to resist any movements toward entering the fray (America did not enter the war until April 1917).[15]

His comments did stir more debate that Wilson intended to seek a second term, particularly when he noted, "There may come a time when the American people will have to judge whether I know what I am talking about or not," a line that drew thunderous applause from the Democratic faithful. Perhaps realizing the sentence sounded a lot like someone ready to submit himself to the voters once again, the president added, "I did not mean to stir up anything. That was merely preparatory to saying that for at least two more years I am free to think I know the American people."[16]

The bulk of the president's remarks distinguished his record and that of the Democratic Party from what he viewed as a still splintered Republican Party. He began with remarks that drew a laugh. "It is rather lonely living in Washington," he said. "I have been confined for two years at hard labor and even now I feel that I am simply out on parole. Our sinews consist in your sympathy and support, our renewal comes from contact with you and with the strong movements of public opinion." Wilson added, "I get very tired of staying in Washington and saying sweet things. I wanted to come out and get in contact with you once more and say what I really thought."[17]

Wilson offered up some traditional red meat for the party loyalists. He stated, "The trouble with the Republican Party is that it has not had a new idea for 30 years. I am not speaking as a politician; I am speaking as a historian."[18] He moved quickly, however, to making the point that neither the Democratic nor the Republican Party held a majority of American voters and those independent voters were the key to success. He told his fellow Democrats, "I have come to ask you how we can best prove to the independent voters that the instrument that he needs is the Democratic Party, and that it would be hopeless for him to attempt to use the Republican Party. I do not have to prove it. I admit it."[19]

Wilson said he spoke to independent voters more as an American than a Democrat, declaring, "I have been bred in the Democratic Party, I love the Democratic Party, but I love America a

great deal more than I love the Democratic Party, and when the Democratic Party thinks that it is an end in itself, then I rise up and dissent. It is a means to an end, and its power depends, and ought to depend, on its showing that it knows what America needs and is ready to give it what it needs."[20]

Turning to concerns about the war, the president said that "we are living at an extraordinary moment. The world has never been in the condition that it is in now, my friends. Half the world is on fire. Only America, among the great powers of the world, is free to govern her own life, and all the world is looking to America to serve its economic need."[21]

In comments that raised more than a few eyebrows, including Republican editors in Indianapolis, the president said, "With all due respect to editors of newspapers, I have to say to them that I never take my opinion of the American people from editorials. So when the great dailies, not far from where I am temporarily residing, thunder with scorn at 'Watchful, Waiting Woodrow,' I sit back in my chair and chuckle, knowing that he laughs best who laughs last, knowing in short what were the temper and principles of the American people. . . . So I feel, my friends, in a very confident mood today. I feel confident that we do know the spirit of the American people; that we do know the program of betterment which it will be necessary for us to undertake, that we do have a very reasonable confidence in the support of the American people."[22]

The question of whether Wilson would seek a second term was resolved by the time he made his way back to Indiana for more political purposes later in 1916. Wilson was in the fray for a second term with his full effort. When his train made a quick stop at Richmond on October 11, 1916, the stop was not particularly noteworthy, with brief greetings offered from the train's rear platform, but the actions of Wilson and a Secret Service agent to save a fervent supporter from certain injury, or worse, death, made the biggest headlines. As the Associated Press reported, "The train to which the President's car was attached backed into a crowd . . . and several persons were nearly caught under the President's car. John Q. Slye, a Secret Service man, pulled one woman out of the way just in time."[23]

The *Richmond Evening Item*'s version of the story noted that after the president's train came to an initial stop, "and without warning a large crowd swarmed to where the President stood . . . Mr. Charles Gagen, an aged but enthusiastic supporter of Wilson, was the first to rush to the rear of the President's car just as the train started to back up. . . . Suddenly realizing his predicament, Gagen, with the other hand, clung to the (train) railing. . . . The President held tight, while a Secret Service agent and local patrolman Harry Vogelsong, came to the rescue. They grabbed Gagen and hefted him to safety."[24]

Once in Indianapolis, Wilson strongly defended the Democratic Party against charges from Republicans that it engaged in "sectionalism" and that "any man who believes the issue of sectionalism in this country is not worthy of the confidence of the nation, he shows himself a provincial."[25] The president avoided any direct reference to his GOP challenger, Charles Evans Hughes, but said he sought to bring the nation together. "After this war, we must be ready with a united force and with a single object," he said. "So long as one group of Americans is pulling in one direction and one group in another, we can get nowhere. We must get together on nationalization and mobilization. We must move together as a single overwhelming force, and we must have cooperation."[26]

Wilson won election to a second term as president, a term quickly overwhelmed by the growing conflicts of World War I. In the years before the United States officially entered the conflict, Wilson and many other political leaders had pushed for American preparedness, while doing what they could to avoid or delay entry into the conflict.

An armistice to end the war was reached in November 1918, and along with focus on rebuilding the devastated portions of the world, political concern quickly turned to efforts to promote peace and prevent any future devastation. In the fall of 1919 Wilson brought the full force of the presidency in support of the proposed League of Nations before a tough fight in Congress. As the months wore on, the league proposal languished in Congress as Senator Henry Cabot Lodge and a coalition of conservative and increasingly isolationist Republicans held firm in their conviction about removal or alteration of Article 10 of the agreement. That article, the Republicans claimed, allowed the league to commit U.S. military forces to conflicts in various parts of the world, removing critical powers assigned to Congress. Wilson was caught in a tough political position, having won the Nobel Peace Prize for his championing of the need for the league as a bold move to prevent further world war and having committed

Wilson (center) meets with members of the Democratic National Committee at the White House, 1916.

American support to the plan without assurance of two-thirds congressional backing. As a result, he set out on September 3, 1919, for an eight thousand-mile campaign that would take him to twenty-two states, including Indiana, to win popular support for the pact.

The second day of Wilson's trip brought him to Indianapolis. While at Union Station, the president and his wife walked between rows of Company H of the Indiana State Militia standing at attention and stood for the national anthem in Jackson Place outside the train depot. The president's motorcade made its way north around Monument Circle and up Meridian Street to Thirty-eighth Street and then east to the fairgrounds, where the president was greeted by a large and enthusiastic crowd of about 15,000 at the fairgrounds coliseum.[27]

The crowd's enthusiasm contributed to awkward moments before the president was introduced. Indiana governor James P. Goodrich, a Republican, had agreed to introduce the Democratic president, but not before making a few remarks of his own. As the *New York Times* reported, "The crowd was anxious to see and hear the President and had no patience with Governor Goodrich, Republican, who presided at the meeting, and tried to speak. Goodrich . . . had a long speech which he wished to deliver but the crowd would not let him. He had been speaking less than five minutes when there were shouts of 'Wilson, we want to hear Wilson!' rose from all parts of the building."[28]

The national news account continued, "The Governor waited a few minutes for the shouts to subside, but when it was apparent that he had no intention of granting the request to introduce Wilson, the cries were reviewed with increased volume. Finally, the governor turned away and another man on the platform jumped up and

while the crowd was cheering, called out that he wished to present the President."[29] The *Indianapolis Star* was a bit more generous to Goodrich in his embarrassing predicament, simply noting that the enthusiasm of the crowd brought his remarks to an "abrupt end."[30]

The rowdiness of the crowd apparently continued, as several hundred people in the audience reportedly left the facility moments into Wilson's speech when they realized they could not hear his voice sufficiently. "After a few minutes, many men and women on the outskirts of the crowd who had satisfied their curiosity to see the president and could not hear him, started for the side doors. The meeting was interrupted about 10 minutes while those who wished made their way out, then the doors were closed and locked by the police, and President Wilson again began his address."[31]

"I want to say to you in all seriousness and soberness that I have not come here to make a speech in the ordinary sense of that term," Wilson told his Hoosier audience. "I have come upon a very sober errand indeed. I have come to report to you upon the work which the representatives of the United States attempted to do at the conference of peace on the other side of the sea, because, my fellow citizens, I realize that my colleagues and I in the task we attempted over there were your servants. We went there upon a distinct errand, which it was our duty to perform in the spirit which you had displayed in the prosecution of the war and in conserving the purposes and objects of that war."[32]

Wilson addressed the level of confusion and misinformation he said existed in the public debate, to date, about the League of Nations pact, particularly Article 10. He said:

> The great bulk of the provisions of the covenant contain . . . engagements and promises on the part of the states which undertake to

become members of it: That in no circumstances will they go to war without first having done one or other of two things, without first either having submitted the question to arbitration, in which case they agree to abide by the results, or having submitted the question to discussion by the council of the League of Nations, in which case they will allow six months for the discussion and engage not to go to war until three months after the council has announced its opinion upon the subject under dispute. The heart of the covenant of the league is that the nations solemnly covenant not to go to war for nine months after a controversy becomes acute.[33]

Wilson said "nine days of discussion" could have saved the nation from World War I. "If there had been nine days upon which to bring to bear the opinion of the world, the judgment of mankind, upon the purposes of those governments, they never would have dared to execute those purposes," he said. "So that what is important for us to remember is that when we sent those boys in khaki across the sea we promised them, we promised the world, that we would not conclude this conflict with a mere treaty of peace. We entered into solemn engagements with all the nations with whom we associated ourselves that we would bring about such a kind of settlement and such a concert of the purpose of nations that wars like this could not occur again. If this war has to be fought over again, then all our high ideals and purposes have been disappointed, for we did not go into this war merely to beat Germany. We went into this war to beat all purposes such as Germany entertained."[34]

Wilson acknowledged that the American people "have heard a great deal about Article X of the covenant of the League of Nations. Article X speaks the conscience of the world. Article X is the article which goes to the heart of this whole bad business, for that article says that the mem-

bers of this league (that is intended to be all the great nations of the world) engage to respect and to preserve against all external aggression the territorial integrity and political independence of the nations concerned."[35] He added:

> That promise is necessary in order to prevent this sort of war from recurring, and we are absolutely discredited if we fought this war and then neglect the essential safeguard against it. You have heard it said, my fellow citizens, that we are robbed of some degree of our sovereign, independent choice by articles of that sort. Every man who makes a choice to respect the rights of his neighbors deprives himself of absolute sovereignty, but he does it by promising never to do wrong, and I cannot for one see anything that robs me of any inherent right that I ought to retain when I promise that I will do right, when I promise that I will respect the thing which, being disregarded and violated, brought on a war in which millions of men lost their lives, in which the civilization of mankind was in the balance, in which there was the most outrageous exhibition ever witnessed in the history of mankind of the rapacity and disregard for right of a great armed people.[36]

Delving deeper into the various aspects of the league pact, Wilson's speech bogged down at times into detail that likely escaped most Americans, particularly the intricacies of economic sanctions that were possible via a new league. And perhaps the strongest argument for the league—its ability to prevent war—was one that had to be qualified: "Nobody in his senses claims for the covenant of the League of Nations that it is certain to stop war, but I confidently assert that it makes war violently improbable, and even if we cannot guarantee that it will stop war, we are bound in conscience to do our utmost in order to avoid it and prevent it," Wilson noted.[37]

Calling the treaty "the first treaty in the history of civilization in which great powers

CAMPAIGN NUMBER

PUCK BUILDING, New York, October 23rd, 1912.

VOL. LXXII. No. 1860.   Copyright, 1912, by Keppler & Schwarzmann.   Entered at N. Y. P. O. as Second-class Mail Matter.   PRICE TEN CENTS.

PUCK

FOR PRESIDENT
WOODROW WILSON:
OF NEW JERSEY
FOR VICE-PRESIDENT
THOMAS R. MARSHALL:
OF INDIANA.

LIBRARY OF CONGRESS

ON TO WASHINGTON!

A Puck magazine cover highlights 1912 Democratic presidential candidate Wilson and his running mate, former Indiana governor Thomas R. Marshall.

have associated themselves together in order to protect the weak," Wilson said he wished to defer point-by-point examination of the treaty, and instead asked the audience to pay attention to the larger ideals embodied therein. "I am discussing this thing with you, my fellow citizens, as if I had a doubt of what the verdict of the American people would be," he said. "I have not the slightest doubt. I just wanted to have the pleasure of pointing out to you how absolutely ignorant of the treaty and of the covenant some of the men are who have been opposing them. . . . My errand upon this journey is not to argue these matters, but to recall you to the real issues which are involved. And one of the things that I have most at heart in this report to my fellow citizens is that they should forget what party I belong to and what party they belong to. I am making this journey as a democrat, but I am spelling it with a little 'd,' and I do not want anybody to remember, so far as this errand is concerned, that it is ever spelt with a big 'D.' I am making this journey as an American and as a champion of rights which America believes in" and "we are ready to insist that everywhere men shall be champions of liberty."[38]

Not all of the president's remarks were on the high road. He referred to the league's opponents on one occasion as "absolutely ignorant," questioned their ability to read the English language, and said they "amaze me by their inability to understand what is plainly expressed."[39]

Wilson said, "When you look at the covenant of the League of Nations thus, in the large, you wonder why it is a bogey to anybody. You wonder what influences have made gentlemen afraid of it. You wonder why it is not obvious to everybody as it is to those who study it with disinterested thought, that this is the central and essential covenant of the whole peace." Recalling his com-

"*We are citizens of the world,*" *noted Wilson.* "*The tragedy of our times is that we do not know this.*"

mitments to American "doughboys" from the just-concluded great war, the president said, "I can come through a double row of men in khaki and acknowledge their salute with a free heart, because I kept my promise to them. I told them when they went to this war that it was a war not only to beat Germany but to prevent any subsequent wars of this kind. I can look all the mothers of this country in the face and all the sisters and the wives and the sweethearts and say, 'The boys will not have to do this again.'"[40]

The president concluded his lengthy statement by declaring, "I look forward with profound gratification to the time which I believe will now not much longer be delayed, when the American people can say to their fellows in all parts of the world, 'We are the friends of liberty; we have joined with the rest of mankind in securing the guarantees of liberty; we stand here with you the eternal champions of what is right, and may God keep us in the covenant that we have formed.'"[41]

Wilson's speech was particularly well received in normally Republican—and marginally isolationist—Indiana, which must have cheered the president. National news reports from Indianapolis, however, emphasized one portion of the president's speech that was not contained in the written text prepared for the occasion—a "put up or shut up" challenge to his opponents.

"You would think to hear some men discuss this covenant, that it is an arrangement for sending men abroad again just as soon as possible," Wilson said. "It is the only conceivable arrangement which will prevent sending our men abroad again very soon. And if I may use a very common expression, I would say, 'If it is not to be this arrangement, what arrangement do you suggest to secure the peace of the world? It is a case of put up or shut up!'"[42]

The Republican opposition, however, had also organized a campaign against the treaty. A week after Wilson appeared in Indiana, Senator Hiram W. Johnson of California spoke before an overflow crowd at Tomlinson Hall in downtown Indianapolis in which he held up "for ridicule" the president's address on the League of Nations and "left no doubt about his conviction that the whole covenant is a bad piece of business. . . . The speech throughout was with caustic comment on the President's course, and this seemed popular with at least part of the audience," reporters noted.[43]

Johnson said, referring to Wilson's Indianapolis speech, that the president addressed Indiana's residents "with his usual confusion of detail and facts. In his declaration of the autonomy of the league he supplied it with three hearts, presumably all beating in unison." He said certain provisions of the treaty "makes America underwrite every territorial grab of every other nation, every wrong and injustice done to peoples, every bargain by which human beings have been handed about from one sovereignty to another, every

violation of natural right and self-determination, every oppression of the strong over the weak."[44]

"Naively, the President remarks that secret treaties hampered him at the peace conference and embarrassed the whole settlement," Johnson barked. "He conceded the wickedness of these secret treaties, but he was neither hampered nor embarrassed to such a degree as to cause him to stand manfully and courageously for his official expressed principles."[45] Pointing to continued concerns of Republicans that the League of Nations treaty took away key powers from America (and other nations), Johnson quoted Wilson as "bravely and boldly proclaiming" in the Paris peace talks key sentiments that Republicans also supported: "No people can be forced under a sovereignty under which it does not wish to live; no territory must change hands except for the purpose of securing to those who inhabit it a fair change of life and liberty. No peace can last or ought to last which does not recognize and accept the principle that governments derive all their just powers from the consent of the governed. No right anywhere exists to have people about from sovereignty to sovereignty as if they were property; and peace which does not recognize and accept this principle will inevitably be upset."[46]

Johnson said the president has "forgotten" and "abandoned his principles" and that "he did more than violate America's high purpose, so eloquently voiced by him. He not only made us *particeps criminis* in such fraud . . . but guaranteed America's treasure and blood to Article X of his league to the eternal preservation of infamy."[47] It was tough talk and simple language that fed into existing American fears of another great war—fears that the nation had not held the boot of victory on the neck of the Germans long enough at the close of World War I.

After leaving Indianapolis, Wilson continued his cross-country trek trying to sell the League of Nations. The *New York Times* made special notice that "the President appeared to be in excellent health" as he departed from Columbus, Ohio, for Indianapolis, and noted that the special train the Wilson party was using was "perhaps the most elaborate ever provided for a Presidential tour. For the first time, an 'office car' in which much of the White House business will be carried on en route, was attached. Each of the 20 newspapermen was provided with a compartment. Representatives of telegraph companies were also on board in order to arrange wire facilities at the stopping places. . . . More newspapermen accompanied the President than have ever made a Presidential tour. There were also representatives of four motion picture concerns on board the special."[48]

Wilson's health would not hold, however, and by the time his train started back east and reached Pueblo, Colorado, on September 25, 1919—just twenty days after he left Indiana—the president appeared weak and was unable to complete his speech. Rushed back to Washington, D.C., it was clear Wilson had suffered a stroke as a result of hypertension (for which no significant medical treatments existed at the time) and remained infirm for the balance of his term in office. In the months and years that remained in his second term, Wilson appeared in public infrequently, and the Senate never ratified the League of Nations treaty. By early 1920 most Americans had become aware of Wilson's physical infirmities, but the Twenty-Fifth Amendment to the Constitution that codified the issues of presidential succession did not yet exist. Wilson left office in 1921 and made only two public appearances while in retirement, one at the state funeral for his successor, President Warren G. Harding, on

August 8, 1923. Wilson died at his Washington, D.C., home on February 3, 1924. He was sixty-seven years old.

William H. Taft

Although Taft's forces had officially "won" the Republican primary delegate voting in Indiana in the spring of 1912, the bitter fight that ensued between his campaign and that of former president Roosevelt ensured the Indiana GOP would remain terribly splintered. Taft enjoyed good support in Indiana, but focused his efforts elsewhere, all the while watching the campaign slip away from both him and Roosevelt as the Democratic nominee, Wilson, surged ahead of the bickering Republicans.

Taft was invited and expected to attend the National Conservation Congress meeting in Indianapolis just after Labor Day in 1912, but as the *Indianapolis Star* reported in a dispatch that reflected Taft's growing distaste for campaigning, Taft "overruled nearly all of his closest friends and advisers . . . who thought it would be a splendid idea from a political standpoint for him to attend this meeting. The president, however, felt that he needed rest and that a trip to Indianapolis at this time would interfere too much with his vacation plans."[49]

Though he served only one term as president—heartily dismissed by voters in the 1912 election with the "help" of his onetime-ally, Roosevelt—Taft remained in public life, including efforts during World War I to help fund war bonds and to support the efforts of the American Red Cross. Both of those campaigns brought Taft back to Indiana as a former president on April 5, 1918, for a war bond-loan drive event at Crawfordsville that included a parade featuring more than 2,300 Montgomery County schoolchildren marching under the theme of "Swatch the

Kaiser." Taft was also feted at a special reception in his honor at the "Supreme Tribe of Ben Hur building" on Main Street and with dinner in the home of the local president of the Chamber of Commerce.

For his evening remarks Taft spoke under the theme of "The Menace of a Premature Peace" in the Wabash College gymnasium, and he presented medals to four local Boy Scouts for their success in selling Liberty bonds.[50] An audience of more than 3,000 heard Taft declare that the United States should "speedily send five million men to France if that number is needed to crush German militarism." He said, "Our cause is right in every way and we have no apologies to make, no lust of gain in this war, but we are fighting for the rights of humanity and justice and Christian civilization . . . the Kaiser [Wilhelm II] and [Paul von] Hindenburg and [Erich] Ludendorff must be crushed and so beaten that the German people will realize that they have been following a false ideal. Then the people of Germany will see the folly of their ways and finish the job for us." Taft also urged Americans to resist violence and "lynch law" in response to pacifists.[51]

A subsequent trip to Evansville in March 1919 focused on raising money for the American Red Cross and its efforts in World War I and the League of Nations. "Now in order to keep the war won," Taft said, "we want to keep Germany on her knees in order to make her repent for all the crimes she has committed. We propose to establish seven or eight republics there where the people have never before known what self-government is. If we merely sign the treaty and run away from the scene, we will have a continuation of the war." Taft said the only way to keep the peace was to keep the coalition of nations together and questioned whether it was wise for America to resist the League of Nations. "Are we a slacker nation? Are we going to retreat and let the other nations go it alone? . . . Will we withdraw now and permit another war to be brought in a few years or will we join the League of Nations to insure universal peace?"[52]

In 1921 President Harding appointed Taft Chief Justice of the U.S. Supreme Court, a position from which he retired from just five weeks before he died on March 8, 1930.

Theodore Roosevelt

By the spring of 1912, the open warfare between Roosevelt and Taft was on full display as both men flexed their political muscle to try and capture the Republican presidential nomination. Perhaps under other circumstances Taft would have walked away from the fight, but it was not to be and he took on the popular Roosevelt in a battle that would ultimately divide and conquer the GOP in November. In deciding to enter the race, former president Roosevelt said, "So far as a personal victory is concerned, I don't care," but said many of his supporters came to him saying they needed his leadership and responsibility in the party.[53]

In sizing up his own chances, Roosevelt said he felt confidence almost everywhere, except Indiana. On that count he was now taking the counsel of Beveridge and Congressman Fred Landis of Logansport on "the Indiana situation." As the Associated Press reported from Roosevelt's home at Oyster Bay, New York, "The Indiana situation was gone over at length. Colonel Roosevelt said that Indiana was the weakest of the Western states from the viewpoint of the Roosevelt forces. If the issue could be put to a popular vote, he said, he believed a majority of the enrolled Republicans would favor his cause. But as there was no primary system in Indiana for the expression of preference as Presidential nominees, he said, the result was in doubt."[54]

Later in March, Roosevelt appeared in Fort Wayne and began a theme he would carry on for months. He believed that the political bosses of the Republican Party were forcing party members in Indiana to support Taft—voters who if given a choice would support his candidacy instead. "If in such contests as these in Indiana, they (the people) are against me, all right," Roosevelt declared. "But if they are for me, I object to the bosses taking them away."[55] Indiana Republicans voted by congressional district that month, and Roosevelt delegates won a slight plurality over delegates pledged to Taft. However, state GOP leaders were signaling they planned to award "at large" delegates to Taft, thus tipping the majority of the Indiana delegation at the upcoming Republican convention to Taft.

In April 1912 Roosevelt rolled across Indiana with stops at Lafayette, Logansport, Peru, Wabash, Huntington, and Fort Wayne, where his comments reflected the paralyzing struggle within the Republican Party for the hearts and minds of the party members. "If, after hearing me, you decide against me, very well, I'll try it again another time and try to get you," he told an audience in Peru from the rear platform of his campaign train. He added, "My hat is in the ring and it is going to stay in the ring. . . . If you are against me in a fair vote, I shall have nothing to say; but if you are for me and the bosses record you as against me, I shall have a great deal to say."[56]

At Fort Wayne Roosevelt charged that the Taft forces were using unfair tactics to try and defeat Republican delegates in Indiana loyal to Roosevelt. "Our opponents apparently are willing to proceed to any lengths to nullify the will of the people," he charged. "When they descend to methods of that sort they forfeit all rights to represent the Republican Party or beyond it."[57] Reporters in Fort Wayne noted that "women were particularly prominent in the throng" at Fort Wayne for Roosevelt as he was "greeted with prolonged cheering."[58]

"We are fighting for the government by the people and not by the combinations of crooked politicians," Roosevelt said. "We are fighting for the right of every man to cast his vote as he wishes it, and to have it count the way he wants it to." Elaborating, Roosevelt openly charged that frauds led by "the Taft machine had attempted to throw the state against me."[59]

At Logansport, things did not go well for Roosevelt. Beyond a smaller than expected audience of far less than one thousand citizens, he had just begun speaking from the rear platform of the train when it began slowly moving away from the assembled crowd. "Roosevelt frantically motioned to the crowd to follow and when the train again stopped, he resumed his speech," the *Indianapolis Star* reported. While he was able to continue to speak, it was only for a few moments more and was still speaking when the train pulled out for good, Roosevelt shouting behind him, "And remember, this fight has just begun!"[60]

At Lafayette, a larger crowd of more than two thousand eventually assembled, although Roosevelt's train arrived at the station twenty minutes ahead of schedule, and so Roosevelt had to wait for the crowd to gather. Once everything was together, the former president thanked his Tippecanoe County supporters and said that "no strong arm work was used here, as had been used in other counties in Indiana" and that a spirit of a "square deal" should prevail as the issues facing the nation were the most important since the Civil War. Speeches that followed at Peru, Wabash, and Huntington would last little more than two to three minutes, news reports indicated, with Roosevelt declaring, "I am content to let my case rest with the people."[61]

Ultimately, Taft won the fight in Indiana with the Republican National Committee voting to seat delegates pledged to the president. Roosevelt was more than displeased, offering an open letter to Taft that said, "In Kentucky and Indiana, in New York City and elsewhere, Mr. Taft knows well that the delegates elected for him represent barefaced frauds. He stands guilty of conniving at and condonation of these frauds; he stands guilty of approving and encouraging fraud which deprives the people of their right to express their will as to who shall be nominated."[62]

Before the Republican convention was complete, however, Roosevelt and progressive members of the party bolted for the new Progressive or Bull Moose Party and gained important support in Indiana, including that of Beveridge.[63]

For the fall campaign, with Republicans clearly divided between forces loyal to Taft and those loyal to Roosevelt, he showed his campaign was for real as he barnstormed across the nation, with particular emphasis on the Midwest. For mid-October, several campaign stops were planned across Indiana during a two-day swing, the highlight being a large nighttime parade in Indianapolis and a major address at the State Fairgrounds Coliseum. Train stops were planned for Hammond, Gary, Indiana Harbor, Covington, Veedersburg, Hillsboro, Crawfordsville, New Ross, Greenwood, Whiteland, Franklin, Amity, Edinburgh, Taylorsville, Columbus, Walesboro, Jonesville, Rockford, Seymour, Crothersville, Austin, Scottsburg, Henryville, Memphis, Sellersburg, and Jeffersonville.[64]

Despite the elaborate plans, none of the stops would be made, as fate intervened in Roosevelt's campaign when a gunman approached him as he exited his hotel in Milwaukee, Wisconsin, en route to make a campaign speech. The gunman, a man who said he was op-posed to any president seeking a third term, got off one round that struck Roosevelt in "the fleshy part" of his right chest, before being wrestled to the ground. Roosevelt insisted on going on to his scheduled speech, although a small amount of blood had surfaced through his shirt and was creating a small stain on his white waistcoat.[65] Once at the auditorium where he was to speak, Roosevelt stunned the audience to silence when he announced, "An attempt has just been made to kill me. I am carrying the bullet in my body now, and so I will have to cut my speech short." Adding to the dramatics, Roosevelt held up the manuscript that had absorbed much of the bullet's strength from his inside breast pocket and declared, "You see, it takes more than that to kill a bull moose."[66] Roosevelt's blood loss appeared to be affecting his speaking ability, and he said to no one in particular, "Give all assurances to Mrs. Roosevelt," and was assisted from the stage and transported to a local hospital. The remainder of Roosevelt's Indiana appearances were canceled as he recuperated from his wound.

By Election Day, it mattered little. Roosevelt finished second in Indiana with 25 percent of the total vote behind Wilson's 43 percent. Taft finished an embarrassing third with a little more than 23 percent of the vote.

Roosevelt made his last appearance in Indiana just six months before the end of his remarkable life, as the special speaker for both a war bond rally in Indianapolis and commencement exercises at Indiana University in Bloomington. On June 12, 1918, Roosevelt addressed a large crowd at the State Fairgrounds Coliseum in an event designed to help meet a $5 million war savings pledge campaign in Marion County. Local media reports indicated the former president was interrupted several times by cries of "Roosevelt in 1920," which caused him to depart from his prepared remarks: "Friends, this is nothing but an American meeting, at which we are discussing Americanism and all it means, preparedness and putting the war over. We must stand by every public servant as he develops and uses the strength of the country. We should stand against him precisely to the degree that he fails to develop and use the war strength of the country."[67] Roosevelt's prepared remarks discussed the importance of supporting the American military and the need to discontinue the use of German in American schools and newspapers.

Reporters noted the ex-president appeared ill and uncomfortable during his Indianapolis speech, but by the next morning, June 13, 1918, he appeared refreshed, although he was delayed in his departure for Bloomington because a doctor visited him at his hotel room. Behind schedule after the doctor's examination, Roosevelt arrived on the IU campus in time to speak before the conclusion of the graduation exercises. He praised the university, noting that "we need the institutions that teach the broad cultural development which this nation needs more than it needs anything else," he said, "if it is to be worthwhile that this experiment in free government should have been tried on this continent."[68]

Before an audience of more than 8,000, Roosevelt acknowledged the Class of 1918 contained more "girls" than "men" and made particular notice of Civil War veterans present in the crowd declaring that "you proved that valor could go hand in hand with tenderness and friends, there were plenty of men then who cried, 'peace, peace' when there was no peace, and I know that you men who wore the blue would be the first to bear testimony to the valor and the high devotion to the right, as it was given to them to see the right, of the men who wore the gray. All fought for the truth that was in them; we are proud of them all,

but we are not proud of the men who didn't have enough conviction to fight on either side."[69] Always a colorful speaker, Roosevelt drew applause when he declared, "There is only one person I cordially despise more than I do a German militarist, and that is an American pacifist. I will shoot a wild beast, but I will step on a snake."[70]

Explaining why he was late in arriving for the ceremonies, Roosevelt said he had planned to make no stops between Indianapolis and Bloomington. "We struck Martinsville," he said, "and they had a drum and fife corps and an automobile and there were two Grand Army men in it and two veterans of the Spanish-American War--my war. It was only a little war, but it was all the war there was . . . a man was there with two stars on his pin that he wore for his two sons, both of them in the army, one of them having just been wounded, belonging to the same division of troops to which my boy, Archie, was wounded and belonged, and he was wounded not far from where Archie was wounded." Roosevelt said, "When I saw those five men (at Martinsville), I said, 'By George, I am going to speak. I don't care what happens now,' so we stopped and I just said a word to the men and women who had gathered there. Aye, friends, it was fine to look in their faces--the faces of the American type--of the type we like to think of as personifying what is best and truest in our country, of the type that is slow to anger, but that, having been roused, does not sink back until the end has been attained."[71]

Roosevelt next directed his comments to the position of immigrants in America and the need to end sectionalism and for all Americans to live under one flag. His remarks rang particularly important in Indiana, where growing anti-German feelings continued to percolate. He said, "Mind you, I am not blaming the immigrant as much as I am blaming ourselves. We have failed to give the immigrant the chance to become American-ized as he should become. We have permitted him to be exploited. We have failed to see that he was taught English and, on the other hand, we have failed to demand from him a full allegiance, not merely in name, but in deed, to the flag."[72]

The former president suggested that America "reverse policy" and "hereinafter treat each im-migrant not merely as a labor unit, but as the possible father of the American citizens, which whom our children and children's children are to inherent this land. If he isn't the right type to make us think, that his children's children will be fit co-citizens of ours, then keep him out. If he is the right type, admit him on a full equality. . . . Require him to learn and speak and read English. It will immediately increase his chance of being able to earn a livelihood in American standards. It will free our workingmen."[73]

Declaring that he loved peace, not war, Roosevelt made a strong argument for American preparedness and the honor of military service by all men. That said, Roosevelt said he wanted "America to act as an honorable man should act" and supported military action to support Amer-ica's interests if that is what situations required. "Let (America) do all it honorably can do to keep out of a war," he said. "When it has gone in, let it fight the war through. We have got to humble Germany now or prepare for a more dangerous war in the future. If we don't win now with our allies, sometime in the future we will have to fight to a finish without allies."[74]

News reports indicated that Roosevelt was suffering from a fever while in Bloomington and asked to be returned to Indianapolis immediately after his speech, bypassing a scheduled alumni luncheon in his honor in order to rest at a hotel before departing by train for New York City. Roosevelt died in his sleep at his New York home on January 19, 1919. He was sixty years old. Reflecting on the towering figure that Roosevelt had been for his entire public life, former vice president Thomas R. Marshall of Indiana com-mented, "Death had to take Roosevelt sleeping, for if he had been awake, there would have been a fight."[75]

Eugene V. Debs

Amazingly during the highly divided na-ture of the 1912 election with Wilson, Taft, and Roosevelt struggling to grasp the White House away from each other, the acknowledged "father" of the Socialist movement in America, Debs of Indiana, conducted his most successful campaign ever for the presidency. "Successful," however, represented capturing just 6 percent of the national vote on Election Day, approximately 900,000 votes, the highest number of votes accu-mulated by a Socialist Party candidate—a record never again matched. In Indiana, Debs matched his national performance, gathering 6 percent of Hoosier ballots.

Born in Terre Haute in 1855, Debs started his political career as a Democrat, but was always interested in the efforts of organized labor. Elected to only one office in his life, a single four-year term to the Indiana Senate between 1855 and 1859, Debs became more and more involved in the labor movement and more disenchanted with the approach of the two major parties. By 1900 Debs won his first nomination for presi-dent by the Socialist Party, but received less than 1 percent of the national vote. He tried again in both 1904 and 1908. Both efforts resulted in slightly more votes—3 percent of the total nationally—but still far from a factor. Beyond his radical anticapitalistic ideas, Debs's open embrace of equality for African Americans put him at odds with many of his countrymen. In June 1903 the editors of the *Indianapolis World*, a newspaper for "colored people," invited Debs to write an article titled, "On the Color Question." Debs acknowledged that railroad men, for whom he had always been a champion, had resisted efforts by "the colored man" to gain jobs in the industry, but he said they did so only in mistaken service to the corporation "whose interest is to have working-men at each other's throats that they may keep them all, black and white, in subjection."[76]

He noted that "in spite of all such influence, the labor movement in general, in America and throughout the world, stands unequivocally committed to receive and treat the Negro upon terms of absolute equality with his white brother, and where this is not the case the genius of unionism is violated and investigation will disclose the fact that corporate power and its henchmen are at the back of it."[77] Explaining what he understood to be the desires of American blacks, he said, "What the Negro wants is not charity, but industrial freedom and then he will attend to his own education. There is no 'Negro problem,' apart from the general labor problem. The Negro is no one worse off than thousands of white slaves who throng the same labor market to sell their labor-power to the same industrial masters."[78]

Socialist Eugene V. Debs at his desk, 1909.

In Indiana Debs's 1904 campaign gathered more attention, mostly because the Socialist Party held its national convention in Indianapolis at the Masonic Lodge. Debs came to Indianapolis on September 1 to deliver the opening speech of the convention, a lengthy address focused on labor issues, most especially wages paid to American workers. "There has never been a free people, a civilized nation, a real republic on the earth," Debs declared in his characteristic provocative manner. "Human society has always consisted of masters and slaves, and the slaves have always been and are today, the foundation stones of the social fabric. Wage-labor is but a name; wage-slavery is the fact. Twenty-five millions of wage-slavery in the United States is twenty-five millions of twentieth century slaves."[79]

Debs said that all consumers in this so-called civilized society perpetuate the slave-labor relationship and said, "The workers (of America) have but one issue in this campaign, the overthrow of the capitalist system and the emancipation of the working class from wage-slavery." He announced that the capitalist-loving Republicans and Democrats could have the discussions of tariff, finance, imperialism, the gold versus silver standard, "and other dust-covered and moth-eaten issues entirely to themselves. The rattle of those relics no longer deceives workingmen whose heads are on their own shoulders. . . . Their eyes are open and they can see; their brains are in operation and they can think. The very moment a workingman begins to do his own thinking he understands the paramount issue, (and he) parts company with the capitalist politician and falls in line with his own class on the political battlefield."[80]

Debs said the 1904 campaign represented a "life and death struggle between two hostile economic classes, the one is capitalist, and the other is the working class." Further, he brushed aside

LIBRARY OF CONGRESS

the Progressive Bull Moose Party and the Prohibition Party efforts as "elements which propose to reform the capitalist system without disturbing wage-slavery, a vain and impossible task" and as such, he sought to ignore them "despite their good intentions." Often referring to the Republican and Democratic Parties by one name—the Republican-Democrats—Debs said the two parties differed little, were equally corrupt, and "are one in their subservience to capital and their hostility to labor."[81]

Calling out to Americans to reconsider their views of the Socialist Party, Debs said:

> The Socialist Party, the party of the working class, the party of emancipation, is made up of men and women who know their rights and scorn to compromise with their oppressors; who want no votes that can be bought and no support under any false pretense whatsoever. The Socialist Party stands squarely upon its proletarian principles and relies wholly upon the forces of industrial progress and the education of the working class. The Socialist Party buys no votes and promises no offices. Not a farthing is spent for whiskey or cigars (to buy votes). Every penny in the campaign fund is the voluntary offerings of workers and their sympathizers and every penny is used for education. What other parties can say the same?[82]

Spending considerable time describing his specific problems and concerns with both the Republican and Democratic parties, Debs also offered commentary on why each of the party's leaders was unsuitable to American workers. About his fellow Hoosier, Fairbanks, the GOP nominee for vice president, Debs said: "Mr. Fairbanks . . . is a corporation attorney of the first class and a plutocrat in good and regular standing. He is in every respect a fit and proper representative of his party and every millionaire in the land may safely support him." The other Hoosier

on a national ticket, Thomas R. Marshall, the Democratic nominee for vice president, escaped any mention by Debs.[83]

Hitting on themes that appealed to many Americans afraid of the growing industrial revolution that put more and more workers out of formerly skilled positions, and equaling growing concern over new social issues, Debs said:

> The hand tools of early times are no more. Mammoth machines have taken their place. A few thousand capitalists own them and many millions of workingmen use them. All the wealth the vast army of labor produces above its subsistence is taken by the machine-owning capitalists. . . . Hence strikes, boycotts, riots, murder, suicide, insanity, prostitution are on a fearful and increasing scale. The capitalists can do nothing. They are a part, an iniquitous part of the foul and decaying system. There is no remedy for the ravages of death. Capitalism is dying and its extremities are already decomposing. The blotches upon the surface show that the blood no longer circulates. The time is near when the cadaver will have to be removed and the atmosphere purified.[84]

By 1912 the prospect of being nominated for president having become familiar, Debs avoided the traditional "notification ceremonies" and "in a marked contrast to the notification ceremonies practiced by other political parties, the Socialist nominee . . . accepted his nomination by simply informing the newspapers that they were at liberty to print his address of acceptance which he had sent to them in printed form. No committee called on Mr. Debs and there was an entire lack of ceremony of any kind."[85]

In the years after the 1912 election, Debs remained active in the Socialist Party but refused requests that he once again represent the party nationally. He instead focused on writing and speeches that kept his political ideas in play,

In running for office Debs said he was trying "to do away with the rule of the great body of people by a relatively small class and establish in this country industrial and social democracy."

LIBRARY OF CONGRESS

including a controversial June 16, 1918, speech in Canton, Ohio, that placed his liberty in jeopardy. Running afoul of the law was nothing new for Debs. He had been convicted of violating an injunction against the Pullman railroad strike and served six months in jail many years earlier. His second jail sentence came as a result of the Canton speech, officially for violation of the Espionage Act of 1917, and he was subsequently sentenced to ten years in prison. During his speech at Canton, Debs spoke out directly against American involvement in World War I and urged men to resist the draft. He was arrested June 30, 1918, and was tried and sentenced less than six months later. As he was sentenced to prison, Debs told the judge, "Your Honor, years ago I recognized my kinship with all living beings, and I made up my mind that I was not one bit better than the meanest on earth. I said then, and I say now, that while there is a lower class, I am in it, and while there is a criminal element, I am of it, and while there is a soul in prison, I am not free."[86]

In a mostly symbolic effort, the Socialist Party nominated Debs once again for president in 1920 as he sat in a federal prison cell, and he won about 2 percent of the vote nationally, despite the reality that if he *had* been elected, he would be unable to serve. During his time in prison, despite continued efforts to win his pardon and release, Wilson refused to act, sticking with his earlier assertion that Debs was a traitor to the nation. Finally, in December 1921, Harding commuted the remainder of Debs's sentence, and he was released from a federal prison at Atlanta, Georgia.

In his hometown of Terre Haute, feelings for Debs contrasted dramatically with those of many other Americans, and a local "welcome home" ceremony was planned with Charles Hunter, the city's Republican mayor, named as the chair of the committee. Hunter told reporters that the political significance of Debs's conflicts with the law "would be lost in a socially and neighborly welcome" and that more than 1,200 Socialist Party members also planned a special demonstration. It was a spectacle rarely matched in Terre Haute—crowd estimates indicating as many as 30,000 supporters—and the curious showed up to see Debs as he left the train and made his way to his modest Indiana home.[87]

Debs continued to inspire strong feelings among many, and a January 1922 speech by Indiana governor Warren T. McCray before a meeting of the American Legion represented how many felt. McCray, who would later serve a federal prison term of his own, declared that he was "sorry that the one arch-traitor of our country should reside in Indiana" and was further quoted as saying that members of the then-powerful Ku Klux Klan should rise up and "endorse the plan to use mob force, if necessary, to break up all labor meetings addressed by Eugene V. Debs." In response, Debs offered a lengthy call for "the jury of the people of Indiana" to try McCray for inciting criminal activity.[88]

After his prison time, Debs never again accepted entreaties to lead his party nationally and in 1926 entered an Illinois sanitarium for rest; he died there on October 20, 1926, at the age of seventy.

Charles Evans Hughes

For the 1916 election, the Republican Party turned to a moderate, compromise choice, a true patriot and well-known national leader, former New York governor Charles Evans Hughes, who resigned after six years' service as an associate justice on the U.S. Supreme Court to run for president. Hughes's candidacy succeeded in helping heal any remaining internal Republican wounds from the bitter 1912 election between Taft Republicans and Roosevelt Progressives. Hughes won the endorsement of both former presidents Taft and Roosevelt. As the nominee, Hughes tapped Roosevelt's former vice president, Fairbanks, as his running mate. With Fairbanks's nomination, Indiana demonstrated its political importance to both parties. Wilson was running for re-election with a Hoosier running mate of his own, Marshall.

Hughes was already well known to Indiana voters. As the governor of New York he had campaigned in the state for Roosevelt in 1908, including delivering speeches on behalf of the Republican ticket at South Bend, in which he directly addressed William Jennings Bryan's question about "Shall the people rule?" Hughes answered it by declaring, "The people have ruled, and they have never had a better representative ruler that stood so high in public esteem and justified himself as well as a representative of the people as our present President, Theodore Roosevelt."[89]

A *Boston Evening Transcript* dispatch indicated that Hughes offered in Indiana a "straightforward meaty talk that made its instant appeal to such intelligent rural audiences as came out to hear the governor in Indiana" and cited an incident at Elkhart as evidence of this: "The governor's train was not scheduled to stop (at Elkhart), and it was after dark when it arrived, but despite these two circumstances, a great crowd had gathered. When the train stopped there, instant cries of 'Hughes! Hughes!' arose and the governor was forced to leave his dinner and show himself on the rear platform. He was cheered lustily."[90]

For his own candidacy in 1916, Hughes undertook an ambitious two-day schedule of September speeches across Indiana—thirteen in his first day in the state. His focus was on the more heavily populated northern half of the state, with stops conducted at New Castle, Anderson, Muncie, Elwood, Tipton, Frankfort, Kokomo, Marion, North Manchester, Warsaw, Goshen, Elkhart, and South Bend. At Goshen, local Republicans were disappointed when a telegram arrived saying Hughes would be unable to leave the train and mount a special stand constructed on the east steps of the Elkhart County Courthouse because of his failing voice.[91] "A very brief stop was made in this city and the nominee made a few remarks which were not heard by many in the crowd assembled to hear him," a partisan report carried in the *Goshen Daily Democrat* indicated. "It was impossible for the nominee to leave the train and proceed to the business section of the city as he was pressed for time and his voice was poor. Headed by Rogers' Goshen Band, the crowd that had assembled in the park moved to the railway station. . . . The Goshen meeting was a sore disappointment to the party managers who had worked for a couple of weeks on the arrangements. There was no enthusiasm and those who met him at the train did so mostly out of curiosity."[92]

Goshen's Republican newspaper, the *Weekly News-Times*, was more generous in its coverage of Hughes and quoted his brief remarks in total:

> Fellow citizens: I cannot commit myself to speak in this damp air, although I deeply appreciate the interest which brings you out at such a time. This is a very important campaign for the business interests of the country. I desire to see our prosperity placed upon an enduring path. I stand for a reunited party. We must have protection to American industry. We cannot succeed, either in agriculture or in industry unless we have proper recognition of the requirements of competition between labor paid at one rate in this country and labor paid at a lower rate abroad.

LIBRARY OF CONGRESS

Charles Evans Hughes

The tariff for revenue only is not an American doctrine. I say that good naturedly, as we want cooperation of all in this campaign, and I am talking for the benefit of Democrats as well as Republicans. When we desire to have prosperity in this country that will endure, we cannot base our enterprise upon war orders. I stand for the protection of American citizens throughout the world—American lives, American property and American commerce; for American rights, fearlessly and unflinchingly maintained. That is the way of peace and not the way of war.[93]

His stop at nearby Elkhart was equally short and complicated by the fact that the train stopped in such a way as to divide the gathered crowd in half, making it impossible for some to hear Hughes.[94] The longest stop of the day was at Marion, where Hughes visited with locals for forty-five minutes.[95]

The *Fort Wayne Journal-Gazette* reported that Hughes reached his last stop of the day at South Bend "almost minus his voice." Local organizers gave up on the idea of having Hughes speak in the night air despite a crowd estimated at 20,000, and instead moved their event to a nearby high school auditorium. Even inside, Hughes "talked to his audience here tonight at times in a hoarse whisper. Utterly wearied, travel strained, worn by the day's exactions, which included shaking thousands of Indiana hands, the nominee faced here a large audience and his chief speech of the day."[96] News reporters focused on Hughes's voice problems, but noted, "He had only himself to blame, the managers of his tour said, for he took the program into his own hands and fashioned it anew to make it include a speech at every stopping place. . . . His doctor stood beside him at almost every station and applied throat sprays freely between talks, but his voice was frayed and ragged long before he reached South Bend."[97] The

problems with his voice were no secret. One of his campaign aides openly "tugged at the nominee's coat to signal him to stop speaking, but Mr. Hughes, with an emphatic gesture, signified that he intended to finish his address" and received dozens of Republican officials between each of the stops along the way.[98]

Hughes's speeches covered a variety of topics, including taking issue with congressional spending. "The recent session, which constituted only one-half of the 64th Congress," he said, "appropriated in cash $1.6 billion, and specially authorized the expenditure of an additional $231 million," some of that money wasted in rivers and harbors appropriations on "rivers that had little water" to recommend them to commerce.[99] The *New York Times* called Hughes's voice "husky and uncertain," his inability to amplify his voice "was a keen disappointment to Mr. Hughes. He plainly showed the signs of wear and tear, but the reception accorded him (at South Bend), easily the greatest demonstration since his nomination, had been medicine to jaded nerves and tired body."[100]

Earlier in the day, while Hughes's voice was still intact, news dispatches from Muncie quoted him as saying, "We desire peace and prosperity. We desire peace with honor. We desire peace consistently with the maintenance of American rights. I am for the protection of American industry; I am for the protection of the American wage scale; I am for the extension of social justice in giving strict consideration to every honorable undertaking in the United States."[101]

He added, "I am for the maintenance of American rights throughout the world, without fear and unflinchingly with regard to American lives, in regard to American property and American commerce. I am for the dignity of American citizenship and to uphold the honor of the American flag. I am for peace and prosperity through firmness and sagacity. I am not for peace that surrenders through an ignoble desire to keep out of trouble. The way to keep out of trouble is to stand erect, to be firm and to be just."[102]

Hughes departed the next day from South Bend for Indianapolis, where he was an overnight guest in the Fairbanks home. En route, Hughes's train made its first stop at La Porte, where he left the train and spoke from a stand erected downtown. "You cannot expect progress if the people are not disposed to recognize and enforce their just rights; that means a loss of self-respect and patriotic energy; that means decadence and disaster," Hughes said. "Therefore, I say to you, not in the interest of a campaign candidacy but in the interest of the American people, that we must fearlessly enforce American rights throughout

From 1930 to 1941, former presidential candidate Hughes served as Chief Justice of the U.S. Supreme Court.

the world and stand unflinchingly for the dignity of American citizenship throughout the world."[103]

At Valparaiso the candidate's remarks were interrupted as the train started ahead for its next stop at Michigan City. At Michigan City, Hughes left the train and spoke to 4,000 workers at the Haskell car shops, most of them members of a labor union, the *New York Times* reported. At Gary, Hughes spent two hours observing a parade and spoke to a crowd of about 7,000 in a city park "against the advice of his physician." Moving south, Hughes's train also stopped at Plymouth and Rochester, where crowds and bands greeted him. "Mr. Hughes, however, kept his remarks within a few words of greeting, saving his voice for the big meeting in Indianapolis tonight," the *Times* reported.[104]

Once in Indianapolis "a remarkably impressive political demonstration" was offered, and "traffic about the railroad station was held up by a throng. A dozen brass bands increased the tumult, and 10,000 marchers were ready to escort the nominee through the crowded streets made brilliant by red fire, rockets and gay banners."[105] Hughes and Fairbanks rode through downtown Indianapolis in a GOP parade, and news reports continued that he appeared "weary in mind, body and voice" and kept a physician at his side who applied a "spray" to Hughes's mouth regularly after he spoke. By his second evening in Indiana, he had regained his voice for an evening speech at Tomlinson Hall in which he attacked the Wilson administration for broken promises.[106] Huges said:

> I want a splendid patriotic sentiment in this country. America cannot provide work, America can never be successful and prosper if we do not have a splendid patriotic sentiment. We are all Americans, whatever race, whatever creed, wherever we come from, whether foreign-born or born here, we are

LIBRARY OF CONGRESS

all here as Americans. American means your attitude toward things not where you were born or what is your race. It is a word of the spirit; it is not a word of the flesh, and I stand here to say that if we are going to have America of the future realize these great ideals I have been talking about, we have got to enforce American rights throughout the world and dignify ourselves.[107]

With just days to go before Election Day, Hughes made more stops in Indiana at Columbus and Evansville on October 31, 1916, where he faced a few hecklers at both stops in the crowd near his train platform. "His answers (to the hecklers) brought tremendous applause from his audience," the AP reported. "Mr. Hughes told a friendly heckler at Columbus, Indiana that a war munitions embargo and warning Americans off belligerent ships would constitute 'a very thoughtless policy'; and that he stood 'for the maintenance of right, including the right of travel and the right of shipment.'"[108]

The final result was as close as they come. Hughes narrowly carried Indiana over Wilson by a margin of 1 percent (less than 7,000 votes separating the two men statewide). Indiana was one of fifteen states where the outcome was determined by a difference of less than 5 percent of the vote, representing 129 electoral votes. Wilson won thirty states overall to Hughes's eighteen, but the Electoral College vote was closer, with Wilson winning by 277 to 254.

Despite his good showing in the 1916 election, Hughes refused appeals to be the GOP nominee again in 1920. He did, however, return to public life in 1921, accepting President Harding's appointment to be secretary of state. Between 1925 and 1930, Hughes returned to private law practice (including arguing several cases before his former colleagues on the U.S.

Supreme Court), and on February 3, 1930, was tapped by President Herbert Hoover to be chief justice of the nation's highest court (replacing Taft). He served until retirement in July 1941, leading the inaugural oaths for President Franklin D. Roosevelt in 1933, 1937, and 1941. He died in Massachusetts on August 27, 1948, at the age of eighty-six.

Charles Warren Fairbanks

In 1916 Fairbanks made his mark in history as one of only two former vice presidents to come to power and was once again the Republican nominee for vice president along with conciliatory GOP nominee Hughes. Fairbanks made as much sense for the Republicans as did Hughes. While Hughes was successfully smoothing over any residual hard feelings from the fierce intraparty battle between Roosevelt and Taft in 1912, Fairbanks was viewed as potentially attracting Democratic voters away from President Wilson. It was an interesting strategy. Wilson and Fairbanks had appeared together in Indianapolis, and Fairbanks even expressed comments somewhat favorable to the president's policies in Mexico during an early September speech before the Indiana State Press Association. Fairbanks's comments before the Indiana journalists were used by both Republicans and Democrats for their own means. Fairbanks said:

> I have no doubt that the disturbances in Mexico during the last few years have been due in a greater or less degree to an effort on the part of ambitious, cunning men to force intervention and possibly annexation to the United States. The exploiters of public utilities and of the mineral and agricultural resources of our neighbors have undoubtedly thought that they would gain much if they could force intervention by the United States. These are soldiers of fortune in Mexico who

The Republican presidential team of 1916—Hughes and Fairbanks.

would undoubtedly welcome such a contingency. President Wilson is dealing with the situation as best he can. We may not entirely agree that his course is better than that of his distinguished predecessor, nevertheless, we should endeavor to uphold his hands. There should be no difference of opinion as to that. By doing so we shall make his task a comparatively easy one. It is not an hour for either little politics or sensational journalism. . . . The President of the United States is a safer guide than sensationalists and the soldiers of fortune who come to the surface whenever international controversies arise.[109]

In 1916 Fairbanks was sixty-four years old, and as occurred in 1904, questions arose about his ability to campaign actively on behalf of the Republican ticket. In mid-September Fairbanks's aides announced he was canceling a scheduled speech at Chicago due to an attack of "gastritis" and would return to his home in Indianapolis for

rest.[110] While Fairbanks had to suspend campaigning temporarily, Hughes paid him a visit at Indianapolis on September 24, 1916. An Associated Press report indicated that "Mr. Hughes today followed his usual procedure of resting on Sunday. He spent the day at the home of Charles W. Fairbanks, his running mate; slept tonight on his private car in the railroad yards and will leave early tomorrow to open his campaign in Ohio at Dayton." Hughes and his wife accompanied Fairbanks to church on Sunday morning in Indianapolis and then "took a motor ride" in the afternoon and attended a closed reception at Fairbanks's home for his friends and neighbors.[111]

By mid-October Fairbanks was back on the campaign trail in several western states and stopped off in Indianapolis before resuming campaigning in Ohio, Kentucky, Missouri, Wisconsin, and Illinois before Election Day.[112] On October 31, 1916, the Hughes-Fairbanks campaign in Indiana got a big boost via an event hosted by the "Crusaders for Hughes," a women's group organized for the election, even though women still did not have the vote. Elisabeth Freeman, a nationally known suffrage leader and early white advocate for the National Association for the Advancement of Colored People, appeared in Indianapolis on behalf of Hughes and Fairbanks. "A rally for colored voters held in Tomlinson Hall was attended by Miss Freeman," the *New York Times* reported. "She appeared waving an American flag, and whipped up enthusiasm for Hughes by blaming President Wilson for the lynchings in the south."[113]

On the same day Freeman and others were leading the big rally in Indianapolis, news reached Fairbanks as he campaigned in western states that his mother had died unexpectedly back in Indiana. Fairbanks's on-and-off campaign was off for good with the sad news from home as he suspended campaigning altogether. News reports indicated he retired early on Election Day after issuing a statement indicating he thought Hughes had been elected and he was about to be elevated to the nation's second highest office for a second time. It was not to be so. Late returns from California sealed the decision for Wilson and *his* Indiana running mate, Marshall.

Having been wrong about the election outcome (although he had helped Hughes win Indiana), Fairbanks made the first move and sent a wire to his fellow Indianapolis resident, Marshall. "My Dear Mr. Vice President," Fairbanks's note said, "I will avail myself of the earliest opportunity since the ascertainment of the California vote to extend to you my cordial personal congratulations upon your re-election as Vice President. My very best wishes go with you always." Marshall was equally cordial in victory, replying to Fairbanks, "Dear Mr. Fairbanks, I thank you sincerely for your kind letter of congratulation. As a partisan it is worth much to know that we have won. As a man it is worth more to know that the years of personal friendship have not ended with this campaign, and to feel that there are left a few men at least who may differ in politics and yet wish each other well. I rejoice to believe that you always have been of that chosen few. Long life and serene content for you."[114]

His political life now officially ended, Fairbanks had intended to return to private law practice in Indianapolis, but his declining health limited his work. Fairbanks fell ill from nephritis, a kidney ailment, and died at his Indianapolis home on June 4, 1918. He was sixty-six years old.

Thomas R. Marshall

Former Indiana governor Marshall's elevation to the national stage as the Democratic vice presidential nominee in 1912 started with a bang. On August 20, 1912, Judge Alton B. Parker, the party's 1904 nominee for president, led the official delegation to notify Marshall of his selection for the ticket to run alongside Wilson, the governor of New Jersey. Marshall's path to nomination was considerably easier than Wilson's. Marshall was nominated on just the second convention ballot, while Wilson was not selected until the forty-sixth convention vote.

The "notification" of Marshall was a major event, filling the streets of Indianapolis with thousands of visitors who made their way to University Park at the corner of Vermont and Meridian Streets, where a special stand was constructed. Parker offered a lengthy speech in which he praised both Wilson and Marshall as governors of important states "who know how to create and apply needed governmental remedies and whose lives give abundant surety that the pledges of their party and their own promises to the people will be fully kept."[115]

Parker's remarks, however, were interrupted by the collapse of a grandstand seating about three hundred guests on hand for the ceremonies. As many as forty-five people were injured, although none seriously. Thomas Taggart, state Democratic boss, calmed the crowd, and the festivities went forward once order was restored. As the *New York Times* reported, "The exercises were hurried somewhat in view of the accident, so, after Judge Parker had concluded his address, Gov. Marshall, with little formality, advanced to the front of what platform there was left to begin his acceptance speech."[116]

For his remarks, Marshall spoke to creating commonality between the two parties of America and the role citizens play in a democratic republic. "American Democracy in its purity was intended to mean, and I believe it does mean, something more than voting, something more than selecting officers," Marshall said. "American Democracy does not depend upon caste or creed or condition, upon race or color, upon wealth or poverty, upon success or failure. But unerringly, it does depend upon the inner life of the individual citizen. It is an inspiration and an aspiration. It does not always depend upon the ticket which a man votes. It does depend always upon the motive back of the ballot. At its best, human nature is weak. The cares of the world and the deceitfulness of riches oftentimes stifle generous impulses. Great crises are necessary to awaken many men to their sense of duty."[117]

Marshall added:

It was because I thought a crisis to be at hand that four years ago I made the statement that 80 percent of the people of Indiana were Democrats at heart even though they did not know it. I now enlarge that statement and declare that 80 percent of the entire country believes in the historic Democracy of Thomas Jefferson. This campaign is going to rid the Democratic Party of every man who does not believe in its principles and it's going to add to the party's ranks, I hope, every man, who does believe in them. This campaign calls upon some for justice, upon others for charity, upon all for patriotism. It does not call for the bandying of epithets nor an appeal to the personal. We may safely leave to that senile dementia which has seized the so-called Republican Party the personalities of this campaign. Its unfitness to rule the Republic is disclosed by its inability to keep its temper. It was cohesive so far as its leadership was concerned, while it was engaged in looting the public, but when its leaders are now disorganized while quarreling over the loot.[118]

Marshall proved an effective campaigner. His speaking style and ability to turn a phrase caught the attention of reporters and played well in front of many audiences. His presence on the Democratic ticket was credited with helping Wil-

son carry Indiana against the splintered Republicans. Marshall's style, although contrasting with Wilson, was such that the more academic Wilson was quickly turned off and basically relegated Marshall to a role of little or no importance in his two tumultuous terms as president.

Indianapolis residents, despite party affiliation, were excited about the day's activities for the Marshall notification ceremony, and large crowds lined the streets as Marshall and Parker led a parade from downtown to the fairgrounds. Evidence of the excitement was the presence of Fairbanks, the former Republican vice president, who attended the ceremony for Marshall. Once at the fairgrounds, Marshall and his wife, Lois, spent a considerable amount of time shaking hands and greeting well-wishers until Lois indicated it was time to go home.[119] Interestingly, al-

LIBRARY OF CONGRESS

Thomas R. Marshall and his wife, Lois Kimsey, at their home in Indianapolis at 1229 North Pennsylvania Street, 1915.

In spite of his many political accomplishments as Indiana governor and U.S. vice president, Marshall is best known today for his offhand quip: "What this country needs is a really good five-cent cigar."

LIBRARY OF CONGRESS

though Fairbanks attended the 1912 ceremonies for Marshall, in 1916 he found himself directly in competition with Marshall when Fairbanks won the Republican nomination for vice president on the ticket led by Hughes. Fairbanks won the match and helped Hughes carry Indiana by a margin of less than 1 percent, while Wilson and Marshall were reelected nationally by a narrow margin of just 3 percent. Little noticed in the several days it took to determine the outcome, Marshall's re-election was the first time a sitting vice president had won a second term since 1828.

Marshall's role in the 1916 Wilson campaign was again somewhat limited, though he spoke everywhere he was invited (and continued to do so in support of the sale of Liberty Bonds in the lead-up to World War I). One amusing report emerged in early September reflecting Marshall's impatience with the latest technology of the day. The Democratic Party had hired film makers to make motion pictures of both Wilson and Marshall, although Marshall's turn in front of the camera did not go well. After eight takes Marshall told the cameraman, "I have marched in front of the thing eight times and that is enough, this is getting to be silly." Democratic senators surrounding Marshall in the film told him he should try again "in the interest of the party," but Marshall said no, eight times was enough.[120]

Marshall briefly sought his party's nomination for president in 1920, but unable to solicit support beyond the Indiana delegation, he gave up his bid. Marshall finished out his term with the virtually incapacitated Wilson having never made any attempt to usurp the president's authority despite his infirmity. In May 1920 Indiana Democrats invited Marshall to be the keynote speaker at their state convention at Tomlinson Hall in Indianapolis. Still pushing for passage of the League of Nations and for resolu-

tions between entrenched differences between Wilson and Senate Republican leaders, Marshall declared that "equal and exact justice to all men" was needed to ensure peace among all American interests at home and abroad. Referring to World War I, Marshall said, "This was, as I understand it, an American war. The peace should be an American peace. The war could not have been fought successfully as either a Democratic or a Republican war. The peace cannot bring that real peace which the American people want if it be made either as a Democratic or Republican peace. I still hope the President and the Senate will reach an accord upon such terms as will enable the treaty to be ratified and a demure peace be made with the government of Germany." Marshall said he did not intend to add to the conflict between the parties, but noted that "I give my unqualified endorsement to the altruistic views of the President, in the defense of which use he has broken his body."[121]

Marshall also addressed the recent enactment of the Eighteenth Amendment five months earlier in January 1920 that prohibited the production, sale, or transportation of alcoholic beverages. He said he opposed any "let up" in the enforcement of prohibition and cautioned his fellow Democrats that the party would "merit the contempt of the people if it ever stands for the flaunting of a law because certain citizens do not believe in it. While the prohibition amendment remains, it must be enforced in accordance with its provisions."[122]

After he left office, Marshall remained a distinguished Hoosier, and his hometown of North Manchester sought to honor him by inviting him as the May 1925 commencement speaker at Manchester College. It would be Marshall's last public appearance and address. Addressing the graduates of the college affiliated with the United

LIBRARY OF CONGRESS

Vice president Marshall tosses a ceremonial first pitch at a baseball game, possibly the home opener for the Washington Senators.

Brethren Church, Marshall's comments reflected the freedom of being retired from public life offered him. He noted, "If you are expecting the usual thing in commencement addresses, you are bound to be disappointed. That kind of address is delivered by a reputed wise man and attempts in 40 or 50 minutes to give enough sound advice and philosophy to last a lifetime. Now that I am out of politics I am old enough to tell the truth. The world never had, has not now, and never will have any great men save those who do something for their countries and for their God."[123]

Marshall declared his Christianity and noted that "the earnest Christian of today has a harder time to be true to his convictions than did our forefathers who were directly under the supervision and direction of another church. Now church and state are separate, and I am not asking that they be reunited to the sense they once were. I believe in an eternal God. I am a blue-stockinged Presbyterian. . . . I can't believe in a God who couldn't do everything told in the Bible; then if He could do it, I believe He did. I am not much of an advocate of the theory of evolution. If anyone

here believes in evolution or takes pleasure in thinking his grandfather was an ape, I have no quarrel whatever with him, but I *knew* my grandfather."[124]

The former vice president said his life had given him the opportunity to meet many great men, including the leaders of France following the close of World War I—a war that had cost France more than one million dead men, women, and children and more than four million injured citizens. "A great philosopher and professor said that the great war was worth as much to France as it had cost her," Marshall said. "I thought of all the ruin and death so evident in that country as a result of that war and said, 'What do you mean?' He said, 'It was worth what it cost because it brought the French people back to God.' The hope of the world is the gospel of Jesus Christ. We have tried laws, ordinances and diplomacy, and to what they come? Documents are as idle as a painted ship on a painted ocean."[125] Marshall also referred to the young men charged in the infamous Leopold and Loeb murder case ongoing in Chicago and asked the graduates to resist contemporary thinking that purports that "I'm just a machine—I'm not responsible to God or man for what I do—I cannot be called to account until I run amuck. They used that kind of argument in the case of two boy murderers in Chicago. If that philosophy obtains in this country, this will be but another example in the long line of ruins that strew the paths of the past."[126]

Marshall's remarks reflected his growing faith in God and his realization over the course of his life that his careers in law and politics had not led him to any answers greater than those he found "in the life and teachings of Jesus." He added, "I left the law for the more honest profession of politics and then after a time changed my mind for I became convinced I had made a mistake. . . . I am saying these things about God and His kingdom because of the things I have seen and watched and because I believe before God that the world cannot come to peace and fraternity except through Jesus Christ."[127]

In closing comments directed to his hometown brethren, Marshall said, "I thank God that here in North Manchester there is an institution that says, 'As for me and my house, we are the Lord's.'"[128] Following the graduation ceremony, the campus newspaper, *Oak Leaves*, captured the last known photograph of Marshall as he walked across campus under a straw hat with the help of a cane. Many in attendance that day reported that Marshall appeared frail and weak. His death on June 1, 1925—just two weeks after his North Manchester appearance—prompted a local memorial service at the college chapel, where his hometown friends remembered him and his life of service. He was seventy-one years old at the time of his death in Washington, D.C.

William Jennings Bryan

Bryan remained a popular figure among many Democrats and was called upon in selected instances to help the party and the man he had helped win the party's nomination, Wilson.

In April 1912, "the Great Commoner" headlined a Jefferson Day banquet of about 1,000 Indiana Democrats at Indianapolis. Bryan's speech was titled "Democracy's Triumph," and the event also included remarks by U.S. Senator John W. Kern and Marshall.[129] Appearing again in the state on the lecture circuit at the Jefferson Theatre in Goshen on July 20, 1912, Bryan addressed the growing temperance movement (and drew a large group of Women's Christian Temperance Union members) and told his audience that "the people must have entertainment, and unless good entertainment is furnished, they are apt to find entertainment not so good."[130] Bryan spoke earlier that day at Angola in Steuben County and received a rousing welcome in South Bend as he made his way north to a speech in Niles, Michigan (although he did not speak in South Bend). His support of Wilson's 1912 presidential campaign won him appointment as secretary of state in the administration, a position he held until 1915.

For more than a decade after his political campaigns had ended, Bryan's notable oratory skills won him hundreds of paid speaking engagements across the nation. One of Bryan's last visits to Indiana had nothing to do with presidential campaigning, but rather was to record forever a piece of history attached to his name. On July 3, 1923, Bryan visited Gennett Record Company in Richmond to make a sound recording of his now

LIBRARY OF CONGRESS

Notification ceremony for Marshall's vice presidential nomination, 1912, Indianapolis.

famous "Cross of Gold" speech from the 1896 Democratic National Convention, a period during which he switched his support for women's suffrage (after women won the vote in 1920) to the growing temperance movement.[131] Bryan's deeply held religious views also guided his opposition to the teaching of evolution in public schools, and he was a participant in the famed Scopes trial in Tennessee. Bryan died in his sleep just five days after the conclusion of the trial on July 26, 1925, at the age of sixty-five.

J. Frank Hanly

By the time he accepted the Prohibitionist Party nomination for president in August 1916, former Indiana governor J. Frank Hanly was convinced that his friends in his original party—the GOP—and his foes in the Democratic Party had no reason whatsoever not to support his candidacy. "There never was a better time in the history of the country for a man dissatisfied with the attitude of either the Republican or the Democratic Party or of the candidate of either, upon question of state and national prohibition, to sever his party affiliations and vote his convictions, registering thereby his protest against his party's unrighteous attitude," Hanly declared from the front lawn of his home at 1202 North Alabama Street in Indianapolis during his "notification" ceremony. "He can do this in this election knowing that nothing will be imperiled by his doing it."[132]

Hanly, who served as governor of Indiana for one term between 1905 and 1909, had become an outspoken and articulate advocate for temperance and intended to make it the center of his presidential aspirations (no matter how slim his chances may have been). A 1915 self-published book written by Hanly, titled *Fallacies Exposed*, was based off a speech in which Hanly

dismantled the arguments against prohibition and provided the basis for his antisaloon feelings, which were also reflected in policies undertaken during his tenure as governor.[133] Hanly successfully pushed legislation allowing local communities to vote to ban liquor sales and eliminating horse-race betting at the Indiana State Fair. A devout Methodist lay leader, Hanly warned that "the liquor traffic brooks no restraint. It knows no law. . . . In Indiana, it breaks over every legislative enactment, respecting neither hour, holiday nor Sabbath." He said he favored laws "against all [liquor] sales, carrying severe penalties, making it an offense to run or operate a place where illicit sales of intoxicants are made. . . . I do not desire that it shall be understood that I am opposed to other restrictive measures. . . . Such is not my attitude. The business is so utterly indefensible from any standpoint, moral or economic, that I am prepared to give executive approval to any measure looking to the further regulation . . . of the traffic which I believe to be a valid enactment."[134]

Taking special aim at his Republican brethren headed by their nominee for 1916, Hughes, Hanly said, "The leaders of the Republican Party are in the midst of a frantic effort to convince the electorate that an emergency, a crisis is confronting the American people in the impending election. They have wrought themselves into a veritable frenzy of alarm lest 'Americanism shall become extinct and the honor of the republic be lost.' But nothing could be further from the truth."[135] While acknowledging war-torn portions of Europe, Hanly suggested that "this danger inheres in the condition there, and is in no wise dependent upon the Presidential choice to be made here in November. The same danger will inhere in the conditions there whoever is elected here. The election of Mr. Hughes will not eliminate or minimize it. The election of Mr. Wilson will not intensify or hasten

IHS, BASS PHOTO COMPANY COLLECTION, P 130

J. Frank Hanly served as the twenty-sixth governor of Indiana after service as a state legislator and congressman.

its immediacy. To contend that it will is mere party fustian, indulged in for the sake of temporary party advantage. In this regard there is no crisis." Hanly said that "both Mr. Wilson and Mr. Hughes are intensely American" and both were interested in protecting the nation's honor and were "lovers of peace," but said both would sacrifice such peace "to save the nation's honor or in defense of American ideals. From this standpoint, it will not make the slightest difference which of the two is elected."[136]

Devoting so much of his acceptance speech to his opponents likely reflected the position the Prohibition Party found itself in Indiana and nationally—it was a nonfactor. Hanly's notification of his nomination came at an interesting period in Indianapolis, as similar notification ceremonies were slated for Fairbanks and Marshall, two Indianapolis men nominated to oppose one another for vice president of the United States. In Hanly's speech, he also took the unusual step of declaring he refused to support the party's platform allowing for voter referendums or recall of elected officials and said he would not uphold it in his campaign, but if elected, he could support women's suffrage for the vote.

During his campaign, Hanly did not spare his Republican brethren from pointed critique. During a speech at South Bend on October 17, 1916, he assailed Hughes's attitude on liquor laws as governor of New York. "I have no desire to butt into the delectable controversy going on between Mr. Wilson and Mr. Hughes," Hanly said, "but that the record may be kept straight and the country not misled. I take issue flatly with Mr. Hughes' statement that while he was governor of New York there was no 'invisible government.' There was no hour during his administration when 'invisible government' was not triumphant at Albany, nor has there been an hour since when

it has not been. The only defense Mr. Hughes can make to this charge is to answer that President Wilson is also mute and obedient to the same element of 'invisible government.'" For Hanly, 'invisible' or 'shadow' governments were part and parcel of the type of corruption he had railed against during his own tenure as governor of Indiana.[137]

Hanly's campaign caught little attention nationally and ended where it started—in Indianapolis. On November 5, 1916, two days before Election Day, Hanly arrived home and made one more speech from his home with his running mate, Ira J. Landrith of Tennessee, at his side. Hanly and Landrith were ending a 20,000-mile campaign that had taken them from coast to coast, but had fashioned very little excitement among voters. "The Prohibition Party stands for the eight-hour day, not for a few, however, but for all of you," Hanly said. "We would appeal to reason. We would not bow to a bludgeon wielded at Washington."[138] Hanly argued for preparations for the millions of men engaged in the battles of Europe to transfer them to productive lives of commerce and manufacturing. On Election Day, Hanly drew only 1.2 percent of the national vote as Wilson was reelected. In Indiana he did slightly better, with 2 percent of the vote, but even finished fourth overall in the state behind Hughes, Wilson, and the Socialist Party nominee, Allan Benson. In his remaining days, he published a national prohibition journal from Indianapolis but was killed on August 1, 1920, while on a prohibition speaking tour when the car he was driving was struck by a train at a crossing near Dennison, Ohio. He was fifty-seven years old.[139]

Warren G. Harding

For 1920 both parties turned to little-known political figures from Ohio, as the death of former president Roosevelt in 1919 and the debilitating stroke of incumbent president Wilson the same year left both parties without the expected top-tier candidates. The 1916 GOP nominee, Hughes, decided not to run again, and the Democrats seemed disinterested in yet another run by Bryan. Among the other possible candidates for 1920 were two Hoosiers who decided to sit out the festivities. Both men had been vice presidential standard-bearers for their parties four years previous—Marshall and Fairbanks.

Although 1920 was the first year in which women were allowed to vote in all states, the campaigns seemed to pay little special attention to the new block of voters. The Republican nominee, Senator Warren G. Harding of Ohio, also decided to pay little attention to his opponent, Ohio governor James E. Cox. Instead, Harding and the GOP calculated correctly that in the aftermath of World War I Americans had grown weary of the dreary Wilson administration that was crawling to an end. The president was mostly out of sight, and with the defeat of his League of Nations proposal, generally neutered in power. Harding eventually settled on a succinct campaign slogan ("a return to normalcy") that accurately reflected the mood of the nation.

Harding's selection as the GOP nominee, however, was anything but a foregone conclusion, and it was not until brokered "smoke-filled room" deals delivered the nomination to Harding on the tenth ballot at the Republican National Convention on June 8, 1920, in Chicago. On the first nine ballots, a plurality of Indiana's GOP delegates backed Major General Leonard Wood of New Hampshire, a former chief of staff of the U.S. Army and a Medal of Honor recipient. Two other blocks of Indiana Republicans backed Illinois governor Frank Lowden and U.S. Senator Hiram Johnson of California. In fact, Harding did not receive any of the Indiana delegation

votes until the third ballot, and it was not until the tenth ballot that Harding finally bested Wood among the Hoosier delegates by a vote of 21 to 9. Among the losing Republican hopefuls at the 1920 convention, incidentally, were two future presidents—Calvin Coolidge and Herbert Hoover—although neither were considered as serious a challenge to Harding as Wood and Lowden. Coolidge was nominated, however, on just one ballot to be Harding's running mate.

Generally unknown in Indiana, Harding made his first foray into the state prior to the May primary for a March 26, 1920, address before members of the powerful Columbia Club of Indianapolis. He immediately clarified that if Indiana Republicans had produced their own candidate, he would have stayed out of the state in respect to any favorite son candidate. "I stand before you as a candidate for the party nomination for the Presidency," Harding told his luncheon audience. "A rather unwilling one, let it be said, but a very confident one."[140]

While praiseworthy of Indiana's native son Marshall, whom Harding declared "has a lot more sense than some of the eminent men of his party,"[141] Harding saved his wrath for the increasing isolated and unpopular Wilson. Harding said the president had pursued a policy of "my will or none" and maintained that despite the silence of weapons from World War I, Wilson's policies had assured that America technically remained at war with Germany.[142]

"Everybody wanted formal peace and a new understanding," Harding said. "Europe was ready and America was eager, but a President, unmindful of the Senate and the sentiment of our country, insisted on a battle of rhetorical pens, for the glory of a personal victory and defiantly bartered our nationality, which the Senate was sworn to preserve and has preserved. A President who told us he kept us out of war has literally kept us out of peace—formal peace duly covenanted—and the American people and the world may charge it to the Presidential usurpation of power and attempted dictation where party counsel and co-ordinated government would have led to instant understanding."[143]

Harding added, "I do not come to Indiana in a spirit of opposition or hostility. My mission is one of cooperation and unity. Ohio and Indiana are neighbors and have neighborly interests: we share much of your pride and have mingled our tears with your sorrows; but if we lived 2,000 miles apart we should have mutual and identical party interests this year, when the nation is call-

Warren Harding's wife, Florence, places a flower on his suit from her garden.

ing for return of the Republicans to power."[144]

It was a scathing assault on the Wilson record, but one that was beginning to gain traction for Americans weary of the Treaty of Versailles that officially had ended World War I, and the inability of Wilson to further make his case to the nation.

Later in April, Harding was the only Republican contender who accepted the invitation to address a large Wayne County GOP gathering at Richmond. Harding focused his speech not on his absent Republican challengers, but instead on concerns about the rising cost of living. "Senator Harding asserted that the cost of living will never go down until workmen give greater efficiency for the high wages they are receiving and until production is increased and less extravagance is practiced by the people generally," the *Rushville Republican* reported. Harding told the gathering, "A return to the simple modes of living is the one great need of this country. We can't go on spending money like a drunken sailor and not expect chaos to come eventually."[145]

Harding's GOP opponents Wood and Lowden eventually joined him in Indiana, with all appearing in Indianapolis on the same day, April 26, 1920. While Wood and Lowden remained popular in Indiana, Harding felt confident in his support in Ohio and, as a result, made an all-out effort in Indiana (at the encouragement of his Senate colleague, Harry New of Indiana), with preprimary speeches in eighteen Indiana communities—Bedford, Columbus, Connersville, Elkhart, Evansville, Fort Wayne, Indianapolis, Kokomo, Logansport, Madison, New Albany, North Vernon, Plymouth, Vincennes, Shelbyville, South Bend, Terre Haute, and Washington.[146]

For his April 17, 1920, speech, Harding spoke at the Nelson Theatre in downtown Logansport. Harding said the purpose of his speech was "chiefly one of cheer and greetings with more thought

LIBRARY OF CONGRESS

GOP presidential candidate Warren G. Harding greets Marie Edwards of Peru, Indiana, who served as treasurer of the League of Women Voters, at Social Justice Day in Marion, Ohio, October 1920. Edwards helped plan the event, where Harding called for equal wages and the creation of an eight-hour work day.

about a Republican victory next November than somebody's personal triumph at Chicago in June. The country is concerned with the party policies and the Republican Party's return to power and sponsorship."[147] Quickly unveiling his "return to normalcy" theme, Harding said, "Every experience following all the great wars ever recorded proves there is just one way to recover from its wastes and altering burdens. Nothing has ever availed, save work and trade, attended by thrift and persistence. High wages come as a war inheritance. They will abide. I think they ought to abide. But high wages are of no avail if living costs grows higher. Money has lost its standard of value. We can't restore it until we recover our poise and get to thinking and acting soberly again. We must strive, all together, for approximately normalcy."[148]

Harding continued:

We ought to favor only the perfected Americanization of the republic, but to hold it wholly American thereafter. We ought to have

it understood from this time on, this is no mere collection of peoples calling themselves Americans, but one people, with one spirit, one soul, one allegiance, and one flag. We might well pledge ourselves never again to be so unmindful of our national defense. We ought to have an ample navy, as our first line of defense. We ought to more than keep apace—we ought to lead the world in the development of aviation, and be stronger in the air than we are on the sea. We ought to have an ample army to have all the young manhood of the republic know the benefits of discipline and physical betterment that come of military training, but it ought to be voluntary, not compulsory; supported by the government in camp, in the national guard, in schools and colleges. It ought to be made so popular and so helpful that young America would seek it as a privilege rather than accept it as a duty of compulsory requirement.[149]

Near the conclusion of his Logansport speech, Harding added, "It hardly seems necessary to allude to women's suffrage, because it is a thing accomplished. I joined those who submitted the amendment, and when the ratification is proclaimed, I want the women of the republic to exercise their new rights and duties of citizenship, and join our parties and enter into full political fellowship and give of their convictions and aspirations and influence them toward the making of the ideal republic."[150]

Historian John Wesley Dean wrote that "Harding was so confident about the Ohio contest with General Wood that he went over to Indiana to campaign for his next primary. As it turned out, he might better have spent his time in Ohio." The April 27, 1920, Ohio primary was a narrow Harding win over Wood, and in Indiana, "things only got worse. . . . On the night of the primary, the returns rapidly showed that Harding was getting trounced." Harding had made a mistake and won not a single delegate in Indiana.[151]

IHS, LEAGUE OF WOMEN VOTERS OF INDIANA RECORDS, 1908–1978, M 612

For the fall campaign, Harding planned to employ a front-porch strategy that had been popular near the end of the nineteenth century, and still had many political advocates. Harding's handlers believed bringing voters and Republican supporters to his home at tiny Marion, Ohio, would provide a solid hometown, folksy image for Harding that would stand in positive contrast to the erudite Wilson. Among the backers of Harding's strategy was Indiana's own Will H. Hays, Republican National Committee chairman. It was a strategy, however, that left Harding worried about the level and type of contact he was having with voters. Despite more than 500,000 visitors (including several Hollywood celebrities and American industrialists) making their way to Marion between July and September 1920, Harding still set out to make speeches in several key states, including twenty in Indiana and dozens more in Illinois, Iowa, Kentucky, Missouri, New York, Oklahoma, and West Virginia. "Those who claim that Harding was kept on his front porch by his handlers to avoid shooting himself in the foot have obviously overlooked these 112 speeches delivered throughout the country" in the 1920 campaign, wrote John Wesley Dean.[152]

For his mid-September sweep across the Midwest, Harding was accompanied by General John J. Pershing on the train as it traveled across Indiana from Chicago, and the campaign made its way back to the front porch in Ohio. Pershing later told reporters his visit with Harding was simply a courtesy call and held no political significance.[153]

A Harding speech in October from the rear platform of a train in Greencastle drew controversy and the attention of lame-duck President Wilson. In that speech, Harding said:

> I noticed in the morning papers that the Secretary of State has said that the kind of world association I am proposing cannot be made with anybody except the nations now out of the president's league. Secretary (Bainbridge) Colby speaks for the State Department of our own America and he ought to be prudent and thoughtful about what he says.
>
> But, he says that America under a proposed association can only associate with the central empires and Turkey, and a few other nations with whom we are engaged in war. Why, my countrymen, Franco is asking: France has sent her spokesman to me informally asking America in its new realization of the situation to lead the way for an association of nations. England has said through Lloyd George and Earl Grey that America must revise and amend and make the League of Nations possible. If there is to be a League of Nations of the world, it ought to be one big enough and broad enough to take in all of the nations, else one group will be organized and arrayed against another.[154]

Wilson was angered by Harding's suggestion that the French government had made contact with him, rather than the White House. Harding explained that he had not been approached by an official of the French government, and instead he had spoken with "spokesmen" or "those who spoke a sentiment which they represented to be very manifest among the French people" for America to lead a new effort for a coalition or "fraternity" of nations. He denied assertions and reports of his speech that more-than-suggested he had been approached by official representatives of the French government.[155] Wilson was unimpressed with the reports of Harding's remarks at Greencastle, sending him a telegram that said: "I need not point out to you the grave and extraordinary inference to be drawn from such a statement saying the government of France (which is a member of the League of Nations) approached a private citizen of a nation which is not a member of the League with a request 'that the United States lead the way to a world fraternity.'" Wilson added that the State Department reported that France remained "most honorably mindful of its international obligations and punctiliously careful to observe all propriety of international intercourse" and said he sought Senator Harding's clarification about his remarks.[156] Harding's reply to the president included a reminder that he was not simply a "private citizen" but was a sitting member of the U.S. Senate Foreign Relations Committee and that "an informal expression to me is rather more than that to a private citizen."[157]

It was clear, however, that Harding was attempting to finesse the League of Nations issue. He appeared as supportive of world peace efforts in front of audiences where it benefited him, all the while not insulting or challenging the solid-wall of conservative Republican opposition in the Senate where Harding served that had derailed Wilson's league proposal. In an October 16, 1920,

speech in Indianapolis at Tomlinson Hall (a day before his remarks at Greencastle), he asserted that he had on several occasions suggested the league proposal could be "amended or revised" and added, "When elected, I will immediately summon the best minds of America to consult and advise as to America's relationship to the present association of nations, to modifications of it or substitutes for it. The Senate and our party have recognized much good in a new world fellowship and cooperation, but we insistently reject all that menaces America. We must separate the wheat from the chaff."[158]

The Indianapolis speech came after a long day of campaigning across southern Indiana and Kentucky. In Indiana he spoke at Jeffersonville, New Albany, Speed (in Clark County), Scottsburg, Seymour, Columbus, Edinburgh, and Franklin.[159]

Once elected president, in June 1923 Harding followed the tried-and-true political advice—

Erie locomotive Number 2933 is shown draped for Harding funeral train, August 8, 1923.

LIBRARY OF CONGRESS

when in trouble, travel—and set out for a western swing away from growing scandals in Washington for a tour dubbed the "Voyage of Understanding." Among his western visits were two historic first-ever visits of a U.S. president, one to Alaska (a U.S. territory until 1959, when it became the forty-ninth state) and the other to Canada. As Harding made his way back south, his health had deteriorated noticeably. When he reached San Francisco, doctors examined the president and believed he may have been suffering from pneumonia. Their diagnosis, however, did not indicate how seriously ill Harding was. He died suddenly while talking with his wife, Florence, in the presidential suite at the Palace Hotel in San Francisco on August 2, 1923. He was fifty-seven years old. Florence refused suggestions that an autopsy be conducted to determine why the president had died, instead accepting a general assessment from doctors that he had suffered heart failure. Wild speculation raged for years that Harding had either committed suicide or was poisoned by his wife (as a result of an alleged extra-marital affair). Investigation into Harding's life and administration, however, was made more difficult after Florence returned to the White House and summarily burned all of the president's official papers, and his personal papers at their home in Marion.[160]

The train carrying Harding's casket from San Francisco to Ohio was eventually greeted by crowds estimated as exceeding one million Americans, including large crowds that caused the train to slow as it exited Illinois and was viewed by residents of Hammond and Gary as it made its way back to Marion.[161] During his short presidency (the fourth shortest in U.S. history, lasting only two years, four months, and thirty days), Harding never made an official visit to Indiana (though he often traveled through the state by train).

James M. Cox

As extraordinary as Harding's nomination for the Republicans after ten ballots, Cox's nomination as the Democratic candidate was even more amazing. A total of forty-four ballots were required before delegates selected Cox over other candidates, including Secretary of the Treasury William McAdoo and Attorney General Mitchell Palmer. Cox won the nomination with the help of Indiana's Democratic power broker, Thomas Taggart, who backed an "anyone but McAdoo" effort from the start. As a result, McAdoo, who eventually fell in line and campaigned for Cox for the fall election, personally scratched Indiana off his list of stops as a payback to Taggart, who was running as the Democrats' nominee for the U.S. Senate in Indiana.

As governor of Ohio, Cox was familiar to many voters in Indiana, but it did not stop him from making a push in the state, including a long series of speeches in mid-October that took him to both Indiana and Illinois. On October 9, 1920, alone, Cox made twelve separate speeches (almost entirely from the rear platforms of trains) in Indiana and heavily emphasized his support of the League of Nations that the waffling Republicans were engaging in, appearing to be for the league in some instances and opposed in others. "It was a day of remarkable experiences for the Governor," the New York Times reported. "At every stop along the line, crowds had assembled, even in territory which has been strongly Republican in the past. At times the meetings assumed the aspects of evangelistic gatherings as the Governor gave his message. It was with difficulty that the Governor was torn away from some of the crowds and his special train was more than two hours late in arriving (at Terre Haute). The Governor was then voice-worn and weary, but he said he was very happy."[162]

In his Terre Haute speech, Cox warmed up on former president Taft for his support of Harding saying, "for the sake of a party victory he has sacrificed principles to partisanship in associating with the reactionary candidate." Cox also took aim at Indiana's senator James Watson, whom he said was a part of the "Senate oligarchy" and declared he had "been in the Senate long enough. Any man who signed the round robin against the most humane instrument in the world does not deserve a place in the United States Senate" and urged Hoosiers to turn Watson out of office in favor of Taggart.[163] Cox said he considered it a "crime" that the issue of the League of Nations had been held hostage by the "Senate oligarchy" and implored, "Men and women ought not to be asked to pass upon a question so important in the heat of the partisanship of a campaign. The Senatorial oligarchy defied the interests of America and of civilization when it did it."[164]

Cox took the unusual step, for the time, of taking questions from the audience, including a pointed one in which the questioner asked whether he owed his nomination to "wets," or those who favored overturning the Eighteenth Amendment creating Prohibition. Cox said he felt "under obligations to nobody, and in consequence of that, I am absolutely a free man in this campaign." He added, "I am opposed to the enactment of any law which in any way is in conflict with the Eighteenth Amendment."[165]

At Bloomington, Cox sounded similar themes, accusing Harding of misleading the American people about Wilson's interactions with Senate Republicans on the league proposal. "I affirm without fear of contradiction that anyone who says the president never heeded the advice of the Senate is either crassly ignorant of contemporary history or grossly insincere," Cox stated. Adding that Harding "simply did

not know what he was talking about" regarding Wilson's interactions with the Congress, and said it reflected Harding's "habit of dodging roll calls (votes)."[166]

"There was more than one frank exchange of views between the President and Senate," Cox said. "Suggestions as to amendments were offered by senators and made a part of the covenant. Reservations were proposed by members of the Senate and accepted by the President. And these things were not alone in a corner. It is true that Senator Harding dodged 163 roll calls which might explain his absence from the Senate when important questions were being discussed and important matters decided."[167]

In a stop at Sullivan, a southwestern Indiana county seat about twenty-five miles south of Terre Haute, Cox again invited questions from the audience. One question on "the Mexican question" dealt with whether American investors should have their property purchases protected by the U.S. military. Cox said to a roaring cheer, "A lot of people in this country have bought oil and pasture tracts in Mexico for nothing practically because it is dangerous to live down there. If you remove the danger, the property will be very valuable, but you can't remove the danger unless we go in and shed a lot of American blood. I'm not going to turn the blood of American soldier boys into coin of the realm for a group of American oil investors."[168] Cox also took questions about Prohibition, repeating his commitment to keeping the Eighteenth Amendment in place and supporting American entry into the League of Nations.

At New Albany, despite an 8:30 a.m. Saturday morning start, media reports indicated a crowd approaching 5,000 showed up to greet Cox. In making his argument for the League of Nations, Cox said he intended to "impress the religious elements" of the league's principles. He asked his audience, "Should we turn our faces away from the suffering of the world and live in isolation? Are we to lay aside the creed of Christ and adopt the creed of Cain who asked, 'Am I my brother's keeper?' Can we hope to keep God's favor by such a course?"[169]

Expanding on the theme, Cox said, "We believe that God almighty intended that the great compensation for this war should be an agreement among the nations to bring war to an end." He said the United States went into World War I with the purpose of preventing wars in the future. "I ask the mothers of Indiana: Was not that the pledge? You will find the League of Nations published in the Democratic campaign book. You will not find it printed in the Republican campaign book. Now I will ask you whether it is fair not to present this greatest question. I contend you are entitled to both sides."[170]

The *Sullivan Daily Tribune* reported the Cox campaign train was "almost an hour behind schedule when it reached Salem (Washington County) at 10:30 o'clock, where an open air audience of more than 4,000 persons awaited the candidate. The governor stood on a truck in a hot sun and again devoted his time to the League of Nations, inviting and arguing questions from audience members. He asked one himself and it was whether there was an Irishman here. 'Yes, Tom, Tom,' several shouted. Mr. Taggart was sitting on the truck near the nominee for president and he stood up and acknowledged the greeting . . . (and) Mr. Cox renewed his promise if elected to bring the freedom of Ireland before the League of Nations under provision of Article 11."[171]

"We were agreed spiritually in those days that we ought to end the war," Cox said in support of ratifying the League of Nations. "The element of social responsibility was the creed of Christ Himself" and added "that the soul of Indiana has been aroused as it always has been when vital questions of the nation are at issue."[172] During his remarks at Salem, a baby began to cry, and Cox noted it, saying, "Don't worry about that baby, it is music to my ears. Every time I hear a baby, I am nerved for this fight, for we are fighting for the babies."[173]

At tiny Orleans in Orange County (about fifteen miles south of Bedford), a healthy audience of 2,500 gathered to hear Cox declare, "Your sons shot to end war; it is your duty to vote to end war." Referring to his boyhood on an Ohio farm, Cox said he had "husked as many rows of corn as any man here."[174] He made a quick argument for how the League of Nations could help improve markets for Indiana farm products and moved north to Bedford, where another 4,000 gathered to hear his remarks. "I am in favor of creating a new order and a new day in the world," Cox said in the Lawrence County seat. "I am in favor of it with all the strength of my body and my soul. I am in favor of the thing that will promote the happiness of nations in years to come. I am in favor of going into the League of Nations."[175] Asked again about Prohibition during the question-and-answer session following his formal remarks, Cox told one Bedford man who asked, "Not until I became Governor of Ohio did the front and back door of every saloon close on Sunday and remain closed."[176]

A day later, Cox's campaign train continued to move north, and he told a crowd of more than 15,000 at the Tippecanoe County Courthouse in Lafayette that Harding had now taken eleven separate positions on the league question. "The vacillating attitude of Senator Harding justifies neither the American people, nor the nations of the world, in taking him seriously," Cox proclaimed. "It is apparent that he hasn't a single deep-seeded conviction upon the subject and that he wobbles about from one day to another in the aimless hope that this group or that group of voters can be pleased. It is the most pitiful spectacle in the political history of America. I can understand why the sentiment of wiggling and wobbling has been emblazoned over the billboards of America with the picture of the senator. The candidate of the senatorial oligarchy has a monopoly on that process and he ought to be privileged to advertise it."[177]

Cox argued that the need for the League of Nations was great. "The old order in the world won't do," he said. "It has been a great failure. Under it wars come overnight because it recognized the principle of the divine right of kings and it had the authority without consulting the will or wish of the men and women of the nations to order the sons of men into the trenches of battle. Now, I stand for a new order in the world. I am opposed to the old order, because it has not only been a great failure, but it has brought upon the sons of men the tragedies, which can no longer be justified in the eyes and light of a modern civilization."[178]

In his Lafayette remarks, the governor again mentioned former president Taft and his support of the GOP nominee. "Judge Taft, who is trying to keep the Republican candidate steady, says the new association of nations is not practical, that it will not work, that it cannot be attained. Forty-one nations of the world have already joined the League. It is a going concern, and they will not abandon it at the mere wish and caprice of a group of senators."[179]

Following the Lafayette stop, Cox's special train moved on to additional stops at Delphi, Logansport, Peru, Wabash, and Huntington, all producing large crowds. The *New York Times* reported that the autumn weather was cooperating with Cox's campaign and added, "The Governor

is brown as a berry as a result of exposure to the sun. He is a bit tired by his efforts, but is standing the strain well."[180]

Reaching Fort Wayne, "throngs totaling thousands welcomed Governor Cox in northern Indiana. . . . At most of the cities today, the governor spoke from specially built stands on court house squares. He encountered numerous difficulties, including strong winds, with dust, noisy small boys, roaring airplanes overhead, and confusion in the rear of today's crowds. Brass bands and automobile parades, fireworks, siren whistles and a Democratic women's quartet from Huntington accompanied him to Fort Wayne."[181] Cox made two separate speeches in Fort Wayne, one at the Temple Theatre and another at an open-air rally at Court and Berry Streets downtown, where a crowd of more than 15,000 struggled to hear him speak. Delivering eight speeches in one day had worn on Cox's voice, but as the *Fort Wayne Journal-Gazette* reported, "Never before has a Presidential candidate in this city gone so close to the people. Questions were invited and asked in a manner that did not leave a doubt that his plea would have a telling effect on Election Day . . . cheers went up as the candidate gave his rapid-fire answers to many questions from the audience regarding the League of Nations and carried on his own heckling with many of his listeners in order that he could better explain the workings of the league."[182]

He told his Fort Wayne listeners, "If I should be elected, the plain inference would be that the American people want the League. If Harding should be elected, the inference would be just the reverse. Yet (former President) Taft says that the way to assure going into the League is to vote for the man who is against it."[183]

"Poor old Judge Taft," Cox said, "tried to apologize (for Senator Harding) and tried to defend him, but he moves so fast that Taft can't keep up with him."[184]

Cox's remarks again focused on his support of the League of Nations saying, "I cannot understand how the men who deliberately and mischievously and hypocritically oppose the League of Nations can sleep nights. I would think their dreams would be disturbed by the suffering of millions and millions of children whose bodies have been starved and whose souls have been seared in the furnace of a great war."[185]

"The League of Nations is based on the primary objective of preventing war," Cox declared. "No league can send our boys to war, no president can do it, Congress alone can declare war."[186]

Speaking to the women in the audience, eligible to vote for the first time in U.S. history, Cox said, "The mothers of America will have something to say about governmental policies in the future. The mothers of America know what war is better than the men."[187] Despite Cox's efforts, and those of his running mate Franklin D. Roosevelt, Harding and Coolidge swept to an easy victory in Indiana, capturing 55 percent of the vote.

After his loss, Cox returned to the private sector building a successful chain of newspapers and radio and television stations. He campaigned actively for each of Roosevelt's campaigns. Cox died July 15, 1957, at his home in Kettering, Ohio, at the age of eighty-seven.

Franklin D. Roosevelt

In 1920 the name Franklin D. Roosevelt was hardly a household name. Known as an effective speechmaker, a former state senator in New York, and as a staunch supporter of President Wilson, he had won appointment as the assistant secretary of the navy during World War I. He lost a Democratic primary in 1914 for a U.S. Senate nomination from New York, but benefited from his famous last name (as a fifth cousin to former president Theodore Roosevelt) and his fervent support for Wilson. At just thirty-eight years old, Roosevelt was tapped to make the nominating speech for Cox at the Democratic National Convention and was later named at the Ohio governor's running mate by acclamation. Roosevelt's 1920 campaign for vice president was unlike anything millions of other Americans would know later in his life. It was not until a year after the election, while on vacation in August 1921, that he contracted polio that resulted in permanent paralysis of his legs.

In 1920, however, Roosevelt was a tall, striking figure with a commanding and confident speaking voice, and he visited Indiana for a key campaign swing in October 1920 as it appeared the election was slipping away from the Democrats. During an October 13, 1920, stop in Terre Haute, Roosevelt repeated his theme of accusing Senator Watson (and by extension the GOP presidential nominee, Harding) of a campaign of "falsehoods" about the implications of the United States approving the League of Nations pact so desired by Wilson. In all, Roosevelt made ten speeches combined in Indiana and Illinois, and at Crawfordsville said the Republican Party was experiencing a "revolt of silence" that would cost Harding the election. "A few prominent men have come out openly and said that, though Republicans, they would not support Senator Harding," Roosevelt said. "Their number is small, compared with the hundreds of thousands who are saying nothing but who will poll quietly and unostentatiously for Cox on Election Day. They believe in real leadership."[188]

Roosevelt's speech at Crawfordsville gained some national notice, however, for a different reason when reports moved on national news wires that he "narrowly escaped injury when an automobile in which he was riding from Crawfordsville to Greencastle lost a tire and went bumping over the road."[189] An Associated Press dispatch indicated "the car was going at only moderate speed and did not leave the road. Roosevelt was transferred to another car and proceeded on his journey, stopping at Roachdale and Bainbridge to give short talks."[190] News reports indicated Roosevelt also spoke at Brazil and Clinton.

Wrapping up his tour of Indiana at Marion on October 15, Roosevelt addressed whether the United States should accept the League of Nations pact just as proposed at Versailles, or address provisions that were not supported by all Americans. "Repeatedly, the Republican charge has been made that Governor Cox and I are demanding the acceptance of the League, as fashioned at Versailles, with the crossing of a 't' or the dotting of an 'i,' and repeatedly we have branded this as untrue," Roosevelt declared. "In almost every speech I have made in the last two months I have stated that we are not only willing, but prefer to put in black and white our ratification of the treaty a provision that nothing contained therein shall be in any way superior to our Constitution, or in any way interfere with the rights of Congress to declare war or save our soldiers overseas."[191]

Roosevelt said Harding's back and forth position on the League of Nations reflected "near panic in the Republican ranks," which is evidence of "a desperate attempt to head off further defections from Republican ranks—disgruntled members of the party who are coming more and more convinced that their only hope in getting the United States into the League is to vote for Governor Cox."[192]

In the closing days of the campaign, Roosevelt told reporters he believed interest in the League of Nations and the Democratic Party's support of it could be a key to winning the election. Roosevelt stated that "I have marveled at the interest displayed among audiences I have addressed which are made up of people who live far away from big cities and daily newspapers."[193] Citing as typical, Roosevelt said, was a meeting at Ridgeville, Indiana, a tiny Randolph County town about thirty-five miles north of Richmond. "This is a very small community," Roosevelt explained to New York reporters. "We were roused out of our berths at 5 in the morning. After a hurried early breakfast in a small private house in the town, I was rushed to a stand in the open air and began speaking at 6 o'clock or shortly thereafter. One might think that hour too early for a campaign meeting, but there was a crowd of automobiles and horse-drawn conveyances through which we could make our way to the platform only with the utmost difficulty. Something like 400 farmers had driven to this meeting, many starting from their homes long before daylight in order to hear the League of Nations explained. They listened patiently, asked a good many questions, and were most generous in their applause."[194]

Calvin Coolidge

"Silent Cal" Coolidge was true to his name in Indiana, speaking on only one formal occasion in the state as president, and smiling and waving on other occasions. He had visited the state as vice president, on January 27, 1922, in Indianapolis to speak before a meeting of the Indiana Republican Editorial Association. During his speech, Coolidge said the Republican Party was responsible for "wiping away the tears of the world and healing the nation," noting that when Harding assumed control from Wilson, "the nation had been without responsible leadership for a year and a half."[195] Coolidge called Harding an "inspirational" and "great president" who had amassed "an honorable record of achievement which no sophistry could misinterpret, no misrepresentation could obscure and which was bringing peace and tranquility to the nation."[196] Coolidge cited the ratification of treaties with Colombia and Mexico and a successful special session of Congress to reduce federal spending. Further, he said, "The temporary law restricting immigration has relieved pressure from without when there was already fear of unemployment within and thus had protected the working man."[197]

Becoming president on August 2, 1923, upon Harding's unexpected death, the little-known Coolidge set about introducing himself to the nation, although in a manner that quickly earned him the moniker, "Silent Cal." Contrasting directly with Harding's more outspoken and gregarious nature, Coolidge reflected the patrician, quiet confidence of many of his fellow Vermonters. Coolidge was easily nominated by the Republican Party in 1924 and sailed to victory in the general election against two opponents, Democrat John W. Davis and Progressive Robert W. LaFollette.

It was not until Coolidge was far into his own term as president that he made his first visit to Indiana, on November 10, 1926, as he was en route to Kansas City to give an Armistice Day address. Apparently Coolidge planned to save his voice for that occasion, as while his train made a brief stop before a large throng near the Pennsylvania Depot in Richmond, Coolidge smiled and waved, but did not speak. Coolidge's wife, Grace, however, did speak, asking a young Richmond boy about his dog. Later at Indianapolis, Coolidge remained silent, media reports offering: "Mr.

Coolidge, who stood on the rear platform, bowed and smiled as the cheers resounded. There were calls for a speech, but the President declined."[198]

Several thousand more Hoosiers turned out to greet the president and his wife during a ten-minute stop at the depot in Terre Haute. Again, "there were frequent calls for a speech, but the President adhered to his program of not making impromptu addresses."[199] Lacking any remarks to report upon, reporters for the *New York Times* gave details about a new Pullman train car carrying the presidential party west: "The President's car is a combination sleeping and observation car, equipped with baths and a phonograph. Provisions have also been made for the entertainment of the chief executive and his immediate party by the installation of a moving picture machine, and after the train had left Terre Haute tonight several of the newest reels were exhibited under the direct supervision of Jack Connely, representative of the film industry."[200]

Coolidge's elevation to the nation's highest office had been, after all, only as a result of Harding's death in 1923. Coolidge had made history as the first vice president to attend cabinet meetings as part of the Harding administration, but had done little to distinguish himself as vice president. Coolidge's reluctance for public life, however, took an even deeper turn in the summer of 1924 just after he was nominated by the Republican Party for a full term as president. Coolidge's son, sixteen-year-old Calvin Jr., died on July 7, 1924, just days after developing a deadly infection in a foot blister from playing tennis on the White House courts without shoes. Coolidge acknowledged that his participation in the 1924 campaign was "delayed by the death of my son Calvin. . . . He was a boy of much promise, proficient in his studies, with a scholarly mind, who had just turned 16. He had a remarkable insight into things." Coolidge added, "We do not know what might have happened to him under other circumstances, but if I had not been President he would not have raised a blister on his toe, which resulted in blood poisoning, playing lawn tennis in the South Grounds. In his suffering he was asking me to make him well. I could not. When he went, the power and the glory of the Presidency went with him. . . . I do not know why such a price was exacted for occupying the White House."[201]

Coolidge's only official address in Indiana came again while he was en route to somewhere else, this time for a three-month-long vacation in the Black Hills region of South Dakota. At Hammond on June 14, 1927, Coolidge led a massive Flag Day parade from the train depot to the site of the new Wicker Memorial Park dedicated to the sacrifices of the doughboys of World War I. While his reputation had been one as a man of few words, Coolidge offered a lengthy speech at Hammond and opened his remarks by commenting on the amazing growth of the northwest Indiana region as the industrial revolution continued to grow the American economy. "This section (of our nation) represents a phase of life which is typically American," Coolidge said. "A few short years ago it was an uninhabited area of sand and plain. Today it is a great industrial metropolis. The people of this region have been creating one of the most fascinating epics. The fame of it, reaching to almost every quarter of the globe, has drawn hither the energetic pioneer spirits of many different races all eager to contribute their share and to receive in return the abundant rewards which advancing enterprise can give."[202]

After reciting the history of Lake County and its growing communities, Coolidge turned his remarks to the veterans for which the 226-acre Wicker Park was intended to honor. "Patriotism is indigenous to this soil; not the visionary variety which talks of love of country but makes no sacrifices for it, but the higher, sterner kind, which does and dares, defending assaults upon its firesides and intrusion upon its liberty with a musket in its hands," Coolidge said. "Yet they are orderly, peaceable people, neither arrogant nor quarrelsome, seeking only those advantages which come from the well-earned rewards of enterprise and industry. Such a people always respond when there is need for military service."[203]

The president added:

> It is peculiarly appropriate for a public recreation field to be dedicated as a memorial to those who served in the World War. Perhaps the chief issue in that great conflict was the determination of whether an autocratic form or a republican form of government was to be predominant among the great nations of the earth. It was fought to a considerable extent to decide whether the people were to rule, or whether they were to be ruled; whether self-government or autocracy should prevail. Victory finally rested on the side of the people. A great step forward was taken in more firmly establishing their rightful sovereignty. This park is a real memorial to World War service because it distinctly recognizes the sovereignty and materially enlarges the dominion of the people. It is a true emblem of our Republic.[204]

Reflecting on the prosperous period the nation found itself in the 1920s, Coolidge reminded his audience that "our hearty pioneers crossed the mountain and the plain, extending our dominions from ocean to ocean. We have opened up an enormous expanse of agriculture, reared great cities, organized mighty industries, and created an immense commerce. Materially, we have prospered, intellectually we have advanced, morally and spiritually we have improved. It is scarcely too much to say that all of this increase has gone to the benefit of the people at large. In spite of all this progress, we are still a great distance from what we would like to be. Too many of our people are unprovided with the advantages of education. The number who are lacking in religious devotion is altogether too large. While we have reached the highest point in material prosperity ever achieved, there is a considerable class of unskilled workers who have not come into full participation in the wealth of the Nation."[205]

Coolidge admonished the audience that "too many of us disregard the obligations of citizenship by neglecting to vote, and violence and crime are altogether too prevalent. Our delinquencies are sufficient to require us to put forth all our efforts to work toward their elimination. But we should not be discouraged because we are surrounded by human limitations and handicapped by human weakness. We are also possessors of human strength. Intelligence, courage, fidelity, character—these, also, are our heritage and our mark of the Divine Image."[206]

As the presidential party left Hammond and moved through Illinois and Wisconsin, reporters shared details about the menagerie traveling with them. On board the train, "Rebecca, the pet raccoon, was brought from her cage in the baggage car and fed by Mrs. Riley, the White House housekeeper. President Coolidge visited with her while Mrs. Coolidge looked after her pet canaries, while en route."[207]

Perhaps not surprisingly, as Coolidge later confirmed, "the power and the glory" of the presidency had left him following his young son's death, and he opted out of running for re-election in 1928. He eventually supported Hoover's candidacy as the Republican nominee and made radio speeches again in 1932 supporting Hoover's failed re-election effort. Coolidge died unexpectedly of a heart attack on January 5, 1933, at Northampton, Massachusetts. He was sixty years old.

John W. Davis

Davis of West Virginia, former U.S. ambassador to England and the solicitor general in the administration of President Wilson, was hardly a consensus choice of the Democratic Party for its 1924 nomination. On the first of 103 ballots at the Democratic National Convention in New York City, Davis finished an unimpressive seventh with just forty-one votes from delegates. Former treasury secretary McAdoo of California led during most of the early voting, including among Indiana Democrats, as he had patched together a powerful coalition of southern and midwestern Democrats loyal to the Ku Klux Klan and Prohibition-supporting "drys." The Klan's shadow over the proceedings were so significant, in fact, that the convention would later become known as a "Klanbake" as northern Democrats pushed hard for resolutions denouncing the Klan and southern and midwestern party members resisted.

Davis was popular among anti-Klan delegates because of his aggressive treatment of their attempts to subjugate black Americans during his tenure as solicitor general. By the fifteenth ballot, Davis had moved up to third among the delegates behind McAdoo and the 1920 Democratic nominee Smith. On the hundredth ballot, Davis had moved into second place as candidate attrition finally began to take its toll on the list of hopefuls, including McAdoo. Finally, on the 103rd vote, a record for any party convention in American history, Davis finally secured the nomination.

Davis had work to do in Indiana in 1924. It was a state controlled openly and defiantly by the Klan from the Indiana Statehouse to courthouses and city halls up and down the state. Regardless, the Davis campaign attempted to reach Hoosier voters despite the popularity of Coolidge and the still-to-be-exposed graft and corruption emanating from Klan-backed Republicans in Indianapolis.

The 1924 presidential campaign is known as the first to rely on radio speeches with any regularity, and Davis and the Democrats took advantage of the new technology. As a result, Davis ended his monthlong train tour of the "west" with a swing through Indiana in September 1924 that took him primarily across northern Indiana, including stops in Fort Wayne, South Bend, and Gary. He skipped the more Klan friendly portions of the state in central and southern Indiana.

It is unclear if Davis had planned to make his opposition to the Klan the centerpiece of his remarks for his Fort Wayne speech on September 20, 1924, but the party's nominee for governor, Carlton McCulloch, left him little choice after opening a Democratic rally with a stern denunciation of the Klan and the "shadow government" it had imposed on Indiana. In answer to a question shouted from the audience, McCulloch said he opposed the Klan "or any other organization seeking to discriminate against Americans because of race, color or religion,"[208] and was in the midst of his reply when Davis joined him on the platform before a large audience.

Davis did not mention the Klan by name in his remarks, but vehemently denounced corruption in the Coolidge administration and ideas of privilege that pervaded Republican political philosophies and said he would serve the nation on the basis of honesty, justice, and courage and would grant equal rights to all men. "We are charging what every man knows," Davis said, "that corruption has crept into high offices and defiled it. We are charging for all candid men must admit it, that privilege has had its way in the writing of the laws, and we are charging what is manifestly true, that between the President on one side and the membership of his party in Congress on the other, there has been a discord, a division, an incoherence, a lack of discipline, which proves that no government, so led on one hand and so indisposed to be led on the other, can work out a consistent policy for the people of the United States."[209]

Turning to the aftermath of World War I, Davis said, "President Wilson never looked upon the treaty of Versailles as a finished document. He realized the animosities and revenge that lay behind the writing of that document, but he knew that the hatred and malice could be modified through confidence and conciliation in the years to come. It was only a starting point for him."[210] Davis said that if Wilson's "principles of peace had been followed and had the United States participated in the councils of Europe these last five years of ruin, starvation, misery and disaster, the stifling of Germany and the crushing of Europe's commerce would have been avoided. There would have been peace, healing and fair dealing among men."[211]

Davis's Fort Wayne stop made headlines nationally, while his visits to Gary, La Porte, and South Bend were little noted outside the state. In Gary, Davis spoke before a receptive audience of 3,500 ironworkers at a union hall and said the nation needed a new commitment to "the principles of human equality, personal liberty and popular sovereignty" and pledged to battle in every state against "privilege in government."[212] Davis said members of the Coolidge administration were "brought up in the school that government consists of not what you put into it, but what you get out of it."[213] He also briefly appealed to labor union members, a powerful force in northwest Indiana, saying he opposed the right of courts to interfere with strikes. "Labor's complaint in this matter is well founded," he said.[214]

At La Porte, Davis made brief remarks from the train's rear platform, and news dispatches from South Bend indicated a large and enthusiastic crowd waited—not uncommon for the Democratically controlled Saint Joseph County seat. While in South Bend, Davis addressed a noon luncheon meeting of business leaders at the Oliver Hotel downtown. Davis told the gathering that if he and the Democratic Party were selected to lead the nation for the next four years, they would move the nation forward with equity and honor. "The road (ahead) is a road of equality and not one of privilege," Davis said.[215] He said, "I do not concede a single state to the adversaries of the Democratic Party. I want the word to go out that there are no lost Democratic battalions cut off from headquarters."[216]

After his remarks at the hotel luncheon, Davis was led on a short parade along Jefferson Boulevard to Howard Park on the banks of the Saint Joseph River, where a crowd estimated at 10,000 heard him offer his vision for the next four years. The Republicans, Davis said, were operating the nation under a tollgate system "under which the proceeds of taxation were devoted primarily to the comfort and well-being of those riding in limousines." He questioned this theory, he said, that assumed that those riding in the limousine were cared for "while all the pedestrians and those riding in less expensive cars eventually would be benefitted by the resultant era of prosperity."[217]

On October 11, 1924, Davis brought his campaign briefly to Richmond, with comments from the train's rear platform to an audience of about 5,000 citizens, where he challenged not only the Republicans, but also Progressive nominee LaFollette, the latter of which Cox said would be unable to lead because of his inability to capture any sort of majority without the other two

parties. Davis suggested apathy among voters resided with Republicans, not with Democrats, and stemmed from the fact that "when men can no longer be pleased by performance, when they become so skeptical that they cannot be deluded by promise, nothing is left but fear to play."[218]

Davis's next stop was Indianapolis for an address before an audience of 10,000 at the Cadle Tabernacle. In his speech Davis took pains to demonstrate the differences between the Democratic and Republican platforms, reminded the audience of Teapot Dome scandals emanating from GOP deal making, and that the Republican economic policies had harmed the nation. "Let us compare the last three years under Wilson with the first three years of the Harding-Coolidge administration," he said. "Take bank failures, for instance. In the years 1918, 1919 and 1920, there was a total of 139 bank failures; in the years 1921, 1922 and 1923 a total of 1,221 and during the first six months of 1924 a total of 4,428 banks failed, with liabilities more than double those of the last three years under Wilson."[219] Davis added:

> Figures of this sort are more eloquent than any campaign oratory or the voodoo hymns sung by those who see in a prohibitive tariff the source and origin of American prosperity. It has long been the claim of the Republican Party that it is the trustworthy guardian of sound business activities that make for the general welfare of the whole country. They have attempted to support this claim by deprecating the worth of Democratic measures whenever it was possible to get a hearing from the public and by ignoring those Democratic measures for the safeguarding and promotion of business whose worth was so evident that attack upon them would have reacted against those who made it.[220]

The *New York Times* reported that Davis received a delegation of "15 Negro leaders" representing clergymen, teachers, and editors before he departed Indianapolis. They told him about an "Independent Negro Voters' League" that was formed for the 1924 campaign in Indiana and had endorsed the Democrats based on their opposition to the Klan. The meeting was noteworthy and perhaps one of the earliest signs in Indiana that black voters were moving away from the party of Abraham Lincoln, which was openly and rigidly controlled in Indiana by the Klan in the 1920s.[221]

Following his Indianapolis speech, Davis went on to make stops in Lebanon, Lafayette, Greencastle, and Terre Haute. At Lafayette a crowd of 8,000 gathered at the Tippecanoe County Courthouse to hear his remarks, uplifting the hopes of Indiana Democrats who felt political fortunes may be turning their way in the late going. "The Democratic Party is marching this year, my friends," Davis said, "with a harmony and a unity and a solidarity that I, in my short life have never seen surpassed. I have been across this country from the Atlantic to the Rockies, and I have found no disposition among Democrats to shirk or to falter in the support they are giving this year to their candidates. I read in the papers constant accounts of apathy. . . . For myself, I see none of the apathy that they talk about. I do not see it here this afternoon in this stupendous gathering in the city of Lafayette."[222]

Davis enjoyed his heaviest applause for his attacks on growing reports of corruption in the federal government and said pointing to the courthouse behind him, "And for a lawyer, the saddest chapter in the whole story is that the secret processes of the law, that make this building here the sign and symbol of security and the guaranty of order and peace to every citizen of this county, and which ought to be as pure and untouched as the divine altar itself, were polluted not only to personal gain, but were polluted also to partisan and political revenge."[223]

In late October, Davis returned to Indiana for the third time with speeches scheduled in Vincennes and Evansville. At Vincennes, a large crowd of 5,000 showed up to hear Davis pledge "a thorough housecleaning in Washington" if elected and declared that the Republican Party was "afflicted with a creeping paralysis" and said the nation could not be cured by another injection of the same virus—the Republicans—that caused the nation's disease. "There is but one method by which (the American people) can disassociate themselves from those crimes and those who participated in them," Davis continued. "And that day is the fourth of November, and that instrument is the ballot, and that event is an election. And when their sons and daughters after them recite the history of the United States and these events, I think it will be a source of satisfaction if they can turn to their children and say, 'I disapproved of those things and because I disapproved of them, I voted to chastise my own party, that no party in the United States and no officer in the United States might ever dare to bring a similar disgrace upon the government of my country.'"[224]

Later at Bosse Field in Evansville, Davis asked his large audience:

> What will you do as patriots and as Americans? Is there no relief? I stand here to offer one. In the name of the democracy, the oldest political organization existent today in all the world, I offer you a sane, a forward-looking and a progressive liberalism that knows no class or section, no petted favorite; that believes it is not the business of those in office to either give favors to their friends or to use official power to punish their personal enemies, but to so administer the affairs of the government that every man, be he a laborer, farmer or businessman or what not,

may feel that he is an equal citizen resting under equal laws and with the equal care and consideration of his government addressed toward his needs.[225]

In both speeches in southern Indiana, Davis returned to themes that the Republican Party was owned and operated by a "third party," a veiled reference to the Klan. The bulk of his remarks, however, were about removal of corrupt bureaucracies in Washington and relief for American farmers.[226]

After his unsuccessful presidential campaign, Davis returned to his law practice. His most famous case, *Briggs vs. Elliott* (a companion case to *Brown vs. the Board of Education*), was unsuccessfully argued before the U.S. Supreme Court, Davis defending the "separate but equal" effort by southern states to keep local schools segregated. He died March 24, 1955, while on a visit to Charleston, South Carolina, at the age of eighty-one.

Robert M. LaFollette

Wisconsin Senator LaFollette had earned the name "Fighting Bob" for his fiery—and often effective—speaking style and progressive ideas. His fighting attitude included taking on members of his own party and initial opposition to American involvement in World War I. In 1924, disappointed that his own Republican Party was again backing a conservative candidate, Coolidge, LaFollette accepted the Progressive Party nomination.

For his presidential campaign, LaFollette made a few strategic visits to specific areas, including California, but had planned a mostly front-porch campaign based out of both his base in the U.S. Senate in Washington, D.C., and his home in Madison, Wisconsin. In Indiana

LaFollette relied primarily on surrogates, including his running mate and his son, to make speeches to Hoosier audiences. He was not, however, a complete stranger to the state. He made a notable appearance in the state in 1912 in support of Theodore Roosevelt's Progressive Party campaign for the presidency. He was also a frequent visitor to the warm springs at French Lick to get relief for his arthritis, but those visits included no public appearances or utterances.

LaFollette's 1912 speech in Terre Haute stood out even in the senator's own mind. In his autobiography published years later, LaFollette said, "I spoke once in Indiana, at Terre Haute, on my way back to Washington. It was the most remarkable series of mid-winter meetings ever held. The weather was bitterly cold; yet there were immense audiences everywhere for both the day and night speeches and I never found people more responsive or more deeply and earnestly interested."[227]

The *Indianapolis Star* sent a correspondent to cover LaFollette's January 6, 1912, speech at the Knights of Columbus Hall before an audience of 600. His campaign had previously announced it was canceling his scheduled appearance later in Indianapolis due to illness. The reporter, George W. Stout, noted that LaFollette had "faced below-zero weather, snow drifts, late trains and other adverse physical conditions" to make his speech. During his remarks, LaFollette struck on familiar themes, including warning Hoosiers about the power of big corporations and consolidated banks, railroads, and other major industrial interests. He also denounced the Payne-Aldrich Tariff and said the American people were continually seeing their power and control of the government being seized by the power of corporations. As part of his effort to restore power to citizens, LaFollette advocated for the direct election of U.S. senators by voters and for the recall of judges in instances of malfeasance. The *Star* report indicated "the man of the famous pompadour and aggressive public record was late in arriving in this city," but "the audience was patient, however, and having greeted LaFollette warmly, showed its appreciation of his snappy speech in many ways."[228]

"The railroads have been consolidated, the franchise holding companies have been combined and industries have been combined, and at last the power has laid its hands on the big banks of the country," LaFollette stated. "A big speculating organization of banks is being formed for purposes of promotion. This big combine of banks plans to draw the money from the local communities to New York to be used in Wall Street for stock gambling operations and to promote concerns which issued watered stocks to be sold to a gullible. If you want the proof of this, drop me a card at Washington and I will furnish the proof."[229] LaFollette warned that "no legitimate industry is safe today with these giant combines built on stilts. There is a menace in over-capitalization. Let a real financial panic—not a manufactured one like that of 1907—but let a real panic come and these over-capitalized concerns will go down with a crash and carry everything with them to their fall. These combines menace the country with the danger of the great panic the world has ever seen. This is not radicalism , it is sober business sense."[230]

Perhaps LaFollette was wise in not spending time in Indiana for the 1924 campaign. He finished third with 6 percent of the vote, most of it apparently having drawn off support from Democratic nominee Davis. In Indiana, Coolidge rolled up 56 percent of the vote, while Davis captured 39 percent. Nationally, LaFollette's showing was stronger—17 percent of the national

vote, and he carried his home state of Wisconsin. LaFollette suffered a heart attack and died on June 18, 1925, in Washington, D.C. at the age of seventy.

Herbert Hoover

Hoover made more than one attempt at the White House, his first coming in 1920 as the Republican Party pulled itself back together again after the revolt led by Theodore Roosevelt and the Bull Moose movement in the 1912 election. Hoover firmly declared himself a Republican and joined the California primary for president, but lost what was considered his home state and withdrew with barely a notice in a GOP contest eventually won by Harding. Hoover's candidacy made some sense at the close of World War I. The *New York Times* had declared Hoover one of the "Ten Most Important Living Americans" for his leadership in bringing food relief to war-ravaged areas of Europe. A native of Iowa, Hoover attended Stanford University and was briefly courted by the Democrats as a possible successor to Wilson.

On October 9, 1920, Hoover spoke before a gathering at the Columbia Club of Indianapolis, in its era a Republican rite of passage for any serious candidate for the presidency. Speaking about the ongoing League of Nations debate, Hoover said, "My personal view is that some of the articles in the present treaty must be abandoned and some must be modified; but a great many parts of the present treaty are good and are intertwined with the ability of the world."[231] Hoover said he sought to reaffirm that the Republican Party (including its presidential nominee, Harding) was committed to "undertake the fundamental mission to put into living being the principle of an organized association of nations for the preservation of peace. Inasmuch as 40 nations, comprising three-quarters of the people of the globe have embraced the League of Nations as a term expressing certain ideas, I prefer that term, but I care little for the terminology."[232]

In comments that suggested what many whispered quietly—that Wilson was so incapacitated from his League of Nations battle and his October 1919 stroke—Hoover stated, "We have simply drifted for the past two years. In political leadership, the Democratic Party has, at least for the present, ceased to function." Hoover declared Wilson's administration a "failure in statesmanship" and that "in the bitterness of the quarrel over the peace, the administration has so disintegrated as to be incapable of a developed program for the great measures of reconstruction which must, must follow the war."[233]

Hoover's notoriety brought him to Indiana for another early visit on June 6, 1922, for a Diamond Jubilee luncheon at Earlham College in Richmond. Hoover's prospects of becoming president grew upon the unexpected death of Harding on August 2, 1923, and with the elevation of the uninspiring, Coolidge, to the presidency. Harding had rewarded Hoover's political loyalty by appointing him commerce secretary, a position he retained under Coolidge. Hoover's relationship with Coolidge, however, often appeared strained publicly and privately. When "Silent Cal" announced he would not run for another full term in the 1928 election, Republicans quickly turned to Hoover as the heir apparent. Coolidge's lukewarm attitude toward Hoover was not helpful, however, and a few would-be challengers emerged to Hoover for the GOP nomination, including Indiana's senator Watson.

Encouraged by the anti-Hoover movement, Watson staged one of the last efforts to stop Hoover's nomination by entering (and winning) the May 1928 Indiana Republican Primary and initially controlling the state's thirty-three del-

egates to the GOP National Convention. As one political writer noted, "If (the anti-Hoover forces) can hold Indiana away from Hoover they will still have a chance to 'stop' him," but he noted that pressure was building to end the Hoover challenge and coalesce around his nomination.[234]

Hoover seemed reluctant to enter the Indiana primary and risk losing to a favorite-son candidate such as Watson, but eventually did so.[235] His Indiana campaign, however, consisted almost entirely of surrogates—such as the governor of Michigan and a former governor of Iowa—crisscrossing the state on his behalf. For his part, Watson staged a vigorous campaign built strongly on his opposition to Hoover's farm policy. Watson relied on in-state surrogates for his southern Indiana strategy and focused himself on the northern half of the state, including Hammond, Gary, South Bend, and Fort Wayne (where Hoover support was believed to be strong).[236] Watson's campaign reportedly employed the same "whisper fight" used against Hoover in Ohio by trying to raise doubts about Hoover's "Republicanism" by noting "his long residence abroad, his international tendencies, his alleged discrimination against agriculture, and even his marriage by a Catholic priest."[237]

With both sides predicting victory going into the primary vote, reporters noted that "political observers agreed that Tuesday's primary would bring out one of the largest primary votes Indiana ever has had. They gave as reason for their prediction their belief that Indiana voters embarrassed by the scandal of corruption and political irregularities would make their demands for a 'new deal' at the polls."[238] The "scandal" referred to the widespread and ultimately destructive influence the Klan had held over Indiana politics in general, and the Republican Party in specific. Ugly corruption accusations involving the state's governor and the mayor of Indianapolis (in addition to the murder conviction of Indiana's Klan Grand Dragon D. C. Stephenson) put Republican voters, some believed, in the mind for new faces (Watson and Hoover included). As the *New Republic* analyzed: "Outside interest in the Indiana contest is largely stimulated by the political degradation of the state. In recent years it has become synonymous with corruption. The belief that the decent people of the state would welcome an opportunity to register resentment against the crowd that has shamed Indiana before the nation constituted the principal reason why the Hoover managers put their horse in the race there."[239]

When the votes were counted, Watson had won a narrow victory over Hoover among Indiana Republicans, with both sides claiming victory. Hoover's surrogates noted his strong vote total, even in losing, in a state where he ran against a popular favorite son. They further openly predicted Watson's challenge was not one he would sustain, and eventually the Indiana delegates would go to Hoover. Hoover's Indiana campaign manager, James W. Good, noted, "That Mr. Hoover should have been able to roll up so great a vote in a contest with a powerful, well-entrenched organization in the home state of an opposing candidate is one of the most striking evidences yet adduced of Secretary Hoover's strength with the Republican rank and file."[240]

After safely securing the Republican nomination, Hoover's 1928 campaign brought him to what was supposed to be friendly territory, Fort Wayne, in July 1928. As the *New York Times* reported, "The Fort Wayne crowd was not so large as had been expected, for that city was the stronghold of the Hooverites in their losing fight against Senator Watson for the Indiana delegation to Kansas City. At Fort Wayne, Mr.

Hoover for the first time responded to the call for a speech. It was his first utterance since leaving Washington. 'This is not an occasion for a political speech,' he said. 'It is Sunday morning. However, I do appreciate greatly the sentiment and the courtesy of your coming down to the station.' That was all the nominee said. Mrs. Hoover also expressed her appreciation of the welcome. It seemed that the cheers for her were just as hearty as those for her husband."[241] Despite a slow start among Indiana Republicans (many of whom had supported Watson in the primary), Hoover went on to easily carry Indiana in the November 1928 election with 60 percent of the vote over the Democratic nominee, Governor Smith of New York.

As president, Hoover made a special visit to Indiana with a stop at Madison along the Ohio River in southeastern Indiana in October 1929. Hoover's visit came during a series of ceremonial visits, including a stop at Dearborn, Michigan, to visit with automaker Henry Ford to join a celebration of the fiftieth anniversary of Thomas Edison's invention of the incandescent light. From there the president's party moved south through Ohio to Cincinnati, where he presided over ceremonies celebrating the opening of the Ohio River for first-class traffic from Pittsburgh west to the Mississippi River. Following remarks at a Cincinnati riverfront park, Hoover boarded a river steamer "for a leisurely journey down the Ohio River to Louisville, Ky., where tomorrow night he will inform the country more completely as to his policies for inland waterways development."[242]

The residents of Madison were quite excited about their day in the spotlight as Hoover planned a quick stop on the Indiana side of the river. Even the arrival of Governor Harry G. Leslie from Indianapolis warranted a nineteen-cannon salute, offered from an old stone quarry east of Madison. "Nineteen guns were fired by Battery E gunners when it was determined the governor is entitled to 19 instead of 17 guns in his own state," the *Madison Daily Herald* explained. "The big gun will be pulled into position on Telegraph Hill tomorrow morning to be fired 21 times on the arrival of President Hoover."[243] The newspaper's editors assured residents that warning shots would be fired as soon as the president's flotilla was within view, allowing all local public and parochial schools to dismiss so that schoolchildren could make their way to the river to greet the president. "Each and every child will be expected to have a small American flag to wave when the President steamer lands," the newspaper account instructed. "Since the crowds tomorrow will be enormous and it will be impossible for school authorities to look after all children, an appeal is made to parents to meet their children at the schools and personally look after them in so far as possible."[244] Madison's mayor, Marcus R. Sulzer, predicted that Hoover's quick visit to the city would be the biggest event in the city's history and added, "People who have never before knew there was a Madison, Indiana, will know it now and the benefit that this will be to Madison in the future cannot be measured at the present time."[245]

Despite all the excitement and preparations, nothing could prevent the weather from being poor, with a cold drizzle falling throughout the day and the day's schedule thrown off by the earlier-than-expected arrival of the president's flotilla. For thirty minutes, however, Madison was the center of attention as Hoover and his wife, Lou Henry, gamely "braved a downpour of rain and a chilling west wind to stand on the open deck of the government steamer, *Greenbrier*, and extended greetings and paid their respects

to the large crowd of people who thronged along the levee."[246] Hoover raised his hat and acknowledged the crowd estimated to be about 5,000 gathered near Mulberry Street, a crowd that moments before was not present since a tragic accident had thwarted the plans for the twenty-one-gun artillery salute, and factory whistles and church bells were used instead to notify townsfolk of the approaching guests on the Ohio River. "President Hoover, Mrs. Hoover and their entire party and the governor and his party stood on the open deck of the steamer the entire time in the downpour of rain without as much as an umbrella to protect them from the elements," the *Daily Herald* reported. "The president and his wife were exposed to the rain for a full half hour, a high mark of respect for Madison which would be received with much gratitude by the entire community."[247]

Even though a reported 5,000 people made it to the riverfront to greet the president, the *Daily Herald* lamented that "one of the major disappointments connected with Mr. Hoover's visit was the fact that the fleet was here and home again before many people had time to hurry to the river. . . . The levee was practically deserted a few minutes before the whistles sounded, but in the space of a short time, people began swarming to the river from every side street. . . . A squad of (state) motor vehicle police were in the city to assist local police in handling the crowds, but the way matters developed their services were hardly needed."[248] No actual account of Hoover's remarks was reported beyond a mention that he urged his Hoosier friends to listen to his address from Louisville, Kentucky, that evening by radio.

A page-two story of the *Daily Herald*, however, told of a horrific event related to Hoover's visit. The "accident" that had prevented the scheduled twenty-one-gun artillery salute had actually been deadly. "A bit of burning waddling, which was shot from the big gun, was carried by the wind and fell in the box of powder that had been placed several feet behind the field piece. The explosion that followed was terrific."[249] Nineteen-year-old Robert C. Earls, a Madison resident and a member of Battery E of the Indiana National Guard, died as a result of massive burns and blunt-force injuries a few hours after the president's visit at King's Daughters Hospital in Madison. Six other members of the crew were seriously injured, suffering from burns and broken bones. Only two of the men present escaped injury.[250] After returning to Washington, D.C., Hoover was informed of the tragedy at Madison. The president and his wife sent a special telegram to Earls's parents from the White House that read, "Mrs. Hoover and I send you deepest sympathy and feel distressed beyond measure over the unfortunate accident which resulted in the loss of your son. Our prayers are with you."[251] A second telegram sent to Sulzer read, "Mrs. Hoover and I are sad to learn of the unfortunate accident which resulted in the death of Robert Earls and injuries to the other members of the saluting battery. We have expressed our sympathy to the mother and father of the boy who lost his life and ask you to convey to the families of those injured our earnest hope that they may speedily recover."[252]

Less than a week after Hoover's visit to Madison, the Stock Market crash of 1929 occurred—Black Tuesday, October 29, 1929—when a record 16 million shares of stock were traded, and the market dropped more than thirty points in one day. The impact of the financial struggles was not completely known at the time, but it soon would signal the arrival of the Great Depression that would haunt the remainder of Hoover's time in the White House.

The Great Depression and the economic woes that continued to grip the nation were motivations for a Midwest swing the president undertook in June 1931, which included dedication of a "Grecian temple" to honor former president Harding at Marion, Ohio, and later, a first-ever stop by a U.S. president at the tomb of President Abraham Lincoln at Springfield, Illinois. In between was Indiana, and Hoover's train made a momentary stop at Greensburg in Decatur County en route to Indianapolis for a major address before the Indiana Republican Editorial Association. Although several thousand local residents showed up and the American Legion staged a welcoming celebration for the president, his Greensburg remarks were succinct: "Mrs. Hoover and I want to express our appreciation for this beautiful greeting. It is a fine welcome to the State of Indiana. It is encouraging to be a President, to receive such a greeting and such a welcome as this. Thank you."[253]

Hoover was apparently saving his voice—and his ideas—for his address before 5,500 people gathered inside a hall at the Indiana State Fairgrounds in Indianapolis for an address carried nationwide via both CBS and NBC radio. "It is a genuine pleasure to meet the Republican editors of the State of Indiana and their guests," the president said. "The editor in an American community has a most serious responsibility today. It is upon him, in a large measure that the responsibility rests of molding and interpreting public opinion in his community. It is upon him also that we lean for leadership in every civic movement—political, economic, and social. And, above all, it is in you, the editors, that we must rest the first defense of American idealism. I can say in all fairness that our editors fulfill these responsibilities in a fashion which entitles them to the gratitude of the country."[254]

Dispensing quickly with recognizing fellow Republicans gathered, including Watson, now the Senate majority leader, Hoover said:

> The business depression is the dominant subject before the country and the world today. Its blight stretches from all quarters of the globe to every business place and every cottage door in our land. I propose to discuss it and the policies of the government in respect to it. Depressions are not new experiences, though none has hitherto been so widespread. We have passed through no less than 15 major depressions in the last century. We have learned something as the result of each of these experiences. From this one we shall gain stiffening and economic discipline, a greater knowledge upon which we must build a better safeguarded system. We have come out of each previous depression into a period of prosperity greater than ever before. We shall do so this time.[255]

Hoover's optimistic predictions notwithstanding, he insisted that the basis for the Depression did not lie alone with wild speculation and inflation of stock prices, loose business practices, or the drought. He declared if those "had been our only disasters, we would have recovered months ago."[256] The president noted that problems in Europe, including war and destruction of democratic and free open economies in key parts of the world, were also impacting the American economy. He further blamed a growing fear on the part of Americans themselves—many of whom had reserves of their own—but were reluctant to spend them and became even more reluctant to invest them in bonds and savings with the banking industry after bank failures began to emerge.

The sanguine tone continuing, Hoover said, "We must bear in mind at all times our marvelous resources in land, mines, mills, manpower, brainpower, and courage. Over 95 percent of our families have either an income or a breadwinner employed. Our people are working harder and are resolutely engaged, individually and collectively, in overhauling and improving their methods and services."[257] Hoover pointed to predictions that "idle money" held by Americans would soon be invested because of his efforts to shore up trust in the nation's financial systems (including the farm loan program), his "steady urging" of maintenance of wages and salaries, his "organized cooperation" with business and industry to distribute work, and "reversal of the traditional policy in Depression of reducing expenditures upon construction work." Hoover's abstract, however, may have been missing a key note with working Americans. Most of what he discussed as responses to the Depression were efforts focused on business and industry, while the Democrats continued to promote an agenda that included direct relief for the unemployed and destitute. What working family in Indiana could be particularly reassured by Hoover's assertion that "I would be remiss if I did not pay tribute to business, industrial, labor and agricultural leaders for their remarkable spirit of cooperation" at a time when many Americans were already weary or outright distrustful of those very same leaders?[258]

Further deepening the divide between his world view and that of his fellow citizens, some of whom he referred to as "timid people, black with despair" or "agitators," Hoover almost chastised Americans when he added, "While we are fostering the slow but positive process of healing our economic wounds, our citizens are necessarily filled with anxiety, and in their anxiety there is the natural demand for more and more drastic action by the federal government."[259] Hoover derided as "experimental" or "theoretical" panaceas being offered by some amidst the economic strife and placed ideas for recovery in one of two camps properly highlighting the differences between Republican and Democratic proposals: "The first is whether we shall go on with our American system which holds that the major purpose of a state is to protect the people and to give them equality of opportunity, that the basis of all happiness is in development of the individual. . . . The other is that we shall directly or indirectly regiment the population into a bureaucracy to serve the state, that we should use force instead of cooperation in plans and thereby direct every man as to what he may or may not do."[260] It was familiar territory, setting up one side of the argument as consistent with true democratic freedoms, and the other side as reflective of a more socialistic (and thereby antidemocracy) approach. He concluded not by outlining any further specific efforts his administration or any part of the government or private sector could do, but instead turned to the people: "Our immediate and paramount task as a people is to rout the forces of economic disruption and pessimism that have swept upon us" and that government should work to "inspire cooperation in the community to sustain good will and to keep our country free of disorder and conflict."[261]

Alfred E. "Al" Smith

Elected to four terms as governor of New York in the 1920s, Al Smith made history as the nation's first Roman Catholic nominee of a major party for president. His religion was ultimately among the "three P's" (prejudice, Prohibition, and prosperity) that most analysts blamed for Smith's noteworthy failure in the 1928 general election against Hoover. Despite his Catholicism and widespread belief among many Americans that a Catholic president would feel obligated to answer first to the Pope, and second to the American

people, Smith won the first Democratic National Convention held in the south (at Houston, Texas) since the close of the Civil War. His running mate, U.S. Senator Joseph Robinson of Arkansas, helped Smith carry a handful of Democratic-stronghold states in the South, but the November tally held little other joy.

Smith's campaign likely had little reason to believe Indiana could be helpful, but it did not stop him from making a plea for Hoosier votes, convinced by advisers that some of the Republican voters who supported Watson over Hoover in the primary may be wooed to the Democratic ballot. His late October 1928 swing through the state "amazed" and "puzzled" Smith's campaign advisers as crowds were larger and more enthusiastic than they had been led to believe was possible in Indiana.[262] At Lafayette, thousands were reported to have turned out to see Smith and his famous brown derby hat, and the governor waved it happily for the crowd from atop the back of a truck he climbed onto near the train depot. He spent only five minutes, however, in Tippecanoe County before his train started again for Indianapolis.

"I never saw a sight like that in my life," Smith said to bystanders as he overlooked the large throng gathered to see him at Monument Circle from a balcony at the English Hotel in downtown Indianapolis.[263] "The governor appeared deeply moved by the evidence of his popularity . . . when a multitude of Italians broke through the thick lines of soldiers and acclaimed him, was so carried away by the scene that he threw kisses to those tens of thousands of shouting and gesticulating partisans of his."[264] News reports indicated that "in Indianapolis the police lines gave way after the governor had been ushered through (Union Station), and the crowd came trooping along in the street, brushing against the cars which carried the nominee and his party."[265]

During his brief open-air remarks in Indianapolis—noted as his first open-air rally of the entire campaign—Smith said he had "carefully refrained during the campaign from delivering open air addresses. I have been 25 years campaigning. I have run for public office every two years for practically the last quarter of a century and I know the effect of open air talking upon my vocal cords. I assure you that I want to preserve them for the next two weeks, for the battle of the Atlantic seaboard. I have, further, made up my mind that it is the duty of the Democratic Party to talk out clearly, plainly and honestly to the American people. With the exception of a very few subjections contained in the Democratic national platform, I have in my swing around the United States, dealt definitely and fairly conclusively with all the big problems that are facing the American people today."[266]

He added, "I would love to talk to this large assemblage at great length, but I know the possible and positive consequences, and for that reason I will ask you to just listen in next week. The subjects not already covered will be taken up and treated in an exhaustive way during my trip along the seaboard from Massachusetts to Maryland. Since I came into Indianapolis, I have been impressed by the size of the gathering. Certainly, no man could fail to be impressed by this great gathering that I have the honor, the pleasure and the great satisfaction of looking down upon. I am doubly grateful, from the bottom of my heart, for the cordial and I might also say, affectionate welcome that you have given me. . . . I am glad to be with you in Indianapolis!"[267]

Other stops in Indianapolis included remarks before a combined group of farm, education and business leaders at the Claypool Hotel, where he accused the Republican Party of failing to keep its promises and that Democrats would bring farm relief. He told the farmers, "The Republican candidate holds out no hope of positive relief. What the farmers got in the last four years they may expect to get in the next four years."[268]   For the teachers in the audience, Smith highlighted his record of supporting public education in New York, declaring himself "the greatest friend that education had ever had in the governor's chair."[269]

He also said, "Now the problem of education is a simple one. "You buy education. You get the quality and to the degree that you buy. You don't get any more, and it is your business to see that you do not get less. We are buying education for the children of the public schools in New York state at a large figure, and that is the reason we have contented school teachers and progressive school teachers. The standard of the classroom will not arise above the standard of the teacher. I am perfectly satisfied in my heart and soul that education, and the public schools providing the education, are the cornerstone upon which must rest for all time to come the success of this great republic."[270] Smith told his fellow Democrats that he was optimistic about the coming election: "In no time during my political career of a quarter century has the outlook for Democratic success been brighter than it is today. I am satisfied that the people of this country want a change."[271]

Reporters estimated the open-air crowd for Smith's appearance at the Circle to be in excess of 50,000, while party officials said it was closer to 100,000. Regardless of the exact number, the excitement was high, and news accounts indicated that Smith "had some difficulty navigating the crowd" downtown in order to visit Methodist Hospital, where the state's powerful Democratic "don," Taggart, had been a patient for several weeks, suffering a stomach ailment. Taggart reportedly told Smith he had listened to all of his radio speeches from his hospital bed and encouraged him: "Just keep on the way you are going, my boy, you are going to win."[272] Smith's wife, Catherine Anne, was rather frank when asked by an *Indianapolis Star* reporter what she thought of the campaign trail: "To tell the truth, it isn't going to make a bit of a difference to me which way the election goes. I'd really be just as happy at home in Albany with the Governor as I would be in the White House."[273]

The rousing visit at Indianapolis, however, came only after another kind of "welcome" Smith received when his train crossed into Indiana from Ohio en route to Chicago before his swing back to Indianapolis. "A fiery cross was burned in a field 100 feet from the special train of Governor Alfred E. Smith shortly after it crossed the Indiana state line tonight," the United Press reported. "A shot was fired as the train passed the spot and the flash of light brought passengers to the car windows. . . . Gov. Smith was at the dinner table when he heard the shot and caught only a glimpse of the burning cross as his train rushed past. No one could be seen near the spot in the light of the burning cross. Only half a cross bar had caught fire and members of the Smith party were not aware of its significance until the other half began to blaze."[274]

Smith died in his beloved New York City on October 4, 1944, as a result of a heart attack. Aged seventy years, Smith had been in a rapid decline throughout 1944, following the death of his wife five months before his own.

6

The New Deal Era and World War II, 1932–45

Franklin D. Roosevelt

Franklin D. Roosevelt's first visits to Indiana came as part of his campaign in 1920 after having been nominated by the Democratic Party for vice president on a ticket led by Ohio governor James M. Cox. Roosevelt, then serving as assistant secretary of the navy in the Woodrow Wilson administration, made one stop at Crawfordsville on October 13, 1920. After eating breakfast at the Crawford Hotel, Roosevelt spoke at the Montgomery County Courthouse and gave the qualified support he and Cox were offering for the United States to join the proposed League of Nations.[1]

Eleven years later, as governor of New York, Roosevelt appeared in June 1931 at the annual meeting of the National Governors Association at French Lick. By then, he had been crippled by polio, a condition he had been living with since he fell ill in 1921. His 1931 visit to Orange County reportedly was not his first, or last, visit to the mineral springs at French Lick, which some doctors believed were therapeutic for individuals suffering paralysis. Democrat Roosevelt and Governor Gifford Pinchot of Pennsylvania, a Republican, were the keynote speakers at the conference, and both men's remarks were reported nationally, as they were expected to be presidential candidates in 1932.

In his remarks Roosevelt cautioned that when the nation's economy was strong, America could "overlook the defects of organization and danger signals from industry and agriculture, but in times such as the present, these symptoms attain new importance and show us the urgency of the new problems we have to face. A century ago, 75 percent of the population lived on farms and 25 percent in cities; today the figures are exactly reversed. Hitherto, we have spoken of two types of living—urban and rural. I believe we can look forward to three other than two types in the future, for there is a definite place for an intermediate type between the urban and the rural, namely, a rural industrial group." He added, "There are without question many industries which can succeed just as well, if not better, by bringing them to rural communities and at the same time these rural communities will be given higher annual income capacity. It is my thought that many of the problems of transportation, of over-crowded cities, of high cost of living, of better health for the race, of better balance of population as a whole, can be solved by the states themselves during the coming generation."[2]

For the 1932 campaign, Roosevelt was an active candidate, going to Chicago to personally accept the nomination of his party for president, and he campaigned in thirty-eight states. The Roosevelt camp was eager to show that despite his disability, the governor was physically able to meet the demands of the presidency (and the requisite campaign for the office). On October 20, 1932, Roosevelt brought his campaign to Indiana. His schedule called for him to make a speech in Pittsburgh, Pennsylvania, and then proceed directly to Indianapolis. However, news reports emerged that indicated the "Roosevelt Special" got lost in Ohio and traveled from Pennsylvania to Indiana by way of Cincinnati, including bypassing a crowd waiting for him to stop at Springfield, Ohio.[3]

Once in Indianapolis, Roosevelt spoke to an incredible throng estimated at between 80,000 and 100,000 Hoosiers at Monument Circle. Joined by his wife, Eleanor, from the balcony of the English Hotel, Roosevelt outlined his plans for the nation: "It will be the purpose of the new administration to bring order out of chaos, to institute sound and progressive and humane policies, to repair the damage that has been wrought, to return, if you will the people of the United States to the ways of economy, soundness and more widely distributed prosperity." Asserting that President Herbert Hoover's administration had brought "terrible retribution" on the nation, Roosevelt said Hoover's "economic heresies have all come home to roost, and this administration stands convicted of having produced this brood of disorder—producing gambles with national prosperity. These ways of prosperity and soundness are assured if we will order our economic and governmental life properly. In spite of the ruinous policies of the present Republican administration, the country still stands as the richest in the world—a nation of the greatest opportunities and potentialities."[4]

Roosevelt accused Hoover of lacking a unified, national grasp of the economic problems gripping America. While trying to make the case that Hoover had led the nation astray, Roosevelt seemed to understand the need to temper his rhetoric to avoid complicating the delicate nature of financial markets, stating that:

> I want to add, too, that the financial system of the United States in October of this year, while badly managed by this administration, is still, in spite of the action of this administration, capable of repair. Nothing but unreasoning and groundless fear and hysteria can chip away the granite foundations on which our fiscal system is based. Thanks to Democratic measures, extending back to 20 years, created by a group of statesmen in our own party, who are still honored leaders in the American Congress, we have flexibility and power of our central banking system, making for basic security.[5]

Sensitive to Republican claims that he was proposing a Socialist approach that would handcuff free enterprise and cripple American enterprise, Roosevelt added, "I have warned the country against unwise governmental interference with business. I have pointed out that the policies of the present leadership of the Republican Party in the past few years has constituted dangerous back-seat driving. It encouraged wanton and dangerous speculation. It refused to encourage those sound and patriotic masters of finance who sounded a warning and who tried to save the financial soundness of the United States from a crash that they saw all too imminent. This from a party that has advertised itself as the friend of true business and true prosperity. I am opposed to their kind of governmental interference with business."[6]

During his remarks Roosevelt also addressed the ongoing debate in the nation about the efficacy of Prohibition. He repeated Democratic Party positions that expressed a desire "to acquire, through a sound federal policy of federal taxation on beer, some of the countless wealth now going into the pockets of racketeers."[7]

The Roosevelt campaign was well pleased with the showing in Indianapolis. Associated Press and New York reporters noted that "his speech from the balcony of the English Hotel, in almost the same spot from which [Alfred E.] Smith spoke in 1928, was heard by one of the largest crowds that has seen the candidate since he started his active campaign for election. Estimates of the crowd by police officials varied from 50,000 to 75,000 and even more. Men and women stood loosely packed in the wide circle, wedged tightly into every vantage spot afforded by the war memorial peaked by its statute of Miss Indiana."[8]

En route to Springfield, Illinois, from Indianapolis, Roosevelt's train stopped briefly to address a huge outdoor crowd at Terre Haute. Speaking to the vibrant mining industry in

southwestern Indiana, Roosevelt reminded his Hoosier friends that when he campaigned in the state in 1920, "most of the coal mines in this part of the state were in operation, most of the farmers were able to pay their taxes and keep their farms. I am afraid now if I traveled through this part of Indiana I would see a different picture." He promised that "I'm not going to appoint a lot of commissions when I go to Washington, but I'm going to undertake to get the coal industry stabilized and not just have a lot of talk."[9] Roosevelt added, "I believe that by restoring old-fashioned common sense economies in our government things are going to be much better after the fourth of March. I feel strongly that this country will bring back the level of farm prices and can do much to aid the coal industry."[10]

In December 1935 Roosevelt made his first stop in Indiana as the nation's chief executive for an event at the University of Notre Dame to receive an honorary degree. "A gymnasium full of Notre Dame students gave Mr. Roosevelt a noisy

IHS, MARTIN'S PHOTO SHOP COLLECTION, P.129

Democratic presidential candidate Franklin D. Roosevelt's campaign train makes a stop at the Central Station in Terre Haute, Indiana, 1932.

football welcome late yesterday afternoon when he stopped at South Bend to receive an honorary degree," the Associated Press reported.[11] Reporters also noted that Roosevelt's voice "almost broke with emotion" when he departed from prepared remarks to note, "In the conflict of policies and of political systems which the world today witnesses, the United States has held forth for its own guidance, for the guidance of other nations, if they will accept it, this great torch of liberty of human thought, liberty of human conscience. We will never lower it. We will never permit it, if we can help it, the light to grow dim. Rather through every means legitimately within our power and our office, we will seek to increase that light, that its rays may extend the farther; that its glory may be seen even from afar."[12]

During his prepared remarks, Roosevelt said, "I am most happy to be so honored. The honor places upon me an additional obligation to try to live up to the citation—both for the sake of my country and as a 'new alumnus' of the University of Notre Dame." The president made special mention of his efforts to preserve America's role in the sovereignty of the Philippine Islands. "The acceptance of sovereignty

A smiling Roosevelt meets with Indiana governor Paul McNutt, circa 1936.

was but an obligation to serve the people of the Philippines until the day they might themselves be independent and take their own place among the nations of the world," he said. "We are here to welcome the Commonwealth. I consider it one of the happiest events of my office as President of the United States to have signed in the name of the United States the instrument which will give national freedom to the Philippine people."[13] Roosevelt praised the genius of the Philippine people. "Subject to the government of a country other than their own, they generously adjusted themselves to conditions often not to their liking; they patiently waited. They forfeited none of that freedom which is natively theirs as a people, and which they have so definitely expressed with due regard for the fundamental human rights in their new constitution. . . . Through our power we have not sought our own. Through our power we have sought to benefit others."[14] Roosevelt added, "This university from which we send our welcome to the new commonwealth exemplifies the principles of which I speak" and praised Notre Dame's founders for their commitment to freedom of education and freedom of worship.

Roosevelt spoke again in Indiana on one of the state's most important occasions, the dedication of the new George Rogers Clark Memorial at Vincennes on Sunday morning, June 14, 1936, before a massive crowd estimated at more than 40,000. Accompanied by Governor Paul V. McNutt and Eleanor, Roosevelt's visit came during his campaign for a second term as president, but was dubbed by the White House as an official presidential visit, not a campaign trip. "Events of history take on their due proportions only when viewed in the light of time," Roosevelt said. "With every passing year, the capture of Vincennes, more than a century and a half ago when the Thirteen Colonies were seeking their independence, assumes

LIBRARY OF CONGRESS

greater and more permanent significance."[15] The president also said that conducting the dedication on a Sunday morning was consistent with the religious freedom sought in the American Revolution. "Today, religion is still free within our borders; it must ever remain so," he said.[16]

"Today, morality means the same thing as it meant in the days of George Rogers Clark, though we must need to apply it to many, many situations of which George Rogers Clark never dreamt," the president observed.[17] Roosevelt added that "George Rogers Clark did battle against the tomahawk and the rifle. He saved for us the fair land that lay between the mountains and the Father of the Waters. His task is done. Though we fight with weapons unknown to him, it is still our duty to continue the saving of this fair land. May the Americans who, a century and a half from now, celebrate at this spot the three-hundredth anniversary of the heroism of Clark and his men, think kindly of us for the part we are taking today in preserving the nation of the United States."[18]

After the Vincennes stop, Eleanor broke from the president's entourage to tour coal mining operations in southern Indiana, Illinois, and Kentucky. Ending her tour in Indianapolis at Governor McNutt's residence, she was greeted by a delegation of Indiana Girl Scouts and attended a dinner party hosted by the governor and his wife, Kathleen. Later Eleanor gave a "town hall lecture" at the Murat Theatre in downtown Indianapolis, where she discussed the need to provide better housing for the nation's citizens. The next day she visited Purdue University at West Lafayette to discuss the Purdue Housing Research Project and spoke before an audience of about 6,000 at the National Guard Armory. Before she left Indiana, she made one more stop in Indianapolis for the local Works Progress Administration sewing

Roosevelt adviser James Farley (left) signs autographs during a campaign stop in Terre Haute, Indiana.

project, which involved more than 900 women at the RCA Building near Michigan and LaSalle Streets on the city's east side.[19]

Roosevelt was back in Indiana in August 1936 for two quick stops. The first came near the Indiana-Ohio line at tiny Garrett in De Kalb County. A 1,000 citizens turned out, and the president spoke for only a few moments, noting that "Governor (McNutt) says I don't have to be introduced to an Indiana crowd. That's fine. In fact, I remember coming through Garrett two years ago, but it was pretty late and I think I had gone to bed, so I didn't see anybody,"[20] drawing a friendly laugh. "I am going out, as you know, further West and up into the Northwest, to see some of the worst drought conditions," said Roosevelt. "I must say this, though, as a Hudson River farmer, that I have been looking at the corn in Indiana today and I think our corn is a little better than yours this year—but this year only, because you generally raise better corn than we do. I am, of course, very much disturbed about these parts of the country that have practically a total crop failure, and that is why I am going out to look at it and get information first hand."[21]

Before departing Indiana, the president's nine-car special stopped for lunch in Gary, and he spoke to an audience of more than 20,000 from the rear of the train saying, "I am not talking politics on this trip, and I shall not talk drought to you. I have been doing that for nearly two weeks." Instead, Roosevelt grew reflective for a few moments, drawing a contrast to his current train tour of the nation to the one he took in 1932 during his first campaign. "I shall always remember, in going almost every day through the country districts and in the manufacturing districts, not only the garb, the clothing of the people, but the faces of the people," he said.[22] Roosevelt said the 1932 trip was "a harrowing experience as I campaigned in that year, because there was such obvious want in almost every part of the country. As Alben Barkley and I were going across the state of Kentucky, he would say, jokingly perhaps, to the people who thronged around the end of the train, 'You have on the same clothes that you had in 1928 when I was through here.' And it was all true; there was not enough clothing to go round, and there was not enough food to go round."[23]

Roosevelt felt that regardless how difficult the earlier years had been, "I am thankful, as an American, that today the faces of the people and the clothing they wear show that their mental condition and their physical condition are a whole lot better. . . . I think everybody who goes through the country at the present time feels that we have come through a very dangerous and a very sad experience."[24] Roosevelt said the spirit of hope that now filled many Americans transcended party labels and mere politics. "Even though people have been hard hit by the drought, we have a new courage to go through the year without losing hope," he said. "This is true not only in the drought years, but here in the state of

Governor Paul McNutt addresses the crowd during President Franklin D. Roosevelt's appearance at the 1936 Indiana State Fair.

Indiana, where I am happy to say, conditions are much better with regard to crops."[25]

As part of his extended return trip to Washington from the West, Roosevelt's return train brought him to Indianapolis, officially for a meeting with a handful of midwestern governors to discuss drought conditions in their respective states, but also to do a little campaigning during the opening days of the 1936 Indiana State Fair. Before stopping at the fair, the first U.S. president to ever do so, Roosevelt took a nearly two-hour open-car tour of various Works Project Administration sites in greater Indianapolis. Those WPA projects included a new "slum clearing" housing complex at Lockefield Gardens (where a mostly all-black audience approaching 20,000 people greeted him), the new National Guard Armory, parkland boulevards and levees near the White River, a new Ball Residence Hall for nurses at the Indiana University Medical School campus, and an enclosed therapeutic swimming pool at the James Whitcomb Riley Hospital for Children.[26]

While at the hospital, the car carrying Roosevelt pulled up close alongside a hospital window so the president could "greet" some of the children there face to face. Eventually, Roosevelt's motorcade made its way onto the race track in front of the fairgrounds grandstand, where he saw three other WPA projects, the under-track tunnel, a model farm home, and an educational building. Roosevelt spoke while seated inside an open car to a crowd of more than 15,000 at the fairgrounds grandstand that "I wish I could stay here and see everything at your state fair but, one of the penalties of being president is that you cannot go to state fairs. I even missed my own county fair this year. I was brought up in the atmosphere of state fairs. When a small boy, my father was still sending trotting horses to the fairs and I miss this very much."[27]

One of the more political events for Roosevelt's Indianapolis stop included a "small luncheon" arranged by McNutt at the Athletic Club, which quickly swelled to more than 2,000 guests. Roosevelt said, "I told my old friend, Governor McNutt, that I would say a few words of greeting and thanks for this most delightful day. I shall always remember these visits to Indianapolis. In the 1932 campaign, I think the thing that stands out most clearly in my memory was that wonderful meeting in the Circle with that sea of faces—they seemed millions—in front of me. On this visit I have been glad to see more of the city and more of the fine work that has been carried on in the recent past."[28] Further recalling the 1932 visits he paid to Indiana, Roosevelt said (in remarks that closely matched what he had said before other Indiana audiences) that "those were difficult years that we went through. I am thankful, as an American, that today the faces of the people and the clothing they wear show that their mental condition and their physical condition are a whole lot better than they were at that time. I think everybody who goes through the country at the present time feels that we have

come through a very dangerous and a very sad experience."[29]

Without ever acknowledging he was a candidate for re-election in the polling to take place in less than two months, and the fact that his audience was overwhelmingly Democratic Party faithful, Roosevelt said, "It is not a question, in my judgment, that ought to be brought into politics, into the partisan give and take of a campaign—it is a fact. Today the people of the country, of all parties and in every section, are looking forward to the future with a great deal more hope than they could possibly have looked forward to in 1932. For that reason this trip of mine has been a happy trip. So, at the end of this trip of nearly two weeks, I am going back to Washington in a happy frame of mind."[30]

The world would change dramatically between that sunny September day in Indianapolis, where Roosevelt affirmed his "happy frame of mind" and the conditions present when he visited the state again for an official function. There were other happy moments along the way. Residents of Richmond remember Roosevelt's train stop on May 13, 1937, more for what the president did than what he said. Roosevelt made a special effort to hoist his granddaughter Ruth onto his lap so that she could see out the train car window and wave at the large crowd. But the world and America faced dramatic change after December 7, 1941, with the Japanese bombing of Pearl Harbor and the official draw of the United States into World War II, which had been raging since the German invasion of Poland on September 1, 1939, followed by Germany's advance on France beginning in May 1940, and the Soviet Union in June 1941.

As the demands of World War II continued to overtake nearly every moment of the president's official life, his travels outside of Washington,

D.C., were limited to addresses in major cities, visits to his home in Hyde Park, New York, and to a vacation villa at Warm Springs, Georgia. Hoosiers, like most Americans, heard their president via his frequent radio addresses and on newsreels shown at movie theaters.

In April 1943 Roosevelt undertook his second wartime tour of the nation, this one more than sixteen days, twenty states, and 7,600 miles that included visits to military encampments and training facilities and the growing industrial complex needed to support the war effort. His trip also included a visit to Mexico to meet Mexican president Avila Camacho. On April 27 Roosevelt visited the Jefferson Barracks at Saint Louis before arriving at the Republic fighter plane plant in Evansville for a quick tour of the interior and exterior of the plant while riding in an open-air car. It was the next-to-the-last-day of Roosevelt's tour, ending with a visit to Fort Knox, Kentucky, before returning to Washington. The *New York Times* reported that "with some of the world's fastest and most powerful fighter planes in a murky sky overhead, President Roosevelt inspected today the Republic Aviation Corporation's fabrication and assembly lines for P-47 Thunderbolts. The Chief Executive obviously was impressed with the planes and the plant that is turning them out on a spot where a cornfield stood 13 months ago."[31] Employees of the plant presented Roosevelt a replica model of the P-47 as a memento of his visit.

Media reports of Roosevelt's activities were delayed a day or more as a security measure during a critical war period. One news dispatch reported that a little Indiana girl, estimated to be eight or nine years old, quizzed a Secret Service agent at the train station in Evansville asking, "Is the President there?" As the United Press reported, "The Secret Service man just shook his head.

'Well, I don't care if he is a military secret,' the child said, running along beside the slow moving train, 'I want to see him anyway.'"[32]

The president made no formal speeches during most of his trip, instead engaging in one-on-one contact with those he met and talking with smaller groups of troops and manufacturing employees. The Associated Press reported during an informal meeting with a small group of reporters in Indiana that the president thought the country was "catching on to the advantages of the training which men and women are getting in the service, as well as in war industries. He commented on a marked gain in their health and physical well-being and on the way a portion of them who missed much of their formal schooling are now learning reading, writing and arithmetic as well as skilled trades."[33]

News dispatches paraphrased Roosevelt as saying that "when you see all the tremendous camps with a capacity of maybe three or four million men, you can't help wondering what will happen to them when the war is won and whether some type of training should continue partly to avoid a net loss on equipment on which millions have been spent." He particularly noted the Republic facility at Evansville, telling reporters that the plant is actually "only making half an airplane" and that "the other parts are supplied by the automotive industry." He acknowledged production delays for the plant that opened in August 1942, but that "the situation has straightened out to a great extent . . . (and) overall production of combat planes would continue to increase every month for the rest of the year."[34]

Evansville historian Darrel E. Bigham noted that the P-47 Thunderbolt was built in Indiana after Republic Aviation Corporation relocated its manufacturing facility from Long Island, New York, to a more secure location away from the nation's coastline. It was an amazing story. Ground was broken for the plant in April 1942, and the first P-47 rolled off the line at the end of September, just five months later. At its peak, the plant employed more than 5,500 workers and produced more than 5,000 Thunderbolts, used heavily in the Pacific theater of the war as an escort fighter, dive-bomber, and long-range fighter. As impressive as the Republic Aviation output was, Evansville's Ohio River shipyard employed more than 19,000 workers at one time and produced the first Landing Ship Tanks (LSTs) used in the war.[35]

Roosevelt made his very last appearance in Indiana for a memorable event in Fort Wayne on October 28, 1944, while the nation remained locked in the ravages of World War II. For Roosevelt, he was locked in the closing days of his fourth—and last—campaign for president. The demands of being a war president had kept him from venturing into many states, and Indiana had been no exception. The stop in Fort Wayne was not only rare, but a "dress rehearsal" of sorts for a major address to follow at Soldier Field in Chicago. For his address, a special trackside stage was constructed at the crossing near Harrison and Pennsylvania Streets in downtown Fort Wayne. The stage, constructed at the same level as the rear of his train, allowed Roosevelt to "walk" from the train to the stand where he spoke. "The area surrounding Harrison Street

IHS, BRETZMAN COLLECTION, P 338

A crowd estimated at 100,000 packs Monument Circle in Indianapolis to hear a speech Roosevelt made from the balcony of the English Hotel, 1932.

is to be blocked off to traffic, thus permitting a large throng to see and hear the President," the *Fort Wayne Journal-Gazette* reported. "The platform on which the President will appear is to be decorated and a special platform for the accommodation of both local newspapermen and those aboard the special likewise is being constructed."[36]

Easing into his remarks, Roosevelt stated the obvious that Indiana was just one of the then-forty-eight states and noted regardless, "I am glad to have a chance to come here, to my friends in Indiana."[37] The president cracked a joke about Republicans and how they had misunderstood his earlier remarks, the GOP claiming that Roosevelt said he would not actively campaign for re-election because of the war. "However, they conveniently overlook what I actually said in my speech of acceptance last July," the president said. "I said I wasn't going to conduct the usual campaign. I said however, 'I shall, however, feel free to report to the people the facts about matters of concern to them and especially to correct any misrepresentations.'"[38]

"I have a conviction," he said, "that the people of Indiana, the majority of the voters of Indiana, know that I am the same Franklin Roosevelt who started in campaigning 12 years ago. . . . I know you will find me just the same, and I wear the same-sized hat."[39]

The president praised the workers of Fort Wayne for their production of goods used in the war effort and the great railroad workers in the state who made sure the goods were shipped quickly and efficiently. One of those railroad workers, "a brakeman named Morrison," was especially called out as he was a Democratic candidate for the Indiana General Assembly. Roosevelt said he had read the polls that placed Indiana as "doubtful" in terms of going for the Democrats,

"but there is one thing that is not doubtful about this state, and that is the ability of its people to produce. That goes for Indiana's industries and Indiana's farms. You have all been greatly helpful in conducting, with other states, the greatest war effort that this world has ever seen in all the centuries. And I hope that regardless of which party you support on Election Day, you will produce a record crop of votes."[40]

His ego showing—or perhaps just an attempt at humor—the president told the Fort Wayne audience that "I would hate to be re-elected by a little bit of a vote," he said smirking. "That wouldn't spell democracy. If I am re-elected, I want it to be a big vote." At the same time, however, he added that he hesitated to "campaign in the usual sense" as that was "not the thing to do, I am in the middle of a war, and so are you. We are all in it. We are going to win it, if we keep on with the same splendid cooperation that we have had in the past. It is quite a job, but I am perfectly able to take it, and you are too, until we win."[41]

Roosevelt concluded his remarks to an audience estimated to be at least 30,000 by saying, "And so let me tell you that I am glad to see you, and I hope to come back once more in the next four years—as President of the United States. And as I said before, you will find me just the same, and I'll wear the same sized hat."[42] His good wishes for another four-year term and his hopes for a victory in the great war were both visions he would not live to see. Roosevelt drew the last breaths of his remarkable life on April 12, 1945.

Herbert Hoover

Roosevelt's path to the presidency would be made easier, in the estimation of many, by the presence of Hoover, one of the nation's most unpopular presidents, elected to a single term in 1928.

Going into the 1932 election, Republicans were not blind and deaf to the idea that they faced an uphill battle in holding on to power amidst the deep and damaging economic Depression that gripped the nation. Some of those problems were surfacing as early as June 1931 when reporters noted that Hoover's forays into states such as Indiana, Ohio, and Michigan had been met with apathy. As United Press appraised the situation, "While the 5,000 at the Republican chicken dinner in Indianapolis Monday night were more enthusiastic than any audience he has addressed since becoming President, there was again, as he drove through the city preparatory to leaving for Marion (Ohio) Tuesday, the same apathy and lack of demonstration experienced upon his arrival Monday. Few persons were out to see Mr. Hoover depart, although his (Indianapolis) schedule was widely published. Persons on the curb lifted their hats respectfully, but only occasionally was there a cheer or friendly shout."[43]

Hoover was not going to lose the election for a lack of trying, and he and his wife Lou Henry Hoover made multiple whistle-stop train tours of the nation, having to focus more effort than normal on traditionally Republican areas of the Midwest (including Indiana). One of those stops came on October 5, 1932, in Fort Wayne, where Hoover addressed a surprisingly small crowd estimated at only 2,000 from the rear platform. Declaring that he believed in sportsmanship and statesmanship, Hoover said he sought to address a series of troubling accusations that he believed Roosevelt and the Democratic Party were using against him, particularly in the middle portion of the nation, struck hard by both the Depression and drought. "I regret that the character of these personalities necessitates a direct word from me," the president said. "I shall say now the only harsh word that I have uttered in public office. I hope it will be the last I shall have to say. When you are told that the President of the United States, who by the most sacred trust of our Nation is the President of all the people, a man of your own blood and upbringing, has sat in the White House for the last three years of your misfortune without troubling to know your burdens, without heartaches over your miseries and casualties, without summoning every avenue of skillful assistance irrespective of party or view, without using every ounce of his strength and straining his every nerve to protect and help, without using every possible agency of democracy that would bring aid, without putting aside personal ambition and humbling his pride of opinion, if that would serve—then I say to you that such statements are deliberate, intolerable falsehoods."[44]

Hoover's train also made a stop at Connersville in Fayette County. In brief remarks there, he said, "Tonight I shall speak to you over the radio. I am in hopes that most of you may have an opportunity to listen. I shall then deal with the questions which I believe are necessary to be understood by our people in coming to the judgment which will be required by them within another 10 or 12 days." Hoover said he planned to speak to the "guidance and leadership of the Republican Party which has maintained this nation in its stable form since the days of Abraham Lincoln." Before his train pulled out moments later, the president said, "I thank you for this reception. I tell you again that it is encouraging, and I believe it indicates where your hearts lie."[45] Less than an hour later, in even shorter remarks at Rushville, Hoover praised Senator James Watson (his onetime opponent), "I am glad to have the opportunity of seeing the faces of men and women who sent Senator Watson to Washington to cooperate with our administration. I would like to spend a half an hour with you to tell you of the service that the Senator has been to his country and to the State of Indiana and the friendship that he has shown for me. . . . I shall speak to you tonight from Indianapolis. I hope you may be able to listen in on the radio. This is not a time to talk of national issues, but it is a time to express to you my appreciation for your greeting."[46]

As the 1932 campaign drew to a close, it was apparent from most polls that Hoover was not only going to suffer a defeat, but also possibly a massive rejection by the voters—a collective voice of anger against the economic struggle in the nation. Hoover's forces knew Indiana was friendly territory, and so it was not surprising to find the president in Indianapolis during the final days of the campaign—a place where he had always been able to surface a large audience. Perhaps more surprising was the crowd of more than 15,000 and a noisy torchlight parade of Democrats in Indianapolis on October 28, 1932, who turned out to hear Maryland governor Albert C. Ritchie make the case for the election of Roosevelt and declare that the Hoover administration had "mismanaged" the nation and the only hope for America was in "putting in a Democratic administration which can succeed."[47] Ritchie said Hoover's farm policies had personally harmed thousands of Indiana families and noted, "The Republican administration has had its opportunity. Its policies are in great measure to blame for the unhappy conditions which exist in this land of plenty. . . . The man who tramps the streets looking for work will not put up with the Republican administration any longer; the farmer who has no market for his crop will not; the merchant who finds himself without customers will not; the factory owner whose fires are banked will not."[48]

Hoover's campaign equaled the effort, backing Ritchie's remarks later the same day with a large parade where "ticker tape and scraps of paper rained down on the President and Mrs. Hoover as they were carried through the business section. The President sat back on the folded top of his automobile at times to wave more readily."[49] Leaving downtown for the north side, Hoover then addressed an overflow crowd of 22,000 at the Butler Fieldhouse and gave a lengthy, more than 9,000-word address proclaiming Roosevelt's plans for the nation "all equally untenable." Hoover declared that if he had time, he would "drive his opponent from every solitary position he has taken in this campaign." Reporters noted that "Mr. Hoover received a nine-minute ovation from a colorful crowd that jammed the huge indoor stadium at Butler University to the rafters, and was frequently interrupted as he directed most of his speech to Governor Roosevelt's campaign positions."[50]

Stopping short of calling Roosevelt a liar, Hoover said he took exception to many of the governor's claims, most especially that he had done nothing to remedy the nation's economic woes. "It seems almost incredible that a man, a candidate for the Presidency of the United States, would broadcast such a violation of the truth," Hoover said.[51] While most of his comments were focused on Roosevelt's positions on farm tariffs and currency policy, Hoover remarked that he was disturbed by Roosevelt's positions regarding the Supreme Court and who controls it. "He implies that it is the function of the party in power to control the Supreme Court," Hoover said. "For generations, Republicans and Democrats have made it their most sacred duty to respect and maintain the independence of America's greatest tribunal."[52]

Hoover also fought back against blame Roosevelt was attempting to place on him regarding bonding and loan policies of America's banks.

He said Roosevelt was "trying to establish the idea in the minds of the American people that I am responsible for the bad loans by American bankers and investors in foreign countries. The governor does not inform the American people that most of these bonds are issued from New York State and that governor has done nothing to reform the evil."[53]

Hoover said Roosevelt "ignores the fact that today real wages in the United States are higher than at any other depression period, higher in purchasing power than in any other country in the world. And above all, he dismisses the healing effect of that great agreement by which this country has been kept free from industrial strife and class conflicts." He said Roosevelt's campaign was focused on suppressing "from the American people the knowledge of the undertaking brought about within two months after the (stock market) crash amongst the industries of the United States to divide the existing work in such fashion as to give millions of families some measure of income instead of discharging a large portion of them into destitution, as had always been the case in previous depressions and was the case abroad. He ignores the fact that these agreements have held until this day for the staggering of employment."[54]

"The Governor says nothing had been done," Hoover charged. "The Governor would also suppress the fact of the mobilization of the American people under my direction during the winters of 1930 and '31 of private charity and of public support to relief of distress in every town, village, and hamlet in the United States through which we carried them over these winters without serious suffering or loss, as is proved by the public health statistics of today."[55]

Making his comments personal, Hoover said, "And again the Governor, despite every proof,

keeps reiterating the implication that the measures taken by this administration have had no fruitful result to the common man. He has been told, at least by some of the men who advise him in this campaign, that the gigantic crisis with which the United States was faced was escaped by the narrowest margins and that it was due to unprecedented measures adopted by this administration. . . . Would it not be well that every American citizen should take pride in the fact that America carried this Nation through this crisis safely and soundly and did it as a matter of national and united action? Why cannot the Governor of New York be frank enough to recognize the successful care of the distressed in the United States?"[56]

Hoover cited statistics that employment growth had come as a result of "cooperative action amongst our citizens"; more than 95 percent of the savings deposits in banks are secure; that 20 million borrowers "who otherwise would have been bankrupt by destructive pressures from forced selling of their assets in order to pay their debts have been protected"; that seventy million life insurance policies have been sustained in their vitality; and foreclosure of hundreds of thousands of home and farm mortgages have been prevented. "Those are national accomplishments for which the whole American people are proud," Hoover said.[57]

Making one last pitch for Indiana votes, Hoover's campaign train rolled across northern Indiana on November 4, 1932, just four days before the election, for four stops in De Kalb, Elkhart, La Porte, and Lake Counties. Starting out with greetings before about 500 people assembled at Garrett at 6:30 a.m., the president's train reached tiny Nappanee (about fifteen miles southwest of Goshen) at 7:31 a.m., where Hoover spoke from the train to an audience that included a small smattering of Amish residents. The audience of about 10,000 more than doubled the normal population of Nappanee. As the *Elkhart Truth* reported, "It was a thrilling sight as the presidential special came into sight in the east. The sun had risen just far enough to show above the buildings east of the station. The crowd peered down the track toward the approaching engine, which was enveloped in steam and white smoke on which the sun's rays glinted prettily."[58]

Hoover said, "I want to express to you the appreciation I have for your coming out so early and coming down to the station to give us this greeting. It is encouraging, and it is very heartening." He added, "This is not an occasion for a political address or a discussion of national issues. I am going to try to do that this afternoon and again tonight, and as most of you, I have no doubt, are able to get to the radio, you will hear a lot of it then."[59]

Before Hoover's train pulled out of the station after a less than five-minute visit, local Republican leaders prevailed upon him to shake the hand of ninety-four-year-old Charles Klaus of Nappanee, who told the president he had voted for every Republican nominee since 1860. Hoover asked him for his vote again, noting that like President Lincoln in 1864, he was seeking a second vote from Mr. Klaus.[60] A thirty-piece Nappanee High School band played as the Hoover special moved on, and one local report indicated that "the first impression made by President Hoover on many who were at such vantage points that they saw him closely was that he appeared very worn and tired. His face was deeply lined."[61]

A short time later, Hoover's train made a "water stop" at the La Porte County settlement of Wellsboro (about ten miles south of La Porte), and he noted the early hour of the occasion: "I have to get up pretty early to do my job ordinar-

ily, but you get up earlier than I do. Don't you think this is pretty early in the morning to begin to make a speech?"[62] A farmer in overalls standing near the train asked the president to "give a speech," and Hoover smiled and invited him to listen to his radio broadcast later that day from Springfield, Illinois. As the train moved west, it slowed near the settlement of Woodville, outside of Chesterton, so the president could wave at Hoosiers who sat and stood on their cars and trucks "lining the country roads and fields for some distance."[63]

By 9 a.m., Hoover's train had reached Gary, and he expanded upon his remarks to "the greatest audience in Gary history" from a platform a short distance from the rear of a Baltimore & Ohio special train inside Gateway Park. "The crowd variously estimated from 30,000 to 50,000, heard a vigorous defense of the Republican tariff and immigration policies as protecting American manufacturers and American workers from foreign attacks," the *Gary Post-Tribune* reported. "Amplifiers carried the President's voice to the crowd that formed a sea of faces below his speaking platform. The thousands spread out toward Fourth Avenue, jammed like sardines along the highline at the rear of the platform where police were almost powerless to handle the press of humanity."[64]

"I doubt whether any President has ever received such a greeting as you are giving to me this morning," Hoover said. "It is heartening. It is encouraging in this fight. It is an indication of the action which you will take on the 8th day of November."[65]

Hoover, recognizing he was in the heart of the steel belt, declared that "the workers, the backbone of the nation, must support the Republican Party, its protective tariff policies and its immigration policies to protect itself."[66]

"We have passed through three long years of national crisis," the president said. "These difficulties of our nation were brought on us from abroad. The administration in Washington has taken unprecedented measures calling into action the full powers of the federal government in the protection of our people from this invasion. We have succeeded in the defense of our people from the invasion of fear and interference from abroad, and we have preserved the institutions of the United States. We first fought a great battle of defense. We have turned our great instrumentalities and measures into an offensive all along the economic front and are restoring employment and agriculture to the United States. We are able at this moment to say to you that men are returning to their jobs at the rate of 500,000 per month, that, since the adjournment of the Democratic House of Representatives and the cessation of their interferences with our program of recovery, we have returned over 1 million men to their jobs."[67]

Hoover said there was "one fundamental difference between our program and that of our opponents (and) . . . that is, the continued protection of our industries from foreign goods. If it were not for the protective tariff today there would be millions more unemployed in our country. If we were to let down the tariff barriers which surround you and which protect you, we should have a new and worse depression."[68] He concluded by reminding the assembled voters that tariff and immigration policies protected jobs and warned those who might possibly be wooed by Roosevelt's message of change: "If you desire a change by which immigration shall be lifted and men entered into this country to apply for jobs at the gates of your factories with you, you only have to vote for our opponents"[69]

"We are fighting for the protection of the American people in their homes and firesides," Hoover explained. "We have no other interest than to maintain the stability of our own country and restore its employment from the shocks which it has received from outside our borders. We have built up protection to you in a score of directions, and those protections and those measures are at this moment working steadily for the restoration of our country."[70]

When the end of the 1932 campaign came on Election Day, the results were staggering. Roosevelt had pulled a rare upset win in Indiana, with a victory margin rivaling what Hoover had posted just four years earlier in dispatching Alfred Smith. In addition, Democrats were swept into virtual control of all of Indiana state government, and voters also retired Hoover's onetime foe-turned-ally, Watson.

As Roosevelt faced his first re-election campaign in 1936, Republican speculation arose that perhaps Hoover would be willing or interested in making a second run at Roosevelt. Hoover's widely reported Fort Wayne speech on April 4, 1936, offered his assessment of what he viewed as the failures of the New Deal and began to articulate for the Republicans the idea that the New Deal was "an invader of private liberty and a corrupter of clear thinking."[71] While in Fort Wayne, the former president addressed two audiences—one a supportive group of Young Republicans and another larger audience of about 4,500 at the Gospel Temple (the latter speech broadcast nationally by NBC and Mutual Radio).

"The most dangerous invasions of liberty by the New Deal have not been in the economic field, as violent as they are," the former president said. "The Supreme Court has the power to check that. The corruption of clear thinking is in the long view far more insidious and destructive to the safeguards of America."[72] Advocating for a "free, alive and unpolluted" society, Hoover said the nation "slumps whenever this is mis-informed, suppressed or intimated. That is the most certain lesson of history. They who have the thirst for power over the daily lives of the people in order to protect themselves from the political consequences of their actions are driven irresistibly and without peace to a greater and greater control of the nation's thinking."[73]

Adding to his thesis, Hoover said, "Those who seek for power thus move easily from propaganda to raucous denunciation. From that it is but a step to intimidation. And we witness today the seizure of private communications of innocent persons and the press. That is gross violation of the spirit of the Bill of Rights. But Americans are not easily intimidated. A number of the unter-rified have taken to sending me pungent tele-grams, expressing the prayer that some New Deal agency will seize them and commit every word of them to memory. This may be the modern method of constitutional right of petition—at least of bringing petitions under the eyes of the New Deal."[74] Hoover said Roosevelt and his "New Deal subordinates" were using smoke screens and "squirt guns of propaganda" to stifle disagreement or dissent. "These are not the answers that add to understanding," he said. "They are not the bold answer of responsible leaders expounding their point of view and offering their solutions. And slogans do not even pinch hit for facts."[75]

Hoover said he and many others had attempted in the last election to charge their opponents "with the intention to introduce these foreign creeds of regimentation, Socialism and Fascism into America. They denied it. No proof is needed after three years of these attempts to so-called planned economy. This government in business; this breaking down of constitutional safeguards by centralization of power; this reduction of Congress to a rubber stamp; this substitution of personal government of men for government laws, and these attacks upon the Constitution. The American people have a right to know and to know whether the New Dealers will abandon these attacks upon the American system. They should stand up and repent or they should defend their intentions."[76]

In remarks that likely fueled speculation that Hoover was contemplating a run in 1936, he sought to "set the record straight" about the nation's economic conditions in 1932–33, his last year in office. He said credible economists believed in that year that "America was shaking itself clear of the Depression . . . and it was the uncertainties following the election (of Roosevelt) that set back this progress. We alone of all great nations were set back (in 1932–33). Most other nations continued upward."[77]

Hoover was not a candidate in 1936 but remained an active public speaker. He made a June 1939 speech at Earlham College in Richmond, the contents of which suggested he was continuing a personal campaign to redefine the record of his presidency and his time in public life.

Near the end of his life, Hoover made an appearance on a nationwide radio program hosted from South Bend by former University of Notre Dame law school dean Clarence E. Manion. During his remarks, Hoover offered " unwavering support" to President Dwight D. Eisenhower regarding American and Western involvement in managing Berlin amidst Communist forces in post-World War II Germany. Hoover said Eisenhower's position of "firmness can bring a halt to the creeping Communist conquest of western Europe" and again criticized failures to hold Russia to agreements to support free elections in Poland, Czechoslovakia, Hungary, Yugoslavia, and Romania. "We stood by and witnessed the death of freedom in five nations," the now eighty-six-year-old Hoover said. "At this moment we are again confronted with precisely the same Communist concept of agreements. The principles of decent relations between nations and the moral standards vital to a peaceful world are at stake."[78]

Hoover said that "as never before in my recollection have our leaders and the American people been so united in their feelings that the time has come for a determined stand. . . . The unity of the free world is at stake today. The agreements as to Berlin must be upheld. They can only be modified by mutual consent in a fashion which truly protects the free people of Berlin and gives hope of a step toward peace."[79]

The South Bend appearance was typical of the former president, who remained active in Republican Party politics for many years and at one time held the record as the longest-living former president. Hoover died in New York City on October 20, 1964. He was ninety.

Alfred M. Landon

Kansas governor Landon gained national attention for the first time by being the only Republican governor to win re-election in the Democratic landslide of 1932. Less conservative than other Republicans, Landon supported certain aspects of the Roosevelt New Deal and enjoyed the support of some labor organizations in Kansas. Landon became the GOP standard-bearer in 1936, not by winning the most primaries—the few that were held were dominated by conservative Senator William Borah of Idaho—but by dominating the Republican National Convention in Cleveland. When Landon selected Chicago publisher Frank Knox as his running mate, a handful of other Republicans withdrew and threw their support behind Landon, thus ending the bid of the seventy-year-old Borah.

Going into the fall campaign, Landon faced a huge task in trying to keep Roosevelt from winning a second term, along with galvanizing a splintered Republican Party struggling to counter the aggressive New Deal programs the Democrats had pushed through to address the lingering Depression—entering its eighth year in 1936. Although parts of his New Deal program were still locked up in congressional or court battles, Roosevelt had initiated both unemployment benefits for the staggering number of Americans out of work and the nation's first Social Security program for the elderly. Both programs were popular and added to the growing affection for Roosevelt. The positive feelings toward Roosevelt, however, were not universal, and there were many Indiana Republicans who were eager to end Roosevelt's run at one term. Both parties focused on Indiana for 1936—a state both campaigns considered "crucial" according to Indiana historian James Philip Fadely. As Fadely wrote, "The Great Depression had stirred up politicians and voters. . . . The Hoosier connection to the national campaign derived from Indiana's electoral importance and status as a borderline state in the political battles of the 1930s. The presidential contest of 1936 in Indiana was characterized by the substantial influence of newspaper editors, by campaign whistle stops along the railroads to bring the candidates close to the people, and by the old-fashioned excitement of politics evident in colorful parades and political symbols."[80]

Landon's campaign made fourteen total stops in Indiana in 1936, many speeches via the rear platform of the "Sunflower Special" (named for the famous state flower of Kansas), and also through spectacular parades in both Indianapolis and Peru. On September 11 Landon's train made quick stops in Gary, Valparaiso, Plymouth, Warsaw, and Fort Wayne, drawing large crowds at each stop. This was the era of radio, not television, and large masses still turned out to see the candidates in person.

For the first stop at Gary, a smaller-than-expected crowd of 3,000 showed up to hear Landon promise a "fighting" and "fiery" campaign. At Valparaiso, more than 6,000 citizens jammed the area around the Pennsylvania depot, including the city's two lone surviving Civil War veterans. As the *Valparaiso Vidette-Messenger* reported, city and county police were in charge of handling the crowd with the "conspicuous absence" of the Indiana State Police (the latter fact reflecting Indiana's highly partisan position of the 1930s and state government and its agencies fully in control of a powerful Democratic Governor, McNutt).

Things did not go so well at Valparaiso, however, as the train conductor missed the mark and went past the bulk of the gathered crowd. "Handling of the train by Pennsylvania trainmen brought severe criticism from the crowd," the *Vidette-Messenger* reported. "Instead of stopping the observation coach somewhere near the depot, the train halted so that the rear coach was in proximity to the freight depot some 200 feet away from the main crowd. Report was current that the conductor of the train signaled the engineer to proceed ahead, but the order was not obeyed for some reason. As a result, only about one-fifth of the crowd was able to hear the governor."[81] Problems persisted. The public address system attached to the train to amplify Landon's voice to the large crowd worked at Gary, but quit working at Valparaiso and did not work at any of the other stops that day, and so only those closest to the train could hear his remarks.[82] News reports indicated Landon remarked about the nature of his whistle-stop campaign, "I know all you folks came to town to look me over. Well, it works both ways. I am glad to see you, too. I know you couldn't all come to visit me on my front porch in Topeka, so I am coming to you for a visit and bringing my back porch with me. This will be the back porch campaign and a fighting campaign for good government in which all Republicans, Independents and Democrats will take part."[83]

In remarks perhaps reflecting the GOP's struggle to define its collective reaction to Roosevelt's New Deal agenda, Landon said, "The government we are striving for will be a fair, just and honest government concerned with the rights and economic opportunities of the average man and concerned with how much it will take out of our pockets. You know we all pay taxes whether we know it or not."[84] A statement about the value of "good government" and "low taxes" was nothing new, but perhaps not the strongest statement to draw voters away from a Roosevelt plan many felt was helping the nation to turn the corner.

Not everything went wrong in Valparaiso. The local media reported that rain held off until Landon's train had pulled out of the station and most of the crowd had begun to disperse. Further, "Landon and his famous smile made a distinct hit with the crowd," the *Vidette-Messenger* reported. "One lady was heard to remark, 'Hasn't he a sweet face?' . . . Yesterday's crowd was a distinctly Republican gathering. A sunflower badge, emblematic of the state of Kansas, graced the person of practically every man, woman and child in the vast throng."[85]

Landon's stop in Warsaw coincided with a meeting of the Indiana Republican Editorial Association taking place elsewhere in Kosciusko County at nearby Lake Wawasee. Landon acknowledged the editors in his remarks at the Warsaw depot: "I know that the Indiana Republican Editorial Association is meeting near this city today. Indiana and Kansas have the reputation of producing the best newspaper men of any two states in the Union. I am not saying this as the trite expression of a campaign orator trying to curry favor with the local community, but every newspaper man in the country knows that it is true. We are proud in Kansas of our country press. It has been one of the great influences in making Kansas the fine state it is and I know the same thing is true in Indiana."[86]

Later at Fort Wayne, Landon told a gathering of 25,000 Hoosiers, "I don't blame this present administration for trying to hide behind a non-political campaign plea," referring to Roosevelt's "non-political" campaign in Indiana and elsewhere that was filled more with "official" visits and duties rather than political rallies. Landon said he would take such an approach himself "if I had to defend such a record as they have made in Washington in the last three years. It is easy enough to go out and promise this and that to cure all our economic ills in one fell swoop. But big talk is always easy."[87]

"To me this is serious business," Landon continued, "so I have weighed very carefully every word and every pledge that I have made in this campaign. I shall continue to do so. Party platforms to me are not to be thrown away in the waste paper basket after the election."[88]

A little more than a month later, the Sunflower Special was back in the Midwest for a series of stops. His train passed Roosevelt's along a rail line outside Grand Rapids, Michigan, while the two men crisscrossed Indiana and Michigan. In Indiana on October 15, Landon's train made stops in Attica, Lafayette, Logansport, Peru, Wabash, Huntington, Fort Wayne, and Kendallville. Entering Indiana from Sturgis, Michigan, his first stop was Kendallville in Noble County, where 3,000 locals gathered to hear Landon return to his theme of warning about the cost of

Roosevelt's New Deal. He declared: "The bonded indebtedness of government is in reality a first mortgage on every home and farm in this nation. It is just as real and far more certain of collection than if it were recorded in your courthouse. It rests largely on the backs of property owners, farmers and wage earners. I am opposed to waste and debt because I am opposed to the ultimate confiscation of farms and home."[89]

Telling the assembled audience at Kendallville that as Roosevelt had "played Santa Claus" via New Deal with the hard-earned money of farmers and workers, Landon said, "New Deal misadministration has hurt the farmer more than anyone else. Its wasteful practices are in direct contrast with the good farm methods of Indiana agriculture. The present administration has piled up an intolerable burden of public debt. It rests largely on the backs of the property owners, farmers and wage earners. They cannot pass taxes on to someone else as other income producing groups can."[90]

Subsequent stops at Huntington and Wabash drew audiences estimated between 7,000 and 8,000, but it was Peru that managed to capture the pageantry of the campaign. There, thirteen circus elephants (and the GOP's favorite mascot) were arrayed around the large downtown crowd, each bearing a letter spelling out the words, "Welcome Landon." Landon noticed, telling the crowd, "They say an elephant never forgets. Well, I never will forget the cordial reception given me by the citizens of Peru and its vicinity."[91]

The elephant idea worked so well in Peru that it was repeated later in October for a two-day visit in Indianapolis that brought larger-than-expected crowds for the Republican nominee. While not stopping in Delphi in Clinton County, Landon's train slowed so he could wave to several thousand supporters gathering along the rail line. As the *Indianapolis News* reported, "The swing down the Wabash valley, with its familiar sycamores, seemed to capture the fancy and admiration of Landon."[92] The tone of Landon's speeches was harsher than his first Indiana tour, reporters noted, as it became more evident that catching Roosevelt was proving every bit as difficult as originally feared.

Days later Landon's two-day stop in Indianapolis represented what Fadely and other historians considered the "high point" of the GOP campaign for 1936. In town to give a speech outlining his foreign policy positions, the campaign was overwhelmed by the large and enthusiastic crowds that appeared, exceeding what they had experienced in other cities before Indianapolis. Landon was welcomed to the capital city by a blue-ribbon welcoming committee that included Indiana's own Will H. Hays, president of the powerful Motion Picture Producers and Distributors of America. Fadely reported, "Indianapolis Republicans gave a parade for the nominee in the afternoon that ranks as one of the city's premier political events. The crowds along the parade route were described as 'tremendous' by the *New York Times*, while Monument Circle was packed with approximately 100,000 people. The crowds were not only large but enthusiastic as well in their support for Landon, with the only booing, which was mixed with cheers, coming in the black district of the city."[93]

"Landon himself led the parade for twelve blocks," Fadely found, "from the Walker Theatre to the Circle, waving his hat to acknowledge the roar of cheers, and then reviewed the procession from a balcony of the Claypool Hotel."[94] Fadely wrote that the Indianapolis appearances "stood in stark contrast to the lackluster reception Landon had received in many areas of the nation during the autumn months of 1936," with some Republicans openly distancing themselves from what was shaping up as a Democratic landslide that would bury Landon. Landon, suffering from a "throat irritation" because of the grueling nature of his campaign, "made no rear platform appearances on the way to Indianapolis . . . and left the train with a muffler wrapped around his throat." While scheduled to rest at the hotel until his evening speech in Indianapolis, he briefly changed course and attended a local Republican luncheon and made a few remarks.[95]

After the big, rousing parade through downtown Indianapolis, Landon addressed an audience estimated at 14,000 gathered inside the Coliseum Building at the Indiana State Fairgrounds. Landon said he did not intend to be "a talkative man" related to foreign policy, "But I do propose to appoint as Secretary of State a competent man grounded in sound American principles. I do propose to build a morale in the department and the foreign service by regarding merit as it deserves. I shall encourage with all my power the cause of peace. I shall not merely talk about my hatred of war."[96]

Quoting President Theodore Roosevelt, Landon warned against the nation becoming "a meddlesome Matty," supporting a more isolationist approach to world affairs. Landon said, "Only last year Mr. Roosevelt over-rode the neutrality legislation he himself has sponsored. His action made it probable that if war had come, we could have been involved" and noted that under Roosevelt Americans were left in question about what the nation's foreign policy actually is. He accused Roosevelt of "attempting to put the United States in the forefront of the sanctionist powers against Italy," thereby making the probability of war more likely.[97]

Landon said his agenda included mediation and arbitration to settle disputes, lowered trade barriers, and abandonment of the League of Nations. Declaring the League of Nations a failure, Landon said the nations of the world were more divided into "two great camps" than ever before, and "if the method provided in the League covenant were really adopted, these two camps would become hostile alliances, more or less equal, in another terrible war tragedy. We cannot use war to end war" and that America must remain "an oasis of peace" standing against the totalitarianism of Communist and Fascist dictators. He added that development of a neutrality policy was "not an absolute guarantee of peace." He said it was "one of the great hopes" for America and noted that "isolation is unfair to our own people and impossible."[98]

"In these high resolves, God helping us, we shall protect America against war," the governor said. "And we shall do our full part to maintain the healing of peace throughout the world."[99]

Landon's Indianapolis speech was broadcast nationally by CBS and NBC Radio, and Hoosier Republicans made sure the audio included repeated breaks for applause in Landon's speech. The next morning Landon attended worship services at Broadway United Methodist Church in Indianapolis before departing the state. His best effort behind him, Election Day brought not only the expected loss to Roosevelt across the nation, but also a rare defeat in normally Republican Indiana, where Roosevelt rolled up a 57 to 42 percent victory over Landon, the latter carrying only twenty of the state's ninety-two counties. While Landon's totals were better than those produced by Hoover four years earlier, it was still nothing short of a devastating loss.

Landon never again ran for public office, and after his term as governor ended, he returned to the oil industry. He enjoyed a long life, living until the age of one hundred, passing away on October 12, 1987, in Topeka, Kansas.

Wendell Willkie

Republican Willkie and other presidential hopefuls in 1940, including Indiana's powerful former Democratic governor McNutt, stood waiting to learn what Roosevelt planned to do about seeking a third term. GOP backers of Willkie were incensed that Roosevelt would consider breaking tradition and running for a third term in 1940, but with world events changing rapidly from the September 1939 overrun of Poland by Nazi German forces from the west and Communist Russian forces from the east, issues were unsettled. As historian Ross Gregory wrote, "Roosevelt of course did not designate anyone as his successor, or perhaps it could be said that he endorsed everyone. It is at least remotely possible that Roosevelt all along wished to run again. He confided a clear intent to no one, preferring instead

IHS, MARTIN'S PHOTO SHOP, P 129

A Terre Haute woman proudly stands by a portrait she painted of GOP presidential candidate Wendell Willkie, August 1940.

to 'divide and conquer,'"[100] especially among Democratic hopefuls such as McNutt.

By spring 1940, events in Europe had changed dramatically as the Nazi advance continued, and open warfare broke out between Germany, France and England. France would soon fall, and Americans grew in worry about their British brethren seemingly next on the Nazi agenda. Enter Wendell L. Willkie. A Hoosier by all accounts—raised in Elwood, married to a Rushville woman, and holding degrees from Indiana University—Willkie had gained a national reputation as "a vigorous fighter, an eloquent and perceptive defender of private enterprise, and a generally gracious contestant"[101] for his work battling the Tennessee Valley Authority on behalf of his employers at Commonwealth & Southern Corporation. Gregory concluded that "by arousing the interest of 'movers' within the Republican party and by sparking his own thoughts about changing careers, Willkie's quarrel with TVA became the avenue for his entry into politics."[102] Willkie's appeal, sometimes based in part on his disheveled appearance with a wrinkled shirt or suit, his hair out of order, but with an exuding level of confidence, seemed to grow amidst a lackluster field of Republican alternatives.

The expected GOP field included Senator Robert A. Taft of Ohio and New York City District Attorney Thomas E. Dewey. Taft was the undisputed leader of the party's conservative and isolationist wing, while Dewey had carved out a reputation as a tough law-and-order politician who battled the New York mob. A few others waited "in the wings" for whatever opportunities may arise, including Senator Arthur Vandenberg of Michigan, Senate Minority Leader Charles McNary of Oregon, and Governor Arthur James of Pennsylvania. Only twelve Republican primaries were slated for 1940—Indiana not among

them—meaning that only about a third of the total delegates needed for the GOP nomination could be earned via retail politics. Not surprisingly, an "outsider" candidate such as Willkie, with no prior political campaign experience, did not enter any of the primaries and only began to emerge as a more palatable alternative as events in Europe went from bad to worse with the fall of France. Taft's isolationist message about staying out of the war stood in stark contrast to Willkie's vocal support of being the supplier of the battle for democracy and that America's value came in standing with and supporting her militarily (but stopping short of declaring war and enjoining the battle with Germany). It was Dewey, however, who did best in the primaries, rolling up wins in ten of the twelve contests and more than doubling the popular vote Taft attracted.

When the GOP convention opened in Philadelphia in late June, the nomination was still considered "wide open," and a true convention battle was expected. Dewey led on the first three ballots taken, with Taft and the "We Want Willkie" backers in the mix. By the fourth ballot, however, the matter was settled in favor of Willkie, as he took his first lead with the defection of delegates from Michigan, Pennsylvania, and New York and held on to win the nomination on the sixth and final ballot. McNary was easily nominated for vice president on a single ballot. Many of the nation's influential editors had made a big difference as well, spotlighting Willkie as a good alternative to the still young thirty-eight-year-old Dewey and the perceived as too unyielding Taft. Analysts believed Willkie's favorable views of some portions of the Roosevelt's New Deal program and his forceful support of Britain, sans direct American military involvement, bode well for the GOP's chances to deny Roosevelt a third term as voters would feel less dissonance moving from Roosevelt to Willkie since their world and domestic views were not that sharply contrasted.

In terms of campaigning, it was Willkie who actually engaged the process, not Roosevelt. Willkie campaigned heavily north of the Ohio River and east of the Mississippi River, with only a few occasional trips West. Roosevelt visited only four states, Indiana included, for "inspection trips" to assess the ongoing drought in the nation, attempting and succeeding in a purely "Rose Garden strategy." Willkie's campaign would start, of course, in Indiana on a blistering hot day on August 17, 1940, in Elwood.

As the headlines of the *Elwood Call-Leader* carried the troubling news of resumed German bombing of various sites in England, details were emerging about the hometown send-off the Willkie campaign had planned. "A few crews of 150 men began work today on the mammoth semi-circle platform which will seat Wendell L. Willkie and numerous other notables when he returns to Elwood," the *Call-Leader* reported. "The platform is located on the east edge of Callaway Park. The structure will face the shaded groves in the west, will be 149 feet long in front and 57 feet at the deepest point in the rear. One shade tree has been left standing near the inside center of the platform. A huge awning will hang overhead to protect the dignitaries from the sun."[103] Workmen were also setting out thirty thousand folding chairs, trimming trees, leveling the ground in various places in the park, and constructing footbridges over the creek for the expected throng.

Before arriving at Elwood, Willkie's plane carrying him from a short vacation at Colorado Springs, Colorado, arrived in Indianapolis on August 16, 1940, to a surprisingly large welcoming party of 55,000. As the *Indianapolis Star* reported, "In spite of efforts of police, the crowd closed in around the plane when Willkie appeared in its doorway. There were wild cheers and the nominee, his face beaming, waved a salute. Republican dignitaries there to greet the nominee officially were shoved around in the jam as the police took charge of Mr. and Mrs. Willkie and edged them to automobiles to take the entire party to Rushville."[104] Willkie's party later drove a fourteen-mile motorcade from the airport along Washington Street (US 40) to the east side of Indianapolis before departing for Rush County. The *Star* reported the caravan was stopped briefly at Irvington, where more than 10,000 people jammed the area of Washington and Ritter Streets for a chance to see Willkie.[105]

Back in Elwood, the town fathers had granted 138 permits for vendors, more than 100 who planned to sell food, drink, and other concessions in the park, and the others who planned to set up along State Road 15 for the Willkie parade downtown. The local newspaper, however, was quick to

Willkie campaign button, circa 1940s.

point out the city already had thirty-eight eating establishments permanently located in the city. The parade was a simple, yet grand affair. Only eight cars were in the official parade, led by the Indiana University marching band and flanked by Indiana State Police troopers on motorcycles. *Life* magazine published one of its most memorable political photos on August 26, 1940, with a beaming Willkie standing up in his open-air car in the blazing 102-degree sunlight, surrounded by a crowd estimated at more than 200,000 that choked tiny Elwood. The parade stopped briefly at Central High School along Main Street, where Willkie greeted a large crowd and then moved on to the park north of downtown.

At Callaway Park, once in place upon the specially constructed stand, Willkie stated his intent: "Here I give you an outline of the politi-cal philosophy that is in my heart. We are here today to represent a sacred cause—the preservation of American democracy. Obviously, I cannot lead this cause alone. I need the help of every American—Republican, Democrat or Independent—Jew, Catholic, or Protestant—people of every color, creed and race."[106] Willkie made clear that he was not your typical Republican nominee: "Party lines are down," he said. "Nothing could make that clearer than the nomination by the Republicans of a liberal Democrat who changed his party affiliation because he found democracy in the Republican Party and not in the New Deal party. And as the leader of the Republican Party let me say this—We go into our campaign as into a crusade. Revitalized and reunited, and joined by millions who share in our cause, we dedicate ourselves to the principles of American liberty,

Women supporters of Willkie gather outside of the Vigo County Willkie Club in Terre Haute.

IHS, MARTIN'S PHOTO SHOP, P 129

and we shall fight this campaign on the basis of those principles, not on the basis of hate, jealousy, or personalities. The leaders of the Republican Party, in Congress and in the party organization, have made me that pledge. I have given that pledge to them. And I extend it to all who will join in this cause. What we need in this country is a new leadership that believes in the destiny of America. I represent here today the forces that will bring that leadership to you."[107]

Willkie said he had come to Elwood because "I have an engagement to keep in this town. It was made a long time ago with a young man I knew well. This young man was born and raised in Elwood. He attended the Elwood public schools. He worked in your factories and stores. He started the practice of law in your courts. As I look back upon him, I realize that he had plenty of faults. But he had also three steadfast convictions. He was devoted to the ideal of individual liberty. He hated all special privileges and forms of oppression. And he knew without any doubt that the greatest country on earth was the United States of America."[108]

Willkie said, "I still adhere to those convictions," and "today I pledge my word that I shall never let them down. In former days America was described as a country in which any young man might become President. It is still that kind of country. . . . We must fight to preserve America as a country in which every girl and boy has every opportunity for any achievement."[109]

Recalling that his grandparents lived in Germany and fought for their democratic rights there, he quickly turned his remarks to concerns across the sea. "Today, also, people are being oppressed in Europe," he said. "The story of the barbarous and worse than medieval persecution of the Jews—a race that has done so much to improve the culture of these countries and our

Front page of the October 29, 1940, Indianapolis News *featuring articles on Willkie's visit to the city.*

own—is the most tragic in human history. Today there are millions of refugees who desire sanctuary and opportunity in America, just as in my grandparents' time . . . their misery and suffering make us resolve to preserve our country as a land free of hate and bitterness, of racial and class distinction. I pledge you that kind of America."[110]

Looking out across his massive Elwood audience, Willkie said, "Today we meet in a typical American town. The quiet streets, the pleasant fields that lie outside, the people going casually about their business, seem far removed from the shattered cities, the gutted buildings, and the stricken people of Europe. It is hard for us to realize that the war in Europe can affect our daily lives. Instinctively we turn aside from the recurring conflicts over there, the diplomatic intrigue, the shifts of power that the last war failed to end. Yet instinctively also—we know that we are not isolated from those suffering people. We live in the same world as they, and we are created in the same image. In all the democracies that have recently fallen, the people were living the same peaceful lives that we live. They had similar ideals of human freedom. Their methods of trade and exchange were similar to ours. Try as we will, we cannot brush the pitiless picture of their destruction from our vision, or escape the profound effects of it upon the world in which we live."[111]

Willkie said it was unwise to commit the nation to a course of action regarding its position in the world with so many issues unresolved and so many "unknowns" still at hand. "The best that we can do is to decide what principle shall guide us," Willkie said. "For me, that principle can be simply defined: In the foreign policy of the United States, as in its domestic policy, I would do everything to defend American democracy and I would refrain from doing anything that would injure it. We must not permit our emotions—our sympathies or hatreds—to move us from that fixed principle."[112]

Saying he was supportive of Roosevelt's position that the nation keep its commitment to Britain and its battle with Germany, "But I cannot follow the President in his conduct of foreign affairs in this critical time. There have been occasions when many of us have wondered if he is deliberately inciting us to war. I trust that I have made it plain that in the defense of America, and of our liberties, I should not hesitate to stand for war. But like a great many other Americans I saw what war was like at first hand in 1917. I know what war can do to demoralize civil liberties at home. And I believe it to be the

first duty of a President to try to maintain peace. But Mr. Roosevelt has not done this. He has dabbled in inflammatory statements and manufactured panics. Of course, we in America like to speak our minds freely, but this does not mean that at a critical period in history our President should cause bitterness and confusion for the sake of a little political oratory. The President's attacks on foreign powers have been useless and dangerous. He has courted a war for which the country is hopelessly unprepared—and which it emphatically does not want. He has secretly meddled in the affairs of Europe, and he has even unscrupulously encouraged other countries to hope for more help than we are able to give."[113]

Willkie said the nation required candid talk. "We have been sitting as spectators of a great tragedy" in Europe and "the action on the stage of history has been relentless." Declaring that "the French people were just as brave and intelligent as the Germans" with strong armies and material resources needed to protect themselves, "yet the Germans crushed France like an eggshell."[114]

"The reason is now clear: The fault lay with France herself," Willkie said, "opening the way to Hitler."[115]

"In this tragedy let us find our lesson," Willkie said. "The foreign policy of the United

Willkie campaign postcard showing the change in Rushville, Indiana, since the candidate made the town his campaign headquarters in 1940.

IHS, JAY SMALL POSTCARD COLLECTION, P 391

IHS, J. C. ALLEN AND SON COLLECTION, 1926–52, P 490, GIFT OF THE CENTER FOR AGRICULTURE SCIENCE AND HERITAGE, INC.

Likenesses of the 1940 presidential candidates were made from pure lard and displayed in the Agriculture and Horticulture Building at the Indiana State Fair.

States begins right here in our own land. The first task of our country in its international affairs is to become strong at home. We must regain prosperity, restore the independence of our people, and protect our defensive forces." Seeking to draw a distinction between himself and Roosevelt, despite Willkie's at least partial support of certain aspects of the New Deal, the Republican nominee was bold to say: "The promises of the present administration cannot lead you to victory against Hitler, or against anyone else. This administration stands for principles exactly opposite to mine. It does not preach the doctrine of growth. It preaches the doctrine of division. We are not asked to make more for ourselves. We are asked to divide among ourselves that which we already have. The New Deal doctrine does not seek risk, it seeks safety."[116]

In remarks that would reflect the still influential progressive attitudes in the Republican Party (later to be replaced by evermore conserva-

tive views in elections to follow), Willkie outlined his vision of what being a liberal meant, including support for appropriate business regulation and the opposition of monopolies; collective bargaining for workers; maintenance of minimum wage standards and maximum safety standards for workers; federal regulation of interstate utilities, securities markets, and banking; federal pensions and "adequate old age benefits"; unemployment insurance; policies that "equalize the lot of the farmer, with that of the manufacturer"; and full extension of rural electrification.

"When the present administration came to power in 1933, we heard a lot about the forgotten man," Willkie declared. "The government, we were told, must care for those who had no other means of support. With this proposition all of us agreed. And we still hold firmly to the principle that those whom private industry cannot support must be supported by government agency, whether federal or state. But I want to ask anyone in this audience who is, or has been, on relief whether the support that the government gives him is enough. Is it enough for the free and able-bodied American to be given a few scraps of cash or credit with which to keep himself and his children just this side of starvation and nakedness? Is that what the forgotten man wanted us to remember?"[117]

Willkie said he had a "grave charge" to make against the Roosevelt administration: "I charge that the course this administration is following will lead us, like France, to the end of the road. I say that this course will lead us to economic disintegration and dictatorship. I say that we must substitute for the philosophy of spending, the philosophy of production. You cannot buy freedom. You must make freedom. This is a serious charge. It is not made lightly. And it cannot be lightly avoided by the opposition."[118] The latter remark—about avoiding a discussion—reflected Willkie's growing frustration with Roosevelt's approach that he did intend to engage in "purely political" exchanges in 1940.

It was a remarkable speech, one in which Republicans across the nation listening by radio and later viewing by newsreel were excited and intrigued about their chances to retake the White House. Willkie's strategy would be greatly tested, however, as Roosevelt retained his strategy of tending to the nation's business, too busy and too concerned about the world's growing troubles to engage in the political discourse presidential campaigns require.

The day after all the hoopla in Elwood, the *Call-Leader* reported that five hundred people "were treated for prostrations, cuts inflicted by broken bottles, blisters and heart ailments" during the Willkie event.[119] A corps of one hundred out-of-town doctors assisted Elwood officials both at Callaway Park, where many fainted

from heat exhaustion, to those more seriously ill transported to Mercy Hospital. Police were also busy, as thirty-seven "drunks" and two "nationally-known pick-pockets" were arrested by local and state police.[120] "Elwood removed its Willkie day dress suit today and settled down to normalcy for the first time in six weeks," the *Call-Leader* reported. "Workmen were clearing Callaway Park of scattered papers, tin cans, pop bottles and all debris this morning. There was little to indicate that 200,000 people have been here only two days ago. The show was over, but the memory will remain. It will endure forever as the greatest day in Elwood's history."[121] For his part, Willkie boarded a train for the short ride south to Rushville, where he "inspected" his five Indiana farms. A United Press correspondent reported, "The tour of his 1,403 acres of farmland today was planned primarily to give newsreel cameramen an opportunity to portray Willkie, lawyer, former school teacher and utilities executive, as a man of the soil. He refused, however, to pose milking cows, driving tractors or pitching hay because he said he never did such things before he became a presidential candidate."[122] He later appeared at a smaller, but still enthusiastic Rushville version of welcoming home its favorite son at Memorial Park, where he spoke for ten minutes. There he told his friends he would make "any personal sacrifice" to keep the nation out of war and "to preserve at all hazards the kind of life we have here in Rush County. While the bombs are raining down on England today, I feel an overwhelming sense of humility that I have been called to a position of leadership in one of the most critical periods of world history. People who live and think as we do are being destroyed in their way of life."[123] Before he concluded, Willkie said he wanted to correct any false impression created by the introduction of

Portrait of Willkie from the July 21, 1940, Chicago Tribune

IHS

him as "a Rush County farmer" by the welcoming committee: "I am a purely conversational farmer. I have never done a stroke of work on a Rush County farm," he said, drawing a big laugh. "And I hope I never have to. I merely do the talking."[124]

Still hopeful he could engage Roosevelt in an actual debate or even one via dueling speeches on the campaign trail, Willkie told reporters, "I am going to keep on asking for the debate, boys. Lincoln did not think it was unworthy or undignified to debate and neither did Daniel Webster."[125] After leaving Rushville, Willkie's campaign planned a 7,200-mile visit to eighteen states with forty-three rear-train platform speeches and twenty-six "city park speeches" scheduled.

Later in September, after the Willkie campaign opened a storefront headquarters in downtown Rushville, the campaign unveiled a film prepared for theaters across America, showing Willkie and his running mate, McNary, on their respective farms. At Rushville, Willkie joined in the "premiere" of the film shown outdoors at Memorial Park. While there, Willkie declared he represented the "party of peace" and said, "I shall never lead this country into any European war."[126] On October 28, 1940, Willkie made another Indiana stop before a massive crowd estimated at 100,000 at Monument Circle in Indianapolis. "Willkie was driven through the business district with Mrs. Willkie and spoke from a platform in Monument Circle," the Associated Press reported, "which was jammed with cheering men and women. Confetti and paper streamers showered down from windows. A band behind the speaker's platform played 'Back Home Again in Indiana.' Willkie, cheered loudly, told the audience that never had he been 'so moved and touched as I am today at this great outpouring of the people.'"[127]

Although his campaign ended in defeat, historian Gregory believes Willkie and Indiana "had no reason to be embarrassed that a native son had lost the presidency in 1940." He noted that in losing, Willkie won 22 million votes, 7 million more votes than Hoover in 1932, 5 million more votes that Landon in 1936 (and ultimately more votes than Dewey would attract in either the 1944 or 1948 races). "He had presented himself as a man of charm, wit, intelligence, and extraordinary excitement," Gregory wrote. "Willkie's manner of running for the presidency and the grace with which he accepted defeat left the nation far less divided than it might have been. He sparkled as the brightest star in Republican presidential politics during two decades of Democratic domination."[128]

A year after his loss to Roosevelt (and in the final months before the U.S. would be drawn into World War II), Willkie accepted an invitation to speak before a joint session of the Indiana General Assembly in Indianapolis. There he ridiculed isolationists and advised legislators that "if the totalitarian powers prevail in this war, Canada and the United States will be surrounded by a totalitarian world. Democracy must be dynamic or it cannot live."[129] Willkie, though he lived most of the time in New York City, returned to Indianapolis again in February 1943 to headline a Republican Lincoln Day dinner. He told his fellow Hoosiers, "There must never again be any question of the right of workers to bargain collectively through representatives of their own choosing, or of the fundamental right of all our citizens to be free of racial discrimination." He argued against division of groups along racial and economic lines and said, "We must recognize that we, through our government, have a duty toward every citizen in this land to protect him or her against economic calamity. For every citizen owes to every other citizen basic protection against the hazards of unemployment, old age, accident and ill health."[130]

In the years after losing to Roosevelt, Willkie became an informal ally of the president and joined First Lady Eleanor Roosevelt in founding "Freedom House," a democracy, freedom and human rights advocacy organization. Roosevelt dispatched him as a "personal ambassador" four times in 1941 and 1942, including trips to Britain, the Middle East, the Soviet Union, and China. He flirted with another candidacy in 1944, but was viewed as too progressive for the increasingly conservative Republican Party and quickly abandoned his ambition. Willkie died October 6, 1944, days after suffering a massive heart attack while en route by train from Indianapolis to New York. Upon his death, Roosevelt remarked, "The nation will long remember Wendell Willkie as a forthright American. Earnest, honest, whole souled, he also had tremendous courage. This courage which was his dominating trait prompted him more than once to stand alone and to challenge the wisdom of counsels taken by powerful interests within his own party. In this hour of grave crisis, the country loses a great citizen through his untimely death."[131] He was buried at East Hill Cemetery in Rushville on October 17, 1944.[132]

Thomas E. Dewey

By 1940 Dewey had already built a solid reputation as a no-nonsense prosecutor for the people of New York. Although only thirty-eight years old, he was even being mentioned as a viable Republican candidate for president. Despite losing his 1938 campaign for governor of New York, many still considered his intellectual manner and law-and-order record a good contrast to President Roosevelt, who faced the prospect of running for an unprecedented third term in 1940. His noninterventionist views regarding the growing tensions in Europe were popular among many Americans, particularly conservatives, who dreaded the thought of a second world war.

On April 16, 1940, Dewey accepted the invitation of Indiana Republican leaders to address a rally at the Butler Fieldhouse. As the *Christian Science Monitor* reported, Dewey's "out-in-the-lead candidacy for the Republican presidential nomination is on the march again, and as he swings across the continent on another speech-making, hand-shaking, get-acquainted tour, every indication is that it is continuing to move ahead. . . . He has convinced the Indiana Republicans that he is a vivid and vigorous political campaigner. He has convinced them he is wielding a powerful force in the renewing and revitalizing the rank-and-file confidence of the Republican Party."[133]

Upon arriving at Indianapolis, Dewey spoke to reporters and reiterated his isolationist views regarding Europe and said that "the paramount obligation of our government is to consider every word and every fact from one standpoint— to make absolutely certain—that this nation is not involved, directly or indirectly, in any aspects of the war or any negotiations between the warring nations."[134]

For his speech at Butler, Dewey focused on the "unsound economic policies" of the Roosevelt administration, which he said crippled businessmen from reemploying workers and specifically penalized small business owners. "There is an emergency in this country," he said. "The emergency is the necessity for restoring employment and the system of private enterprise by getting rid of the New Deal—and quickly." Dewey said 10.5 million men were listed as unemployed in 1935, and that number had not changed in five years. "There has only been a steadily increasing national debt and a decline in our productive plant and equipment. Our national economy has actually gone backward under the New Deal," he said.[135]

In contrast, Dewey said he had a seven-point "Fair Play" plan that would revitalize the nation's economy. The seven points he identified were: treat businesses as allies and not enemies of government, stop "bureaucratic interference" in private enterprise, reform the Securities and Exchange Commission, redesign the federal tax structure, improve credit opportunities for small businesses, end "defeatist" and "ill-conceived experiments" and "frantic improvisions" in domestic and foreign policy, and stop governmental abuse without making unnecessary grabs of power by the federal government. "These moves," Dewey said, "will bring us again to the normal course of progress. They will start again to point the American ship straight ahead and away from those dangerous rocks on the left and away from those rocks on the right."[136]

Dewey went into the 1940 Republican National Convention with the most pledged delegates in his pocket, but still lacked enough to claim a nomination victory on the first ballot. Other contenders, Taft of Ohio and Vandenberg of Michigan, shared Dewey's isolationist views regarding the brewing problems in Europe, but each had their own strengths. The May 1940 German invasion of France, Belgium, and Luxembourg (which followed its previous aggression against Poland, the Netherlands, and Denmark), came just a month before the start of the GOP convention and seriously eroded support for Dewey, who had no prior experience on the national level and no expertise in foreign policy. When balloting opened at the conven-

tion, Dewey led on the first three votes but still lacked enough to claim the nomination. On the fourth ballot, Willkie had drawn off enough of waning support from Dewey, Taft, Vandenberg, and a handful of other hopefuls to take his first lead. On the sixth ballot, Willkie claimed victory with Taft a distant second and Dewey's support dwindled to nearly nothing.

Robert A. Taft

Just two years into his first term as a United States senator from Ohio, Taft had already set his sights on the office once held by his father, President William Howard Taft. During the 1940 campaign, Taft traveled the nation as the champion of conservative Republicans, who vehemently opposed American intervention in Europe, and brought his campaign to Indiana, friendly territory for the Ohioan. On May 21, 1940, Taft wrapped up his preconvention efforts with important speeches in both Saint Louis and Indianapolis in which he admonished Americans to "stop playing with the idea that we may enter the war and devote ourselves to a genuine program of defense" and that "if we abandon our position as a neutral, which we always have maintained with respect to wars between nations, if we admit that our safety and defense are at stake in the European war, then we cannot go half way."[137]

Taft said, "If we are justified in spending billions for the allies and supporting their navies, then it would be cowardice not to support them also with men" but added, "our going to war would be more likely to destroy American democracy than to destroy German dictatorship."[138] Taft told his audience that he doubted Germany would ever gain enough strength to mount any successful invasion of North America, particularly if the nation remained focused on a strong national defense at home. After his Indianapolis appearance, Taft made his way to adjacent Boone County to the Ulen Country Club in Lebanon, where he and former Indiana governor and ambassador Paul V. McNutt (a Democrat) were honorees for a special bipartisan "Governor's Day" banquet.

7

The Postwar Era, 1946–59

Harry S Truman

Although he was the incumbent candidate in 1948, coming at the end of a long run of sixteen years of Democratic control of the White House, Harry Truman did not let that—or his favorite target, the "Do Nothing Congress"—stop him from turning himself into the outside challenger for the presidency.

Widely viewed as out before he even started his campaign, Truman picked up the banner of the Democratic Party in much the way he had the presidency—because it was presented to him. It was not as if the party or the nation had a long love affair with the former senator from Missouri. In fact, a great many Americans knew little about the thirty-third president. Serving in obscurity in a short vice presidency with little power or authority, it was not until President Franklin D. Roosevelt died that Truman even learned of plans to develop an atomic bomb. The shadow cast by the nation's longest-serving and beloved wartime president, Roosevelt, would not be easy for Truman to outshine.

Overlooking and underestimating Truman had been a well-worn and regretted tactic. He had often proven critics wrong. In 1948, with low approval ratings among those who knew Truman, and no approval rating among those who hardly knew his name, Democrats looked around

for someone else to head the ticket. Democrats were unsuccessful in their effort to lure General Dwight D. Eisenhower to run as a Democrat, and Truman began to lock down his needed support for nomination. However, an historic and noteworthy move by Senator Hubert H. Humphrey of Minnesota to include a groundbreaking plank regarding the rights of African Americans into the Democrats' platform initiated a southern revolt from the convention. Even those who remained did not support Truman and tried to topple him with Senator Richard Russell Jr. of Georgia. Truman prevailed, but without a large chunk of traditionally Democrats from the South along (most of whom supported Senator Strom Thurmond of South Carolina and his third party Dixiecrat candidacy).

Limping out of his own convention Truman faced off against, New York governor Thomas E. Dewey, who had turned back the Old Guard of the GOP (and General Douglas MacArthur) to win his party's nomination. Truman started out behind. Early opinion polls showed Dewey leading Truman, and Thurmond having no support outside of the Deep South. None of that scared Truman. Now his own man, free of the Roosevelt strings (Roosevelt's eldest son, James, had been a part of the "anyone but Truman" effort),

Truman's campaign was on, with the sitting president spending a remarkable amount of time away from Washington, D.C., campaigning for re-election.

In Indiana Truman made an unusually large number of appearances in his now famous "whistle-stop campaign," perhaps analyzing that the state's heaving manufacturing base of hourly wage workers, farmers, and small-town values would find a connection with the president from Independence. The counsel of former senator Sherman E. Minton of Indiana, one of Truman's closest friends from his Senate days (and to whom he later appointed to the U.S. Supreme Court), may have also played a factor. But Indiana was in Truman's playbook.

A parade of stops emanated from the 1948 Truman campaign—Crawfordsville, Elkhart, Evansville, Fort Wayne, Garrett, Gary (twice), Greenfield, Hammond, Indianapolis (twice), Kokomo, Logansport, Mount Vernon, Noblesville, North Judson, Richmond (twice), South Bend, Terre Haute (twice), Tipton, and eventually Vincennes (just days after his re-election while en route back to Washington, D.C.). In each of his stops at train depots, Truman's message was essentially the same. He claimed the mantel of accomplishment for the economic recovery and the victory in World War II that had come as part of, and since, the Roosevelt administration. And he lectured relentlessly about the economic and political reforms he had attempted to undertake, only to find a blockade in the Republican-controlled eightieth Congress.

In Fort Wayne on June 4, 1948, just as the campaign was getting started, Truman invoked memories of Mad Anthony Wayne as a person who did not know the world cannot. "Whenever he was given a job to do, he did it," Truman peeled. "These northwest territories are very

much beholden to him for being a part of the greatest republic in the world."[1] Truman said that in those early days—even before Indiana statehood—"people were thinking just as they are now. They were anxious for peace and security, and they themselves contributed to making that peace and security. They usually had their own squirrel rifle up over the door, the bag full of powder and shot, and a King James version of the Bible (but) it took all those things to make this great community what it is now."[2]

"Permanent peace" in the world was possible, Truman said, if the United States took the role "God Almighty intended" as the leader of the United Nations. Beyond the UN, the elements needed for peace in the world, the president said, were the success of the European recovery program for sixteen nations ravaged by World War II and a universal military training program so "that we have the strength to maintain that peace."[3]

Later that same day, while in Gary, Truman lamented that his stop did not permit him to visit the great industrial complexes the city boasted—"the youngest town in America over a hundred thousand inhabitants," he proclaimed to the delight of the locals. "You have done some great things here in this town," he said. "I made some investigations here during the way, and the plants in this city made a magnificent contribution to that war effort."[4] Truman reminded the audience that worry had spread across Indiana and the rest of the nation that after V-J Day, "everybody wondered whether he was going to have a job or not . . . whether he was going to have enough to eat . . . and when he was going to be able to get what he needed to live. Well, that worry about the job went out the window!"[5]

Jobs were not the issue, Truman said, but the rising cost of living was, noting skyrocketing

IHS, MARTIN'S PHOTO SHOP COLLECTION, P 129

President Harry S Truman waves to the crowd at a campaign stop at Terre Haute's Union Station, 1948.

prices in the nation for basic goods since the end of the war. He used this reality to introduce his struggle to get Congress to address price and production controls in order to hold down inflation. He expressed fear that Congress would adjourn in 1948 without addressing these issues. "I am hoping when we get a new Congress, and we are going to get one this fall, maybe we'll get one that willl work in the interests of the common people and not in the interests of the men who have all the money," he said to warm applause.[6] The economic stability of America was directly tied to the peace needed in the world, he said: "Whether we like it or not, (we) are the leaders

in the world, and in order to get a lasting peace, the economy of this country must be absolutely sound and solid."[7]

Later that same month, on June 17, 1948, Truman's train stopped in Terre Haute, and he reminded the locals that it was not his first time to visit their city. "I have been through this city and stopped here on numerous occasions," he said. "When I was in the Senate, I was there for 10 years, I used to drive back and forth from Independence, Missouri to Washington by way of highway number 40—and I usually always stayed on that highway in Terre Haute going one way or the other."[8]

Truman bridged from his familiarity with Terre Haute to his love of the Indiana farms along the way. He noted that his policies had benefited farmers, citing a statistic that in 1932 farming income was only $4.7 million but had risen to $30 billion in 1947. He reminded Hoosiers also that when Roosevelt came to office, more farms were held on back-due mortgages or in foreclosure than ever before in the nation's history. "The farmers didn't know which way to turn," he said.[9]

In Terre Haute and later in Indianapolis, he reminded Democrats in particular that when they do not show up to vote, "you get just what you deserve," such as a Republican Congress. "If all of you don't come out this time and decide what is best for this country, you can't complain about what you get for the next four years,"[10] Truman said. At Indianapolis, he boasted that his travels by train had placed him before more than two million Americans with growing crowds along the way. He reminded the overflow crowd of nearly 8,000 present at Union Station that the Republican Congress had rebuffed his efforts to address housing shortages and price controls in the nation.

By 7:45 p.m., Truman's train made one more Indiana stop, this one in Richmond. Remarkably, no one apparently had told the mayor that he was coming. "I am told he is out of the city, and didn't know I was coming," Truman said, to nervous laughter from the locals. He reminded Richmond's residents, as he did in Terre Haute, that he had visited their city many times via his east-west travels on US 40, the National Road. "I sometimes stayed at the Richmond-Leland Motel," he said. "I ought to get something for that plug, don't you think?"[11]

Months later, Truman was back as the campaign hit its homestretch, and his train made a brief stop on September 30 at Mount Vernon, the county seat of Posey County in the southwesternmost tip of Indiana. He asked residents there to "vote for themselves" as "when you vote for yourselves, you vote the Democratic ticket straight because the Democrats are for the people. The Republicans are for special privilege."[12] Apologizing for departing after speaking only a few moments, Truman explained he was overdue for a national radio broadcast emanating from Louisville, Kentucky, further down the line. He did not tell the Posey County residents that between their town and Louisville, he also planned to stop at Evansville, where a large and enthusiastic throng had gathered to hear him. "Judging from the crowd before me, I would say that Evansville is pretty prosperous these days," Truman said.[13]

Truman said prosperity was "the main issue of this political campaign, whether we are going to stay prosperous with the Democratic Party, or fall back on the boom and bust politics of the Republicans. There are many fine Republicans in this country, many Republicans who vote the Democratic ticket because they know the leaders of their own party haven't learned anything since the days of Warren G. Harding."[14] As example of that, the president asked his audience to consider the record of Congress. "For two years I have been trying to get the Congress to do something for the people," he said. "But the Republican leaders were too busy protecting the interests of big business and the bankers. They didn't have time to do anything *for* the people, but they did plenty *to* the people."[15] Hammering hard on his efforts to help improve the rights of workers and labor practices, Truman told his audience that they should not vote for him, "but vote for yourselves. Vote for the welfare of the country. Vote for the future of this great nation by voting the Democratic ticket straight."[16]

Just under two weeks later, Truman was back in Indiana for an October 12 whistle-stop at Richmond, his second visit to that city in 1948. He retold his travels on US 40, but also recalled attending a ceremony sponsored by the Daughters of the American Revolution. He told his audience that "Richmond is a fine example of the balance that we want to see between the farms and the cities. It is a good example of the way that farm prosperity makes for industrial prosperity, and the way industrial prosperity helps the farmers."[17]

Not mentioning Dewey by name, Truman nonetheless had sharpened even further his assault on the Republicans and Congress. "The Republican candidate for President has put his stamp of approval on the record of the eightieth Congress," Truman said, noting that Dewey had expressed pride on how Congress had delivered. "I'll say it delivered," the president bellowed. "It delivered for the special interests 100 percent! There isn't much reason to hope for continued prosperity, or for good housing, or for better education for our children, or a genuine national health program, or for lower prices, as long as these backward men lead the Republican Party."[18]

Truman's criticism was not limited to Dewey. He also attacked the third-party candidacy of former vice president Henry A. Wallace, noting that "the Communists are doing everything in their power to beat me" and that with the help of Republicans, Wallace's presence on the Indiana ballot "they have taken over the third party and are using it in a vain attempt to split the Democratic Party. The Republicans have joined up with this Communist-inspired third party to beat the Democrats. They finance the situation right here. The Republicans financed the third party to get them on the ballot right here in Indiana."[19] It was a provocative claim, with no evidence offered by the president to support it.

Later that morning, in a quick stop at Greenfield, "Give 'em Hell Harry" may have been showing the signs of the long, grueling campaign when he inartfully raised again his argument that Hoosiers should go and vote Democratic to preserve their own interests. He noted, "You know, the farmer, like everybody else when things are easy for him, he tends to neglect his political duties. He becomes fat and lazy and won't go to the polls on Election Day. He did that in 1946—and look what he got! The Republican Congress immediately began to try and turn back the clock, and the first one they took a whack at was the farmer."[20]

Voters—farmers or not—were likely not used to being called "neglectful" and "fat and lazy," but Truman was known to speak his mind. He reminded the Greenfield audience that he had fought hard for farm programs, such as soil conservation, and federally sponsored school lunch programs to help Hoosiers know "the tremendous prosperity they enjoy today."[21]

Truman thanked his audience, and perhaps realizing he had spoken bluntly to them, tried to end on a self-deprecating note: "You don't have any trouble finding out where I stand. I tell you frankly where I stand on all these issues which affect the people," he said. "Try to get the other fellow to do that, and you'll be a good one if you can get it done!"[22]

Skipping Indianapolis, Truman's train next made a stop at Crawfordsville, drawing a large amount of college students from both nearby Wabash College and DePauw University. Calling the upcoming election one of the most important in a generation, he said, "I don't think there is any Republican who could accuse me of 'pulling punches.' I am telling facts, and they can't stand facts! They like to talk about unity and give you a little soothing syrup and make you believe that they are all right, but if you will study the record, you will find that they are anything but right!"[23] He reminded the farmers present that the Republicans had even opposed the Rural Electrification Act, which had brought electricity and modern conveniences to even the farthest reaches of rural Indiana. "Before REA began, only one farm in 10 in Indiana had electricity," he said. "Now, nine out of 10 Indiana farmers have electricity on the farms. One-hundred and three thousand Indiana farm homes have REA electricity. Imagine what that means to a hungry world? It means food for people who would otherwise starve to death."[24]

Turning to the group of college students standing nearby, the president said, "I appreciate very much these young men and women, these college students, who are here this morning, because they are interested in the welfare of the country, or they wouldn't be here. And this country is yours. You are going to take over the operation of this country in the next generation, and I am most happy to see you interested in things that are pending now in the campaign because your future is wrapped up in the results of this campaign."[25]

Three days later, as Truman's campaign train continued to move in and out of Indiana from stops in Ohio, Michigan, Illinois, Wisconsin, and Minnesota, he made a brief visit to Hammond on October 15. There he congratulated the city's workers for their part in supporting the war effort and briefly reviewed the importance of the Fair Labor Standards Act that he supported. "That act established a minimum straight-time hourly wage for all workers," he said to the laborers gathered. "It required payment of time and a half for all hours over 40 hours a week. It outlawed oppressive child labor. The Fair Labor Standards Act now covers an estimated 20 million American workers."[26] Truman reminded

the workers that the Republican Congress had continually fought him on his efforts to increase the minimum wage to seventy-five cents an hour. Reminding his audience that his GOP opponent, whom he did not name, was running on the record of Congress, he said, "He won't come out and say what he believes the minimum wage ought to be. He is ducking the issue. He says he believes in the minimum wage, but as I said at St. Paul (Minnesota) the other evening, I think the smaller the minimum the better the Republicans like it!"[27] Reminding his northwest Indiana audience that when Democrats showed up in 1944, Democrats won. But when Democrats "were lazy and stayed at home" in 1946, the Republicans won. "You can't afford to let that happen this year," he warned.[28]

A short time later, the tiny Starke County community of North Judson had its rare moment in the spotlight as the Truman train stopped there, also on October 15. The hometown of Governor Henry F. Schricker, Truman told the audience, "I know you must be exceedingly proud that you are the native city of one of Indiana's greatest governors, and the next Governor of Indiana."[29]

An hour later, the whistle-stop campaign made its way into Logansport, where a large, enthusiastic throng gathered. There Truman said he was "most happy" to be "on the banks of the Wabash River. I have heard of the Wabash River all my life, and I have crossed it a dozen times, but I have never been at this point on the Wabash. I wish I could stay longer."[30] He reminded the large group of railroad workers present that the entire teams of engineers on his campaign train were Democrats, including the conductor who was the Democratic candidate for Cass County Sheriff. Truman often heaped praise on the crews operating the trains for his campaign, especially after Dewey had been overheard criticizing his train crew for jolting to an abrupt stop elsewhere in Indiana.

"You people here in Logansport know what great benefits the railroad brotherhoods have brought to all of you," he said. "The brotherhoods have been responsible for bringing very much better incomes to all railroad workers. I think there are about 4,000 railroad men in this good town. And higher pay means better living standards for themselves and their families, more business for the merchants here in town, and better markets for the farmers in the surrounding community."[31]

Later that afternoon, Truman's train pulled into nearby Kokomo, and he declared to the large, enthusiastic crowd: "I thought I had seen all the people of Indiana at the first two stops today, but I evidently hadn't seen a third of them! You're all here! It shows conclusively that you are interested in the welfare of this country or you wouldn't come out like this to hear what your president has to say."[32] Truman again made a pitch for Schricker in his bid for a second (non-consecutive term) as governor. He added, "Kokomo is a manufacturing town famous for its farm machinery, stoves, and furnaces, and many other products. A great deal of your prosperity comes from your factories. At the same time, you are in the middle of one of the richest agricultural areas in the whole world. Business here is good when farmers are prosperous, as they are now."[33]

The president advised, however, that "we can enjoy genuine prosperity only when all groups of the American people are well off. But this simple fact seems to escape the Republicans. They think the farmer is getting too much for his crops, and they tell the people in the towns that this is the reason for high prices. Then they go and tell the farmer that prices are high because wages in the city are too. Neither of these two statements is correct. The Republican remedy for high prices seems to be to pull everybody down in a crash all together, like they did in 1929."[34]

Truman's Kokomo stop would set in motion an incredible story that most Hoosiers and Americans never knew about. The story was prompted after Truman spotted a sailor in the crowd at the rear of the train. The young man in uniform was a member of the U.S. Navy crew that operated the *Williamsburg*, the presidential yacht docked on the Potomac River in Washington, D.C. "The President motioned to the boy to come up and shake hands, which the young man did," recalled Truman campaign aide William J. Bray. "The President asked the young man what he was doing in Kokomo, and he said he was home to visit his parents and also to be inducted into the Masons. This made the President very happy because he was a Mason himself."[35] Truman invited the young man and his father to join the presidential train as it made its way south to Noblesville (en route to Indianapolis). "The President instructed us to bring the young man and his father back to the President's private car for a visit," Bray recalled. The young man's father mentioned that it would be nice if the president could attend the Masonic induction ceremony, and it apparently was an idea that caught the president's fancy. Truman told his aides that he would go forward with his full schedule of events that evening in Indianapolis, but afterward wanted the Secret Service to coordinate a private "escape" to Noblesville to attend the sailor's Mason ceremony. "The President had indicated that he wanted no publicity about this matter, but we advised the President that the newspaper people travelling with us would probably get the story and make much of it," Bray said. "The President was insistent. He said he was not interested in the details but to work it out and bring it about."[36]

After leaving Kokomo, Truman's next stop was in Tipton, where the president emphasized the benefits of the Commodity Credit Corporation and the International Wheat Agreement. He declared, "The Republican Party has consistently opposed the Democratic farm program."[37] His final whistle-stop of the day took him into the heart of Republican territory at the Hamilton County seat of Noblesville. In his introduction, Schricker predicted that he would be the next governor and Truman would be the next president. He repeated earlier themes of how Republican members of Congress did not stand for working people but were for "special privilege," noting that "the first they did when they got in there was to pass a rich man's tax bill."[38] A couple of Secret Service agents left Truman's train after his brief remarks at Noblesville to make arrangements with the local police for the president's secret visit to the Masonic Hall.[39]

In Indianapolis, Truman made two important stops after a brief open-car ride up Meridian Street from Union Station to the Indianapolis Athletic Club. There an overflow audience of Democratic Party faithful and precinct workers received personal thanks from the president, who declared them "necessary to make a great party function." He added, "We have to go forward and I know that when the Democratic workers in Indiana are willing to turn out as you have turned out this evening, just to see the president and the next governor, and your able and distinguished Democratic mayor of Indianapolis [Al Feeney]. I know, after meeting all these wonderful people today that Indiana is going along with the president and try to keep the clock running forward and not backward."[40]

After dining with fellow Democrats and briefly resting, Truman and Schricker made their way to the Indiana War Memorial along North Meridian Street for a 9:00 p.m. address that was broadcast nationally by radio. For Truman, it was an important moment to help "seal the deal" with voters about what the difference was between him and Dewey. In his introductory remarks, Truman noted that "the people of Indiana all during this day have given me a wonderful reception. I never saw anything like it anywhere. From the bottom of my heart, I thank you all for your real Hoosier hospitality."[41]

The president offered an "apology" of sorts to his Republican challenger, who "apparently I have offended. I'm afraid I have startled him by talking about issues and depressions. Republicans don't like people to talk about depressions. You can hardly blame them for that. You remember the old saying: Don't talk about rope in the house where somebody has been hanged."[42] Truman said he resented Republican suggestions that talking about a possible depression could give aid to the Communists. He said, "I've been trying to prevent a depression," and said the 'Do Nothing Congress' had been no help in addressing runaway inflation, lower wages for workers and farmers, and housing. "That is why I have been saying that we must never return to the policies of Harding, Coolidge and Hoover," Truman added.[43]

Drawing the economic distinction even further, Truman said, "The basic difference between the two parties in economic matters is simply this: The Republican Party, as it operates in Washington, favors the interests of a few, small, powerful groups at the expense of the rest of the people. . . . The Democratic Party, on the other hand, consistently works for measures which increase and protect the purchasing power of the great majority of our people."[44]

In a precursor to Democratic platforms that would follow for decades, Truman made a strong pitch for health-care benefits for Americans, blasting the Republican Congress for actions that he said dumped a million workers from health care. He urged extension of "old age insurance benefits" by at least 50 percent because "we need more doctors, more nurses, more hospitals. We need a system which will enable the average American family to pay for proper medical care. Each year, because of a lack of proper medical care, we lose more people than we lost in all the fighting of World War II. Listen to that! Each year, because of a lack of proper medical care, we lost more of our people than we lost in all the fighting in World War II!"[45]

Truman said the nation lost $27 billion each year "through sickness and disability. We can do something about it, and we must do something about it."[46] He said that because "the best health facilities and the finest doctors in the world are not much help to people who cannot afford to use them, I proposed a national system of health insurance in 1946, and I have urged it repeatedly since that time. There is no other way to assure that the average American family has a decent chance for adequate medical care. There is no other way to assure a strong and healthy nation."[47]

The president's remarks next turned to education, where he urged more funding to prepare more teachers and build more schools—schools at all levels across the nation that had already begun to "bulge at the seams" as the postwar baby boom got into full swing. "Knowledge is not only the key to power, it is the citadel to human freedom. We must maintain and expand our schools or we shall surrender our liberties without even fighting for them," he declared.[48]

"Following the speech [at the War Memorial], the party returned in cars to the train (at Union Station)," recalled Truman's aide Bray. "The car that the President was supposed to ride in at the head of the procession, however, was occupied by two members of his party and his personal Secret Service bodyguard. The car containing the president and several Secret Service people proceeded [to Noblesville] where the President had insisted that he wished to be at the installation of the boy from [the] Williamsburg."[49] Truman's security detail informed reporters there would be no further public appearances that evening and that the train would depart Indianapolis in about ninety minutes. "The President was then in the Masonic Lodge in (Noblesville). About an hour later the President returned to his railroad car, very much pleased that he 'maybe' had made several people happy," Bray said. "Of course, he had made many, many people happy, especially the boy and his father. It was not until two days later that word 'leaked out' about the President's detour and it did not make the press very happy that they had missed quite a scoop."[50]

Truman's major barnstorming of Indiana was far from over. Ten days later, on October 25, as the campaign reached its final days, the Truman train reached Garrett. The campaign almost over, he noted, "It has been a good campaign for me. It has been a hard campaign. I have traveled from one end of the country to the other, telling millions of people about peace, prices, and places to live, and the other issues which face the nation today. My opponent has talked a great deal too, but he has said almost nothing about where he stands on the major issues."[51]

The president asked Hoosiers to disregard "lies" about how the Democrats would make the threat of Communism more real. "They believe that if you tell a big enough lie, somebody is bound to believe it," he said. "Don't fall for their cheap promises."[52]

Later that day, Truman delivered a major address to an overflow audience packed into the

Memorial Auditorium in Gary. He opened with a familiar joke among Democrats—about a young Republican Party worker assigned to try and round up votes in Democratically controlled Lake County. Truman said, "I can think of no harder job than to try to sell the Republican Party to the men and women of Gary who lived through those dark years of the Republican depression."[53]

He reminded the labor friendly audience that the Democratic Party had stood for workers wanting to organize for better wages and working conditions and restored collective bargaining across the board. He noted that average American wages had risen from a level of forty-five cents an hour in 1932 to a rate of $1.33 in 1948. "I don't know how any man—any farmer—any laboring man—can go to the polls on November 2nd and do anything else but vote in his own interests—and if he does that, he will vote the Democratic ticket," the president declared to roaring approval.[54]

He concluded, "Now, I trust people. Every good Democrat does. I trust their commonsense, their decency, and their sense of justice. That's why I'm talking to you right now. We beat this Republican outfit in 1932, beat them in 1936! We beat them in 1940! And we beat them four years ago! We'll do it again!"[55]

Truman spent the night in Indiana and departed early on October 26 to head back east to campaign in Ohio. Before he did, however, his train stopped twice more, once in South Bend and once in Elkhart. In both places he sounded familiar themes, although he spoke of the fight of immigrants to the United States to build a better life for themselves in his South Bend remarks (perhaps a nod to the city's significant Catholic and Serbian Orthodox populations of Polish, German, Irish, and Serbian descent). "When we tell the world that we believe that all men are

entitled to earn a decent living," he said, "without regard to race or national origin, or religion, we have got to live up to what we say."[56]

At Elkhart the president warned of Republicans who were used to helping the rich "skim the cream off the top and leaving the leftovers for the rest of us" and said if they were elected, the nation would have a government "for the benefit of the wealthy, privileged, special interests" and not the working people of Elkhart County. "Every time business snaps its fingers, the Republican leaders in Congress obey orders," he added.[57]

Truman's final stop in Indiana prior to Election Day came on October 30 at Terre Haute, as his campaign train made its way west from Ohio to Illinois, ending just before Election Day near his hometown of Independence. "By this time, I think all of you know where I stand," Truman said. "There is a good reason why I can be frank and honest with the people. That is because I made no secret deals with the lobbies of big business. I have made no commitments except to the people. I don't have to double-talk to conceal what I stand for or what I propose to do."[58]

Were all the stops and visits to Indiana making a difference? Reporters and political analysts did not think so, remaining convinced that Truman would not only lose Indiana but also the presidency. As Roscoe Drummond, head of the *Christian Science Monitor*'s Washington bureau, noted, Truman faced "a puzzling paradox: The presence of large Truman crowds throughout his trip and the evidence in all the public opinion polls of a losing Truman vote on Nov. 2." They added that Truman appeared "buoyed and elated by the throngs which are turning out to see him," including several in Indiana. The analysts were quick to note that Truman was able to draw such crowds more out of a combination of curiosity and his willingness to stop at communities large and small. "This has been evident all along the itinerary," Drummond wrote. "Almost the entire population of Logansport and Kokomo, Indiana turned out when the presidential train pulled up at the stations. It suggests that a predominant pulling factor is interest in and curiosity to see the President of the United States in towns where a President has rarely, if ever, appeared in the flesh."[59] Drummond concluded, "These factors may account in part for the disparity between the present Truman crowds and the prospective Truman vote, for few politicians on either side, in candid moments, are seriously questioning that Mr. Truman is going to lose."[60]

Two days after the election, in which Truman shocked pundits by defeating Dewey, Truman was back in Indiana as his "victory train" reached Vincennes, where the victorious candidate joked that he had just been handed a banknote on the First National Bank of Independence for $10, "and the gentleman who gave it to me told me that if I ever went broke, he would redeem it! I can't thank you enough!"[61]

Declaring his election as "a great victory, my friends, for the people," he said, "We must not do anything that will reflect on the judgment of the people—so when we get back to Washington and are sworn in on the 20th of January, we will continue to work for the people and in the interests of the country. I do not feel elated at the victory—I feel overwhelmed with the responsibility. Just bear that in mind. Now, good luck to all of you and I hope—I sincerely hope—that you will not be disappointed in the result."[62]

In 1951 the Twenty-second Amendment to the Constitution was adopted, which provided that "no person shall be elected to the office of the President more than twice, and no person who has held the office of President, or acted as President, for more than two years of a term to which some other person was elected President shall be elected to the office of the President more than once." A second sentence in Section 1 of the amendment exempted it from applying to Truman, noting that "this article shall not apply to any person holding the office of President when this article was proposed by the Congress, and shall not prevent any person who may be holding the office of President, or acting as President, during the term within which this article becomes operative from holding the office of President or acting as President during the remainder of such term."[63] Truman, suffering from extremely low public approval ratings, briefly contemplated running for another term as president, but eventually opted out of an active campaign to gain the Democratic nomination. Truman eventually backed Illinois governor Adlai Stevenson II for the party's nomination.

Despite his absence from the ballot in 1952, Truman renewed his whistle-stop campaign efforts on behalf of the Democrats and made visits to Indiana on Stevenson's behalf in Indianapolis, Anderson, Muncie, Garrett, Terre Haute, and Gary. His appearances were intended to help Stevenson, but also to help Democrats running for House and Senate seats. There was also a hint of Truman attempting to protect and preserve his record as president. Just after 7:00 a.m. on October 9, 1952, the president addressed a Union Station crowd in Indianapolis explaining, "I am out here campaigning because I believe it is essential for the welfare and progress of the country to help elect Adlai Stevenson and John Sparkman. You know the fine, liberal record Adlai Stevenson has made as governor of your neighboring state . . . he has shown that government can be used to improve the lot of the average man."[64] The lame-duck president said that "the Republican Party has opposed every progressive measure for the good of the people in this country for the last 20 years. They tell me the Republicans are squealing like stuck hogs and saying I have been unfair. Well, I don't think I've been unfair. I know them too well. You see, I have been with the administrations in Washington for the last 18 years. They can't tell you that I don't know the facts about it."[65] Urging Hoosiers to resist "falling for the hooey the Republicans are giving you," Truman told them to vote Democratic.

An hour later, in Anderson, Truman spoke to a large crowd at the railroad depot and noted, "I appreciate most highly this turnout at this hour of the day" and apologized that "the last time I was through Anderson we didn't stop, and I have regretted it ever since."[66] Truman proclaimed that "we have as able a man in Adlai Stevenson as I have ever met. . . . Governor Stevenson is the finest new civilian leader to come along since Franklin Roosevelt back in 1932. He will look out for you and your interests. Roosevelt did, just as I have tried to do."[67]

About forty minutes later in Muncie, Truman said, "I guess it's no secret why I am here today" and added that Stevenson "really understands the problems of the everyday man in the country, and he knows how to handle the job of running a civilian government. He will make a great president."[68] Having some fun with the Republicans, Truman said, "They like to call themselves the GOP. Now, let me tell you what that really stands for. It stands for the 'General's Own Party'" and confirmed he was not talking about General Motors, General Electric, General Mills, or General Foods, all familiar brands to the people of Muncie. The president reminded his audience that the Democrats were the party of privates, not generals. Offering a surprisingly negative remark against the popular Eisenhower, Truman said, "The way he has been acting has been a terrible

disappointment to me. I once thought he might be a good president, but that was a mistake. In this campaign, he has betrayed almost everything I thought he stood for."[69]

"Don't turn our country over to the generals of big industry, or even over to the military generals, either," he said. "We don't want a military government. We want a civilian government . . . the President of the United States ought to be a civilian, so he can tell the generals and the admirals to stand down—and I have done it. You will get the same kind of program if you put Adlai Stevenson in the White House."[70]

Weeks later, on October 27, Truman made two stops—one where he again spoke from the back of a train to an audience at Garrett and another during a lengthy speech at the Memorial Auditorium in Gary. During his remarks at Gary, Truman made frequent references to Eisenhower's apparent unhappiness with the rigors of the campaign trail. He said Eisenhower "either doesn't understand the political facts of life, or he is trying to pull the wool over your eyes when he gives you the fine promises of what he and his team will do" and added, "let him cool off, let him look at the record, then he may understand some things."[71] Scaling back some earlier salvos fired at Eisenhower, Truman did openly question the GOP presidential candidate's statements about the Korean conflict. Truman said Eisenhower's most recent statement on Korea "contained so many misquotations or quotations out of context that it was clearly an attempt to deceive the American people" and described his remarks "a combination of falsehood and truth so interwoven as to create a completely false impression."[72]

For the 1952 campaign, the Democratic Party tapped Truman to appear in selected areas to help lead the "low road" attack on the popular hero figure created by Eisenhower and the Republicans. It was a role well suited for Truman, who had made more than 350 speeches in the closing weeks of the 1948 campaign to surprise everyone with a win. He hoped to create similar magic for Stevenson, though the men were not particularly close and Stevenson had made major changes within the Democratic Party in the post-Truman days. Just days before the 1952 election, Truman made a stopover in Terre Haute while en route by train to his home in Independence and spoke from the rear platform of a train to a crowd of 5,000. In September U.S. Senator Richard M. Nixon had delivered his famous "Checkers speech," which had saved his position on the GOP ticket with Eisenhower, but Truman was in the mood to remind voters of Indiana and Illinois about the issues behind Nixon's speech. He held back no punches, accusing Nixon of being sponsored directly at a "millionaires' club" that had raised an $18,000 expense fund for Nixon and that he had returned the favor with votes beneficial to his benefactors in the Senate. "That 'millionaires' club' included men whose business interests were oil, real estate, big manufacturing, banking and insurance," Truman said. "Now, I urge you to compare these interests with the way the Republican vice presidential candidate has voted in Congress. You'll find out why they thought he was worth a little subsidy."[73]

Referring to Nixon as "one of the most thorough-going reactionaries in our public life today" and "frequently an isolationist on foreign policy," Truman said voters should carefully consider whether they wanted him "a heartbeat away" from the presidency. He backed up the worry with a note that drew heavy criticism from Republicans (and reporters) by noting that "only three presidents in our history were older when they were inaugurated than the Republican can-didate for president would be if he were elected. He would be only one year younger than President Roosevelt was when President Roosevelt died. Seven of our Presidents have died in office and have been succeeded by their vice president." Eisenhower's age, sixty-two years old, was an issue, Truman said, because "this is a time of crisis and decision. This is not a popularity contest. This is a matter of bread and butter—your bread and butter. It is a matter of your safety and your children's safety in the atomic age."[74]

In the hot summer of 1953 Truman fired up his new Chrysler sedan for a motor trip from his home. That trip took him through Indiana in an era when a former president and his wife could travel the country without Secret Service protection (and without a presidential pension). In June 1953 Truman and his wife, Bess, set out from Missouri on their car trip to visit their daughter, Margaret, at New York City and a subsequent trip to Washington, D.C., for a reunion of former Truman administration staff. As part of their trip, Truman took US 40 through Indiana and stopped in Indianapolis at the North Meridian Street home of Frank McKinney, former Democratic National Committee chairman, for a private luncheon that included McKinney's wife, Margaret, and the couple's teenage children, Frank Jr. and Claire. Before departing, the Trumans posed on the front steps of the McKinney home for a photograph, although temperatures were climbing above one hundred degrees.

After leaving the McKinney home, the Trumans set off again, driving through the streets of Indianapolis, catching US 40 on Washington Street and continuing east. Apparently by accident, the Trumans encountered an Indiana State Police "traffic safety" zone near Greenfield, the Hancock County seat about twenty-one miles east of Indianapolis. At first the Trumans had made it through the safety stop basically unnoticed until one state trooper was curious about the shiny new car, and another state trooper, Carroll Mohr, called out, "Hey, that's Harry Truman!"[75]

The former president was in a friendly mood, despite the delay, and agreed to pose for pictures with the troopers present, while his wife remained inside the car waiting for about twenty minutes. "I certainly endorse your program," Truman told the troopers before resuming his travels.

In his book *Harry Truman's Excellent Adventure*, Matthew Algeo noted that the Trumans went unnoticed many places they traveled, and the Indiana publicity was the last they encountered while making their way east for more than seven hours. While in Washington, D.C., Truman seemed to enjoy his everyday interactions with citizens, walking the Mall in the nation's capital and showing up elsewhere and shaking hands with regular citizens.[76] By the time the Trumans started their return trip to Missouri later in July, locals along the route (particularly sheriffs and police departments) were spreading information about their travel route. Shared information from the Ohio State Police about Truman's route was helpful to Wayne County sheriff Ora Wilson, who ordered a deputy sheriff, coincidentally his son, Lowell, to watch US 40 for the Trumans' vehicle and bring them into town. The sheriff's deputy just happened to have a photographer from the *Richmond Palladium-Item* along for the ride, permitting photographs to be taken of the famous former First Couple with the sheriff and during their lunch at the Leland Hotel.[77] Later that day the Trumans reached Indianapolis to be overnight guests of the McKinneys and guests of honor at an outdoor garden party attended by prominent Indiana Democrats and at least one Republican, Indianapolis mayor Alex M. Clark.

The next morning news reports indicated Truman and McKinney took a twelve-block walk around the Meridian-Kessler neighborhood at around 7:20 a.m. before the Trumans resumed their trip. Legendary *Indianapolis News* political reporter Edward Zeigner accompanied Truman and McKinney and reported that the former president was adamant that he was not interested in seeking another term as president. "I'll never be a candidate again," he said, tamping down a rumor that he would be interested in running on a ticket with Stevenson for 1956. The former president did say he was more than happy to serve as an adviser to the party in its plans to regain the White House following Stevenson's loss to Eisenhower a year earlier. "Democrats will always be out to win," he said. "They wouldn't be Democrats if they weren't." He attributed the 1952 loss to complacency and letting "glamour and demagoguery get the best of them." (Truman did not specify whether he was referring to Eisenhower's star status as a World War II hero or Stevenson's bookish campaign style).[78]

While Truman's loyalty to McKinney was widely known, when asked whether he supported making McKinney the national Democratic chair again (a position McKinney had lost under the Stevenson campaign), Truman said, "Indiana politics is none of my business. Now if you asked me something about Missouri politics, I might be able to tell you."[79] Truman declined lengthy remarks about hopes for a truce in the Korean War but said, "I'm always optimistic about the future of this great country of ours. It's the greatest country the world has ever seen, and it will be for generations to come."[80] Despite known differences between the two men, Truman offered a word of encouragement to his Republican successor, Eisenhower: "I have sympathy for any man sitting in the White House, because I know what he is up against."[81]

In August 1955 Truman was the headline guest for the seventy-fifth annual Indiana Democratic Editorial Association meeting in French Lick, where he spoke before an overflow audience of 1,300. Truman's remarks were of the classic "Give 'em hell Harry" variety that made him a popular draw among Democratic Party faithful. The former president spared no words when discussing the current president, saying Eisenhower "has never missed a chance to befuddle the real issues in every speech he reads" and alleged the Republican administration was "dominated and controlled by big business—which it allows to plunder our natural resources . . . [and] is infiltrated with servants of the special interests— those who put the interest of the few ahead of the welfare of the many." Truman added that he believed Eisenhower "went so far as to use misrepresentation and demagoguery in his message on the State of the Union in January 1953."[82]

Making his case for more Democratic newspapers in the nation, and more objective reporting, Truman said, "As you all know, I am somewhat interested in the Democratic Party. Its history is long and glorious, and I believe that the Democratic Party is the best means we have for bringing representative government to this country. I have always thought so, and the last three years have made me more certain of it than ever."[83] Perhaps channeling the coming demonizing of the word "liberal" in American politics, Truman said that the Democratic Party "was the only hope of liberalism in the United States of America. The Republican Party is attacking liberalism as such, and is even trying to make the word 'liberal' an ugly or subversive word. If Democrats in Congress do not and cannot put across all the liberal measures we would like, be-

cause some few Democrats stray away from their party's platform and program, the answer is not to attack both parties indiscriminately."[84]

"We are in the midst of revolutionary changes in the country," Truman said. "The development of atomic energy and other technological advances have given us the means to produce an abundance of goods and services hitherto undreamed of. If our economy is made to function properly for the benefit of all the people, and if its products are used and distributed wisely, we can have a great era of growing prosperity. But, on the other hand, if a severe imbalance is allowed to occur, and if our economy is operated primarily in the interest of big business or any other narrow group, the results may well be serious for everyone in the country."[85]

Eisenhower never directly responded to Truman's visceral criticism, including charges of purposefully misrepresenting facts to the American people. Eisenhower left that to Republican National Committee Chairman Leonard W. Hall, who fired back in response to Truman's French Lick speech: "Harry Truman, whose administration was noted for high taxes, unemployment and a vacillating and ineffective foreign policy which culminated in the Korean 'police action,' sounded like a bitter, frustrated man. He is jealous of President Eisenhower's accomplishments and can't stand the comparison with Eisenhower's tremendous popularity. It's a good thing that Truman knew when to quit his office, but it's unfortunate he can't take retirement with dignity and grace. He doesn't present a pretty picture with his name calling and brickbats (and) he hardly fits the role of elder statesman which he tries to assume."[86]

Despite what the Republicans thought of him, Truman remained a popular draw for party fund-raisers and events, and Allen County

Democrats hosted him for their campaign kickoff in September 1958. Truman drew 13,000 to the War Memorial Coliseum in which the seventy-four-year-old former president showed no signs of letting up on his "Give 'em hell" reputation, despite the reality that the Democrats had lost both the 1952 and 1956 elections to the popular Eisenhower. Hitting a familiar theme, Truman told his fellow Democrats, "you got fat and lazy from 20 years of Democratic administrations, and you wanted a change. Well, you got just what you deserved." In a sarcastic tone, he added, "It's fantastic that Indiana has supported Republicans as long as it has. Do it again and you'll get just what you've got coming—nothing."[87] Despite his frank talk among his Democratic friends, Truman held most of his "hell" for the Republicans and Eisenhower, who he said had let the nation down in the areas of highway construction, small business tax relief, public housing, and unemployment compensation. He said the GOP continued to follow a policy of "do as little as possible and as late as possible." As an extra measure, he added a somewhat controversial reference to Eisenhower's "surrender" in Korea for the truce negotiated there in the year after Truman left office.[88]

Truman delivered another Indiana speech in support of Stevenson's second try on October 18, 1956, at the Memorial Auditorium in Gary. Truman thanked Lake County voters for their support, but noted the rest of Indiana had disappointed him and voted for the Republican ticket in 1948 and 1952. "The people that voted those Republicans into office have been getting just what they deserve," he said. "But the sad thing is that the rest of us have been suffering with them. We have all been getting a government that gives us a lot of talk but very little action. We've been getting government that's long on promises but short on performance. We've been getting a gov-

ernment that looks after the coupon clippers and lets the men and women look after themselves."[89]

Referring to the Eisenhower-Nixon administration as "Ike and Tricky Dicky," Truman said their policies are hurting farmers, small business owners, and working people. "The Republicans brag about prosperity," he said, "but their kind of prosperity is lopsided and does not apply to all the people or all parts of the country. Unless we can make sure that everyone participates in this prosperity, it will run the old Republican course of boom and bust. If we let the Republicans run things for another four years, we are bound to have a bust."[90] Turning to foreign policy, Truman said his successor had made a "mess of things at home and a worse mess of things abroad," in particular by allowing the Russians to "get a foothold" in the Mediterranean. "The Russians are now in the Middle East, and our vital interests are in danger," he warned.[91]

Known for never holding back (and for his long-term loathing of Nixon), Truman then launched into a lengthy passage about the impact and importance of the presidency and the growing demands of the office. Without alluding to Eisenhower's first-term heart attack, Truman did say the presidency "is not a part-time job, and it can't be run from a golf course. . . . The people are thinking about this, and they are worried, even the people who still like Ike are worried. More and more of them have misgivings every day as we near the election. They wonder whether he can withstand the exacting demands of the Presidency. They wonder who would control the next administration if Mr. Eisenhower were re-elected. They think of Mr. Nixon, and are frightened at the possibility of turning the government over to him. This is something to be frightened about, for remember this and remember it well, you cannot elect Ike without electing Tricky Dicky."[92]

Truman said he spoke as a former vice president who had become president upon Roosevelt's death and noted voters must pay attention to who is elected vice president. "The Republican Party, in this campaign, is offering a Vice Presidential candidate who could never possibly be elected President in his own right. They are offering a man who has neither the qualifications nor the standing in the eyes of his fellow-citizens to hold that exalted office," Truman said, labeling Nixon as "reactionary" and "not half the man Senator [Robert] Taft was."[93] Still not done, Truman asked his audience "to go home tonight, just sit down quietly by yourself, and think whether you want Dick Nixon to be President of the United States. . . . Picture Dick Nixon with all that authority over your lives and over the destiny of this country. Think it over."[94]

Truman finally got to an endorsement of Stevenson near the end of his speech, saying, "Governor Stevenson has demonstrated in this campaign a broad understanding of the issues and a thorough comprehension of the responsibilities and functions of the office he is seeking. It is to his everlasting credit that he has refused to compromise on the issue and is insisting on a full debate before the American people."[95] Truman reminded the gathering, "I am here tonight talking to you in the interest of this country we all love so well," he said. "I am asking nothing for myself and am seeking nothing. I have had the highest honor the people can give to a man. . . . Certainly, in the perils that confront us today, I cannot sit idly by. I cannot sit by without raising my voice while the country drifts toward disaster abroad and depression at home. I am telling you now, as I feel I ought to do, you must make a change in Washington."[96]

Robert A. Taft

U.S. Senator Robert A. Taft of Ohio was a young man in his twenties when his father, William Howard Taft, served as the nation's twenty-seventh president between 1909 and 1913. As a son of one of the nation's most prominent and best-known families, Robert Taft's success in being elected to the U.S. Senate from Ohio (and his rise in Republican leadership in the Senate) was not altogether surprising. A highly partisan man deeply loyal to the GOP, Taft emerged quickly as an opposition leader to the New Deal policies of President Roosevelt (Taft having won his first of three terms of the Senate in 1938). He could, however, prove to be a complex figure, challenging his fellow Republicans for their support of the Ku Klux Klan in the 1920s, supporting the development of federal public housing programs and Social Security for the nation's elderly, while vehemently opposing American involvement in World War II.

In 1940 Taft represented the conservative wing of the Republican Party and challenged more progressive forces backing Wendell L. Willkie for the GOP presidential nomination. Taft sat out the 1944 Republican nomination battle, backing a fellow Ohioan, Senator John W. Bricker, who failed to wrest the nomination away from Dewey. Regardless, Taft's opposition to New Deal policies continued to make him a "sweetheart" of the anti-Roosevelt forces and was summed up primarily in an Indianapolis address he delivered on March 11, 1944, before the Indiana Republican Editorial Association. Taft's speech, titled "How Long Shall We Submit to the Usurpation of Power by the President" was so popular among conservative Republicans that it was entered in its entirety to the *Congressional Record* just days later. At the center of Taft's remarks was concern by many Americans about Roosevelt's plans to seek a fourth term, as unprecedented in U.S. politics as had been his third term. "If the president is elected to a fourth term, with a Congress disposed to do his bidding," said Taft, "the people can only expect one course to be pursued—that is the course of steady enlargement of the executive power. That means the subjection of the states and localities to the federal government. It means the subjection of the individual to the arbitrary decrees of a hundred bureaus. It means the removal of every check upon the arbitrary power of a single executive."[97]

Taft said that "whatever powers the commander in chief of the Army and Navy may be given by the constitution, among those powers is not the right to represent them, in civilian affairs or appear for them before Congress. More and more the judges of the courts owe their appointments to President Roosevelt, and are naturally inclined to support his policies. More and more the executive departments look to him for their support, and not to the people."[98] Taft made special note of powers granted to the president because of emergency or war needs: "If one man makes the laws, can execute the laws, and can judge the violations of the law, liberty cannot long exist." He noted, "There can be little doubt that the President completely lacks respect for the legislative process and for Congress as an institution."[99]

Taft lamented the support Roosevelt had enjoyed in the Congress. "For years Congress followed the President without protest," Taft said. "Now Congress is the only barrier between the president and complete power."[100] Taft added that "all of our lives we have heard of the division of powers prescribed by the Constitution of the United States. It has become such a commonplace that any discussion of it is regarded as

elementary and uninteresting. People assume, because they see a President, a Congress, and a Supreme Court of the United States all in existence, that the division of powers is fundamental and unimpaired. But today it is impaired, and unless we change the course we are pursuing, the independent organization of the courts and the legislature will become a mere shell."[101]

Taft delivered a long, comprehensive review of both domestic and foreign policy arenas for his Indianapolis audience, outlining his view that Roosevelt had overstepped his bounds. "We are apparently asked now to elect Franklin Roosevelt to a fourth term," Taft said. "The very length of sixteen-year tenure is an invitation to arbitrary action. No man now has ever been President of the United States for more than eight years. . . . Now Congress is the only barrier between the President and complete power. Because only Congress has recovered its independence, we see today a determined assault upon that independence."[102] Taft's arguments against a fourth term for Roosevelt, however, fell on deaf ears.

In 1948 Taft made another run at the GOP presidential nomination, challenging Dewey's second attempt to be the party's standard-bearer. Taft's plans for 1948, however, were complicated by the success of former Minnesota governor Harold Stassen. Only twelve states (not including Indiana) held primaries in 1948, and Stassen did surprisingly well among voters, winning direct contests against Dewey and Taft in Wisconsin, Nebraska, Pennsylvania, and West Virginia. Stassen also had strong showings in New Jersey and Taft's home state of Ohio (although Taft held on to win the Ohio vote). At the convention in Philadelphia, it took only two ballots for Dewey to garner enough delegates to be the nominee for the second time (Taft finishing second on both ballots, ahead of Stassen, who finished in third).

By 1952 Dewey carried the unfavorable label of having lost two consecutive races for the White House, and Republicans were hungry for a win (something that had eluded them since Roosevelt's first victory in 1932). Taft made perhaps his strongest effort for the GOP nomination, calculating that although Eisenhower was widely popular among many Americans, the general lacked political campaign experience and deep roots in the party's infrastructure. Further driving Taft for the tough primary fight against Eisenhower was his distaste and vitriol for Truman, who was everything he was not— an unpolished, plainspoken man who had been elevated to the presidency by fate more than by working his way up through the ranks.

Of his multiple runs for the Republican nomination for president, Taft counted on 1952 as his best, and perhaps last, chance to succeed. Heavily favored by conservatives and many other party insiders, Taft's campaign was in place years before more progressive elements of the GOP successfully recruited Eisenhower to seek the nomination. In Indiana, most political reporters and analysts agreed that Eisenhower was wildly popular among rank-and-file Republicans and among independents and some Democrats, but that Taft had locked up the support of the state's GOP hierarchy. Unlike Eisenhower, Taft had worked Republican Party insiders in states such as Indiana for years and months leading up to 1952.

In June 1951 Taft was a special guest of Republicans in Indianapolis, where he delivered a characteristic scathing attack on Truman and the incumbent Democrats. "We have plunged into the European army project without adequately considering the capacity of our allies to contribute their share of a European army," Taft charged, "although everyone agrees that they must con-

tribute the bulk of that army." He also opened up on Truman administration policies in Korea and the president's withdrawal of General MacArthur from command there. "This shows there was no plan to deal with the Korean crisis," said Taft. "Is there any program to deal with a Communist attack in Indo-China or India or Iran or Yugoslavia?"[103]

Taft said that Truman "started the Korean War on his own responsibility" and is risking a "war with China and a war with Russia." Truman's approach to the Korean War had "practically invited an attack by the Communists," Taft said, adding, "If we had kept our troops there [in Korea], or if we had really armed the South Koreans or if we had given notice that we intended to return, as we actually did later, it is doubtful if war would ever have occurred." He said, "Even if [the President] makes an appeasement peace, he can hardly claim credit for ending without result the war which he began."[104]

Drawing applause from his partisan audience, Taft said, "All-out war and all-out mobilization are an easy method of socializing a country, and that socializing can easily be made permanent. It is a part of Joseph Stalin's plan to weaken this country's economy by his constant threats that he can accomplish his purpose by breaking up our economy from within, and make easy the path of renewed Communist infiltration."[105]

In June 1952 more than 2,000 Indiana Republicans gathered at the Indiana State Fairgrounds for a convention to select their national delegates and pledge them to either Taft or Eisenhower (Indiana did not enact a primary system until four years later). Indiana Republicans flexed their muscles in 1952, holding the last major state party convention prior to the Republican National Convention in Chicago. The state convention was swept by

Taft forces, giving all thirty-two delegates to the Ohio politician. With the Indiana sweep, Taft inched ahead of Eisenhower in unofficial delegate tallies kept by the Associated Press by a count of 462 to 389. The *New York Times* reported that "pro-Eisenhower forces were caught off guard by the [convention] motion to instruct all of Indiana's 32 delegates to vote for Senator Taft," and reflected that Eisenhower's strength with party members seemed limited to Indianapolis Republicans and not more rural party members. Reflecting that divide, the convention's keynote speaker, State Senator D. Russell Bontrager of Elkhart, took open aim at Eisenhower, calling his supporters "a paper-doll army" and that "in due time, and perhaps to our utter amazement, we will come to realize that the talents and energies of General Eisenhower have been assigned to the shadow high command of a skeleton army" and that his positions "put more cannons and more gift dollars for Europe ahead of more and cheaper bread for America." Among those angered by the move was one influential GOP delegate, Eugene Pulliam, the powerful publisher of the *Indianapolis Star* and the *Indianapolis News*, who told reporters that the delegates would go to Chicago "and vote as we damn please."[106]

A day before the convention opened, Taft arrived in Indianapolis to speak before an enthusiastic rally of 4,500 supporters at the Claypool Hotel. Amidst questions that he and Eisenhower were headed for a harmful floor fight at the Republican convention, Taft said he was "open" to negotiations on how to settle delegate disputes, including any delegates that the Eisenhower forces claimed were stolen. Taft's statements, however, were a little hard to take seriously as he appeared at a news conference surrounded by members of the state's College Republicans chapters, including two members

in costume—one with a big moustache to look like Dewey and another (a woman) dressed like Eleanor Roosevelt—both sporting "I Like Ike" buttons as Taft smiled smugly. Before leaving town, and despite temperatures climbing above ninety degrees, Taft stayed and shook hands with each of the 4,500 supporters as they filed past him for more than two hours in the lobby of the Claypool Hotel. "Coatless and with perspiration rolling off his brow, the Ohio Senator had a smile and a warm handshake for each man and woman, many of them Republican delegates," the *New York Times* reported.[107]

Taft's success among Indiana Republicans notwithstanding (their first ballot vote held for him but by a lesser count of 30–2), things grew progressively more difficult for him at the national convention. Republicans were hungry and desperate to win the presidency. Polls showing Eisenhower's popularity among Republicans and possible crossover voters contributed to a drift away from Taft. On the first ballot, Eisenhower held a slim ninety-five-vote lead over Taft, a lead that grew substantially on the second (and final ballot), as Eisenhower was nominated for his first political campaign ever.

The vanquished Taft took several weeks to overcome the disappointment of his loss, but was true to his title of "Mr. Republican" by showing up in the fall campaign to assist Eisenhower on a twenty-four-state tour to inspire the party faithful. Among the states where Taft was popular, including Indiana, he made a strong pitch for Eisenhower's election, along with other members of the GOP ticket. On October 9 and 10, 1952, Taft made a swing through the state with stops at Indianapolis, Bloomington, La Porte, and Elkhart. In Indianapolis, Taft warned a Republican audience at the Columbia Club that it must not underestimate Truman's influence on the presidential race, even though he was not a candidate. Taft had reason to have Truman on his mind. Both men spoke in Indianapolis just six hours apart on October 9. Taft said Truman's "give 'em hell" charges against the GOP could appeal to "know nothing" voters, but not intelligent voters. Taft urged Republican candidates to focus "on all the issues which people are concerned [because] the people are on our side. There is no enthusiasm for the Korean war, for mink coats, for freezers, or for big spending." Taft declared the Truman administration "the worst and more general, corrupt and immoral government we've ever had," and that Democratic presidential candidate Stevenson "is with these people hand and glove."[108]

During the evening, Taft spoke to an audience estimated at 2,000 at Bloomington and urged the election of Eisenhower as "the only way to clean out all Communist influence from the government."[109] Declaring that Secretary of State Dean Acheson had a tendency "to love Communism," Taft said that the "pro-Communist sympathies" of the Truman administration would continue if Stevenson were elected. "Stevenson has stood with Acheson," Taft said, "he's had the same tendency to love Communism" and that both men were "blind to Communism in the government itself."[110]

The next day in Elkhart, Taft told another GOP audience at the high-rise Hotel Elkhart that the Eisenhower campaign had effectively succeeded in outlining winning issues for the November election. "I have talked with General Eisenhower several times," Taft said. "He has frequently stated his belief—long before the convention—in the same American principles which I think are essential to achieve continued progress in the United States and protect the liberty of our people." Taft repeated now common themes thrown at the Democrats that Truman and Acheson had "demonstrated softness to Communism"—typical of many "left-wingers in this country"—and said "the Republican Party has always known the doctrine of international Communism for exactly what it is."[111]

Following his speech as he was departing from the hotel via a freight elevator to avoid a crowded hotel lobby, Taft was among six people shaken up as the elevator dropped to the hotel's basement in a grinding stop at the bottom of its shaft after the operator was unable to engage the car's break at the street level. "Taft was the calmest man on the elevator," said Wallace Sheridan, one of his aides. Hotel and campaign officials used the operator's stool to assist the passengers out of the crashed car. A nearby reporter quoted Taft as saying sarcastically, "This is a nice welcome" and described him as "unruffled" by the fall.[112] Taft seemed to recover quickly, later in the day speaking before more than 6,000 people gathered at Rice Field at Elkhart High School to hear him rail against "Communism and socialism in our government" and to praise American labor leaders for their efforts to help "weed out acknowledged Communists and Communists-controlled unions," and then indicted the AFL-CIO political action committee as "a socialist political organization trying to elect Stevenson President."[113]

During a stop at La Porte before arriving in Elkhart, Taft told a rally audience there that the Truman administration had "set up the Communists in both Europe and Asia" and claimed Russia held "the power to attack us any time." He pledged that Eisenhower would make firing Acheson one of his first priorities. Taft said Acheson and "his fellow New Dealers" had dealt with "the Chinese Communists as peace-loving agrarians with whom any New Dealer would get along and love."[114]

Following Eisenhower's election in November 1952, and the accompanying Republican majority in the U.S. Senate, Taft became majority leader of the upper chamber. It was a short-lived tenure, however, as by April 1953 growing pain from what Taft believed was arthritis caused him to check into the Walter Reed Hospital in Maryland. A few weeks later with a diagnosis that he was suffering from a debilitating form of bone cancer, Taft stepped aside as majority leader but retained his Senate seat. He never returned to the Capitol, however, dying of a brain hemorrhage on July 31, 1953. He was sixty-three years old. Upon news of his death, his onetime opponent, Eisenhower, released a statement that said:

> The passing of Robert A. Taft is a tragic loss to America. The brilliant son of our twenty-seventh President, Senator Taft served the people of Ohio and the nation with distinction and integrity. He will be greatly missed on Capitol Hill where his unimpeachable character and his vast knowledge of the business of good government played such an important part in Congressional decisions over many years.
>
> The Senate has lost one of its leading members of all times, the American people have lost a truly great citizen and I have lost a wise counselor and a valued friend. Mrs. Eisenhower and I extend to Mrs. Taft and the family our heartfelt sympathies in the personal loss that they have sustained.[115]

Thomas E. Dewey

The contrast between the Truman and Dewey campaigns of 1948 was perhaps no more exemplified than in Indiana. While Truman's campaign train seemed to stop at every community along the rail line, Dewey apparently took Indiana as solidly Republican and not needing much of his attention. News reporters noted the differences between the Truman and Dewey campaigns,

particularly on how the separate candidates conducted their whistle-stop efforts. As Truman aide Bray noted, "Perhaps the best way to describe the atmosphere on the [Truman] campaign train during the trips is to use the characterization of the newspapermen. On the Dewey train, the newspapermen played bridge and drank martinis and manhattans. On the Truman train they played poker and drank scotch and bourbon."[116]

Dewey's less-than-engaged attitude about Indiana was exemplified in his rather reluctant late campaign stop in Rensselaer for "Charlie Halleck Day," while the candidate was en route to his mother's home in Owosso, Michigan, for some much-needed rest. It would be Dewey's only formal campaign appearance in Indiana, though his "Victory Train" special rolled into and out of Indiana many times as he moved back and forth across the nation. *Time* magazine reported that Dewey seemed disengaged about his Indiana visit until the last moment. *Time* reporters noted that Dewey did not leave his private rail car to greet U.S. Senator William Jenner of Indiana as he joined the train at Chicago, and Dewey refused to emerge from his private quarters until the train came to a stop in Jasper County, where he promptly ignored most of the local Republican dignitaries and focused most of his effort on repairing his friendship with Halleck, who felt betrayed by Dewey and his campaign. Halleck believed if he delivered the entire Indiana delegation to Dewey at the Republican Convention, he would be assured a spot on the ticket as the party's vice presidential nominee. No such nomination came (it instead went to California governor Earl E. Warren), and Dewey stopped off in Rensselaer on a widely viewed "peace-keeping mission" with the powerful House leader.

As *Time* magazine reported, Halleck joined Dewey on the rear platform of the Victory Special, but "he was not invited to board the train and he looked more disconsolate than usual when the candidate majestically appeared. But Charlie cheered up later when Mr. Dewey, making a speech at the town's little Saint Joseph's College, referred to Congressman Halleck as 'one of the oldest friends I have in public life.' During the rest of the speech Charlie beamed, clapping at every opportunity."[117]

James Reston, political writer for the *New York Times,* openly referred to Dewey's stop in Indiana as "a 150-mile detour which indicated what he is really worrying about. Mr. Dewey, who feels more confident about winning the election than winning the support of some Republican leaders in Congress, made a special trip here to see Charles A. Halleck, Republican leader in the House of Representatives and disappointed also-ran for the Republican vice presidential nomination." Reston reported that Halleck had "seldom shown much enthusiasm for many of the progressive foreign and domestic policies supported by Mr. Dewey," but remained a key figure in the Republican Party and would help determine the success of the expected Dewey administration. At least publicly, Halleck seemed to share Dewey's strong confidence that the November election was sewed up for the Republicans and declared, "We will all work together as a team in meeting our problems." Dewey added, "I can think of nothing I look forward to with such pleasure as working with him [Halleck] for the benefit of the entire American people."[118] Reston emphasized the Dewey confidence level, reporting, "The Dewey organization, therefore, is beginning to think not only about Nov. 2 but about Jan. 20, when, if elected, Mr. Dewey will have to deal with powerful members of his own party who have, in the past, taken positions directly opposite to those favored by the Republican candidate."[119]

For his speech at the Saint Joseph College Fieldhouse, Dewey addressed a crowd of 7,500, and loudspeakers were used to broadcast his remarks to those gathered outside who could not fit inside.[120] Dewey complimented the slew of Indiana Republicans on the stage with him and the local band on hand for the festivities, a joint effort of Rensselaer and Morocco High Schools. He promised "a spring housecleaning in January [in Washington], the biggest and the best and the healthiest housecleaning this government has ever had."[121] Dewey's speech was typical of his campaign style—a bureaucratic review of his ideas for a reorganization of parts of the federal government. Dewey said the nation's welfare programs needed to be gathered up under one Cabinet level office, an office to manage the nation's programs for unemployment compensation, old age assistance, the public health service, minimum wage enforcement, and a federal study of guaranteed annual wage. "One of the great and solemn tasks before us is to care for the security of our people," he said. "Services which the government must perform for the people are now so scattered and in so many hands that nobody is getting the service in which he is entitled."[122] Dewey also addressed the need for soil conservation and support for rural electrification programs in other parts of the nation.

On foreign policy, Dewey said, "It is our obligation to lead in peace. If we make our purpose clear to all the world that we want peace, we can and we will succeed."[123] Dewey said the United States carried a postwar obligation to lead all free nations of the world in a coalition for peace and to deter any dictator's desire to impose restraints on freedom. Dewey called for a future of "peaceful progress" as "a rightful heritage to our sons and daughters."[124]

The *Rensselaer Republican* noted that "Governor Dewey made a distinct impression on his audience. His address was forceful and direct. His speech was clear cut and concise, and delivered in a very pleasing and homey manner, with many extemporaneous, humorous sidelights."[125]

After having paid his "party dues" to Halleck in a stop at Rensselaer that lasted little more than an hour, Dewey's train made a brief stop at Hammond, where he addressed a small crowd from the rear of his train. He said he was pleased to see the large amount of schoolchildren at the rally, until several of them yelled back that it was Saturday and that they were out of school anyway. "Well, then, it shows that you came down here because you wanted to and nobody made you do it," Dewey said.[126]

The Rensselaer stop was noteworthy for the fact that it represented one of the last campaign appearances by Dewey outside of New York. Polls showed that Dewey was on his way to a major victory over President Truman.[127]

Henry A. Wallace

Dumped by Roosevelt as his running mate for the 1944 election, Wallace, the former secretary of agriculture and later the secretary of commerce, was not ready to step from the limelight in 1948. Wallace accepted the nomination of the Progressive Party, a third-party effort launched in response to the more conservative Democrats led by Truman. Wallace, as it played out, had missed becoming president via the route Truman did by only a few months.

In 1948 Wallace shed all pretense about trying to placate southern Democrats and worked hard to pull the agenda to the left on a variety of issues, including the ongoing effort to win World War II and civil rights. At the other end of the scale was Senator Strom Thurmond of South Carolina and his States' Rights Democratic Party nomination effort. For Truman, it appeared the Democrats were splitting apart at the seams—Wallace to the left and Thurmond to the right. Wallace's 1948 campaign never gained much traction (polling approximately 2 percent of the popular vote in November, just behind a similarly unimpressive showing by Thurmond), but it was not for a lack of trying, and Indiana was a key, if not newsworthy, player in Wallace's effort.

Wallace's campaign scheduled three visits to Indiana in April 1948—at Evansville, Indianapolis and Gary—and generated national headlines for a handful of ugly incidents that surrounded his appearances. Days before Wallace's arrival in Indianapolis, controversy erupted when Howard Maxwell, the adjutant general of the Indiana National Guard announced that the Guard had canceled a reservation by the Indiana Citizens for Wallace Committee for use of the National Guard Armory in downtown Indianapolis for a rally. Maxwell, told reporters that "certain individuals" were not welcome to appear inside the armory building, including "noted Negro singer" Paul Robeson. Wallace's campaign officials objected and said they intended to carry on their meeting as planned, but Maxwell was not backing down. "I have no objection to Mr. Wallace," Maxwell said. "The armory was rented so that he could make a speech. Now I find that a number of persons in the 'radical fringe' are scheduled to appear on the platform. I reserve the right to say who shall appear on the platform."[128] Governor Ralph Gates eventually intervened, and Maxwell backed down. Wallace's speech, "Peace, Security and Abundance," was allowed to go forward.

The troubles did not end, however. Upon arrival in Indianapolis for a fund-raising luncheon before departing for Evansville, the Wallace campaign found its luncheon reservation had been canceled by the manager of the Hotel Warren in downtown Indianapolis because of Robeson's appearance. Major hotels in downtown Indianapolis were mostly segregated in 1948. Three hundred guests were eventually routed to a new venue, but overnight accommodations also became difficult for Wallace, Robeson, and their party to arrange in an inhospitable capital city. Wallace's top campaign aides openly accused leaders of the Ku Klux Klan and the American Legion (a claim denied by Legion officials) of placing hurdles in front of Wallace's campaign. Robeson's rude welcome was not new. In January 1948 local officials had successfully blocked a planned speech by Robeson at Roosevelt High School in Gary, believing that a public school building should not be used to allow remarks by a "Communist sympathizer."[129]

As ugly as the reception in Indianapolis had been, things were worse in Evansville, where a protest crowd of more than 2,500 surrounded the War Memorial Coliseum to protest Wallace's presence. Many of them were angry union aircraft workers, who heartily disliked Wallace's call to scale back aviation construction in the postwar years. Union opposition to Wallace was so strong that the Indiana Industrial Union, a national affiliate of the CIO, suspended eight of its twenty-four executive board members for "refusal to follow policies" by publicly stating support for Wallace's candidacy.[130]

While waiting for Wallace to arrive, two of his national campaign aides and an auditorium usher were injured in a variety of skirmishes that broke out among the protesters (some of whom attempted to crash into the auditorium in order to interrupt Wallace's speech). "The altercation developed when a group which had been picketing the Coliseum attempted to enter," the Associated Press reported. "Mr. Wallace's campaign

manager was struck in the face . . . a national field representative suffered a black eye and a cut over the other eye, and . . . an usher was slugged in the face."[131]

Wallace eventually spoke to a paltry crowd of less than 800, which was easily dwarfed by the protesters outside, but, according to the Associated Press, "Mr. Wallace did not pass through the line, remaining at his hotel until the marchers had been disbanded. City police cleared the foyer of the Coliseum after the exchange of blows, but the crowd continued to mill around outside the building. Mr. Wallace's supporters inside the auditorium barricaded the doors with metal chairs. The third party candidate was brought in a side entrance of the Coliseum by police."[132]

For his Evansville speech, Wallace noted that April 6 was "Army Day" and took the occasion to salute "the professional military men of our country. They have performed valiant services in both peace and war. As an American who is proud of their records and grateful to them, I salute them from the heart." But Wallace then added, "I must also express the hope that the day is not too far distance, when our children and our children's children shall observe Army Day purely for its historical significance."[133] Wallace declared that the men guiding the nation's foreign and domestic policies in 1948, however, "have embarked us on a dangerous course, which will postpone the achievement of that new kind of Army Day. I won't want to see them make everyday Army Day—yet that is precisely the course on which we are launched." He charged the Truman administration's foreign policy had "earned the enmity of many people, and if it continues, we shall not have any substantial number of friends left in the entire world, save the out-and-out fascists."[134]

Referring to the angry protesters outside the arena, Wallace said it was difficult for most

Americans to understand the truth of the problem. "Our foreign policy is dressed up in all the right words—freedom, justice, democracy. But the clothes don't make the man; nor words the foreign policy," he said. Wallace noted that the aspirations of Americans reached far beyond the desire for peace, however. "They hope for products of peace; for the economic and social justice of which hundreds of millions of them have been deprived. The growth of Communism in Europe is not a result of something evil in the hearts of the workers and farmers. It is a reflection of their desperate needs."[135] Hitting on a major theme of his campaign, Wallace asked his audience to consider who "profited" from war and declared that the Republican and Democratic parties "are no more interested in the welfare of the people abroad than they are of the great mass of people here at home. They don't become humanitarians in dealing with foreign countries after opposing measures for the advance of health, education, housing, and social security here at home. Their purposes abroad, and their purposes in getting through the misnamed foreign aid bill are the same as their purposes here—they are interested in profits, and the general welfare be damned."[136]

Adding a local flair, Wallace noted that "here in Evansville, where you produced one of our great tools for victory in the last war—the Thunderbolt plane—I was to discuss an industry which is helping to foment the present war hysteria and urge a course of action which will provide some safety to the people of the United States. I speak of the aircraft industry. It is dependent on our money—yours and mine—as taxpayers to keep going. As presently operated, it needs huge military contracts. To get those contracts, it has helped foment the war hysteria." He accused aircraft manufacturers of being "unable or unwilling to adapt their operations to peacetime civilian

needs; and they want easy and big profits such as they enjoyed during the war years." To underline his case, he noted that the Republic Aviation Corporation that operated the Evansville Thunderbolt plant enjoyed profits of $9 million after taxes over an initial investment of only $1 million. "That represents a 150 percent profit per year for the six years from 1940 through 1946," he said.[137]

Alternately, Wallace advocated turning over the aviation industry to the federal government and out of the hands of "warmongers," "defanging" their profit motive for war. "The war makers would make a Frankenstein of the airplane," he said. "To hundreds of millions of people the airplane is a nightmare symbol of sudden death. We can make the airplane a symbol of progress and good living."[138]

Veering into territory that often brought Wallace controversy, he asked his audience to distinguish carefully between Adolf Hitler's defeated dictatorship in Germany and Stalin's Russia. "We lost too much [in the war] to blindly accept that they are the same," Wallace stated. "When we are willing to accept the factual difference between fascism and communism; when we have stopped the circulation of the myth that the two are the same, we shall find that we can live at peace with Russia without jeopardizing our own hopes for an economy of abundance based on a system of progressive capitalism in a democratic society."[139] He concluded by declaring that "people everywhere are demanding that our science, our resources, and our energies be used to meet human needs. War is not a human need. The world wants peace. If we enlist for peace and act for peace, we shall have peace!"[140]

Back in Indianapolis after his rough night in Evansville, Wallace and Robeson found shelter in the homes of local supporters after hotel rooms remained unavailable. Speaking to reporters about the violence the night before, Wallace said, "We must avoid being drawn into acts of violence. That is what they are trying to get us to do. We are not going to roll around in the gutter with them."[141] For Wallace's evening speech, twenty-five Indianapolis Police Department officers patrolled in and around the armory, but no incidents were reported before from a small group of protesters who gathered outside the armory, who quickly dispersed as a thunderstorm rolled in.[142] Wallace spent the better part of his speech lamenting the lack of coverage his remarks in Evansville had received. Instead, the local media there attempted to cast him as a Communist appeaser. "I am certain that the Evansville newspaper, which quite justly criticized the press of the Soviet Union for biased selection of the news,

never printed the substance of my criticism of the policies which are leading us toward war. But they have doubtless printed many columns of attacks, slanders and distortions. I could feel happy and hopeful for the future if the newspapers of America allowed me a single line to state my position for every two lines they spend criticizing me," Wallace declared.[143]

Wallace again promoted America as the greatest, richest, and most powerful nation in the world, "Yet we meet as citizens of a nation which is shaking with fear. We haven't been struck by bombs. We haven't felt the onslaught of invading forces. We aren't shaking because our shores, our land, our people have been attacked. We are trembling from the attacks of headlines and commentators. We are victims of a deliberate campaign to create fear. It is a campaign designed

Secretary of Agriculture Henry Wallace shakes hands with Senator George Norris of Nebraska, after Wallace explained details of his "ever normal granary" proposal to members of the Senate Agricultural Committee in November 1937.

LIBRARY OF CONGRESS

to win support, the support of frightened people, for policies which would put our economy completely at the mercy of the military."[144]

Without mentioning the ousted Indiana union leaders directly, Wallace told his audience of 3,500, "I am in the fortunate position where I can afford to speak out. I am privileged to enjoy free speech. But millions of my fellow Americans who wish to speak openly, frankly and forthrightly about the problems of our time cannot afford to speak out. Speech which costs a man his job isn't free." Wallace did not know it as he spoke, but within days another Hoosier would lose his job for his vocal support of Wallace and his positions. Doctor George Parker, a professor of philosophy and religion at Evansville College, was asked for his resignation days after having served as emcee and introducing Wallace for the controversial Evansville speech and for his role as Vanderburgh County chairman of the Wallace campaign. The college's president, Doctor Lincoln P. Hale, was open about Parker's departure from the faculty, noting that the school's executive committee believed Parker's "usefulness to the school is at an end" because of his "political activities both on and off the campus."[145]

In his Indianapolis speech, Wallace restated his views from the night before about turning over the aviation industry to the federal government and said, "I said this industry has shown it is incapable of profitable peacetime production, which is the only justification for private enterprise. I said that industries depending on war and unlimited preparation for war must not remain in private hands. There is nothing new or radical about this proposal."[146]

Concluding, Wallace added to his prepared remarks in a handwritten sentence that read, "The immediate prospects are not that pleasant. Today under the guide of a war threat, our civil liberties are in jeopardy; writers, artists and scientists are afraid to speak up; workers see the revival of government-by-injunctions, as they fight for decent wages and better working conditions." His most widely reported remark was a provocative claim that the "war scare tactics" of the Truman administration represented an "aping act" of the fear the Nazis employed in Germany.[147]

For his stop in Gary on April 8, 1948, Wallace said he viewed the industrial steel center of America to be "a perfect symbol of industrial America. It is a symbol of our strength, of our democracy. It is a city which has been built, as our country has been built, by people who fled from tyranny, and hunger abroad, to the freedom and the promise of freedom here in the United States. Gary is a symbol of our almost limitless industrial power—the power which, if properly harnessed, would bring plenty to all our citizens and contribute so greatly to the peace and prosperity of the world. And Gary is important as a symbol of the century-long fight of American workers for a better life through strong, free trade unions."[148] Wallace quickly moved to railing against the Taft-Hartley Act, noting that its authors and supporters "are not interested in humanitarian purposes abroad. They use all the right words to describe a foreign policy which the people would approve, but they don't mean what they say any more than they mean 'freedom for labor' and 'industrial peace.'"[149]

Wallace said the steelworkers of Gary know the meaning of the word monopoly. "They know what I mean when I speak of 'the use of force'— economic force, political force, yes, and physical force as the weapons of monopoly. The steel trust was the great champion of the open shop, sweated labor, low wages, labor spies, and private police. The steelworkers of America have not forgotten the 18 years of bloody battles that marked their efforts to organize from the end of the first war until 1937 when they forced U.S. Steel to recognize their union and sign a contract—an historic contract—for higher wages and better (working) conditions."[150] Absent from Wallace's prepared remarks was any mention of civil rights, although the rough-and-tumble reception his campaign had received in Indiana remained on his mind and in his remarks in days later in New York City, when he told the audience there:

> Every time a Negro citizen is forced to use Jim Crow facilities or attends a segregated meeting, he is suffering from a police state. When Paul Robeson, myself and other members of our party were denied hotel rooms in Indianapolis, we were experiencing the effects of the psychosis which will lead to a full police state here. . . . You say that these are small incidents. They are. But they are straws in a very dangerous wind. And the victims of violence in Evansville or intimidation by the House Un-American Committee can't be counted. These incidents are intended to frighten other people into silence; they place a high price on speech which should be free.[151]

During a September 1948 speech in South Bend, Wallace urged Truman to "throw the weight of his office behind the Progressive Party practice of refusing to participate in un-American meetings—in segregated meetings." Wallace said, "Mr. Truman has the opportunity to make a historic contribution by speaking to real [integrated] meetings in the South, and I hope he takes the opportunity. It will help restore some of our moral strength in world affairs."[152] Speaking before a small crowd of 1,500 supporters at South Bend, Wallace again derided the Marshall Plan to restore postwar Europe as "a gigantic pork barrel" project meant to benefit big business and accused Truman and the military-industrial complex of always looking for a new world crisis.[153]

Wallace's campaign appearances in Indiana

for the 1948 campaign contrasted greatly with his stops in 1940 as Roosevelt's running mate. In 1940 the president's disability limited his physical campaigning in the states, and so it was left to Wallace to work the campaign trail. Not coincidentally, Wallace began a 7,000-mile tour of the nation from Indiana—Republican nominee Wendell Willkie's home turf—before an overflow audience of 10,000 Democrats assembled at the Cadle Tabernacle in downtown Indianapolis on September 24, 1940. There Wallace spoke on "Democracy and Capitalism," saying he had come to Indiana "to speak to the farmers, the workers, and the businessmen of Indiana about democracy and freedom."[154] Wallace said, "In this dark year of the world, many free nations and millions of free people like ourselves have lost their liberty, and we know only a little of the outrages that they suffer. But we know that unless we are wise as well as brave, we too may lose our right to democratic government and our right to personal freedom."[155] As he spoke, German invaders continued their march across Europe, fully engaged by British and Russian troops, while Japanese forces began their encroachment upon portions of China and other parts of Asia. Inside Germany and other European nations controlled by the Nazis, orders were arriving that required all Jewish citizens to wear special arm bands identifying their faith to Nazi forces.

Although most of his remarks were focused on domestic and economic issues, Wallace repudiated Republican congressmen from Indiana who had defied their party's presidential nominee, Willkie, and voted against the military draft proposed by the Roosevelt administration. He noted to heavy applause, "Those who chose to vote the Republican ticket may be in some doubt whether their votes will count for national defense, or against it."[156]

"We all pray the war should end happily before we are forced to defend our own shores," Wallace said. "(But) you and I know that the danger will not be over. We must then go on with the long struggle that has engaged our country for 70 years, the struggle to preserve freedom against internal forces that break it down and wear it way. To keep the name of democracy is not enough. We must be careful lest we lose the substance."[157] Wallace said he believed protecting democracy meant "protecting the interests of the vast majority of Americans," specifically farmers, workers, small businessmen, and big business leaders who showed good judgment, fairness and responsibility for the general welfare of others. He warned that this type of democracy was what the founding fathers intended and what was threatened by the financial collapse of 1929, fueled by excesses of the few in the decade prior.

Drawing applause he said, "It is the kind of democracy that has been saved, restored, and set upon the road to new strength and security by our great democratic leader, Franklin D. Roosevelt."[158] Continuing his populist appeal, Wallace said freedoms such as speech, worship, and the ability to criticize the government were not at risk, but a real problem existed in ensuring not only political liberty, but also economic liberty. He warned that the "field for free enterprise" continued to shrink in America and that business people were particularly "fenced in by the great financial empires, and most of us cannot get into those fields unless the men who hold power there are pleased to give us a job."[159]

He also warned of the dangers of trusts and combines, monopolies and holding companies, and the rising influence of high finance. "There is a difference between business and finance, which some people sometimes try to make you forget," he said. "Capitalist enterprise is a familiar process of producing and selling food, clothes, automobiles, and other useful goods and services. . . . But high finance is not much concerned with producing real things. It is concerned rather with manipulating stocks, weaving an intricate web of controls—a web that the ordinary working business man cannot understand."[160] Wallace said the nation was replete with examples of small businesses "snared in the meshes" of big business rendering the small man helpless. "He never knows what happened to him, except that he is out of business, or is reduced to a salaried job as the servant of some unseen distant power."[161]

Wallace turned next to a review of public battles between the Roosevelt administration and large corporations and monopolies, many of them tied to utilities and transportation. He cautioned that Abraham Lincoln and Thomas Jefferson would never recognize or understand "this labyrinth of corporate organization as the kind of democracy to which they dedicated their lives. Any one of these men would have done just what Roosevelt has done: They would have tried to put the people back in control!"[162]

Acknowledging his former Republican roots, Wallace said he, like many, had fled to the Democratic Party in the depths of the Great Depression of the 1930s. He said Roosevelt had "labored at the painful task of repairing the devastation that had resulted from financial mistakes" of previous Republican administrations. "We have not yet cleaned up all the dangerous monopolies and financial monstrosities that overhang the capitalist system in this country, but we have made progress," he declared.[163]

Wallace touted the success of the Civilian Conservation Corps, the National Youth Administration, and the Works Progress Administration that had put many Americans back to work. "We have built highways, airports, bridges and dams, designed for peace, but extremely valuable in case of war," he said. "Even in direct military preparedness, the President, who foresaw the rising storm long before the rest of the country was willing to recognize the danger, used his powers under the 1933 Public Works appropriation to lay down large additions to our Navy."[164] Promotion of a safety net for seniors, via Social Security, and through labor laws intended to protect workers and ensure fair wages, had all benefited Indiana's citizens, Wallace said. Enactment of the federal Food Stamp Plan was also highly beneficial to Hoosier farmers, he added.

Concluding his lengthy remarks, punctuated by applause from his partisan audience, Wallace said the election of 1940 presented voters with a critical choice: "Shall we turn our destiny in this critical period over to the same forces of monopoly and high finance that so blindly threw us into the ditch in 1929? Or in the interest of Main Street and with its democratic point of view, shall we keep on finding ways for business, labor, and agriculture to act in true partnership with a people's government!"[165]

Effective at delivering the populist appeal, Wallace won election as the nation's thirty-third vice president in November, but struggled to keep the support of the president and his fellow Democrats. Often clashing over wartime policies at home, Roosevelt eventually pulled power away from Wallace, who was unceremoniously dumped by his party to be a nominee for re-election in 1944. Instead, Roosevelt allowed convention delegates to name Truman as his running mate. Sworn into office in early 1945, Truman replaced Wallace as vice president and became president himself just eighty-two days later.

Truman made the rare move of appointing Wallace as Secretary of Commerce, but eventually fired him for political differences that continued

to surface between the two men. Wallace abandoned the Democratic Party in 1948. Wallace retired to rural New York and resumed farming and occasionally dabbled in politics. He died in Danbury, Connecticut, on November 18, 1965, at the age of seventy-seven.

Dwight D. Eisenhower

Considering his historic role in the Allied victory in World War II, it is not surprising that both major parties in the United States were eager to woo General Eisenhower to lead their ticket for president. It was the Republicans who won the rights to have Eisenhower be their candidate for president.

Eisenhower's 1952 campaign found him in the Hoosier State early in the going for the fall campaign. Lucky Hoosiers at Richmond had gained an even earlier glimpse of the popular war hero. He and his wife, Mamie, made a brief stop by the back of a train just after the close of World War II on June 24, 1945, with Eisenhower calling Mamie to the platform to accept a large bouquet of roses in Richmond, "the city of roses."[166]

Just after Labor Day 1952, Eisenhower made a quick visit to Indianapolis to speak before a noisy audience of 16,000 supporters at Butler

IHS, O. JAMES FOX COLLECTION, P. 266

GOP presidential candidate Dwight Eisenhower campaigns on Indiana Avenue in Indianapolis during the 1952 election.

Fieldhouse. An overflow audience of Republican fans and the curious were sent to the adjacent Butler Bowl football stadium, where they listened to Eisenhower's speech via a loudspeaker. Upon arriving in Indianapolis, Eisenhower overlooked the fact that Indiana Republicans had pledged their support to Taft at the Republican convention just weeks earlier and that he was introduced to the audience by Senator Jenner, one of his most loathed Republican counterparts. Jenner had won Eisenhower's scorn, and that of many across the nation, for his 1950 remarks that General George C. Marshall was "a front man for traitors" and "a living lie" as "either an unsuspecting stooge or an actual co-conspirator with the most treasonable array of political cutthroats ever turned loose in the executive branch of the government."[167] Eisenhower opened his remarks by noting that his last visit to the city, in 1950, came at a time when he never expected he would one day be a candidate for president of the United States. "But no American can stand to one side while his country becomes the prey of fear mongers, quack doctors and barefaced looters," he said. "An American doesn't twiddle his thumbs while his garden is wrecked by a crowd of vandals and his house invaded by a gang of robbers. He goes into action. When the same sort of thing happens to his country, an American goes into action by getting into politics—fast and hard. I'm

in politics just that way, my friends. And I'll keep on bombarding the administration until you, the voters, lick them for good in November."[168]

While asking his audience to support the entire Republican ticket, although avoiding mentioning Jenner by name, he declared, "We Republicans are not servile puppets of a dictated party line. We don't have loyalty oaths. . . . We want independent minds and men who speak their minds."[169] With Mamie looking on and smiling, he suggested further that the men in the audience exercise some ultimate patriotism by babysitting the children and "washing the breakfast dishes on Election Day, if in that way a wife is enabled to cast her vote. And may I point out to the wives of America that postponing a shopping tour or keeping the supper warm an extra hour on Election Day will be equally an act of patriotism, should thereby a husband be enabled to vote." The remarks represented a clear push by the Republicans in 1952 (and again in 1956) to court the female vote—a rarity in American politics to that point—and to contrast the happily married Eisenhowers to the divorced Democratic nominee, Stevenson. Returning to familiar themes of needing to root out entrenched bureaucrats and accompanying graft after twenty years of Democratic rule in the White House, Eisenhower invoked a biblical theme noting that "there is a time to keep and a time to cast away"

Eisenhower on the campaign trail somewhere in Indiana, 1952

IHS, GIFT OF EMMA WOLFANGER FORLER

and that he would cast away "the incompetent, the unfit, the cronies and the chiselers. Next we shall cast away the alien philosophy that our national destiny lies in the supremacy of government over all."[170]

On September 15, 1952, Eisenhower appeared at Indiana Harbor in Lake County, the starting and ending point for an initial twelve-day, twelve-state whistle-stop tour. To open his remarks he repeated his Labor Day promise that he hoped that if he were elected president that "at the end of the four years, every working man in the United States—of whom I have always been one, was raised as one—would be able to say about me, 'He was our friend and he was fair.'"[171] He sought to contrast himself with his Democratic opponent questioning the now commonplace campaign wit and humor that Stevenson used to connect to his audiences. Eisenhower asked: What's so funny about the Korean War, national debt, high taxes, and inflation that reduced the spending power of working American families? "I have found," Eisenhower said, "in this business of going around the country carrying a political message to your friends and neighbors wherever you may meet them, it would be very, very fine if one could command new and amusing language, witticisms to bring you a chuckle. Frankly, I have no intention of trying to do so. The subjects of whom we are speaking these days, my friends, are not those that seem to me to be amusing."[172]

Eisenhower, obviously hoping to create an image of Stevenson as witty, but out of touch with the American public, continued by noting that 117,000 Americans had already been killed or wounded in Korea. "Is it amusing that war seems to be no closer to a real solution than ever; that we have no real plan for stopping it; is it amusing that we now have a debt so great that

the thousands of babies born today in the United States, each one of them, gets as his first present an $1,800 debt that it has to pay to the government?" Eisenhower asked.[173]

The Republican whistle-stop campaign included the state's two U.S. senators, Jenner (running for re-election) and Homer E. Capehart, both usually identified with Eisenhower's vanquished GOP challenger, Taft. Eisenhower visited seven Indiana communities during those September days, with police estimates indicating a crowd of 55,000 at Fort Wayne; 3,000 at Indiana Harbor; 2,500 at Warsaw; 2,000 at Gary, Plymouth, and La Porte; and an stunning 30,000 jamming the streets of downtown South Bend surrounding the Saint Joseph County Courthouse. The size of the South Bend crowd apparently surprised Eisenhower (given the city's Democratic track record). People were "crowded onto the tops of near-by buildings until they seemed to be in peril of their lives and screamed his name until he finally responded to their calls," the *New York Times* reported. "Along South Bend's downtown streets, too, the people were so numerous that almost all downtown traffic was stopped while his 50-auto caravan rode out to the University of Notre Dame." Eisenhower waved happily to packed crowds along the downtown streets from atop an open-top Studebaker (made in South Bend).[174]

While at Notre Dame, Eisenhower spoke to a group of enthusiastic male students. He told them "never forget for one second this is the one country where you can do and act and think and worship as you please. Perhaps I dwell on this subject a little more than most of my friends think I should, but I have lived too many years in those places where government tells you what you may do, where you may go, how you are going to spend your lives. Treasure it and keep

Crowd gathers to greet GOP presidential candidate Dwight Eisenhower at the Weir Cook Airport in Indianapolis, 1952.

it and work and fight for the United States of America. You not only can do it but you will have the richest and fullest possible life doing it."[175] En route to the campus, Eisenhower asked his driver to take his car into the driveway of the Northern Indiana Children's Hospital "where the nurses had rolled the patients' beds outside so that they could see the nominee."[176]

Eisenhower's remarks in downtown South Bend were delivered with some difficulty, reporters noted, since the size of the crowd far outdistanced the ability of loudspeakers installed. As a result, shouts of "We like Ike!" continued at times when the retired general was trying to speak. The audience did not miss, however, his heartfelt declaration that although he lacked the wit and ability to turn a phrase that his opponent possessed, "The only single dedication I should like to make is this: I am one of you and to you and those like you in all this broad land, whatever I have of spiritual, intellectual strength is yours to use as you please."[177] Eisenhower said the people of the United States had paid him a tremendous compliment by entrusting to him "thousands, literally millions of their young men and women, to lead them in a crusade in Europe in order that a threatening dictatorship could not impinge

upon our free way of life. The assignment of that responsibility was the greatest thing that ever happened in my life to that date." He added a special message for the children and young adults in the throng. "In this crowd and out at the university I saw and see now a tremendous proportion of young people. The most we can do for them is to point out such mistakes as we have made, give to them such wisdom as we may have picked up along the line. But it is their idealism, it is their fervor, it is their determination to work for a cause that is going to make this America what it must be."[178]

Speaking from the steps of the Allen County Courthouse in Fort Wayne, Eisenhower repeated his shots at Stevenson, declaring that the campaign issues of 1952 were too important to be treated as jokes or fodder for quips. Eisenhower said he would like to offer speeches that included only "some bright and new words" but, "Of that, I am not capable. I can't be amusing in this business because primarily—and completely outside any capability on my part of that kind, or lack of capabilities—these are not laughing matters of which we are speaking."[179] He also noted corruption problems arising in the Truman administration that he said were unlikely to be cleared in another Democratic administration. "You have it in your power to change things in the November voting," Eisenhower said.[180]

Among the serious issues Eisenhower said needed addressing was the situation in Korea, "a war into which we were fumbled without any plan for winning that war; a war in which we have had already 117,000 casualties, killed and wounded. . . . We must turn our hearts and minds to bringing it to a close so that your sons and mine can either come home or don't have to go."[181]

"The one single personal dedication I should

like to make is this," he concluded at Fort Wayne, "I am one of you and to you and those like you in all this broad land, whatever I have of spiritual, intellectual strength is yours to use as you please."[182]

At Warsaw, Eisenhower talked about the need for peace in the world and drew comparisons between Warsaw, Indiana, and Warsaw, Poland, and the desire for peace in both places. Warsaw, Poland, he said, was the greatest picture of destruction he had visited in all of Europe. "Think of that capital," he said, "ground under the heels of a despotism that has no concern for the

human that exists only to glorify the state and to perpetuate the power of the central government, the dictators in the Kremlin. We have one job in the world today—to promote and maintain peace."[183] He decried the Communist forces ruling portions of Eastern Europe in the aftermath of the war, saying they existed in a system where they "must deny God" while America served as a symbol of "godliness" in the world. Being in Warsaw, Indiana, also inspired Eisenhower to recall one of the area's most famous residents, evangelist Billy Sunday, who built a religious movement from nearby Winona Lake. Eisenhower

IHS, BASS PHOTO COMPANY COLLECTION, P 130

Former U.S. Army general Eisenhower is besieged by fans upon his arrival in Indianapolis at Weir Cook Airport, 1952.

said he had many memories of listening to radio broadcasts by Sunday from his boyhood. "Unless we acknowledge the existence of God," he said, "unless we acknowledge the fact that all men are created in His image, there is no sense to free government. Once we have gotten that thought in our minds so that we can never forget it, ladies and gentlemen, we can clean out corruption [in government]. All of this drift toward socialism, centralization of government, into your private lives will be defeated because you and I, each of us, is a being created in the image of our God."[184]

At Plymouth he said, "All of us know that a prosperous agriculture depends upon a prosperous world trade, where peace and security exist in the world and we can trade freely with those who need the products of our farms." He also argued for wage increases for industrial workers and made strong links between a strong industrial segment of the economy and a strong agricultural program. "Workers must get the highest possible wages that a prosperous industry can afford to pay them, and then we will have a prosperous agriculture because we will eat better and we will eat more," he said, trying out some very simple economic policy on the audience made up mostly of Marshall County area farmers.[185]

In Gary, Eisenhower made an appeal for some of the region's ethnic voters by repeating an earlier claim noting that, "There is nothing the United States can do of a belligerent nature that will cause the beginning of another great conflict. But the conscience of America will never be at peace until our friends and relatives who are living under the whip are free again."[186] At nearby La Porte, Eisenhower commented, "You know, ladies and gentlemen, this business of politicking is not all fun. There is a lot of work and study and scratching the head and all of that. But the chance to meet Americans is really a wonderful experience." But he quickly added his commitment to cleaning up corruption in Washington and strengthening the nation's economy. "When we find that our dollars will no longer buy a decent basket of food or a suit of clothes in the levels that we used to pay for them or anything like it, we say it is time to do some cleaning up," he said.[187]

On Election Day, Indiana delivered an easy victory to Eisenhower, who polled 58 percent of the popular vote to Stevenson's 41 percent. The numbers would be virtually the same four years later, as Eisenhower rolled up 60 percent of the vote to Stevenson's 40 percent.

As president, Eisenhower's official visits took on a far more formal approach and included little of the "ticker-tape" style motorcades that had punctuated his 1952 campaign run in the shadow of the just won war. In October 1954 Ike returned to Indiana as the guest of both Butler University and members of the Columbia Club. An overflow crowd of about 17,000 filled Butler Fieldhouse on the university campus to hear Eisenhower address agricultural issues, noting that his administration was committed to building "a foundation of enduring prosperity" for American farmers.[188] Eisenhower reminded his hosts, the National Institute of Animal Agriculture, that farmers had suffered tremendous losses in buying power under the previous Truman administration and that he had taken "bold, progressive steps" to improve the lot of farmers. "The welfare of 163 million Americans is bound up with our nation's agriculture—just as every farmer is affected by all national and world affairs," said Eisenhower. "Our farmers, like the rest of us, want and need peace. They want their boys at home, and not at war. So, it is important to all of us that the seemingly endless and frustrating war in Korea was ended 14 months ago. Today we have peace, for the first time in 20 years, there is no active battlefield anywhere in the world."[189]

He also declared, "I pledge to you that every resource of this country is being tirelessly used to make it a lasting peace. Our nation extends the hand of friendship to all the world who will grasp it in honest and good faith. We will confer on this subject with any and all—if only we can have some assurance of sincerity of purpose, which underlie all progress toward permanent peace. In this I know I speak for every American, regardless of partisan or any other consideration."[190]

Although his Butler speech was described as being "nonpartisan," Eisenhower nonetheless encouraged his Hoosier audience to support Republican candidates for Congress: "Opportunity is ours if we continue to reject policies that lead to even higher taxes, to regimentation, to depen-

Candlelight vigil for Eisenhower on Monument Circle in Indianapolis following one of his medical scares as president, circa 1950s.

dence on a government far from our homes. Opportunity will be ours if we keep a government of teamwork—a government not of partisan rivalries, but of harmony and good will. To continue to advance along the course charted 21 months ago, we need a Congress and an executive department both guided by leaders of the same political philosophy. They must be dedicated to the same broad program and objectives."[191]

Before his remarks at Butler, Eisenhower visited the Columbia Club in downtown Indianapolis, joining a long line of Republicans who had addressed the club's members since its formation in support of Benjamin Harrison's presidential campaigns. Eisenhower returned to his days as an army general by noting that the club's members were desperately needed to ensure a Republican congressional sweep in 1954. "I had several years of rather exciting experiences in the recent war," Eisenhower said. "And I learned one thing: a victory is not won until every objective for which you are struggling has been attained. Time and again, you found units, having gotten off to a good start, everything going pretty well, suddenly being surprised—driven back—sometimes suffering quite a reverse, as at Kasserine Pass in Africa. Because, in that first flush of victory, they forgot there were no rules applied to his game except winning—in war, I was talking about. I hope I am not partisan enough that I put any thought of winning above honor and decency. And I don't think the Republican Party does."[192]

Eisenhower told his fellow Republicans that "in the 1952 campaign we started something in which we deeply believed" about the need to control the growing penetration of government into the lives of American citizens. "So we set about reversing this trend," the president said. "And we have got the new trend started. It started well. . . . But maybe that pride is just not of the kind to stir us to the action that will let the Congress, under the same leaders, [to] carry forward and finish the job. That is what we are trying to do now. We have got to stir up and obtain the same kind of enthusiasm we had in 1952."[193] He encouraged party leaders to "regain the flame" from the campaign two years previous, and with that, "America can continue to grow and be great, (and have) the kind of government that respects the human, respects him as an equal before the law and before God. That is the thing in which we must believe—by which we do believe—but which we must build up again into such a cause for which to fight. . . . Now, I should make myself clear: I have never made any claim, and I am certain no one in this room does, that all the patriotism in America is the exclusive property of any one party."[194]

The president concluded his remarks by apologizing for the absence of his wife: "Mrs. 'Ike,' who is still on the plane, charged me with making her apologies. But a long plane trip is a thing that throws her out of kilter a little bit, so I made her stay on the plane and take a nap. So she is not here, not because she did not want to come, but because just the spirit's willing; the flesh is just a bit weak."[195]

Adlai E. Stevenson II

The erudite Stevenson was so admired by Democrats they tried not once, but twice, to elect him president of the United States. The grandson of the nation's twenty-third vice president tried even a third time, in 1960, but it was not the charm. Regardless, Stevenson is often regarded by political scholars as one of the most able Americans who failed to win the nation's highest office.

Biographer Jean H. Baker's posit on the Stevensons of Illinois is apt when considering Adlai

II: "Like all families, the Stevensons' elaborate various issues and themes were central to history and culture, though they are by no means typical Americans." Acknowledging that Adlai II came from "a special American family," they were, in reality, "more often losers than winners, like other also-rans, the Stevensons reveal possibilities of what might have been."[196]

Stevenson was elected governor of Illinois in 1948 and quickly distinguished himself as one of the nation's most gifted politicians. But his White House ambitions eventually matched those of his grandfather, ending in failure. Stevenson's son, Adlai III, was elected to the U.S. Senate from Illinois from 1970 to 1981, but failed in two later bids (1982 and 1986) to be elected as Illinois's governor.

But it is Adlai II and his place in public life in the 1950s and 1960s that most Americans remember, and Hoosiers were lucky to have had up-close contact and attention from the shoe-leather candidate. In fact, one of Stevenson's most famous quotes, "In America, any boy may become president. I suppose it's one of the risks he takes," was uttered during a September 1956 speech in Indianapolis.

A strong wit and a brilliant mind helped propel Stevenson to the top of the Democratic ticket for 1952 to challenge the presumptive and seemingly unbeatable Republican nominee. It was not as if the line was long seeking to take on Eisenhower. Even Truman, constitutionally eligible to run for another full four-year term of his own, took a pass. Among Stevenson's most ardent backers was former First Lady Eleanor Roosevelt, who seemingly campaigned as hard for him as she ever did for her late husband. She was not alone—enthusiasm for Stevenson among Democrats was strong. He struggled, however, to connect with everyday voters and stood little chance to overcome the hero status gained by Eisenhower in World War II. Amidst the growing threat of a Cold War with the Soviets, Eisenhower's position seemed to gain strength daily.

For his part, Stevenson said he was introducing himself as a candidate for president in the same way as the Indiana farmer of lore introduced himself: "I am an Indiana farmer and I want it understood that I make an honest living and my reputation's good."[197] The start of his 1952 campaign found Stevenson actively campaigning in Indiana. On September 26 Stevenson made major stops in both Evansville and Indianapolis. In Evansville he told about 7,500 locals gathered for a midday rally downtown that he was present because Vanderburgh County voters had selected the winning presidential/vice presidential team every year since 1896. "In 1892, you only missed by nine votes in the whole county," Stevenson said. "But unfortunately, that was the year in which my grandfather was running for Vice President. Now I have come here to ask you people of Evansville to find the nine votes that my grandfather lost here just 60 years ago!"[198]

While in Evansville, Stevenson toured both the International Harvester and Chrysler plants (where he saw a few workers donning "I like Ike" buttons) and thanked the area's workers for their efforts in support of America's victory in World War II. He said the success of both companies in the postwar years were clear evidence that the Democrats had served America with distinction. "You people here in Evansville know what is going on in the world," Stevenson said. "In this city you are making aircraft parts, steel bridges and rifles for our men in Korea. You know we are fighting for our country, willing to die for it if need be. You know we are working furiously to build up the strength of our armed forces to prevent the Kremlin from starting another world war. You know, as

well as I do that this is the only way to win peace in this world where the Kremlin plots the slavery of us here, and if you are looking for a man who promises to buy your security in a bargain basement, I can tell you right now you better not vote for me."[199]

Stevenson took on directly claims by the Republicans that the Democratic proposals for price controls equated to Socialism and that the Democrats would be slaves to organized labor—backers of sometimes violent union protests in the nation. "I say to you, my friends, that we don't want Socialism, and I think that goons and violators, and property damage are as wrong and as intolerable in labor disputes as it is everywhere else," he said. Stevenson declared that "no labor bosses are ever going to boss me."[200]

Later that evening Stevenson spoke before a packed audience of more than 12,000 inside the Indiana State Fairgrounds Coliseum in Indianapolis. There he again shared the stage with Governor Henry F. Schricker, of whom he proclaimed: "I shall never know a gentler, kinder, wiser man than the great and beloved Hoosier that governs this state."[201] Schricker was the Democrat's nominee for U.S. Senator against incumbent Jenner, a race he lost by a slim margin. Hoosiers were creative in their campaign signs, including ones that said, "Protect your pay with Adlai!" and "We need Adlai badlai!"

The Indianapolis speech focused more on keeping a rein on the nation's budget, with Stevenson suggesting an idea adopted by many candidates to follow him: Give the president the power of a line-item veto over the federal budget. To connect with his conservative Democratic audience, Stevenson called up an old yarn about "a Hoosier has always been a hard man with a dollar—his own dollar or anybody else's. I think of a Hoosier as a down-to-earth, prosperous, rather generous, neighborly fellow—but one who knows where every piece of string is in the pantry. He is a hard-to-beat man. And he's hard to fool."[202] Stevenson joked that evidence of this can be found in the fact that the original Indiana Territory included the state of Illinois, the latter formed by men who were not shrewd enough to keep up with the original Hoosiers.

Stevenson also took a swipe at Eisenhower's coronation as the GOP nominee by saying, "Nomination to office and a round of speech-making do not automatically qualify anyone as an economic administrator."[203] He elaborated by noting that "in Washington, civilian leadership is most important in relation to the military, because that is where the great bulk of our tax dollars are spent. We must make sure that wastage of our silver is not a privilege of our high brass. In this connection I am obliged to say that I think the Republican suggestion that a general can best cut down on military waste deserves examination."[204]

Other themes in Stevenson's remarks were a nod to states' rights, although he said, "I have never believed in states' rights when they are used as a cover for states' wrongs." He also asked

his audience to resist Republican cries of Socialism about every idea the Democratic candidates raise to improve life in America. "You know how it is, anything that helps the other fellow is extravagance; anything that helps you is a necessity," he said.[205]

During a quick swing through northern Indiana late in October 1952, Stevenson's rear-platform appearance in downtown Elkhart drew a crowd of 5,000, who heard Stevenson make a strong pitch for the use of Indiana farm products to help promote peace and stability in the world. He noted the role Elkhart County farmers played in shipping goats, heifers, and other farm animals across the globe. His quick stop in Elkhart made headlines, however, less for what he said than for a egg thrown from the crowd. "An egg hurled from the crowd splattered the canopy over the rear platform of the Illinois governor's private car as he was concluding his speech," the Associated Press reported. "It was the first incident of the kind during his presidential campaign. The egg struck far above Stevenson's head and he gave no indication that he noticed." Elkhart police later detained twenty-two-year-old Lola Banghart of Michigan, who attended the speech and said she threw the egg after hearing things she did not agree with. Her mother told reporters that the egg was "a nice, fresh brown one, not a rotten egg," and Banghart was later released and not charged with a crime.[206]

Despite the egg throwing in Elkhart County, Stevenson was back there again between the 1952 and 1956 elections, but literally by accident. On December 21, 1955, Stevenson's young son, John Fell, age nineteen, was seriously injured, and two of his Harvard University classmates were killed in a grinding head-on collision near Goshen. Stevenson's son was traveling home for Christmas break with classmates

IHS, BASS PHOTO COMPANY COLLECTION, P 130

Democratic presidential candidate Adlai Stevenson II arrives at Weir Cook Airport for a campaign stop in 1952.

from Harvard to the family home in Chicago when a semi crossed the center line along US 20 northeast of Goshen. Upon learning of the crash, Stevenson immediately left Chicago by plane and arrived at Goshen and stayed at Goshen General Hospital to check on his son, who had a host of injuries—a broken kneecap, a broken lower jaw, five teeth knocked from his mouth, and numerous lacerations. His classmates had died of blunt-force injuries in the collision between the truck and the car, driven by John Fell.

Local political leaders scrambled to house Stevenson at the home of Goshen's newly elected Democratic mayor, as the *Elkhart Truth* reported: "For the great, near great, or the common man, tragedy is tragedy. In whatever category you put Adlai Stevenson, he has reacted as most parents would if their children were involved. The great difference is the tragedy which struck Thursday around the Stevenson family is that it has attracted nationwide interest because of his name." As his son was transferred from the Goshen hospital to a Chicago facility, Stevenson asked photographers to not take a picture of him and his son because "I have been spared tragedy, the other fathers will not be seen with their boys again."[207]

In 1956 Indiana moved to a preferential primary system to select delegates for the national Republican and Democratic conventions, but as an inaugural run the Indiana primary was a yawn. As expected, Eisenhower was virtually unopposed for the GOP nomination, and the only major Democrat to tip his toe in Indiana was Senator Estes Kefauver of Tennessee. Backers of Stevenson indicated early on that they would skip Indiana in favor of other key primary states and indicated even if Kefauver won all of the state's convention delegates, he would not be a serious challenger to Stevenson.[208] Stevenson's supporters were right about winning the nomination,

but were wrong about how close Kefauver would come. After several close calls in primaries (and outright victories by Kefauver in New Hampshire and Minnesota), Stevenson engaged in a rare televised debate with his Tennessee opponent prior to the Florida and California primaries, and by the time the Democratic National Convention opened in August in New York City, Stevenson was in charge and threw open to the convention the selection of his running mate. Kefauver prevailed in the "Veepstakes," defeating two fellow U.S. senators, John F. Kennedy of Massachusetts and Albert Gore Sr. of Tennessee.

For the fall campaign, Democrats were interested in winning, but surely had doubts about being able to do this time what they could not do four years earlier. The only wild cards were nagging questions about Eisenhower's health (the president had suffered a massive heart attack in 1955) and the role of female voters. For the first time since women gained the vote in 1920, women voters were expected to constitute more votes than their male counterparts. What role women would play—whether they would simply follow the voting patterns of their husbands or fathers or would strike out on their own—was an unknown. The Stevenson campaign was betting on the idea that women would view issues differently and place higher priority on domestic issues, including the cost of living.

The cost of living was front and center for Stevenson's September 28, 1956, noonday speech from the south face of the Soldiers and Sailors Monument in downtown Indianapolis, which drew a crowd estimated at 15,000. Claiming the cost of living had reached an all-time high, Stevenson said Eisenhower had failed to deliver on his promise to "do something" about the cost of living. "Moreover, economists are now forecasting that prices will go even higher," Stevenson

Stevenson delivers a speech in Indianapolis during his second run for the presidency in 1956, an effort that saw him defeated by the incumbent, Eisenhower.

IHS, INDIANAPOLIS RECORDER COLLECTION, P 303

said. "Your rent is likely to go up; your car is almost sure to cost you more; and so are television sets, refrigerators, clothing and nearly everything else you buy."[209]

A tight money policy proffered by the Republicans, Stevenson said, had done nothing to stop inflation but had "tightened the screws even tighter" on working people, farmers, and home buyers. Stevenson said the administration's policy "has given a bonanza to large financial institutions," and while the cost of living goes up, farmers' income "has been going down, down, down." Endorsing an idea of allowing the Federal Trade Commission to investigate "price spreads" (an idea the Eisenhower administration had nixed), Stevenson said, "It isn't the farmer who is getting more money because your grocery bill is going up. Ten years ago, the farmer was getting 52 cents out of every housewife's dollar spent on food; now he gets about 40 cents, and meanwhile, his costs have gone up too."[210]

Remembering he was speaking in the heart of farm country, even from the busy downtown streets of Indianapolis, Stevenson made strong links between the fate of farmers and the rest of the economy. "A farmer doesn't know what price he will get when he plants a crop, or when he harvests it, or even when he loads it on a truck and takes it to town," he said. Stevenson told his listeners that prosperity on the farm "means jobs in the city and money in the storekeepers' cash registers. I want to remind you the depression on the farm has always spread to the city—and that it could again. Any attempt to set consumer against farmer and the farmer against workingmen is malicious politics."[211]

Stevenson traveled into downtown in an open-car motorcade and drew laughter during his speech after several loud explosions were heard in the background. "You missed," he said. The

explosions, part of a celebration for a national convention of American Legion youth occurring elsewhere in downtown Indianapolis, were not aimed at the governor.

In late October 1956 Stevenson was back in the state for a speech before 5,000 students at the University of Notre Dame, where he cautioned that Republican efforts to block social and economic reforms in the nation played into the hands of the Communists. Stevenson said, however, he was stopping short of "doing as their leaders do me, (alleging I am being) soft on Communism. But I do say that, it seems to me high time the leaders of the Republican Party—or at least one wing of it—start realizing that their opposition to the programs of social justice in America is opposition to the building of our strongest defenses against Communism."[212] Stevenson said the only cure for the "disease of Communism" was "social justice" and added that despite Eisenhower's direct appeal for black votes in Indiana and elsewhere, "We don't know whether the Republican candidate really believes what he says about civil rights—whether he means what he says in the north or what he says in the south."[213]

On Communism, Stevenson said, "The quackery of medicine men who claim to cure the disease with words of hate and loud accusations" will never banish Communism from America. The former governor said he took issue with Republican claims that he would "coddle Communists" and noted that those same Republicans were the ones who voted against "every proposal of the Democratic administration to destroy Communism by pulling out—in America and the free world—the roots of poverty and ignorance and insecurity from which it grows." Stevenson contrasted this approach to the one he said reflected the values of the Catholic Church:

Your church leaders have approach this disease, Communism, not with a politician's bombast, but with the care and method of a doctor. The effectiveness of anti-Communism is measured not in words, but in deeds—deeds of courage when the force of Communism must be met by force; deeds of patience and sacrifice when Communist strength must be met by strength controlled by restraint; deeds of charity and generosity when the roots of Communism may be best attacked by establishing social justice.[214]

Before traveling to the Notre Dame campus in the company of Senator Kennedy, Stevenson spoke briefly during a light rain and fog from the steps of the Saint Joseph County Courthouse in downtown South Bend to a crowd estimated by local police to be 15,000, impressive, but shrunk by more than an hour's delay getting Stevenson's plane on the ground because of the heavy fog. Stevenson led off with a strong pitch for one of his former aides, twenty-nine-year-old John Brademas, who was seeking election to the U.S. House of Representatives from South Bend, and local Democrats presented Stevenson with an antique 1892 campaign ribbon from his grandfather's campaign for vice president. In his remarks, Stevenson declared that it was time "to take this government away from General Motors and give it back to the Joe Smiths."[215] Stevenson likely knew the GM reference would be popular as South Bend struggled to hold on to one of the nation's last smaller automakers, Studebaker-Packard, within earshot of the train station where the governor spoke. Making a joke of Republican charges that Stevenson's campaign speeches were "irresponsible," the governor said, "What some people do speaks so loudly you can't hear what they are saying. Why did the Republicans oppose a $1 minimum wage? Why did they oppose Democratic efforts to relieve unemploy-

ment in some distressed areas?" He said Republican candidates often ridicule domestic policy programs promoted by Democrats as empty "pie in the sky" promises, until the programs are put into place. "Then they pretend to have invented them," Stevenson added. "I sometimes think that a Republican idea is a Democratic idea, two generations old." Concluding, Stevenson reiterated his support for an international agreement to stop hydrogen-bomb tests as part of a "supreme effort" to slow the arms race.[216]

Later during the Notre Dame-Michigan State football game, reporters noted that students hoisted a "We Like Ike!" sign a few rows above the governor, and a woman seated in front of him also wore an "I Like Ike!" button. Stevenson was photographed smiling and chatting in a "friendly fashion" with the Eisenhower supporter.

Stevenson made one more attempt to become the Democratic nominee for president in 1960, but quickly abandoned the effort when it became clear party regulars were not interested in tapping him for a third try. His interest in a third consecutive run kept him from endorsing Kennedy before the Democratic Convention in July 1960, a move that later cost him his desired role as secretary of state in the Kennedy administration. Instead, Kennedy tapped Stevenson to be the U.S. ambassador to the United Nations, a post he held from 1961 through the Kennedy and Lyndon B. Johnson administrations until his unexpected death on July 14, 1965, after suffering a massive heart attack while on a stroll in London, England.

Richard M. Nixon

Richard Nixon enjoyed outstanding electoral success in Indiana throughout his political career—loyalty from Hoosiers earned through years of hard work. He appeared frequently in the state not only in his eight years as vice president, but also in earlier years as a U.S. senator and rising star in the Republican Party.

An early appearance in Indiana by Nixon came while he was serving in his very first years in the U.S. House of Representatives and was named ranking member of the House Committee on Un-American Activities. Invited by his fellow Quakers to speak before the Foreign Affairs Institute meeting at Earlham College in Richmond in May 1949, Nixon railed against the Truman administration and "lax" oversight by the State Department of Communist subversives operating in America. Nixon took a provocative posture among his fellow Quakers, noting that "tolerance and nonresistance" were ineffective in confronting the Communist menace.[217] Nixon said that "a course of tolerance and nonresistance with the Communists would inevitably lead to war and complete defeat for the democratic nations. As a Friend [a term fellow Quakers use to describe themselves], I wish that this approach were a possible solution of our present difficulties, but this is not the case."[218]

"The Communist movement presents the same problem to the civilized world which the Nazi and Fascist movements presented 10 years ago," Nixon declared. "We tried tolerance, compromise and appeasement then. We learned that totalitarian dictators consider such treatment only as a sign of weakness and that the only language they understand is firm resistance to their program for world domination."[219] Nixon said he supported the proposed Atlantic Pact but warned it may not be fully effective against the Communist "program for world domination" and added, "But unless the free nations of the world do enter into such an agreement, there is no question but that Soviet aggression will continue."[220]

Nixon said he was convinced western democracies would ultimately win the Cold War with the Soviets, but added, "We must realize that even though the Communists are unable to defeat us militarily or economically, they still are counting on their eventual ability to infiltrate and weaken us ideologically and accomplish their purpose without warfare."[221]

Three years later, in 1952, as the GOP vice presidential nominee, he made three stops in Indiana to discuss "the Korea situation" in speeches at Kokomo and Evansville and attended a "Youth vs. Communism" meeting of the Young Men in Government organization at Indianapolis. In mid-October Eisenhower's campaign dispatched Nixon to Indiana for a whistle-stop tour of his own. It was vintage Nixon with his well-earned title as a hatchet man, calling Stevenson "Adlai the Appeaser." For extra measure, Nixon told his Evansville Coliseum audience that the Illinois governor was a PhD graduate of the "Dean Acheson Cowardly College of Communist Containment." Nixon said ideas proposed by Democrats to appease or contain the Communists were the equivalent of "writing the ticket for another global war."[222] Nixon bitterly remarked that Stevenson reminded him of "other little men" who had once attempted to contain and/or appease German dictator Adolf Hitler. "The appeasers thought they could 'contain' him . . . [and according to Nixon] it brought the bloodiest war in the history of mankind.[223]

Nixon's whistle-stop campaign took him from Evansville to Vincennes, Terre Haute, Lafayette, Frankfort, and Kokomo, with crowds estimated at between 5,000 and 6,000 at each stop. At Logansport reporters estimated the crowd numbered only 1,500 and was "unenthusiastic" about Nixon's remarks, noting the audience was dominated by union organizers and railroad workers.

Appearing with Nixon were Indiana's U.S.

senators Jenner and Capehart, and Nixon did not shy away from endorsing Jenner's re-election campaign, although Eisenhower had attempted to distance himself from the nominee in the preceding days. Jenner's remarks that General Marshall was "a front man for traitors" and "a living lie" won him widespread scorn, not only from Eisenhower, but also from Eleanor Roosevelt.

Nixon was back in Indiana late in the campaign for a big October 25 Republican rally at the Indiana State Fairgrounds in Indianapolis. There he declared Stevenson was "color blind on the Red issue" and added, "Mr. Stevenson has lined up consistently with those who minimize and cover up the Communist threat. . . . Mr. Stevenson (is) a body-and-soul captive of his environment. He is color blind on the Red issue."[224] Declaring that "the tragedy of Mr. Stevenson and his advisers who surround him is that they really believe that Communists in the United States are 'phantoms' and not very important." He said the Democratic nominee does not recognize "the cold facts of life," and as a result, he was unqualified "to lead the fight for a free world against atheistic Communism."[225]

Once elected vice president in 1952, Nixon did not speak again in Indiana until September 1954 in the lead-up to the midterm elections before a full house at Butler Fieldhouse in Indianapolis. He asserted that the Eisenhower administration had "put the Reds on the run in America" and that the administration had dealt "firmly, sanely and effectively with the Communist threat in the United States. We have established a magnificent three-way record to strengthen our internal security after so many years of ignoring and under-estimating the peril by other administrations."[226] He said the administration had employed existing and new laws and a variety of federal agencies, including the Federal Bureau of Investigation and the Justice Department, as "effective weapons against the Communist conspiracy" and that the strict "security risk program" undertaken in federal hiring had driven Communists and their sympathizers from the federal payroll. Earlier in the day Nixon visited Community Hospital on East Sixteenth Street to help break ground for a new $12 million hospital.

In September 1955 Nixon drew a typical vice presidential assignment as the administration's representative at the National Plowing Contest under way in Wabash County. Despite media reports that Nixon's hay fever was greatly irritated by the dust stirred up in the plowing competitions, the vice president smiled broadly for pictures with the winners named in two plowing categories. The *Warsaw Times-Union* did report that "Nixon's hay fever was aggravated by the dust at the plowing contest and he had to resort to a nose inhaler while handshaking his way through well-wishers among the 10,000 farmers and politicians gathered."[227]

Nixon told the Indiana farmers that more should be done to help them because they "are not getting their fair share of America's unprecedented prosperity. There is no farm depression in the United States, but farmers are undeniably caught in a squeeze. The prices of the things they sell have gone down faster than the prices of the things they buy."[228] He added, "It is time to talk sense on the farm issue and stop the demagoguery. There has been too much of a tendency in recent months to make a political football out of this issue. The new flexible parity law cannot by any stretch of the imagination be held responsible for the drop in prices. Almost two-thirds of the drop took place before the Eisenhower administration took over in 1953. The cause of the drop in prices is not the law but the market. If we want to get at the cause of lower prices, we must find a way to reduce the surplus."[229]

Before departing Wabash by private jet for a Republican fund-raising dinner in Indianapolis, the vice president and his wife, Pat, "sat on a bale of hay on a tractor-drawn flatbed wagon for a leisurely tour of an array of farm demonstrations on the 1,800-acre tract northeast of Wabash," the Associated Press reported. He told the farmers, "We do not believe that America's farmers are getting their fair share of America's unprecedented prosperity. We shall continue to explore every possible program which will remedy the inequity that exists."[230]

For the 1956 re-election campaign, Nixon maintained the low road, and some of his history as a bare-knuckled campaigner came back to haunt him. Upon landing at Weir Cook Airport in Indianapolis on September 18, 1956, Nixon denied claims by Eleanor Roosevelt that he had labeled his Democratic opponent for the U.S. Senate in California, Helen Gahagen Douglas, a Communist. "I was rather surprised that Mrs. Roosevelt made such a statement," Nixon said. "She was misinformed. I did not call Mrs. Douglas a Communist. I questioned her judgment, but not her loyalty." Trying to turn his comments into a softer review of Mrs. Roosevelt's continued political influence, he added, "One thing that has impressed me is the amount of good will Mrs. Roosevelt has created in other countries I have visited."[231] During his political speech before local Republicans, Nixon said the Eisenhower administration deserved a vote of confidence because it "got the United States out of one war, kept it out of others and offers the best hope for peace without surrender" and assailed Democrats, saying, "It probably is not surprising that those who defend [the Truman administration] which refused to admit that the war in Korea was a war, might not know the

difference between war and peace. But the American people know the difference."[232]

On economic issues, Nixon said take-home pay for workers was at its highest level in the nation's history and openly declared that prior to the Eisenhower administration, the American people had "never had real prosperity except in war or as a result of war." Perhaps recognizing the political land mines he was stepping near, Nixon quickly added that he did not mean to suggest "that our national leaders got us into war so that we would have prosperity" but said that New Deal and Fair Deal planners "were never able to find the secret to the problem of creating prosperity during peacetime."[233] He added, "The great majority of the American people have enjoyed the best four years of their lives under the Eisenhower administration."[234] During his visit in Indianapolis, Nixon visited with executives at Eli Lilly and Company and the Pitman-Moore Company, human and veterinary laboratory companies, respectively.

On October 23, 1956, Nixon visited South Bend just a week after Stevenson had been in town. The target was again the repeat Democratic presidential nominee, whose proposals to halt testing on hydrogen bombs and ending the military draft, Nixon said, would pave a path to another war. "A vote for Stevenson is a vote for weakness, for indecision and for inexperience that would lead to war," Nixon said before about 3,500 people in the gymnasium of John Adams High School. Again he linked Stevenson's "good intentions" to efforts to appease and contain Hitler prior to World War II and accused him of helping perpetuate a lie that Soviet leaders, whom he dubbed "merchants of misery," were more dedicated to peace than their American counterparts.[235] Nixon's visit included a stop at Notre Dame, where he spoke on similar themes.

He added, "If we were to agree to the Stevenson plan for stopping nuclear tests, without insisting on the Eisenhower plan for (mutual) inspection (of arms) to guarantee that the agreement would be kept, we would be playing right into the Communists' hands."[236]

Nixon visited DePauw University at Greencastle, to receive an honorary Doctor of Laws degree in May 1957. The vice president was accompanied by Pat, Senator Capehart, Congressman Winfield K. Denton, and Governor Harold W. Handley, and drew an overflow and supportive crowd on a sunny late spring day.

The remarks offered that day were classic Nixon:

> We hear a lot of dire predictions about what's going to happen to the world these days. The Soviet Union is immensely strong, the free nations are having their difficulties, and sometimes I think there's too much pessimism as to the eventual outcome. Oh, I wouldn't underestimate for one moment the serious world danger that we confront. But I would not want to leave this college campus today without expressing a faith as to the future and eventual outcome of this tremendous conflict of ideas in the world. There isn't any question about the outcome. We are going to win. And we're going to win fundamentally because we're on the right side.[237]

Nixon's last major appearance in the state as vice president came in October 1959 when Republicans gathered at Rochester in Fulton County to honor long-serving House Minority Leader, Representative Charles A. Halleck. A Hoosier native and successful Rensselaer attorney, Halleck joined the U.S. House in 1935 upon the death of another congressman and held the seat from the second district until 1969—an incredible thirty-four-year span. He rose to the rank of Republican Minority Leader for several terms in the House, but also during three separate stints (1947–49, 1953–55, and 1959–65) served as the powerful House Majority Leader. In 1959 Halleck had visions of joining the 1960 Republican ticket as Nixon's running mate. Halleck was eventually passed over by Nixon and the Republican Convention (in favor of Henry Cabot Lodge), similar to the slight he suffered in 1948 from Dewey.

The event to honor Halleck (and hopefully impress Republicans nationally about his popularity in Indiana and beyond) found Rochester going all out "to receive the most distinguished guest in its 123-year history—the Vice President of the United States." The *Rochester News-Sentinel* excitedly reported that more than 20,000 guests were expected to greet "Richard M. Nixon, the nation's No. 2 executive, . . . [during] a busy five hours in the city Tuesday afternoon and evening for the purpose of honoring his longtime friend. . . . The occasion is the Second District Republican organization's tribute to Halleck, for 25 years as U.S. Representative and for his recent elevation to the post of House Republican leader."[238]

In the end, a cold rain kept crowds closer to 10,000 as Nixon made a quick stop at the Fulton County Courthouse in downtown Rochester before proceeding onto the Athletic Field at Rochester High School, where tents were set up serving fried-fish dinners. Nixon told the throng that he had discerned from his just-completed visit to the Soviet Union that the Communists were "borrowing" capitalistic methods to keep up economically with the U.S., a welcome move, he said, which could raise the standard of living for many impoverished peoples in the Soviet Union. Nixon said he hoped the USSR would put more of its power to this effort rather than seeking to extend Communism around the world. "Russia is making progress by leaving some of the theories of Communism," Nixon said. "They are paying more to the people in the factories who produce more."[239]

Estes Kefauver

Nixon's direct opponent for the 1956 campaign—at least his counterpart as the number two man on the ticket—was Senator Estes Kefauver of Tennessee, who gained fame in the Senate for his anticrime crusade. Unable to wrest the Democratic nomination for president away from Stevenson, Kefauver joined the ticket and set off on what was ultimately another unsuccessful effort for Stevenson. But before he did, his own campaign brought him to Indiana, mostly by way of fierce support from Andy Jacobs Sr., father of a young Andy Jacobs Jr., who would later go on to represent Indianapolis in the U.S. House for all but one two-year term between 1965 and 1997. Kefauver was no dynamo on the campaign trail, but was respected and well known. He lives forever in the history of Franklin, however, for a mix-up on where he actually was. Confusing the name of the city, Franklin, with the name of its mayor (Alexander), Kefauver quickly declared to his confused audience how pleased he was *to be in Alexandria!* A Franklin native and recent Franklin College graduate on hand that day was Bill Bridges. He described Kefauver's visit as "a striking and memorable moment" and noted the following:

> There is something awe-inspiring in the sudden appearance of a great man, even a third- or fourth-rate great man like the senior senator from Tennessee, Estes Kefauver. To many of the three hundred or so persons who gathered on the Courthouse lawn in Franklin, Indiana, a little before four o'clock Saturday afternoon, the idea that a national figure and prominent contender for the presidency of the United States was about to materialize before them must have seemed a little unlikely.
>
> Kefauver looked tanned, healthy, and confident as he moved slowly from his automobile up the Courthouse walk, smiling slightly, shaking hands, and imparting his much-publicized impression of down-to-earth friendliness. But somehow it seemed that the senator left the Square with considerably less of the glamour, at least, which had been his when he arrived. A large part of the loss was that which always occurs when the great man reveals himself not only as an ordinary human being, but also—horrors!—as a politician. Before he came, one knew him largely from newspaper and commentators, who generally featured him as an underdog fighting an uphill battle against the party bosses—a corn-fed friend of the common man with charm and intelligence but short on political savvy.[240]

Bridges concluded, noting that Kefauver "turned out to be a rather quiet man, a so-so public speaker who called the town 'Alexandria' and stumbled over his words occasionally, a heavy hand at political humor, and, apparently, a political thinker at about the level of the *Democratic Digest*."[241]

During an Indianapolis speech before a small group of Democrats, Kefauver raised eyebrows with his suggestion that President Eisenhower tap former President Truman as a special "European ambassador," noting that it was time "that politics be forgotten once more—and the future of America be placed above petty partisan advantage." Kefauver said he was making the Truman suggestion because he was "beloved everywhere—this side of the Iron Curtain."[242] He said his Truman suggestion was his own idea and that he had not talked to the former president about it "and he may not like my suggesting it."[243]

Alben W. Barkley

In the lead-up to the 1952 race, it was clear Vice President Barkley was *not* in the running for the Democratic nomination, not only because of his advanced age (he was seventy-four in 1951 and died five years later), but also because of his close ties to the increasingly unpopular Truman. Among party faithful, however, Barkley remained a draw as the sitting vice president and as such arrived for the August 1951 meeting of the Indiana Democratic Editorial Association at French Lick. Barkley took the unusual task of directly addressing emerging stories of corruption in Washington, condemning them as "petty, though inexcusable and reprehensible," but quickly turned to ask how Republicans felt any entitlement to claim the high road when it came to corruption.[244] "We speak of morality in government, and some of our opponents are uttering anathema against the present administration on the grounds that it has permitted morality in the government to decline," Barkley said. "I do not condone wrongdoing on any level in the government of our country though that level be national, state or local. I have spent most of my life combatting public immorality and seeking to punish it wherever it lifts its hideous head. But no party has, or ever has had, a monopoly on virtue or vice."[245]

Barkley took aim at the GOP by noting that "it might be well for our people to recall when the Republican Party was last in power it brought about an era of corruption and misconduct in high office which shook the very foundation of our society and of our political institutions," citing corruption that, among other things, cost American veterans needed benefits.[246] He said it was time to ask "all political parties to be as direct and as truthful and as fair in their efforts to regain power as we were in telling the public what we have done, and we ask that the voice of the American press be a fair and truthful voice. No permanent good can come from misrepresentation or character assassination. . . . In this day of the widely read newspaper, and widely heard radio, and the widely observed television, it is more difficult than ever to deceive the people, but sometimes it is also easier to confuse them."[247]

Before his speech before Indiana Democrats, Barkley met with reporters at the famous French Lick Springs Resort Hotel and said he was in good health, but dodged all questions about whether he would be a candidate in 1952 or beyond. "He volunteered a statement that he felt just as good today as he did 40 years ago," the New York Times reported. "He said he weighed no more, that he had never had a headache or a stomach ache in his life."[248]

John F. Kennedy

In the years before the 1960 presidential race, Kennedy a young, dynamic senator from Massachusetts, had become known nationally for his 1957 Pulitzer Prize–winning book, *Profiles in Courage*. The book helped lay the groundwork for a national campaign, including several key stops in Indiana.

Kennedy's earliest official visit to the state came on October 16, 1953, less than a year after he entered the Senate, in a comprehensive speech at Indianapolis before the executive committee of the American Legion. Sounding more hawkish than he would in later exchanges, when he would emphasize paths of diplomacy to avoid the "folly" of the arms race, the newly minted Senator found "there is, of course, good reason to believe that the ultimate reliance of the Soviet Union will be on the weapons of subversion, economic disintegration and guerilla warfare to accomplish our destruction, rather than upon the direct assault of all-out war. But we cannot count on it. So long as the Soviet Union and her satellites continue to dedicate the large percentage of their national production to the preparation for war—so long must the United States recognize the peril to which we are now subjected in increasing quantities."[249]

Kennedy said the nation was entering "the most critical period in our long history" and that "the time is rapidly approaching when the Soviet Union will have the long range planes to carry to the United States the weapon capable of infinite destruction."[250] Clearly well prepared by his advisers, the young senator fleshed out intricate details of U.S.-Soviet relations and defense systems in place on both sides of the equation. Kennedy offered a four-point agenda to address the growing Soviet menace by calling for renewed efforts to enhance the nation's continental and civil defense systems, to monitor closely Soviet efforts to improve their air power and atomic and hydrogen weapons, to commit U.S. resources to a fully developed "Strategic Air Force" with "sufficient retaliatory powers to threaten a global aggressor with havoc and ruin," and major buildups of the U.S. Air Force to match the growth rate seen among the Soviets. Kennedy said, "I do not see how a country which is productively the most powerful in the world with its people enjoying the highest standard of living in our history can be satisfied with anything less than an Air Force second to none. Today we do not have it."[251]

In April 1959 Kennedy visited Indianapolis for two events—one to commemorate National Library Week and the other to address the national convocation of the United Negro College Fund meeting in the Circle City. Black voters were an increasingly important constituency that still had to be wooed away from "the party of Lincoln" and their strong ties to Eisenhower. Democrats and African Americans were making similar transitions to meet on the same road, as the nation's civil rights movement made slow gains during the 1950s. This lack of progress was surely in Kennedy's sights. Perhaps unwill-

ing to let Senator Hubert Humphrey of Minnesota gather in the bulk of black voters among Democrats based on his early support for civil rights, Kennedy said he appeared for the purpose of placing "the importance of education and of Negro education in particular in proper perspective as we view it against the background of our troubled world."[252] Kennedy praised the UNCF for its efforts that allowed "the full potential of so many millions of our young citizens whose skills might otherwise be lost to our nation by the irrationality of racial discrimination." He called "Negro education" not only "an essential act of justice" but also "an urgent requirement of national security."[253] Predicting that black college graduates would join their white brethren in playing a key role in shaping the course of the world into the 1960s and beyond, Kennedy said college education must be considered "in the context of the demands for American leadership in world affairs, for American contributions to peace, for American assistance to the undeveloped nations of the world, and for American strength in the face of harsh threats from around the world."[254]

In a speech peppered with academic quotes and other remarks from Abraham Lincoln and Woodrow Wilson, Kennedy cited growing democratic movements in Africa and Asia as demanding of American skill, sympathy, and compassion. "Our graduates must all be men of their time regardless of any specialized training they may receive," said Kennedy. "Some of our education for world responsibility comes from the harsh logic of events. Some can only come through the experience of actually engaging in world-wide activities—for we still learn by doing." The senator suggested that "here, it seems to me, you can play an increasingly important part. For Negro colleges and universities share the general crisis of American education at the same time they face a special crisis of their own" amidst the growing reality of court-ordered desegregated schools. "In the transition period to an integrated society," Kennedy added, "you will, of course, have to play an increasingly important role in remedying the results of inferior education at the lower levels due to continued segregation. This will be an era of ordeal. In some states you will have to continue to carry the main burden of Negro education for some years. With the rise in school population which is already bursting your existing facilities, your great responsibility will grow greater." Kennedy offered hope that America would arise to the challenge not only of national security but also increased freedom for all of its citizens stretching from "the far side of space to the inside of men's minds."[255]

While Kennedy's two Indianapolis appearances were billed as nonpartisan events, he did not leave the state before making political remarks meant to build up his name recognition and support among Indiana Democrats heading into 1960. At a Democratic event in Decatur in Adams County, Kennedy focused his criticism on the Eisenhower administration by noting "it has no new ideas and has taken no bold action" to solve the nation's problems. Citing the nation's housing crisis, wasted natural resources, and more than four million Americans "driven from their farms" by corporate farming, Kennedy said, "These are some of the reasons why I cannot agree with those who regard the election of 1958 as merely a reward to the Democratic Congress for a job well done. It represents, instead, an opportunity to do the job that still needs to be done."[256] The senator urged his fellow Democrats to be resolute in the need to recapture the White House in 1960 and said, "The problems are not all solved, the battles are not all won, and the issues are not all gone. . . . We are challenged by prob-

lems which were never even foreseen by Franklin Roosevelt."[257]

In October 1959, just four months before he would enter the Indiana primary in earnest, Kennedy made three days of strategic political stops at Evansville, Huntingburg, Jasper, West Lafayette, Fort Wayne, and Indianapolis. His first stop was the Murat Shrine in Indianapolis for a $10-a-plate dinner intended to boost the re-election campaign of Mayor Charles Boswell, a fellow Democrat. During his remarks, Kennedy expressed concern about Soviet Premier Nikita Khrushchev's statement about America upon returning home, when he declared that "capitalism is a sick and dying horse." He said of Khrushchev's visit and subsequent statement, "We have learned that he is a formidable, energetic and confident opponent. It should be a warning to us."[258]

Kennedy said, "Our aspirations as the most powerful leader of the free world conflict with their aspirations as the most powerful leader of the Communist world. No negotiations can end these differences. No exchange of personal visits can cause either side to compromise away its fundamental position in Germany, Europe or the world community."[259] While he acknowledged that nothing "justified any relaxation on our part" in the Cold War with the Soviets, he suggested that "both nations would like to be free of the crushing burden of the arms race and neither wants a nuclear war that would leave not one Rome but two Carthages. Neither wants too many other nations, friendly, unfriendly or neutral—to join the Atomic Club and hold the power of life or death. Neither country wants to breath radioactive air—we do not want the atmosphere we share polluted by an excess of nuclear tests. Both nations seek to advance their economics and scientific achievements—and would benefit by a much greater exchange and pooling of ideas, goods, and personnel between our two nations."[260]

The next day Kennedy attended part of the Notre Dame-Purdue football game at Ross-Ade Stadium as the guest of Purdue president Frederick L. Hovde. From West Lafayette, he flew to Fort Wayne for a speech at the Scottish Rite Cathedral. He sounded familiar themes, predicting the arrival of the 1960s would prove a pivotal time in the nation's history. "The American people cannot turn to the Republican Party to lead them through these tense, critical years," Kennedy told Allen County Democrats. "The Republican Party has traditionally been the party of the status quo and in 1959 and 1960 there will be no status quo." He further predicted that the Democratic Party would lead the nation toward "peaceful revolution and change" in areas where Americans stood in need. "We have been the party of new ideas, new experiments and new approaches," he said.[261]

On his third day in Indiana, Kennedy traveled south in the state in the company of U.S. Senator Vance Hartke, visiting Jasper and Huntingburg for Democratic Party functions and to raise funds. Kennedy flew into Evansville aboard his own Convair plane, but transferred to a smaller plane owned by the Huntingburg Furniture Company for a short flight to Dubois County, which had a runway too small to accommodate Kennedy's personal plane. At the American Legion post, Kennedy met with local Democratic leaders and also talked to reporters. A "chuck wagon" box dinner was offered later with local Democrats gloating that "over 600 chickens will be barbequed near the 'big top' and will be served 'hot' to the crowd'" via an open-pit barbeque operated by Flav-O-Rite Barbeque of Leavenworth, Indiana.

While in Jasper, Kennedy met with local reporters at the American Legion Home and discussed a variety of issues, including the Cold War and Khrushchev. "We cannot continue to let the Soviet Union be first in science, first to the moon, first in outer space," Kennedy said. "It will take a greater public effort if our system is going to prove the system of the future."[262] Kennedy played it coy about whether he actually planned to run for president in 1960, although no major analysis was necessary to conclude he had already decided to do so by appearing in remote southern Indiana months before the state's primary. Asked about whether his Catholic faith would impair his chances about winning the nomination, Kennedy said, "My experience has been that most people make their judgment of a man on his competence to do a job. There are so many issues. The question is: How does he meet them? It's not a question of where he goes to church on Sunday."[263]

8

The New Frontier and Great Society, 1960–67

Author and political pundit Chris Matthews noted that the 1960 race for the presidency—pitting Vice President Richard M. Nixon against U.S. Senator John F. Kennedy of Massachusetts—stands out not only as one of the nation's most interesting, but also closest, presidential races in history. "But behind this snapshot," Matthews wrote, "lurks a darker, more enduring saga that began with their election to Congress in the months just after World War II, then crept for fourteen years along those old Capitol corridors where politicians, even rivals, share the small space."[1] Matthews details a "complex" relationship between the two men, complicated by Nixon's fast rise from a member of the House, to a surprise senator from California, to vice president for two terms in the shadow of President Dwight D. Eisenhower. Kennedy, on the other hand, was a failed Veep choice in 1956 and was viewed as an upstart challenger to Nixon. "During the early years, Nixon was the man to beat," Matthews writes. "He was the best politician of his time, articulating more ably than anyone else the nervous post-World War II America."[2]

Richard M. Nixon

Vice President Nixon made an interesting, if not altogether unwise pledge, for his 1960 presidential campaign—vowing to visit all fifty states, and Indiana was near the start of his list (likely because the state was solidly Republican and was not expected to be in play come November). A massive crowd of Republicans—and the curious—packed Monument Circle in downtown Indianapolis to see the sitting vice president and his wife, Pat, on September 12, 1960. It was Nixon's first major campaign stop after spending eleven days in the hospital for an injured knee that left him unable to stand for long periods of time and was the start of a marathon run of rallies in nine major cities in fourteen days. Nixon personally scrapped plans to limit his Indianapolis stop to an airport tarmac event, saying he wanted to visit Monument Circle as he had in the 1956 campaign.[3] "Since this is more or less the first formal appearance of the campaign, I think it is an appropriate occasion for me to indicate to you the kind of appeal I expect to make during the course of this campaign, not only to the people of Indiana, but to the people of this nation," he said.[4]

Nixon expressed particular gratitude for the large turnout in a state he acknowledged having skipped during the primary election. "For that wonderful vote in the primary when we didn't even visit the state, we thank you," he said.[5] Nixon emphasized that a principal issue for voters was to answer the question: Is the candidate qualified "by experience, by background and on his stand on the great issues before the world"—a veiled reminder to voters that Nixon's opponent, Kennedy, was too young and inexperienced for the nation's highest office. "I know Mr. [Nikita] Khrushchev, and I know when you're dealing with a man like this that when he engages in the kinds of activities that he does, the wrong thing is to make concessions to him, because those concessions will never satisfy him," said Nixon. "They will only lead him to demand more."[6] Nixon took issue with suggestions that the United States should ever apologize for its role in the world and defense of the security of the nation. "We have difficult times ahead," Nixon said in lengthy remarks reported nationwide as the GOP nominee returned to the campaign trail from Indiana. "We must have a President who will be firm, who will not be belligerent, and we are going to have difficulties in the years ahead, but we can avoid the twin dangers of appeasement and surrender on the one side and war on the other side if America can be strong militarily, strong economically, and strong also in our faith in our country and in ourselves."[7]

Nixon expected that economic issues were to be of great importance during the election. He cited successes of the previous eight years under Eisenhower, but noted that those issues "aren't going to make any difference if we're not around to enjoy it. And so, I say peace without surrender, the extension of freedom—this is the great issue."[8]

"Under the leadership of President Eisenhower, we have ended one war, we have kept this nation out of other wars, and we have kept the peace without surrender for America for eight years—and we're proud of that as we stand here today," Nixon said.[9] He acknowledged that the United States was not perfect but urged voters not to overlook "the things that are right about America, and when we consider the things that are right, my friends, just remember this: America is the strongest nation in the world militarily. We have the most productive economy, far ahead of the Soviet Union . . . we have the best education in America . . . in other words, those who say that America is second best just don't know what they're talking about!"[10]

He concluded his remarks in Indianapolis, "For the many times I have come to Indiana and you have welcomed me and Pat, as you have today, I thank you. . . . But, above all, we urge you: go forth and in these next eight weeks—if you believe in our cause—vote for it, work for it, and talk for it, remembering you are not just working for a man or for a party, but you're working and voting for America and for peace and justice for all peoples of the world."[11] Nixon's speech lasted about thirty minutes, but he and his wife remained for another twenty minutes shaking hands, even though an *Indianapolis Star* reporter said it appeared the vice president was still favoring his sore knee. The Nixons were a hit with several they met, most especially a young Lois Edelman of Indianapolis, who was able to shake Nixon's hand and was excited when she noticed that one of Pat's earrings was about to fall and kept her from losing it.[12]

Nixon was back in Indiana less than a month later, on September 21, for a rally at the Allen County Courthouse in Fort Wayne before an enthusiastic crowd of more than 20,000. Nixon noted he was so impressed by the growth of the state's "second city" that Indianapolis should take notice.[13] The Fort Wayne Central Catholic High School band provided the music as "crowds lined the downtown streets cheering and waving at the Nixons as the motorcade neared the courthouse. Confetti and torn paper was thrown from business building windows and by some of the crowd lining the route," the *Warsaw Times-Union* reported.[14] Nixon singled out the band and a chorus of "Singing Nixon Girls" on hand for the downtown rally and noted the difficulty of trying to reach all fifty states in an eight-week campaign. "We have found this is a pretty big country," he said. "So that is the reason for the very fast pace and fast schedule, because I can assure you that coming home to Indiana is always a great pleasure to me."[15]

In what would become a frequent speech tactic for Nixon, he referred to his Hoosier-born mother, Hannah Milhous. Drawing applause, the vice president noted that "during the years I was growing up, my mother used to talk about 'back east' and that meant Indiana, where she was born, on a farm down in Butlerville, down in Jennings County. And during those 12 years that she lived there, it must have made a tremendous impact because while the rest of her 75 years she's lived in California, and you know how Californians feel about California, my mother is still for Indiana. This is her state!"[16]

Nixon said he gained two major "Indiana qualities" from his mother—her Quaker faith and its commitment and desire for peace and a fighting political spirit. "This is the great American tradition, where we all gather together to listen to the man that some of us are for, and listen to the man that some of us may be against, but listening because we want to be sure that the decision we make . . . is made on the basis of what is best for America," he said.[17]

Issues of "peace without surrender" and the need to "extend freedom throughout the world" were familiar themes in Nixon's Fort Wayne speech. He said there was "one issue" Americans were concerned about in electing their new president in 1960, and that is "which of the two

candidates for the Presidency can give America and the free world the leadership that will keep the peace without surrender and extend freedom throughout the world."[18]

"We want our children to grow up in a land of peace and freedom such as we have had under the leadership of President Eisenhower, who ended one war and has kept America out of another war," he said.[19] He reminded his audience that America had fought three wars in the twentieth century: "For what? Talk to you legionnaires, your VFW people, they'll tell you. We didn't get an acre of territory. We didn't ask for a concession. We fought why? One, to keep our own freedom, and two, because we were interested in the freedom of others, and we realized that when it was threatened, ours was as well."[20]

Nixon told his Fort Wayne audience that "you can play your part and play your part well by strengthening the moral and spiritual fiber of this country, by striking down prejudices and hatred whenever you see it" and reminded the massive audience that "what we feel about the respect for God, by recognizing the rights that we have do not come from men but they come from God and must be respected. For that we reason what we feel about the universal right of people to be free, what we deeply feel in our hearts about peace, what we feel about loyalty to our country, that must come from you . . . from the hearts of the American people."[21]

The vice president noted that Western democracies were not interested in extending domination over others—unlike Communist leaders in Russia and China—and that America wanted for the world what it wants for itself: freedom. Nixon said that because Khrushchev and Mao Tse-tung sought to "conquer the world," they naturally only "respect power and strength, and they have nothing but contempt for weakness, they have nothing but contempt for those who are naïve in dealing with them." It was a frequent Nixon theme, openly suggesting that the younger, inexperienced Kennedy would approach such situations with world leaders with either naivety, or appeasement. "If America is to keep the peace," Nixon said, "if we are to extend freedom, we must first start by seeing to it that America remains as she is today, the strongest nation in the world militarily and that we will pay the cost to see that America retains this military strength."[22] He added that he would continue the strong position Eisenhower had established when dealing with the Soviets: "In dealing with a man like Mr. Khrushchev, when you make a concession without getting a concession in return, you don't serve the cause of peace. You work against it. You don't serve the cause of freedom. You work toward the cause of surrender, because in dealing with a Communist leader, any dictator, whenever you engage in activities that are not, at the same time, matched by concessions on their part, the inevitable result is that they are not satisfied. They ask for more. They demand more. And so President Eisenhower was right in this respect."[23]

On October 1, 1960, Nixon returned to Indiana for a rally attended by an estimated crowd of more than 14,000 at Roberts Municipal Auditorium in Evansville, and for one of his toughest attacks on Kennedy thus far, reflecting national polling that showed the Nixon-Kennedy matchup was very close. Nixon's remarks fell between the first and second nationally televised debates between the two candidates and allowed him to declare Kennedy as "reckless and irresponsible" in his assessment of how Eisenhower had conducted himself before the United Nations in relation to Cold War interactions with the Soviets. Nixon said, "If Mr. Kennedy would stop looking so hard for things that are wrong with America's position

and America's prestige he would not have made such a reckless and irresponsible attack on the President. If he would talk less and read more he would have learned that the President has been giving dynamic leadership in this situation to the cause of peace and freedom. He has been applauded by the entire world."[24] To further buttress his argument, Nixon added, "What Senator Kennedy should realize, and what virtually all of the free peoples of the world can clearly recognize, is that the future of the United Nations itself and of its powerful influence for peace is being preserved by American leadership, by the leadership of President Eisenhower. He should recognize what the world sees—that the hopes of the free nations, those which now exist, and those which are coming into being, are relying on this leadership."[25]

Nixon said Kennedy was failing to realize that "Mr. Khrushchev's efforts to sabotage the U.N. and these hopes of the world have been overwhelmingly rejected by the representatives of the nations in New York. Senator Kennedy has a right and a responsibility, as the opposition candidate, to criticize the administration record. But he also has a responsibility when he criticizes to be right about what he says. I cannot allow this attack on the President's leadership and his prestige to go unanswered when it carries with it the hopes of the entire world at this crucial moment. The Senator owes it to his party and to his country to cease these irresponsible attacks on the President of the United States."[26]

Press reports from Nixon's Evansville stop were unanimous. It was a tougher edge showing than before, with the Associated Press reporting that the speech "was the toughest Nixon has made so far in the campaign" and cited it as "evidence that the vice president intends to slug it out with his challenger."[27]

Nixon would come to love his relationship with Indiana Republicans. For 1960 they delivered him an impressive vote total in the May GOP Primary, set up by the media and some campaign insiders as a "test run" of Nixon against Kennedy, as both men ran virtually unopposed in their respective primaries. Nixon racked up more than a million votes in the May primary among Republicans, gathering 95 percent of the ballots cast, dwarfing Kennedy's total of less than 800,000 votes, gathering only 81 percent of the Democratic ballots cast against token opposition.

John F. Kennedy

Primary elections in 1960 were not supposed to matter much among Democratic Party faithful. In fact, only sixteen states were conducting primaries that year (including Indiana). Most of the states had decided on caucus or internal party convention strategies to determine delegates to the Democratic National Convention in Los Angeles. Via the latter route, U.S. Senate Majority Leader Lyndon B. Johnson of Texas was among the presumed favorites. Deemed "next in line" among Democratic hopefuls—and a clear step away from two-time losing Democratic nominee Adlai Stevenson II in the previous two cycles—Johnson stayed in Washington for the primary season and worked internal channels to secure the nomination. Johnson's move left the primaries open to others who hoped to challenge him, and among those who wanted to do so were two major hitters in the party—Senator Hubert H. Humphrey of Minnesota, a self-made politician and former mayor of Minneapolis, and a rather fresh face, just entering his second term in Senator Kennedy of Massachusetts.

Kennedy had assembled a mediocre record for himself both in earlier terms in the U.S. House and Senate but had gained national attention by finishing second for the 1956 vice presidential nomination at the Democratic convention. Party regulars were lined up behind Johnson—as the titular party head by virtue of his leadership position in the Senate—and Johnson was the man to beat. Humphrey, meanwhile, had presidential visions of his own, previously gaining a national reputation for his eloquent call to Democrats in their 1948 convention to "walk into the sunshine of human rights."[28] As Johnson waited out the winter and spring thaw in Washington, the success of Kennedy no doubt began to cause him and his supporters some nervousness. By February, in Indianapolis for the state's Jefferson-Jackson Day Dinner, Johnson made news by taking a few more obvious steps toward an open candidacy by telling reporters he expected to head the Texas delegation to the upcoming Democratic convention and added this nugget: "And I hope it will be committed to the support of my candidacy."[29] Just a week earlier Johnson told a Democratic audience that he would not seek the nomination. As Associated Press political analyst James Marlow wrote, Johnson wanted "the nomination all right, but until this past weekend he's been as coy as an Alice-blue gown. Sens. John F. Kennedy of Massachusetts and Hubert H. Humphrey of Minnesota, both out-and-out candidates, can butt heads in state primaries and crisscross the country, looking for support, until their tongues hang out. That's not Johnson's way."[30]

Kennedy and Humphrey vigorously engaged on the primary circuit, most notably in Wisconsin (where Kennedy narrowly defeated Humphrey on the basis of a heavy Catholic vote from selected urban areas of the state) and West Virginia. For Kennedy, the primaries were a key test to prove his chance of election despite his youth and Catholic pedigree, a hurdle New York

John F. Kennedy

LIBRARY OF CONGRESS

governor Al Smith had tried to clear nearly a half century earlier to little success. Kennedy ended up on the Indiana ballot without Humphrey. The latter focused more on West Virginia, where 95 percent of the voters were Protestant. In Indiana, Kennedy could count on pockets of heavily Catholic precincts in South Bend, Fort Wayne, Indianapolis, and the ethnically diverse communities of northwest Indiana. In the middle of the showdown primaries of Wisconsin and West Virginia stood the Indiana Democratic Primary on May 3, 1960.

Kennedy had traveled the state extensively as early as February 1960, stating his intentions to enter the Indiana primary. During a series of stops in Indianapolis, Gary, East Chicago, and Terre Haute, Kennedy made the case for the importance of the primary process in selecting a presidential nominee. In opening his Indiana primary campaign, Kennedy stopped first at Indianapolis for an airport news conference to declare his intent to enter the Hoosier primary and noted that "I cannot believe that serious consideration will be paid to claims of popular strength in this state on behalf of any candidate unwilling to test his record in the voting booth."[31] Recalling the state's important role in electing presidents in many prior election cycles (although most of them almost a half century or more before Kennedy's time), Kennedy said, "I have no reason to doubt that once again, in 1960, the President elected in November will have entered the Indiana primary this May. I have no reason to believe that a candidate by-passing the Indiana primary can, for the first time in history, be elected President."[32]

Kennedy said he intended to talk directly to primary state voters, including those in Indiana, about achievement of world peace and freedom "in place of the fantastically dangerous and

expensive arms race in which we are now falling behind"; spurring the national economy "to provide a more secure life for all Americans, regardless of race, creed or national origin," including increasing wages for workers, social security and medical care for seniors, and "a better break for the mentally ill"; increasing weapons to fight monopoly and racketeering in key economic sectors; lowering interest rates for borrowing money for homes; increasing income for farmers by activating U.S. food surpluses to create markets and promote peace abroad; and seeing "whether the children of Indiana and the nation can obtain safe, decent, adequate public school facilities with competent, well-paid teachers."[33]

Kennedy's February 1960 visits to Indiana were referred to by one reporter as "a sortie into normally Republican Indiana."[34] *Chicago Sun-Times* political reporter Justin Fishbein wrote that "despite a youthful appearance that belies his 42 years, Kennedy showed he is a mature politician, candid and intellectually able" during multiple stops in the Hoosier state. His schedule was ambitious—stops for news conferences and receptions in Indianapolis and Gary the first day (the latter being a benefit banquet for the Greek Hellenic Center at the International Center of Gary) and additional meetings in Gary, East Chicago, West Lafayette, and Terre Haute (including a well-received breakfast with a large gathering of Lake County Democratic Women's Clubs, a tour of the U.S. Steel Corporation Gary Works, and a speech at Indiana State University). Fishbein noted that Kennedy seemed apt at forming meaningful bonds with local audiences, reminding a Purdue University alumni group gathered at West Lafayette that he knew the university's president and had enjoyed the most recent Purdue-Notre Dame football scrap. "Someone pointed out that I received an honorary degree from Notre Dame, but he was sitting on the Purdue side of the field," Kennedy told the small gathering. "They suggested that I should cheer for Purdue and pray for Notre Dame."[35] Moving on to a larger evening gathering of 800 Democrats from Tippecanoe County and surrounds, Kennedy joked that he had always wanted to speak before a cocktail party, "especially one that's been going on since 4:30."[36]

Earlier in Gary in an appearance that played up the ethnically diverse nature of Northwest Indiana, Kennedy told the benefit audience at the International Institute of Gary that "no issue confronting the next President of the United States will be more complex or more difficult than the issue of Eastern Europe" and added, "and no issue in a Presidential campaign is in more danger of being exploited in a demagogic fashion, by easy promises and easy slogans, by playing on the hopes and fears of relatives and friends, than this same issue of Eastern Europe."[37] The senator then set about to unbraid the Eisenhower-Nixon record in Eastern Europe throughout the postwar years, noting that "pious" and "eloquent and moving phrases" about the desire of America to stop the oppression of rights by the Soviet Union were basked with "no plan of action, no intent to help those who struggled for freedom, no forceful role for the United States" that left millions of Eastern Europeans free of Nazi rule, only to be replaced by Soviet domination.[38]

Kennedy said it was not too late for the U.S. to lead an effort to restore true liberation to Eastern Europe, "a freedom without war . . . and without encouraging rebellions which would only force Soviet intervention." He said, "There is much in Eastern Europe to give us hope that the future could be better. Under the surface gloss of unwavering ideology, of automatic obedience to Moscow rule, domestic problems are being given equality with the aims of international Communism." He predicted younger Soviet leaders who had replaced the now-deceased Joseph Stalin were more concerned with dealing with local economic, social, and political issues directly affecting the quality of life of those living in a Communist system. Kennedy called for "vigorous, imaginative and continual pressure" to bring about peaceful advances in freedom for Eastern Europeans and recalled Thomas Jefferson's belief that "the disease of liberty is catching." He offered a four-part plan for the next decade he intended to lead, including recognition and support of growing divisions among Communists in Europe to help "wean the so-called captive nations away from their Kremlin masters"; refusal to accept or acknowledge Soviet domination of Eastern Europe and to hold them to their commitments at Potsdam and Yalta; adopt policies that recognize and encourage connections between all Europeans, whether east or west, regarding their history, culture and economy; and elimination of residual fears of the west, and particularly of Germany, in many parts of the region that stand in the way of trusting a new day where differences are settled by peaceful negotiations.[39] As he was prone to do, Kennedy ended his speech by quoting poet Henry Wadsworth Longfellow and his words about the role of Polish immigrant Casimir Pulaski, who left Poland and joined the American Revolution for freedom: "Take thy banner! and beneath, The battle-cloud's encircling wreath, Guard it, 'til our homes are free! Guard it, and God will prosper thee!"[40]

The following morning at a breakfast meeting of the Lake County Democratic Women's Club at the Hotel Gary (where the senator and his party had lodged overnight), Kennedy's reception was reported in excited, breathless terms. His youth and good looks were winning over many, particularly women voters, a key demographic in elections since 1952, as the number of registered female voters continued to swell in America. Kennedy's remarks at the breakfast were more partisan than other stops, urging his audience to find promise in recent election returns that showed gains by Democrats in House and Senate races across the nation, and the importance of the upcoming campaign that "will determine whether a Democrat will once again lead this nation in the most important office in the world, the President of the United States."[41]

A word of caution was thrown in, however, as Kennedy noted that "local victories do not make a national victory" and that the GOP held a major advantage as the incumbent party to steer defense contracts, patronage, purchase of surplus commodities and bring federal criminal indictments—all to their benefit. "The Republicans, in addition, have a great asset and a great campaigner in the current President of the United States. And Mr. Nixon himself is a skillful campaigner, an experienced political fighter and a candidate with tremendous financial and newspaper backing." Working in favor of the Democrats, he said, was a record of eight years of Republican politics and the fact that after "eight gray years" of Eisenhower's leadership, the nation was hungry for the Democratic Party's tradition of nominating "a dynamic, progressive man to the White House, a tradition which the sixties demand."[42]

Kennedy continued to acknowledge Eisenhower's personal popularity, but said he was certain Nixon's plan to run on Eisenhower's record of "tired policies" was a doomed effort. Noting that Nixon's oft-stated claims of "Republican peace and prosperity" throughout the 1950s "is a myth," Kennedy said, "We are not enjoying a period of peace, only a period of stagnation

and retreat, while America becomes second in missiles, second in space, second in education, and if we don't act fast and effectively, second in production and industrial might." He said the Republican promise of prosperity was one "for some, but not for all" and that its focus on "abundance of goods, not of courage" had resulted in a nation where "we have the most gadgets and gimmicks in our history, the biggest TVs and tailfins, but we also have the worst slums, the most crowded schools, and the greatest erosion of our national resources and our national will. It may be for some an age of material prosperity, but it is also an age of spiritual poverty."[43]

In additional remarks before another friendly audience of Lake County Democrats at the Elks Building in East Chicago, Kennedy was in a reflective mood, recalling author Carl Sandberg's tales of a young Abraham Lincoln growing into a man on Hoosier soil and staring up into a moonlight Indiana sky and declaring, "We lived the same as the Indians, 'ceptin we took an interest in politics and religion." Kennedy attempted to connect his Lake County friends to Lincoln's time noting that "the people of Indiana still take an interest in politics and religion. . . . And there are still pioneers (here), there are still new frontiers, some of them (now) on the moon itself. But the moon has to look hard to find Americans on this new frontier. It sees a Soviet rocket to the moon, and Soviet missiles soaring through space." Kennedy quickly moved on to fueling a growing flame of doubt among many Americans in the post-Sputnik days: "We are asked today to forget about the missile gap, to forget about our dwindling prestige abroad and our dwindling defenses at home. These are of no importance to the 1960 election, we are told. According to the Vice President of the United States, Americans are 'living better than ever before and they are going to vote that way.'"[44] Expanding his earlier theme about prosperity, Kennedy said, "We have more swimming pools, freezers, boats and air-conditioners than the moon has ever seen before, but 'the test of our progress,' as Franklin Roosevelt said, 'is not whether we add more to the abundance of those who have much; it is whether we provide enough for those who have too little.'"[45]

Taking a closer aim at Eisenhower than Nixon, Kennedy said the president had offered his annual State of the Union address "painting a picture of a fat and complacent nation, a nation of wealth and abundance, a satisfied nation; satisfied with what it had and satisfied with where it was going. But the truth of the matter is that behind the President's contented phrases are facts that give us no cause for satisfaction (and ones) that do not meet the Roosevelt test," including seven million American families struggling with annual incomes below $2,000; certain areas of the country where unemployment rates had reached 25 percent; seniors trying to survive on substandard incomes; 17 million Americans suffering from malnutrition; 5 million American homes lacking indoor plumbing; and overcrowded school classrooms. He concluded by offering that "we *are* increasing our wealth, but we are failing to use that great wealth to meet the urgent needs of millions of our citizens, and the demands of our growing nation."[46]

Later that evening at Terre Haute (following his quick stops in Tippecanoe County), Kennedy gave what was dubbed a "nonpolitical speech" that was advertised as a push to get Americans engaged at the polls via primary voting, but it was a carefully crafted appearance to allow him firsthand, press-the-flesh contact with Hoosier voters in a heavily Democratic area. His speech, titled "The Presidential Primary and Your Vote," was given in the Student Union building on the

Indiana State University campus as part of the Wabash Valley Lecture Series Dinner. Drawing heavily on Indiana's formerly great past in selecting presidents, Kennedy said the state's voters could play a similar role in 1960 because of the primary being offered in the state. He lamented the lack of competition in the Indiana primary from other potential Democratic candidates because "primary contests not only educate the public, they educate the candidate as well. For if a candidate wishes to understand the needs and aspirations of the people he seeks to serve, he must go among them. He must view the cities and towns and factories and farms first hand, not merely read second-hand reports from local supporters or look at the nation through the wrong end of a television camera. . . . If he is to understand the problems of all sections (of the nation) and not merely his own, he must listen as well as talk, see as well as be seen, learn as well as teach. And the primary is the greatest instrument there is for that kind of education."[47]

In the question-and-answer session that followed Kennedy's remarks, questions ranged from the silly ("Why had he changed his haircut?") to the more serious ("Was he worried that his Roman Catholicism would negatively impact his campaign?"). Even more serious questions were raised by a member of the "nonpartisan" audience who asked him whether he was concerned he would have to engage in "dirty politics" in order to successfully take on Vice President Nixon—the questioner referring to Nixon as "Dirty Dick." Kennedy took the high road—and drew applause—by responding to the questioner by saying, "It seems to me you are indulging in the very tactics you find so objectionable in Mr. Nixon."[48]

Kennedy was back in the state again a month later in March 1960, and the "religious" issue came front and center as a group of Indiana

Baptists staged a demonstration outside the Indiana Statehouse as Kennedy arrived to file his primary candidacy papers at the Indiana Secretary of State's Office. The picketers held a sign challenging Kennedy to a debate under the theme: "Resolved that a Roman Catholic President cannot impartially defend the Constitution and advance the true welfare of the United States while remaining true to his religion."[49] Kennedy politely accepted a leaflet from one of the protesters, but did not engage him in debate. Later, when he faced reporters from a podium at the front of the chambers of the House of Representatives, Kennedy said, "These demonstrators are entitled to their views. I believe in the United States Constitution and in freedom of speech. I also believe in the First Amendment, which provides for the separation of church and the state. I also believe in Article VI, which says there shall be no religious test for qualification for public office."[50] Not satisfied with Kennedy's polite brush-off, a few of the Baptist demonstrators who had infiltrated the otherwise mix of Democratic partisans and reporters in the chambers stood and reissued their debate challenge directly. Drawing enthusiastic applause from his supporters and recalling his noteworthy record as a World War II veteran, Kennedy retorted: "Why didn't you issue this challenge when I joined the United States Navy?"[51]

After Kennedy left the statehouse, the leaders of the "Indiana Bible Baptist Fellowship" commandeered the podium the candidate had just used and elaborated on their views. One of the protest organizers, Reverend Doctor Hendon M. Harris Jr. declared, "We would have a safer and quieter country if we were free of Vatican politics. I like Kennedy better than Nixon, but I will have to vote for somebody else than Kennedy. Some of his statements sound more like a young

Irish thug than a statesman." One of Kennedy's supporters who remained in the room had had enough. Francis Roland, a Democratic precinct committeeman from Indianapolis, leaped to his feet and told Harris, "You are a rabble-rouser. You are arousing hate."[52]

A handful of additional Kennedy stops would be made in early April, a month out from the Indiana vote, as national reporters began to focus on the fact that with Kennedy and Nixon virtually unopposed in their respective party primaries, the "vote total" for each candidate could serve as an interesting barometer on where each stood for a possible November matchup. Kennedy made stops in Alexandria, Anderson, Marion, Muncie, Lafayette, and West Lafayette on April 7 and was scheduled for stops in Plymouth, Michigan City, Elkhart, Mishawaka, and South Bend on April 8. Earlier in the day Kennedy spoke before a "Farm Forum" at Beulah Park in Alexandria where he declared that "no domestic problem is of more concern than the steady decline in farm income. Farm close-out sales are reaching new peaks, young farm operators are leaving the land, bank deposits are down and loans are up in rural areas, there is despair and discontent in the midst of claims of prosperity."[53]

Declaring that "we cannot have prosperity in the city without prosperity on the farm," Kennedy claimed that under the Eisenhower-Nixon administration corporate profits and factory wages had all increased, while farm income had dropped 20 percent in the same period. He noted that he suspected some wanted more farmers pushed out of the market to eliminate crop and grain surpluses. Saying there were no easy answers, Kennedy said he had heard from Indiana farmers that "they were getting tired of hearing from politicians in either camp about some new short-term experiment, a wonder drug aimed at treating some current symptom instead of getting at the real problems" facing agriculture.[54] At the center of Kennedy's ideas for agriculture, however, remained a key link between the incredible producing power of American farmers with the need for bargaining chips in international diplomacy and the hope increased food supplies could mean to starving nations on Earth. Agriculture, he said, "can support a foreign policy dedicated to winning the cause of democracy (in) the uncommitted nations of the world, and can be a powerful source of military and economic strength." Key policy provisions to reduce surpluses and preserve farm incomes, Kennedy said, could be found in production controls, price protections for farmers, elimination of government-held surpluses, promotion and preservation of the family farm, and increased efforts at worldwide food distribution. Part of the expanded distribution, he suggested, could start at home with greater contributions from American farmers to support school lunch, school milk, and public welfare programs.[55]

Kennedy repeated similar themes in his remarks before a Farm Bureau meeting at the Farm Unions Clubhouse in Lafayette. Elsewhere in the state, Kennedy toured the Warner Gear Plant and attended a Democratic Women's Breakfast at the Hotel Roberts, both in Muncie; visited a farm in Madison County and make brief remarks at the Eagles Lodge in Anderson; attended an informal reception in the City Auditorium at Marion; stopped by an Alcoa Union Hall at Lafayette; and returned to Muncie for a community leaders' luncheon and remarks before a student assembly at Ball State University. That evening, Kennedy's ambitious schedule included a stop by at the Purduvian Club on the campus of Purdue University and at Saint Elizabeth's Hospital in West Lafayette, before ending the day with a

political speech before the Tippecanoe County Jefferson-Jackson Day Dinner at Central Catholic High School in Lafayette. In his remarks before the party faithful, Kennedy said that "today our very survival depends on that man in the White House—on his strength, his wisdom and his creative imagination," and added, "Mr. Nixon has repeatedly stated that he intends to carry on the policies of this administration. Let us hold him to that—because I predict on November 8 the American people are going to reject that tradition. After eight years of the administration, the nation needs a strong, creative Democrat in the White House."[56]

Kennedy was scheduled to use his second day in Indiana for a mix of public service and political activities, first shaking hands at a Studebaker plant gate in South Bend and later attending a convocation at the Marshall County combined junior and senior high school in Plymouth. His senatorial responsibilities, however, provided for an abbreviated swing through the state with planned stops at Plymouth, Nappanee, Elkhart, and Mishawaka all shelved. One "late night" speech in South Bend at an event intended to support the re-election of Congressman John Brademas did go forward at the University of Notre Dame dining hall in South Bend, but not before the audience waited in excess of three hours for Kennedy to return from Washington. As he finished campaigning in Lafayette, Kennedy was to go next to Plymouth, but instead diverted back to Washington, D.C., using his own plane in order to participate in a roll-call vote on a civil rights bill. Although the Senate vote cost him time with Hoosier voters, its topic and his desire to keep his voting attendance record high came first. The advantages of a well-financed campaign also showed. Unlike other candidates who had to rely primarily on commercial flights to get back and forth, Kennedy had the luxury of jumping out of the state, only to dip back in later for a patient crowd of more than 1,000 Democrats at South Bend. Kennedy's remarks did not start until almost 11:00 p.m. as a result, and he promised he would be back in the state before the primary. The *South Bend Tribune* was still impressed, its Saturday editions proclaiming in a banner headline that "Kennedy Turns on the Charm" and noted "his charm and the zeal of his supporters came close to overwhelming the announced purpose of the dinner—to kick-off the re-election campaign of U.S. Rep. John Brademas."[57]

Speaking for only sixteen minutes—having abandoned prepared speeches he had ready for his original schedule—Kennedy focused on what he said were the major issues facing the nation in the decade ahead, including economic growth, technological revolutions in agriculture, atomic disarmament, and aid to underdeveloped nations in Asia and Africa. Kennedy said the American people must answer a variation on Lincoln's question of old, "Can the world exist half slave and half free? No people since ancient Athens have had such responsibility."[58] After his remarks when reporters asked him for more details about his farm program, the late hour and long taxing day may have shown through in his reply, "If you think I'm going to write a farm bill for you tonight, you're mistaken."[59]

Post-South Bend stops at Walkerton, LaPorte, and Michigan City were later shelved as well as Kennedy left Indiana to campaign in Arizona.[60]

In late April Kennedy was back in Indiana for additional stops that included Indianapolis, Kokomo, and Richmond on April 29. This foray found Kennedy tiring under the realities of a national campaign, and local reports indicated

that by the time he reached Richmond he was rendered literally "speechless." His voice worn out, a small audience of supporters at Richmond heard one of Kennedy's aides read the remarks the senator had prepared. While in Richmond he visited students and faculty at Earlham College and had an impromptu speech delivered to parishioners at Holy Family Church. At Earlham, Kennedy offered a lengthy speech focused on disarmament talks begun among ten nations of the world, a topic his advance staff undoubtedly told him would be popular among a mostly Quaker and decidedly pacifist audience. Kennedy expressed concerns about a "hurriedly prepared" disarmament plan that "compounded old proposals" and lacked "new, creative thinking" about how to address the arms race.

"Modern science has created weapons of fantastic destructive power," Kennedy said, not mincing words. "A single nuclear weapon today can release more destructive energy than all the explosives used in all the wars throughout history—the radioactive fallout from that single bomb can destroy all higher forms of life in an area of 10,000 square miles. And the powerful new gases and deadly bacteria which are now being developed for war promise suffering and devastation in many ways more horrible than even the threat of nuclear destruction."[61] It was his belief, Kennedy said, that while modern science has made arms control essential, "it has also made arms control more difficult," citing the development of underground missile launch sites, growth of nuclear stockpiles in the U.S. and the Soviet Union, evolution of new techniques to launch surprise attacks from beneath the earth or under the seas or in the air. These "have all multiplied the difficulties of achieving arms control—of developing an effective inspection system."[62]

There remained hope, Kennedy said, in the

certain knowledge that the Russians knew as well as the Americans that the spread of nuclear weapons "upset the balance of power and increases the danger of accidental war" and that "a war of mutual destruction would benefit no one nation or ideology." Kennedy said there was no reason to believe that the Soviets would abandon their desire for more Communist rule in the world, but that history provided examples where "fanatic Islam and crusading Christiandom generally transformed themselves into centuries of perpetual truce, although both parties retained their universal goals."[63] Careful to avoid stepping into an area that opened his remarks to ongoing criticism from Nixon and the Republicans that he was soft on Communism and naïve of the Soviet threat, Kennedy said we must not minimize the Russian threat and their desire to "bury us economically, politically, culturally and in every other sphere of interest," but that the post-Stalin Soviet leaders "may realize that the path of Russian self-interest permits—and perhaps compels—them to agree to some steps toward comprehensive arms control." While not referring to Nixon by name, Kennedy did suggest many within the Eisenhower administration's State Department still viewed disarmament as "a fuzzy ideal for fuzzy idealists." He added, "Of course, the President is sincere when he says we want disarmament, but I am also afraid that the rest of the world is justified in wondering whether we really do. There are, of course, many powerful voices in the government—both in and out of the Pentagon—who do not want disarmament, or professing to want it, do not really believe in it."[64]

Also during his Richmond stop, Kennedy spoke to a Wayne County Jefferson-Jackson Day Dinner of Democratic loyals and sounded similar themes to his Earlham speech, but added in more partisan jousts, such as providing comparisons between the Eisenhower approach to dealing with the Communists with that which existed when President Harry S Truman left office in 1953. Then, Kennedy said, the United States was the undisputed leader in economics, military, and all other spheres, "a record we intend to match—and surpass—when we have a Democrat in the White House in 1961." Noting that "the Russians beat us into outer space. They beat us around the sun. They beat us to the moon" and that "half of Indo-China has disappeared behind the Iron Curtain"—the record of the last eight years must be broken.[65] Seven years of reduced forces, cut military budgets, and "held back" missile programs under the Republicans placed the nation at the risk of falling behind the Soviets, as had "harassment" of the nation's scientists and underpayment of teachers. Finally, he cited economic woes that "for seven years has kept our sights low, fluctuating between inflation and recession, handicapped by serious pockets of high unemployment, low purchasing power, and declining farm income." Kennedy added that "I do not say the picture is all bad. I do not say that the other side of the ledger is all blank, but neither can we afford to ignore these facts and their implications any longer. . . . Eight 'gray years,' years of drift, of falling behind, of postponing decisions and crises, and as a result, the burdens that will face the next administration will be tremendous. The gaps between ourselves and the Soviet Union will be many—and dangerous—and still growing."[66]

Earlier at the Howard County Courthouse in Kokomo, Kennedy repeated earlier ideas about melding challenges facing agriculture with those of world peace and democracy. Perhaps recognizing Howard County's locale in the heart of Indiana farm country (but missing its centrality as an industrial manufacturing base), Kennedy said the two challenges facing agriculture domes-

COURTESY JOHN LIVENGOOD

Kennedy stopped for dinner in Richmond, Indiana, during the 1960 presidential campaign. Fort Wayne's WOWO radio station broadcasted the Democratic candidate's appearance.

tically and peace internationally "merge into a single challenge, at one point at least, summed up in three powerful words: Food for Peace."[67] Covering once again the realities of farm surpluses driving down prices at home, and the reality of malnourished and starving nations abroad, Kennedy said "only America has too much food in a hungry world." The senator noted that Public Law 480, which allowed the United States to trade, donate, or barter agricultural surpluses for foreign currency, did not go far enough. "It is time, therefore, for this nation to try a bold new expansion of our food for peace program—with new goals, and new steps forward, to relieve our

farm surpluses, and to turn our great agricultural abundance into a blessing—for ourselves, and for all the world," Kennedy said. He offered a three-step proposal that would allow storage of up to one-half of the nation's grain surplus abroad (making it more readily available for transport to needed areas and shifting storage costs to the recipient nations), expanding uses of the foreign currencies the United Sates receives to include investments in schools and teachers in developing nations, and the formation of new partnerships with Canada and Australia who also had large food surpluses. Once again highlighting how he was a different candidate than most had heard before, Kennedy quoted Norman Cousins that "'when I enter my home, I enter with the awareness that my table is only half set, for half the men on this earth know the emptiness of want.' Tonight, all tables in America are only half set in this sense—and they remain half set until we can begin to use our richness, our abundance and our great resources to drive want away from the tables of men everywhere."[68]

As 1960 unfolded, Kennedy wrestled the Democratic presidential nomination away from Johnson (who he later added to the ticket as his vice presidential running mate), and Kennedy crisscrossed the nation, mostly bypassing Indiana. By October 1960, however, Democrats in the state remained hopeful for a chance to move Indiana into the Democratic column (despite an impressive rally and massive crowds for Nixon at Indianapolis, Fort Wayne, and Evansville). Key stops were scheduled for Kennedy on a busy two-day swing on October 4–5 into solidly Democratic pockets of the state, including Indianapolis, Evansville, Terre Haute, Pendleton, Anderson, and Muncie. It is not clear if the Kennedy campaign actually believed it had a chance in Indiana or viewed the visits as key to the campaigns of Matt Welsh for governor and Democratic candidates running in the state's then-eleven congressional districts.

At Terre Haute, Kennedy was accompanied by Welsh and Senator Vance Hartke and others on the steps of the Vigo County Courthouse and mixed comments about the opening of the 1960 World Series between the Pittsburgh Pirates and the New York Yankees with concerns about repeated recessions that "this country cannot afford. The demands placed upon us [during a recession] are too great. Every time we fail to meet our problems, every time we fail to move our economy forward, we fail not only our own

people, but we fail all those who look to us for leadership."[69] Kennedy reminded his audience that "Indiana does not exist by itself." and the desire of Hoosier parents for their children to have better lives is shared across the nation. "I believe the issue is very clear," he said, "and the issue is whether the American people are satisfied with things as they are, whether they feel that the 1960s are a time to really conserve and stand still and gather our energy, or whether the 1960s are a time to move forward again."[70]

Kennedy said he believed, rather, that Hoosiers and most Americans would invest in new leadership for the decade ahead and took on directly Nixon's claims that Kennedy's assessment of the recent past was based in negativity. "Mr. Nixon says I downgrade America," Kennedy said. "I have served the United States just as long as he has, and I have just as much affection for it and just as high an opinion of it. I downgrade his leadership. I downgrade the Republican leadership, and anyone who thinks the prestige of the United States is increasing as fast as it needs to should look around us."[71] The sharpness of Kennedy's remarks reflected not only the late hour of the campaign—voters would go to the polls in just under thirty days—but the immediacy of the historic Nixon-Kennedy debates, the second of which occurred just forty-eight hours after Kennedy spoke in Indiana.

In Indianapolis, coverage for Kennedy's visit was decidedly downplayed by the city's dominant Republican daily, the *Indianapolis Star,* which focused its coverage on the size of street-side crowds assembled for the Kennedy motorcade and Governor Harold Handley's role in leading the Indiana version of the "GOP Truth Squad" that followed Kennedy around the nation. The *Star*'s coverage included a street-by-street description of the Kennedy motorcade, a practice that at the time seemed innocuous, but in retrospect looks frightening considering Kennedy's assassination in a well-publicized motorcade route through the streets of Dallas three years later. Kennedy made a quick stop at the Claypool Hotel in downtown Indianapolis, although the motorcade from the airport to the hotel (and the one later to the State Fairgrounds) reportedly produced disappointing crowds, "thinly lined by supporters," the *Star* noted. Among those who did show up, some were sporting "Nixon for President" signs for Kennedy to see.[72]

"The crowd thickened at some intersections in Wayne Township and along Capitol and Indiana avenues as the motorcade neared the hotel," the *Star* reported. "A crowd estimated at 1,000 to 1,500 persons jammed the first block of North Illinois Street and the Claypool Hotel lobby to see the Massachusetts senator."[73] The determination of *Star* reporters to poke holes in Kennedy's visit continued: "Newsmen and Kennedy staff members expressed amazement at the meager crowds which greeted the Massachusetts multi-millionaire. The staff members' amazement was mixed with chagrin at the 'indifferent' reception their candidate received on his caravan from the airport into downtown Indianapolis. Visiting newsmen were also surprised, they said, at the small size of the crowds lining Kennedy's two parade routes, the second being his tour to the Coliseum from the Claypool Hotel. They said the numbers had been far exceeded in cities of smaller size to Indianapolis earlier in his campaign."[74]

Crowds on the street may have been smaller than some expected, but nearly 10,000 Democrats packed the Coliseum for Kennedy's remarks—an impressive showing in Republican-leaning Indiana—although the *Star* again dutifully quoted unnamed Nixon campaign officials as saying the crowd for Kennedy was only half

of what the vice president had drawn on Monument Circle in September. Regardless, Kennedy delivered perhaps his most eloquent campaign speech to date in the state, rising, perhaps, to the formality and awe of the large audience. He opened by recalling Franklin D. Roosevelt's words at his 1936 renomination acceptance speech when he said, "Governments can err, Presidents do make mistakes, but the immortal Dante tells us that Divine Justice weighs the sins of the coldblooded and the sins of the warmhearted in different scales. Better the occasional faults of a government living in the spirit of charity than the consistent omissions of a government frozen in the ice of its own indifference."[75]

"I think that is the test for the sixties," Kennedy said to rousing applause. "Where Franklin Roosevelt set before our country its unfinished business, the agenda of our nation, the things that we must do if we are going to realize our potential, this administration has set ceilings and limitations, and we now move from stage to stage in the most difficult time in the history of our country, when the challenge is clearly laid upon the United States. We move into 1960 not with vigor and energy and foresight, but instead being dragged along, year after year, without any recognition of how serious are the problems that face us at home and abroad." Kennedy said he was unimpressed with "leap-year progressivism which comes upon the Republican Party every four years, when they support and sustain programs which they fight against year after year in the Congress."[76]

Kennedy made his agenda clear:

I think it is time the United States began to stir itself again. You cannot possibly be satisfied to move from a recession in 1954 to a serious recession in 1958, to a slowdown in 1960, which promises a hard winter in 1961, and feel that the United States is living up to its capacity. You cannot be satisfied when there are 15 million American homes which, according to the last census, are substandard, five million American homes in the cities of the United States which lack plumbing of any kind. You cannot be satisfied as an American when the average wage for laundrywomen in five cities of the United States is 65 cents an hour for a 48-hour week, and most of them are Negroes. You cannot be satisfied to see our steel capacity at 50 percent, to know that last week the Soviet Union produced more steel than the United States with one-half of our capacity, because our machines and men are not being used to the fullest. I think this is a somber time for us all.[77]

Kennedy, borrowing quotes from diverse sources such as Oscar Wilde, Abraham Lincoln, and Robert E. Sherwood, said, "I don't run for the office of Presidency saying if I am elected life will be easy, but I do believe that a new administration composed of new people inheriting a great tradition of intellectual vitality, can move this country further ahead."[78] Acknowledging the huge task before Indiana Democrats to turn a decidedly Republican tide in the other direction for 1960, Kennedy concluded, "Here in this state of Indiana, it is not an easy job. This is a long, tough, uphill fight, even though I am confident that you are going to elect Matt Welsh as Governor. But I am under no illusions that this election on my part is easy in the state of Indiana. It is uphill. But I am confident that the tide is moving in our direction. I am confident that the people of this state recognize that there are serious issues which affect the two parties, that the history of the two parties is entirely different. My judgment is that a majority of the citizens of this state are going to choose the Democratic Party and choose to move again, choose to go ahead again, rather than standing on dead center."[79]

Following his remarks at the Coliseum, Kennedy spent the night in Indianapolis and embarked the next morning on whistle-stop campaign rallies in Pendleton, Anderson, and Muncie and flew to Terre Haute and Evansville for rallies on October 5. Anderson was the second stop and the candidate drew laughter and got in a dig at the heavily pro-Nixon coverage he was receiving from the state's largest newspaper when he said, "I understand this town suffered a misfortune this morning when the bank was robbed. I am confident that the *Indianapolis Star* will say that Democrats arrive and bank robbed. But we don't believe that!"[80] Kennedy said he was there on a different mission, one that hoped to move Indiana into the Democratic column for the first time in twenty-four years. "If there is any merchant in this town who thinks his business is good this fall, who looks to the future of 1961 with optimism, who thinks that agricultural prices are going to go up, who thinks that the tide is rising in Indiana and the nation, who believes that our position is more secure in the world than it was five years ago . . . I believe they should vote for Mr. Nixon," Kennedy explained. "In the winter of 1961 and 1962, unless this country moves again, this state won't move. I don't care what happens in Indiana by itself—unless the rest of the country is going ahead. Who buys the products of General Motors? Not the citizens of Indiana alone, but the citizens of the United States. Therefore, in this state, which for 24 years has sustained the Republicans, I think you should give us a chance. I think you should give us a chance to lead."[81] In short, Kennedy asked his Hoosier audience "to say 'yes' to the sixties" and embrace new leadership.

In brief remarks from the back of the train at Pendleton, Kennedy began his remarks curiously introducing himself, saying, "My name is Kennedy. I am here running in Indiana and I just wanted to stop here and ask for your help in this campaign. I think that this is a difficult and important election. I think the fight in this state is going to be close and hard fought. I have come here today to ask for your help."[82] Later at his last train stop, the downtown depot in Muncie, a much larger gathering was present to hear Kennedy say he could not believe that Indiana voters could be fooled into supporting a Republican campaign trying to sell voters on the idea "which says you never had it so good. I believe we can do better, and I come here to Indiana today and ask for your support as the Democratic candidate for the office of the Presidency."[83] Kennedy joked that "Mr. Nixon the other night in Boston said that I was another Truman, and I regard that as a compliment, and I returned it to him, and I suggested that perhaps he was another Dewey."[84]

Kennedy blasted the GOP for viewing as "too extreme" an increase to the nation's $1.25 minimum wage, improvements to social security and medical care for the aged, and combatting farm prices. His public remarks at Muncie ended with a theme that would become familiar—a reference to "moving ahead to the New Frontier" and by quoting Lincoln: "One hundred years ago in the campaign of 1860, Abraham Lincoln wrote a friend, 'I know there is a God, and He hates injustice. I see the storm coming, and I know His hand is in it. But if He has a place and a part for me, I believe that I am ready.' Now, 100 years later, in the most trying period in the life of this country, when freedom is undergoing its most severe test, *we* know there is a God and *we* know He hates injustice, and *we* see the storm coming. But if He has a place and a part for *us*, I believe that *we* are ready. I ask for your help."[85] Later Kennedy spoke to a small group of workers and union leaders outside the Muncie Gear Works factory where

he hit on similar themes to his larger speech in downtown Muncie, and noted, "I think we can win in Indiana and we can win in the country. . . . I believe the American people are going to choose to go with the Democrats again. I come here today to ask for your help in a tough fight here in Indiana. If we can win in this state, we can win the election."[86]

At Evansville on the steps of the Vanderburgh County Courthouse, Kennedy said he was pleased to be visiting the city just four days after Nixon because of the importance of the coming election decision, one that represented "a turning point in our history" and noted that "the whole world in the next four or eight years will be entirely different than it is today."[87] Kennedy then addressed what advisers no doubt had warned him that conservative Hoosiers, even Democratic ones, often cast a weary and suspicious eye toward Washington. "I know there are those in this state who say that Indiana should cut its ties with the government, that Indiana should move its own separate way," he said. If Indiana did so, Kennedy asked, who would buy the products of the state's impressive manufacturing and agricultural prowess? "Indiana is not a separate state, it is part of the United States, and Indiana and Evansville and the United States will rise or fall depending upon the leadership which is given to his country in 1960," Kennedy declared.[88] He said his candidacy presented the people of Evansville with "a clear alternative" between himself and Nixon—between a vision of progress and one of standing still. "I ask for your help in this campaign, not merely because it affects our party, but because, as this is the most dangerous time in the life of our country. I don't think we can possibly afford to stand still," he said. "Now in 1960, and in the sixties, we are asked to live in the service of this country. We are asked to contribute to it.

We are asked to build a stronger and better society, and I come here today to this community to ask you to join us."[89]

Throughout his visits in Indiana, members of a "GOP Truth Squad" went where Kennedy went. Comprised of Republican congressional leaders and governors loyal to Nixon, the Truth Squad held news conferences and raised pointed questions about Kennedy's proposals. Reminiscent of the "take no prisoners" campaign style Nixon had employed in being elected to the House and U.S. Senate in California, the Truth Squad scored a front-page attack in the *Indianapolis Star*, courtesy of Indiana's Republican governor, Handley, who posed seven loaded "questions" or "challenges" to Kennedy, including suggesting that Kennedy favored appeasement with the Soviets and wanted Eisenhower to apologize to Khrushchev, questioned his leadership, attendance, and experience in the Senate, alleged plans for higher taxes and bigger government, and "schemes" that would harm Indiana farmers.[90] The Kennedy campaign ignored the lame-duck Handley, and no response was offered to the Truth Squad badgering.

Kennedy ultimately won the election, one of the closest presidential elections in U.S. history. He failed to carry Indiana, however, with Nixon earning a comfortable 55 to 45 percentage win among Hoosiers. Kennedy's fall campaign partner, Welsh, fared better and won a narrow-thin victory to be elected governor. Welsh's victory ensured him access to the new president in the years ahead, including one-on-one meetings in August 1961 at the White House, discussing the upcoming 1962 election and Kennedy's deep desire to defeat Senator Homer Capehart, a virulent Indiana Republican critic. Consistent with that, Kennedy made a last-minute campaign swing through Indiana in October 1962, just three days before he would receive "unmistakable evidence

[that] established the fact that a series of offensive missile sites is now in preparation on that imprisoned island"[91]—the words he would use to explain Soviet military buildup in Cuba. In fact, it was not until the day after Kennedy appeared at Weir Cook International Airport in Indianapolis that American military intelligence began to uncover the Soviet activities ninety miles off the coast of Florida.

Kennedy's remarks that day appear to confirm subsequent historic reports that the president was not informed of the situation until three days after he left Indianapolis. For his highly partisan audience of more than 18,000, Kennedy reminded them that he had correctly predicted Welsh would be elected governor and had correctly predicted his own overall victory to move America forward.

"I can report to you with some satisfaction that this country is moving again, that we have put idle men and resources back to work, that we have cut back on waste and decay, and that we are building the economic, scientific and military strength of this country to a level which no foreign power can overcome or endanger," Kennedy said.[92] Outlining defense budget increases of more than $8 billion, Kennedy included reference to Southeast Asia (not Vietnam specifically) by noting, "Recognizing that the time had come to stop the decline of free world security in Southeast Asia, we committed 15 times as many men to assist in the defense of that area."[93] Beyond his military and defense budget brags, Kennedy also praised Peace Corps volunteers now serving in thirty-seven nations across the globe and the newly independent "Food for Peace" programs in other developing nations. In addition, "We have increased both our power and our prestige by shifting our space program from low gear into high," he said, "sending twice as many satellites into orbit in the last 20 months as were launched in all the preceding years, and making the decisions necessary to achieve world prominence in space before this decade is out."[94]

Kennedy quickly turned to his real agenda—the defeat of Senator Capehart, who strongly opposed Kennedy's efforts to topple the Communist Castro regime in Cuba, had missed 130 of 225 Senate roll-call votes, including a key Cuban resolution, despite heavy criticism of the administration's policies in Cuba and elsewhere in Latin America. The president's brother, Attorney General Robert F. Kennedy, later confirmed that his brother loathed Capehart and formed a fast friendship with the GOP senator's upstart novice challenger for 1962, a little-known young farmer and ambitious state legislative leader from Shierkeville, Indiana, by the name of Birch Bayh. The president, without referring to Capehart by name, said, "This is no time for rash and irresponsible talk which strengthens the claims of our adversaries. This is no time for confused and intemperate remarks on the part of those who have neither the facts nor the responsibility to determine this nation's course. This is a time for men who talk softly and carry a big stick—and that is the kind of man you have in Birch Bayh!"[95]

Again drawing a sharp contrast between Bayh and Capehart, the president noted that Bayh was an army veteran, as contrasted to "those self-appointed generals and admirals who want to send someone else's sons to war, and who consistently voted against the instruments of peace, [who] ought to be kept at home by the voters and replaced in Washington by someone who has some understanding of what the twentieth century is all about." Kennedy said Bayh, unlike Capehart (but again, without mentioning Capehart's name), "would not be using the Senate floor for speeches which embarrass this nation abroad and embarrass most members of the Senate from both parties. . . . In Birch Bayh, Indiana will have a Senator who understands the importance of strength and understand the importance of peace."[96]

Kennedy was not finished. He noted continually that Bayh would not have taken the approach of the incumbent Capehart on issues as diverse as the minimum wage, agriculture, education funding, Social Security, and trade agreements. "And he would not have voted to permit an endless filibuster against the bill to ban literacy tests as a means of discrimination against Negro voters," Kennedy said, alluding to Capehart's vision as one more appropriate to the nineteenth century.[97] He added a strong pitch for Democratic House candidates in Indiana, noting that seven of the state's eleven congressional districts were represented by Republicans and that all seven had voted lockstep against progressive trade agreements, increases in the federal minimum wage, housing programs for seniors, urban renewal programs for Indianapolis, and expansion of federal home loan programs.

Kennedy's last visit to Indiana on that sunny October day in 1962 was successful. Bayh narrowly defeated Capehart in the November 1962 election, the beginning of a distinguished eighteen-year career in the U.S. Senate for Bayh. Kennedy, who never again visited Indiana as president, prepared for a 1964 re-election campaign that never occurred. Kennedy was assassinated on November 22, 1963, in Dallas, Texas.

Lyndon B. Johnson

In the 1960 campaign Johnson was an active crusader for the Kennedy effort. As was characteristic, he took on the role of "attack dog," delivering some of the strongest punches against Nixon and the Republicans. In late September

Johnson made a five-city sweep across Indiana with stops at Columbia City, Wabash, Evansville, Fort Wayne, and Indianapolis.

At Evansville he appeared at the Vander-burgh County Courthouse for a rally before a crowd of 4,000, but was slightly behind schedule after stopping to talk to schoolchildren at String-town Elementary School. During his remarks, Johnson "scoffed" at the idea that Nixon was best prepared to deal with the Communists: "Nixon went to a Midnight conference with Rocky [Nelson Rockefeller] in the Waldorf-Astoria Hotel in New York and when it was over, Rocky had turned him around 180 degrees on the Republican platform. If Rockefeller can do that in one Midnight conference, what could Khrushchev do if he had him all day?" Reporters at Evansville asked Johnson whether he thought Kennedy's Catholic faith could cost him votes among conservative and Protestant voters. Johnson said that religion should never influence a vote and quoted Kennedy as saying, "I don't tell the Vatican what to do and the Vatican doesn't tell me what to do."[98]

As Johnson departed Evansville, his flight was delayed by a burned-out starter. The Electra plane would not start (eventually causing the entire party to switch planes). Before that decision was made, however, one of Johnson's traveling companions, Senator Hartke, bailed out on the flight. A vocal critic of the Electra safety record since the deadly March 17, 1960, crash at Tell City that left sixty-three people dead, Hartke told a reporter, "No sir, I'm not about to ride in an Electra."[99]

Finally at Fort Wayne, Johnson was amused by one of his greeters, ten-year-old Jack Kennedy of Fort Wayne at the airport holding a sign that said, "Jack Kennedy welcomes you to Fort Wayne." Johnson made his way to both Wa-bash and Whitley Counties for airport rallies. At Columbia City he blistered Agriculture Secretary Ezra T. Benson:

> We are going to get a secretary of agriculture who understands farm problems and who will sit down with farmers and work with them, not against them. We are going to set up a price support system for basic crops with better prices for farmers which will protect the family-size farm and offer larger farms a chance to compete in world markets. We are going to distribute more of our abundance to the needy and underfed people at home. We are going to put our surpluses to work for peace through a world food bank. We will share our surpluses with the millions and millions of people who go to bed hungry every night. We are going to find a new use for farm products through concentrated research programs.[100]

At Wabash, Johnson asserted before about 1,000 supporters that "net farm income has dropped one-third while farm mortgages have increased 58 percent" under President Eisenhower and that GOP fiscal policies are "deliberately designed to reduce buying and reduce business expansion." He also took swipes at Nixon, saying the vice president "has bitterly opposed Democratic proposals for a world food bank, a strategic food reserve, and a food stamp plan for our needy" and that Nixon is acting like "a political schizophrenic" in his talk about disposing of farm surpluses.[101]

"Now in the clutches of a campaign and with his back against the wall, the Republican nominee draws 'Operation Consume' out of his pocket," Johnson proclaimed. "He is trying to steal for campaign use the Democratic proposals he has fought since 1953."[102] Regarding the just completed first debate between Kennedy and Nixon, Johnson said Kennedy had won. "You can take it at face value—one fellow fell on his face," he said with a smile.[103]

As vice president, Johnson visited Indiana just over a month before Kennedy's assasination. Media reports regarding Johnson's appearance in Indianapolis for an October 1963 Indiana Democratic fund-raising dinner focused on whether Kennedy planned to keep Johnson on the ticket for the upcoming 1964 election. As he arrived at Indianapolis's Weir Cook Airport, Johnson said any question about his role in 1964 was "pure speculation without any foundation whatever" and added, "The 1964 Democratic National Convention will decide about my renomination." Back in Washington, Kennedy had already stated his support of keeping Johnson on the ticket and dismissed any rumors to the contrary.[104]

"Today's new radicalism does not dress in shabby clothes or wear short beards," Johnson told about 1,800 of his fellow Democrats, "but it is radicalism all the same when men seriously propose that we abandon the income tax which supports our government, our dollar and the arms which keep us free."[105] The vice president did not mention conservative Republicans specifically, but his partisan audience understood who he was talking about, especially in the midst of a Liberty Amendment suggested by conservatives to eliminate the federal income tax.

Johnson said "radical" conservatives were undermining the federal government, its courts, the military, and even sought to withdraw the United States from its role in the United Nations. "The American people have made it decisively clear in election after election that they do not want and will not accept the leadership of those who seek only to turn back the clock," Johnson said. "If this is to be the issue of the election at this particular period in our history, Democrats should welcome the opportunity to accept that challenge and carry their cause to the people."[106]

In themes that suggested how he and

Kennedy planned to run in 1964, he listed thirty-one months of "what promises to be the longest peacetime expansion in our history," with more than seventy million Americans employed and average factory wages more than $100 a week. "The overriding fact of our times is that never before in any land have so many people of one nation lived so well, had so much, enjoyed so many opportunities, found so many of their rights protected or so many of their hopes fulfilled as do we in this generation of Americans," Johnson said.[107]

Johnson praised the Kennedy administration's efforts to draw the line against Communist expansion in Europe. Regarding the emerging issue of America's involvement in Vietnam, Johnson said, "The guerilla wars of Communism against independence in Southeast Asia have failed to crush the freedom-loving people of the area."[108]

Before he departed, Johnson joked about his previous presidential aspirations and noted that he "had no real cause to complain about other ambitions which may not be fulfilled" and that "since becoming Vice President I have more or less resigned myself to the probability there is one great honor I may never have—the honor of becoming a Hoosier."[109]

Henry Cabot Lodge Jr.

Former Senator Lodge of Massachusetts was entering his sixth year as ambassador to the United Nations—at the appointment of President Eisenhower—when he accepted Nixon's invitation to be his vice presidential running mate in 1960. Lodge was likely Nixon's second choice. His first choice, New York governor Nelson Rockefeller, declined an invitation to run. The Nixon campaign saw Lodge, although not a very effective campaigner, an appropriate choice given his credentials in international relations, which might give Nixon the edge in a campaign dominated by foreign policy. Lodge's political base in Massachusetts might also require Kennedy to spend time in his home state to preserve those electoral votes.

In September 1960 Lodge undertook a campaign swing through Democratic territories in northern Indiana. At South Bend, reporters noted that no local officials were on hand to greet him for remarks at the Saint Joseph County Courthouse, since none of them were Republicans. Regardless, Lodge spoke before a crowd estimated at 5,000 before moving on to a second speech on the campus of the University of Notre Dame, where an audience of another 3,000—a mix of students and faculty—listened to the former ambassador. During his downtown speech, Lodge said the nation needed to adopt a civil rights program "with no discrimination of race, creed or color" and that America could only "go forward together, and leave no one behind."[110]

At Notre Dame, Lodge spoke from the steps of the historic Administration Building and took questions from students in the audience. One female student from nearby Saint Mary's College asked why he had given up his post at the United Nations to run for vice president. Lodge said this was the first time he had been asked that question. He said Republican Party leaders had convinced him he could "add much to the ticket," and Lodge said he was enticed to leave his ambassadorship to run with Nixon because of his belief this provided him a better opportunity to serve the cause of world peace. "Mr. Nixon said that if elected to the Presidency he would give the Vice President the job of leadership in the non-military aspects of the world struggle," Lodge stated. "The threat today isn't on the military side. They [the Communists] are not going to take over

the United States. We're strong enough to stop them. Khrushchev himself has said that if there is a third world war, Russia will be hurt as badly as anyone." Lodge said America must establish "a new, high plateau of peace."[111]

A male student asked Lodge whether the nation had lost prestige in the world in the last few months. "We have more prestige than any other country in the world, and that's the truth of the matter," Lodge said. "The best place to measure a nation's prestige is in the United Nations. We have never lost a vote in the U.N."[112]

Another student asked what were the primary differences between the Democratic and Republican platforms and nominees. Lodge replied that both parties and their nominees "have roughly the same social goals, but there are two major differences. First, the Republicans want a program that will work, and second, we want a program that won't cause a rise in prices because of inflation." Lodge added there was no reason to treat Khrushchev as "a bosom friend" and in responding to a question about the Communist revolution in Cuba, he urged "patience and restraint" in dealing with Premier Fidel Castro and said relations between the U.S. and Cuba appeared to be improving.[113]

An Associated Press report about Lodge's Indiana campaign emphasized two incidents that interfered with his day. At Notre Dame, Lodge waved with his right hand, but quickly shoved it into his coat pocket with a strong grimace. As he greeted students, he switched to shaking hands with his left hand—the result of an incident moments earlier when a campaign aide slammed his right hand in a car door as they were arriving on campus. Although not broken, Lodge's hand was badly bruised and too injured to endure handshaking. At a quick stop at the Northern Indiana Children's Hospital in South Bend, Lodge had his hand x-rayed, which revealed no break. It was bandaged and Lodge soldiered on.[114]

Following South Bend, Lodge moved on to Lake County, where some of his bad luck persisted. He navigated an awkward situation and eventually declined to enter the U.S. Steel Corporation's Gary Works after union officials stood him up and did not come to greet him.[115] Finally, as he attempted to retire for the day later at a downtown Gary hotel, Lodge was briefly trapped in an elevator as it stopped between the sixth and seventh floors of his hotel. An aide forced open the doors of the car, and Lodge reportedly climbed about two feet down to get out of the situation.

Lodge's main purpose for visiting northwest Indiana was to emphasize his views on immigration policies before a meeting of the International Affairs Society of Lake County at East Chicago High School. Before an overflow audience of 1,800, Lodge said, "Unfortunately, our immigration laws have not kept pace with our admirable concept of the United States as a new and welcome home for people from other lands. We should modernize the quota system by basing it on the 1950 rather than the 1920 census. We should also permit the pooling of unused quotas by geographic areas. If, for example, France has not used up its quota of immigrants, these could be added to a general pool."[116]

"This is a matter of simple justice and a means of showing the world that we do not have a rigid and limited view of democracy," he continued. "Immigration helped to make this nation great, and the constant infusion of other peoples will keep us a strong and vibrant democracy. . . . Here I am particularly conscious of what a wonderful melting pot the United States is. In Gary alone, 55 different nationalities are represented—and many of Gary's fine citizens are refugees from Iron Curtain tyranny."[117]

Lodge said the nation's immigration laws have not kept pace with "our admirable concept of the United States as a new and welcome home for people from other lands. These laws are riddled with outmoded and discriminatory provisions which should be eliminated." Lodge said his experience as United States ambassador to the United Nations had left him "deeply concerned" with the fate of "captive Communist nations" and said the U.S. must stand steadfast against Communist forces and noted "the world watches us to see how we will make democracy work."[118]

Lodge later canceled news conferences and appearances in Anderson and Muncie, sending a telegram to his Republican hosts there saying he had to be back in New York for the taping of an NBC television program.

Nixon and Lodge lost a close campaign, but Lodge was later tapped by Kennedy to serve as U.S. ambassador to South Vietnam in 1963, a post he retained under Johnson until 1966. Lodge later became a special "Ambassador at Large" for Johnson, and with the election of Nixon in 1968 was tapped by his former running mate as ambassador to West Germany and went to Paris as head of the American delegation in peace negotiations with North Vietnam. He died in his Massachusetts home on February 27, 1985, at the age of eighty-two.

Hubert H. Humphrey

Humphrey's hopes for the 1960 Democratic nomination were fading fast by the time the May 1960 Indiana primary arrived. Kennedy had easily dispatched him in their head-to-head battle in Wisconsin, and Humphrey generally skipped over Indiana and tried to create a fire line against the Kennedy campaign in West Virginia's primary, held the week after Indiana's vote. Regardless, Humphrey had laid important groundwork in the state, including a fiery January 30, 1960, address before the Young Democrats of Indiana at the group's annual Roosevelt Dinner in Indianapolis. Humphrey told the youth of the party that the biggest advantage they had in 1960 was the Republican nominee—"Mr. Republican himself," Nixon—but quickly added, "It will be impossible for Mr. Nixon to rise above the party, as his predecessor [Eisenhower] has done. He has been in Congress 13 years . . . and he is Mr. [Herbert] Hoover without the dark beard, Mr. [Thomas] Dewey without the mustache."[119] Humphrey said Nixon was on the wrong side of the Taft-Hartley Act, minimum wage, Social Security, housing, small business, farm price supports, wage standards, interest rates, tax policy, labor control, and especially civil rights.

"Of course Mr. Nixon will try to escape his Republican past," Humphrey said. "But I remind you that [the Republicans] expect Mr. Nixon to carry out their policies and never a peep from Mr. Nixon to the contrary."[120] Nixon was contributing to a spirit of fear, caution, and uncertainty in Washington just as the nation entered an important new decade, the 1960s. "What America needs most today is to regain its vigor, its youthful enthusiasm, its greatness—and it pleases me to say this before a gathering of Young Democrats," Humphrey declared. Calling the GOP a party dominated by "Old Fogeys," Humphrey said, "My friends, we are not going to send rockets to the moon as long as we are led by a bunch of Fogeys—old or new! And we're not going to close the science gap or the space gap with the Russians as long as we're led by Fogeys—old or new!"[121]

Like many others who sought the nation's highest office, Humphrey had put years of work into building a base in Indiana. Two important appearances scheduled to support his expected 1960 campaign in the summer of 1958 were greatly altered by Senate proceedings that prevented him from leaving Washington. Undeterred, Humphrey delivered two "speeches" to Indiana groups that year via telephone—the first a lengthy address focused on "works for peace" given to the National Christian Education Conference meeting at Purdue University in August 1958, and the other to the opening session of the annual Indiana Democratic Editorial Association meeting at French Lick, also in August 1958.

Labor Day 1958 finally freed Humphrey from Senate duties, and he appeared before a large and friendly gathering for the annual Jefferson Democratic Club picnic in Anderson on September 8, 1958. While there, Humphrey fired up the Democratic base by predicting that "the American voters will call the Eisenhower-Nixon administration to account in November for the failure of Republican leadership at home and abroad," adding, "We are not going to let them change the subject and campaign against a false set of manufactured scarecrows of their own making. The Eisenhower-Nixon administration in less than six years in office has brought America into the worst recession since World War II at home, and to mortal danger of war and worldwide defeat abroad."[122] Recognizing the heavy labor vote to be found in Madison County, and other parts of central Indiana's automotive manufacturing belt, Humphrey lamented the Republican lack of respect for labor leaders (except Jimmy Hoffa) and their creation of false issues related to "racketeers" and Communists in the American labor movement: "The Republicans do not want the American people to look at the real story of who is doing an honest job of trying to protect America's working men and women by cleaning up the blooms, who with management collusion, infiltrate labor movements."[123]

During a well-received December 1955 speech at Notre Dame, Humphrey accused Eisenhower's administration as lacking in the ability to deal with the Soviet Communists and their growing influence in the world, saying, "There are three great areas of danger in foreign policy today. These are Germany, Japan and the east, Israel and India" and that America must not underestimate the power or desire of the Soviets to spread their domination into each of these regions. He also addressed the ongoing "Red scare" going on in Washington, noting that "there is ample evidence to prove that the Administration is misrepresenting the facts about

workers ousted from their government jobs as 'security risks' . . . the Republicans have collected incompetents and other undesirables of any sort and have dismissed them all as 'security risks.' In reality, the reasons for their dismissals were in no way connected with the workers loyalty or lack thereof."[124]

One of Humphrey's earliest speeches in Indiana came on January 29, 1951, in South Bend before a meeting of Americans for Democratic Action. At the meeting, Humphrey suggested that America lead an effort to move the Russian people "away from their Soviet masters . . . an Emancipation Proclamation for the Russian peo-

Hubert H. Humphrey meets with African American supporters in Indianapolis, April 11, 1964.

IHS, *INDIANAPOLIS RECORDER COLLECTION, P 303*

ple." He noted, "The Russian people are the first victims of Communist aggression, our potential allies of the American people, and all strive toward liberty and equality. They could, in fact, be our most important ally."[125] Humphrey continued his theme of a "democratic peace offensive" for the United States before a second meeting of Americans for Democratic Action later the same day in Indianapolis. "We of the democracies of the world," he said, "must capitalize on the discomfort, the poverty, the bitterness, and the potential disloyalty of the Russian people. This is the Achilles' heel of the Soviet structure."[126]

Humphrey also sounded a humanitarian note, encouraging Congress to move forward on plans to approve India's request for two million pounds of grain to help combat starvation in parts of that democratic nation. "Whether we agree with the present foreign policy of the Indian government or not, India remains one of the few democratic strongholds left in Asia, and we must respond, as we always have, to a humanitarian appeal," he said.[127]

In the fall of 1964, with Johnson's forces having successfully dispatched the challenge from the right represented in Alabama governor George Wallace, the Johnson-Humphrey campaign went forward with the relative ease that front-runners often enjoy. Humphrey was seeking election to the office of vice president; Johnson had served without a vice president since Kennedy's murder in November 1963. Humphrey made no less than eight stops in Indiana in 1964, a luxury the campaign could afford (along with additional stops by Johnson himself) as dreams of a rare Democratic win in Indiana became closer and closer to reality. Humphrey came to Indiana during the primary season for the Indiana Gridiron Dinner in Indianapolis in April and again in early May to deliver a speech on "human

and civil rights" at Shortridge High School in Indianapolis. On September 23 Humphrey made three campaign stops in Fort Wayne, Terre Haute and Evansville.

On October 10 Humphrey was back for a speech at Notre Dame covering an array of topics related to war, peace, arms control, Latin America, and the United Nations. Speaking before a packed meeting of Young Democrats at the Stephan Center, Humphrey chided Republican presidential nominee, Senator Barry Goldwater of Arizona, for his assertion that war was inevitable. Humphrey claimed Goldwater had "forsaken his right to the presidency" because of his failure to recognize that "peace must be the plan of the nation, the peace called for by Pope John [XXIII] in his encyclical, the peace that President Kennedy had striven for. But peace is best preserved through strength—strength used with restraint, with wisdom, and with a clear sense of perspective."[128] Humphrey reminded his audience that Goldwater had opposed the bipartisan nuclear weapons testing ban treaty and also U.N. calls for prohibiting the placement of nuclear weapons in space.

"Today, in the great tradition of Pope Paul VI and John F. Kennedy, President Johnson has asked that we look beyond the Cold War," Humphrey said. "President Johnson knows that most Americans—indeed, most people on this plant—yearn to build a world where peace is more than simply a hiatus between wars. To those who ask, 'Why not victory?' we reply, 'Why not victory, indeed?!'—victory over war itself, victory for peace, victory for mankind."[129]

Humphrey made two more Indiana stops for the 1964 campaign. On October 16 he spoke at the Murat Shrine in Indianapolis on the use of nuclear weapons, the value of the Peace Corps, and the "War on Poverty," and again on October

21 at the Armory in Gary, attempting to drum up support for Johnson's election. Once elected vice president, Humphrey was a frequent visitor to Indiana, making two speeches in the fall of 1966 for the midterm congressional elections at both Indiana University in Bloomington and Democratic Party rallies at Indianapolis and Evansville. Humphrey's three visits in 1967 were for more serious topics—the highlight being a Notre Dame speech he offered on January 16, 1967, on the promise of science and technology in the new decade ahead and the need to address issues of poverty and racial discrimination in America. That year he also made stops at a "civic luncheon" in Indianapolis, as well as a testimonial dinner for Indiana's retiring United Methodist Bishop Richard C. Raines at DePauw University in Greencastle.

Nelson A. Rockefeller

The progressive New York governor seemed to be making all the moves of a Republican presidential hopeful leading into 1960, but never seemed to engage the retail level of politics that his chief rival, Nixon, had mastered over many years of tough campaigning. Rockefeller always seemed to be ready, or willing, to *accept* his party's nomination, but never seemed altogether comfortable with the process of *seeking* the nod.

In the waning days of 1959, Rockefeller embarked on what would now be known as a "listening tour" of Indiana, Missouri, Minnesota, Wisconsin, Oklahoma, Texas, and Florida, assessing his chances for the 1960 GOP nomination. One of those stops brought him to South Bend, where he attempted to make news by addressing pending labor strikes affecting steel production in Indiana and elsewhere. He told reporters he was "basically opposed to compulsory arbitration" but added, "In an event of an extreme case

of complete stalemate which affects the health and safety of our country, it seems to me we should trust the president, regardless of party, with his discretionary authority." On the issue of whether he planned to enter upcoming Republican primaries, he was more circumspect: "I ought to give my decision sometime before the middle of January."[130] Theodore H. White, author of *The Making of the President 1960*, concluded that Rockefeller's effort lasted a total of only eight weeks. "His speeches . . . were excellent, he discussed our foreign policy, our need of economic growth, always with good sense and fine tailored eloquence," White wrote. "He made two serious scouting trips, the first in November, the second in December. . . . The citizen wing turned out to see, listen and be charmed. The regulars, who controlled the delegate machinery, ignored him."[131] Rockefeller concluded, White wrote, that there were "pockets of strength" for his campaign in Indiana, Washington, and Minnesota, but not enough to overcome the amount already locked up by the Nixon campaign.

Dwight D. Eisenhower

Although not a candidate in 1960, Eisenhower made a significant visit to the state as the guest of Notre Dame for its June 1960 commencement exercises, where he was awarded an honorary Doctor of Laws degree. Eisenhower became the first U.S. president to speak at a Notre Dame graduation ceremony and the second to earn an honorary degree (the first being Franklin D. Roosevelt).[132]

In his remarks, the president took on world events before a large audience of more than 7,000 on the Notre Dame mall, emphasizing that America had a great need for more talent in government and called on the Notre Dame graduates "to help the political life of the nation soar as high as human wisdom can make it" and reminded them that the United States operates "on a relentless timetable which we must race to keep events from overwhelming us."[133] Without referring to Soviet Premier Khrushchev by name, Eisenhower said, "The enemies of human dignity lurk in a thousand places—in governments that have become spiritual wastelands, and in leaders that brandish angry epithets, slogans and satellites." But he cautioned against the growing commercialization engulfing many Americans, noting that "where peoples worship material success, (they have) become emptied of idealism" and that "peace with justice cannot be attained by peoples where opulence has dulled the spirit—where indifference has supplanted moral and political responsibilities. Neglect of our civic responsibilities will be a greater danger to a free America than any foreign threat can ever pose; but an enlightened, dedicated people, studiously and energetically performing their political duties, will ensure us a future of ever-rising standards of spiritual, cultural and material strength."[134]

Returning to his theme about the importance of civic engagement by the young people graduating that day, but also all young people, Eisenhower said, "Too many of our ablest citizens draw back, evidently fearful of being sullied in the broiling activity of partisan affairs. This must change. We need intelligent, steady political leadership as at no time before in our history. There must be more talent in government—the best our nation affords. We need it in county, state and Washington."[135] The president made no reference to his own vice president running to succeed him or the young Massachusetts senator who also wanted to lay claim to the White House, but seemed generally interested in embracing his role as senior statesman, even before leaving office. After his Notre Dame speech, Eisenhower returned to West

Point for the second time in a day to attend a reunion of his 1915 graduating class.

As a former president, Eisenhower returned to Indiana again in September 1962 for Charlie Halleck Day in Rensselaer in support of U.S. Representative Halleck, speaking from the steps of the Jasper County Courthouse and later helping lay a cornerstone for the new Halleck Center at Saint Joseph College. The *Rensselaer Republican* dubbed Eisenhower's visit as "Rensselaer's Greatest Day," and although initial estimates of 25,000 guests were not met, more than 16,500 chicken half dinners were served at the college, representing an overflow crowd. Eisenhower reminded his Jasper County audience that it was just a decade ago that he had asked for its vote for president, but he was present now to ask their support for his friend, Halleck. "This is my first opportunity to thank you personally for the confidence you then displayed in me," Eisenhower said. "And I am deeply grateful for that, in that office, you provided me with a loyal, fighting, and deeply patriotic legislative leader, Charlie Halleck. He was and is my warm friend and a staunch supporter and a champion of Republican principles and programs."[136]

Eisenhower said he purposefully was avoiding a lengthy list of personal memories of working with Halleck in lieu of focusing on important national issues and the need for all voters to participate. "I address those who, because of a blind assumption that the American system will automatically work forever," he said, "who deny themselves the right and privilege of a voice in the conduct of political affairs. The non-voter stupidly steals from himself his most priceless heritage."[137] Understanding he was in the heart of farm country, Eisenhower addressed agricultural policy and warned against those "who presume they can blueprint the entire economy to the slightest detail, particularly in agriculture," noting that "I concede that such theorists are masters in propaganda. But in a corn field, they would likely wax polish a tractor until it outshone the sun, and fail to put fuel in the tank—and then wonder why it would not run." Republicans, he said, recognize the "fuel of American agriculture, as in every area of our economy, is individual energy, ambition, pride in work, confidence in self, and a decent hope for reasonable reward honestly rewarded."[138]

The former president said "a disturbing trend" continued to grow in Washington, where more and more power was centered in the federal government. "At times it seems we are losing sight of a fundamental principle in our political institutions—a simple principle, basic to democracy. . . . Political leaders in a democracy are not the source of power, they merely direct it."[139] Without directly referring to the Kennedy administration by name, Eisenhower did elude to a challenge to representative government found in "those who treat government as a paradise for theorists; the country as a playpen for the exercise of their notions and abstract fantasies; the people as a captive horde to be manipulated—benevolently, of course, for their own great good. . . . In public life, too many men confuse dreaminess with a vision, wild fancy with foresight and wisdom; fluency in words with clarity in ideas. They do have a knack in concocting slogans; but the slogans are slick rather than profound."[140]

Eisenhower said that President Kennedy's theme of "Get America Moving" misses the fact that the nation is not sitting still and immobile. "I should like to propose a question to the slogan makers: This is it, Get America Moving where? In what direction and to what purpose? . . . With all our hearts we say: Keep America moving ahead!" Eisenhower said.[141]

While at Saint Joseph College, Eisenhower and Halleck laid the cornerstone for the new Halleck Student Center, and the school's board of trustees named the solidly Presbyterian Eisenhower "honorary president" of the Catholic college for a day. "I'm not so certain where this sort of thing will lead," Eisenhower joked, "but I do know it's useless to run for Pope on the Presbyterian ticket."[142] During his remarks, Eisenhower took up his normal practice of addressing himself to young people, asking them to pattern their lives after two great Hoosiers—Halleck and Abraham Lincoln: "Be clean and strong in body and filled with learning and your future will be most exciting."[143]

Before arriving in Rensselaer, Eisenhower rode for several blocks in an open-air car through the streets of West Lafayette after landing at the Purdue University Airport, where he was greeted by a crowd of about 1,000, including the Purdue University Marching Band.[144] During his Indiana visit, despite expectations that he might elaborate on his White House visit with Kennedy just three days earlier, Eisenhower made no references to his private meetings with the president and his behind-the-scenes efforts to assist Kennedy in his relations with Berlin following Eisenhower's just-completed six-week tour of Western Europe.[145]

His 1962 foray on behalf of Halleck was Eisenhower's last visit to Indiana. Eisenhower spoke at the 1964 Republican National Convention and offered a tepid endorsement of Goldwater's candidacy, but four years later was too ill to actively campaign for Nixon. Eisenhower died of congestive heart failure at Walter Reed Army Hospital on March 28, 1969. He was seventy-eight years old.

Harry S Truman

Although he was seventy-six years old and slowing down his political activities, former president Truman accepted two major campaign swings for the 1960 cycle—to Michigan and Indiana—before being advised by doctors to curtail plans for a long West Coast swing. One of Truman's first stops was at Marion for Labor Day-related events. A luncheon, attended by more than 1,000 labor union members, started off the day, followed by a short parade through downtown. An evening public rally before a crowd estimated at 10,000—despite ninety degree temperatures still roasting the Hoosier State—concluded the day. Truman started off with, "I'm for John F. Kennedy and Lyndon Johnson all the way." It was the former president's first public pronouncement of support for the Kennedy-Johnson ticket since the conclusion of the Democratic convention. Reporters covering Truman's Marion appearance noted, "He refused to backtrack on statements he'd made before the Democratic convention in opposition to the candidacy of Senator Kennedy, saying, 'I'm from Missouri and I have to be shown. He [Kennedy] showed me.'"[146]

Truman's "cheerful mood" during his day-long, seven-hour Indiana stop changed when he discussed the Republicans. At a party fund-raising dinner before his rally speech, Truman sounded his familiar theme: "If Indiana votes for the Republicans, you'll get what you deserve" and elaborated that Indiana farmers had particularly suffered under Eisenhower administration policies.[147] Following the visit, despite well-laid plans, aides to Truman indicated he was growing increasingly unhappy with the level of "manhandling" he would receive from members of the large crowds. "I have never heard him complain as much about this situation as recently, except for the experience at the National Democratic Club reception, where they tried to get a thousand people into rooms that would hold 400 or 500 people," reported former Truman aide Tom Gavin. "That was an occurrence that incensed all of us and left the mark on the President in the form of a broken rib. Apparently this kind of thing has happened to him on a number of occasions. Although the arrangements made in Marion were excellent for his protection. . . . I heard him since refer to Marion as one of the places where he was pushed and shoved by the crowds, although he moves into and through situations with the same good humor and smiles."[148]

For the 1962 midterm congressional elections, an even older Truman was back in Indiana for a massive Democratic Party dinner and rally at Roberts Memorial Stadium in Evansville, attended by more than 6,000 party loyalists. Clearly not slowed by age, Truman seemed to relish the attention heaped upon him as a party celebrity stumping for the promising U.S. Senate campaign of Bayh, who was seeking to unseat Republican incumbent Capehart. Still able to draw headlines for his rather blunt delivery of his opinions, Truman said he felt the nation was "still vulnerable to a hero worship for some of our most glamorous military figures," resulting in unnatural support that kept Eisenhower in office for eight years. Truman revealed that he had "serious misgivings" about Eisenhower when he left the White House in January 1953. He said Eisenhower had broken faith with the nation as a "grandfather figure," who presided over a period of inaction and had as many scandals and corruption problems he had said were prevalent among the previous Democratic administrations. "We may as well face up to the fact that we are now paying the penalty for eight years of a do-nothing administration," Truman said. "We must realize that the new administration has had its hands full in doing some major repair work that needed to be attended to."[149]

Truman told reporters that he was proud to back Bayh for the U.S. Senate and took special exception to Capehart's "wrong" position on eliminating Soviet missiles from Cuba. He said, "If Senator Capehart is right on anything, I'm mistaken. I know that old sidewinder better than any of you fellows do."[150] Truman offhandedly made a remark that turned Capehart red and brought the threat of a slander suit against Truman. The former president said that when he was president, Capehart had come to the White House to help solve a labor issue that would benefit him and his friends as owners of a coal mine. Truman said he had dismissed Capehart from the Oval Office upon hearing the request, considering it influence peddling. Capehart vehemently denied that any meeting had ever occurred, or that he had ever made any request, and denied he had any business interests in a coal mine. Capehart said Truman had issued a "fantastic lie" and vowed "to make Truman pay for that statement." No slander suit was ever filed, however.[151]

Most of Truman's dinner speech, however,

Former president Harry S Truman draws the interest of some amateur photographers during a visit to Evansville, Indiana, in September 1962.

assailed the Eisenhower administration and praised Kennedy's work, singling out his careful and thoughtful handling of emerging civil rights issues in southern states. President Kennedy had handled the Mississippi "integration crisis . . . exactly like it ought to be done" and added, "He didn't fool around with it the way President Eisenhower did in Arkansas."[152] He did not elaborate at length on the growing Communist influence in Cuba, instead noting that a man whose initials were "JFK" held responsibility for guiding the nation through this period.

Upon his eightieth birthday, Truman addressed members of the U.S. Senate in 1964, but after a fall at his Missouri home in 1965, his public schedule shrunk dramatically. Johnson went to Truman's Presidential Library and Museum at Independence, Missouri, on July 30, 1965, to sign the nation's Medicare program into law. Truman and his wife Bess received the nation's first two Medicare cards from Johnson in recognition of their efforts to support health care for the nation's elderly. Truman fell ill with pneumonia in December 1972 and was admitted to a Kansas City hospital where he died on December 26, 1972. He was eighty-eight years old.

Lyndon B. Johnson

In the mid- to late-1960s, Indiana could not escape the turmoil and strife that spread across the American political landscape like locusts. Through acrimonious campaigns that brought dire predictions of doom for the nation, to ugly and violent endings for some of the nation's political leaders, Hoosiers took in the scenes in this era with a sense of awe and dissonance. An assassin's bullet had done its worst, taking the life of a young President Kennedy and ushering in a determined progressive, Johnson. But as the

Johnson era drew to a close, a remarkable record of achievement in the areas of domestic policy and civil rights was being blotted out by the daily blood flowing from across the sea as the Vietnam "conflict" would take more than 58,000 American lives and physically and emotionally injure scores more before the fighting ended. At home, African Americans, still widely referred to as "Negroes" in this era, began a painful and difficult struggle to live out the promises of American freedom.

By 1964 Johnson was poised to win a full four-year term of his own. Johnson, who had taken the oath of office in the aftermath of Kennedy's murder, had successfully brought the nation together emotionally and was backed by a strong Democratic majority in the Congress on a variety of important public policy issues. From all indications, Johnson was unbeatable in 1964, finding two powerful Republicans, Rockefeller of New York and former vice president Nixon, both sitting out of the race. Nixon's fortunes had been damaged by his stunning defeat in the 1962 California gubernatorial contest. Rockefeller briefly opened a "campaign headquarters" in Indianapolis, presumably to gain Indiana GOP delegates on a second or third ballot at a possibly deadlocked Republican convention. The colorful New York governor, however, did no active campaigning in Indiana in 1964 beyond talking to reporters and keeping his name alive as a Goldwater alternative.[153]

Perhaps Johnson's most historic domestic victory was the enactment on July 2, 1964, of the Civil Rights Act.[154] As President Johnson signed the act into law alongside civil rights icon Doctor Martin Luther King Jr., many Americans cheered this advancement (and the Voting Rights Act that followed a year later).

Johnson's first visit to Indiana as president came on April 24, 1964, just four months after

Studebaker Corporation had given the expected—yet heartbreaking—announcement that it would cease operations at South Bend. Nine thousand workers faced their jobs disappearing, and Indiana leaders were frantic to try and find a way to either save Studebaker and its operations or find some new purpose or manufacturer for the operation. Heavily lobbied by Senators Vance Hartke and Birch Bayh, along with rising star Congressman John Brademas from South Bend, Johnson agreed to visit the city on a mission of promoting job development. Eventually the Kaiser Corporation acquired portions of the Studebaker facility to manufacture military vehicles, but ultimately would employ only about 10 percent of the original Studebaker workforce.[155]

Johnson's visit was to the Lulu V. Cline School in South Bend, where a workforce training and employment help center had been established. Accompanying the president were the First Lady, Lady Bird; Bayh; Hartke; Governor Matthew Welsh; and three key members of the Johnson administration—Secretary of Commerce Luther H. Hodges; Secretary of Health, Education, and Welfare Anthony J. Celebrezze; and Housing and Home Finance Administrator Robert C. Weaver. The president's remarks were preceded by those of the First Lady, who said, "On the way in from the airport, we saw signs that say 'We're for South Bend,' and I just want to tell you that Lyndon and I, we're for South Bend too, and we thank you for this marvelous welcome." She added, "Statistics only come alive when you see the people behind them, and it's been thrilling this morning to see people with the initiative and the get up and go to attack problems and to learn new skills and set about finding new ways in life."[156]

For his part, President Johnson said, "I have had some familiarity with your problem, particularly since Studebaker closed down, so this morning we got up early in Chicago to come here and to shake your hands and to look into your faces and to talk to you about the problems that exist in South Bend because South Bend's problems are our problems. The reason we are here is, we want to see what good work you are doing, in the hope that we can get other people to follow your fine example. The reason we are here is to try to tell you that in a good many places in America there are more jobs open than there are unemployed people, but we don't have the people trained for the jobs that are open."[157]

Johnson said he had enjoyed his tour of the job site and said, "We have been stimulated and inspired by what we have seen—men and women who I have talked to who have lost their jobs have not lost their determination. Men and women that I have talked to that have gone off the payroll, have not gone out of existence. They are here working and preparing themselves to do a better job tomorrow than they did yesterday, and I am here to see what the federal government can do to work with you to help us all improve the lot of our fellow Americans."[158]

Johnson said he had proposed a major anti-poverty and unemployment program to Congress and urged again for its passage. He said, "It's been a real inspiration to me this morning to come here and see these young people, these middle-aged people, these older people that have not taken discouragement and said 'there's nothing we can do about it,' but have come in here and rolled up their sleeves and stuck their chin up and their chest up and are doing something about it, and it is going to stimulate us to do more about it in our own work. And when I go back to Washington I am going to say to the leaders of that great Capital, that I wish they could come here to the heartland of America and

see what the people are doing for themselves, see what the people want to do for their families, and we are going to try to refuse to take 'no' for an answer and get in here and do something ourselves about it."[159]

While Johnson's South Bend stop had officially been as president, his timing was immaculate, coming just days before the Democratic Primary in Indiana, and his visit was widely viewed as his part to shore up support for his 1964 stand-in candidate in Indiana, Welsh.

Johnson's next visits to Indiana were more overtly political in nature, as he was now officially the presidential nominee of the Democratic Party and was determined to win a rare Democratic victory in Indiana. On October 8 the president addressed a crowd estimated at 25,000 gathered for a morning rally at the Washington High School football field in East Chicago. While en route to his speech, reporters noted that an enthusiastic Johnson "had barely reached East Chicago when he climbed to the roof of his shiny new bubble-top limousine to wave at placard carrying crowds that pressed in around his motorcade. Standing bare-headed and coatless in the brisk morning air, Johnson brandished a microphone and told his welcomers how pleased he was to see them. And, as customary, he threw in words of praise for the Hoosier state and its Democratic office holders. In his off-the-cuff speech to a street crowd, Johnson said 'we're all going to put our shoulder to the wheel and get the job done Nov. 3.' He added, 'We can't take anything for granted. So let's get going.'"[160]

Quickly setting his agenda, Johnson said, "Our business here this morning is politics, so let us get right down to business. I understand that there have been some other political speeches around here recently. Well, this one is going to be different. I am not going to tear down anybody or anything. . . . I haven't come out here to sling mud and say ugly things."[161] His latter remark was an open reference to Goldwater's appearances in Lake County. Continuing, Johnson said, "If we are honest with ourselves, and we have to be, political issues affect us all personally. It does not degrade our hopes for peace in the world that we want most of all to be alive, and to be sure that our sons and our daughters have the right to live. It does not degrade our hopes for prosperity."[162]

Referring to East Chicago, Hammond, and Gary as "economic boom towns," the president claimed victory over past economic problems and noted: "Unemployment is down. Profits and production are up." In addition to heaping praise on Indiana's Democratic leaders, Johnson praised his press secretary, George Reedy [an East Chicago native], as "one of the best human beings I have ever known."[163]

Understanding the ethnically diverse nature of Lake County, Johnson turned his remarks to immigration policy. He declared, "We must do something about our immigration laws," he said. "Two-thirds of the total immigration quota goes under that law, to people who never use all their quota. President Roosevelt, with a good Dutch name, proposed the immigration law be changed. President Truman, with a good English name, proposed the law be changed. President Eisenhower, with a good German name, proposed the law be changed. President Kennedy, with a good Irish name, proposed that the law be changed. And now a President, Lyndon Johnson, with an English name, and with an Irish name, and with German and Scottish and French forebears, proposes this law be changed!" Johnson's plan specifically would eliminate "discriminatory quotas" over a five-year period and raise the nation's overall immigration levels, which "would permit families to unite which have too long been

broken. We stand for a compassionate nation, not a callous nation. Will you stand up with us and help us in that fight? We stand for uniting our country instead of dividing it. Will you stand up with us in that fight?"[164]

Briefly addressing peace issues, civil rights, collective bargaining for workers, and education, Johnson said that prosperity goals for America must be matched with other goals, such as "trying to see that every child has a schoolroom to attend, and a teacher to teach him. Try to see that every father has a job to send that kid to school. Try to see that he is paid decent wages. In this election, all of those things are at stake. We fought for Social Security 30 years ago. Twenty million Americans today draw Social Security. We don't want it to go down the drain. That is why you better go vote on November 3rd if you don't want Social Security to become voluntary."[165] He concluded by remarking, "Don't talk about how proud you are to be an American and how you want your boy to avoid war, and then sit home and not vote. You go and vote, and you vote for the man in your judgment, and the ticket in your judgment, that is most likely to protect your job, your prosperity, and your home and your children. You go vote for the man and the ticket that in your judgment is most likely to preserve peace in the world. If you do that, if you vote for peace and prosperity for yourselves, according to the dictates of your own conscience, Lyndon Johnson and Hubert Humphrey will be mighty happy."[166]

Before he departed East Chicago, Johnson surprised the family of Raymond and Lois Pozywio at 4023 Grand Boulevard, across the street from the high school, by accepting Lois's invitation for a cup of coffee. The president told his hosts, "I feel just like I'm with my home folk." Raymond, a twenty-one-year-old laborer in a steel plant, said Johnson's unexpected visit "was like Christmas and New Year's Eve and all the holidays rolled into one." Lois said, "If I live to be a hundred, I'll never forget today. It was like a dream—something that always happens to somebody else—and then it happened to me."[167] Lois, also age twenty-one and married only five months, said the president drank two cups of coffee, both of them black. As for the coffee cup the president used? "I'm going to put it away," Lois said. "It will never be used again. It'll be enshrined in our house."[168]

Johnson's party flew from East Chicago to Indianapolis for a noon rally on Monument Circle, where he joked with his large audience:

> Indiana on other occasions has voted for another party, but I know that you want to consider this very carefully this time. In the first place, I am not just sure whether there is a real Republican candidate to vote for this year. Then, I think probably you will want to think back to when Indiana did vote for a Democratic President. That was back in 1936. The choice that year was something like the choice this year—between the past and the future. Indiana in 1936 voted for the future, and Indiana in 1964 is going to vote for the future again.[169]

Quoting I Corinthians 3:13 that "Every man's work shall be made manifest," Johnson said, "seldom has an administration's work been made manifest more abundantly than this one. We promised four years ago, under the leadership of that beloved, great champion of this country, John Fitzgerald Kennedy, that we would get the country moving again. Well, it is moving!"[170]

Again invoking the name of Kennedy as a man with "foresight and the vision and the courage and the love of humanity," Johnson said it had been his honor to carry on the work of the slain president. He added:

> Ten months ago, in a moment of tragedy, I was called upon to assume the awesome responsibilities of the Presidency. Our great leader had fallen, and the rest of the world and the rest of this country looked to America during that transition period. I told you then that I would do my best to embrace his program and lead America forward as best I could. I could promise you only that I would do my dead level best. I have done that. On that day, the 22nd of November, our beloved President, John Fitzgerald Kennedy, had 51 major recommendations pending before the Congress of the United States. Last weekend I sat in the White House and looked down that list, and observed that we had passed every single one of those 51 measures through the Senate of the United States. And the three or four that didn't pass through the House of Representatives are going to pass through the House of Representatives when we get this election behind us.[171]

In remarks designed to contrast directly with the increasingly strident and harsh tone of Goldwater's campaign, the president said, "I have faith in people. I have hope for the future. I have no doubt that freedom is going to survive and democracy is going to win. But we are not going to win by talking about each other, and using a lot of ugly names, and slinging a lot of mud, and chewing on each other. America cannot win by dividing brother against brother, sister against sister; we must have a united America—united we stand; divided we fall."[172]

Johnson was in good spirits for his Indianapolis stop. Reporters noted that he temporarily took over conducting duties for the band playing "Hello Dolly," shook hundreds of hands as he worked the crowd, and climbed a photographer's platform and tossed his $25 Texas Stetson hat into the crowd as he pumped his fingers in a V for victory.[173]

Johnson made one more stop in Indiana on October 27, 1964, just one week before the election, for a rare late night Democratic Party rally—beginning at 11:00 p.m.—at the Evansville Memorial Airport. The stop represented the intensity of the Johnson campaign, the president having personally visited forty-three of the fifty states between Labor Day and Election Day. The Evansville stop was originally scheduled just to allow the president and his wife to join together on one jet for the remaining days of the campaign. Lady Bird's speaking skills were used heavily in southern parts of the nation, where Johnson was generally unwelcome due to his advancement of the Civil Rights Act. Johnson said, "But I guess as long as I am here, we might as well talk a little politics. I never saw a Hoosier, or a Texan, who minded talking politics. I didn't come out here to say anything bad about anybody. I am not mad at anybody. I don't want to fight anybody. I want to unite. I want to unite this nation. And we do have a story to tell in Evansville, in Indiana, and in the country. It is a story of the greatest peace-time prosperity in the history of any land. It is the story of peace, and I think you are going to keep it that way—by your votes next Tuesday." In what was becoming a regular feature of Johnson's campaign speeches, he again referred to his Republican opponent, but not by name, when he remarked, "I didn't stop by here tonight to talk about petty little things or little men."[174]

Johnson said that for him the choice voters faced was simple. "We want to go on to the Great Society where there is full employment for our workers, where there is maximum development for our industry, where there is full education for our children, where there is adequate protection for our parents, and where there is full opportunity and equal opportunity for all of our citizens," he said. "We are going to have to unite and start working with each other instead of fighting each other, start loving each other instead of hating each other, start uniting with each other instead of dividing with each other."[175]

In the years following the 1964 election, Johnson embarked on two memorable visits to Indiana, one in April 1965 following the devastating Palm Sunday tornadoes that claimed 271 lives across the Midwest, 138 of those in Indiana. At Dunlap (an unincorporated settlement between Elkhart and Goshen), the president viewed the massive devastation that claimed sixty-two lives in Elkhart County. A solemn Johnson told reporters upon arriving at the South Bend airport that "all of our Nation was stunned and shocked over the weekend by the tragedies which struck so many families and communities in so many of our states. I am visiting in three of the states which were stricken and inspecting from the air the damage caused in six states here in our great Midwest. I am beginning the visit here so that we may go to your neighbor communities of Elkhart and Goshen, where the loss of human life was the highest. Neither our presence nor our programs of assistance can do more than symbolize the sympathy of the nation for those who have lost their loved ones in these grim disasters. But I know that all Americans, in all their homes across the land, are here with me this morning to extend their sympathy and a helping hand."[176] Once in Elkhart County, Johnson visited with survivors of the storm in the Sunnyside neighborhood and stopped to thank emergency workers and volunteers marshaling their efforts at the Concord Township Volunteer Fire Department in Dunlap.

Johnson returned to Indiana on July 23, 1966, as the state celebrated its sesquicentennial with observances at both Indianapolis and Vincennes, the latter being the site of the George Rogers Clark Memorial dedicated three decades earlier by Franklin Roosevelt. Johnson faced a full day—two speeches in Indianapolis, one each in Vincennes and Jeffersonville, and a separate speech at Fort Campbell, Kentucky.

The summer heat baked the audience gathered at Monument Circle in Indianapolis as Johnson declared, "I am happy to be out here among you on this summer day at what I like to think is the crossroads of America." He noted that he had "a busy, long hot day" ahead of him in Indiana. "One hundred and fifty years ago the great State of Indiana entered our Union," the president said. "We were a young and a very weak nation in those days. But we faced an uncertain future on an untamed continent with one unfailing asset: our strength, then as now, was in the people of this country. That hasn't changed in 150 years. It is from these people that the President of this country gathers his own strength. So today I have come back to Indiana."[177]

Despite Johnson's purpose of being in Indiana to celebrate the state's 150th birthday, the ongoing Vietnam War remained on his mind and in his remarks. Events in 1966 seemed particularly troubling. American prisoners of war were attacked by angry mobs as they were paraded through the streets of Hanoi, North Vietnam, in early July, days after Johnson had authorized Operation Rolling Thunder, which unleashed American B-52 bombers on Hanoi beginning on June 29, 1966. More than 300,000 sorties were flown over North Vietnam during the operation, representing more than 865,000 tons of bombs and an estimated 52,000 fatalities.[178] Recalling his multiple visits to Indiana during the 1964 presidential campaign, Johnson said "the world has changed since 1964. The Communist leaders in North Vietnam listened with only one ear as we spoke. They heard only half of what we said. They misjudged our deep desire for peace as a sign that they could take over South Vietnam

while we looked the other way. . . . And so they acted. They pushed the accelerator of aggression to the floorboard. They drove straight for their destination: the independent nation of South Vietnam."[179] He made clear his view that the increasingly ugly war in Southeast Asia was driven by "guerilla warriors inspired, organized, directed, and supplied by Hanoi."[180]

Making his case for the increased attacks on North Vietnam, Johnson said, "When the Communists took over North Vietnam, more than a million people—double the city population of the great city of Indianapolis; one-fourth of the entire population of the great State of Indiana—packed up and went south to live. They voted against communism the only way they were permitted to vote, with their feet. Their journey and their agony would have been in vain if the Communists conquer the South. So, in South Vietnam almost a million people have moved out of their villages to escape the terror of the Vietcong. They are living as refugees until they can return to their homes. They would never be safe if the Communists move in."[181] He added:

> So I ask all of those who wonder if South Vietnam is 'worth it' to think about what would have happened to the millions of South Vietnamese who want to build their own country? They may not look like we do. They don't speak the same language that we do. They may not even think like we do. But they are human beings. We promised them, by treaty, to help protect their independence. And America doesn't break its promises. We are going to stay there. If the American people need any reminder of the kind of enemy we face, the kind of enemy that seeks to take over South Vietnam, they can read reports this morning in their morning paper, they can hear it over their radio—where the Vietcong attacked, on yesterday, the United States Naval Hospital in Danang. At least three of our men who were patients in that

hospital were injured. That is typical of the way the Communists fight. Because they cannot hope to win on the battlefield, they rely on terror and on attacks against the wounded and the innocent.[182]

After his lengthy remarks at Monument Circle, the president joined state business and labor leaders, along with Democratic Party leaders, for a luncheon at the Indianapolis Athletic Club. Johnson opened his remarks by noting that Indiana's sesquicentennial was a good time to remember that "the building of a Great Society [involves] embracing the talents of all Americans. Every man sees the Great Society through his own eyes. But I think we all mean about the same thing. We mean a nation where man can enlarge his reach and realize his full potential. We mean a nation that is free of those things that afflict a man's body and restrict his mind—crime and ignorance, disease and poverty. We mean a nation that is free of those brutalities that rob him of his real happiness in the great cities of this land where we live. We mean a nation where men set aside their prejudices and work together in common tasks, uniting the land."[183]

While the bulk of the president's address dealt with economic issues, Johnson acknowledged ongoing dissent in the nation over issues of war and peace and civil rights, including recent racial violence in Brooklyn, Cleveland, and Chicago. He noted:

But there are ways of protesting that any civilized society can tolerate. There are also ways of protesting that are unacceptable. The ballot box, the neighborhood committees, the political and civil rights organizations— these are the means by which Americans express their resentment against intolerable conditions, their design to reform society, but not to rip it apart. Riots in the streets will never bring lasting reform. They tear at

the very fabric of the community. They set neighbor against neighbor. They create walls of mistrust and fear among fellow citizens. They make reform more difficult by turning away the very people who can and who must support their reforms. They start a chain reaction the consequences of which always fall most heavily on those who begin this chain reaction. So it is not only to protect the society at large that we refuse to condone riots and disorders. It is to serve the real interests of those for whose cause we struggle. Our country can abide by civil protest. It can improve the lives of those who mount that protest. But it cannot abide by civil violence.[184]

New York Times coverage of Johnson's Indiana swing noted that "the President did not mention Negroes in his appeal for an end to violence in America's cities but the context of his remarks made clear that he was referring directly to the riots in which Negro youths have been the principal participants. Mr. Johnson expressed sympathy for the plight of the poor, ill-housed Americans. The Government, he noted, has been working to relieve their circumstances, but 'all of this takes time.'"[185]

Following his two major addresses in Indianapolis, Johnson's party moved on to Vincennes to sign the act creating the George Rogers Clark National Historic Park. (Later, on November 5, 1966, Johnson signed an act creating a second new national park in the state, the Indiana Dunes National Lakeshore.) "This is going to be a very beautiful park," Johnson said. "It will include the memorial to George Rogers Clark that the people of Indiana built, with federal help back in the 1930's. This will be the first park in our entire national system to commemorate the Northwest Territory. Yet if that were all it did it would not inspire us with thoughts of the enduring strength of the American people. For George Rogers Clark was more than just a great soldier of the Revolution. In him there blazed a courage, a tenacity, and a devotion to liberty that brought a band of frontier fighters through hardship to ultimate victory—that, really, later brought a rich new land into a new Union."[186]

The president's remarks moved quickly, however, from the bravery of Clark (and references to Abraham Lincoln) to the Vietnam War. In thoughtful remarks he said, "As we meet here in this peaceful, beautiful scene this afternoon, in this heartland of America, thousands of miles out yonder, across the Pacific, American fortitude is again being tested. Our men are being tested in a harsh and deadly struggle. And here at home American conviction is being tested, too. This is the conviction that the integrity of men and the independence of nations must be defended. It is the conviction that peace just cannot endure if aggressors are allowed to succeed."[187]

"I honestly believe that the American soldier in Vietnam tonight is as brave and as resourceful as any man who forded the rivers of Illinois behind George Rogers Clark, and I have evidence of that fact," he said. "I saw it on the faces and on the bodies of the boys of the 101st just a few miles back just a few minutes ago. I could read to you from a number of the citations of the men that we decorated, some who had given their eye, some who had given their arms, some a leg, some both legs, but I am not going to take the time to review all of those citations that we went over this afternoon."[188] He did recount, however, the story of Charles William Bosley, a young fighter he met from Fort Wayne who had more than 1,800 flying hours in a helicopter, "most of it under fire," he said. "He had two Silver Stars and six Air Medals. He was rather bored while we were over there because he wanted to get back to Vietnam to fight for that flag. Every commanding officer of his had recommended that Indiana boy for a decoration."[189]

Quickly dispensing with comments related to the purpose of his visit, the remainder of Johnson's remarks concerned the war, with the president remarking that "freedom is not easily won, nor is it held without sacrifice. We have won it and we have held it because there are a good many among us who were willing to risk our lives and our fortunes in order to preserve our freedom and our liberty. We were willing to endure the times of confusion and uncertainty to fight in battle and to build in peace."[190] He noted:

> We look today to the conflict that rages in faraway Vietnam, where our men and our flag are committed. We are confident enough to believe that from the long travail of that land will emerge a free and a hopeful nation. We are wise enough, I hope, to know that more fighting, more trouble, and more uncertainty lie ahead before its aspirations are fulfilled. I cannot give you this evening an assurance of the hour or the day when this conflict will end. I can assure you that we have sent word to North Vietnam, through every means available to us, of our earnest willingness to negotiate the terms of peace. Twice, with great doubt, with reluctance, but with hope and with prayer, we stopped our bombing to the North to signal to the entire world our plea and our prayer and our hope for peace. We waited . . . but the answer we received from Hanoi was always the same story: a stony and contemptuous reply while more battalions were sent into their neighbor's land to join the fighting to kill their neighbors and to kill our soldiers.[191]

Johnson said he had heard the calls of many Americans to "stop the bombing," but distinguished American bombing raids from those of the North Vietnamese, asserting that American efforts had avoided targeting embassy or hospital locations, while the Communist north had held no such reserve. Quoting John Steinbeck, Johnson said, "I want to stop bombing. I want to stop the war on both sides. But I don't want to talk about half a war. I want to talk about all the war. So when you hear these voices in the days to come, the men who exercise the right to dissent, I hope you will ask yourselves the question: 'I just wonder why we don't talk about all the war? I just wonder why they are so anxious to get us to stop bombing to protect our men and they never say a word about stopping them from infiltrating and killing our men? Why don't we talk about both sides sitting down?' Your President is ready."[192]

Perhaps showing the weariness of a long, hot day in Indiana, Johnson opened his remarks just before 9:00 p.m. outside the Jeffersonville Post Office by noting, "I came here to Jeffersonville for two reasons: to please my wife and to please myself. Postmaster General Larry O'Brien has been telling Lady Bird that the Jeffersonville Post Office has been in the forefront of the beautification program." The Jeffersonville Post Office was one of sixteen honored across the nation for its efforts to beautify its property as part of the First Lady's Beautification Program. Once again, however, the Vietnam War dominated the president's remarks as he moved quickly away from honoring the local post office for its efforts and dove into a lengthy defense of his policies in Southeast Asia. He noted, "We do not want to be strong in order to be able to wage or win wars. We want to be strong so we can prevent war and bring peace. Your government, and your administration, is ready at this hour, as it has been every hour since I have been President, to talk instead of fight, to negotiate instead of bomb, to reason instead of try to force. But this is not a one-way street. It takes two to enter into an agreement. You can't have a unilateral treaty. You can't stop everything you are doing unless the other fellow will stop some of the things

that he is doing. So we continue to hope and work and try to hold our hand out, but keep our guard up."[193]

Lamenting that the media seemed to overlook the advancements his administration had brought in the areas of education, civil rights, and health care for the elderly, he noted, "I know there are some that like to keep (those accomplishments) a secret, but I take great pride in talking about what we are doing to educate little children, what we are doing to help older people when they are sick, what we are doing to try to increase the freedom of the farmer and increase his income at the same time, and what we have done in five years to get seven million more people jobs at an average factory wage in this country of $112 a week, the highest that was ever realized by any industrial nation. I am proud of those things."[194] Johnson added, "I am sorry that we have our men in Vietnam. But I had rather have them there with honor, doing their duty, keeping their commitment, carrying that flag with pride and honor, than to tuck their tail and come running home and break their word. And if I know anything about those men, they had rather be there doing it, too."[195]

George C. Wallace

Alabama governor Wallace's presidential ambitions in 1964 seemed inspired almost entirely by his opposition to the 1964 Civil Rights Act and his self-constructed battle to carry on the battle for states' rights originally taken up a century earlier in the U.S. Civil War. But not all Americans cheered. Inhabitants of the southern states—roughly the remnants of the Confederacy—raised strong objection to the act and feared the forced integration that they were certain would follow. The undisputed leader of the segregationist movement that winced at the advance of the civil rights agenda by President Johnson was Wallace, sworn into office as governor of Alabama in January 1963 declaring, "In the name of the greatest people that have ever trod this earth, I draw the line in the dust and toss the gauntlet before the feet of tyranny, and I say segregation today, segregation tomorrow, segregation forever."[196]

As part of his stand against advancements in civil rights, Wallace staged his meaningless, yet highly symbolic, "stand in the school house door" in June 1963, attempting to block the admission of black students to the University of Alabama under federal court orders. Later, upon the passage and enactment of the Civil Rights Act, Wallace dubbed President Johnson a "Texas sellout" and began referring to the act as "the Civil Wrongs Act." Wallace angrily warned that the impact of Johnson's actions would be to "destroy every neighborhood school in the country."[197]

But Wallace's theatrics were about to take on a larger scale as he gathered together a group of Alabama loyalists and launched a Quixotic run for the Democratic nomination for president in 1964. No one, possibly including Wallace himself, believed he was any serious challenger for the

BALL STATE UNIVERSITY, UNIVERSITY LIBRARIES, ARCHIVES AND SPECIAL COLLECTIONS

Alabama governor George Wallace waits backstage at his speech at Ball State Teachers College (today Ball State University) during a visit to Muncie, Indiana, in May 1964.

nomination. The move, however, was viewed by many to demonstrate to less-than-steel-boned members of Congress that American support for the Civil Rights Act was soft, even in northern enclaves such as Indiana. For all his faults, the short, stubborn governor had notable political instincts at times and had accurately picked up on anger among majority whites—whether their anger was based on blatant racism or couched in more civic-based concerns, such as limiting the scope of the federal government or states' rights. Wallace even successfully co-opted white conservatives who viewed this latest move by the federal government as too much, especially in light of federal court rulings that kept prayer out of public school classrooms.

Beyond Indiana's rather straightforward requirements for collecting signatures of registered voters in each of the state's congressional districts in order to qualify for the presidential ballot, Wallace successfully exploited hidden, often whispered, fears and bigotry still held in the hearts of many Hoosiers. The 1960 census showed 274,000 black citizens in Indiana, most of them concentrated in two communities, Indianapolis and Gary. By the spring of 1964, Wallace was on the ballot for president, and Johnson's plans to have "favorite son" stand-in candidates run for him in several states began to look like a risk. In Indiana, term-limited Governor Matthew Welsh had accepted Johnson's invitation to stand in for the president on the ballot, but was the Democrat governor popular enough to withstand an ever-increasingly serious challenge from Wallace on Hoosier soil?

In March 1964 the die was cast and the Wallace challenge was no longer a possibility but a reality. Welsh pledged "every effort" to roll up a large vote for Johnson in the state's May 5 presidential primary. "The [Indiana primary] election, which binds the delegates to the national conventions only on the first ballot, has become a free-for-all," the *New York Times* reported.[198] Wallace was coming to Indiana—whether Democrats liked it or not—and likely with a good head of steam from the Wisconsin primary, just ahead of Indiana's on the schedule. "Governor Wallace's avowed purpose in Wisconsin—and obviously also in Indiana—is to gather a large enough vote to hurt the civil rights bills pending in Congress. He hopes to demonstrate to northern Senators that there is voter opposition to the bills in their own states," the *Times* said.[199]

Interestingly, as Indiana Democrats gnashed their teeth over the obvious racial overtones of the Wallace campaign, the state's Republicans were having an easier go of it, although they would have a chance to vote for one of the nation's first African-American candidates for president, attorney Frank Beckwith of Indianapolis, who polled 20,000 votes in his previous GOP primary challenge to Nixon in 1960. Widely favored candidate Goldwater of Arizona was placed on the Indiana ballot, and beyond token

Protesters greeted Wallace with signs honoring victims of racial violence during his May 1964 appearance at Ball State Teachers College.

opposition from Beckwith and former Minnesota governor Harold E. Stassen (the latter a perennial candidate), the Republican slate was set. New York governor Rockefeller was not on the ballot, but still staged a late and unsuccessful move to wrestle Indiana delegates away from Goldwater.

All eyes remained focused, however, on Wallace and any damage he could do to Johnson in Indiana. Coming off a better-than-expected performance in Wisconsin, where he polled more than 250,000 Democratic primary votes, Wallace, upon his arrival in Indianapolis, was in high spirits. He refused to speculate about whether he could match his Wisconsin performance in Indiana. "If we get any votes at all, we have won," he said. "If I get any significant vote, it will not only shake the eye teeth of the liberals in both parties, it will make them drop out."[200]

Wallace was met with mostly stony silence when he addressed faculty and students at Earlham College in Richmond. At Notre Dame, where Wallace had gladly accepted an invitation to speak in the final days before the Indiana primary, he found a mixed and far less polite reception than the Quakers had given him at Earlham. While an audience of more than 5,000 packed into the Knute Rockne Fieldhouse to hear Wallace's speech, about 500 of those repeatedly interrupted Wallace's remarks. Wallace was undeterred and approached the podium repeatedly with confidence. "The men students, some women students from nearby St. Mary's College and a few nuns took part in the protest . . . [as Wallace] was booed and hissed for more than an hour. Midway in his speech a shouting, pushing effort and walkout that included the singing of the integration hymn, 'We Shall Overcome,' stopped [Wallace] for 10 minutes. The students carried picket signs that said such things as 'Christ made us all one race.'"[201] But Wallace also won "rousing

BALL STATE UNIVERSITY, UNIVERSITY LIBRARIES, ARCHIVES AND SPECIAL COLLECTIONS applause" for some of the points in his speech defending segregationist policies, and "he never lost his composure," the media reported.[202]

Wallace's "welcome" at Fort Wayne was even less cordial than that afforded him at Notre Dame, as news reports indicated he was booed and heckled throughout his remarks. United Press International reported that the heckling was accompanied by bomb threats phoned in and 200 sign-waving demonstrators making it difficult for any pro-Wallace supporters to even hear the governor's remarks. Wallace was making a last-minute pitch for Republican crossover votes in his Democratic primary versus Welsh, since the GOP contest was virtually decided already for Goldwater. "While the police battled the pickets, an anonymous caller reported that a bomb had been planted at the Van Orman Hotel, scene of [the Wallace] news conference. Police and fire officials searched the building but found no explosives."[203] Wallace's remarks were intended for a group of business leaders at the Fort Wayne Country Club and drew criticism for his "illegal" appeal for Republicans to vote in the Democratic Primary from Welsh, who said it was evidence of Wallace's lack of appeal among Indiana Democrats. [204]

Moving on to Ball State Teachers College in Muncie, Wallace addressed a student assembly of about 1,500, about half of them more than willing to boo and jeer at not only his introduction, but his speech. Another large crowd of students remained outside Emens Auditorium, staging an active protest heavily guarded by Muncie police and the Delaware County Sheriff's Department. Several audience members held anti-Wallace or pro-Johnson signs, "but the governor had one sturdy backer. A crop-haired student waved a placard declaring, 'Wallace is here to stay,'" the *Charleston (SC) News and Courier* reported. Seeing

BALL STATE UNIVERSITY, UNIVERSITY LIBRARIES ARCHIVES AND SPECIAL COLLECTIONS

Ball State students protest Wallace's visit to the university.

the signs, Wallace said, "Why, just the other day a fellow hit me over the head with a placard that read, 'God is love,' what about what? And then some people accuse me of favoring violence."[205] Wallace's comments about the federal government throwing tax dollars "down a rat hole" drew heavy applause, but his follow-up remarks that Alabama operated segregated schools "because the overwhelming majority of our people want separate schools,"[206] drew a loud chorus of boos. Recalling the post-Reconstruction days in states such as Alabama, he recalled for students how southern whites had faced widespread economic discrimination following the Civil War. "We were relegated to be hewers of wood and drawers of water in an agrarian society," he said.[207]

Protesters outside of Wallace's speech grew more vocal as the governor went back and forth with unfriendly questions from the audience for almost an hour. Muncie police quickly surrounded the governor as he left the auditorium and swept him into a waiting car. Indiana State Police motorcycles surrounded Wallace's car as he was escorted from the campus to the Muncie airport, and no incidents were reported.

At Indiana University in Bloomington, about 500 students picketed outside the IU Auditorium, where Wallace spoke before about 4,000 listeners. Of those, about 400 students inside, a mix of black and white, waited until he started to speak before turning their backs on him and silently leaving the room. "His speech was repeatedly interrupted by derisive laughter but was greeted just as frequently with enthusiastic applause from other segments of the student audience," the Associated Press reported.[208] The portions of Wallace's speech that drew most applause included his belief that many nations of the world were more than willing to accept foreign aid from the United States, but would cooperate on little else, and accused the State Department of acting like "a petted poodle." He added, "They ought to be worrying about what we think of them instead of what they think about us."[209]

Later in his speech, Wallace defended the "separate but equal" approach to public education Alabama had adopted as an artifact of treasured states' rights and said, "I suggest we enhance educational opportunities for all people. That's going to be the ultimate solution."[210] Again developing his theme that the pending civil rights bill would usurp state authority, Wallace told students in an IU dormitory dining hall during a question-and-answer session, "we are convinced in Alabama that segregation is the best in Alabama, for both Negro and white. You can have what you want in Indiana, but just decide it for yourself."[211]

Although Wallace had been invited to speak on a Sunday afternoon at the Freemont Street Baptist Church in Crawfordsville, more than 200 protesters gathered outside the church and booed and jeered portions of his speech broadcast over a loudspeaker set up outside the church. Once his

remarks were finished, Wallace emerged from the church and shook hands with more friendly members of the crowd and made a quick exit for Indianapolis.[212] At a later speech there, Wallace had his receptive audience fired up when he threatened to drive over "any silver spooned brats who will lie down in front of our car."[213] While not as dramatic as throwing themselves in front of a car, one report from Terre Haute indicated a female protester attempted to shove her protest sign inside the open window of Wallace's car, striking the governor in the forehead. At nearby Vincennes University, college administrators initiated an interesting policy by refusing to allow Wallace to make his remarks from the stage inside a school auditorium, and instead insisted that he remain on the seating level floor, the same as the students he addressed. The university also chose to allow only VU students and faculty to enter the auditorium.[214]

National news reporters followed Wallace's Indiana campaign closely for indications of how deep and wide were the cracks in Johnson's Democratic base as a result of his efforts on the Civil Rights Act. "President Johnson's political prestige has been committed" to the campaign in Indiana, the *New York Times*'s Claude Sitton reported, noting that the Indiana primary "could have fateful consequences for the civil rights bill" with a sampling of voters that indicated "surprising" strength for Wallace among Hoosiers. "With the approval from Washington, the state Democratic organization is seeking to drive home the point that Mr. Wallace's opponent is the President and not Gov. Matthew E. Welsh. . . . The Democratic strategy is underscored by the slogan emblazoned on buttons, literature, posters and other campaign paraphernalia: '*Clear the Way for LBJ: Vote for Welsh the Fifth of May.*'"[215] Johnson campaign officials never took Wallace's challenge for the nomination seriously, but they did worry that a strong showing by Wallace in primaries in Indiana, Wisconsin, and Maryland could create vulnerability in getting the Civil Rights Act through a still skeptical Congress.

During a later appearance at Butler University in Indianapolis, Wallace appeared to tone down the rhetoric that had grown ugly in the prior Wisconsin primary and told about 350 faculty and students, "I don't run on segregation. I'm not a racist. I make the same speeches in Wisconsin and in Indiana that I make in Alabama." He added, "A racist is one who hates another person in his heart because of his color. I would not be a segregationist president. I would be a state and local rights president."[216] At an Indianapolis news conference, he elaborated that "not even the left-wing press can show that I have ever made any statement reflecting on anyone because of his race, creed or national origin"[217] and said, "I have no objection to Indiana having integration. I feel that it is a matter to be decided by the states. . . . Anyone who believes in the turn to constitutional government that we're trying to bring about in this country, we welcome their support."[218] Generous donations from back home in Alabama and Mississippi loaded Wallace's campaign with about $50,000 to buy newspaper, radio, and television ads across the state—a figure dwarfed by Welsh's supporters.

As primary day approached, southern newspapers in Alabama, Mississippi, Georgia, and South Carolina reported heavily on Wallace's "northern invasion" and projected an optimistic governor. Wallace told the *Charleston News and Courier* that he hoped he could survive the mud being hurled at him by the Democratic establishment. "I feel that the people have the ability to detect the truth and that they recognize mud-slinging," he said. "The smear and invective is the standard tactic of the left wing. You've got to take it or get out of the

fight. They can hand it out, but they can't take it."[219] Wallace said his ten-day campaign across Indiana to Vincennes, Richmond, Terre Haute, Bloomington, South Bend, Fort Wayne, Muncie, Indianapolis, and Crawfordsville had given him a chance to show Indiana's strongly pro-labor Democrats that he was their friend. He readily pointed out that picketers at his appearances had been organized mostly by college and university agitators.

Wallace's last appearance in Indianapolis just before the primary vote was described by southern reporters as "a slashing attack on the federal civil rights bill" delivered by "the spunky little Southerner."[220] Wallace warned a veterans group of about 150 men that passage of the Civil Rights bill would mean that states like Indiana might as well abolish their state and local governments and that the Justice Department and twenty-three other federal agencies would take over control of the states. "I predict the Civil Rights bill will not remain on the books, even if it is enacted," he said. "It's going to be replaced by the people of Indiana, New York and Pennsylvania, because they're going to wake up and realize it isn't aimed only at the heathen in Alabama and Mississippi" and that the bill represented "10 percent civil rights and 90 percent federal power grab."[221] Wallace said the federal law was designed by liberals to "pre-empt control" of the states. "You are intelligent enough to run your own schools in Indiana," he said. "There's no need to turn them over to 23 federal agencies. Why should you turn the schools of Indiana over to a bunch of social engineers in Washington?"[222] Wallace said Hoosiers had been welcoming to him and that "a good vote for me Tuesday is going to make those liberals in both parties realize that the huge mass of people who have been tranquilized is to be reckoned with."[223]

Matthew Welsh

Indiana Democrats backing Governor Welsh pulled out all the stops as a counter to what they considered the embarrassing spectacle of Wallace's segregationist views. The normally genteel and friendly Welsh blistered Wallace with his declaration that he was "the man who tolerated the presence of billboards in his state before the assassination [of President Kennedy] which demanded: 'Kayo the Kennedys.' This is the man whose beliefs were responsible for the deaths of innocent children in the bombing of a Sunday school class. This is the man who stood by while dogs were set upon human beings and fire hoses were turned on groups of peaceful demonstrators. This is the man who even today is actively denying Negro children access to the University of Alabama. This is the man who is trying to destroy the political system in the United States as we know it, and who seeks to discredit President Lyndon B. Johnson. This is the man who flies the Confederate flag over the Statehouse in Alabama in place of the Stars and Stripes."[224]

Unaccustomed to the spotlight that a presidential campaign would bring—even if he was a stand-in for Johnson—Welsh had his campaign pull no punches. The governor brought in two southerners who presumably knew Wallace well—Charles Morgan Jr., a former Birmingham, Alabama, attorney, and James McBride Dabbs of Mayesville, South Carolina. Reporters described Morgan as "most vociferous" in his attacks aimed at Wallace on behalf of Welsh, with the *News and Courier* noting that the "tubby attorney has been a nightly performer on television, accusing Gov. Wallace of riding political 'tail wins,' of holding Alabama under a reign of terror, and of engineering the release of a man convicted of castrating an inoffensive old Negro."[225] Welsh's campaign also counted on a $75,000 investment from the Democratic National Committee that paid for television and radio advertising across the state, with the television ads including images of black protesters being sprayed with fire hoses, police dogs attacking African American men, and images of a Birmingham church bombing that left four young girls dead.

Wallace's presence in Indiana even produced a rarely repeated public show of support for Johnson by members of the late President Kennedy's family. At the urging of Senator Bayh, Senator Ted Kennedy of Massachusetts appeared at the Democrats' annual Jefferson-Jackson Day Dinner and invoked the name of his deceased brother in asking for support for Johnson. He asked Democrats who "believe in President Johnson" to support Welsh, saying the Indiana primary had become "a test of the entire record of the Democratic Party" and offered Hoosiers a chance to declare to the world whether the state was "the home of extremism or the home of common sense." Kennedy challenged what he called Wallace's "distortions and half-truths about civil rights."[226] He added that he and his family were devoted "to the continuation of the principles and programs for which the President lived and the elimination and eradication of the hatred and extremism that took him away."[227]

Bayh and fellow Democratic Senator Hartke both sent thousands of letters to Hoosiers, reminding them that a vote for Welsh was a vote for the memory of President Kennedy. Wallace supporters openly complained that the Welsh campaign flexed its incumbent muscle by warning state patronage employees that they risked their jobs if they backed Wallace over Welsh. "Indiana was George Wallace's stand-or-fall battle," author Rick Perlstein wrote. "Party loyalty was sacred in Indiana. If Wallace could peel off significant numbers from Johnson's stand-in, Governor

Matthew Welsh, it would mean that the backlash was for real."[228]

More familiar with Indiana's political landscape than anyone else on the ballot, Welsh barnstormed the state, asking voters to "Clear the way for LBJ." Indiana Democrats worked hard behind the scenes to tamp down protests and demonstrations planned for Wallace's Indiana appearances—appearances that helped gain him additional media coverage. Further, Welsh had been instructed to downplay civil rights, with top Democratic aides telling a reporter off the record that keeping black demonstrations at a minimum and deemphasizing issues of segregation and civil rights would help hold together a

fragile alliance of black Hoosiers ready to vote for anyone but Wallace, and traditional working-class, union, and mostly white Democratic voters in key pockets of the northern parts of the state. In an unusual flourish of pointed rhetoric, Welsh told an audience in Gary that "thousands of Negro and white families are moving north [from Alabama] to escape [Wallace's] modern tyranny" and said Wallace had transformed his state into "a police state ruled by the iron fist of would-be dictators."[229]

In the end, Wallace polled 30 percent of the Democratic vote against Welsh, enough to lay claim to a symbolic victory. Wallace had come to fame on the back of a symbolic victory in

Indiana governor Matthew E. Welsh attends a press conference with John F. Kennedy.

IHS, GIFT OF JACK L. NEW

the schoolhouse door. He would gladly take his showing in Indiana. As he gloated to reporters, "The noise you hear now are the teeth falling out in Indiana."[230]

Years later, Welsh wrote an article for the *Indiana Magazine of History*, detailing his 1964 campaign. In it, Welsh said, "What particularly concerned me was the impact a large Wallace vote would have on the people of Indiana—on their perception of themselves. I felt very strongly that a powerful showing by Wallace would surely affect—adversely—the political and social climate of Indiana, perhaps for a generation, as it would revive and give credence to a racist philosophy my administration had worked very hard to defuse."[231] In his postscript, Welsh acknowledged that he ran mostly because the state's two Democratic senators, Hartke and Bayh, were unwilling to risk their own re-elections and urged the lame-duck governor to take on Wallace instead.

Constitutionally barred from seeking a second consecutive term, Welsh did return in 1972 as the Democratic nominee for governor, but lost to Republican Otis R. Bowen. Welsh later retired to Vincennes and died while on a visit to Indianapolis on May 28, 1995, at the age of eighty-two.

Barry Goldwater

Goldwater had a tough time in 1964 as the presumptive Republican nominee, even in a normally hospitable state for conservatives such as Indiana. In the May GOP primary, Goldwater's token challenger, Stassen, was positioned as the "anyone-but-Goldwater" and the "middle-of-the-road" candidate. However, as historian Perlstein noted, "That was all it took for oafish Stassen to siphon off an embarrassing 27 percent of the vote from Goldwater in one of the most conservative states in the country. . . . Commentators

continued to refer to Goldwater's 'wretched showing' in [the Indiana] primary where he won upwards of 70 percent of the vote."[232] It was not for a lack of strong ties to Indiana. Goldwater's wife, Margaret "Peggy" (Johnson), was a native of Muncie, and the couple met when Peggy's family was on vacation in Arizona and visited the Goldwaters' store in Phoenix. Peggy eventually made her first and only political appearance on behalf of her husband in Muncie, but she reportedly loathed campaigning. She told reporters during the early October stop in her hometown that she would not be making any speeches or discussing any issues. "One speaker in the family is enough," she said.[233]

It was no surprise Peggy did not enjoy campaigning, and her husband could not have been enjoying himself, either. As the *South Bend Tribune*'s Jack Colwell reported, pundits openly discussed that Goldwater was "feared more than respected by a larger segment of voters. That included many Republicans."[234] Of particular interest was "whether the Republican nominee for governor of Indiana would greet Goldwater at the South Bend airport or dodge an appearance with the controversial presidential nominee."[235] The GOP's gubernatorial nominee, Lieutenant Governor Richard O. Ristine, decided to join Goldwater in South Bend.

Despite the weak knees of fellow Republicans, more than 3,000 supporters showed up to hear Goldwater speak on September 26, 1964. During his speech, Goldwater denounced Johnson's Great Society initiatives as "fairy tales so ridiculous that if anyone asks for equal time, it is going to be Snow White." And, as was normal for his stump speech, Goldwater railed against the evils of Communism in the world.[236] Large crowds gathered along the streets of South Bend as Goldwater made his way to an outdoor rally at nearby Niles, Michigan. The motorcade ironically delayed, among many others, Muriel Humphrey, the wife of Johnson's running mate, as she made her way to the South Bend airport after wrapping up Indiana campaigning.

A subsequent appearance before an audience of about 6,000 supporters on October 1 at the Civic Center Hall in Hammond solidified Goldwater's growing image as being too extreme for the presidency. Author John William Middendorf reported that "nuclear war . . . was so much on [Goldwater's] mind that he couldn't stop talking about it. At a campaign stop in Hammond, Indiana, he mentioned nuclear weapons, war, 'destruction,' and 'holocaust' twenty-six times in about as many minutes."[237] He told the otherwise receptive Hammond audience that "we will not start a war against anyone. And the Communists must be certain that any holocaust they unleash will result in their own destruction and the end of their system," speculating that such a strike by the Communists would likely take out Washington, D.C., and "in all likelihood, the President of the United States and the Vice President would not be around at all to push the button."[238] Goldwater said America needed "to elect a President who will consistently keep before the Communists a clear-cut picture of what will happen if they push the button that starts war. This country must always maintain such superiority of strength, such devastating strike-back power, such a strong network of allies that the Communists would be creating suicide for themselves if they push the button." Goldwater said the choice between him and President Johnson was one of "peace through strength or the increasing possibility of war through weakness."[239]

Goldwater was relentless in his attack on his opponent: "President Johnson thinks we can negotiate with the Communists . . . curtail our national defense [and] he believes that peace will prevail if we talk nice to the Communists, if we expand our trade with them. He thinks that Khrushchev will no longer want to bury us if we avoid taking a firm stand against the Communist program of expansion." The senator insisted that America must provide "adequate security for our freedoms" and that "there is no other way."[240]

Before reaching Hammond, Goldwater's campaign train made seven other stops across the state, including Jeffersonville, Seymour, Columbus, Indianapolis, Frankfort, Logansport, and Crown Point.

At Indianapolis before an enthusiastic downtown crowd near Union Station estimated at 15,000, Goldwater again called Johnson "soft on Communism" and said the incumbent was more interested in gaining votes than securing the nation's safety. Goldwater said the nation "faces a bleak future, and so does peace, but the leader of this Administration is happy so long as his personal polls are bright. How can anyone who truly wants to keep the peace trust a man to whom everything is just a political game?"[241]

Goldwater showed his anger at a devastating and historic television ad the Johnson campaign was running nationwide that showed a small girl pulling the petals of a flower in front of a nuclear mushroom cloud. "The homes of America are horrified and the intelligence of Americans is insulted by weird TV advertising in which this Administration threatens the end of the world unless all-wise Lyndon is given the nation for his own."[242] Goldwater said Johnson was conducting "a lie-filled campaign" and referred to him as "an interim President," a risky reference to Johnson's ascension to the presidency just a year earlier upon Kennedy's assassination. "This interim president who seeks to win an election by talk of war doesn't understand the first thing about keeping the peace," Goldwater said to roaring applause. "How can anyone who truly wants to keep the peace trust a man to whom everything is just a political game? We want peace and we know how to keep it far better than the present administration with its policies of drift, deception and defeat. The cause of peace is too precious to be entrusted to men who have a wishbone where they need a backbone."[243]

His bitterness seeping through still, Goldwater told his Indianapolis audience that "I will not be a wartime President" and reminded them that "this nation has gone to war three times in this century, but not under a Republican President." He added that efforts to cast him as an extremist were "nothing but a big lie. This is nothing but the administration's version of the old tactic of spend and spend and spend and elect and elect and elect. This time, it's lie and lie and lie."[244]

Declaring that Johnson "lacked the guts for his job," Goldwater openly questioned the administration's support of "military advisers" in South Vietnam. "They cannot defend this nation against Communist bullies because they don't know bullies when they see them," he said. "They are plainly and simply soft on Communists. They live in a dream world where Cold War problems don't exist. . . . The result is a policy of weakness. The result is a war in Vietnam--Lyndon Johnson's war."[245] Goldwater said Johnson's approach in Southeast Asia had collapsed America's strategic position in the region and is resulting in the deaths of American soldiers there. He claimed U.S. troops were poorly prepared for combat in Southeast Asia and that Johnson had engaged in "double talk" about his Vietnamese policy, including "foolish" moves that have signaled the North Vietnamese Communist forces of American moves in the region.

Despite big-picture discussions of nuclear weapons and national security abroad, Goldwater did not cede white fears about growing civil rights unrest around the country, telling a Crown Point audience that the election would decide what level of "protection you and your family have on the streets" and noted that in some places in America, a person was "safer being a criminal than being a law-abiding citizen."[246] Goldwater left out any reference to Civil Rights in Lake County, his campaign officials estimating that too much emphasis on such a divisive issue could boomerang, despite diverse populations in Hammond and Gary (including many black voters) and focused instead on "law and order" issues meant to appeal to heavy concentrations of Serbian, Polish, Croatian, and Hungarian communities elsewhere in northwest Indiana.[247]

In earlier stops at Columbus and Seymour, Goldwater slid easily into his earned persona as the grouchy old man. "Too many Americans are interested in the buck than they are their freedom, and, let's face it, that is true," Goldwater lectured. "This is the way freedom goes. It doesn't appear overnight. You are not going to bed some night free people and waking up the next morning slaves. It is going to be chipped a little bit here, chewed on a little bit there, taken a little bit here, until one day you wake up, and say, 'By golly, we are not free anymore.'"[248] His smallest audience was in mostly Democratic Jeffersonville, where less than a 1,000 voters showed up. Crowds were larger in the more heavily GOP areas that followed. At Logansport, Goldwater said Johnson, "the very man who claims to be the friend of the Social Security recipient," was on track to bankrupt the system. He said the administration's plan for a so-called Medicare amendment would cost too much and made no provision for direct care by a doctor. "It just lets you into a hospital. As it is, by 1970 the Social Security program will take 10 percent of an employee's wages, half of which will be paid by the employee, and half by the employer. The Medicare plan would be so expensive it would wreck the entire Social Security program." Turning to a group of teenagers in the crowd, Goldwater sternly warned that "you are the ones who are going to pay for these follies."[249]

Goldwater's push in Indiana, a normally safe Republican state he should have sewed up early in the fall campaign, was important to the nominee. "Indiana has a very special importance to Mr. Goldwater exceeding the value of its 13 electoral votes," the *New York Times* analyzed. "It is in the heart of 'Goldwater Country' in the Midwest."[250] Because of what the *Times* called the "psychological importance" of Indiana to Goldwater, Johnson's campaign also focused on Hoosier voters. "President Johnson made a carnival-like triumphal entry into Indianapolis . . . and his running mate Senator Hubert H. Humphrey made his third foray into the state," the *Times* reported. "The critical element in the campaign in Indiana is this: Whether white resentment over civil rights, as a political force, outweighs a widespread distrust of Mr. Goldwater. The white backlash is almost impossible to measure, statistically, but competent observers [in Indiana] say it occurs in its most aggravated form among industrial workers, many of whom are of foreign extraction . . . and there is reportedly a widespread belief among factory workers that under the recent Civil Rights Act of 1964 a certain proportion of white employees in every factory can be dismissed to make way for Negroes."[251]

Despite Goldwater's efforts, the Johnson-Humphrey team made Indiana history as one of only three Democratic tickets in the twentieth century to carry the state in the November election.

Goldwater's 1964 run for the White House

caused him to have to give up running for another term to his U.S. Senate seat from Arizona. Subsequently, he ran for the Senate again in 1968 and was easily elected and served there until 1987. In the years after he left the Senate, Goldwater was a sought-after speaker for both Republican and Democratic audiences, particularly because of his outspoken nature that continued to win him followers. In 1996 Goldwater suffered a massive stroke, and shortly thereafter it was disclosed he was suffering from Alzheimer's disease. He died at his home in Paradise Valley, Arizona, on May 29, 1998, at the age of eighty-nine.

Richard M. Nixon

While Goldwater struggled to keep his head above water against the growing Johnson tide in 1964, former vice president Nixon licked his wounds from a devastating loss in the 1962 California gubernatorial campaign and began a strategic effort to collect political chips that would help him four years hence. Among the stops he made that year for literally dozens of Republican congressional candidates was a quick stop in Elkhart on October 1, 1964, for the candidacy of Robert L. Miller of South Bend. "We didn't have any money to speak of at all, and we were having a terrible time getting someone to head a fundraiser," Miller said. "It was a very difficult time to get a name Republican to come out here with Goldwater as the party's nominee."[252] Nixon's help was not enough, as Miller joined a long list of Republicans who were swept under by Goldwater, losing the seat to incumbent Congressman John Brademas, a Democrat. Nixon also made an October 1964 stop in Marion on behalf of Republican congressional nominee John Feighner, who also eventually lost to incumbent Democrat J. Edward Roush.

9

Civil Rights and Vietnam, 1968–71

Lyndon B. Johnson

Despite an admirable domestic agenda that could rival almost any administration in U.S. history, President Lyndon B. Johnson's efforts at home were continually dragged down by the quagmire of Vietnam. By 1967 it was clear that American support for the war was beginning to wane. Fueling the sag in support was a critical lack of confidence expressed by the mainstream media—dubbed a "credibility gap"—between what the Johnson administration reported about the American efforts in South Vietnam and the reality of a bloody, difficult war. Indiana's senator Vance Hartke joined a growing chorus of legislators who questioned the objectives in Vietnam, although his counterpart, Senator Birch Bayh, did not break ranks with the president on Vietnam during Johnson's term in office.

In January 1968 Johnson suffered an embarrassing "win" in the New Hampshire Democratic presidential primary, polling 49 percent of the vote and leaving another 42 percent to a virtual unknown challenger, fierce antiwar Senator Eugene McCarthy of Minnesota. Then, on March 31, 1968, tucked in at the end of a long speech on the American effort to sustain South Vietnam from Communist takeover, Johnson slipped in a statement that caught the world by surprise:

Fifty-two months and 10 days ago, in a moment of tragedy and trauma, the duties of this office fell upon me. I asked then for your help and God's, that we might continue America on its course, binding up our wounds, healing our history, moving forward in new unity, to clear the American agenda and to keep the American commitment for all of our people. United we have kept that commitment. United we have enlarged that commitment. Through all time to come, I think America will be a stronger nation, a more just society, and a land of greater opportunity and fulfillment because of what we have all done together in these years of unparalleled achievement. Our reward will come in the life of freedom, peace, and hope that our children will enjoy through ages ahead. What we won when all of our people united just must not now be lost in suspicion, distrust, selfishness, and politics among any of our people. Believing this as I do, I have concluded that I should not permit the Presidency to become involved in the partisan divisions that are developing in this political year. With America's sons in the fields far away, with America's future under challenge right here at home, with our hopes and the world's hopes for peace in the balance every day, I do not believe that I should devote an hour or a day of my time to any personal partisan causes or to any duties other than the awesome duties of this office—the Presidency of your country. Accordingly, I shall not seek, and I will not accept, the nomination of my party for another term as your President. But let men everywhere know, however, that a strong, a confident, and a vigilant America stands ready tonight to seek an honorable peace—and stands ready tonight to defend an honored cause—whatever the price, whatever the burden, whatever the sacrifice that duty may require.[1]

Johnson finished out his term in office during a tumultuous 1968, being called upon to make statements upon the assassination of Doctor Martin Luther King Jr. in April, and again in June upon the murder of Senator Robert F. Kennedy of New York. Johnson returned to Texas in January 1969 and opened his presidential library and museum in 1971. He endorsed Senator George McGovern's campaign for the presidency in 1972, but did not actively campaign for the party or its nominee. His last public appearance came on December 28, 1972, in Independence, Missouri, at the funeral of former President Harry S Truman. Less than a month later, on January 22, 1973, he suffered a massive heart attack and died at his home in Stonewall, Texas. He was sixty-four years old.

Robert F. Kennedy

Johnson's stunning departure from the race changed the political landscape dramatically. While normally McCarthy should have been viewed as the greatest recipient of Democratic support after the president's withdrawal, the best bet was on Robert F. Kennedy, the deceased president's younger brother and the former attorney general for both Kennedy and Johnson. It was only a matter of time before Robert Kennedy made the decision to join the race, and join he did, in Indiana.

Kennedy's quick entry into the 1968 Democratic Primary in Indiana brought political attention the state that it had not seen for a long time. But the road was not clear. McCarthy was going nowhere, having come so close to the prize. And Johnson loyalists quickly rallied behind Vice President Hubert Humphrey by lining up "favorite son" candidates to support him. Years later, Kennedy's brother, Ted, said "the risks were high. Indiana was a conservative and pro-war state, despite having elected two antiwar Democratic senators. It was the home to the Ku Klux Klan, a stronghold of the Teamsters, whose membership still resented my brother's investigation of Jimmy Hoffa, and a large conservative agricultural community."[2]

For Kennedy, the Indiana contest was shaping up similarly to his slain brother's 1960 showdown against Humphrey in West Virginia. Kennedy had more to lose, however, now tasked with putting the family's golden political name on the line but with plenty of Kennedy cash to give it a good shot. Depending on where he spoke, Kennedy adjusted his message, talking about issues of law and order before white audiences by reminding them he had been "the nation's chief law enforcement officer" as attorney general, and vowing that if elected, "lawlessness and violence will not be tolerated."[3] He later reminded black audiences, "Violence won't get you better housing, or better jobs or better education for your children."[4]

Oakland (CA) Tribune reporter Mary McGrory wrote about the contrast Kennedy's campaign brought to the race in Indiana. "The difference between the Kennedy and McCarthy campaigns is the difference between the old politics and the new," McGrory wrote. "Kennedy is pressure, McCarthy is infiltration. Kennedy's [campaign] has strong direction from the top. He has a high-powered, star-studded staff, led by veterans of his brother's battles. McCarthy's [campaign]

IHS, BASS PHOTO COMPANY COLLECTION, P 130

Robert Kennedy leaves after giving a speech to Indianapolis Democrats during the Indiana primary. Behind Kennedy is his aide, Fred Dutton.

has strong direction from the bottom, with few chiefs."[5] She added, "Kennedy's crowds come out to see him, and if possible to touch him and they are mammoth. McCarthy's come out to hear him. They are, except in the small towns, not comparable."[6] A difference in Kennedy's campaign rhetoric was also noted. McGrory reported that Kennedy downplayed his antiwar views among "hawkish Hoosiers," while McCarthy continued his national themes that it was time for America to end the war in Vietnam.

On April 4, 1968, Kennedy made stops at South Bend and Muncie, the latter for a speech before an overflow crowd of 9,000 students and community members at the Men's Gymnasium on the campus of Ball State University. Three persons were injured in the mad crush of admirers to shake Kennedy's hand, and his wife, Ethel, was briefly knocked to the floor along with toppled press tables—the latest in crowd-crushing incidents that continued to happen during Kennedy's campaign. During his speech Kennedy invoked the words of his brother JFK by reminding the students that:

> You must help in all of these complex questions because you will bear the burdens of errors or misjudgment. President Kennedy once said . . . that you, the younger generation, you have the least ties to the past and the greatest stake in the future. So what happens in the decisions that we make are going to have the greatest stake in your lives, the greatest effect on your lives. . . . The question of what kind of lives we're going to lead— the quality of life that's going to exist in the United States—whether there is going to be these tremendous divisions between blacks and whites, between various age groups, on our foreign policy, the quality of life that's going to be. . . . These are the questions that are being decided and these, it seems to me, have the greatest effect on you more than any other generation. We have made mistakes in

the past. As I have said before, I was involved in mistakes—the mistakes made during the administration of President Kennedy—undoubtedly mistakes that were made regarding Vietnam, for which I was intimately involved. But what I hope is that we look to the past. . . . And we see where we've erred and where we've done right, and we benefit by the mistakes that we have made.[7]

Following his remarks, during a brief question-and-answer session, a black student rose and remarked: "Your speech implies that you are placing a great faith in white America. Is that faith justified?" Kennedy said it was and added that "faith in black America is justified, too" and that there "are extremists on both sides." Another student asked the Senator about his views on laws banning cannabis (marijuana). It's unclear if Kennedy was just joking, or truly did not hear the student, but he replied, "Laws against what? Cannibalcy? Eating your fellow human beings? You've got me. I don't know. You're right, that's one I haven't got an answer on."[8]

Kennedy's campaign made unexpected history later that evening with a speech he delivered

Kennedy uses a microphone to address a crowd gathered to hear him speak at Twenty-first and Harding Streets in Indianapolis, May 4, 1968.

IHS, KATIE PALMER COLLECTION, P 123

to an outdoor campaign rally near Seventeenth and Broadway Streets in Indianapolis. The mostly African American crowd gathered at the site waiting for Kennedy to speak was mostly unaware of tragic events unfolding about five hundred miles away in Memphis, Tennessee. There, Doctor King was slain as he stood on the balcony of the Lorraine Motel. Kennedy had been told of the King shooting shortly after news of it broke, as Kennedy was preparing to leave Muncie, and by the time he reached Indianapolis by plane the news was official: King was dead. A dramatic story has unfolded over the years about efforts by local officials to convince Kennedy to cancel his planned appearance in a mostly black Indianapolis neighborhood, with fears rising that civil unrest would surely follow the news of King's murder. Kennedy and his campaign were undeterred, and the speech went forward. Once at the rally, Kennedy abandoned his prepared remarks and told his audience, "Ladies and gentlemen, I'm only going to talk to you just for a minute or so this evening. Because I have some very sad news for all of you, and I think sad news for all of our fellow citizens and people who love peace all over the world, and that is that Martin Luther King was shot and was killed tonight in Memphis, Tennessee."[9] Kennedy added:

> Martin Luther King dedicated his life to love and to justice between fellow human beings. He died in the cause of that effort. In this difficult day, in this difficult time for the United States, it's perhaps well to ask what kind of a nation we are and what direction we want to move in. For those of you who are black—considering the evidence evidently is that there were white people who were responsible—you can be filled with bitterness, and with hatred, and a desire for revenge. We can move in that direction as a country, in greater polarization—black people amongst blacks, and white amongst whites, filled

Kennedy's car is mobbed by spectators as he campaigns on Indianapolis's Monument Circle on May 1, 1968.

> with hatred toward one another. Or we can make an effort, as Martin Luther King did, to understand and to comprehend, and replace that violence, that stain of bloodshed that has spread across our land, with an effort to understand, compassion and love. For those of you who are black and are tempted to be filled with hatred and mistrust of the injustice of such an act, against all white people, I would only say that I can also feel in my own heart the same kind of feeling. I had a member of my family killed, but he was killed by a white man. But we have to make an effort in the United States; we have to make an effort to understand, to get beyond these rather difficult times.[10]

Historians later noted that Indianapolis was the only major U.S. city that did not experience serious rioting after King's murder. Perhaps it was Kennedy's remarks that helped:

What we need in the United States is not division; what we need in the United States is not hatred; what we need in the United States is not violence and lawlessness, but is love and wisdom, and compassion toward one another, and a feeling of justice toward those who still suffer within our country, whether they be white or whether they be black. So I ask you tonight to return home, to say a prayer for the family of Martin Luther King, but more importantly to say a prayer for our own country, which all of us love—a prayer for understanding and that compassion of which I spoke. We can do well in this country. We will have difficult times. We've had difficult times in the past. And we will have difficult times in the future. It is not the end of violence; it is not the end of lawlessness; and it's not the end of disorder. But the

vast majority of white people and the vast majority of black people in this country want to live together, want to improve the quality of our life, and want justice for all human beings that abide in our land. Let us dedicate ourselves to what the Greeks wrote so many years ago: to tame the savageness of man and make gentle the life of this world. Let us dedicate ourselves to that, and say a prayer for our country and for our people.[11]

Kennedy and the other candidates temporarily suspended their campaigns until after King's funeral in Atlanta, Georgia. By mid-April, Kennedy was back in the state for a speech at Indiana University in Bloomington on April 24 and a Democratic Party rally in Indianapolis the

Kennedy rides with Gary mayor Richard G. Hatcher (left) and East Chicago mayor John B. Nicosia (right) on a campaign swing through northwest Indiana on April 29, 1968.

CALUMET REGIONAL ARCHIVES, INDIANA UNIVERSITY NORTHWEST

same day. At Bloomington, Kennedy rode in an open convertible (though temperatures were only thirty-eight degrees), and "the wind was making a haystack of his famous mop top."[12] A noteworthy speech before medical students at the IU School of Medicine in Indianapolis on April 26 followed a few days later. It included a spirited question-and-answer session in which Kennedy was pointedly questioned by a medical student who clearly was not a supporter. In the exchange, Kennedy confronted the student who worried who would pay for the social programs the candidate advocated. "You will," Kennedy replied, and asked the future doctors present to think about the privilege of their lives and how they could use that to benefit others.

Kennedy advocated before a sold-out luncheon organized by the United Auto Workers in Indianapolis on April 30 for changes in the nation's Social Security program, including increased benefits, not penalizing retirees who wanted to return to work after retiring, and basing benefits off a worker's highest ten-year average of wages. After the downtown event, Kennedy's open-car motorcade moved slowly around Monument Circle and was quickly overwhelmed by thousands of admirers reaching out to shake his hand. Kennedy did not speak on the Circle because no permit for a public event had been obtained from the city. One man carrying a Teamsters sign supporting Kennedy earned a special handshake from the senator—and a wink, given Kennedy's successful prosecution of former Teamsters boss Jimmy Hoffa while he was attorney general.[13] Other stops in Indianapolis that day included informal visits to the Christian Theological Seminary, the Marion County Home, a local UAW hall, and the General Motors plant on South Tibbs Avenue.

Kennedy kept up the pace, many times

making stops in parts of Indiana unaccustomed to much attention, including Anderson, Bedford, Brownstown, Crawfordsville, East Chicago, Elkhart, Evansville, Fort Wayne, Gary, Greensburg, Hammond, Lafayette, Madison, Mishawaka, Muncie, New Albany, Oolitic, Scottsburg, Seymour, South Bend, Terre Haute, and West Lafayette. At Oolitic, he stopped briefly to shoot a few baskets with some children playing on a school yard. At New Albany, despite the continued temperatures in the thirties, Kennedy sat atop a convertible for a three-mile ride through town. Downtown at Pearl and Market Streets, Kennedy addressed an enthusiastic crowd of Democrats, saying he would hold the American-backed South Vietnamese leaders to a strong program of assuming more leadership and spoke out against organized crime, violence, and disorder plaguing the nation's cities.[14]

At Kokomo, Kennedy visited his campaign headquarters downtown and spoke from the lawn of the Howard County Courthouse. The Kennedy appearance was a big deal for Kokomo. "The warm sun, the high school band's pop music, and the drama of attempts to chase young enthusiasts off the roofs across the street held the crowd together," reporter Charles Bartlett wrote. "Then he appeared, sunburned, squinting and perched with his wife on the back of a convertible. He wore the look of a man who stepped into a warm pool as he descended into the swarm of admirers. The speech was short and distinguished, chiefly for the strong, clear voice which cut through the persisting hubbub and occasional heckles. He spoke tersely and with elaboration, responding more to the restlessness at the core of his crowd than to the thoughtfulness on its edges."[15]

At Fort Wayne, Kennedy spoke out against the violence and rioting still rocking the nation's cities and noted that America needed to change

INDIANAPOLIS STAR

Kennedy is flanked by his wife, Ethel, and Indiana campaign coordinator Gerard Doherty, during a victory celebration with his volunteers at the Sheraton Lincoln Hotel in Indianapolis, May 7, 1968.

"so everyone has an equal opportunity no matter where they live." He distinguished the problem of poverty as not one of race and noted that more whites in America lived in poverty than did blacks. He reserved his only criticism for the presumptive Republican nominee, Richard Nixon, who continued to elude requests to offer a specific plan to bring peace to Vietnam. "All [Nixon] said on Vietnam is that everybody should keep quiet," Kennedy said. "That's a good suggestion by somebody who doesn't have anything to suggest."[16]

At Terre Haute, Kennedy repeated his theme that Hoosier Democrats could play an important role in determining the party's nominee for 1968. "Indiana really can decide who is going to be the nominee of the Democratic Party," he said. "It's that important. Indiana can make that judgment. Not because it has 63 votes in the convention in Chicago. Not because of that, but because of the psychological effect of this primary. That's why it's so important that you listen to the candidates who are running for the Presidency of the United States—those who are genuine candidates—who

will come here and talk about the issues and debate them and discuss them with you."[17] Kennedy confirmed for the crowd that he had received a haircut before arriving in Indiana and followed the advice of a sign he saw as he landed at the Terre Haute airport that said, "Help Beautify America: Get a Hair-Cut."[18]

Making a quick stop in South Bend for its annual Dyngus Day celebration, reporters noted the crowds there were smaller and less enthusiastic than he encountered later in the day at both Michigan City and Gary. Enthusiasm could be found in pockets, however, as one report from South Bend indicated: "Kennedy grasped hundreds of outstretched hands from his moving car, but one held on too long," the Associated Press reported. "Kennedy was pulled to the pavement from the back seat of the slowly moving convertible. Kennedy hopped quickly back into the vehicle and moved on. Later, he exhibited a puffed upper lip."[19]

Reporters and others had begun pointing out Kennedy's tendency to pronounce the name of the state as "Indian-er," as he did in Columbus. By the time he reached Gary, Kennedy (accompanied by Mayor Richard Hatcher, who officially endorsed none of the candidates) had made a concerted effort to correct his speech, carefully denunciating, "I'm delighted to be here in Indiana. In-dee-an-uh!" he said. "There was some fellow from Massachusetts that was here the other day that called it 'Indian-er.' That was my younger brother Teddy. He looks like me, but I call it Indian-uh! And we're going to elect a President of the United States who knows how to pronounce the name of this state!" The crowd roared with approval.[20]

In Indianapolis, despite major addresses that made headlines in the state and nationwide, Kennedy did not skip retail politicking, spending his last day in the state before the primary hold-ing an early-morning coffee for teachers at the Hotel Sheridan-Lincoln and stopped in several predominantly black and working-class white neighborhoods in Indianapolis, including King Avenue and Michigan Street, the Speedway Shop-ping Center, Blake Street and Indiana Avenue, Twenty-first and Harding Streets, Twenty-sixth and Harding Streets, Twenty-seventh Street and Northwestern Avenue, Twenty-second and Tal-bott Streets, Thirty-ninth and Illinois Streets, the Glendale Shopping Center, the Meadows Shop-ping Center, the Eastgate Shopping Center, and the Southern Plaza Shopping Center. *Village Voice* reporter Jack Newfield quoted Kennedy as hav-ing been satisfied with his exhausting effort to gather Hoosier votes: "I like Indiana. The people here were fair to me. I gave it everything I had here, and if I lose, then, well, I'm just out of tune with the rest of the country."[21]

As the votes were tallied on that spring eve-ning in May 1968, it was clear a record number of voters (764,000) statewide had requested Democratic ballots. In the final tally, Kennedy polled 42 percent, while Roger D. Branigin kept McCarthy out of second place, garnering 31 per-cent to McCarthy's 27 percent. Reporters noted "the time of [Kennedy's] first-place finish and his surprisingly broad base of support gave the New Yorker's campaign a solid, if less than meteoric, boost."[22] Kennedy won nine of the state's eleven congressional districts, 56 of the 92 counties, and won 90 percent of the "Negro vote," yet still did well among white voters "and succeeded in the face of several handicaps. Indiana is basically a conservative state. The Democratic organization, labor-union leadership and the state's two largest newspapers did their best to torpedo Kennedy."[23]

In the final analysis, Kennedy's win did not settle the race or eliminate McCarthy or the

Humphrey challenge, but "it demonstrated his survival power in hostile territory."[24] McCarthy tried to put his best face on the loss: "We've test-ed the enemy now, and we know his techniques. We know his weaknesses."[25]

All of the excitement, energy, and atten-tion the Indiana primary battle created between Kennedy, McCarthy, and Branigin was soon a moot point. Kennedy went on to win subsequent primaries in Nebraska and California, but mo-ments after the California primary result was announced, Kennedy was shot and killed on June 5, 1968, as he exited a victory rally at the Ambas-sador Hotel in Los Angeles. He was buried three days later, eulogized by his brother, Ted, in Saint Patrick's Cathedral in New York City, his voice cracking with emotion as he said:

> My brother need not be idealized, or enlarged in death beyond what he was in life; to be re-

IHS, INDIANAPOLIS RECORDER COLLECTION, P 303

Kennedy informs a crowd gathered for a political rally at Seventeenth and Broadway Streets in Indianapolis that civil rights leader Martin Luther King Jr. has been shot and killed in Memphis, Tennessee, April 4, 1968.

membered simply as a good and decent man, who saw wrong and tried to right it, saw suffering and tried to heal it, saw war and tried to stop it. Those of us who loved him and who take him to his rest today, pray that what he was to us and what he wished for others will someday come to pass for all the world. As he said many times, in many parts of this nation, to those he touched and who sought to touch him: "Some men see things as they are and say why. I dream things that never were and say why not."[26]

Kennedy's assassination and McCarthy's inability to coalesce Democrats around his candidacy opened the door for Johnson's late-game stand-in, Vice President Humphrey, who later told reporters, "The President's withdrawal meant a very important decision in our lives. If I was ever going to run for President, I would want to do it now."[27]

Roger D. Branigin

In Indiana, for the second time in two consecutive election cycles, the state's governor, this time the popular Branigin, served as a stand-in for the "mainline" or "old guard" Democratic interests. Branigin told reporters that Johnson's surprise departure from the race "left candidates

Union leaders and local officials listen to a speech by Indiana governor Roger Branigin in Highland, Indiana, on April 27, 1968.

shadow-boxing in the ring, hunting for an issue. He left pundits speechless. And he left me a favorite son."[28]

"Known for his ready wit and lauded as one of the state's premier public speakers," according to historian Ray E. Boomhower, Branigin was a force to be dealt with all on his own—stand-in or not. The Franklin native attended Harvard for law school, but maintained a common-man's approach to his office and told Indiana audiences in the spring of 1968 that "national issues are not at stake here. What is at stake here is who is going to represent the state of Indiana in Chicago" at the Democratic National Convention.[29] Branigin said he sought to "project the most effective image for the state of Indiana and the national convention" and to do so "with prudence, good taste and good judgment." He added, "We don't know what the facts are going to be in August. The political situation now is very fluid, yet we have some guests in our midst who would have ourselves commit ourselves today. I believe we should not attempt to make any firm commitment for outsiders."[30]

The dramatic turn of events set in place an incredible and frenetic primary race that found Kennedy, McCarthy, and Branigin popping up in almost every city, town, and hamlet in the state almost every day in April and May leading up to the primary. Branigin had his work cut out for him, with McCarthy headed to Indiana with a strong wind at his back with impressive primary showings (sans Johnson) and the media focused mostly on the Kennedy-McCarthy matchup: "The Indiana confrontation will be [McCarthy's] first direct square-off at the polls with the formidable Kennedy and his first opportunity to prove himself as a genuinely viable presidential candidate," *Time* magazine analyzed.[31] Branigin frequently reminded his Hoosier compatriots that their vote

INDIANAPOLIS STAR

As Indiana's forty-second governor, Branigin set a record by vetoing 100 bills passed by the state legislature.

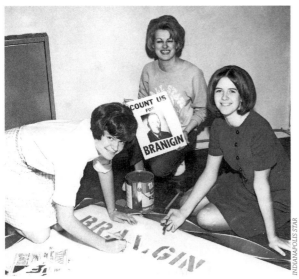

(Left to right) Karen Rariden, Annie Moore, and Carolyn Himes prepare campaign signs and posters at Branigin campaign headquarters in Indianapolis.

was too precious to be entrusted to the "alien hands of tourists and guests" from New York and Minnesota. "No one can speak for Hoosiers except a Hoosier at the national convention," Branigin said. "National issues are not at stake here. What is at stake here is who is going to represent the state of Indiana in Chicago."[32]

Branigin's campaign showed signs of its inexperience at the national level. Strangely, he turned down multiple requests to appear on national news programs to discuss his views along with Kennedy and McCarthy. It must have been a surreal experience for Branigin, just four years removed from his own successful campaign for the 1964 Democratic nomination (and eventual election) to governor, having to watch Indiana Democrats being wooed and choosing sides sometimes against him. As he shook hands in downtown Kokomo, Branigin told reporters that "I believe the majority of our people will support me" and once again referred to Kennedy and McCarthy as strangers to most of his fellow Hoosiers.[33] As the governor crisscrossed the state he knew

well—south to Salem and north to Hammond— he picked up important endorsements from the state's labor unions, but struggled to generate the media or public interest that Kennedy did. For the most part, Branigin took the high road and left State Democratic Chairman Gordon St. Angelo to take shots at his opponents, particularly Kennedy and his spending. His campaign headquarters inside the Claypool Hotel in downtown Indianapolis was advertised as more than an office. The Branigin campaign also planned to sell soft drinks, popcorn, hot dogs, and six-cent cigars.

Branigin also benefited from the vitriolic opinion Eugene C. Pulliam, publisher of the state's largest newspaper, the *Indianapolis Star*, held for Kennedy. The *Star* heavily promoted Branigin's campaign moves and trumpeted on its editorial pages questions about the amount of

Branigin reaches out to shake hands of Hoosier voters at a campaign stop in Delphi, Indiana, on April 22, 1968.

money the Kennedy campaign was expending—a likely exaggerated figure of $2 million. A *Star* editorial urging Hoosiers to support Branigin said such a vote would tell the nation that Indiana was not "for sale." Kennedy's spokesman, Pierre Salinger, said Pulliam's newspapers should be investigated for biased reporting, and Pulliam replied in kind: "Bobby Kennedy is like all spoiled children. When he doesn't get what he wants, he bellyaches."[34]

In the end, Branigin's take was pure Hoosier: "I got whipped. I got taken to the woodshed."[35] Upon the completion of his term as governor in January 1969, Branigin returned to his law practice in Tippecanoe County and died on November 19, 1975.

Eugene McCarthy

If ever a man's candidacy represented the best-laid plans gone awry, it was that of McCarthy, a soft-spoken and thoughtful man from Minnesota. As he started his run for the presidency in 1968, based almost solely on his opposition to continued American involvement in the Vietnam War, most viewed McCarthy's effort as symbolic and a balm for unhappy opponents of the war who did not want to support President Johnson, but also found no respite among the Republicans. No other Democrats were willing to challenge Johnson, including Robert Kennedy, but McCarthy was. McCarthy may have never had very serious ambitions about being elected president, but he was rock-solid serious about turning the Democratic Party around to opposing the Vietnam War.

Focusing his entire effort on the first-in-the-nation New Hampshire primary and backed by an army of antiwar and pacifist college students who got "Clean for Gene" (cutting their long hair short to go out and talk to voters on Mc-

INDIANAPOLIS STAR

U.S. Senator Eugene McCarthy laughs as he prepares to answer a question from a reporter at a press conference at the Marott Hotel in Indianapolis on April 22, 1968.

Carthy's behalf), the little-known Minnesotan rolled up 42 percent of the New Hampshire vote to Johnson's 49 percent. Johnson had won the primary, but in winning by such a narrow margin put in motion quickly spreading speculation that despite his impressive array of domestic achievements, his attachment to and identification with the war in Southeast Asia was likely to cripple Johnson's chances of winning a second four-year term. With Johnson's surprise withdrawal from the race, McCarthy continued to roll up impressive primary wins, winning contests in Wisconsin, Pennsylvania, and Massachusetts leading up to the Indiana primary on May 7. By then, Kennedy had entered the race, and McCarthy's campaign dynamics were forever changed. His army of more than 7,000 imported college students—so warmly received and engaged by New Hampshire voters—were no contest for Kennedy's barnstorming of Hoosier voters (backed by Kennedy largesse that kept his advertising running day and night on Indiana television and radio stations). The enthusiasm of the college students seemed to energize McCarthy personally, as reporters noted when he addressed a group of them at Butler University in Indianapolis as colleagues: "I do not exactly thank you," he said, "because we are serving a common and mutual cause."[36]

Also sharing the cause with McCarthy was a handful of Hollywood celebrities that his campaign dispatched across the state, headlined by popular film actor Paul Newman, who was already known in the state for his love of the Indianapolis 500. Other celebrities appearing in Indiana on behalf of McCarthy included actress Myrna Loy, actor Dustin Hoffman, comedian Garry Moore, and singing duo Paul Simon and Art Garfunkel. Often speaking from the tailgate of a station wagon, it was not always clear if audiences were showing up to hear what Newman had to say about McCarthy, or to get a look at the famous actor. The welcome was not universal. The *South Bend Tribune* reported that Newman's seventeen-year-old son Scott (working as a McCarthy campaign volunteer in South Bend) was struck in the head by a thrown rock at his father's

McCarthy supporters at a rally for the candidate in Indianapolis's University Park on March 18, 1968.

car. The *Tribune* report included details that "200 voting-age housewives, many in hair curlers and with baby strollers, waited patiently in the drizzling rain" at the Town & Country Shopping Center in Mishawaka, where Newman was scheduled to speak. Recognizing his celebrity status may be getting in the way, Newman declined to sign autographs and instead earnestly attempted to engage voters with information about McCarthy's agenda.[37]

Newman told an Indianapolis neighborhood gathering, "I feel I'm the better man, win, lose or draw, for having been part of [the McCarthy] campaign. I wear this button with considerable pride and, for the first time, with a great deal of hope."[38] It was one of eleven stops in Indianapolis, four in Lafayette and West Lafayette, and one in Crawfordsville, all on one busy day in April. Neighborhood stops were smaller, but Newman drew more than 3,000 for a stop at Purdue University and another 1,000 for twilight remarks he made near the Montgomery County Courthouse in Crawfordsville. Standing atop a station wagon tailgate, Newman declared, "I am indifferent to your political persuasion. I am not a public speaker. I am not a politician. I'm not here because I'm an actor. I'm here because I've got six kids. I don't want it written on my gravestone, 'He was not a part of his times.' The times are too critical to be dissenting in your own bathroom."[39] McCarthy himself made a stop at Crawfordsville about a week later, jumping aboard a busload of bowlers headed for a tournament to shake each of their hands and spending about an hour walking around the downtown business district greeting potential voters.[40]

Beyond his inability to access the amounts of money that the Kennedys could tap, McCarthy's lack of experience as a national candidate often showed. McCarthy himself admitted to a *News-*

INDIANAPOLIS STAR

McCarthy talks to newsmen at Indianapolis's Weir Cook Airport during a campaign visit for the Indiana primary on April 25, 1968.

week reporter that by his own estimate he was wasting more than 80 percent of his time in Indiana talking to small groups of people in very out-of-the-way locations and making little headway. In one instance, an unplanned stop by McCarthy to play a pick-up baseball game with reporters delayed him so long that 250 people waiting at his next stop dispersed before he could arrive.[41] One magazine described McCarthy's Indiana effort as "more than normally disorganized," with McCarthy appearing late for speeches and finding small and unresponsive audiences.[42] One writer noted, "Senator McCarthy [headed] for the Whitlow Community Center where he talked to precisely 12 people. During the afternoon, he visited Kokomo, Peru, Wabash, Marion, and Gas City. It was snowing at Peru. Most of the partisans were under the age of 15. At one point,

the audience consisted of three farmers in a tool shed."[43] At Peru, a handful of adults and almost 150 schoolchildren withstood a mix of cold snow and rain at the Miami County Courthouse. Local Democrats in "Circus City" presented him with a commemorative box of "circus sawdust." He commented, "Take a good look at me for the next two weeks, then decide who you want to be president. If you are satisfied, vote for me," a line of children followed him as he went in and out of stores on the courthouse square, shaking hands.[44] At Kokomo, McCarthy attended what was referred to as "an interracial tea" at a private residence and shook workers' hands at the General Motors plant. After a quick tour of the Howard County Courthouse downtown, McCarthy greeted about 250 schoolchildren and then stopped by his local campaign headquarters. At Wabash, a mostly

McCarthy addresses a crowd of supporters at University Park in Indianapolis on March 18, 1968.

INDIANAPOLIS STAR

college-age audience heard him opine, "I feel like a relay runner. Every time I go around the track, they put another candidate in against me."[45]

As he went along, McCarthy seemed to gain more footing, telling reporters at Vincennes that he believed that "as Indiana goes, I think that's the way the Democratic Party [convention] will go in Chicago."[46] But he had barely made the statement and was quickly backtracking from it with new polling showing Kennedy pulling ahead of both him and Branigin. McCarthy's objective was a new one, analysts noted. "McCarthy could no longer simply run *against* Johnson; he now had to run *for* himself, a very different prospect," author Dominic Sanbrook wrote. McCarthy seemed to understand the change, telling Hoosiers: "I think the question becomes one of which of us you think could best administer the government—which one of us could best unify the country and provide what is called leadership for the days which are ahead."[47]

In the closing days of the campaign, McCarthy reminded a South Bend audience that his campaign represented "a politics of participation and grass-roots activity by millions of Americans" and retorted that Humphrey—via the Branigin candidacy—was "offering us homogenization—unity without validity and variety." Of Kennedy, McCarthy said, "He seems to be seeking to reconcile Americans by setting up special committees representing ethnic and economic groups—an approach which assumes that divisions in America are somehow inevitable and permanent."[48] McCarthy's remark reflected the growing support Kennedy seemed to be rolling up among the state's black voters in Indianapolis, Fort Wayne, Evansville, South Bend, and the Calumet Region. McCarthy was unable, and perhaps unwilling, to openly court black voters. Hurt in part by his 1965 vote in Congress to

maintain poll taxes in southern states, McCarthy noted his small-town Indiana audiences did not want to hear about civil rights. Talking up civil rights and pursuing black voters "was pointless," McCarthy said in the years after the Indiana campaign concluded. "I couldn't get the Negro votes away from Bobby Kennedy. I could have moved into the ghetto and stayed in them through the whole campaign."[49]

During the campaign, however, McCarthy bristled at a reporter's suggestion during an appearance at Michigan City that he might take a stronger stand on civil rights. "I've been taking a strong stand on civil rights since 1949," he said testily. "I've supported every civil rights bill in the Senate. I've supported the old civil rights and the new civil rights, so I don't know what you mean by a stronger stand. I've been committed to civil rights for 20 years without hesitation and without apology."[50]

Undeterred by his small crowds, McCarthy casually toured La Porte's downtown, stopping for coffee and a donut at one shop and accepting the gift of a new tie from a men's store owner there. In Michigan City, a stop at a local elementary school was unsuccessful, the principal unwilling to allow him to come inside to visit students and also unwilling to allow the students to come out to greet him.

Later at Valparaiso University, more than 1,000 audience members listened politely to a McCarthy speech. "I did appreciate what I thought was a genuine love affair between me and the students," he said. "I became a little bit worried at one point when someone came in and tried to make it into a triangle," the latter remark a reference to Kennedy's campaign in Indiana.[51] Openly acknowledging the financial lead Kennedy enjoyed in spending for television and radio ads, McCarthy said, "I believe if we can raise as

Guests In The House—!

INDIANAPOLIS STAR

Editorial cartoon "Guests in the House!" that appeared on the front page of the April 24, 1968, edition of the Indianapolis Star *depicting Kennedy and McCarthy as unwelcome visitors attempting to woe Indiana voters. Governor Branigin is depicted warily watching the two interlopers.*

much as one-fourth as much money as Senator Kennedy intends to spend, we can tell the people of this state all they need to know about me."[52]

In a separate appearance at Anderson College, McCarthy reminded his audience that although Kennedy had joined the race, the basic issue of the campaign—the war in Vietnam—remained the same. Sounding a theme that America was facing many tests at home and abroad, a small audience showed up at Markleville, and about a hundred supporters waited for him outside the Henry County Courthouse in New Castle.[53]

On Primary Day, although the vote tally showed Kennedy's name, personality, and money had made all the difference, McCarthy's sup-

porters were wildly supportive of the senator as he made his concession speech at the Claypool Hotel in Indianapolis. He reminded them to cheers of appreciation, "I didn't come here to dismiss the troops," and pledged his campaign would go forward.[54]

In spite of Kennedy's assassination in June, the party turned away from McCarthy at its raucous 1968 convention and nominated Humphrey as its presidential candidate. McCarthy entered the 1972 Democratic presidential primaries, but withdrew after early losses. In 1976 he staged an independent candidacy for the presidency, but received less than 1 percent of the national vote. In 1982 he sought a Senate nomination from Minnesota, but lost. Ten years later, in 1992, he entered the Democratic primary in New Hampshire, and although gaining attention for the novelty of his effort, secured few votes and ended the effort soon thereafter. He died as a result of Parkinson's disease at a retirement home in Washington, D.C., on December 10, 2005, at the age of eighty-nine.

George C. Wallace

By 1968 Wallace's standing among voters was more legitimate than perhaps anyone wanted to admit. Skipping a try at his party's nomination, noting that there was not "a dime of difference between the Democrats and the Republicans," Wallace trudged on, carrying the banner of the conservative American Independent Party in the general election. A *New York Times* analysis of his August and September 1968 visits to industrial northwest Indiana was typical of the "increasingly segregationist appeal" Wallace's campaign inspired.[55] Wallace attacked what he referred to as "left-wing, liberal beatniks," who he said had pressured passage of the Civil Rights Act. "You people are going to treat some national politicians to a big surprise in November," he said.[56]

During his August Lake County swing, Wallace had polished his populist themes of the little man versus the government. He asked "the little folks" in Hammond to help him bring down "the smart folks who have been looking down their noses at you in Washington."[57] Wallace's campaign packed in four hundred supporters at twenty five dollar a plate to the Ukrainian Hall, among them "a white-haired retired carpenter, who would not give his name [to reporters], who arrived in a short-sleeved shirt with a certified check for $100 sticking out of his pocket." The man told a *Times* reporter, "I have children and grandchildren and I don't want them growing up in this country the way it is now, the way newspapers like yours made it."[58]

Later, at a well-attended rally of about 4,500 at the Hammond Civic Center Hall, Wallace denied he was a racist, noting that, "They say it is racist to oppose those federal guidelines that would tell us how to run our lives. Well, when you can't talk about upholding the Constitution without being called a racist, this country has come to a sad day."[59] He added, "They say it's racist what I say, but they're really using this as an excuse to defend their effort to get control of your heart and mind. Some of these liberal newspaper editors are saying one reason the Wallace philosophy is so popular is he says what the people want to hear. And they're saying it in such a manner that it sounds like what the people want is bad. Their trouble is these liberals created a Frankenstein in this country, and now their chickens are coming home to roost and they don't like it."[60]

Wallace had reason to focus on the Calumet Region, having carried both Lake and Porter Counties in the 1964 Democratic primary. "His tour here was a clear success," the *New York Times* reported. "There is little doubt that the Wallace campaign on the American Independent Party ticket is gaining momentum nearly everywhere. He is drawing large and enthusiastic crowds, 'rebels' Mr. Wallace calls them, even for here in Indiana."[61]

Returning to Hammond a month later in September, Wallace said "The people are tired of big government in Washington pushing them around. And the liberal left-wing beatniks have captured the leadership of government and denied us a choice."[62]

The 1968 version of the Wallace campaign had grown up a bit, often having the candidate appear with a band from Alabama's Troy State University rather than gospel or country singers typical of his first campaign. Wallace also arrived more in style than before, now aboard his own chartered DC-7 aircraft. His campaign reported distributing more than three million Wallace bumper stickers nationwide, but still only requested a minimum $5 donation from supporters at its Indiana rallies. Reporters noted that the Wallace rhetoric had been toned somewhat, but when protesters during a Fort Wayne rally began shouting a four-letter word at the governor, he responded: "What you need is a good haircut" and added, "These free-speech folks know all sorts of four-letter words except w-o-r-k and s-o-a-p."[63]

On October 3, 1968, Wallace announced his running mate, retired General Curtis E. LeMay, former chief of staff for the U.S. Air Force and head of the Strategic Air Command. The news conference where Wallace announced LeMay's selection was considered a fiasco by most observers. Showing his hawkish ways and inexperience with national political campaigns, LeMay walked into a hornet's nest on day one when he entertained reporters' questions about the possible use of nuclear weapons in Vietnam, saying, "There are many occasions when it would be most efficient to use them," but adding that he did not think they

During his independent run for the presidency in 1968, George Wallace blasted foreign aid, describing it as "money poured down a rat hole" and called for allies of America to pay more for their own defense.

were needed in Vietnam. LeMay's remarks were startling:

> If necessary, I would use anything we could dream up to end the war. I know I will be misquoted, it has happened before. I'll be damn lucky if I don't appear as a drooling idiot whose only solution is to drop atomic bombs all over the world. I think to most military men, a nuclear weapon is just another weapon in the arsenal. Nuclear war would be horrible. To me, any war is horrible. To me, if I had to go to Vietnam and get killed with a rusty knife or get killed with a nuclear weapon, I would rather get killed with a nuclear weapon.[64]

Wallace, standing next to LeMay as he made the hawkish remarks, quickly attempted to distance himself from the nuclear comment, with Wallace declaring he "flatly ruled out" the use of nuclear weapons in Vietnam and added, "General LeMay shares my views completely."[65] Wallace described LeMay as "a man of great courage," and he admired him for his "willingness to speak his mind. The keystone of our campaign is courage."[66]

Moving on to friendly political territory, Wallace and LeMay made one of their first joint appearances at a noon rally on Monument Circle in Indianapolis, an event that drew 10,000, a mix of supporters and detractors. Wallace's campaign aides told reporters that Indiana played a key part in his plan to win enough Electoral College votes to play a role in deciding the election, and that Indiana ranked fifth out of all states in terms of financial support given to their independent candidacy. "Mini-skirted young women passed buckets through the crowd, seeking cash contributions," the Associated Press reported. "Observers said they collected a substantial amount."[67] While Wallace supporters cheered his speech—and his introduction of LeMay (who did not speak)—as was typical of a Wallace rally, loud protesters were present. Police reported nine arrests of "Democratic Party demonstrators" and that "at one point, police scuffled with a group of 20 to 30 anti-Wallace demonstrators."[68] During his speech, Wallace hit on familiar law-and-order themes, shouted at one heckler that "Boy, you need a haircut!," and said he believed if current peace negotiations with North Vietnam were to fail the war should be "concluded militarily with conventional weapons."[69]

In mid-October, Wallace stopped off for a rally before about 5,000 loud supporters outside the Vanderburgh County Courthouse, where he had two items on his agenda, trying to make news by announcing he was dispatching his running mate on a "fact finding" mission to Vietnam and railing against national pollsters. On the former point, Wallace said his running mate would make a four-day trip to South Vietnam and report back in time for a "major address" Wallace planned to give on television on October 20. "I am particularly interested in getting the views of the American servicemen in Vietnam and, of course, General LeMay will consult leaders of the various branches of the military service now engaged in the Vietnam fighting," Wallace said. "When he returns, General LeMay will make a full report to

me and I will then make a report to the American people."[70]

LeMay's credentials to assess a military operation were not in question. The Wallace campaign hoped LeMay's mission to Vietnam would remind voters of a similar trip taken by General Dwight D. Eisenhower in 1952 to Korea as he sought the presidency. LeMay, however, lacked the standing or respect that Eisenhower had engendered over the course of his military career, and his increasingly hard-line approach in Vietnam worried many voters. Wallace, on the other hand, was articulating a more middle-of-the-road approach, suggesting he would support the Paris peace talks.

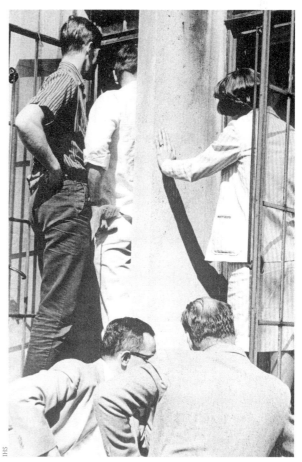

Spectators scramble to find perches to hear Wallace speak at an appearance in Indiana during the 1968 election.

Trumping his own news from his Evansville appearance, Wallace took the occasion to rant against national pollsters and what he viewed as "big eastern moneyed interests" that conspired to rig the polling against his third-party effort and wanted Nixon to win. Wallace claimed a conspiracy was in the works and suggested a congressional investigation of "rigged" national political polling was appropriate, not suggesting this idea, however, until his poll numbers began to drop dramatically after naming LeMay as his running mate. "In my opinion [the polls] are rigged," Wallace said in his Evansville remarks. "Mr. Nixon gave it away up in Michigan when he said that George Wallace would start to go down," saying that Nixon would not have made such a statement if he did not know in advance of a "fix" in the polling numbers.[71]

Wallace declared, "I have no inside knowledge of what the next national poll is going to show, but if the next one doesn't show me going down, then the following one will, and if that one doesn't, then the one after that. You can count on it! I told you in September it was going to happen, and I think it's about to happen."[72]

Despite his rocky start, LeMay was set loose by the Wallace campaign for independent appearances, mostly in safe places in the South and in Indiana—quick stops in Indianapolis and Evansville on October 27. LeMay focused his comments on the peace talks under way between the Johnson administration and the North Vietnamese government. He said there were "indications that the North Vietnamese have no intention of ending the war" and that his tour of American military operations in Vietnam had convinced him the war was the most important issue in the election. He said that American troops were doing "remarkably well" in fighting the war and that sufficient American forces, combined with the South Vietnamese military, existed to "win the war" and added, "I think the South Vietnamese *are* winning the war" and objected to the war's critics who he said viewed themselves as "the ruling class" of the nation.[73]

Hubert H. Humphrey

As the unpredictable and troubling events of 1968 unfolded, among those who found their life changed dramatically was Vice President Humphrey. First elected in the Johnson landslide of 1964, the former U.S. senator from Minnesota likely had no plans to be leading the Democratic ticket four years later. But time and events had changed dramatically. By the time the Democratic National Convention opened in Chicago in August 1968, the political landscape was set for Humphrey's unexpected run.

Johnson was a lame-duck president, engulfed by the Vietnam War. The strongest contender to succeed him as the party's leader, Robert Kennedy, was dead from an assassin's bullet, and still standing was Humphrey, who had made his way to the nomination via a circuitous course—collecting delegates from stand-ins originally signed up for Johnson—and left to preside over a heartbroken and deeply divided party and nation. Historian Carl Solberg wrote that Humphrey, despite a strange array of circumstances unfolding, traveled the country in the weeks following Johnson's withdrawal as a candidate, seeking to present himself, as he termed it, "the candidate as man and statesman, a leader of wisdom and compassion." As he officially entered the fray, Humphrey called up an interesting turn of a phrase noting that, "Here we are, the way politics ought to be in America, the politics of happiness, the politics of purpose, the politics of joy, and that's the way it's going to be, all the way, from here on out."[74]

Solberg described Humphrey's statement as words "uttered in an outburst of shared exhilaration. . . . It was pure Humphrey, bubbly, extemporaneous, but it was an inappropriate note to strike when wooden boxes are arriving from Vietnam, when flags still flew at half-mast for the murdered Dr. King, when wild-eyed students were occupying the president's office at Columbia University, when the cities ripped apart by racial hatred quaked in fear of renewed arson and looting."[75] Criticism of Humphrey's take on "the politics of happiness and joy" was swift and ugly. Newspaper editorial writers across the nation lampooned the remarks, while Kennedy (still campaigning in Indiana) told reporters that "it is easy to say this is the politics of happiness— but if you see children starving in the Delta of Mississippi, despair on Indian reservations, then you know that not everyone in America is satisfied."[76] Kennedy was relentless in his attack on Humphrey's take, telling voters, "You can't say we have the politics of joy and happiness when you look at television sets and see rioting and violence in our cities," and then, "I don't think we can be joyous and happy when 562 American boys were killed in Vietnam last week."[77]

Humphrey's campaign struggled from the start, from the fact he was the nominee basically as a result of being the last man standing and also from a highly fractured and ugly Democratic National Convention in Chicago. Polling showed that despite claims to the contrary, the third-party candidacy of Wallace seemed to be hurting Humphrey more than Nixon, as the GOP candidate showed a consistent lead in the polling. Wallace likely was drawing off the last of the Democratic votes in the South that would eventually move to the Republican Party. Humphrey denied claims he was engaged in any bidding process to woo away Wallace electoral votes. The

campaigns of both major party nominees worried that Wallace's presence in the race could throw the election into the House of Representatives with no one candidate winning the necessary 270 electoral votes on Election Day. Humphrey was adamant, "I for one would not make such a deal," he said at Evansville. "There will not be a Humphrey-Muskie deal with Wallace and General LeMay." Nixon made similar denials, and in the end no such deals were needed as Nixon won a clear Electoral College victory.[78]

In an October 1968 appearance in Evansville, Humphrey came out swinging, comparing Nixon to a "mechanized kewpie doll that says what he is programmed to say when his powerful clients push the button"[79] and declared he was "willing to go any place, to talk to anyone to see that an honorable peace comes in Vietnam."[80] Sensing that time was slipping away and polling continued to show Nixon in a solid position to win, the vice president reminded his audience of 14,000 Democrats at Roberts Memorial Stadium that "the greatest single threat of a Nixon victory is what he would do with the [Supreme] Court"[81] and that the next president will likely have at least one, if not more than one, high court appointment, placing progress on social justice and economic development at risk. Humphrey's welcome in Evansville had been positive, so much so that a writer for United Press International declared that "it was one of those nights that could easily make Hubert H. Humphrey forget that he is trailing in the polls, is desperately short of money, and faces a difficult uphill battle to beat Richard M. Nixon."[82]

Prior to his speech, Humphrey used his Evansville news conference to once again challenge Nixon and Wallace to a three-way debate. Humphrey said he had even paid for and reserved television time on the CBS network for the upcoming Sunday night to make it happen. "He is afraid to ask the real Richard Nixon to stand up," Humphrey said. "I'd be afraid too to put a computerized, mechanized, slicked-up Madison Avenue kewpie doll that says what he is supposed to say when his powerful clients push the button up against a flesh and blood human candidate who is willing to stand for something."[83] During his speech at the Roberts arena, Humphrey drew loud approval when he accused Nixon of lacking the courage to debate and place his views before the American people and vowed to "smoke Mr. Nixon out—with the help of the American people—who want to know what they're voting for."[84]

Humphrey also revived earlier claims that Republican senator Strom Thurmond of South Carolina was serving as a "lifeline" between the Nixon and Wallace camps in an effort to control the election and to assure southern voters that a vote for Nixon would help ensure their wishes for a conservative Supreme Court. Humphrey's warning about what the court could look like under Nixon or Wallace was well received among the partisan Democratic crowd, but his attempts to ingratiate himself to Hoosier basketball fans fell flat. First acknowledging he was happy to be in Indiana, "a basketball hotbed," a few unexpected boos caused him to add praise for the University of Evansville's Purple Aces team as well. A few more boos persisted, and Humphrey shielded his eyes from the spotlights and finally noticed a large section of "Kentucky for Humphrey" signs in the crowd, and added, "Kentucky has had many fine teams as well," at last settling the friendly rivalry issue, alive and well on the banks of the Ohio River, the Indiana-Kentucky state line.[85]

Elaborating on his Vietnam policies, Humphrey underlined his "go anywhere, talk to anyone" pledge and said to polite applause, "I'm going to be a peace President, first and foremost.

I have placed on top of my agenda—if peace has not come by that time—the full authority, the full prestige of the Presidency to bring about peace speedily in Vietnam."[86] The Evansville visit was to be Humphrey's only campaign stop in Indiana for the fall 1968 campaign, polling confirming on Election Day that Indiana was solidly Republican territory. On January 20, 1969, Humphrey stood by and watched his opponent, Nixon, take the oath of office as president.

Edmund S. Muskie

The broken and challenged 1968 Democratic National Convention in Chicago did not provide Senator Edmund S. Muskie of Maine much of a major introduction to the national stage as Humphrey's running mate. His nomination finally confirmed well into the wee hours of the night, most television viewers had gone to bed, and Muskie's convention acceptance speech went mostly unnoticed. In the weeks that followed, Muskie was dispatched far and wide to help lift the seriously sagging Humphrey campaign.

Muskie's campaign swing brought him to Indianapolis for a speech at Lawrence Central High School and to South Bend for two speeches on September 11, 1968, one before students at the University of Notre Dame and another before the West Side Democratic Club. Before the students gathered at the Stephan Center, Muskie attempted to counteract a growing sense of defeat and abandonment among the young in 1968, a year that had brought more violence in Vietnam and even more at home. He said his advice to young people was that young people need to understand the following:

> the part that each individual citizen plays in our public life, that has made our country great. There are many groups in our country today, the young, the disadvantaged, who are

crying out for a voice in the making of public policy, who are urgently seeking a role in the making of public policy. . . . I think for all of those who are now crying out for a role to play in our democracy, and who dislike many of the things they see in our governmental structure, that who, as a consequence at least expressing if they don't believe, expressing distrust in the system itself, that they ought to take a look at America when it was new. When America was new, it was made up of a people who believed in freedom. It was made up of people who understood that freedom didn't work unless we worked at it. It was made up of people who trusted each other. It was made up of people who could disagree with each other, but who finally understood that it was necessary to resolve their differences and to act.[87]

Turning to the Vietnam War, Muskie drew loud applause when he acknowledged that many Americans disagreed about which way the nation should progress, but declared, "There are some things we are agreed upon about the war. The first is that it must end . . . that it must be settled, not by a military victory, but by a negotiated settlement. . . . We are going to end this war and we are going to end it in a way that I think most Americans can accept. But we cannot end it in such a way as to create greater risks to those of our boys who are fighting in Vietnam and we cannot afford to end it by running out on our responsibility."[88]

Across town at the West Side Democratic Club, Muskie proclaimed himself to be "just one of you and you know that," playing up his Polish American ancestry in a part of Indiana that would understand and respect such a connection. "I come from the same place, from the same origin, the same stock," Muskie said. "We all came to this country, or our forefathers did before us, to find opportunity, to make a living, to build a home, to raise a family, and to make a place where they

could have a better life than we do. Now, that is the kind of thing that is understandable to every immigrant or every son of an immigrant, or anyone who has ever come to this shore looking for opportunity."[89] He ended his remarks by noting that he believes he was selected to run for vice president "because I am just average like all of us. That is what this country was made for, the average people, and we're going to keep it that way. That's why I'm running for Vice President."[90]

At Lawrence Central High School in Indianapolis, Muskie addressed a student assembly and joked, "I appreciate your enthusiasm and your applause, but I have had enough experience with school audiences to suspect that part of it has to do with the fact you are getting out of classes! At least that is the reason we used to apply to speakers when I was a student in high school."[91] Muskie addressed the desire of all young people to make a difference in the world, but added, "But this is a more clouded and more complex society today and it is understandable, and I get it is true, that you feel more frustrated about the things that you don't like and less able to do something about them."[92] After encouraging the students to get involved politically, Muskie said he wanted to stop "the filibuster" and instead open the floor to questions—a bold move with high school students in 1968.

Asked whether he supported lowering the voting age to eighteen, Muskie answered that if the young people were allowed to be married at age eighteen and are expected to be fully responsible under law for their conduct, then yes, he supported lowering the voting age, noting that he had five children of his own, and he would be happy to see his oldest—a nineteen year old—being allowed to vote. Another student asked the senator whether he was bothered by the Secret Service officers who surrounded him as he campaigned. "I think that kind of security is the sort of thing Americans are always restive about, and I am also," he said. "I don't like the limitation on my freedom, but I think some of it is apparently necessary in the turbulence of our present times and I couldn't ask for any better men to do this than those who have been assigned to me."[93] Muskie also addressed concerns that Wallace's third-party candidacy would throw the election into the House of Representatives and said voters could avoid that possibility by focusing on choosing between Humphrey and Nixon only.

Another provocative student question recalled the images surrounding the Democratic Convention in Chicago, where street riots were put down by police. Who is to blame for the riots, a student asked? "I think there is blame on both sides," said Muskie. "The police were provoked . . . and this is what you can expect whenever any people undertake to settle the question not by reason, but by emotion. I hope that out of Chicago we learned that lesson—that when you've got this kind of situation, you don't have all guilt on one side and all innocence on the other—you have human beings who can be provoked by what happens instantaneously. You can have perfectly peaceful citizens who react violently. This sort of thing happens. Violence begets violence."[94]

As expected, questions soon turned to the Vietnam War, and Muskie stuck to his standard remark that "I want the Vietnam War ended and ended as quickly as possible," a line which drew heavy applause from the students. A follow-up question about the involuntary draft caused Muskie to note, "I think the present system is filled with inequities. That is understandable because it was developed to meet the manpower needs of total war, which was World War II. . . . Now, this kind of system in

this conflict has inequities. I am troubled by the voluntary draft system . . . and I am interested in the idea of what is called the lottery system, of volunteers with some restriction on deferments. It is the deferments, after all, which work in the inequities. . . . But I think a lottery system, covering a greater limitation of deferment is perhaps the direction we ought to move."[95]

Muskie made one more stop in Indiana on October 18, 1968, to speak before a Jefferson-Jackson Day Dinner in Hammond, with the reality of a Republican victory lingering on the horizon. Defending the Johnson-Humphrey record, Muskie said:

> For the elderly, we have provided the security of Medicare, for the young we have increased five-fold the federal investment in education, for the poor we have provided jobs and housing, for the citizens who are black we have committed ourselves to the request for dignity and equality. I wouldn't suggest that in the next four years, if Humphrey and Muskie are elected, that there will be no more crime, no poverty, no racial tension. These problems are inherent in a modern, crowded, diverse, urban society. But we will continue what we have done, and four years from now, we will have made even greater progress toward the solution of the problems.[96]

Richard M. Nixon

Perhaps derisively, the return of Nixon in 1968 prompted a popular phrase that the candidate himself never uttered—"He's tan, rested, and ready." The reference to being "tanned" was an obvious throwback to concerns that Nixon had looked pale when compared to a tanned John F. Kennedy in the 1960 television debates. The term fit. Nixon had learned his political lessons with his painful, razor-thin loss in the 1960 presidential race and an even more devastating 1962 loss to Edmund G. "Pat" Brown in the

California governor's race. In reality, Nixon had never stopped campaigning, working hard for Republican congressional candidates in the 1964 and 1966 elections and forever keeping his name in contention. The field of competitors included California governor Ronald Reagan, Michigan governor George Romney, and New York governor Nelson Rockefeller, representing the right and left wings of the GOP, respectively. Nixon took to the middle road and successfully captured the nomination.

In Indiana's May GOP primary, Nixon was unopposed with the names of Reagan and Rockefeller absent. It mattered little. All of the attention in the spring of 1968 was focused on the Democratic battle in the Hoosier State among Kennedy, McCarthy, and Branigin. Nixon, however, was unwilling to leave the state untouched, going into his unopposed primary coronation and dropped into Indianapolis, Gary, Fort Wayne, and Evansville a week before the May 7 primary. His timing was perfect. Nixon quickly gathered up all of the state and national media already on the ground in the state, particularly harmful to the cash-strapped McCarthy and Branigin campaigns. As an added measure, Nixon hinted wherever he went that "crossover" Republican voting in the Democratic primary was not only illegal, but unethical, and urged his fellow Republicans to stay with him. The move cut into any progressive Republican votes that McCarthy or Branigin may have hoped for to stem the rising Kennedy tide. Political analysts suggested that the Nixon camp viewed Indiana as a means of regaining credibility and dominance in the party after a good showing by Rockefeller from write-in votes in the Massachusetts primary.[97]

At Evansville, Nixon showed he was ready for the fall campaign, taking clear aim at the Democrats in the race and one who was not, incumbent president Johnson. Addressing an audience of about 2,000, Nixon said, "If you want to stop the rise in crime and reverse the trend, you can't go ahead with the namby-pamby politics of the administration or of those who would follow them. You need new leadership and we will provide that leadership. The men who supported the policies that got us into trouble shouldn't be entrusted with getting us out of trouble."

Earlier, at Concordia College in Fort Wayne, Nixon addressed the Vietnam situation and once again was vague and general in his remarks, focusing on his belief that presidential candidates should be circumspect in their criticisms of American policy in Southeast Asia.[98] As Nixon put it, "Let's not destroy the chances for peace with a mouthful of words from some irresponsible candidate for President of the United States. Put yourself in the position of the enemy. He is negotiating with Lyndon Johnson and Secretary [of State Dean] Rusk, and then he reads in the paper that . . . a potential President of the United States will give him a better deal than President Johnson is offering him. What is he going to do? It will torpedo those deliberations. It will destroy any chance of bringing the negotiations to an honorable end. The enemy will wait for the next man."[99]

In Gary, 4,000 excited and noisy Republicans jammed a hangar at the Gary Municipal Airport for a quick stop by the former vice president. Nixon told his rapt audience, "When I speak of new leadership, I mean more than just a change of men. I mean a change of ideas, a change of philosophy, and a change of direction for America."[100] Among those greeting Nixon at the airport was Gary mayor Richard Hatcher, who had won national headlines just a year earlier becoming the first black mayor of a large American city. Reporters nearby said Hatcher and Nixon had a friendly exchange, with Nixon saying, "I recognize you from your picture. I sincerely appreciate this bi-partisan welcome."[101]

For his brief speech, Nixon said, "If you remove the great issue of Vietnam, the three men running on the Democratic side of the ballot this year are like three peas in a pod. They represent a political philosophy of the past. They can offer us nothing but more of the same. And America can't stand any more of the same—we need new direction."[102] Addressing ongoing concerns about civil unrest and economic struggles in the nation, Nixon said the Democrats' approach "has failed. We must enlist the mighty engine of free enterprise, to build new housing for our citizens and to create jobs that will take people off welfare rolls and put them on payrolls. The time for new action is at every level of the government now. Yours is the decision. Here in this great state, in this great country, you have the chance to change the direction for America with new and vital leadership."[103]

At Indianapolis, Nixon emphasized his proposed plan for tax incentives and loan guarantees to address poverty and to rebuild inner-city neighborhoods in order to "remove the ceiling from black aspirations." Nixon said he would provide leadership that could "reconcile the races and rescue the poor" via new efforts aimed at self-reliance and self-respect to replace "dismaying cycles of despair and dependency."[104]

"The old ways have failed," Nixon said, "because the crisis of the old order is not the crisis of today. In the ruins of downtown Washington, or Detroit and of Newark, lie the ruins of a philosophy of government that has outlived its origins and no longer speaks to its time."[105]

Nixon's one and only stop in Indiana for the fall campaign was brief and uneventful. The GOP had locked up the state and focused its efforts elsewhere in a three-way race against Humphrey and Wallace. Staying focused on keeping any conservative Republican voters from drifting away to Wallace's campaign, Nixon made a quick stop in Indianapolis on September 13, 1968, for a speech before a loud crowd of 7,000 supporters at Monument Circle. Nixon challenged claims made by Johnson and Humphrey that poverty was a leading cause of crime in the nation's cities. Describing Humphrey as "tragically naïve" about "the crime crisis that grips America," Nixon added, "Just like the administration of which he is a part, Mr. Humphrey has exaggerated and over-emphasized poverty in the country as a cause of crime. Certainly, conditions of poverty are the traditional breeding ground of criminals and we should not diminish our efforts to eliminate these conditions. But contrary to what this administration believes and preaches, the 'War on Poverty' is not a war on crime and it is no substitute for a war on crime."[106] Nixon cited statistics that showed growing gross national product and personal incomes "while major crimes have almost doubled" and "dangerously accelerating uses of drugs among the teenagers of affluent Americans," Nixon continued. He concluded, "There are thousands of hardened criminals . . . who steal and rob, not because they are living in conditions of poverty, but because they can make a comfortable and successful career out of crime. I say doubling the conviction rate . . . would do far more to cure crime in America than quadrupling the funds for Mr. Humphrey's 'War on Poverty.'"[107]

Successful in 1968 in a way that had eluded him eight years earlier, Nixon became the nation's thirty-seventh president and visited Indiana for the first time as chief executive on February 5, 1970, to launch his "New Federalism" initiative in friendly territory. As he told reporters as he stepped from Air Force One at the Indianapolis airport, "I stand here again in Indiana, a state that has been very good to me politically, as was pointed out by the Governor [Edgar Whitcomb]; where we did get the biggest majority in 1968."[108] The president directly addressed a group of schoolchildren present for his arrival: "I know that when you get back to school, they are going to want you to give some report on what was said," he stated. "And I did a little studying before coming here, knowing that in your social studies or history classes that you will wonder what Indiana had to do with the federal government through the years in various ways."[109]

Later, Nixon arrived at the new City-County Building as the guest of Mayor Richard G. Lugar (dubbed "Nixon's favorite mayor") and the mayors from ten other American cities. Essentially, New Federalism represented the administration's effort to transfer not only responsibility, but also funding, for various social programs to the state and local level. Nixon brought a lineup of cabinet members with him to the Indianapolis confab, including Attorney General John Mitchell, Secretary of Commerce Maurice Stans, Secretary of the Interior Wally Hickel, Secretary of Housing and Urban Development George Romney, Secretary of Transportation John Volpe, Director of the Office of Economic Opportunity Donald Rumsfeld, Presidential Science Adviser Doctor Lee DuBridge, and Special Counsel to the President for Urban Affairs Daniel Patrick Moynihan.

The president said, "I think I have spoken in every small and medium-sized town in this whole state over the past 22 years, but I want this Cabinet to know Indiana and to love it as I do."[110] Later elected to six terms as senator from Indiana, Lugar said he believed he earned the title as Nixon's "favorite mayor" in a *Washington Post* article that noted the president often cited Indianapolis and Lugar as examples of urban policies

working well. Lugar said he never promoted the label and likely was glad later he did not as the Watergate scandal enveloped and overtook the Nixon administration. "Nixon never called anybody his favorite mayor," Lugar said.[111]

At the City-County Building, Nixon called his visit "unprecedented" and "historic" and said the idea for the Indianapolis confab had grown out of a meeting at the White House involving several of the nation's mayors to address domestic policy issues. "Today, we are bringing Washington to Indianapolis, and to the cities, and this is a theme I wish to emphasize. I believe that it is time that, after over a century and a half of power flowing from the people and from the local communities and the states to Washington, D.C.—let's get it back to the people and to the cities and to the states where it belongs—because the power should be there, because I firmly believe that the people know best. The people of Indianapolis know what is best for them. The people of Indiana know what is best for them."[112] Nixon said he wanted members of his cabinet to know what the needs of citizens are, what they think, and what we ought to do. "That is why we are here," Nixon said.[113] As impressive as the Council of Urban Affairs meeting had been in Indianapolis, people who knew Nixon well said he was rarely interested in the views of a wide swath of people. "Anytime you see R.N. polling people, you can be sure he's not seeking their opinion," said former Nixon said staff member John Sears. "He just wants to substantiate his own views. He's not the kind of man who comes to a situation without an opinion."[114]

Nixon also addressed the ongoing war in Vietnam, noting that "everybody here is interested in the problem of peace in the world, and I can only say this: There is nothing to which this administration is more dedicated, nothing to which I am more dedicated than to continue to make the progress we have made in bringing men home from Vietnam rather than sending them out to Vietnam. I look forward to a time when we will not only end that war, but where we can build a solid basis for peace in the future, a peace we can keep, a peace that Americans can look proudly on because it was a peace that was won, not over anybody else, but a peace providing for the right of people to determine their own future."[115]

The president was back in Indiana on October 20, 1970, before a large and mostly partisan Republican audience in Fort Wayne. Nixon hoped to boost the campaigns of Congressmen Richard Roudebush for the Senate and E. Ross Adair for Roudebush's House seat (both lost their bids). Under a banner of "Welcome to Nixon Country," the Concordia High School band played for the overflow crowd at the Fort Wayne Coliseum. Acknowledging that he was not a candidate in 1970, Nixon told his audience it was essential that Indiana voters promote Roudebush to the Senate (over his Democratic opponent Vance Hartke) and Adair to the House, contrasting their level of support for his political agenda to that of the state's two Democratic senators—Bayh and Hartke. "This is the time for the people of Indiana and the people of the nation to look at the various candidates to determine whether or not they feel those candidates have been carrying out their wishes or whether they have been working in interests that (you) do not approve of," he said to heavy applause.[116]

The president's lengthy remarks focused consistently on the ongoing and increasingly unpopular war in Vietnam. "When we came into office, we confronted a problem," he said. "We had had a war that had been going on for five years—men had been going out to Vietnam in increasing numbers for five years, casualties had been going up. Five-hundred and fifty thousand Americans were in Vietnam. There was no plan to bring any of them home. The casualties were 300 a week. There was no peace plan on the table . . . and then we came into office. We went to work."[117] Nixon said his plan consisted of a rock-solid commitment to "not cut and run," but focused on "instead of sending more Americans to Vietnam, they have been coming home by the tens of thousands, and they will continue to come home under this administration."[118] The president also defended the highly controversial move—"a hard decision,"—to "destroy enemy sanctuaries" in Cambodia and Laos and reported that "as a result of that, the casualties that were 300 a month had been cut down so that it is the lowest in four years."[119]

In particular, Nixon singled out Bayh and Hartke for their support of the Hatfield-McGovern Resolution that called for all U.S. forces to be removed from South Vietnam by December 31, 1971. The resolution ultimately failed under heavy opposition from the Nixon administration, but in 1970 the president used it to remind Hoosiers that he needed more Republicans to occupy the heavily Democratic House and Senate. "This is the time for the people of Indiana and the people of our nation to look at the various candidates to determine whether or not they feel those candidates have been carrying out their wishes or whether they have been working in the interests that they do not approve of," Nixon said, a return to GOP themes that Bayh and Hartke acted like conservatives at home, but sided with liberals once in Washington. Nixon said he agreed with anyone who said it was time to end the war in Vietnam, but "the problem is not to end the war. The problem is to end the war in a way that will discourage those who might start another war.

LIBRARY OF CONGRESS

President Richard M. Nixon

And I say, let's end this war in a way that will win the peace and have a full generation of peace for the young Americans."[120]

Nixon said he felt compelled, due to the large number of high school and college students in his audience, to address the issue of "student protest and student unrest." He noted that on television news each night, "You see a picture of young America, usually violent, bombing, burning, shouting obscenities, shouting speakers down. And you get the impression that maybe that is what young America is. I want to tell you, I have been around this country a bit . . . and I have got news for you. They aren't the majority of young Americans today and they aren't going to be the leaders of America tomorrow."[121]

Repeating his previously designed prototype of "the great silent majority in America," Nixon urged Indiana residents "to stand up and be counted for America. The answer, my friends, the answer is for the great silent majority of Americans—and I believe there is a majority, a great silent majority—to speak out and you can speak out in a very quiet, but with a very powerful voice, the most powerful voice in the history of mankind . . . by walking into that polling booth and you vote."[122]

Before leaving Fort Wayne, Nixon diverted from his normal plans and went to speak to an overflow audience of supporters who could not fit into the 13,000-seat arena. "I wanted to say to all of you that I just couldn't miss the opportunity to come down here and to thank you so much for staying here in this room, and giving me the chance to greet you," Nixon told the overjoyed and enthusiastic Hoosiers. He urged them to "when you think about what is wrong about America, don't overlook what is right . . . we have freedom, we have opportunity, a spirit we have had from the beginning. Believe me, we have still got it in America. Don't you ever forget it! You have got it here in Indiana!"[123]

The reason for Nixon's next visit to Indiana, in June 1971, was one near and dear to his heart. Nixon's mother, Hannah Milhous, was born in Indiana and spent the first dozen years of her life on a Jennings County farm near Butlerville. The president could not resist an invitation from a local junior historical society who had convinced state officials to erect a historic marker commemorating the county's place in Nixon family history. It seems Nixon's mother was often on his mind, and not only during his political trips to Indiana in which he often invoked her name and her Hoosier roots. During his last speech in the East Room of the White House on August 9, 1974, as he gave an emotional speech to members of the White House staff just before departing the presidency in disgrace, he reminded those assembled that "nobody will ever write a book, probably, about my mother. Well, I guess all of you would say this about your mother—my mother was a saint. And I think of her, two boys dying of tuberculosis, nursing four others in order that she could take care of my older brother for three years in Arizona, and seeing each of them die, and when they died, it was like one of her own. Yes, she will have no books written about her. But she was a saint."[124] The reference to a book never being written about his mother was viewed with disdain by many, some noting it reflected Nixon's bitterness that one of the best-selling books at the time was a biography on the life of Rose Kennedy, mother of President Kennedy, Nixon's political foe. While no book had been written about Hannah, a group of young Hoosiers *had* made the president's heart lift with their idea of honoring her with a historic plaque in Jennings County.

Accompanied by Governor Whitcomb, Nixon

arrived on a warm summer day on June 25, 1971, via a helicopter that landed at Jennings County High School in North Vernon. While there, Nixon greeted those gathered and was "temporarily thrown off guard by a pretty 5-year-old girl in a blue dress" who wanted to ask the president about the just-completed White House wedding for his daughter, Tricia, a month earlier. Editors at the *North Vernon Plain Dealer* were excited about Nixon's visit, declaring it not only "the biggest thing that has happened to Jennings County since Morgan's Raiders tried unsuccessfully to breach Union defenses around Vernon back in the Civil War days," but also that his visit "may well be the most impromptu visit that a president ever paid anywhere."[125]

Reports issued following Nixon's visit indicated that local officials were given less than thirty-six hours notice that the president planned to visit, which caused a brief panic involving the Jennings County High School Band. All of its members were out of school for the summer and all of their uniforms were being dry-cleaned. The band persevered, learning to play "Hail to the Chief" in just a few short hours, happily mixing it in with "Back Home Again in Indiana" for Nixon's courthouse appearance.[126]

After a brief stop at the high school, Nixon's motorcade made its way from North Vernon to the adjacent county seat, Vernon, where an overflow crowd (estimated by local media to be as large as 10,000, but by the *Washington Post* to be as small as 4,000) waited on the grounds of the Jennings County Courthouse and braved warm and humid temperatures to hear the president. He told the crowd, "I want all of you to know that this day does mean a great deal to me. I have traveled to much larger cities in America and in the world, but none where I felt that I was more welcome than right here in Indiana."[127] Nixon

reminded his audience that famed British Prime Minister Winston Churchill had visited America in the past, eager to learn the roots of his American mother's homeland. Nixon said he recalled reading Churchill's remarks that "I cannot say that this is my father land, but I proudly say that this is my mother's land." Nixon added his postscript: "And so I say today, I am very proud to be in my mother's land here in the heart of Indiana!"[128]

Indiana never left the heart of his mother, the president said. "From the time that I knew her until she died—and she was eight-two years-old—my mother always spoke with great affection and love about back home in Indiana. . . . She loved the farm. She loved, too, the seasons. You know, my native California does not really have seasons. I remember that I was not in snow to feel it until I was 15 years old. My mother used to miss the change in the seasons, the fall, and the snow, and the summer—a warm day like this."[129] The president said his mother brought with her from Indiana "a deep religious faith, a faith that communicated to us in her quiet way, the Quaker way." He added to applause and laughter, "She had, also, a very great interest in politics. After all, anybody from Indiana has got to be interested in politics, as you can be sure."[130]

Nixon's visit to small-town Indiana, referred to as "Nixon country" by reporters for the large political majorities Hoosiers had always given him, came just days after the *New York Times* began publishing a series of secret Defense Department documents about the conduct of the war in Vietnam. Officially titled, "United States—Vietnam Relations, 1945–1967: A Study Prepared by the Department of Defense," the document eventually became known simply as the Pentagon Papers. Leaked to the media by a contracted military analyst in the Defense Department, Daniel

Ellsberg, the incident marked the beginning of a series of clandestine political maneuvers that befouled the Nixon administration via his Committee to Re-Elect the President. There was no mention of the Pentagon Papers incident during Nixon's Indiana stop, as the *Washington Post* reported, "President Nixon returned to Nixon country Thursday to receive the kind of welcome presidents dream of but seldom get anymore. At the Jennings County Courthouse in Vernon, a small farming community southeast of Indianapolis near where his mother was born, the President dedicated a plaque to her memory."[131]

Nixon's prepared remarks briefly touched on the ongoing war in Vietnam, always a part of the president's speech and his repeated commitment to end the war with honor. He concluded by saying, "I think my mother would want [me] to leave another thought with you. It is very simply this: That what really counts is the spirit of a country and the spirit of an individual. I told you what our heritage was. My parents were not rich people, but they were hard workers. We had to work our way through school, but they helped. And while they were certainly not rich in terms of material goods, they were very rich in character and spirit. And that meant a great deal to all of us as we grew up. Let's look at America today in that same context."[132]

As Nixon departed Jennings County, he made a "snap decision" to forgo the helicopter that had brought him from Indianapolis and instead decided to make the seventy-mile trip back to the capital by car, disappointing a crowd of about five hundred gathered in downtown Indianapolis expecting him to arrive by helicopter.[133] Later in Indianapolis, Nixon spoke at a dinner honoring retiring Purdue University president Frederick L. Hovde and then continued on to Chicago. A month later Nixon shocked the world with news he planned to visit mainland China—the first American president to ever do so.

Spiro T. Agnew

Not long after joining Nixon on the Republican ticket, Maryland governor Spiro T. Agnew, a virtual unknown nationally, began the two-fold task of introducing himself to the country and taking up the traditional role of bolstering Nixon's chances, especially in friendly locales for the GOP such as Indiana. In Indianapolis Governor Agnew accepted the invitation of Eugene C. Pulliam, publisher of the *Indianapolis Star* and the *Indianapolis News,* to appear before a "bipartisan" luncheon of five hundred Indiana business and political leaders at the Indianapolis Athletic Club. The presence of Indiana governor Roger Branigin, a Democrat, helped seal the bipartisan label on the event, although the audience was decidedly a Republican group and seemed supportive of Agnew's attack on the nation's antipoverty programs that he said in some instances had been placed into the hands of "ignorant and dishonest persons," citing instances of financial irregularities in New York and Chicago.[134]

"One of our nation's greatest problems results from the flow of the rural poor to the big cities," Agnew said. "Billions have been spent foolishly in an attempt to cure this situation in which the poor have been crowded into ghettos and dire unemployment has been created."[135] The major problems undermining poverty relief in the United States included spending money on projects "sponsored by people with the loudest voices," reluctance by aid recipients to take available jobs, and lack of standardization of poor relief systems across the states, causing an "invasion of reliefers to the 10 states that pay the highest allowances." He added, "I think it's time for the people in the government to say, forthrightly and honestly, to the militants who wish to run their own destinies and control their own heritage, to the students who are demonstrating in the universities that yes, we will listen to your complaints, you may give us your symptoms, but we will make the diagnosis and we the establishment, for being a part of, will implement the cure."[136]

"The thing that's causing the trouble in this country today is dissent that is out of control," Agnew said. "Nobody is willing to say we have the expertise, we are prepared, we have the responsibility, we are in control and we're going to do the job and if you don't like it, work within the system to change it. Don't try to destroy the system. It's worked pretty well all these years."[137]

Agnew defended Republican messages on law and order, saying they are not a form of oppression, but forms of freedom and compassion. "I am not endorsing poverty and oppression," he said. "Crime is an illegal method to get a share of the system and riots are an illegal method to destroy the system."[138]

Once elected vice president, Agnew set about replacing the title of "Spiro Who?" with one praising his role as the Republican Party's top political fund-raiser. That effort brought him to Indianapolis in September 1970 for the midterm elections and to bolster the coffers of the Indiana Republican Party. During a full day of activities, Agnew headlined a cocktail party reception as well as a rib dinner for 4,000 at the state fairgrounds to benefit the U.S. Senate candidacy of Congressman Roudebush (who was seeking to unseat Democratic incumbent Hartke). Outside the fairgrounds, a little-noticed group of protesters carried signs that read "Hippies for Roudebush," although the Republican faithful greatly outnumbered any naysayers. A reporter assigned to cover Agnew's appearance for the *Valparaiso*

Vidette-Messenger gushed that the crowd "came, saw and was conquered by one of the most dynamic men in American history."[139]

"My friends, I believe the people of Indiana reject the permissive, weak-kneed, short-sighted, free-spending approach of your senior senator 100 percent," Agnew said. "I believe [Hartke] represents some people in Berkeley, California, some people in Madison, Wisconsin, and some people at Columbia University in New York, but he does not represent the views of the people of Indiana."[140] Agnew drew a standing ovation when he declared, "Congressman Roudebush has stated that if a person burns down a building or otherwise destroys property, whether on a campus or elsewhere, he is no longer a demonstrator, he is a lawbreaker and ought to be treated as such."[141]

Hartke, who had emerged under Johnson and continued under Nixon as an outspoken critic of the Vietnam War, supported "topsy-turvy reasoning" that was "absolute poppycock" in how to address the issues at hand in Southeast Asia. "My friends," Agnew said, "the people who have proven themselves consistently wrong do not deserve to be your leaders. You have a President from Middle America, who is proud of his roots. I hope you will send a Senator to Washington who will help him carry out the mandate Indiana gave him two years ago—Dick Roudebush."[142]

Agnew made two more stump speeches in Indiana for Roudebush's campaign, although protesters stole the show when the vice president attempted to give a speech in late October before an audience at Hammond. In his speech, Agnew accused Hartke of "currying the favor of the revolutionary left" prompting about seventy-five "young people" in an audience of more than 3,000 to make a loud exit as Agnew tried to speak. The vice president halted his speech for several minutes and then added bitterly, "Let's forget these people who don't understand what democracy is all about" and urged voters to support law-and-order Republican candidates to "sweep that garbage" of demonstrators out of society.[143]

On Election Day, Hartke squeaked out a 50.1 percent victory over Roudebush, as the Democrats maintained a narrow majority overall in the Senate.

Ronald Reagan

Just one year into his first term as governor of California, Ronald Reagan had already earned darling status among conservative Republicans—first for his strong and articulate support for Goldwater's unsuccessful 1964 campaign and also for his movie-star looks and made-for-television charm. During the spring of 1968, Reagan joined New York governor Rockefeller in sticking a toe into the waters of the Republican nomination for president. Although not a candidate in the May Republican Primary in Indiana, Reagan accepted the invitation of Indianapolis Republicans for a fund-raising dinner and addressed 2,600 party faithful over a $100-a-plate dinner at the Indiana State Fairgrounds. Reagan's appearance came just seven days after Kennedy's assassination in Reagan's home state of California and dominated the governor's remarks and allowed him to showcase his "law and order" pedigree for conservative Hoosier Republicans.

Calling Kennedy's murder in Los Angeles an act of "senseless savagery" and reflective of "the violence of war in the middle east imported by an alien," Reagan resisted the suggestion that the act was the result of a sick society. Of Kennedy's death coming just weeks after bullets silenced King, Reagan said, "Perhaps we are sick, but not in the way they mean it. We are sick with grief, sick with anger, and sick of what has been al-

lowed to go on in this nation for too long a time. In this week of tragedy, six policemen in Chicago have been killed in the line of duty. Two Marine officers were murdered in cold blood in our nation's capital because of the uniforms they wore. It is time for an accounting of the stewardship that has left us a nation where this can happen—a nation whose President [Johnson] cannot reveal his travel plans among his own people because of fear for his personal safety."[144]

Reagan taunted the Kennedy-Johnson administration's efforts to lead the space race, noting that "we talk bravely of sending a man across space to the moon, but we cannot guarantee a citizens' safety on a walk across the park." Reporters noted that Reagan's remarks were more serious than normal and included none of his regular Hollywood stories and anecdotes that audiences enjoyed. "Right now our minds are on the breakdown in law and order, the erosion of old and valued standards, and the violence that stalks our land and we turn to those who are supposed to be our leaders," Reagan said. "The only answers we get are classics of over-simplification. Make it more difficult for the legitimate citizen to retain a gun and assassinations will no longer take place, legislate prejudice out of all men's hearts, confess that we are filled with hatred for our fellow men. But there already was a law against the assassin having a gun and most of us do not feel prejudice or hatred. It is time to review our heritage, time to seek the truth and face the facts. It is time to get angry."[145]

The anger, Reagan said, reflected "a revolution in favor of tyranny" under way in America advanced by "a tiny minority of radical malcontents with a hodge-podge variety of causes rebelling against the people's freedom. They demand that we be made subject to a government which will have the power to redistribute our earnings and possessions, while it denies us the right of even self-protection. In pursuit of this goal, legislators are subjected to coercion by endless marches, demonstrations and acts of mass civil disobedience."[146]

Reagan's remarks reflected his particular role at the head of the nation's largest public university system in California—the site of hundreds of antiwar and other protests. Reagan offered provocative remarks to the level of free speech displayed on campus: "In the name of academic freedom and even free speech some, claiming privilege because of intellectual attainment, encourage students in their charge to deny cabinet members and even the vice president the right to speak on the campus. At the same time, they arrogantly demand that it be offered as a forum for Communist speakers and domestic radicals. If permission is denied, they threaten to burn down the school. They advocate increased welfare not by pleading that we become more charitable, but because the fruit of our toil is not ours to control."[147]

Turning to the ongoing struggle in Vietnam, Reagan declared that "it is time to tell friend and foe alike we are in Vietnam because it is in the national interest to be there and whether it offends friend or foe, we are going to do what has to be done, beginning now." He cautioned, however, that while Americans valued peace, they did not value it at any price. "If [an American's] son is called to fight, he wants his government to say it will be worth winning and he will be allowed to win," Reagan said. "He wants to be told that wherever he walks in the world his country's flag will defend his God-given right to life and liberty."[148]

Reagan also took on Johnson's "Great Society" agenda noting that "quick and easy answers" calling for more money for education and for

social programs to end poverty were not working. "Aid to the poor has increased 290 percent in the last eight years," he said. "Still, your chances of being murdered, maimed or robbed this year are one out of 70. One out of five families will be the victim of a criminal this year. One boy in six will get in trouble before he is 18. Crime is increasing six times as fast as the increase in population." Reagan added, "It is time to stop being our brother's keeper and try being our brother's brother."[149]

Nelson A. Rockefeller

New York governor Nelson Rockefeller sniffed out the possibilities for the 1968 Republican nomination in much the same manner he had in 1960 and 1964, talking about a candidacy and seeking levels of support that could propel him forward. In the end, the result was the same—a Rockefeller campaign was a nonstarter that would make little to no impact. Leaving former vice president Nixon alone for the Indiana primary, strangely Rockefeller kept his options open and visited the state in July just before the Republican National Convention in an attempt to snatch away some of the state's delegates. Rockefeller made the pitch that despite Nixon's complete sweep of the Indiana primary, the commitment of Indiana Republicans only need hold for one ballot at the convention and that Nixon was still as much as seventy delegates away from having sewn up the nomination on the first ballot. "At some point the pledge runs out," Rockefeller said. "At that point, I expect to get some of those delegates." The governor said he had heard reports of possible shifts in the Hoosier delegation, and he enjoyed the support of a powerful political and business force in the state, banker and financier J. Irwin Miller of Columbus. As the *New York Times* reported, "Rockefeller displayed his customary optimism as he campaigned in this northwestern Indiana city [Gary], where the skyline is dominated by sulfurous smoke from the stacks of vast steel mills."[150] The Gary appearance, which included black community leaders, was hurt by a delay in Rockefeller's plane getting to Indiana and part of the audience for a campaign luncheon departing before he arrived. Regardless, he pressed on, flying next to Indianapolis to tape a local television show and meet privately with Republican convention delegates. In the end, it was a wasted effort, as Indiana Republicans stayed with Nixon as he easily rolled up the party's nomination for the second time in a decade.

Strom Thurmond

For the 1968 fall campaign, the Republicans enlisted some unusual help to boost Nixon's campaign in Indiana, though polling indicated he needed little help among Hoosiers and was sailing to an easy grab of the state's thirteen Electoral College votes. Regardless, the Nixon campaign wanted no erosion of support to Wallace's third-party candidacy, which was making some headway among southern voters. Enter Senator Strom Thurmond. An amazing character in American politics, the South Carolina politician was a Blue Dog Democrat for most of his life until 1948, when he launched an ill-fated third-party candidacy for the presidency under a states' rights Dixiecrat ticket. By 1964, with the civil rights battle fully engaged, Thurmond officially switched parties and jumped onboard with Goldwater's quixotic GOP campaign.

Thurmond, who set records for the longest one-man congressional filibuster and the record for oldest serving member of the U.S. Senate at age ninety-four, and the second longest cumulative tenure in the U.S. Senate (47.5 years), could still make news in the 1968 campaign. During a September 1968 stop on the Notre Dame campus, Thurmond told a group of about 500 students that Nixon "is a man who will stand up to Communism and wind up the war in short order."[151] Adding that he favored "equal opportunities for everybody, but not favoritism for anyone," Thurmond's remarks made less news than the reaction to them. Moments into his comments, Dewitt Flemming, a Notre Dame student and member of the Afro-American Society of Notre Dame, stood up and said, "Senator Thurmond, you have a very distinguished record, a record distinguished in racism and bigotry. Since the beginning of your political career you have been an advocate and exponent of the inherent right of the American citizen as put forth by the Constitution. At the same time, you have been a leader in the camp of those who would deny the black man these same fundamental rights. It is for this reason that the Afro-American Society of Notre Dame denounces you and your philosophy."[152] With that, about twenty-five students stood up and walked out. Thurmond did not respond directly to the student protest and instead restated that "every man should be given a job either by private enterprise or by the federal government" and that "jobs are better than welfare handouts."[153]

10

The Watergate Era, 1972–79

Richard M. Nixon

For the 1972 campaign, President Richard Nixon correctly calculated that Indiana was a sure thing for the Republicans and skipped the state entirely, instead dispatching Vice President Spiro Agnew and other GOP surrogates to the state. While Nixon campaigned vigorously at times, with polls showing him enjoying a comfortable margin over his Democratic challengers, his re-election campaign was a limited proposition. Nixon's historic February 21–28, 1972, visit to the People's Republic of China, and his May 22, 1972, summit in the Soviet Union with Russian leader Leonid Brezhnev, reinforced his ideas about a Rose Garden campaign and meant a fifty-state effort was out of the question.

One of the president's surrogates to Indiana in October 1972 was his twenty-three-year-old daughter, Julie Nixon Eisenhower, who attended an Indianapolis rock concert sponsored by a group known as Young Voters for the President. "I don't think anyone in my family is being complacent about the campaign," she said in response to reporters' questions about why her father had skipped campaigning in Indiana. She was focused, she said, on the effort to reelect her father with the help of "selfless, working young Americans" such as those she was greeting in Indiana.[1]

Julie also deflected questions related to Senator George McGovern's claims that the Nixon administration was "the most corrupt in history." She said, "I've made it a practice during the campaign not to make any comments on charges. I think my father's record speaks for itself."[2]

During 1972, beyond his notable trips to China and the Soviet Union, Nixon sought to shore up politically what he correctly viewed as an emerging Republican coalition of traditional conservatives and southern Democrats that were growing increasingly disenfranchised with the more liberal and progressive views of the national Democratic Party. While Alabama governor George Wallace's campaigns continued to stunt Nixon's approaches, the president's friendship and alliance with former Texas governor John Connally (who served as Nixon's Secretary of the Treasury and switched from the Democratic to the Republican Party), buttressed his outreach to southern conservatives via statements opposing federal court intervention to racially integrate the nation's schools and increased bombing of North Vietnamese targets and strategic mining of that country's ports.

Although reelected with almost 60 percent of the vote nationally, and an equally impressive

Nixon meets in the Oval Office with singer/entertainer Sammy Davis Jr., the newest member of his National Advisory Council on Economic Opportunity, July 1, 1971.

LIBRARY OF CONGRESS

showing in Indiana, the next twenty-one months for the Nixon administration were overrun by troubling questions about the president's knowledge of, or participation in, the Watergate affair and the subsequent cover-up. Nixon's attentions were deeply divided during his last months in office between a scandal that was quickly engulfing his administration, but also a stagnant economy and little progress in Vietnam. In January 1974 the Senate Watergate Committee issued subpoenas requesting more than 500 audiotapes secretly recorded at the White House, a request the president continued to fight, citing executive privilege.

In the midst of this struggle, Julie became ill during a meeting with her editors at the *Saturday Evening Post* in Indianapolis in February 1974. First Lady Pat Nixon and Julie's husband, David Eisenhower, grandson of President Dwight D. Eisenhower, immediately flew to Indiana to be at her bedside. Eventually diagnosed with suffering from internal bleeding and severe pain caused by an ovarian cyst, Julie talked to her father by phone before and after a minor surgery and was released from the Indiana University Medical Center days later. On February 18, 1974, Nixon asked Air Force One to divert his return flight from Alabama to Washington, D.C., to stop by Indianapolis to pick up his daughter. As David Eisenhower wheeled Julie from the hospital, followed by a line of doctors and nurses, the Nixons followed and shook hands with each of the medical staff present. The president was overheard telling some of the nurses, "I've always said doctors are important, but nurses are indispensable. Thank you."[3]

Nixon's Indianapolis stop came during a particularly troubling period in his presidency. On February 6, 1974, a House committee had voted to grant broad subpoena powers to Special Prosecutor Archibald Cox to compel the White House to release dozens of audio tapes made in the Oval Office, a request with which Nixon had previously refused to comply.

In the weeks and months that followed, the president was buried under the realities of the Watergate scandal as congressional support continued to erode and a House committee considering impeachment had voted to go forward on three articles of impeachment. On August 8, 1974, Nixon offered unprecedented remarks to the nation via a televised special address. He declared:

> In all the decisions I have made in my public life, I have always tried to do what was best for the Nation. Throughout the long and difficult period of Watergate, I have felt it was my duty to persevere, to make every possible effort to complete the term of office to which you elected me. In the past few days, however, it has become evident to me that I no longer have a strong enough political base in the Congress to justify continuing that effort. As long as there was such a base, I felt strongly that it was necessary to see the constitutional process through to its conclusion, that to do otherwise would be unfaithful to the spirit of that deliberately difficult process and a dangerously destabilizing precedent for the future. But with the disappearance of that base, I now believe that the constitutional purpose has been served, and there is no longer a need for the process to be prolonged. I would have preferred to carry through to the finish, whatever the personal agony it would have involved, and my family unanimously urged me to do so. But the interests of the Nation must always come before any personal considerations. . . . I have never been a quitter. To leave office before my term is completed is abhorrent to every instinct in my body. But as President, I must put the interests of America first. America needs a full-time President and a full-time Congress, particularly at this time with problems we face at home and abroad. To continue to fight through the months ahead for my personal

LIBRARY OF CONGRESS

Nixon meets with Soviet Union leader Leonid Brezhnev at the White House, June 18, 1973.

vindication would almost totally absorb the time and attention of both the President and the Congress in a period when our entire focus should be on the great issues of peace abroad and prosperity without inflation at home. Therefore, I shall resign the Presidency effective at Noon tomorrow.[4]

Gerald R. Ford

In late July 1974, during the final days of the Nixon administration, Vice President Gerald Ford made a noteworthy visit to Indiana barely six months into his new post to support the campaign of his friend, Congressman David W. Dennis of Muncie, a Republican member

of the House Judiciary Committee, which was considering articles of impeachment against Nixon. Dennis left Washington and the ongoing hearings for the Muncie campaign appearance as Ford made his thirty-eighth stop of the 1974 campaign to try and hold off expected significant GOP losses in the November election.

While speculation ran rampant that the Nixon presidency was near its end, Ford told his Indiana audience that impeaching the president would have "a very, very bad impact" on the nation and the world. "I can say from the bottom of my heart that the President of the United States is innocent. . . . He is right," Ford said. He noted that he had read all of the transcripts of the testimony before the Judiciary Committee and talked with individual members of the panel. Ford declared, "Not all, but a substantial amount of the effort against the President, is an attempt to try to undo the election results of 1972 and don't you forget it."[5] Ford, like many Americans, was reluctant to believe the president had done anything wrong, until evidence would eventually raise serious questions about the ethics of the Nixon administration and Nixon himself.

Less than a month after his Muncie stop, Ford took the oath of office as the nation's thirty-eighth president of the United States on August 9, 1974, following Nixon's resignation. In humble remarks resonant of his entire public life, Ford told the nation, "This is an hour of history that troubles our minds and hurts our hearts. Therefore, I feel it is my first duty to make an unprecedented compact with my countrymen. Not an inaugural address, not a fireside chat, not a campaign speech—just a little straight talk among friends. And I intend it to be the first of many." He added:

I am acutely aware that you have not elected me as your President by your ballots, and so I ask you to confirm me as your President with your prayers. And I hope that such prayers will also be the first of many. If you have not chosen me by secret ballot, neither have I gained office by any secret promises. I have not campaigned either for the Presidency or the Vice Presidency. I have not subscribed to any partisan platform. I am indebted to no man, and only to one woman—my dear wife—as I begin this very difficult job. I have not sought this enormous responsibility, but I will not shirk it. . . . In all my public and private acts as your President, I expect to follow my instincts of openness and candor with full confidence that honesty is always the best policy in the end. My fellow Americans, our long national nightmare is over. Our Constitution works; our great Republic is a government of laws and not of men. Here the people rule. But there is a higher Power, by whatever name we honor Him, who ordains not only righteousness but love, not only justice but mercy. As we bind up the internal wounds of Watergate, more painful and more poisonous than those of foreign wars, let us restore the golden rule to our political process, and let brotherly love purge our hearts of suspicion and of hate.[6]

Ford's voice broke only once, as tears welled in his eyes, but he recovered quickly and said, "In the beginning, I asked you to pray for me. Before closing, I ask again for your prayers, for Richard Nixon and for his family. May our former President, who brought peace to millions, find it for himself. May God bless and comfort his wonderful wife and daughters, whose love and loyalty will forever be a shining legacy to all who bear the lonely burdens of the White House."[7]

Ford subsequently granted Nixon a full pardon for any crimes against the nation on September 8, 1974. It was a controversial move, but one Ford defended for the remainder of his life as necessary for binding up the nation's wounds from Watergate. In the aftermath of Nixon's res-

ignation and the Ford pardon, Republican prospects for the looming 1974 midterm elections began to look quite poor. Ford visited Indiana for the first time as the commander in chief on October 16, 1974, just over sixty days after assuming the presidency for an Indianapolis campaign dinner before more than 5,000 sponsored by the Indiana Republican State Committee—an event mostly designed to boost the Senate campaign of Indianapolis mayor Richard G. Lugar, who hoped to unseat incumbent Democrat Birch Bayh (Bayh won the election).

Ford opened his remarks by acknowledging that he remained an unknown commodity to many Americans—having never run for or been elected either vice president or president—and now having served in both offices. "Frankly, I want to be visible, and I want to be an accessible President," Ford said. "And obviously I need it. Let me tell you why. As I was walking through the lobby, a very friendly lady came up to me, shook my hand and said, 'I know you from somewhere, but I just can't remember your name.' So in a friendly way, I tried to help her out, I said, 'I am Jerry Ford.' She said, 'No, but you are close.'"[8]

Ford heaped praise on Lugar and urged the Republican faithful to redouble their efforts to help him defeat the large amount of out-of-state money coming into Indiana in support of Bayh's re-election campaign. He also was praiseworthy of Governor Otis R. Bowen, but joked, "I had planned to meet with Doc [Bowen] at the White House a few weeks or a month or so ago, but I found out that like so many doctors these days, he doesn't make house calls any more. So, I have come to see Doc in Indiana."[9]

In his formal remarks, Ford said, "Americans have been rediscovering a lot of other things, too. In the wake of Vietnam, Watergate, the energy crisis, and the economic challenge, we are learning some of the very basic things that help to build America into the great country it is. I have in mind, for example, things like the need for integrity in government, a need for fiscal responsibility to fight inflation, the timeless balance created by our founders—those great founders of our country almost 200 years ago—between the three branches of government, and the need for a balance in Congress through a viable two-party system."[10] Ford said he did not believe polls and analysts' predictions that voters would punish the Republican Party in the 1974 elections for "the unfortunate deeds of others" (not mentioning Nixon or his formal pardon of him in specific). He warned of the dangers of a "veto proof" Congress dominated by Democrats who could stop any initiatives he might undertake as president.

"I just happen to think that the American people at this critical time, at this serious period in our American history, are willing to do battle today if we are going to preserve our form of government, if we are going to win the battle against inflation and keep a healthy economy," Ford said. "Hoosiers have never backed away from anything, and they are not going to back away from this struggle."[11]

As president, Ford seemed to settle into his role quickly, enjoying support and well wishes generally from both parties, not only as a result of his efforts to unite the nation, but also the respect he had earned via decades of service in the House. As a congressman, Ford had always maintained a strong relationship with his neighbor state of Indiana, headlining 1960s Lincoln Day fund-raising dinners for the Republican Party in Richmond and elsewhere, then invited as a major leader among House Republicans (including service on the Warren Commission investigating the assassination of President John F. Kennedy).

On Saint Patrick's Day 1975, Ford returned to Indiana to keep up a growing University of Notre Dame tradition of hosting sitting presidents. While not a graduation ceremony (at which most presidents had visited Notre Dame), the convocation did give the university a chance to welcome Ford—a well-known alumnus of Notre Dame's arch football rival, Michigan—into the Irish family. Ford quickly thanked the university's president, Father Theodore Hesburgh, for granting "amnesty" to students so they could skip class and hear the president's speech.

Ford noted that "the Fighting Irish of Notre Dame have become a symbol of the tenacity and determination of the American people. But Notre Dame believes not only in might on the football field, or on the basketball court, but in a spiritual response to humanity's struggle for a decent life."[12]

The president praised students who had focused personally on the plight of hunger in the world and said, "I am especially proud to be on a campus that looks up to God and out to humanity at a time when some are tempted to turn inward and turn away from the problems of the world. . . . To conform to apathy and pessimism is to drop out and to cop out. In that sense, I fully reject conformity. In that sense, I am a nonconformist who continues to be proud of America's partnership with other nations and who makes no apology for the United States of America. America's goodness and America's greatness speak for themselves. I believe in this nation and our capacity to resolve our difficulties at home without turning our back on the rest of the world."[13]

Ford reminded the students that he had been elected to the House as part of a wave of military veterans returning from World War II. He said, "Today, as I look back, I am grateful for the op-

LIBRARY OF CONGRESS

President Gerald R. Ford discusses his pardon of Nixon at a House Judiciary Subcommittee meeting in October 1974.

portunity to serve in our government during the third quarter of the 20th century. These past 25 years, while not perfect, were incomparably better for humanity than either of the two previous quarters of this century."[14]

"We are counseled to withdraw from the world and go it alone," Ford said. "I have heard that song before. I am here to say I am not going to dance to it. Nor do I believe this generation of young Americans will desert their ideals for a better nation and a better world."[15]

He concluded, "I am not alarmed when I hear warnings that the tide of history is running against us. I do not believe it for a minute, because I know where the tide of history really is—on this campus and thousands and thousands of others in this great country, wherever you find young men and women who are preparing themselves to serve God and their countries and to build a better world."[16]

Ford's official visits to Indiana would become more complicated in the months to come. Ford wrote in his autobiography about a telephone call he received late in 1975 from former California governor Ronald Reagan. In it, Reagan told Ford that "I am going to run for President. I trust we can have a good contest, and I hope that it won't be divisive."[17] Ford said he told Reagan he was very disappointed and said, "Regardless of your good intentions, your bid is bound to be divisive. It will take a lot of money, a lot of effort, and it will leave a lot of scars. It won't be helpful, no matter which one of us wins the nomination."[18]

Undeterred, Reagan went forward with his challenge from the right, answering the call of many Republicans, particularly conservative ones, not content to leave the GOP nomination to Ford—part of the "Washington establishment"—without a challenge. They worried out loud that Ford's ties to the Nixon administration,

most especially from his September 8, 1974, pardon of Nixon, would be a drag on his candidacy that would deliver the White House to the resurgent Democrats. The Democrats surely felt it could be their year. No less than twelve candidates entered the early primaries to try and gain their party's nod. For Ford, there was only one challenger, and he was as serious as could be.

Reagan, a champion of many arch conservatives since his rousing defense of Barry Goldwater's 1964 presidential candidacy, was everything Ford was not—slick, well-spoken off the cuff, and well-financed with an entirely new level of financial backers from the Hollywood establishment. Ford, an up-from-the-boot-straps former House Republican leader, had just one advantage: incumbency.

Polling showed many Americans knew little about Ford, the so-called accidental president, and he worked hard to define himself after initially having reminded the nation in a too-self-deprecating moment he was "a Ford, not a Lincoln." A Rose Garden strategy was crafted in which Ford sought to woo Republican nominees and votes using the largesse of his office. It was his greatest, and perhaps, only advantage.[19]

In the early going, the Ford strategy seemed to work, as he was able to cast Reagan as an extremist. Ford captured a narrow victory in the nation's first primary in New Hampshire. The president followed that, however, by wider margins of victory in big-state primaries in Pennsylvania, Massachusetts, Illinois, and Florida. By the time the race had reached North Carolina, the Ford camp was certain Reagan (almost out of money and not gaining traction) would withdraw. They figured incorrectly. With the help of North Carolina's fiery arch-conservative Senator Jesse Helms, Reagan scored an upset win in that state's primary. He followed that with a big victory in

Texas, leading up to the Indiana primary. Many analysts, however, wrote off any Reagan wins in the Deep South as nothing more than a protest vote by the conservative wing of the party. As the candidates moved to Indiana, it seemed likely Ford would again prevail in a northern primary. Hoosier Republicans (and more than a few crossover Democrats) were about to prove that analysis wrong.

"I had expected to lose the two Southern states [Alabama and Georgia], but the Indiana defeat came as a complete surprise," Ford wrote years later in his autobiography. "It shocked me as much as anything else that happened during the campaign. Indiana, after all, was next door to Michigan. Governor Otis Bowen and the state Republican chairman, Thomas Milligan, had declared for me, and so had other public officials, and Agriculture Secretary [Earl] Butz was a native Hoosier. At one point, a poll had me leading Reagan by 24 points, but he'd come from behind to win by 17,000 and capture 45 of Indiana's 54 delegates."[20]

Ford was worried. "Suddenly the perception spread that the President Ford Committee was a sinking ship," he wrote.[21] Ford's team abandoned the Rose Garden strategy when it appeared Reagan was making significant headway and dove in to capture the Indiana primary, although late in the going. Ford's first primary appearance in the state came on April 22, with the backing of the Indiana Republican establishment, including Bowen, Indianapolis mayor Bill Hudnut, GOP members of the Indiana congressional delegation, and presumably the editors of the *Indianapolis Star* that provided extensive coverage of Ford's every move in the state. Ford appeared to be the favorite. He also was better financed in the state, able to flood the TV airwaves with ads tagged with his familiar, "President Ford 76" logo.

Asked upon arrival at the Indianapolis airport how important the Indiana primary was to him, Ford said in his often plain, understated style: "Indiana is a very important state. I have a great affection for Indiana. Michigan and Indiana have gotten along together for a good many years. I have a special reason for wanting the support of the people of Indiana. I know many people here. I always enjoy being here. And, aside from the political side, I would certainly like to get a successful campaign here in Indiana so that we could have the delegates when we go to Kansas City."[22] The *Star* reported that Ford "was surrounded by well-dressed, clean-cut Secret Service agents, and Indianapolis and Marion County police lined the nearby rooftops as Mr. Ford stepped from the plane. A bright sun was shining and a breeze ruffled the President's hair as he stood outside Gates 11 and 12 . . . for an open air press conference. Mr. Ford wore a three-piece navy blue suit with vest, a blue shirt and a dark blue tie with a diagonal red stripe."[23] Ford told reporters he was excited to visit Indiana after having just hosted the 1976 Indiana Hoosiers, the unbeaten National Collegiate Athletic Association's men's basketball champions, at the White House a day before. Among the 350 supporters greeting Ford at the airport were fifth graders bused in from Bloomington.

Reporter questions raised to Ford focused on whether he would change any of his campaign efforts in Indiana given Reagan's recent success? "I don't see why it should," he said. "When you look that the overall record, and that is what I am running on, I'm not running on campaign promises, I'm running on the accomplishments of what we have done in the last 21 months. . . . It's a good record and I think it is supported by a majority of the American people."[24]

Ford assured his campaign volunteers that

"we are going to win in Indiana, we are going to Kansas City and we are going to win that nomination, and we're going to win in November 1976. But I must say, a lot depends on what happens in Indiana, and therefore, every one of us . . . should make a maximum effort."[25] Ford also dispatched his popular wife, Betty, to separate visits to Indianapolis, including a rare stroll from Monument Circle along East Market Street to the City Market, accompanied by about 2,000 of her "closest" Indiana friends. She spoke freely about disagreeing with her husband's position on abortion: "My position is that it is the choice of the person herself and she has the right to make the decision . . . it is very important, I think, that abortion should be brought out of the backwoods and into the hospitals."[26]

IHS, INDIANAPOLIS AIRPORT AUTHORITY MATERIALS, 1928–2012, M 1080

Ford waves to the crowd during a visit to Indianapolis in April 1976 to drum up support for his re-election as president against fellow Republican Ronald Reagan.

Acknowledging that she was at least as popular as her husband, Betty said, "I think people relate to me because they know I've had a rather normal life. In fact, I feel like the luckiest woman because I've had the best of both worlds. I've had my career, I've had my wonderful marriage, and four children and home."[27] Freely calling out "Hey" to downtown passersby who yelled out "Hey Betty!," she ate lunch at City Market before meeting with Hudnut.

A typical Ford campaign event, including a selected audience of 1,000 state and local government officials from across Indiana (guaranteeing that most of them were Republicans), gathered at the Murat Shrine in downtown Indianapolis, found the president accompanied by Bowen, Lieutenant Governor Robert D. Orr, and Hudnut. The focus of Ford's remarks was dubbed "new prosperity" by reporters and emphasized the continuation of federal revenue sharing funds that, combined with local funds, had made many local projects possible, as well as federal employment training programs. Following his meeting with local officials, the president took questions from reporters in another room at the Murat Shrine for about an hour.

As expected, questions focused a lot on how Ford thought he would do in Indiana's primary just twenty-four hours away. "We have always considered the Indiana primary a very important primary," he said. "As you well know, I have been in Indiana twice, my wife has been here on one occasion. We have a first-class organization, we have the support of the governor, and we have the support of many public officials as well as many, many volunteers, which is an indication of how important we feel the Indiana primary is."[28] He was asked repeatedly about the level of delegate support he expected to have prior to the GOP convention, especially in light of Reagan's sweep of all ninety-six Texas delegates a week earlier. He also batted down a *Time* magazine poll that showed presumptive Democratic nominee, former Georgia governor Jimmy Carter, as leading. Ford said that in addition to Indiana, Republicans in Georgia and Alabama were voting. "We certainly would be very disappointed, but we don't think we are going to lose all three," he said. "We think are chances are very good here in Indiana, for the reasons that I have given. . . . So, we think Indiana will do very well by us. And the other two states, why, we certainly are underdogs in both Alabama and Georgia, but we are going to make, as we have in the past, a very maximum effort in the time that is allowed. After all, I do have to be president, and that takes a lot of time, so we can't campaign as much as my opponent does in the primaries."[29]

In interactions with the media, Ford seemed to particularly bristle at a reporter repeating claims by Carter that Reagan had successfully "pushed" the president around on the campaign trail. "That's a very inaccurate charge," Ford replied. "There's an old Michigan saying that people who live in glass houses shouldn't throw stones. Let me make an observation how Governor Carter has really been pushed around. For example, when he raised the question of ethnic purity, I think within 24 hours he made a flip-flop. So I think his flexibility in this campaign is pretty well recognized. The minute any of his Democratic opponents hit him on something, he backtracks and takes another position."[30]

Ford declared, "I know of no position that I have taken from the very beginning to now, where I have changed my basic policy or program based on any campaign rhetoric of Governor Reagan."[31] The president did respond to questions about the White House paying the tab for his latest trip to Indianapolis, as it was considered nonpartisan because it included a discussion of federal revenue-sharing funds for local communities. "I should think Governor Reagan would applaud this kind of a healthy economy instead of trying to scare people," Ford said, adding that his Ford administration was "doing the right thing" to strengthen the economy, and "it's getting better."[32] The president told his audience of local leaders, "Perhaps the greatest success of revenue-sharing is this: Washington involvement is held to the absolute minimum in the operation of the program. Only one-eighth of one penny of every revenue-sharing dollar goes to the bureaucracy in Washington, D.C."[33]

Reporters' questions directed to Ford got tougher—whether he could support Reagan if he won the nomination or whether he would consider a vice presidential nomination on a ticket led by Reagan: "Of course not." When asked to elaborate, Ford said, "Well, I think that first, I anticipate winning in Kansas City, and I, therefore, don't anticipate any opportunity to serve as Vice President. I have had that experience."[34]

A reporter also asked Ford if he still believed that Reagan was distorting the economic record of his administration, and other issues, creating a harmful division among Republicans. "When accusations are made without foundation, or there is a distortion of statistics," said Ford, "I think it is my obligation to the American people to tell the truth and to explain what the facts are in the total context. . . . I don't think Republican voters, once they have heard the facts, will think that what I am saying is divisive."[35]

Ford's exchanges with voters and reporters indicated what was becoming clear to anyone paying attention: Reagan had successfully stolen the primary campaign agenda from Ford and had put the incumbent president in the position of responding to, rather than articulating, the issues.

Despite his stated confidence, Ford did change his previously stated position that he would have enough delegates in place to win the GOP nomination on the first ballot at the upcoming convention. On this day the president said, "I *think* [emphasis added] we will have enough delegates in Kansas City to win." When asked if he would have those delegates locked up before he got to the convention, he would only commit, "We expect to win in Kansas City."[36]

At a May 2 rally at the Fort Wayne Memorial Coliseum, the president took questions from selected members of a large audience of more than 10,000, this time about agriculture, the Panama Canal, Social Security, court-ordered school busing, federal aid to cities, defense spending, and services for people with disabilities. The president emphasized law-and-order issues in his opening remarks, no doubt a response to move the agenda farther right as Reagan was doing up and down the state.

The Panama Canal issue, which took several minutes of exchanges, reflected the traction Reagan had begun to make in Indiana on the issue. Ford made a special point to emphasize that his position was consistent with one of the nation's top conservatives, Goldwater, and matched efforts by Lyndon Johnson and Nixon to negotiate a treaty with Panama: "And what are we trying to do? We are trying to establish a long, long-term treaty of about 50 years that would guarantee to the United States the right to defend, maintain, and to operate that canal. . . . So what we are trying to do is to make sure that during the economic lifetime of the canal, we have an absolute control over it. . . . What we're trying to do, as Senator Goldwater says, where he agrees with me and he disagrees with Governor Reagan, we're trying to protect the economic and the military capability of that canal as long as it's

necessary in our national security."[37]

On court-ordered school busing, Ford said, "Court-ordered, forced busing is not the way to achieve quality education" and that "our emphasis should be on quality education and we can do it without those kinds of court orders that, I think, have gone beyond the proper remedy."[38] Again, the nature of the question and Ford's answer reflected his thoughtful, calm approach, but it clearly was a less emotional and less forceful answer than an Indiana voter likely would have received from Reagan (or George Wallace).

Campaigns provide odd and funny moments. Ford had one backstage at the Allen County Coliseum as he greeted members of the Northeast Indiana Kennel Club and acquiesced to a request to present the "Best in Show" trophy to the winner of the 1976 Northeast Indiana Kennel Club Dog Show.[39]

As his campaign volunteers gathered at the Marriott Inn in Fort Wayne and in the company of his volunteers, the president took a little more liberty than he did during his public remarks, pointing out that not only had Goldwater stated his support of Ford's Panama Canal position, "but Reagan would too, if he knew more about it" (a comment that drew laughter at Reagan's expense).[40]

"I think Barry Goldwater is not a bad backup witness on my behalf," Ford said, "and I think it totally destroys the credibility of Governor Reagan with all the charges and comments he has made about the Panama Canal. We are trying to do the responsible thing, and we are not going to give away our national security interests in that canal, I can assure you of that."[41]

For all his assurances, Ford was caught in a classic situation where his explanation was much more lengthy and difficult to articulate than Reagan's original charge. Reagan's charge that the Panama Canal "is ours . . . we paid for it, and we darn well intend to keep it" much more easily connected with voters. Reporters also analyzed that Reagan's message had "emotional appeal" that connected to voters beneath the banner of his Indiana campaign, "Make America No. 1 Again."[42]

In an appearance at Butler University in Indianapolis for the Student Assembly Lecture Series, Ford conducted another question and answer session before a Hinkle Fieldhouse audience of 14,000, where students and other members of the community could ask the president questions. It was consistent with his previously stated style of wanting to be accessible and open to voters. In his introductory remarks, Ford compared his efforts to keep the federal budget balanced (which included forty-eight vetoes offered in a twenty-month period) to those of Butler's president, Alexander E. Jones. He also touted improved unemployment figures, wage increases for American workers, and the increase in consumer confidence that the economy was going to improve (including a slightly reduced inflation rate). Ford even made special mention of the only Hoosier in his cabinet—Secretary of Agriculture Butz—an association that eventually caused the president alarm and heartburn. Ford declared the previous three years as the most profitable for America's farmers ever because "the government left the farmer alone and let him produce without a lot of bureaucratic interference" and that "that is the kind of successful farm policy I plan to have in the next four years." Ford said he had appointed Butz to chair a cabinet-level "Agricultural Policy Committee" and that "with Earl Butz as chairman, you can be sure that his strong, plain-spoken common sense, and his enthusiastic advocacy of the American farmer will be well heard in the highest councils of government—

and Indiana can be very, very proud to claim this great man as a native son."[43]

A wide range of questions were offered, with Ford playing the good sport and staying for a lengthy question-and-answer session involving queries on the economy, gun control, use of an all-volunteer military force, the presidential primary system, the role of Henry Kissinger as Secretary of State, employment opportunities for college students, pollution and clean-air issues, abolishment of a Senate committee on internal security, federal revenue sharing with local government, federal aid to education, inflation and price controls, and even his own image as president.[44] Asked about Kissinger's role in his administration (Kissinger a favorite lightning rod for criticism for arch-conservatives), Ford told a questioner that "he can stay as Secretary of State as long as I am President of the United States." He stated that, "The foreign policy of this administration, as executed by Secretary of State Kissinger, under my direction, is successful. And if you have somebody on a ball team who is successful, you keep him. . . . Our policies are right and good and successful, and as long as he wants to stay, he will be Secretary of State under my administration."[45]

Another questioner asked Ford why he did not back efforts to ban handguns, such as "the Saturday Night Special," often used in urban violence. Ford said he supported efforts to control "the illegal use of guns" and had proposed a mandatory penalty for a person who commits a felony while possessing a firearm. "In addition, I suggested to the Congress that we tighten up the control of these cheap handguns called Saturday Night Specials. . . . But the people who make them overseas, what they did to evade the new law was to send the parts to the United States, and they have been assembled in our country."[46]

Although Ford made a special effort to say

he opposed federal registration of guns and gun owners, his response to the first two questions highlighted the problem he was having with the Reagan insurrection from the right. Staying loyal to Kissinger, a central figure from the Nixon years, and discussing with a well-meaning college student the need to control guns, were not the issues that would win him the hearts of conservative Hoosier Republicans. It was the nature of an open-ended question-and-answer session. While appearing accessible and friendly (and even well informed and glib on important issues facing the nation), it also ensured that the questions asked and the answers given were mostly driven by those in the audience. Any chance to control questions and gear the event's "news" to a Ford agenda was placed in the hands of the audience.

Another problematic question followed, with Ford defending the use of an all-volunteer army and having to remind voters that American forces had been stretched dramatically during the long and difficult Vietnam War.

One student from Evansville drew nervous laughter when he noted that "on several recent episodes of *Saturday Night Live*, you have been portrayed as being, shall we say, clumsy. Do you think that by portraying you this way this has possibly increased your popularity among the average American?"[47]

"Well, I have not quite thought of it that way," Ford said smiling. "But if that is the end result, I am delighted to have that conclusion."[48]

But again, in sharp contrast to his opponent, Ford did not leave the fun aspect of his personality showing with his happy-go-lucky response, adding a too long and too obvious caveat: "To be serious for a moment, I think in the world in which we live you have to expect the bitter with the sweet, and you have to take a little kidding here and there. You have to expect some sharp

barbs in a political campaign, and you have to expect various people in the press and elsewhere to have a lot of fun with those kinds of things. You just have to let it roll off your back, like water off a duck's back, and that is what I did."[49]

Ford made the short trip from Butler to the governor's residence, where he was the overnight guest of Governor Bowen and his wife, Elizabeth. The next day the president made brief remarks to a meeting of the Indiana Broadcasters' Association in Indianapolis, where he said he would consider Reagan, along with ten or fifteen other potential names, as a running mate, but gave a sideways insult to Reagan's comments about the Panama Canal, saying, "When you grab for issues, sometimes you go beyond the facts."[50] Later he flew into Evansville, where reporters immediately asked if his presence in the state was evidence that he was concerned the nomination was slipping away from him. Ford dodged the political strategy nature of the question and gave a bit of a nonanswer, "Well, I decided that because I had such good leadership here in Indiana and so many friends, that I wanted to come to Indiana and to make sure that I supported them as they have supported me. And because we think Indiana is a crucial state, I'm here. And I've had a wonderful trip so far."[51]

Ford made his way to the Vanderburgh County Auditorium and Convention Center, accompanied by Bowen and Evansville mayor Russ Lloyd Sr., via a rare open-car motorcade through the city's downtown. Similar to events the day before in Kokomo and Indianapolis, Ford took questions from members of the audience after making introductory remarks (mostly focused on how federal revenue-sharing dollars had benefited the Evansville community). Questions from the audience were varied, including issues of states' rights, federal housing policy, negotiations for release of the Panama Canal, public employment programs, federal funding of space programs, and foreign policy. The inclusion of the questions on states' rights and the Panama Canal suggested that at least *some* of the audience were disciples of the issues Reagan had been articulating across the state.

On the Panama Canal issue, Ford took his first swipes back at Reagan, noting that "some have alleged, and in this case, my Republican opponent has alleged, that in effect we should break off these negotiations [for turnover of the canal] which were started 12 years ago or more. I think that is a totally irresponsible position."[52]

Ford reminded the audience that Panama Canal discussions had begun in 1964 after a series of riots had left twenty Panamanians and four Americans dead. The negotiations, he said, would not do away with American opperation, maintenance, and defense of the canal in the future. "If you break off those negotiations, as my Republican opponent wants us to do, you will have riots, more bloodshed, and also you will incur the enmity, the antagonism of every one of the 25 Latin and South American countries," Ford predicted, adding that such an outcome could force intervention from American military forces.[53]

"We can avoid all of that by continuing the negotiations for a responsible settlement, and those who advocate breaking off negotiations are irresponsible," he concluded.[54]

The president's answer gave him another opportunity to demonstrate his measured, thoughtful approach to foreign-policy issues, an attempt to contrast with what the Ford campaign hoped voters would view as the knee-jerk, reactionary approaches favored by Reagan.

And while the Evansville audience asked some very serious questions, including Ford's support for building the B-1 bomber, two ques-

tions were asked in fun. In one of them, a young student asked whether Ford was allowed to sit in the chairs behind the velvet ropes that he witnessed during a school tour of the White House. Ford invited the youngster back to Washington and said, "We'll go down there in person" and sit in the chairs. Another person complimented Ford for his brief appearance on NBC's *Saturday Night Live.*

Before departing Evansville, Ford made a quick stop at the Executive Inn Hotel to greet and thank his Indiana volunteers. He offered "a few selling points" for the campaign volunteers to use in their phone bank and door-to-door canvassing in the community. He asked campaign workers to remind Hoosiers how far the nation had come since August 1974, when double-digit inflation ruled the day, and how unemployment continued to fall. "What I say to you is simply that in 20 months," said Ford, "we have made headway at home, we have made great progress abroad, and this administration in the next four years will continue to give us the kind of prosperity that we want and the kind of peace that we need."[55]

Hoping he had dispatched the Panama Canal issue that Reagan continued to raise across the state, reporters' questions turned back to the horse race nature of the campaign. In Fort Wayne reporters continued peppering Ford with questions about his primary performance, including a significant loss in the just-completed Texas primary. When asked what happened, the president said, "Well, I was naturally disappointed with the results in Texas. We expected to get a fair share of the delegates. We didn't. I think the main problem was a great many crossovers from people who ordinarily vote in the Democratic primaries and some apathy on the part of some Republicans."[56]

Despite the performance, Ford said, "I don't

think it will have any serious impact on our winning in Kansas City and winning in November."[57] In all, Reagan won eleven primaries to Ford's eighteen, including five in a row at one point. Reagan also came within less than five percentage points of winning primaries in close contests in North Dakota, Kentucky, Oregon, and Tennessee. But it was Reagan's 51–49 percent win in Indiana on May 4, 1976, that relit the fire and kept the Reagan-Ford battle going all the way to the GOP convention in Kansas City. Coming out of Indiana, Reagan officially held more Republican delegates for the nomination than Ford.

The Indiana primary long past, but the battle for the Republican nomination still very much alive, Ford came back to Indianapolis on June 22, 1976, to speak to an enthusiastic group of more than 7,500 community leaders—the Jaycees. The Jaycees, a community-based group that links young leaders with the Chamber of Commerce on issues of business development, management skills, and community service, was holding its annual confab at the Indiana Convention Center.

Ford's connection to the group was strong. He had joined the Grand Rapids, Michigan, chapter of the Jaycees in 1941. "I have found the philosophy and the spirit of the Jaycees to be a great source of personal strength," he told the conference attendees. Ford added that "if there is one single group of outstanding young Americans that has come to reflect the Bicentennial spirit, it is the United States Jaycees, and I congratulate you."[58]

Ford asked the Jaycee members to continue to ask what sort of future they want for their families and their country, as he said he did when he returned from military service. As the nation's bicentennial approached, he said, "In our third century, I propose that we climb an even higher mountain. Let us fulfill the dreams of the early

fathers. Let us make these new 100 years the ultimate triumph of people of individual freedom in the United States of America."[59]

For Ford, the speech provided another opportunity to remind Americans of his role in healing the nation in the aftermath of the Watergate scandal. He reminded the audience, "Our greatness is because of our goodness. Should we cease to be good, we would cease to be great. Americans have seen too much abuse of the moral imperatives of honesty and decency, the foundations of our civilized society."[60]

Although Ford wrestled the GOP nomination away from Reagan on the first ballot at the Kansas City convention, he limped out of the gate politically wounded. Adding Senator Bob Dole of Kansas to the ticket as his vice president (Reagan refused to consider the idea of running with Ford) was meant to build Ford support in critical farm states of the Midwest and try and cut into Jimmy Carter's southern strength from his base in Georgia. Farm states such as Indiana, expected to be a strength for midwesterners Ford and Dole, were proving a challenge not because of the candidates, but because of the only Hoosier in Ford's cabinet. Butz drew headlines in the critical late-going in October 1976 for a joke based on racial slurs against blacks, a joke Carter declared as "disgraceful" and one Dole called "tasteless." *Newsweek* reported that black members of Congress were particularly angry at Ford for keeping Butz on his team. "Equally offended, the president summoned Butz to the Oval Office and dressed him down with a 'severe reprimand,'" *Newsweek* reported. "But the episode confronts Ford with an awkward political problem. Butz is popular in the Farm Belt, where he has served as Ford's main buffer against the sensitive issue of grain embargoes—deftly opposing them without quite attacking Ford."[61] Political analysts speculated that "if Butz is forced out in disgrace, Ford could be hurt in Indiana, Iowa and Illinois."[62]

Ford's last appearance in Indiana before the critical November 2 general election came on October 28, as he addressed 3,000 supporters at the massive Scottish Rite Cathedral in downtown Indianapolis. The event included appearances by actor Forrest Tucker and NBC sportscaster Joe Garagiola. It was an exciting time in the Ford campaign. Polling data showed that after months of trailing Governor Carter, positive movement was detected that indicated the election could be very close. A Market Opinion Research Poll commissioned by the GOP showed Ford with an uncomfortably close 47–38 lead in Indiana, with 15 percent undecided.[63]

"We have less than a week to go before Election Day," Ford said. "One of the major issues in this presidential campaign has been the state of our national economy. Of all the differences between Mr. Carter and me, none is more important than our differences over economic policy. These differences have a lot to do with contrasting views of what the fundamental role of our government should be in the United States of America."[64]

Ford said his administration had worked hard to gain the confidence of the American people in addressing economic and foreign policy concerns. The president also acknowledged "the rather precipitous decline" in Carter's standing in the polls. "In my view, one very important reason for his decline in popularity is that since his party's convention, he has relied very, very heavily on the discredited old formula of more promises, more programs, and more spending," he said.[65]

Tax cuts, Ford said, combined with reduced federal spending would help rebuild the American economy: "I pledge to the American people that I will seek tax cuts as the number one prior-

ity in the next Ford administration, and I ask for the help of voters in electing a Congress that will work with me toward that end. This is but one of the many important reasons I am a candidate for the Presidency in 1976."[66]

"You know where I stand," he said to the friendly audience. "You know what I've done. You know what we can do . . . and with your support here in Indiana and nationwide on November 2nd, I will never let you down."[67] Ford won Indiana but lost the November 1976 election, despite staging a major comeback in the polls that fell just short.

Ford had been out of office for about a year on December 7, 1977 when he made an appearance as the special speaker for the twenty-fifth anniversary of the Goshen Chamber of Commerce. Just a year removed from his narrow loss to Carter in the 1976 election, Ford was greeted by a crowd of about 4,000 people packed into the Goshen High School gymnasium. Described by locals as "very down to earth," Ford's speech focused on a familiar Republican theme—the idea that tax cuts for individuals and businesses would help spur a stagnant economy. "Don't listen to the prophets of doom, but be aware of the shoals along the way. The economy is neither poised for a boom, nor teetering on the edge of a recession, but it is high on a tight rope," Ford declared.[68]

Ford criticized President Carter's energy policies amidst the first major rise in gasoline prices American consumers had ever faced. Stating that, "[t]he energy crisis we face is the moral equivalent to war."[69]

Ronald Reagan

By the time the May 1976 Indiana primary approached, former California governor Reagan was hardly giving up on his quest to wrestle the

GOP nomination from President Ford and bet heavily on Hoosier Republicans. Hoosiers of all stripes were invited to a $5-a-plate luncheon with the actor turned governor in the 500 Ballroom at the Indiana Convention Center in downtown Indianapolis, where he was "besieged" by autograph seekers following his remarks.[70]

Reagan paid courtesy calls while in Indianapolis on two men who had signaled their support for Ford: Bowen and Hudnut. At the statehouse, Bowen was polite and said he welcomed Reagan's visit and said his long-term support of Ford "doesn't mean I am anti-Reagan or anti-anybody else" and considered his support of Ford "neighborly," given Ford's history as a Representative from southwestern Michigan. "He is a neighbor who has paid close attention to Indiana, and Indiana people feel close to him," Bowen said.[71]

Regardless of the challenges, Reagan showed up everywhere, and for Hoosiers it seemed that the actor-turned-politician still had enough Hollywood flash and finesse to woo a crowd. Everywhere he went were voters who may never have supported a particular candidate, but were immensely curious about Reagan. Hoosiers were not disappointed, as Reagan brought along Hollywood legend and pal Jimmy Stewart to campaign by his side. Stewart appeared with Reagan at both Indianapolis and in stops in northern Indiana. At Gary with Stewart, a member of the Hollywood film elite standing by, Reagan attacked Ford for being part of "the Washington elite" and said, "President Ford has made it plain he places his faith in the Washington establishment. I don't think Washington is the answer. . . . Washington is the problem."[72]

As *U.S. News & World Report* opined, "Suddenly, the battle has taken a new turn. What seemed like a shoo-in for Ford now looks a lot closer. And Reagan strategists think they've found a way to take it all."[73] Ford campaign insiders acknowledged the situation had changed "dramatically" and that Reagan had successfully broken Ford's momentum going into Indiana. Reagan's campaign manager, John Sears, told reporters that the goal in Indiana was "to define what the Reagan candidacy was all about" and cast him as the man able to restore the nation's sense of purpose.[74] A *New York Times* reporter spent a day visiting Republican voters in Plainfield in Hendricks County and came away with a sense of the "Reagan mystique." There, loyal Republicans questioned the fact that Ford always seemed to have "an alibi" for the economy, or for other problems. The *Times* offered, "Mr. Reagan's real appeal is the promise that he might have the force of personality to lead the country back to patriotic values as they are construed in towns like Plainfield and assailed, it has sometimes seemed here, nearly everywhere else. Basically, it is the promise of a revival."[75]

Before 1,200 excited Republicans in Anderson for the Madison County Bicentennial Lincoln Day Dinner, Reagan said the Ford administration was committed to "the Washington establishment" and the growth of the federal government. "Mr. Ford has been a member of the Washington establishment for more than a quarter of a century, congressman, appointed Vice President by Richard Nixon and for the last 20 months, President," Reagan said. "I spent most of my adult life in the private sector."[76] Reagan said the areas in which Ford allowed the government to grow were the wrong areas, ignoring needs in the Defense Department. "The situation goes beyond an imbalance of weaponry," Reagan said. "The real issue is faith in the Washington establishment or trust in the people." Reagan said members of Congress have complained to him that "just since the matter of military preparedness became an issue, a number of them are now going to vote for increased military appropriations."[77]

Reagan also took up differences between himself and Ford on the issue of gun control. "The Ford administration by way of the Attorney General is pushing a bill through Congress that is a gun control bill. It makes it more difficult, if not impossible for the law-abiding person," Reagan charged, advocating for the imposition of additional penalties against criminals convicted of carrying out crimes while armed.[78] He said additional penalties should be imposed and sentences made mandatory for commission of a crime while armed. One other issue, reporters analyzed, was meant to draw wavering George Wallace supporters over to Reagan's campaign. The former California governor joked, "If Joe McDoakes is using his welfare money to go down to the pool hall and drink beer and gamble, and the people on his block are paying the bill directly, Joe is apt to undergo a change in his lifestyle—or get off welfare."[79]

Before his Anderson audience, Reagan revived his concern about the United States giving up control of the Panama Canal, vowing that if he were elected, he never would agree to such an arrangement. "If we have given up sovereignty to the Canal Zone, no scrap of paper can prevent any government of Panama from deciding to come in and nationalize and take over the canal," Reagan charged. "The Panama Canal Zone is every bit as much United States territory as Alaska which we purchased from Russia."[80]

The shadow of Vietnam continued to hang over the nation in 1976, and Reagan drew his heaviest applause from the Madison County Republicans when he declared, "I do not think there is any of our generation—in my lifetime there have been four wars—that does not hope and pray that no generation will ever again have

to bleed the finest young men of that generation into the mud and sand of a battlefield. But a few years ago, this country committed what I consider a great immorality, by way of our government. I pledge that will never be done again. Never again will young Americans be asked to fight and die for their country unless it is for a cause this country intends to win."[81]

Reagan stirred controversy on Vietnam-related issues days later when he alleged the Ford administration of a "hat-in-hand" approach to North Vietnam, via the controversial Kissinger (whom Reagan always derisively referred to as "Dr. Kissinger"). Reagan alleged the Ford administration, via Kissinger, had suggested considering diplomatic recognition of North Vietnam, an accusation that succeeded in putting Ford on the defensive again. Ford said Reagan's claims of U.S. overtures to Hanoi were "unfounded."[82] Ford told Indianapolis reporters, "There hasn't been a serious discussion by me or the secretary of state or anybody in authority in this administration that we were going to recognize Hanoi" and chided "irresponsible others" for making the suggestion.[83] Ford emphasized that his administration was committed to finding American soldiers listed missing in action in Vietnam and added, "We have been working with members of Congress to try and find a way to get our MIAs back. But this government has no intention whatsoever of recognizing North Vietnam—none. I don't know where Mr. Reagan got this so-called rumor, or this so-called news story that we were. He must have pulled it out of the blue someplace because it has no credibility at all."[84] The exchange was more evidence that Reagan had successfully shifted the debate to issues of foreign policy for the Indiana primary. Reagan accused the Ford administration of having weakened military spending and investment to levels that caused the United States to fall behind the Soviets, a claim Ford blasted as "preposterous, demagogic and nonsense."[85]

Time magazine, perhaps sensing the late shift toward Reagan, noted that, "As he hammered at his issues, Reagan's following grew. His acting experience served him well. He was punchier, funnier, more dramatic than Ford, yet at the same time he seemed cooler, more professional and dignified than the president."[86] *Time* noted, however, that the Reagan charm that would be considered key to his later political victories could at times come up missing. They noted, unlike Ford, Reagan declined to kiss a baby noting, "I come in contact with so many people in the course of a day, and there are so many strange bugs going around."[87]

"The often aloof Reagan also passes up many waiting crowds," *Time* reported. "In Fort Wayne, Indiana he rushed past a cheering group of well-wishers. 'We've been waiting 20 minutes in the freezing cold,' complained one woman. Reagan pointed to his wristwatch to indicate he was running late—but he was actually on schedule."[88] While in Fort Wayne, Reagan played the unusual role of a fellow roaster for a Gridiron Dinner sponsored by the Fort Wayne-Allen County Press Club. Reagan represented Republicans present, while Evansville native Jimmy "The Greek" Snyder, a Las Vegas oddsmaker and CBS Sports personality, spoke for the Democrats.[89] Speaking to reporters at Baer Field in Fort Wayne, Reagan said he was "not interested" in serving as Ford's running mate, should the president win renomination, and said, "It was nice of Mr. Ford to consider it. I'm not interested."[90]

En route to a campaign stop at Notre Dame, *Time* noted that Reagan "rarely loosens his necktie or takes off his suit coat" and did not fraternize with reporters. "Once the houselights go on

Regan prepares to board Air Force One after visiting Indianapolis to speak at the National Convention of Counties on July 13, 1987.

IHS, INDIANAPOLIS AIRPORT AUTHORITY COLLECTION, M1080

and Reagan faces a crowd, however, he is all charm and good humor. Given an old football helmet last week at the University of Notre Dame (where red, white and blue banners proclaimed 'Welcome Back Gipper'), Reagan turned the event into a neat jab at (Ford): 'When I played football, I wore one.'"[91]

Reagan waved off claims of polls in Indiana that showed the president prevailing and reports that the state's GOP chairman Thomas S. Milligan predicted Ford would win with 55 percent of the vote. Reagan told Indiana audiences that he offered the Republican Party its best chance of victory in 1976 because of his ability to attract crossover votes from disaffected Independents and Democrats who were poised to abandon the GOP over Watergate-related issues. "There has been a suggestion among Republicans that maybe I have a base so narrow that I could not offer us victory in November," Reagan said. "I was elected Governor in California, a state where Independents and Democrats outnumber Republicans almost 2-1. I won the office by a million votes. If I did not believe in my heart that I offered us the best chance of victory in November, I would not be here asking for your support."[92]

Citing his desire to form "a new majority," Reagan said individual opportunity was the road to making America strong again, stating his support for state and local control over welfare programs and gun laws. He drew some of his strongest applause, however, when he told the Indianapolis audience that "never again will young Americans be asked to fight and die for their country until it is a cause this country intends to win," referring to the Vietnam War. Calling the Vietnam War one of the "great immoralities" of our time, Reagan said, "No other nation will ever be tempted to break the peace and challenge [America's] strength."[93]

Reagan sounded a theme that would traverse

through his entire career in public life, accusing Ford and his supporters of placing their "faith in the Washington establishment" instead of trusting the people. "One of us turns to the government for answers—and I don't happen to believe that those associated with the buildup of problems over the years are best qualified to solve them," Reagan said in a thinly veiled reference to Ford's longevity in the nation's capital.[94]

Coming into Indiana, Reagan described himself as "astonished" at the full sweep in the Texas primary conducted just prior and raised the specter that Ford was too weak to compete against the Democrats. Reagan left no doubt that he thought he was the stronger choice for Republicans. "The issue that now has to be determined by Republicans in these primaries is that it begins to look like Jimmy Carter, who is not a member of the Washington establishment, who is running on criticism of the Washington establishment, is going to be the Democratic nominee," Reagan said in Indianapolis. "Republicans must ask themselves who is better able to run against Mr. Carter? Mr. Ford, who will have to defend administration policies, or someone else who is not a member of the Washington establishment and who has already proven he can win elections in Democratic states?"[95] Reagan told reporters, however, that he still considered himself the underdog in Indiana, despite the wins in North Carolina and Texas, given the support that Bowen and the Indiana GOP "establishment" was granting Ford.

On the Panama Canal issue that he frequently revisited in front of Indiana audiences, Reagan carefully avoided appearing too extreme, while sounding tough. Asked how far he would go as president to preserve American sovereignty of the canal given Ford's oft-raised concerns that violence could erupt in the region, Reagan responded with his own question: "How far would I go from stopping someone from taking Alaska from us or any other part of United States territory? The United States does not dare set a precedent in which it says that anyone that threatens us with violence and force can have anything they want, [or that] Uncle Sam would just roll over and give up."[96]

Reagan seemed to understand he was making progress on issues such as the Panama Canal, but was put in the unusual spot of having to respond to a less-than-supportive remark from his fellow conservative, Goldwater, who said he backed Ford's position on the canal and that Reagan's candidacy ran the risk of splitting the party in harmful ways, as it was in 1964. "I am a little surprised at Senator Goldwater saying such a thing," Reagan told reporters outside an Indianapolis church. "Senator Goldwater knows better than anyone else that his defeat was because the opposition succeeded in picturing him as, not a conservative, but a dangerous kind of radical. Now he seems to be lending himself to this same kind of false image-making."[97]

For his part, Reagan approached Indiana full tilt, but without any guarantee of success. The Reagan camp had reason to lack full confidence in Indiana. Political wrangling in Washington had tied up federal matching funds for the presidential campaign, meaning the former California governor's campaign was running on fumes—almost $1 million in debt—while Ford's campaign could "fly now, pay later" aboard the government-owned Air Force One. Ford deflected Reagan's criticism that he was playing games with the federal funds, advising Reagan and the Democrats (who also were complaining) to take their gripes to Congress. Ford offered that his campaign had "husbanded" its funds. "Some of these other candidates have apparently either wasted their money or have not planned it properly so that

they are in some trouble. But the President Ford Committee, because we spent it wisely, we have handled it well, and we are in the black."[98]

The prophets of the 1976 primaries in Indiana were all wrong, at least for the Republicans. While Carter sailed to a major win among Democrats (seemingly tamping out the last of the Wallace embers in Indiana forever), Reagan squeaked through with a 51–49 percent win amidst a massive move of more than 625,000 GOP ballots cast. A margin of less than 14,000 votes separated Reagan and Ford, but for Reagan, symbolism was terribly important. He had won a large state, an industrial state, and a state in Ford's prized northern tier. Ford's Indiana loss completed the worst series of election defeats for an incumbent president since William Howard Taft's record twelve-primary losses to Theodore Roosevelt in 1912.

With his Indiana loss sinking in, Ford told reporters in a Rose Garden news conference that the Reagan win in Indiana made the race for the GOP nomination even tougher, and conceded he did not know how to stop crossover Democratic votes for Reagan that Ford attributed to giving Reagan victories in Indiana and Texas. Ford also, for the first time, declined to make his normal declaration that he would defeat Reagan on the first ballot at the convention. Reporters at *The Economist* picked up the Ford posit, noting, "Indiana was a state with as many rednecks as Texas, but nevertheless in the north" and estimated as many as 280,000 Democrats dumped Wallace in the Democratic Primary and instead flipped for Reagan.[99]

"A key to Reagan's success in Indiana, as in Texas, was to tie up drifting Wallace voters set loose by the collapse of their former hero," *The Economist* declared. "Taking aim at this frustrated group searching for a new candidate to voice their angry concerns is proving an electoral master-stroke for Reagan's strategists. They were able to exploit the defection from Wallace in Indiana because the state's primary rules, like those in Texas, permit 'crossover' voting."[100]

Time analyzed that "the Reagan crowds in Indiana responded readily to his smooth style. Ford, on the other hand, often got a rousing reception when introduced as the president, but audiences lost enthusiasm as he read his speeches, actually more thoughtful and more varied than Reagan's standard pitch."[101]

As one reporter summed up, "Ford's defeat in Indiana was especially damaging to the president, since it shatters the belief that Reagan was no threat to Ford in the north. The president's political advisers can no longer hope to limit Reagan to doing well in the Sunbelt only."[102]

The Indiana results revealed even more, a *New York Times*/CBS News poll of the state's GOP primary voters revealed. "If voters in the Republican primary in Indiana are any indication, the ideological cleavage between the conservative and moderate wings of the Republican Party is widening," the *Times* declared.[103] The poll demonstrated that in an unusual turn of events, Democrats appeared to be uniting behind Carter, while it was the normally united and "once-subdued" Republicans who seemed prepared for a bloody internal battle. The poll authors noted that "by dividing their vote almost evenly between Mr. Ford and his challenger, the Indiana Republicans showed that they were indeed deeply split along ideological lines. In previous primaries, Mr. Reagan had difficulty punching through on issues he espoused. But in Indiana, a clear demarcation line emerged, with Mr. Reagan scoring exceptionally well."[104]

His Indiana success notwithstanding (and seven primary victories over Ford that followed), the math did not work out for Reagan (despite winning more than five million Republican primary votes), and Ford won the GOP nomination

at a highly competitive convention in Kansas City, the final delegate count an unusually close 117 delegate vote margin for Ford.

Reagan made a brief speech before the Kansas City delegates after Ford's victory was assured, but many viewed it as a stronger pitch for himself as a future GOP nominee than for Ford's upcoming fall campaign. Regardless, Reagan promised to campaign for the Ford ticket where needed, including an October 1976 GOP fund-raising dinner in Indianapolis. Reagan was asked about the close nature of the contest, with neither Carter nor Ford seemingly able to sew it up. Reagan said, "Many things are unprecedented in this campaign. I don't believe it has happened before that this close to Election Day there are people who are actually falling back and saying they are still undecided. It may have been the debates, but I believe President Ford is going to win."[105] At the time of the announcement of Reagan's visit, the Ford campaign said it had no current plans to actively campaign in Indiana. "Indiana is not considered critical enough to warrant spending any of that time here," Milligan, the state's GOP chair, told reporters. "That doesn't mean they don't think Indiana is important. It just means Indiana is a state where they think Ford will do well. I concur with their view."[106] Ford's calculations about Indiana proved true, though his margin of victory, just under 170,000 votes, was narrower than most modern-day Republicans found in the state.

Spiro T. Agnew

No greater evidence can be found that the 1972 general election was never fully engaged anywhere, let alone Indiana, than in the presence of the two vice presidential standard-bearers making themselves at home among Hoosiers.

Having delivered the Nixon-Agnew ticket

their largest margin of victory in 1968, President Nixon could be excused for ignoring the state during the election cycle. His campaign dispatched Agnew to a Fort Wayne appearance in early October, where the always quotable Agnew was in prime form. As the *New York Times* reported, Agnew "abandoned his restrained recitations today for a snappy, off-the-cuff debate with youthful hecklers" who sought to interrupt his remarks.[107] During a noon outdoor rally, the vice president grew impatient with the antiwar protesters and "glaring out across the crowd to the tiny band of protesters standing beneath a large antiwar banner, called them 'bleeding hearts' and dismissed them with a disgusted wave of his hand."[108] Agnew seemed particularly perturbed by a shouted question from the protesters: "How many bombs were dropped today?"[109]

"I will get to Vietnam," Agnew replied. "I'm glad you brought Vietnam up, because I'd certainly do not want to go away without responding to the thoughtless cries of 'How many bombs did you drop today?'"[110]

Agnew launched into a belated attack on Johnson's efforts to scale back bombing as having only motivated the North Vietnamese to increase their efforts. If the North Vietnamese wanted to end the war, Agnew said, "They have only one thing to do: get those thousands and thousands of troops out of South Vietnam, sit down at the bargaining table under international supervision, have a ceasefire, allow the international community to witness a free election so the South Vietnamese people can determine who they want to govern them."[111]

"But what really makes my heart bleed is that these bleeding hearts don't have any sympathy for the people that stand in the South Vietnamese market place when rockets are deliberately aimed at them," he said. Pointing at the protesters, Agnew added, "And these people have no sympathy for the columns of fleeing refugees who were headed south to escape the North Vietnamese tanks and were machine-gunned down as they ran. What about those people? They are entitled to your compassion, too." Building to a finish, Agnew said, "Stop tearing your own country apart and recognize your enemy," invoking a huge ovation from the Republican faithful gathered.[112]

Agnew would not have the last word. On October 10, 1973, Agnew resigned the vice presidency in disgrace as he pled "no contest" to charges of tax evasion related to more than $100,000 of bribes he allegedly accepted while governor of Maryland. He vigorously and bitterly protected his privacy in the years after he left public office, his only major public appearance coming at Nixon's April 1994 funeral. He died September 17, 1996, at the age of seventy-seven after a short battle with leukemia.

George McGovern

Senator McGovern of South Dakota joined the 1972 presidential race with a singular focus on ending American involvement in the Vietnam War—an issue that galvanized a large segment of the Democratic Party, but not all of it. As a result, McGovern won a splintered Democratic primary process, denying the nomination to former vice president and 1968 Democratic nominee Hubert H. Humphrey after party officials stood by their "winner take all" approach for McGovern's narrow win in the California primary.

The Democrats were in disarray coming into and going out of the 1972 convention in Miami—a stark contrast to the organized and united front presented by the Republicans under the Nixon-Agnew banner. To complicate matters, McGovern struggled to find a running mate. Several prominent party members said "no thanks" to an invitation to run for vice president, including Humphrey, Edmund Muskie, and Senators Ted Kennedy of Massachusetts, Birch Bayh of Indiana, and Walter Mondale of Minnesota. Eventually, U.S. Senator Thomas Eagleton of Missouri accepted McGovern's hasty bid— one apparently made quickly without properly checking Eagleton's background. Reports soon surfaced that Eagleton had been hospitalized in the past for depression (a fact he acknowledged he did not disclose to McGovern and the party), and troubling media questions were raised. Psychiatric experts suggested Eagleton's depression could return and impair his ability to serve in the nation's highest office (should something happen to McGovern), with unnamed sources indicating Eagleton had even undergone electric-shock therapy for his condition. Eagleton finally withdrew at McGovern's request, and Sargent Shriver, brother-in-law to former president John F. Kennedy, agreed to serve, and the McGovern campaign limped forward.

Not surprisingly, polls showed Nixon was on his way to an easy re-election. The Nixon campaign (having helped dispatch what they considered their strongest competitor, Muskie) rolled forward, however, with heavy campaigning typical of Nixon. McGovern, too, was a tireless campaigner but struggled to break out beyond issues involving the Vietnam War, as Nixon focused on a broader agenda. McGovern's campaign was further hindered in Indiana by media reports, such as those by conservative Robert Novak, quoting "a Democratic insider" as saying, "The people don't know McGovern is for amnesty [for Vietnam draft dodgers], abortion and legalization of pot. Once middle America—Catholic middle America, in particular—finds this out, he's dead."[113] (Following Senator Eagleton's death

in 2007, Novak told NBC's *Meet the Press* that the source of the quote had been Eagleton.)[114]

Perhaps not surprisingly, McGovern's campaign had little time to spend in Indiana in 1972, waiting until three days before the election for a quick in-and-out stop at Gary before an audience of 6,000 gathered at Gary West High School for a ninety-nine-cent "People's Dinner" that included Coretta Scott King, the widow of Doctor Martin Luther King Jr.; Georgia legislator Julian Bond (later United Nations ambassador under Carter); and Gary mayor Richard G. Hatcher. It would be McGovern's only visit to the state and represented last-minute efforts by Democrats to try and shore up traditional constituencies, including black voters, in Illinois, Michigan, and Indiana. Additional campaign stops in East Chicago and South Bend were scrapped by McGovern's campaign as he focused his efforts on Chicago and Michigan. McGovern was also concerned with taping a national television speech on the Vietnam War in response to a statement meant to highlight Nixon's failure to deliver on a promise to end the war in Southeast Asia during his first term.[115]

McGovern's hardhitting message to the nation about Vietnam, and to his Gary audience, reflected the growing frustration among Democrats who seemed unable, regardless of what they tried, to cut into national polls that showed Nixon in command. "After four years of war, Mr. Nixon has closed the door to peace once again," McGovern said in his television address from Chicago. "If he escapes his responsibility now, do you think he will end the war after the election once he is free from the will of the American people? Mr. Nixon will not end the war . . . [and] the fundamental issues in the war remain unresolved. And because they are not resolved, as Mr. Nixon admits, we have changed nothing in

Senator George McGovern of South Dakota, 1972

LIBRARY OF CONGRESS

the last four years."[116]

During his remarks at Gary, McGovern was loudly applauded as he revived the theme of his Democratic convention speech by inviting black voters of America to "come home from an exile of racial politics" and warned that "never again must political leaders try to win votes while denying black rights."[117] McGovern's appearance caught the attention of Indiana media mostly for its inclusion of former governor Matt Welsh, who was seeking a second, nonconsecutive term in a hotly contested race against then-Indiana House Speaker Bowen. Prior to the Gary appearance, Welsh had seemed reluctant to stand next to McGovern, whom most Hoosiers viewed as too liberal. Reporters quickly noted that McGovern sported a Welsh campaign button on his lapel, and Welsh wore a McGovern button on his lapel. Welsh spoke briefly, offering only that "Indiana needs a President who understands the basic problem of welfare. [McGovern] will put the people to work."[118]

McGovern's remarks—only slightly longer than Welsh's despite a buildup by Mayor Hatcher that the speech would represent a major "human rights address" by the Democratic nominee—focused primarily on issues of race and economy. McGovern said he would "take whatever steps are necessary to see that there's a decent job for every man and woman in this country who's able to work" and that by turning out President Nixon, the nation could focus on policies that would address health care, education, clean water, veterans' rights, and child care.[119]

"I say the only remedy to the list is to veto Mr. Nixon next Tuesday," McGovern said to loud applause. In a veiled reference to the emerging Watergate scandal, McGovern also said voters would take the nation back from war makers, special interests, and "wire tappers." He charged

Nixon was "more interested in perpetuating the power of a military dictator in Saigon" than in solving the nation's problems, adding that seniors, young people, and "blacks, browns, reds, whites and all other Americans have been neglected" under Nixon's leadership.[120]

Although organized in the state, until McGovern's last-minute campaign stop in Gary the only campaign appearances offered Hoosier Democrats came from replacement running mate Shriver and Senators Kennedy and Muskie as McGovern fought the Nixon tidal wave everywhere else. McGovern's campaign failed to engage not only in Indiana, but also across the nation, as he lost forty-nine of the fifty states (including his home state of South Dakota), carrying only Massachusetts (and the District of Columbia) in an election noted for the lowest voter turnout in more than three decades.

McGovern, however, had enjoyed some notable visits to Indiana before and after his 1972 disappointment, including two noteworthy stops at Notre Dame coming before and after his presidential run, in 1970 and 1973. In both, McGovern proved a powerful voice against the Nixon administration and the pro-Vietnam forces, and as a result continued to gain support among those who had always felt, or grown to feel, the Vietnam War was a mistake.

Author Theodore White attributed McGovern's famous "come home" speech that punctuated his 1972 Democratic convention acceptance speech to his 1970 appearance at Notre Dame. White wrote that McGovern "had been perfecting the call for almost a year and a half and had first voiced it in Indiana in a college speech, a long time before, but now he was making it the theme song, come home."[121] At the Miami convention, little was remembered about McGovern's postmidnight acceptance speech, except a remarkable passage that won him praise for decades to follow as he called Americans to come home "from secrecy and deception in high places, come home America. From the waste of idle hands to the joy of useful labor, come home America. From the prejudice of race and sex, come home America. Come home to the affirmation that we have a dream. Come home to the conviction that we can move our country forward. Come home to the belief that we can seek a newer world. And let us be joyful in that homecoming. May God grant us the wisdom to cherish this good land and to meet the great challenges that beckons us home."[122]

McGovern won notice on college campuses, such as Notre Dame, because of his open support of the October 1969 Moratorium protest and teach-in on Vietnam (he was one of the only members of the U.S. Senate to sign on to the effort). McGovern told Notre Dame's *Scholastic* magazine, "I think [the Moratorium] did a lot in the sense that it brought together thousands of people all over the country in a way that the policy makers couldn't possibly have missed. It was a demonstration of the strength and depth of feeling on the war, no matter how much [the Nixon administration was] inclined to dismiss it with their public statements."[123] McGovern said Nixon had slowly moved toward the positions of antiwar leaders, but vehemently opposed the moratorium. McGovern also addressed his distaste for an element of the antiwar movement that resorted to "four-letter words" and violence and acknowledged that "liberals have been slow to recognize the urgency of the law and order issue. Sometimes law and order has been used by demagogues as a device to beat blacks over the head and suppress honest and legitimate dissent."[124]

Asked about Agnew, who had quickly gained

a reputation as a sharp-tongued advocate of the president, McGovern did not hold back: "I think Agnew is an outrageous and obscene person to demean the Vice Presidency as he has. That's the second most powerful office in the land; he's treated it like he was some kind of an irresponsible demagogue running for a courthouse post, willing to do anything in order to discredit his opponent."[125] He added, however, that it would be a mistake to blame Agnew alone: "That would be like blaming Charlie McCarthy for what Edgar Bergen has him saying. Agnew reflects exactly what President Nixon wants him to say."[126]

Back on the Notre Dame campus in November 1973, almost a year to the day after his crushing defeat, the questions posed to McGovern were vastly different and focused a growing concern about the Watergate issue. McGovern said he would "prefer impeachment" of Nixon to any resignation "because [an impeachment] would answer some of the questions which might otherwise never be answered if the President were just to resign and walk off into the night. What I really think the situation requires now is that the President be removed from office, either by resignation or the impeachment route. I think that's what the Constitution most clearly provides. I think it's what the present tangled and confused situation dictates."[127]

McGovern said he believed as many as twenty-two impeachable offenses may be possible against the president and that Congress could not avoid dealing with the issue, even with the president trying to convince the nation he could and should continue to govern. He added, "I don't think there has ever been a time when the White House or high government officials, acting for the White House, broke the law so fragrantly, and misused sensitive agencies like the FBI, the CIA and the Internal Revenue service. . . . I don't think there's any precedent for this."[128]

McGovern denied charges that he was seeking to neuter the presidency in exchange for more congressional power. "I believe in a strong President, a strong activist President, but I think he ought to use all the powers the Constitution provides," he said. "But that will only work if the Congress does the same thing. . . . I would not want to see the Presidency crippled."[129] Regardless, he reminded his Notre Dame hosts "to keep in mind that we've already had two major Cabinet members indicted, including the former Attorney General [John Mitchell]; and people sent to jail who were high in the president's confidence. . . . I do think that the revelation of that kind of shocking conduct can serve a useful purpose, in that it's massive enough to really frighten the country about what happens when you put expediency ahead of principle."[130]

On Vietnam, McGovern called Nixon's claims that the United States' truce with the North Vietnamese represented "peace without honor" was "terrible" and noted even the South Vietnamese government was reporting as many as 50,000 deaths since the cease-fire. "I'm very much disturbed about the continuing slaughter that goes on there," McGovern said. "This is the forgotten war. . . . It may be a peace for us, but it's not a peace for the people who continue to die on both sides."[131]

McGovern remained an active political voice in the years following the 1972 race. He appeared at Indiana University-Southeast in New Albany in September 1979. Part of his trip was meant to buttress the coming 1980 re-election campaign for Senator Bayh, a campaign that ended in failure for both Bayh in Indiana and for McGovern in South Dakota. Revealing that the wounds of his crushing defeat for the presidency almost a decade earlier were still fresh, McGovern said he

wanted "to take just a moment to thank any of you who are here tonight who may have stood with me in the presidential effort of 1972. I gather there are a few survivors! That was a great experience in my life, and I would like to think a worthwhile effort as far as the nation is concerned," he said.

"While we didn't prevail in 1972, looking back on it I have thought for some time that we need a new definition of winning and losing in political contests of that kind," McGovern noted, pointing out that his campaign manager from 1972, Gary Hart, was now a senator from Colorado, and "I'm very sure he would not want to change places with the winning campaign manager, John Mitchell, who has spent most of the time since then in jail. And I can say without any doubt that I would much rather be here on the campus of Indiana University Southeast as the loser of 1972 than to be out there in San Clemente, California with the winner of that effort."[132]

McGovern said he remained close friends with both of Indiana's senators—Bayh and Richard G. Lugar—the latter of whom he said was "in the wrong party, but he's a good man and an excellent senator."[133]

Jumping on the "crisis of confidence" bandwagon that was trailing the sagging fortunes of Carter, McGovern said, "There is, indeed, a crisis of confidence, as the president said in his address to the nation a few weeks ago, and it's a crisis that is obviously complicated by the inaction and bungling of our most critical domestic problem—the energy future of the nation."[134] McGovern said that his visits with constituents in South Dakota and in Indiana convinced him that the American people were angry. "I find them angry about either perceived or actual manipulation by the major oil concerns in our society," he said. "I find them upset about the performance of the federal Energy Department. They are afraid that they are going to have to choose, perhaps this winter, between fuel on one hand and adequate needs such as food and clothing on the other. But most of all I have found them very skeptical and distrustful about the promises of the federal government—not just Jimmy Carter, but the Congress of the United States and the predecessors of this administration—who have displayed a tendency to approach this problem in starts and stops that thus far have got us necessarily little ways down the road."[135]

McGovern said he saw "no relief in sight from the basic energy dilemma" and that Carter's plan to increase oil prices as a solution to the shortages was an ineffective approach. He said, "I find people inquire not only in my state but elsewhere across the country about what's happened to the Alaskan oil pipeline that was supposed to be such a deliverer, what has happened to coal development and the miraculous promise of nuclear power? Why have we failed, I am asked, to take a greater advantage of Mexican and Canadian oil? Why have we failed to develop alternative and renewable sources of energy—a question that I get every day, especially from younger people. And why have we not been able to reduce our dependence on foreign oil?"[136] Synthetic fuel development, reduction in fuel consumption by increasing mass transportation, enhancement of the nation's rail system, and exploration of alternative energy sources beyond coal and gas were on the top of McGovern's agenda. "Although we cannot afford to close the door now on any of the area's forms of energy technology that had been proposed, it has become increasingly clear that conservation and renewable energy sources hold the greatest promise for the immediate future," McGovern said.

McGovern was swept from his Senate seat in 1980 and made one more attempt at the presidency, entering Democratic primaries in 1984, but withdrew before the Indiana primary. He remained active in retirement, promoting UN food programs and died in Sioux Falls, South Dakota, on October 21, 2012, at the age of ninety.

Hubert H. Humphrey

Officially in 1972, Humphrey won more popular votes among Democratic primary voters than any other candidate—more than 4.1 million votes to just 4 million for the eventual nominee, McGovern. Racking up four primary wins, however, was not enough for Humphrey, however, to overcome feelings among his party faithful that he was not only a retread of the unsuccessful 1968 campaign against Nixon, but also carried with him all of the weight and scorn from the Johnson administration's policy in Southeast Asia. Despite Humphrey's long and distinguished leadership on issues such as civil rights, most liberal leaders of the party seemingly could not forgive him for his support of Johnson's war policy. White wrote in his 1972 version of *The Making of the President* that "for the young of 1972, Humphrey was a man of the war, Lyndon Johnson's vice president."[137]

For the first ten primaries in 1972, Humphrey struggled to gain traction, his best showings being a distant second place to Wallace in Florida and a third place showing in Wisconsin behind two Georges—McGovern and Wallace. Humphrey finally broke through with a win in Pennsylvania in a tight race that featured active campaigns by him, McGovern, Wallace, and Muskie. Indiana was Humphrey's next win, but the size of his victory in a head-to-head matchup against Wallace—47 to 42 percent—troubled many and reflected that the Democrats remained deeply divided. Wins in Ohio and West Virginia followed, but McGovern's campaign soon caught steam and finally finished off Humphrey in California.

Humphrey spoke in Indianapolis on January 15, 1972, before a national meeting of the Jaycees as it honored its "Top 10 Outstanding Young Men," as his campaign took on more and more importance as the Democratic field continued to thin—Muskie, Bayh, Vance Hartke, and Congressman Henry "Scoop" Jackson all having faded out. All that remained were Humphrey, Wallace, and McGovern, and McGovern was skipping Indiana to focus his efforts elsewhere. Humphrey made a bid for Muskie's support—that came along with an endorsement from Bayh—to go along with his support from Hartke. Despite his efforts, concerns remained high that Wallace could do well in the state, exposing further division among Democrats desperately needing a united front against Nixon. Eventually, the United Auto Workers, the AFL-CIO, and other labor leaders jumped from Muskie's nonexistent Indiana campaign to Humphrey in an effort to stop Wallace.[138]

Humphrey described Wallace's campaign as "primarily a protest" and said the Alabama governor "has a certain amount of showmanship. He articulates many of the concerns people have and doesn't burden himself with the solutions."[139] Noting that he believed Wallace was unelectable, Humphrey said, "I appeal to every Democrat who wishes to see this party of ours win in November to unite behind my banner and I believe if we do, we can go on to the Miami convention with a considerable degree of unity and support and come out of the convention with a candidate—and I am sufficiently selfish to want it to be myself—who can carry on and win in November." He acknowledged that the Indiana primary was shaping up, "rightly or wrongly by

many people in this country as a test between George Wallace on one hand and a regular Democrat on the other. I want Democrats who wish to see their party win in November to rally to my banner. . . . It will boil down to a contest between those who support Mr. Wallace and the rest of us who are pretty much on the same ideological wavelength."[140]

As the days grew shorter before the Indiana vote, Humphrey made an all-out effort in Indiana, with campaign and media stops in Indianapolis, Terre Haute, Anderson, Gary, Clarksville, and Evansville. He acknowledged the past support Wallace had enjoyed in Indiana, but emphasized that he doubted such a level of support still existed for him in Indiana. At Terre Haute, Humphrey said, "I would hope the McGovern supporters or the Muskie supporters would realize that I stand here in Indiana as the legitimate spokesman for the progressive Democratic Party. I can't imagine that people who want change in

LIBRARY OF CONGRESS

Vice President Hubert H. Humphrey, 1965

America, people who believe we should end this war and end it promptly would in any way try to discourage voting for the one candidate that challenges Wallace. That one candidate is myself."[141]

During his Indianapolis stop, he suggested that if elected he would likely replace FBI director J. Edgar Hoover, noting that "I think the next president would want a younger man," but said he would like to see Hoover "retire with dignity and not under fire." Hoover's future as the head of the bureau was quickly a moot point. Hoover died at his Washington, D.C., home on May 1, 1972, at the age of seventy-seven.[142] In additional remarks before the Indiana Broadcasters Association, Humphrey said he had a plan for the nation's future, rather than just complaints—all that Wallace could offer. "I have a program for the nation, for jobs, for tax reform," he said. "In 1968, I had the solutions. The governor of Alabama in 1968 was standing in school house doors. He isn't going to be standing in any White House doors."[143]

Regarding the ongoing war in Vietnam, Humphrey sounded a vastly different tone than he had in 1968, saying he favored "a prompt and total withdrawal. No amount of bombing is going to make the situation any better. This is an unpopular war and the people want out."[144] The former vice president said he felt that American involvement in Southeast Asia was based on "too little" information while acknowledging that his war position may have cost him the 1968 election to Nixon, Humphery said that as a world power the United States could not operate foreign policy "with a half-world knowledge. I suggest this is part of our problem."[145] In remarks at Clarksville, Humphrey said a "30 to 90 day timetable" made sense for American withdrawal from Vietnam and called for advancement of legislation supporting equal pay for women. "The time

has come to do something about the fact that a nation founded on justice and equality can no longer relegate more than half of its population to second class citizenship," Humphrey said.[146]

Humphrey worked hard to change the focus from the Humphrey-Wallace matchup and reminded voters, "The man to beat is President Nixon. He is the man who has said he could end the war and had a secret plan and would do it in six months and it still rages."[147] The former vice president said that the Nixon policy in Vietnam had escalated the war and "the first thing I would not do is escalate the war. I think we have a policy we are committed to that we ought to follow—namely to disengage from that struggle and as rapidly as possible. If Vietnamization is a success, its testing point is now. Either fish or cut bait. We are going to find out whether Vietnamization really works. It is our duty now to pursue the course that the President said he was launched on—namely disengagement. I want it now promptly, air, land, water and CIA—all of it."[148] In addition, Humphrey said he thought "the conference talks in Paris ought to be reopened. Whether they make progress or not is relatively unimportant. There has to be a channel of communication and that channel of communication between North Vietnam and the United States is in Paris."[149]

Humphrey's Indiana stops included visits to black churches, as well as local TV morning shows. He said he had heard "mixed reports" on his ability to defeat Wallace in the head-on battle in Indiana. "I have reason to believe we will win. I'm the only one that represents the national Democratic Party," he said.[150] A week later, Humphrey won a narrow win over Wallace in Indiana. Humphrey left the analysis mostly to others, for his part summing it up as "winning is winning."[151]

Humphrey never gathered enough delegates to take the party's nomination away from McGovern. He returned to his Senate seat, one he regained in 1970 after Eugene McCarthy declined to run, and won another six-year term in 1976. He was never again a factor in a national race. Humphrey died of cancer on January 13, 1978, in his home at Waverly, Minnesota. The remainder of his Senate term was completed by his wife, Muriel, until a special election could be held.

George C. Wallace

Still questioned about whether he truly wanted to be or believed he could be elected president, Wallace trudged ahead in 1972, gathering up as many conservative and moderate Democrats as he could. Wallace's 1972 campaign became his most successful and was perhaps best characterized as a waiting room for Democrats struggling to understand the changes sweeping America-

LIBRARY OF CONGRESS

Humphrey shaking hands with civil rights leader Dr. Martin Luther King as King's wife, Coretta, looks on at a rally at Harlem's 369th Regiment Armory, December 1964.

-urban problems of crime and poverty, continual racial strife, and opposition to forced school desegregation and Affirmative Action.

While many of the "Wallace Democrats" may eventually have become Republicans, in 1972 there remained enough of them to keep the spirited former pugilist in the fight, punching away, hoping for enough delegates at the Democratic National Convention to be an influence on his party. The "official" Democratic Party in Indiana, however, remained vehemently opposed to the presence of Wallace, with state party chair, Gordon St. Angelo, calling Wallace "a fascist."[152]

Coming into the Indiana primary, Wallace clearly could see the setup was working out well for him. Senators Muskie, Jackson, McGovern, Bayh, and Hartke were all either out of the race or skipping the state. Muskie's name was officially still on the ballot, but mainline Democrats were quickly lining up behind Humphrey in an "anybody but George Wallace" strategy. Wallace vacillated between downplaying his chances in Indiana and openly declaring, "I think I can win in Indiana."[153] He told reporters that he hoped to draw "about 30 percent" of the Democratic vote and emphasized that he lacked the finances and organization of state party officials, who were refusing to remain impartial and jumping behind Humphrey. Despite his challenges, Wallace admitted he was transferring campaign resources from the upcoming Tennessee primary to Indiana. "We want to spend more time in Indiana where it's a head-on race with Mr. Humphrey," he said. "I think I can win in Indiana."[154] Humphrey was also predicting an all-out victory over Wallace in Indiana, although party leaders openly admitted there was a lack of enthusiasm on the part of Democrats for any of the candidates.[155]

Wallace opened his Indiana campaign in mid-April 1972 at Hammond, an ethnically diverse "white flight" community situated next door to an increasingly politically powerful and growing Gary, the latter a community ruled by a newly emerging black political power in the state (the city having elected its first black mayor, Hatcher, in 1967). During subsequent stops at both South Bend and Fort Wayne, crowds were respectable in size and respectful in behavior and seemed to match or exceed the enthusiasm Wallace had drawn in his two earlier forays into Indiana in 1964 and 1968. Before his remarks at the Morris Civic Auditorium in South Bend, Wallace predicted that whomever finished third in Indiana would likely be eliminated as a serious contender for the nomination and predicted that he if were to win first place over Humphrey and Muskie, that the path to his nomination could be a lot more certain.[156]

Wallace was counting on support from working voters, although official UAW leaders followed him around the state reminding voters of their support of Humphrey's candidacy. And though they had originally backed Muskie, they reminded fellow Democrats that a vote for Muskie's now-ended campaign was a vote for Wallace. Wallace's confidence seemed to be wavering, although he told an enthusiastic group of supporters in Indianapolis in late April that he was still confident he could win the party's nomination.[157] In Indiana, however, Wallace's financial situation limited his campaign mostly to news conferences and quick stops in the state. In the waning days of the primary campaign, Wallace said he hoped to grab as many as thirty of Indiana's delegates to the upcoming Democratic National Convention and declared himself as the "only progressive Democrat" on the Hoosier ballot.[158] As the *Milwaukee (WI) Journal* reported, "Wallace is not, however, completely pessimistic about his prospects for capturing some of the

100 convention delegates to be assigned in the primary voting. After all, he reasons, Hoosiers have always 'treated me fairly well' in the past. 'I got 29 percent in the Democratic primary here in 1964 and nearly 12 percent in the general election four years ago. And do you expect that some of those people might still be around?'"[159]

Time magazine reported on Wallace's "characteristically helter-skelter" campaign in Indiana by focusing on a $25-a-plate lunch at the Indianapolis Hilton Hotel, headlined by local leaders of the John Birch Society and the Grand Dragon of the Indiana Ku Klux Klan. Frank Thompson of the Birch Society reminded those at the luncheon that Wallace was "American, he's Christian, and he's experienced."[160] Wallace did *try* for positive coverage while in Indianapolis, a CBS News camera crew tagging along as he rode in a 1972 Oldsmobile Cutlass, the Indianapolis 500 pace car driven around the famous oval by his wife, Cornelia.

For a scheduled Terre Haute speech at the Vigo County Fairgrounds, Wallace's campaign plane arrived three hours late, and he and his wife were met by tight security spurred on by a large group of protesters. Delivering what the *Terre Haute Tribune-Star* described as "a fiery address before a highly partisan cheering crowd . . . Wallace brought repeated applause from thousands in the 4-H building when he called for support from 'you, the forgotten middle Americans.'"[161] As the patient crowd waited, "Wallace girls" worked the crowds for donations and handed out campaign buttons and stickers while a country and western band entertained from the stage. The *Tribune-Star* reported, "Anti-Wallace pickets appeared at the east end of the huge building before the governor arrived, but a major confrontation with the heavily pro-Wallace crowd was held in check by police. Some youths

were escorted from the building by state police. The fairgrounds crowd erupted into a standing ovation when Mrs. Wallace was introduced, but the ovation increased to a deafening roar when Wallace walked onto the stage accompanied by Secret Service agents who took positions on either side of the platform."[162]

Wallace's speech focused mostly on his Democratic primary opponents, and he reminded his Hoosier audience, "I came to Indiana in 1968 and everything you and I said then, the other candidates are saying now. Nothing will make a candidate change his mind faster than seeing crowds applauding George Wallace. The six Democrat senators running for the nomination are calling for tax relief for you the working men and women, but why weren't they talking that way four years ago?" Answering his own question, Wallace declared, "I'll tell you why! They've sat in Congress and taxed you to death and given the money to welfare loafers and everybody overseas!"[163] Not forgetting that his audiences always enjoyed some law and order red meat, Wallace added, "On the streets of our large cities, thugs have taken over. When you go home at night, you have to lock yourself in. And I'll tell you that if you get knocked on the head when you leave this building tonight, the guy who hit you will be out of jail thanks to some judge before you get to the hospital."[164]

Wallace continued his effort in the heart of Indiana's industrial belt, with additional campaign speeches in Gary, Kokomo, Columbus, Bedford, and Anderson. The Wallace schedule reflected the support he was peeling off from large blocks of UAW members despite the union's stated support of Muskie and Humphrey on the state level. "I may not have all the answers, but I represent more of the issues to your satisfaction than any other candidate," Wallace told his

Madison County audience.[165] During his speech at the Anderson Municipal Airport, delivered while standing in the bed of a pickup truck before about 2,000 supporters, he also took aim at federal court orders forcing local communities to bus students in order to achieve racial desegregation of schools and taxes. In addition, he restated his support to keep FBI director Hoover in place, noting, "I think he is a great one" and chastised "false liberals" invading the Democratic Party in Indiana and encouraged his Indiana backers: "You are on the way to having more power than you ever had. It used to be your party and you're taking it back." Later he told reporters that he was hopeful for an Indiana win, but cautioned it with, "I feel we will get a good vote. I think we are going to win delegates."[166]

At his Indianapolis speech at the state fairgrounds, a handful of local UAW members presented Wallace with an honorary UAW member jacket in defiance of their state and national organization endorsements. Wallace's campaign also called on Norman Jones, identified as the chairman of a group known as National Black Citizens for George Wallace, to appear with the governor in Indianapolis to appeal to black Democrats in the city. When pressed by reporters to name any black Democrats in Indiana who were active in his organization, Jones declined to do so, but readily introduced Wallace to the state fairgrounds assemblage. In his remarks, Wallace at least made attempts to gain back black voters that he had long ago lost via the protracted and ugly civil rights struggle in his native Alabama. "People of all races are against wholesale busing," Wallace said. "I want to appeal to the support of all people in [Indiana] regardless of race and color."[167]

On primary day, Wallace rolled up his largest percentage in any northern, industrial state to date, and "ran well in predominantly white, blue-collar districts of the industrial northwest parts of state," and Wallace reportedly also "did well in blue-collar wards, suburbs, and rural counties, benefiting from a strong cross-over Republican vote," with Humphrey's victory attributed to a heavy black vote in Indianapolis, Fort Wayne, and Gary.[168] Although Wallace would later complain loudly that he did not say it, reporters quoted him as saying Humphrey's Indiana win could be attributed to "that big, nigger vote" and that a week earlier he had used the word "nigger" to describe the only Republican challenging Nixon in the Indiana primary—Senator Edward M. Brooke of Massachusetts. Reporters also quoted him offstage as joking following a speech in Boston and saying, "I didn't give them much nigger talk today, did I? Shoot, folks are going to start saying that I've gone soft."[169]

The glow of Wallace's impressive showing in Indiana did not last long. Headed to Maryland for the next primary, Wallace was met with persistent protesters all along the trail. Security remained tight around the outspoken Alabama governor, but was ill-equipped to protect him on May 15, 1972, as he plunged into a crowd at a shopping plaza in Laurel, Maryland. There twenty-one-year-old Arthur Bremer, a deranged gunman who originally had planned to assassinate Nixon, stepped from the crowd and emptied his .38 caliber handgun, striking Wallace four times and paralyzing him for the remainder of his life. Bremer was tried and convicted for the crime and served thirty-five years of a fifty-three-year-sentence before being released from prison in 2007.[170]

Four years later in the 1976 campaign, a very different Wallace approached the presidential primary campaign, this time slowed considerably by the assassination attempt on his life. Generally, Wallace sought credibility and mainstream acceptability back inside the Democratic Party and scaled back and toned down earlier themes, rarely mentioning segregation or busing, and instead championing working people. He did accuse his Democratic opponents, notably another southern governor, Carter of Georgia, of stealing his ideas and campaign themes. With a very unclear path to the Democratic nomination, and showing signs of strain from conducting his campaign as a paraplegic confined to a wheelchair, the *New York Times* asked *the* question in an article titled, "Wallace's Last Hurrah?" The *Times* referred to his latest attempt for the presidency this way: "He is, after all, a 56-year-old, extremely hard-of-hearing paraplegic who has already spent thousands of miles on the road pushing a product that just not enough people wanted to buy, and he has already had three successive political bankruptcies, the last of which left him bleeding on the hot, hard pavement of a Maryland shopping center."[171] The *Times* declared, "What seems even more remarkable, though, is that despite the tragic toll it has taken on him, and regardless of his record for rather consistent failure, George Corley Wallace still sees himself as one of the major figures in the market."[172]

For Indiana, Wallace was the first candidate to file his paperwork for the May 1976 primary with many times the number of signatures required from voters from each of the state's eleven congressional districts.[173] His campaign scheduled five "airport drop in" appearances, basically a chance for Wallace to fly in, gain some media attention, and fly out, at Indianapolis; Terre Haute; Evansville; Fort Wayne; and South Bend. It was about as rigorous a type of campaign one could expect from Wallace, but still did little to remove the lingering doubts that he was not only unelectable based on his politics,

but appeared physically unable to withstand the rigors of the presidency. Perhaps stung by an earlier Indiana appearance at Anderson, where an unknown saboteur had canceled hotel ballroom reservations, confusion reigned among Wallace supporters about whether he would appear. The campaign was tight-lipped about specifics of the Wallace trek.[174]

At Terre Haute Wallace brought his "Trust the People" campaign to a handful of about 150 supporters and said he would engage in some "impromptu speech making" and bypass just answering reporters' questions. Positioned in his wheelchair behind a desk set on the back of a flatbed truck parked on the airport runway, Wallace said he was gravely concerned about the level of crime gripping the nation. "We are at the mercy of thugs and criminals as a result of federal court decisions," he said, decisions that favored defendant rights over those of "law-abiding citizens."[175] Wallace said he opposed efforts to overturn death penalty statutes across the states and said as president he would push for a constitutional amendment to allow death penalties in all fifty states. Moving on to his views about "the welfare state," Wallace said, "I'm tired of people getting handouts from my pocketbook, and yours." He estimated as many as 25 percent of all welfare and food stamp recipients in the nation were frauds and liars—claims that met with enthusiastic applause from his small crowd. He directly addressed whether he was physically able to not only campaign for president but to serve. "The health issue will dissipate as my rigorous campaign continues," he said.[176] At Evansville, Wallace reminisced about a summer job as a teenager that brought him across the Ohio River into southwestern Indiana to sell magazine subscriptions. Wallace campaign aides blamed a misunderstanding about the different time zone for Evansville for the reason the governor drew only a small handful of ardent backers.

Later, at Indianapolis, Wallace said his presence in the race provided a "fringe benefit" to Democrats, allowing them to avoid a sharp turn to the left as in the 1972 race under McGovern. Wallace said the Democrats were returning to their rightful role as "the party of the people after their exotic far-left extremism positions of the 1972 campaign."[177] He reminded doubters among reporters at his news conference that he had polled 1.2 million primary votes in 1976 so far among Democrats, while front-runner Carter had polled 1.8 million votes. Wallace said he was open to being asked to be the running mate of any eventual Democratic nominee, but said he opposed any effort to place a woman or a black candidate in the vice presidential slot purely on the basis of gender or race. Wallace campaign officials called off plans for the governor to stay overnight in Indianapolis and instead took a late flight back to Alabama. They denied it was related to the investigation of a loaded shotgun found in the trunk of an open car trunk at the Airport Holiday Inn where Wallace appeared. Secret Service agents questioned, and later released, an Indianapolis man who had the gun in his car as no federal or state firearms violations were cited.[178]

Wallace made another last-minute stop in Indiana just before the primary voting, but acknowledged his campaign was not attracting the support among Hoosiers he had enjoyed just four years earlier when he won 42 percent of the Democratic vote. "Forty-two percent is a big amount to get when you have lost some momentum and it would be very difficult to approach that figure in Indiana," Wallace told reporters in a voice described in an *Indianapolis Star* dispatch as weak. "But I still believe we will do well here."[179] Wallace signaled that he no longer held much hope of

capturing the Democratic Party's presidential nomination, but that he hoped to influence the Democrats' national platform toward "the views of the great middle class. I said in 1972 that one of the aims of running in that year was to take the Democratic Party back to the people. I want the 1976 platform to be one that is acceptable to the great mass of middle-class citizenry."[180] When a reporter asked Wallace if he had grown discouraged about the fate of his current campaign, the formerly feisty Alabama governor said, "I never get discouraged. With the things that have happened to me, I never get discouraged unless, of course, someone walked up and stuck a thirty-eight in my face" (a grim reference to the bullets that paralyzed him in the May 1972 assassination attempt).[181]

Wallace's last moment on the national stage came in July 1976 as he was carefully wheeled to the podium of the Democratic National Convention in New York City's Madison Square Garden. His speech, a noncontroversial tome on "Government Reform and Business Accountability," stirred more sympathy for his obvious physical struggles than excitement for his ideas.[182] *New York Times* political reporters indicated Wallace appeared "fatigued and bored" in the weeks leading up to the convention and was particularly irritated by defections from his camp to Reagan among Hoosier faithful, costing him the Indiana Democratic primary to Carter.[183] Wallace's opportunity to address delegates came at the invitation of Carter and included an agreement that Wallace would not permit his name to be placed into nomination from the floor of the convention. He was elected to a fourth and final term as governor of Alabama in 1982. He left the governor's mansion for the last time in January 1987, the same year his third marriage ended. The remaining years of Wallace's life were spent in struggle dealing with the pain and the difficulties of his paralysis, and he died of septic shock at a Birmingham hospital on September 13, 1998.

Edmund Muskie

The once-hopeful Muskie candidacy for the presidency was showing serious signs of strain as Indiana's May 2, 1972, primary approached. Although he had obtained ballot access and had an active campaign organization in place, at the last minute Muskie's campaign turned its attentions elsewhere and ordered the Indianapolis office closed.

Before things fell apart, however, Muskie sounded confident of his chances in Indiana. During a media swing through the state in March 1972, as he made his primary filing official, Muskie told reporters at East Chicago: "I hate what George Wallace stands for. I stand against him because he is wrong about social justice. . . . I stand against him because he is wrong about economic justice, because this preacher of prejudice is nothing more than a pretender to populism. George Wallace says he stands for workers, family farmers and the average-income Americans. The truth is that Wallace has spent his entire time in public office in the service of special privilege. We must beat George Wallace and Richard Nixon. Wallace and Nixon joined together to defeat the Democratic Party in 1968. They jointly share the responsibility that we have continued inflation, rising unemployment, and a failure to end the war in Vietnam."[184] Recognizing the past support Wallace had enjoyed in northwest Indiana, Muskie declared, "George Wallace isn't your friend. He isn't your man, and neither is Richard Nixon. There's only one party that has ever concerned itself with the welfare, the well-being of grass-roots Americans. You know that in Lake County, and that's the Democratic Party when it's operated at its best."[185]

In Indianapolis, Muskie kept his focus on Wallace and Nixon and said the two remained "close allies" and that Indiana Democrats could not trust their vote to him. He reminded voters that Wallace's 1968 third-party bid "defeated the Democratic Party and George Wallace now wants the Democratic nomination. I find that incredible."[186] Muskie warned that "what is at stake in 1972 is our chance to change America. We have lost it before . . . in the decision to fight a senseless and immoral war that the Nixon Administration still fails to end."[187]

In the weeks that followed, however, Muskie underperformed in the subsequent primaries, and news reports indicated his campaign was broke.[188] By late April the inevitable was clear, and while Muskie remained on the Indiana ballot, he staged no active primary campaign in the state.

Despite his primary struggles in 1972, the former Maine governor and U.S. senator had made a strong impression on Hoosiers during several previous forays into the state. Once considered by Nixon campaign operatives as their most challenging opponent in a crowded Democratic field, Muskie had the backing of four of Indiana's five Democratic congressmen (despite the slow-starting presidential campaigns of Indiana's two senators—Bayh and Hartke).[189] Muskie's campaign said he was headed to Indiana "with a new image of an aggressive, issue-oriented liberal rather than a soothing centrist and planned to present himself as the only viable liberal alternative to Humphrey."[190] However, Muskie's campaign suffered multiple wounds via a round of Republican-backed dirty campaigning. In the final Indiana primary vote, he still polled 12 percent of the vote, but was a footnote to a too-close race for Indiana's delegates with a narrow win by Humphrey over Wallace.[191]

Muskie's appeal, particularly his strong views on the ongoing Vietnam War, made him a popular choice, so popular that conservative columnists Rowland Evans and Robert Novak opined that Muskie had outshone Indiana's own potential nominee, Bayh, at the 1971 Jefferson-Jackson Day Dinner in Indianapolis. At that event at the fairgrounds, Muskie said his remarks were about "pessimism and party politics" and declared that "some people think the Democratic Party will prosper in direct proportion to the misery in which the country finds itself."[192]

"I hear it said that a strategy for victory of the Democrats in 1972 should be built on the expected failure of President Nixon to get out of Vietnam, on a continued increase in unemployment, and, in general, on the worsening of economic conditions," Muskie said. "It is not enough, however, for Democrats to come before the American people, either today or in 1972, with proposals just to end the war in Vietnam. The American people, and especially the young people of the country, are looking to us to be even more basic than that. They want to know what our ideas are on how to avoid future Vietnams. They want to know how we propose to go about building an enduring peace."[193]

Muskie dug in on the Vietnam War issue, a conflict he termed "a road-block in the way of progress" for the nation. Taking on Nixon's claims that opponents of the Vietnam War and containment of Communism in Southeast Asia were isolationists particularly drew Muskie's ire. "The way to begin is to get out of the quicksand of Vietnam," he said. "But the President says that people who take this position are actually fostering a new form of isolationism. The President has defended his position in Vietnam by saying that America must not retreat from the world. . . . I have no trouble in accepting the position that

the United States is part of the world and that we have the strongest obligations to the keeping of the peace. But I find it difficult to see how intelligent and humane opposition to the war in Vietnam fits in with any reasonable definition of isolationism."[194]

Drawing loud applause from his audience, Muskie said, "The American people are willing to accept their responsibilities to other people in the world, but they do not believe that what we have been doing in Vietnam, in Cambodia, or Laos, is a proper exercise of that world responsibility. I don't believe it is isolationist to protest the dropping of bombs on villages."[195]

Muskie said the Democratic agenda must also include a strong program to address sagging employment numbers across the nation. "I said I was eager to cooperate with the President in getting out of Vietnam. I'd also like to cooperate with him in ending the recession and in helping him to keep his promises of jobs for our war veterans. We cannot tell the boys who have just come home from Vietnam that this country has very clear ideals about what they are expected to do in war, but only the vaguest notions about what they are expected to do for a living when they come back."[196]

His presidential ambitions dashed in the 1972 primary season, Muskie reluctantly backed McGovern's losing effort in the fall and returned to a distinguished career in the Senate until May 1980 when he accepted the appointment of President Carter as secretary of state, a post he held only eight months, as Carter failed to win election to a second term. Muskie retired from public life and died on March 26, 1996, at his home in Washington, D.C., at the age of eighty-one.

Edward M. "Ted" Kennedy

Much of the dynamic of the process the Democratic Party had to undertake for 1972 started and ended with the question: "What will Teddy do?" The last Kennedy brother, and perhaps the best hope of the party to keep a popular President Nixon from winning a second term, Kennedy pondered for months about whether to enter the race and ultimately decided to opt out. Just three years removed from a tragic car accident in Chappaquiddick, Massachusetts, that left a female campaign aide dead, doubts lingered not only about Kennedy's personal character, but also his desire for the office. His decision made, Kennedy did dig in to help the party where he could in senate and congressional races.

Kennedy's close friendship with Bayh brought him to Indianapolis for the state's Jefferson-Jackson Day Dinner in April 1972, his first appearance on the Democratic circuit for 1972 and drew national news coverage. The friendship between Bayh and Kennedy was not only cemented via their combined service in the Senate, but also as a result of their shared tragedy of a June 19, 1964, plane crash in which both men survived, Bayh having pulled the seriously injured Kennedy from the wreckage, although the plane's pilot did not survive.

"The first appearance by Senator Edward Kennedy at a Democratic Party rally this year has demonstrated that the Kennedy vote-getting ability is still strong," the Associated Press reported. "His speech was a party rallying cry to oppose President Nixon on the basis of his 'broken promise'—but the speech was secondary to the impact of the man. Women in expensive gowns and men in evening clothes shoved each other to get autographs from Senator Kennedy throughout the evening and some followed him to the airport to get his signature on the dinner program."[197] Kennedy told reporters in Indianapolis, "I am interested in keeping in contact with Democrats in various parts of the country" and said the crowded Democratic presidential primary field was not necessarily harmful to the party's chances. Kennedy said the presidential primaries had a twofold value: "They give people an opportunity to get a clear, definitive idea of the candidates, and give the candidates a better understanding of what is happening in this country," but added, "It is tiring, it is expensive, and is wasteful in some ways."[198]

Kennedy was back in the state in October 1972 for a campaign appearance to benefit Congressman John Brademas of South Bend and drew a standing-room-only crowd of 6,000 students and citizens inside and outside of the Stepan Center on the Notre Dame campus. In a speech that left many Democratic Party faithful wishing Kennedy was running against Nixon, he said, "The people of America have known scandals and corruption in government before, but rarely in such a steady flow as we have seen in the past four years. It isn't easy to be found with your hand in the till and your foot in your mouth and your tongue in your cheek and your eye on the polls, all at the same time, but the Nixon administration is managing to perform that feat today."[199]

Kennedy's remarks came just as news was developing about a June 17, 1972, break-in at the headquarters of the Democratic National Committee inside the Watergate office building in Washington, D.C., but long before any link to the Nixon White House was made. "Twice before in our history we have had presidents whose administrations were schools for scandal," Kennedy said. "Ulysses Grant had his whiskey ring, Warren Harding had his Teapot Dome. And now Richard Nixon has an administration so full of examples of corruption that future historians will disagree only about which one was the worst."[200]

Kennedy openly criticized recent agreements reached with the Soviet Union, including one that would affect wheat grown by Indiana farmers. He said, "For a hundred years, the Russians have been trying to get even for the way we bought Alaska and now they've finally done it. It took only a few brief bargaining days last summer for the Russians to send Earl Butz back to Washington in a barrel, and make our departments of commerce and agriculture a laughing stock of East-West trade."[201] Kennedy's knock on Secretary Butz, an Indiana native, was no accident and won applause from the audience.

While in South Bend, Kennedy joined Brademas and former governor Welsh, running to regain the state's top office in 1972, to shake hands at a workers' gate at the Bendix Plant in South Bend. He made more stops—Elkhart, Fort Wayne, and Muncie—before arriving the next day in Indianapolis. For his speech at an outdoor rally before 3,000 rain-soaked Hoosiers in Indianapolis, Kennedy focused on the Vietnam War. "People are fed up with a war that will not end," he said. "They are fed up with rising prices, welfare costs and taxes. They are fed up with jobs that don't exist, with tax loopholes that can't be closed, streets that aren't paved. They are fed up most of all with Richard Nixon and Spiro Agnew."[202]

"Just about four years ago on October 9, the nominee for the Republican Party for the Presidency said if we can't win [the war in Vietnam] in four years, we ought to be held accountable and responsible for it," Kennedy said. Declaring that Nixon "hasn't ended the war and we aren't going to give him another chance with four more years," he added, "Every bomb that's dropped is nailing tighter the doors in which our prisoners

of war are held. The prisoners will not be released as long as we continue the policy on which we are embarked."[203]

Kennedy said he was optimistic about Democratic chances to keep Nixon from winning a second term, saying, "There is victory in the air," noting that in his travels with McGovern "I saw the spark of victory out there. There are those people who say the Democrats can't win in 1972. Those same people were saying in 1948 to Harry Truman and in 1960 to John Kennedy they couldn't win, and they went ahead and were victorious."[204] Kennedy's optimism notwithstanding, there was no victory at hand for McGovern and Kennedy's brother-in-law, Shriver, both en route to one of the worst political defeats in American presidential history.

Sargent Shriver

Shriver, experienced a warmer Indiana reception in 1972 than his Republican counterpart, Vice President Agnew, speaking before an overflow student audience in the Stephan Center at the University of Notre Dame at South Bend a week after Agnew's Fort Wayne fracas. Shriver asked students to avoid being "swept along by the cynicism that's so prevalent in this land" and to "create a politics of people to replace the politics of power—a politics of every family in America, a politics of every neighborhood."[205]

"In the seventies, the battle for social justice goes on—not only in the third world of Latin America, Africa and Asia, not only for civil rights in the South, but in Northern neighborhoods where millions of our fellow Americans walk the streets looking for jobs—including, I want to add, 310,000 veterans of Vietnam—where crime has terrified the inhabitants, where substandard houses degenerate and collapse while the United States government under Richard Nixon has become the Number One slum landlord in the nation."[206]

Shriver's remarks were frank and memorable: "Never in my adult lifetime . . . has the presidency of the United States been so blatant, so arrogant, in its tolerance of corruption. They [the Republicans] buy the presidency in 1972, and they buy it cheap. But it isn't just the presidency—they're buying you because the presidency isn't theirs—it belongs to you—to you and all the people. More pious words are not enough, more manipulation of opinion is not enough, mere victory in an election is not enough. What is at stake for America is not one man's success. It is a nation's soul."[207]

Shriver told the 3,000 students present, "This nation needs you, the nation needs your spirit of honesty. The nation needs your willingness to hear the cries of the poor and the lower-middle-class. It needs your resistance to corporate power and wealth. The nation needs the dedication of your lives. The generation of the 1970s . . . will be a toughened generation; it will be at work for the long pull. We don't need an hour's enthusiasm, we need a life's fidelity. We need the daily grind of precinct work, the daily proof to neighborhoods that we are worthy of their trust. We don't need instant righteousness."[208]

From South Bend, Shriver went on to stops

R. Sargent Shriver (left) holds a Peace Corps Week proclamation from New York mayor Robert Wagner at City Hall, watching is James B. Donovan, vice president of the city's Board of Education, June 1962.

LIBRARY OF CONGRESS

in Gary, East Chicago, and Richmond in an effort to do anything to fight back against what was shaping up as a major landslide that would swamp McGovern-Shriver, not only in Indiana, but also across the nation.

Shriver's life would have a major impact on the nation regardless of the outcome of the 1972 vote, with Shriver being a driving force behind the creation of valuable community-based programs such as Head Start, the Job Corps, Community Action Project, Upward Bound, and along with his wife, Eunice, the Special Olympics.

Shriver was diagnosed with Alzheimer's disease in 2003. He made his last two public appearances in 2009, on August 11 for the funeral of his wife, and again two weeks later on August 29 for the funeral of his brother-in-law, Ted Kennedy. Shriver died at a hospital in Bethesda, Maryland, on January 8, 2011, at the age of ninety-five.

Nelson A. Rockefeller

The lengthy struggle Ford experienced in dispatching Reagan for the Republican presidential nomination likely helped make up his mind about the role incumbent Vice President Nelson Rockefeller would or would not play in the campaign. Rockefeller was nominated by Ford for the vice presidency in 1974, only the second person elevated to the nation's second highest office under the Twenty-Fifth Amendment (the other being Ford himself a year earlier in 1973). Conservative Republicans were not enamored with the liberal-by-Republican-standards Rockefeller. He won congressional confirmation for the office without the support of a handful of conservatives and liberals, including Bayh, who voted against his selection.[209]

Rockefeller's place in the Ford administration was in question almost from the start. During his first visit to Indiana as vice president in October

1975, Rockefeller told reporters that the decision about whether he would be Ford's running mate for the 1976 election was up to the president. The Associated Press reported that Rockefeller "side-stepped questions about the possibility of Ford dropping him from the ticket by declaring, 'I am not a candidate,'" but said at a news conference that it was "a fair statement" that his presence on the ticket would help the Republicans draw some labor support that might otherwise go to Democrats."[210]

Rockefeller seemed more certain about another political fact—that Reagan would challenge Ford for the nomination and predicted, "I personally cannot believe that an incumbent president is going to be unseated under these circumstances." He told two groups, one a gathering of state Republican Party leaders and the other the Indiana State Teachers Association, that he was not appearing in a campaign mode for either himself or President Ford, and instead was carrying the message that "we have a great President of the United States." The Associated Press reported Rockefeller received "mild applause" from a small gathering of only 600 GOP leaders, even when he joined in Ford's assertion that federal aid should not be used to bailout "bankrupt" New York City (despite Rockefeller's multiple terms as governor of New York and emerging reports that the two men did not agree on the best approach to help the nation's largest city).[211]

Less than a month later, Rockefeller hand delivered a letter to Ford, indicating he was not interested in being the Republican nominee for vice president in 1976. Rockefeller's letter listed no specific reasons, and it was widely believed it was the result of strong signals from Ford that he was interested in selecting someone else. Ford told reporters that the White House had not asked Rockefeller to step aside and said the vice president's decision "was his own" and that Rockefeller had indicated he would support Ford for renomination.[212] The discussion of whether Rocky had stepped aside on his own or been asked to do so by the Ford campaign subsided as the 1976 election progressed, and Ford lost a close contest to Carter.

Before leaving office in January 1977, Ford presented Rockefeller with the Presidential Medal of Freedom, the highest civilian honor available in the United States. Back in private life, Rockefeller turned his attentions to substantial arts patronage efforts his family had championed, including the Museum of Modern Art in New York City. He died on January 26, 1979, in New York City, the result of a heart attack. He was seventy years old.

Jimmy Carter

The former Georgia governor and peanut farmer, Carter, made his first campaign visits to Indiana in April 1976 in the run-up to the Democratic primary election in May. His first stop was Indianapolis and then South Bend, at both stops predicting Governor Wallace would show considerably less electoral strength in Indiana in 1976 than he had done in 1972 (when he won 42 percent of the Democratic primary vote). Predicting he would have more than a thousand delegates in hand before the opening gavel fell for the Democratic National Convention, Carter said he believed he was becoming "a very difficult candidate to stop" for the nomination.[213] Carter's first Indiana tour included a stop at the University of Notre Dame, where he conferred with head football coach Dan Devine and the football team in spring practice, before addressing an audience of more than 4,000 students. Devine referred to Carter as a "good, young liberal," and Carter noted his excitement in visiting the Notre Dame campus for the first time. "It's a very exciting thing for someone to come to Notre Dame," he said. "Wherever I've been, there is an intensity of interest and appreciation of what Notre Dame means to this country."[214]

Carter's foray into Indiana was not without controversy. His remarks before reporters at Indianapolis raised eyebrows and were quickly seized by two other Democrats still in the running for the nomination—Senator Henry "Scoop" Jackson of Washington and Congressman Morris K. Udall of Arizona. Carter told reporters in response to a question about the role of government in issues of school desegregation, civil rights, and integration: "I have nothing against a community that's made up of people who are Polish or Czechoslovakian or French-Canadian or blacks who are trying to maintain the ethnic purity of their neighborhoods" and that he would "never condone any sort of discrimination against, say, a black family, or any other family, from moving into that neighborhood."[215] He elaborated, "I'm not trying to say I want to maintain with any kind of government interference the ethnic purity of neighborhoods. What I say is that the government ought not to take as a major purpose the intrusion of alien groups into a neighborhood simply to establish that intrusion."[216]

The phrase "ethnic purity" stuck in the ears of many Democrats who were still skeptical of the "New South" Carter represented (as contrasted to the "Old South" still found in the likes of Wallace and former Georgia governor Lester Maddox). Carter's choice of words did not improve by the time he made his second appearance in South Bend where he added, "I don't think government ought deliberately to break down an ethnically-oriented community—deliberately by injecting into it a member of another race" and that "I think it's good to maintain the homogeneity of neighborhoods if they've been established that way." Using words such as "black intrusion," campaign aides finally convinced Carter to step back from his remarks.[217]

By then Jackson and Udall were already pouncing on what the meaning of Carter's remarks could be, and Carter told reporters a day later that his comments in Indiana were "a very serious mistake" and that "what I should have said was neighborhoods with ethnic character and ethnic heritage. What I meant was that people with the same ethnic background have chosen to live together."[218] Udall was not satisfied, saying, "There is no place in this land for thinly veiled hints of the politics of racial division" and openly suggested Carter had made his remark on "ethnic purity" in Indiana on purpose in order to draw away the last of the Wallace supporters among Hoosiers. "There is a Wallace vote [in Indiana], and Carter is raising this issue to get that vote, this may be his motive," Udall said. Jackson was equally critical in his assessment, saying that Carter would "be explaining that (remark) for a long time" and that his apology had only served to further muddy the issue—reflecting a lack of judgment on the part of the Washington outsider, Jackson said. For his part, Carter declared, "I would not take a racial attitude or discriminatory attitude toward any group. If I did, I would withdraw."[219]

Working hard to rebound, the Carter campaign said victories in upcoming Indiana and Pennsylvania primaries would likely end the candidacy of Jackson, once and for all. They did not have to wait until the Indiana vote. Jackson read the tea leaves and withdrew just before the Indiana vote, with the *New York Times* reporting: "Early yesterday evening, Jackson workers in Indianapolis quietly shut down the Senator's campaign office there."[220] Further easing the path for Carter, Udall's campaign fell thirty-five signatures short of getting him on the Indiana ballot. That left just Carter and Wallace, with Wallace becoming increasingly marginalized as southerners seemed to have found their new man in Carter. The sometimes overwhelming rigors of campaigning as a paralyzed man confined to a wheelchair did not go unnoted about Wallace. The *New York Times* described him as appearing "fatigued and bored" as he wrapped up two days of campaigning in Indiana, Texas, and Pennsylvania. Wallace openly complained that many of his supporters in Indiana and Texas appeared to be planning to vote for Reagan in the GOP primary, rather than him on the Democratic ballot.[221]

Carter kept focused on Ford and Reagan, noting that "at this point the country's drifting because there's no leadership," he said. "We don't need a caretaker in the White House, and that's what we've got." Carter's focus beyond the Democratic field seemed appropriate as he picked up the endorsement of his former competitor, Bayh, on the eve of the Indiana primary. Inviting workers to shake hands with Carter outside the Western Electric plant in Indianapolis, Bayh noted, "One thing I learned a long time ago and that's how to count."[222]

Carter made what his campaign dubbed a "non-political" appearance at Second Christian Church in Indianapolis and spoke to a primarily African-American audience where Pastor T. Garrott Benjamin declared Carter had "a lot of soul." Carter told his audience that while his Plains, Georgia, church was segregated and all white during his childhood, "most of my church mates and classmates were white, but most of my friends and most of my playmates were black. We have a lot in common," Carter said. "We have belief in one another and a common faith.

There is a hunger in the minds and hearts of the American people to restore those things we've lost. God knows I don't know all the answers, but I'm trying to learn them."[223] Speaking briefly to reporters, Carter said Ford let Reagan "push him around" in their contest. Carter said, "There is a lot of advantage to being an incumbent President. There is the aura of being President in itself. But along with that there is the responsibility not to let a political opponent in a heated campaign push you."[224]

For his part, Democratic Party stalwart Humphrey popped up in Indiana just before the May primary for the Jefferson-Jackson Day Dinner, but not as a candidate. Humphrey made light of the fact he had come to greet Hoosier Democrats many times before asking for their vote and did not rule out playing a role if a deadlocked Democratic convention emerged in July. Humphrey suggested that having taken a pass on the 1976 primary battle (which included contests in more than thirty states), he might be a useful choice to break any deadlock among Democrats. "It isn't as if Hubert Humphrey just dropped in, you know," Humphrey said in Indianapolis. "It isn't as if I'm saying 'here I am, a brand new boy,' . . . there are no secrets about me." Despite having skipped the primary process, Humphrey noted, "The primaries are intended so that candidates can get better acquainted with the public and the public can get acquainted with the candidates. I am already well known."[225] Humphrey's hopes for a deadlocked convention would not play out. Carter would go on to win the Indiana primary and his party's nomination.

For the fall campaign, Carter spent a considerable amount of time in the months before and immediately after the 1976 election buoyed by polling in Indiana (as in most other states) that post-Nixon Republican fatigue was running

high, and while polling consistently showed him trailing Ford, 15 to 20 percent of Indiana voters told pollsters they were "undecided" going into the final weeks of the campaign. Carter easily won Indiana's Democratic primary election in May, but made return trips to the state in hopes of stealing away a state Ford had been unable to carry in the Republican primary.

On June 19, 1976, a full month after Carter had wrapped up his Indiana win and as the delegate count began to make his nomination in New York City later that summer a seeming inevitability, Carter kept an early campaign promise to address a "Men's Fellowship Breakfast" organized by the Indianapolis-based Christian Church (Disciples of Christ) meeting at Purdue University in West Lafayette.[226] The meeting drew 3,000 men from Disciples of Christ congregations from across the Midwest and gave Carter yet another chance to highlight his commitment to morality and ethical government practices—a scarlet letter that squeaky-clean Ford had to carry for the departed Nixon. Carter noted that he had accepted the invitation to speak to the men more than a year ago, but "I'm very glad that I accepted that invitation, and that you have let me come," noting that it was worth the early flight from Georgia to Indiana just to hear the hymn singing prior to his speech.[227] Clarifying that "I didn't come here to preach to you, I'm not a preacher," Carter said that as a Baptist layman in the traditions of the Southern Baptist Convention, he was very much like the men from the Disciples of Christ Christian churches who sat before him. Recalling stories from his childhood in tiny Plains, Georgia, and his family's peanut farm, he joked that "I had a chance as I moved along the streets of Plains to learn at an early age who the people were, and how to judge the good ones from the bad ones. The good people who were the ones who bought boiled peanuts from me, and the bad ones didn't. I haven't improved at all in my ability to judge people since then, so I didn't come here to preach."[228]

Carter said eighteen months of campaigning for the presidency up until this point had helped him to see the vast diversity of the nation. "We all bring together different viewpoints, different needs, different hopes and dreams, and different aspirations, we even bring our own different prejudices and fears." He said, "Quite often we tend to think that the differences that exist among us are a source of weakness, but that need not be true. I think one of the great innate and natural strengths in our country is in our ability to take different kinds of people and to form a strong nation."[229] Without making a direct mention of the scandal that had plagued Washington politics in the preceding years, he noted that "we have to take what we have learned about Christ and about God, and about ethics and morality, about truthfulness and honesty, and brotherhood, and let that be part of our lives."[230] Americans were longing for the stability that older generations had known, but that "stability in America is changing." He suggested, "This has carried over into a loss of belief in the things we thought would never change. I always thought that my political leaders told the truth and that our nation stood for what was right in the eyes of God. Maybe it was too much national pride? But in the last few years, with the Vietnamese war, with the bombing of Cambodia, with the Watergate tragedy, the CIA revelations, that the goodness of our nation and the rightness of our nation is not assured anymore."[231]

Carter asked his fellow Christian church leaders to consider that none of them were hungry at that very moment—that each of them had access to a warm breakfast—and a promising future for themselves and their families. He said this placed a "tremendous responsibility" upon each of us to remember that "the biggest blessing that we have in our lives is our belief in Christ. This gives us the surety of faith and an unchanging core around which our lives can function. That is an enormous benefit to us, a tremendous blessing."[232] The openness with which the former Georgia governor spoke about his Christian beliefs was new to many voters. The more reserved, less outspoken Christian values expressed via Ford's Episcopalian faith were more common in American political life. Emphasizing that he shared the belief in a strong separation between church and state, Carter clarified "that doesn't mean, however, that we should have a different standard of ethics or morality or greatness or humility or brotherhood or compassion or love in public life than from what we have in our private lives."[233]

For the fall campaign against Ford, Carter crisscrossed the state in late September and again in October, as the polling showed the nation's voters deeply divided between the incumbent Ford and Carter. Even Indiana, traditionally a Republican territory, was viewed as possibly in play by the Democrats, most notably because Ford had failed to carry the state's Republican Primary in May. Carter's running mate, Senator Walter Mondale, often campaigned in Indiana, as did Rosalynn Carter and the Carter's eldest son, Chip. At a Fort Wayne stop, Mondale mistakenly referred to his running mate as "Jimmy Ford, but quickly corrected the error.[234] On September 12, 1976, Carter made a quick stop at the Indianapolis International Airport to talk to reporters and took a shot at Ford's Rose Garden strategy that found Ford in Washington more than on the campaign trail. Carter said that he was glad "my opponent had finally and reluctantly emerged from the Rose Garden" and said that "when a candidate becomes a recluse and refuses to submit himself to the constant cross examination that is inherent in an open campaign, then that indicates a concern by the administration about its acceptance on the basis of trust."[235]

Later in September at Evansville, Carter addressed an audience of about 6,000 at Roberts Stadium after attending a fund-raiser for Senator Hartke's ill-fated re-election campaign. Carter's speech emphasized economic troubles that he said had worsened under Ford's watch and said, "We've set new records in crime," which he related to growing unemployment. Blasting Ford and the GOP for their lack of progress on tax reform, Carter declared the current income tax system "a disgrace" and said the Republicans lacked the will to enact reform because of the influence of special interests. "I owe special interests nothing," Carter said, hoping to emphasize his "outside the Washington beltway" resume. "I owe the people everything."[236] He added, "You can't expect any better from political leadership that has been bogged down in Washington for 25 or 30 years, drawing their advice, their counsel, their financial support from lobbyists, from special interests. They go to the same restaurants, belong to the same clubs, play golf on the same courses. They communicate with each other, they support one another—in the absence of participation, understanding and control of people like ourselves."[237]

Perhaps showing the wear of a grueling period of campaigning before a short three-day rest at his Georgia home, Carter engaged in some unusual glibness in his Evansville remarks when talking about his opponent, saying Ford "serves in the great tradition of Warren Harding, Herbert Hoover and Richard Nixon. When he became president, he said he was not a Lincoln, but a

Ford. He told the truth. Ford's a good automobile that's not doing too well in the White House. It's stuck in the mud with four flat tires, out of gas, gears locked in reserve. If it ever does move again, which I doubt, I'm sure it will try to back into the future."[238]

Carter made another late swing through Indiana on October 10 to normally safe Republican territory. At South Bend, he repeated his claims that the Ford administration's economic record was "absolutely abominable."

"In the South, we've got a great respect for the word stonewall (as in Stonewall Jackson)," Carter said at the Center on Civil Rights at the University of Notre Dame in South Bend. "Well, in this administration a stonewall seems to mean not letting the American people have a right to know what's our own business. Mr. Ford has created in recent appearances—which are very rare—more questions than he has provided answers."[239]

For his October visits, United Press International political writer Hortense Myers noted that Carter made a special outreach to ethnic and racial minorities in Indiana, perhaps as a means of papering over less-than-artful remarks the candidate had made about the preservation of the "ethnic purity" of neighborhoods during an April visit to Indiana. Carter's appearances were buttressed by a major mistake by Ford in the latest head-to-head debate in which the president insisted no part of Eastern Europe remained under Soviet control—something Carter said reflected that Ford "just doesn't know what is going on" and is "terribly misinformed" about the desire for Democratic freedom in Eastern Europe.[240]

Speaking before a crowd of about 10,000 at Garfield Park on the south side of Indianapolis, Carter said, "I believe Mr. Ford was brainwashed when he went to Poland, and I believe it has hurt our country that this hope of freedom of the Eastern European nations is being held in abeyance." As the Associated Press reported, it was some of the toughest rhetoric of the campaign yet as aides close to the Georgia governor conceded that they believed Ford's poor debate performance had provided an opportunity Carter could not pass up. "This was the week we overcame the incumbency," as one aide put it.[241] In his Indianapolis speech, Carter further reminded Hoosiers that Ford had not followed up on his pledge to eradicate from U.S. Department of Commerce records companies that willingly chose to boycott Israel or Jewish-backed businesses. "Mr. Ford said he was going to stop the Arab boycott, which is a disgrace. . . . This lets a foreign country tear apart and bypass the American Constitution and the Bill of Rights. It's a dreadful thing."[242]

During his remarks before large crowds at both the Center for Continuing Education and the Center for Civil Rights on the Notre Dame campus in South Bend, Carter said Ford's confusion about who controls Eastern Europe is reflected in his "abandonment" of the Helsinki Agreement under pressure from the Soviet Union. He said if he was elected president, he would "do everything I can to encourage freedom in the presently dominated Eastern European countries."[243] To further emphasize Ford's debate error regarding Poland's status, Carter operatives lined up Saint Joseph County treasurer A. J. Kromkowski to warm up the audience by speaking in Polish. Sounding a theme he would return to as president during a subsequent visit to the Notre Dame campus, Carter told students and faculty gathered for a Sunday afternoon speech that America's foreign policy needed to include an emphasis on human rights, requiring "a balance of tough realism on the one hand, and idealism on the other. The question is if, in recent

years, we haven't become too pragmatic, too cynical, and have ignored those moral values that have always distinguished America from other countries."[244] While in South Bend, Carter took time to tape a question-and-answer television program with Brademas and attend a Sunday school class with residents with developmental disabilities at the Northern Indiana State Developmental Center.

President Carter made only three visits to Indiana—one to address commencement exercises at the University of Notre Dame on May 22, 1977, one to address the 1979 Jefferson-Jackson Day Democratic Party Dinner in Indianapolis, and the other to call on National Urban League President Vernon Jordan Jr. as he recovered from a gunshot wound suffered in an assassination attempt outside the Marriott Hotel in Fort Wayne.

At Notre Dame, Carter's 1977 commencement visit was his third to the campus in little more than a year and reflected his growing friendship and shared admiration with the university's acclaimed president, Father Theodore Hesburgh. Carter's remarks that day are widely viewed as indicative of the dramatic turn he intended to introduce to U.S. foreign policy. Carter said he had come to Notre Dame to "reaffirm America's commitment to human rights as a fundamental tenet of our foreign policy" and that "for too many years, we've been willing to adopt the flawed and erroneous principles and tactics of our adversaries, sometimes abandoning our own values for theirs. We've fought fire with fire, never thinking that fire is better quenched with water. This approach failed, with Vietnam the best example of its intellectual and moral poverty."[245]

Carter declared, "We are now free of that inordinate fear of communism which once led us to embrace any dictator who joined us in that fear."[246] The speech, described as an embrace of the right-left balance Carter had assembled in foreign affairs by seeking the input of "hawkish" National Security Adviser Zbigniew Brzezinski and "dovish" Secretary of State Cyrus Vance, was a distinct departure from previous American foreign policy and was consistent with human rights themes covered in preliminary remarks that day by Hesburgh. Carter noted the sacrifices of others in promoting human rights around the world and said, "I believe we can have a foreign policy that is democratic, that is based on fundamental values, and that uses power and influence, which we have, for human purposes. We can also have a foreign policy that the American people both support and, for a change, know about and understand."[247] Carter said his approach to foreign policy was based on an "historical vision of America's role" and "is rooted in our moral values, which never change. Our policy is reinforced by our material wealth and by our military power. Our policy is designed to serve mankind. And it is a policy that I hope will make you proud to be Americans." Noting that "we can no longer separate the traditional issues of war and peace from the new global questions of justice, equity, and human rights," the nation must "reaffirm America's commitment to human rights as a fundamental tenet of our foreign policy."[248]

While Carter's remarks were viewed by many conservatives as a reckless move away from strong alliances around the world that had served the nation during the Cold War, they were received well in many parts of the world. Headlines in Scotland announced that "Carter declares an end to Cold War."[249]

Carter had not completely abandoned, however, the need for international relations with leaders who may not have shared American values. A little more than six months after his re-

marks at South Bend, the president paid a fateful New Year's Eve visit to Tehran, Iran, that included a poorly received "toast" of the maligned Shah of Iran, Mohammad Reza Pahlavia, a longtime American ally in the volatile Middle East. In his Tehran toast, Carter noted that Iran and the U.S. "have a close friendship that's very meaningful to all the people in our country. I think it is a good harbinger of things to come—that we could close out this year and begin a new year with those in whom we have such great confidence and with whom we share such great responsibilities for the present and for the future."[250] Carter's open praise of the shah incited simmering revolutionary forces within Iran, particularly those under the control of Muslim cleric Ayatollah Ruhollah Khomeini, who had been exiled from Iran by the shah's forces. A successful Khomenini-led revolutionary coup toppled the shah by February 1979 as the shah and his family went into exile in Egypt and elsewhere. Events continued to unfold as Khomeini's forces staged a successful overrun of the U.S. embassy in Tehran on November 4, 1979, a takeover that eventually lasted 444 days and contributed mightily to the downfall and end of the Carter administration.

Before the defining Iranian crisis was fully under way, Carter was back in Indianapolis on June 2, 1979, for the state Democratic Party's Jefferson-Jackson Day Dinner and likely reflected that the president could ill afford spending any time in Indiana for the upcoming 1980 re-election campaign. Indiana Democrats, it seemed, were willing to take what they could get, even if the president's visit came more than a year before the presidential election. Carter's appearance was the first visit by an incumbent Democratic president to the annual Jefferson-Jackson Dinner in Indiana, and it brought out a record crowd of just under 4,000, including many supporters of Bayh, who faced a tough (and ultimately unsuccessful) re-election campaign in the coming year. Bayh's campaign would unfold in the shadow of sorrow after the April 24, 1979, death of his beloved wife and political partner, Marvella. Carter addressed her death, noting that "her spirit and courage were known here in Indiana, but they were equally well known throughout our nation. She faced the prospects of an untimely death with courage and an inspirational attitude which sustained many others who faced sorrow and tragedy in their own lives."[251] Acknowledging Marvella as a personal friend of both his and Rosalynn, the president said, "I know that Birch, in the memorial service for her, pointed that he did not want to see sorrowful faces as we talk about Marvella. And I do have a spirit of thanksgiving and happiness that she lived among us. And she still lives among us, as far as I am concerned."[252]

Perhaps channeling or previewing his famous "Crisis of Confidence" speech from the White House in July 1979, Carter told Indiana Democrats that his administration had tackled the difficult and controversial issues of our time and that "we have never put temporary political gain ahead of the permanent benefit of the United States of America" and that "after Vietnam and Watergate and the CIA and other embarrassing circumstances, we Democrats have together been able to restore the faith and trust of the American people in their own government." He noted that a platform of peace, prosperity and trust had been built allowing America to "enter the 1980s as a proud, confident, strong and united nation."[253] Providing a framework that reminded his audience of the problems persistent in the Nixon administrations, Carter said "Great changes have taken place. We've demanded a government that does not need to cover up and which actually

deserves the loyalty and the trust of the people. There are no more official government lies. There are no more enemies' lists. There are no more sellouts to the special interest groups."[254]

Directly addressing the "energy crisis" facing Americans as they filled up their gas tanks and asking again for support for the SALT II treaty with the Soviet Union, Carter asked the friendly audience that "if you remember nothing else from my speech," (a lengthy address of nearly four thousand words) remember that "we have a great nation which can meet any challenge if we work together. We can solve the energy problem with the same courage, the same pioneer spirit, the same sense of partnership which has always been exemplified by the people of Indiana. Our economic strength, our military strength, our political strength, our ethical strength, our moral strength, are unsurpassed by any nation on Earth."[255]

Reminding his supporters that during his campaign he promised a government "as good as our people. Some critics said this was just cheap political talk, but you understood what I was trying to say. Our foreign policy is as good as the American people when we speak out for human rights around the world. And we will continue to protect human rights for as long as I am your President. Our foreign policy is as good as the American people when we work to bring peace not just to our own shores but to ancient enemies" (making reference to the Israeli-Egyptian peace accords made possible by "two courageous men"—President Anwar Sadat of Egypt and Prime Minister Menachem Begin of Israel).[256]

Walter Mondale

For the 1976 campaign, Mondale was a loyal and effective surrogate for Governor Carter's upstart presidential campaign and, not surprisingly, was used in Indiana (along with Rosalyn), while the main campaign focused on truly battleground states. Mondale undertook three swings in the state in September 1976, including stops at South Bend, Fort Wayne, and Gary.

While in South Bend, Mondale made an address before a combined group of students and faculty at Notre Dame (including a private luncheon with the university's president, Hesburgh) and later toured the Bendix Corporation plant in South Bend. For his Notre Dame speech, Mondale focused on the nation's foreign policy, which he said "is a mirror image of the lawlessness of Watergate" and said the nation must reaffirm its commitment to freedom and justice at home and abroad. "We still have a government that does not recognize that power alone is not enough, that principle must govern our actions overseas," Mondale said. "Nothing is more disturbing than the gap between the goodness of the American people and the policies being pursued in Washington. A government that believes in itself has the most enduring security of all and no expediency will achieve security if that security is not based on our own principles."[257]

Specifically, Mondale criticized U.S. policy that involved the CIA in secret operations in Chile, Greece, Angola, and Pakistan. He pledged that as president, Carter would not "indiscriminately" provide weaponry to foreign countries, or use intelligence agencies to topple democratically elected governments. Americans "want a government that looks beyond self-interest to the principles that animate American democracy . . . that not only exercises power but exercises it with vision and purpose, with ideals abroad and at home."[258]

In closing, Mondale also pledged a commitment to human rights as a cornerstone of foreign policy efforts and a push to champion equal rights to Apartheid-ruled South Africa. He acknowledged that the experience of the Vietnam War had left "fearful scars on the spirit" of the American people, but that there was reason to be optimistic and hopeful for the future.[259]

Bob Dole

After securing the nomination, Ford tapped Senator Dole of Kansas as his running mate, and Dole's Indiana visit in the closing days of the campaign came amidst a bit of created controversy. In an earlier stop in Rhode Island, Dole drew gasps when he suggested that America's wars had been "Democratic wars," and when pressed by a reporter to distinguish how a Republican president would have handled Nazi and Japanese threats in World War II, Dole got personal. He noted, "I had some reservations at the time. Not about fighting it, but every time I get dressed in the morning, I think about it" (a less-than-subtle reference to Dole's serious physical injuries suffered in combat).[260]

During a vice presidential debate with Mondale, the Democratic veep nominee, Dole bristled at the suggestion that Ford's 1974 pardon of Nixon was a legitimate campaign issue. "If they want to dredge up the past, we can dredge up some of the past," Dole said. "Now if you want to go back and rake that over and over and over, you can do that. I assume Senator Mondale doesn't want to do that. It seems to me that the pardon of Richard Nixon is behind us, Watergate is behind us . . . [the pardon] is not a very good issue, any more than the war in Vietnam would be, or World War II or World War I, or the war in Korea, all Democrat wars, all in this century. I figured up the other day if you added up the killed and wounded in Democrat wars in this century, it would be about 1.5 million Americans, enough to fill the city of Detroit."[261]

Dole kept up the attack in postdebate campaign stops, warning veterans they should "shudder at the thought" of men like Carter and Mondale in power. On October 27 the controversy around Dole's remarks was still swirling as he made a swing through Indiana in Fort Wayne, Terre Haute, and Evansville. He attempted to step back from his earlier claims during a quick stop in Terre Haute. He told reporters that he had never used the term "Democrat wars," and that he had no recollection of having used it, but stated that if it was fair for the Democrats to try and tie Ford to the Watergate scandal, it was fair to tie Democratic administrations to war.[262] Later at Evansville, he attempted to explain that any reference to "Democrat wars," which he now seemed to acknowledge having made, was only an effort to draw a parallel with what he said were attempts by Democrats to use the Watergate scandal against Ford. Dole said his logic was that if it was "fair" to blame Republicans for Watergate, it may be "fair" to blame Democrats for World War II.[263]

Dole seemed to continue to stumble over himself, agreeing to a reporter's suggestion that a vice president was correctly characterized as "standby equipment" for the administration.

Later while speaking at Indiana State University, Dole seemed to miss the happy irony of the introduction of one his supporters in the audience named Jimmy Carter, a longtime Republican supporter. Further, he appeared clearly angered by a group of student hecklers—and Carter supporters—who continued to make their presence known. Dole finally erupted, advising the students to "drink some pineapple juice. Peanut butter sticks to the roof of your mouth. In your case, peanut butter might be better."[264] Dole reminded his mostly student audience that America was at peace and held the respect of the world and that the presidency was too risky to turn over to someone of Carter's judgment, noting that "if his judgment in granting a Playboy interview was that bad, how bad will it be if he has something important to decide?"[265]

Dole's sharp edges showing, he ironically told a Fort Wayne reporter that he resented Mondale's assertion that Dole was serving the role as "hatchet man" for the Ford campaign, declaring instead that it was Mondale who was taking the campaign "on a very low, low road." He added that perhaps "Fritz [Mondale] is a little tired. I wish this campaign would end so he can get some rest."[266]

11

The Republican Revolution, 1980–91

Jimmy Carter

Carter skipped any personal campaigning in Indiana for the May 1980 Democratic primary despite an active, but fading, challenge from Senator Edward M. "Ted" Kennedy of Massachusetts. Instead, Carter surrogates crisscrossed the state, including Vice President Walter Mondale and First Lady Rosalynn Carter. She visited Indianapolis on April 30, 1980, when she appeared with Reverend Billy Graham to help promote his upcoming crusade in the capital city (and to promote her husband in the Indiana primary less than a week away). Graham, traditionally a supporter of Republican candidates, stopped short of endorsing Carter but reminded Indianapolis reporters that he had a long-term relationship with Carter, extending back to 1966 when they worked together to plan one of the first integrated religious crusades at Americus, Georgia. "I want her to carry back to her husband the assurance of our love and our prayers," Graham said.[1] Rosalyn directly addressed the failed rescue effort six days earlier that her husband had ordered in Iran to free hostages at the U.S. embassy in Tehran, Iran, a mission that left eight Americans dead and many others injured. Saying she did not think the failure of the effort would adversely affect her husband's campaign for re-election, she said, "I think [the effort] has made the country proud of the courageous men who are willing to risk their lives to go to Iran to try and save our hostages who were there. Now the Iranians realize we can do something about it and they are getting very nervous. People know Jimmy Carter will do anything he can to free the hostages."[2]

On June 2, 1980, Carter made a quick, unscheduled fifteen-minute stop at Parkview Memorial Hospital in Fort Wayne for a private visit with an injured Vernon E. Jordan Jr., president of the National Urban League, who was shot while standing in a hotel parking lot on May 29, 1980. Carter spoke briefly to reporters after leaving Jordan's side and said, "Vernon has sometimes been a very severe critic" of the Carter administration's civil rights agenda, "but at the same time we've always maintained a friendship. Whenever I've made economic or civil rights decisions in my own administration as President, I've always invariably called Vernon in. I've done this with just a few other leaders in the country."[3] Carter's reference to the shooting of Jordan to be an "assassination attempt" caused a minor stir among reporters who seemed to believe it meant the president had inside information about the motive and details of the still-unsolved shooting. Carter clarified that "I have no way to know what the motive is" for the shooting and that "this is obviously a time for us to recommit ourselves to the protection of poor and minority groups. It certainly is a reminder of the need to redouble our efforts."[4] Carter's assessment that it was an "assassination attempt" on Jordan's life would eventually prove true as serial killer Joseph Paul Franklin, whose crime spree focused violence on African Americans in the Midwest, later admitted he had shot at Jordan with a high-powered rifle while hiding in tall grass on a hill near the hotel.[5]

Able to read polls that showed former California governor Ronald Reagan would easily carry Indiana's electoral votes, the Carter campaign made more than a few Hoosiers angry in mid-July 1980 when Air Force One flew into and out of Evansville Regional Airport in order for the president to attend a $500-a-plate fund-raiser across the Ohio River in Henderson, Kentucky, bypassing any public appearances on Hoosier soil. Carter's Evansville stop was limited to greeting local political dignitaries at the airport, including the wife of slain Evansville mayor Russ Lloyd Sr., a Republican gunned down at his home in March 1980. Genna Lord, the mayor's widow, later told reporters that Carter hugged her and "he told me he had heard about our tragedy and he wanted to tell us that we have a wonderful family. He was very gracious and we were deeply honored that he thought enough about us to do this."[6]

Carter's 1980 struggle in Indiana was mirrored across the nation, with Reagan commanding the momentum of the campaign from the start, and the Independent candidacy of former Republican Congressman John Anderson of Illinois stealing off even more votes from the incumbent president. Defeated by Reagan in the November balloting, Carter left Washington and returned to run his family farm interests in Plains, Georgia, and formed the Carter Center,

which promotes peace and election integrity across the globe.

As a former president, Carter constructed a personal image for himself that exceeded almost anything he accomplished during his one troubled term as president between 1977 and 1981. Widely respected as an international force for good, Carter won the Nobel Peace Prize in 2002 "for his decades of untiring effort to find peaceful solutions to international conflicts, to advance democracy and human rights, and to promote economic and social development."[7]

While the Nobel Prize recognized Carter's work across the world, at home his strong identification with and support of the faith-based Habitat for Humanity program brought him back to Indianapolis a year before he would become a Nobel Laureate for the twenty-fifth anniversary celebration of the Habitat program. Carter spoke at the then-named Conseco Fieldhouse before a crowd of about 10,000 and reported that he and Rosalynn had just returned from a weeklong visit to China, where they had participated in Habitat building programs in small, rural villages there. His remarks came just four days after the terrorist attacks on the United States on September 11, 2001, and just one day after he attended a National Prayer Service with President George W. Bush and his fellow former presidents Bill Clinton, George H. W. Bush, and Gerald Ford. Carter offered that despite the "celebration" of Habitat for Humanity's work for a quarter century, "I think tonight it is good to adopt a sober tone, but not one of despair."[8] Recalling his experience as a young naval officer during World War II and the Korean War, he said, "I've seen our country face crises and I've seen our country not only survive, but grow stronger. Crisis calls for reassessment of life's values, the cherishing of those most precious, the reaching out to others and forming alliances. Crisis calls for the resurrection of hope and a consummation of mutual faith."[9]

Carter reminded his audience that crisis is felt throughout the world each day by mothers and fathers who realize they cannot create or find adequate shelter for their children, situations that can "generate despair and a sense of hopelessness and isolation and abandonment. [But then] comes the element of sharing and reaching out to others and of faith and hope." He called for understanding and vigilance against violence and threats to peace, and particularly for patience for those of faiths other than Christianity. "I teach Sunday school at our little church in Plains every Sunday. . . . I'm there about 35 times a year; the rest of the time I'm out doing things for the Carter Center. When I'm not there, my substitute is a young man named Mashuq Askerzada who came to this country [from Afghanistan] while I was President. . . . He's become an American citizen, and although he was a Muslim, he's become a Christian and he's a member of my church and he teaches every time I'm not there. Some of the regular church members have been heard to say that they're glad when I'm away somewhere!"[10]

Calling attention to a newspaper article he had read en route to Indianapolis about an Arab man in Gary who had windows of his store shot out by an unknown vandal in the wake of 9/11 and another Arab-born American physically assaulted in Indianapolis, he said that the attacks granted the wishes of the terrorists. "Their goal has been to set Christian against Muslim, to set America against the Arab world. If they can do that, they will have been successful," he cautioned.[11] Habitat for Humanity, he said, provided American citizens of all faiths an appropriate, meaningful response. "Habitat not only provides hope and a realization of faith to an individual family, but also provides a means by which we

can expand our religious faith to encompass others and to draw us nearer to God. It's not just governments that have a responsibility to resolve crises, it's really a conglomerate of dedicated individuals; and this is particularly true in a democracy. To demonstrate our faith—our faith in ourselves, our faith in each other and our faith in God—that's what Habitat means to me."[12]

Edward M. "Ted" Kennedy

Going into 1980, Kennedy's primary challenge to Carter may have looked like a good idea on paper, but in reality it further weakened Carter's chances for re-election. Polling in August 1979 showed Kennedy was preferred by a wide margin over the incumbent Carter, but that lead began to weaken amidst missteps, including an underwhelming performance in a November 1979 interview with CBS journalist Roger Mudd in which Kennedy fumbled and stumbled for an answer to Mudd's question, "Why do you want to be president?" Undeterred by that, and with questions about his crumbling marriage and lingering questions about his role in a July 1969 car accident on Chappaquiddick Island, Massachusetts, that left twenty-eight-year-old campaign aide Mary Jo Kopechne dead, Kennedy strode into Boston's historic Faneuil Hall on November 7, 1979, and made it official: he would challenge Carter. Kennedy said he would bank on his nearly two decades of experience in the Senate but placed the real emphasis for his candidacy at the feet of Carter's perceived failures in leadership.

"When public issues grow so large that they threaten the essential confidence of our nation, the energies of our people must be marshaled toward a larger purpose," Kennedy said. "That can only be done from the White House. Only the President can provide the sense of direction needed by the nation. Only the President can inspire the common will to reach our goals. For many months we have been sinking into crisis, yet we hear no clear summons from the center of power. Aims are not set, the means of realizing them are neglected, conflicts in direction confuse our purpose, government falters, fear spreads that our leaders have resigned themselves to retreat. This country is not ready to sound retreat, it is ready to advance, it is willing to make a stand, and so am I."[13]

Kennedy eventually won twelve primary and caucus races against Carter, including big wins in California, New Jersey, New York, and Massachusetts and narrow victories in Michigan and Pennsylvania. Carter proved a more formidable candidate than perhaps originally estimated, rolling up big victories in twenty-six primary states, including Indiana. With cash running low and a Carter victory becoming more and more of a reality, Kennedy abandoned his campaign efforts in Texas, North Carolina, and Tennessee and instead focused on Indiana, a state he knew well from his brother Robert's campaign in 1968. As the *Washington Post* reported, "Kennedy campaigned only in Indiana . . . largely a recognition of political realities. He trailed badly in all three states and lacked the time and money to reverse the situation. His only realistic hope was to hold down Carter's margin, and hope to pick up a few scattered delegates. Indiana was his best shot. Kennedy's brother Robert won there in 1968 and this year it has a high unemployment rate."[14]

Kennedy made quick stops in heavily unionized areas of the state, including Gary, South Bend, Kokomo, Evansville, and Indianapolis and ran a flurry of television ads featuring actor Carroll O'Connor, known to most Hoosiers as Archie Bunker from the CBS sitcom *All in the Family*. In the ad, O'Connor accused Carter of "hiding" in the White House as Herbert Hoover had once

done. "I am supporting Senator Kennedy because he is out there facing the issues, inflation, sky-high prices, an almost worthless dollar, unemployment," O'Connor said. "I trust Ted Kennedy, I believe in him, in every way folks."[15] Another actor, Martin Sheen (lesser known at the time), also made appearances in the state on behalf of Kennedy.

Despite the earnest effort in Indiana, Kennedy suffered from a lack of formal commitment on the part of the state's powerful auto unions (which remained neutral), along with the neutrality of Senator Birch Bayh (who had his hands full with a tough re-election bid of his own). In Indianapolis Kennedy told reporters he viewed Carter's plans to actively join the campaign trail as "a political judgment" and added, "I think probably the fact he has lost five of the last six primaries, he realizes you can't really remain distant from the American people and understand their anguish and their anxiety."[16]

"Mr. Carter is willing now to leave the Rose Garden and face the American people on the issues on which we both are concerned," Kennedy said. "I think the decision quite clearly is a political judgment." He reminded the organized labor members of his audience that he had worked hard for them in the Senate and added, "I need your help now. I believe I am entitled to it," and recalled he knew Indiana well. "There are few communities in this state that I haven't campaigned in over the last 17 years."[17]

"I know we are underdogs. . . . Mr. Carter is the odds-on favorite in Indiana," Kennedy said in assessing his chances in the Indiana primary. "In a few days they are going to have those time trials out at the Speedway. And it isn't always the one that runs the fastest time trial that wins on Memorial Day. With your help, we will win the big one in August in New York City."[18]

Later in Evansville, Kennedy spoke before an enthusiastic group of five hundred supporters, with his wife Joan at his side. "I believe in the American dream, and I believe it should be maintained and kept alive," he said. "Carter wrings his hands and says 'What president could do any better?' . . . I could not stand on the sidelines with the administration turning its back on the people."[19]

By the time the votes were counted, Carter trounced Kennedy in Indiana by a wide 68 to 32 percent margin. Postprimary polling by political analysts showed serious reservations among Hoosier Democrats about Kennedy. As the *Washington Post* revealed, "The Indiana primary also saw the re-emergence of the personal morality issue that has plagued Kennedy in other states in the nation's heartland. Kennedy's loss in Indiana was total and devastating. He lost among almost every population group and in every region, raising serious questions about his claims of a growing disillusionment with Carter's foreign and domestic policies. In large part, the vote was a personal rejection of him in the Midwest heartland. . . . Half the Democratic voters interviewed by ABC News as they left Indiana polling places said they found the Massachusetts Democrat an unacceptable candidate. Only one Democrat in ten found him truthful. About the same proportion approved of his personal morality, an apparent spill over from his marital problems and the Chappaquiddick incident."[20] The same poll of Indiana Democrats who voted showed they rated Carter high on personal characteristics, such as truthfulness, sticking to his principles, and personal morality. "Many Democrats in Indiana apparently don't blame him for inflation, which they regard as the nation's most important issue, or for the Iranian hostage situation," the postprimary poll showed.[21]

Kennedy never again stood for national office, winning continual election to his Senate seat from Massachusetts and becoming the fourth-longest serving member of the Senate in U.S. history, his terms extending from November 1962 until his death on August 25, 2009. Politically active until the very end of his life, Kennedy recovered from a small stroke in order to deliver a rousing endorsement of Barack Obama at the 2008 Democratic National Convention and attended Obama's inauguration as president in January 2009. Kennedy's final cause of death was attributed to brain cancer. He was seventy-seven years old. A champion of universal health care for all Americans, he did not live, however, to see the Patient Protection and Affordable Care Act signed into law by President Obama on March 23, 2010.

Ronald Reagan

For the 1980 campaign, the landscape had changed dramatically for Reagan. Rather than cast as the outside challenger to a sitting president, Reagan was the heavy favorite to win the Republican nomination, even though a crowded field of challengers initially formed, including former CIA director and ambassador George H. W. Bush, Congressman John Anderson of Illinois, Senate Minority Leader Howard Baker of Tennessee, former Texas governor John Connally, Congressman Phil Crane of Illinois, and Senator Bob Dole of Kansas. Bush emerged as the most serious challenger to Reagan, whose initial primary strategy was to stay above the fray and avoid the large "cattle call" events that included the whole lineup of GOP hopefuls. In New Hampshire, in fact, Bush seemed to buy into Reagan's strategy, suggesting a one-on-one debate between the two, an idea Reagan turned on his head when he showed up with Anderson,

Dole, Baker, and Crane in his company for a raucous debate at Nashua, which eventually occurred when the other candidates agreed to step aside and left Reagan and Bush to debate. Bush's short-lived front-runner position (which he festooned as "Big Mo") was buttressed by a first-place finish in the early January 1980 straw poll in Iowa (besting Reagan 32 to 30 percent) and winning a virtually uncontested face-off days later in Puerto Rico (sans Reagan).

By the time the primary parade reached New Hampshire, however, Reagan was fully engaged and swept to an easy victory over Bush and the rest of the field. Bush hung around, however, winning a handful of remaining primaries in Massachusetts, Connecticut, and Washington, D.C., and made surprisingly strong showings in Pennsylvania and Michigan. Indiana, nevertheless, was strongly Reagan country, with the former California governor rolling up 76 percent of the May 6 primary vote in Indiana. Bush received 16 percent of the vote and Anderson 10 percent. The die was cast, however, and Reagan rolled to an impressive showing the rest of the way and stormed into the July 1980 convention in Detroit with a head full of steam and no one with a chance to catch him.

Reagan's strong Indiana showing is perhaps not surprising. Combined with his extensive barnstorming of the state four years earlier in the surprise win over an incumbent president, Reagan did not take the state for granted, despite his apparent lead in 1980. As the Associated Press's Daniel Beegan wrote, "George Bush got the votes in Pennsylvania, but Ronald Reagan had the hearts of many Indiana Republicans during a two-day campaign swing through the state."[22] Although uncommitted in the primary, popular Governor Otis R. Bowen did sit by Reagan's side and introduced him to the Tippecanoe County Lincoln Day Dinner in West Lafayette. "Although Bowen was warm and cordial in his introduction of Reagan at the Purdue Union, he stopped short of an endorsement," the Associated Press reported.[23] While in the state Reagan also visited South Bend, Lafayette, Terre Haute, and Evansville, though Bush and Anderson (still active campaigners at this point) skipped Indiana.

Meeting with reporters in Evansville, Reagan was in fine form calling out Carter for labeling his primary opponent, Kennedy, a big spender. "Well, that's absolutely true," Reagan said, "but look who was talking. I don't know of any bigger spender than we've had than the man who was making the accusation."[24] During a stop in Terre Haute, Reagan advocated cutting federal income taxes and eliminating income taxes on savings accounts entirely. As for his own tax returns, Reagan was not budging in his belief that candidates were under no obligation to reveal their tax return. "I've taken a stand on principle on this," he said. "I will make all disclosures required by law. I believe a bad precedent is indicated if we think anyone who is going to be in public life is going to make disclosures other citizens don't have to make. . . . I feel this very strongly."[25] At Lafayette, Reagan downplayed Bush's impressive win of the popular vote in the Pennsylvania primary, noting that he would net more delegates than Bush. In an unfortunate turn of a phrase, Reagan referred to Indiana's primary as "meaningless."[26]

By July, with the nomination firmly in hand—and Bush now at his side as his running mate—Reagan looked to be a formidable foe to primary-weakened Carter for the November 1980 contest. Indiana was never in doubt, shining bright red on most polling maps, and both campaigns generally ignored the state. The Republicans, particularly, had no reason to spend any time or money in the state, although

IHS, BASS PHOTO COMPANY COLLECTION, P 130

President Ronald Reagan

Congressman Dan Quayle was staging a fierce challenge to incumbent Senator Bayh (who was trying for a fourth term in the upper chamber). Just after Labor Day 1980, and with memories of a Detroit convention that made strong appeals to traditional Democratic voting blocks, Reagan's team set up a "poster child" sort of visit to Kokomo in Howard County on September 8, 1980. In stories that repeatedly referred to Kokomo as "economically depressed" or as "a community with one of the highest unemployment rates in the country," Reagan staged a rally outside the Kokomo Mall, within eye and earshot of the massive Delco-Remy and Chrysler plants along US 31. The staging was no accident. Kokomo was as strong a union town for autoworkers as was Detroit, and Reagan intended to pull some of their votes in 1980.

While in Kokomo under a hot late-summer sun, about 6,000 people showed up to hear Reagan blast Carter's economic programs as too late to repair serious damage to the nation's economy. Reagan said Carter's plans were "cynical, political and too late," he declared, "the damage has been done." He added, "I have talked with unemployed workers all across this country. I have heard their views on what Jimmy Carter has done to them and their families. And I've talked to some more today, and they're not interested in sematic quibbles. They're out of work and they know who put them out of work and they know the difference between a recession and a depression."[27]

Reagan reminded his Indiana audience that unemployment in Kokomo was 19.5 percent, far above the national average of 8 percent, "and up in Flint, Michigan, it's 25 percent. These figures are comparable to the Great Depression of the 1930s. That's not the recession [President Carter] speaks of, that's depression."[28] Reagan suggested that the president "go to the unemployment lines

and lecture those workers who've been betrayed on what is the proper definition for their widespread economic misery. They don't need defining, they need action. With two months to do until the election, (Carter) rides to the rescue with a crazy quilt of obvious election year promises."[29] Carrying forward his "definition" theme, Reagan repeated his increasingly popular applause line that noted, "A recession is when your neighbor loses a job, a depression is when you lose your job, and recovery is when Jimmy Carter loses his."[30]

Reagan spoke for only ten minutes in Indiana, and reporters complained in their stories that they were kept so far away from the nominee that they could not ask him any questions. The Kokomo stop was part of an interesting set of campaign swings for the Republican nominee. Before arriving in Indiana, Reagan stopped off in Philadelphia for breakfast with Cardinal John Krol, an attempt to attract some of the millions of Roman Catholics in America who heretofore were solidly Democratic voters. After he left Kokomo, Reagan visited West Lithuanian Plaza in Chicago, again asking for the votes of traditional Democrats.

While in Kokomo, Reagan made an unscheduled stop at the Howard Township Elementary School near the Kokomo airport. There he stopped and talked briefly with a large group of sixth graders on the playground for recess. Attendance at a $250-per-person fund-raiser, however, at the American Legion Hall drew a disappointing audience of only fifty. "Most of the people in the Legion's meeting room were news media representatives, Secret Service agents, and Kokomo policemen," the *Kokomo Tribune* reported.[31] Among those who were no-shows was Lieutenant Governor Robert D. Orr, running for governor in 1980. Reagan's "doom and gloom" message about job loss may have been helpful to Republicans nationally, but it was not going to help Orr, who was running on the Bowen-Orr record for a first term as governor. Local Democrats did their part to change the subject. City officials told anyone who would listen that they had put the kibosh on plans by Reagan's campaign to shoot off fireworks in the mall parking lot at the conclusion of the speech. Local police and fire officials, under the control of a Democrat mayor, told reporters the fireworks were a dangerous fire hazard because of a nearby gas station.[32]

Reagan was swept into office as the nation's fortieth president in November 1980, which also brought him a rare Republican majority in the U.S. Senate. Although he enjoyed the initial "bounce" in public opinion polls as his term started in January 1981, by March critics had begun to question the Reagan economic policies based on a promised 25 percent tax cut coupled with promises of significant increases in military spending. Tragic events would intercede on March 30, 1981, as Reagan left the Washington Hilton Hotel and was struck by an attempted assassin's bullets that critically injured three others. Amazingly, Reagan survived the attack by John Hinckley Jr. and returned to the White House from the hospital within weeks. The nature of the Reagan presidency, however, was changed forever. Gone were the days when Reagan would meet and greet voters and others in an up-close manner. For the remainder of his eight years in office, Reagan was carefully managed by both the Secret Service and his political advisers. The "great communicator" used television and mass media as much as he did any personal contact with Americans.

In May 1981 the Reagan White House scheduled a trip to Indiana, one of the president's first trips outside of Washington, D.C.,

since the assassination attempt. As the *New York Times* reported, "The White House has sharply increased security measures surrounding President Reagan since the attempt on his life. . . . As a result, Reagan is now increasingly out of sight in his travels."[33] This included special, first-time arrangements for Reagan's planned speech at Notre Dame for commencement. "Those attending the event were screened by an electronic metal detector, and women's purses were checked," the *Times* reported. "The White House staff has also begun supervising virtually every footstep by Reagan and his entire entourage on trips outside the White House. On the trip to Notre Dame in South Bend, all those traveling with Reagan were assigned specific places in automobiles in the motorcade."[34] Perhaps raising the tension surrounding Reagan's security, a gunman had attempted to assassinate Pope John Paul II three days before the Notre Dame event. "This increased the uneasiness of the Secret Service, whose agents poured onto campus," *Notre Dame* magazine reported. Reagan protesters were kept far away from the Athletic and Convocation Center (later renamed the Joyce ACC in 1987), where Reagan was to speak, "but the mood in the arena was overwhelmingly warm for a president who was still recovering from his wounds."[35]

Reagan, accompanied by First Lady Nancy Reagan, was among honorary degree recipients that included Reagan's *Knute Rockne: All American* co-star Pat O'Brien and former senator Edmund Muskie of Maine. Those in attendance were also aware that this was the last commencement for Notre Dame's noted president, the Reverend Theodore Hesburgh. Noting that he was the fifth president to address a Notre Dame graduation, Reagan said, "The temptation is great to use this forum as an address on a great international or national issue that has nothing to do with this occasion. Indeed, this is somewhat traditional. So, I wasn't surprised when I read in several reputable journals that I was going to deliver an address on foreign policy or on the economy. I'm not going to talk about either. But, by the same token, I'll try not to belabor you with some of the standard rhetoric that is beloved of graduation speakers."[36]

Recalling some of the history of Rockne and his Notre Dame legend, the president acknowledged that many seemed to use the phrase "Win One for the Gipper" as a joke. But he noted that it was a statement used only once, many years after George Gipp had actually died. For Reagan, he said the phrase "might sound maudlin and not the way it was intended" and "football is only a game," but asked, "Is there anything wrong with young people having an experience, feeling something so deeply, thinking of someone else to the point that they can give so completely of themselves? There will come times in the lives of all of us when we'll be faced with causes bigger than ourselves, and they won't be on a playing field."[37]

The president also briefly touched on the assassination attempt on John Paul II, noting that "one can't say these words—compassion, sacrifice and endurance—without thinking of the irony that one who so exemplifies them, Pope John Paul II, a man of peace and goodness, an inspiration to the world, would be struck by a bullet from a man towards whom he could only feel compassion and love."[38]

Shifting to the nation's continuing sagging economy, Reagan said, "We're troubled today by economic stagnation, brought on by inflated currency and prohibitive taxes and burdensome regulations. The cost of stagnation in human terms, mostly among those least equipped to survive it, is cruel and inhuman." He joked to the graduates of the Class of 1981 assembled before him that

"now, after those remarks, don't decide that you'd better turn your diploma back in so you can stay another year on the campus. I've just given you the bad news. The good news is that something is being done about all this because the people of America have said, 'Enough already.' You know, we who had preceded you had just gotten so busy that we let things get out of hand. We forgot that we were the keepers of the power, forgot to challenge the notion that the state is the principal vehicle of social change, forgot that millions of social interactions among free individuals and institutions can do more to foster economic and social progress than all the careful schemes of government planners."[39]

Returning to his favorite themes of smaller government, Reagan told the students that "for too long government has been fixing things that aren't broken and inventing miracle cures for unknown diseases." He suggested that his election in 1980 represented that "the people have made it plain already, they want an end to excessive government internship in their lives and in the economy, an end to the burdensome and unnecessary regulations and a punitive tax policy that does take 'from the mouth of labor the bread it has earned.'"[40]

Returning to more traditional graduation themes, Reagan added, "We need you. We need your youth. We need your strength. We need your idealism to help us make right that which is wrong. I know that [in] this period of your life, you have been critically looking at the mores and customs of the past and questioning their value. Every generation does that. May I suggest, don't discard the time-tested values upon which civilization was built simply because they are old."[41]

In February 1982 Reagan followed up his State of the Union address with a trip to Indiana to make the case for a "New Federalism" that mandated returning to states more responsibility from the federal government to a friendly locale. The Republican-controlled Indiana General Assembly was a perfect audience, and the House Chambers of the Indiana Statehouse was packed for his address to a joint session. The few balcony seats that existed were quickly snatched up for this rare appearance of a U.S. president before a joint session of Hoosier legislators.

Reagan thanked his audience, which included current governor Orr and former governor Bowen, as well as the state's two Senators, Richard Lugar and Dan Quayle. "You know, the late Herb Shriner, who was from Fort Wayne, said that he was born in Ohio, but he moved to Indiana as soon as he heard about it," Reagan joked, recalling the career of an entertainer he once knew.[42]

Reagan added a story about *Indianapolis News* columnist William Herschell, who wrote in 1919 about "coming upon another admirer of this state, an old man near Knightstown who was sitting on a log in the warm sunshine, fishing in the Big Blue River. And with a sweep of his arm, the old boy encompassed the whole countryside, and he says, 'Ain't God good to Indianny!' Well, God certainly has been good to Indiana, but unfortunately over the past few decades, the federal government hasn't been quite so kind. If the federal government had been around when the Creator was putting His hand to this state, Indiana wouldn't be here. It'd still be waiting for an environmental impact statement."[43]

Reagan said, "It's not an exaggeration anymore to refer to the almighty federal government. In recent years, power and tax dollars flowed to Washington like water down the Wabash. And yet things didn't get better. We didn't move closer to solutions; we moved farther away. Hoosiers, like citizens all over this country, began to realize that the steady stream of money

and authority to Washington had something to do with the fact that things didn't seem to work anymore."[44]

In his continued folksy style, Reagan said, "the closer you look, the clearer it becomes: The federal government has taken too much tax money from the people, too much authority from the states, and too much liberty with the Constitution."[45] Reagan declared: "This administration seeks nothing less than a realignment of government, a realignment that will give power back to those most responsive to the people."[46]

Reagan boasted about his efforts his first year in office to reduce government spending and to procure tax breaks for business and individuals. He acknowledged Indiana's outrageously high unemployment rate of just under 12 percent, but said, "We have in place an economic program that is based on sound economic theory, not political expediency. We will not play hopscotch economics, jumping here and jumping there as the daily situation changes. We have faith in our program, and we're sticking with it,"[47] drawing applause from the overwhelmingly Republican legislators.

Addressing his critics who raised concern that while domestic spending portions of the federal budget were being slashed, defense spending was increasing, Reagan said, "As President, I can't close my eyes, cross my fingers, and simply hope that the Soviets will behave themselves. Today a major conflict involving the United States could occur without adequate time to upgrade U.S. force readiness. It's morally important that we take steps to protect America's safety and preserve the peace."[48]

Claiming his administration had cut more than 23,000 pages of regulations from the Federal Register, Reagan said he was committed to returning more programs and powers to the states. His argument was that it strengthened home rule and states' rights—something attractive to him as a former governor. The other big argument critics raised was that moving programs to the state level would also reduce the need for additional federal spending, offering help in balancing an already wildly out of whack federal budget. Reagan was ready for that criticism too, noting, "Now, there are those who for their own narrow political purposes say our federalism plan is a mere diversion from our economic problems, or that federalism is simply a means to cut the budget further. Well, don't you believe it. Our federalism plan stands on its own merits, a key to a freer, better America."[49]

The president highlighted several portions of his proposal, "guarantees" he called them, which maintained "the mandatory pass-through to the local governments of some funds, such as for mass transit assistance, and community development. We will ensure civil rights protections and adequate welfare, and the transition period will allow plenty of time for discussion and fine-tuning of the program."[50]

Less than a month later, on March 16, 1982, Reagan made a quick and unscheduled stop in Indiana to visit flood-ravaged Fort Wayne. Reagan's trip was so hastily arranged that news reports indicated both Orr and Ohio governor James Rhodes scrambled to get to Fort Wayne in time to greet the president. The visit to Fort Wayne came at the end of a two-day swing in which Reagan had emphasized the value of volunteerism and provided a perfect backdrop to demonstrate his idea.

For a president and a presidency already gaining a reputation as being "well handled" and

President Ronald Reagan at his desk in the Oval Office, circa 1980s.

LIBRARY OF CONGRESS

packaged (especially since the assassination attempt), the visit to flood-ravaged Fort Wayne was particularly close to the people (security perhaps aided by the fact that his stopover in Indiana was not announced until Air Force One was already in the air en route back to Washington). As the *Milwaukee (WI) Sentinel* reported, "When on the banks of the St. Mary's River, Reagan lost one of his boots in ankle-deep mud and had to be helped by a group of youths. The president congratulated the youngsters who were stacking sandbags, then pitched in . . . as cameras recorded the action."[51] Reporters noted that "it was clear the President derived personal satisfaction from seeing the volunteer efforts—efforts that bolstered his belief in the usefulness of private assistance. 'It's quite a story that's been going on here,'" the president said.[52]

During his visit, Reagan stopped by the Precious Blood Catholic School to speak to volunteers: "It could have been far worse had it not been for thousands of volunteers, including young people, who've been working literally around the clock, sandbagging the dikes and really helping to prevent this from being worse."[53] Reagan then stayed to shake hands with volunteers and told one older man, "I hope we can meet again someday when our feet are dry."[54] As he concluded his visit to Fort Wayne, which included his turn at sandbagging, news reports indicated the seventy-one-year-old president "looked disheveled from the two-hour visit. He heaved a big sigh, as if he were exhausted and exhilarated at the same time. Mud was spattered on his dark blue suit."[55]

The president returned to Indiana on December 8, 1983, to address the National Forum on Excellence in Education meeting at the Indiana Convention Center in Indianapolis. He quickly made ties to his still lingering New Federalism

proposals—stalled in the Democrat-controlled House—but this time with efforts to transfer more educational authority to the states. In his classic style, Reagan opened with folksy humor about the Indiana farmland he had seen as his plane approached Indianapolis. Reagan told of the farmer so proud of his crops that he invited the minister to come see his yield. The minister heaped heavy praise on the Lord for the overwhelming yield, and the farmer responded bitterly, "You should have seen this place when the Lord was doing it by himself."

"Well, maybe it's a little like that with education," Reagan said. "God gives us sons and daughters with bright, eager minds, but it's up to us to cultivate and plant their seeds of knowledge. For more than a century and a half, American schools did that job and did it well. . . . Soon America boasted the finest public school system on Earth. Our rich network of public, church and private schools performed a miracle. With the tide after tide of immigrants thronging to our shores, our schools taught the children of those new Americans skills to earn their livings, a new language, and a new way of life--democracy."[56]

Reagan said he had directed the Departments of Education and Justice "to find ways that [the federal government] can help teachers and administrators enforce [classroom] discipline" and used his speech to launch the President's Academic Fitness Awards. "These awards will be modeled on the Presidential Physical Fitness Awards begun under President [Lyndon] Johnson," he said, but offered few other specific details beyond his desire to present the awards annually at the White House.[57]

Reagan noted the "coming" computer age would confront American students, all while math and science scores for students entering colleges in recent years had continued to decline.

He quoted Thomas Jefferson as saying, "If a nation expects to be ignorant and free . . . it expects what never was and never will be."[58]

"Now, some insist there's only one answer: more money," Reagan said. "But that's been tried. . . . If money alone were the answer, the problem would have been shrinking, not growing."[59] Reagan said total expenditures in American schools for 1983 totaled $230 billion, up 7 percent from the previous year, and more than double of what was spent in 1973. "American schools don't need vast new sums of money as much as they need a few fundamental reforms," he said, advocating six steps "that can and will turn our schools around."[60]

The six broadly defined steps he outlined included restoring "good old-fashioned discipline to schools" so that all students could learn; end drug and alcohol use and abuse by students that affects not only them individually, but all students; raise academic standards; encourage "good teaching"; restore parents and local governments "to their rightful place in the educational process"; and teach the basics because "too many of our students are allowed to abandon vocational and college prep courses for general ones, so, when they graduate from high school they're prepared for neither work nor higher education."[61]

Harkening to his conservative worldview, Reagan also advocated public schools teaching values predicting that "if we fail to instruct our children in justice, religion, and liberty, we will be condemning them to a world without virtue. They'll live in a twilight of civilization where great truths were forgotten."[62]

"One other idea at the core of our basic values, I just have to believe is that the loving God who has blessed this land should never have been expelled from America's classrooms," Reagan said to mixed applause. "When we open ourselves to Him, we gain not only moral courage but intellectual strength. If the members of Congress can start each day with a moment for prayer and meditation, so can our children in their schools."[63]

Reagan singled out several state programs that he believed were making a difference, including Project Prime Time in Indiana, promoted by Governor Orr to emphasize basic skills programs and smaller class sizes for early grades and increased high school graduation requirements for the first time in half a century. "The 50 states taking action to solve problems with efficiency and imagination—this is federalism in action," Reagan said. "You, our nation's governors, legislators, school board members, school administrators, and teachers, are meeting America's educational needs with common sense, vigor, and prudent use of taxpayers' dollars that Washington could never match. On behalf of the American people, I thank you."[64]

Because Indiana was safely in the Republican column for the 1984 presidential matchup between Reagan and former vice president Walter Mondale, the Democratic nominee, Reagan made no appearances in the state during the campaign. He did return to Indiana six months into his second term in June 1985. Reagan put tiny Mooresville, a Morgan County community just outside Indianapolis, on the map as he pitched his new tax-cut proposal at the start of his second term. Speaking before members of the Mooresville Chamber of Commerce inside Mac's Family Restaurant, Reagan said he was there to promote his new tax plan overhaul to "make it fairer and simpler and more compassionate. I wanted to bring the message directly to you in America's heartland. I've been traveling all over the country; the enthusiasm, I must say, for America's tax plan is overwhelming."[65] Reagan said he called it "America's tax plan" because it will "take the load off the back of the long-suffering American taxpayer. It'll take the low-income wage earner and the retired elderly off the tax rolls entirely, and it'll remove the tax distortions that I think are holding the American economy back from reaching its full potential."[66]

"By closing loopholes and ensuring that all big businesses and individuals pay their fair share, we think we can lower the tax burden on everyone," the president declared. "And one of the best things about our tax proposal is the boost it'll give to America's mainstream."[67]

Reagan's remarks were brief in relation to regular presidential speeches. Instead of a monologue, he said, he wanted a dialogue with the leaders of Mooresville. Several specific questions followed about how the tax plan would benefit or harm small and large businesses, seniors, and working families. After Plainfield Chamber of Commerce president Bill Cherry asked his question about the number of tax brackets envisioned, Reagan seemed confused in his reply: "Wow! You know, I may turn my head here to Don Regan again. If you haven't met him, Don Regan was Secretary of the Treasury when this plan was being created and is now the Chief of Staff. For me to try and off the top of my head bring up some of the other benefits—now wait a minute. Again, you asked—about simplification and tax brackets—down to three. Yes, it's 14 tax brackets; it's really down to four."[68] Reagan did better on Cherry's follow-up question about whether anyone's taxes would go up under Reagan's plan, the president replied:

> The only people that we can see that will pay more taxes are those that presently are unfairly not paying their share, those that have been taking advantage of so-called tax shelters and those, as I said, for example, at

the major corporate level where they have found that they can earn a profit and escape paying any tax whatsoever.[69]

Before Reagan left Mooresville, officials presented the president with an Indiana state flag, designed by Mooresville native Paul Hadley. As the president exited the restaurant for his limousine, questions were shouted to him by members of the Washington press corps, particularly Sam Donaldson from ABC News, who asked questions about the release of American hostages held in Beirut, Lebanon. Reagan offered little new information, saying he was limited in what he could say and that he was "praying ceaselessly" for the hostages and slipped away from the reporters. The "exchange" with reporters was one that reflected the rather frustrating distance the media had to keep with President Reagan, with reporters often resorting to shouting questions at public events from a great distance and both sides struggling to hear the questions and the answers. Reagan even said as aides hurriedly moved him toward his car, "They turned out the lights. That tells me I can't talk anymore."[70]

Reagan was quickly whisked from Mooresville to the Indiana Convention Center in downtown Indianapolis, where he addressed the annual convention of the Jaycees, receiving a roaring welcome from the more than 6,000 delegates present, who interrupted his remarks at various points chanting "U.S.A.! U.S.A.!"

The president offered that "before I go on with my remarks for today, let me speak to a concern that I know is on all your minds—our American prisoners in Beirut. We're continuing to do everything that we can to bring all credible influence to bear, to get our people freed and returned home safe and sound. But let me say we must not yield to the terrorist demands that invite more terrorism. We cannot reward their grisly deeds," he said. "We will not cave in."[71] More chants of "U.S.A.! U.S.A.!" filled the room.

Reagan quickly shifted to a pitch for his new tax proposal noting that "trying to tackle the great challenges of our future with today's outdated tax system—that's a little like trying to win the Indianapolis 500 on a bicycle. We're proposing a plan that will say, if I may paraphrase the start of that race: America, start your engines! We're proposing a plan that will tell 238 million Americans: 'Go for it!'"[72] The president added:

> Families are the bedrock of our society, and they're going to receive long-overdue relief. It's a national scandal that Washington sat back for over three decades and let the value of the personal exemption collapse. Well, we're putting an end to benign neglect. Of immense importance to working and middle class families, we will nearly double—to $2,000—the personal exemption for every taxpayer and dependent. . . . As we open the windows of opportunity for all, we're going to start shutting the doors on special privileges that enable some to avoid paying their fair share.[73]

Quoting from the Jaycees motto, Reagan said, "I wish you an America rich in success, rich in our kindness and love for each other. And if I must say goodbye, and I do—because saying goodbye to the Jaycees is pretty hard to do—then I'll do it by leaving you some words I almost feel were written for you—they're from a very noted poet in our background. He said: 'Believe in your mission, Greet life with a cheer; There's big work to do, and that's why you're here; Let the world be better for you, and at last, when you die; Let this be your cry, Come on my soul, carry on.'"[74]

The midterm congressional elections of 1986 brought Reagan back to Indiana to do what he could to even the score in the "Bloody Eighth,"

Indiana's eighth congressional district stretching across southwest Indiana that had bounced back and forth between the Democrats and Republicans and in 1984 resulted in one of the most controversial House elections in the nation. In 1984 a state-level recount indicated Republican Rick McIntyre had defeated incumbent Democrat Frank McCloskey by a margin of thirty-four votes. However, once in Washington, the Democratic majority refused to seat McIntyre and later ran its own recount and declared McCloskey the winner by four votes. House Speaker Thomas P. "Tip" O'Neill swore McCloskey into a new two-year term. McIntyre and the Republicans were determined in 1986 to get back the seat they believed had been stolen from them and enlisted no higher force than Reagan to make the case for McIntyre.

On October 29, 1986, Reagan joined McIntyre and an array of Indiana Republicans at Roberts Memorial Stadium to make a pitch for his election. Reagan told a packed house, "I'm here today because I was hoping you could right a great injustice and send us one more Republican to the next session of the Congress. And I promise . . . as a farmer says, I intend to throw some hay down here where the goats can get at it."[75] Reagan said, "Rick's opponent is a card-carrying member of the tax-and-spend crew. He has voted repeatedly to block our cuts in the federal budget and for higher and higher taxes. But Rick McIntyre and the American people know the truth. They know we don't have a deficit . . . because we're taxed too little; we have it because Congress spends too much."[76]

Reagan said he wanted to talk about his

> most solemn duty as President, the safety of the American people and the security of the United States. Here, too, because of the Republican support, we've been able to

restore America's strength. There's nothing in this job that I'm prouder of than the 2 million young men and women who make up the Armed Forces of the United States. And let me tell you, if we must ever ask them to put their lives on the line for the United States of America, then they deserve to have the finest of weapons and equipment that money can buy. . . . Because of our young men and women in uniform, things really have changed around the world. You know, America used to wear a 'Kick Me' sign around its neck. Well, we threw that sign away and now it reads, 'Don't Tread on Me.' Today every nickel-and-dime dictator around the world knows that if he tangles with the United States of America, he will have a price to pay. And one other thing I'm especially proud of: After six years of this administration, not one square inch of territory in the world has been lost to communism, and one small country, Grenada, has been set free.[77]

Reagan said he remained committed to move ahead with the Strategic Defense Initiative against ballistic missiles, "the thing we call SDI," he said. He said doing so meant that "today we're dealing with the Soviet Union from a position of strength, and it was SDI that brought the Soviet Union to the bargaining table. And let me pledge to you: Our goal is to keep America strong, to save the West from mutual nuclear terror, to make ballistic missiles obsolete, and ultimately to eliminate them from the face of the Earth. SDI is America's insurance policy to protect us against accidents or some madman. . . . And I'll bet on American technology every time."[78] Again singling out McCloskey, Reagan reminded his Hoosier audience that McCloskey had voted seven times to cut or delay implementation of SDI.

The president said his argument was not with all Democrats, he acknowledged "Reagan Democrats" in Indiana and elsewhere: "I've relied again and again when the chips were down, on the support of some of the Democrats, like those who are probably here. And I thank them, because, as you may know, I used to be a Democrat myself. Yes, until I learned that the liberal leadership of the Democratic Party had gone a direction that took them completely out of step with millions of hard-working, patriotic men and women who make up the Democratic Party across the country."[79] In the portion of his remarks that made the most news in Indiana and elsewhere, Reagan added, "You know, my friends, one of the principles that the Democrat leaders have abandoned most dramatically is the principle of fair play. And there's no better example than what happened to Rick McIntyre. Twice—twice the votes showed that he was certified as the duly elected representative of this district, but the Democrats in the House, on a strictly partisan vote, simply refused to seat him. It was an act of unprecedented arrogance."[80] The Republicans filling the room roared their approval.

A loud cry of "Four more years! Four more years!" began to sweep the auditorium. Reagan smiled in his vintage aw shucks manner and said, "Well, there's a little constitutional difficulty there, but if you mean you want me to live four more years, I'm with you. And I'll tell you what I'll settle for: You send Dan Quayle back there so that we've got a Republican Senate for two more years, I'll be happy. You know, my name will never appear on a ballot again, but if you'd like to vote for me one more time, you can do so by voting for Rick McIntyre."[81] Reagan's wish for Quayle's re-election would come true (although the Democrats regained a 55–45 Senate majority), but not for McIntyre, who lost the November 1986 election to McCloskey by an indisputable 53 to 47 percent margin.

On April 3, 1987, Reagan hosted Coach Bobby Knight and the members of the National

Collegiate Athletic Association champion Indiana University basketball team at the Rose Garden for the traditional recognition afforded the NCAA tournament winner. Perhaps it was fitting then that Reagan's next visit to Indiana was just six days later at Purdue University in West Lafayette. While there, the president toured the Knoy Hall of Technology, a computer technology laboratory, and then addressed a packed Mackey Arena audience of students and community members. Upon arrival at the Purdue University Airport via Air Force One, Reagan stopped to make brief remarks to a large crowd gathered there to greet him. He noted that his schedule was tight—he was expected at the campus—"and after I leave the university, I'm heading home for California, and Nancy told me not to be late for dinner." He remarked that visiting western Indiana reminded him of his boyhood home of Dixon, Illinois, and said the nature of his Indiana welcome had made him feel "three inches taller."[82]

After his tour of Knoy Hall, Reagan brushed off questions about allegations of American bugs in the Soviet embassy and made his way to Mackey Arena, the basketball home of the Purdue Boilermakers. He noted, "I understand that the last time there were this many people in Mackey Arena, Purdue beat IU. And as for football, the old oaken bucket has a ray that looks new enough to have been added this past fall. Am I right about that?"[83]

Reagan recited a long list of technological advancements attributable to Purdue and its prestigious record of producing engineers and astronauts for the nation, and added, "For someone who grew up in the era of slide rules, seeing all those computers and robots was one of the most amazing sights of my life. But all this high-technology equipment is being used to train students for jobs of the future. And it's just this,

the need to prepare America for the challenges of the 21st century that I have in mind in speaking to you this afternoon."[84] Reagan expressed his belief that the American economy was changing dramatically, "but one question remains constant, especially among students like yourselves: the question of jobs . . . about how best to prepare for the jobs of the future . . . [and] how best to promote the economic growth that leads to job creation. In preparing Americans for the jobs of the future, perhaps the first matter that comes to mind is education. There can be no doubt that, as we prepare for the 21st century, American education itself must prepare. . . . Today let me simply restate my firm belief that to improve our nation's competitiveness in the world economy, we must strive for new standards of excellence at all levels of American education."[85]

The nation's oldest president turned to rather progressive ideas related to technology and its impact on the American economy "and the deeper question, the underlying question: How can we best foster the economic growth that leads to the creation of jobs in the first place?" He acknowledged the fears that some had that "technological innovations will destroy more jobs than they create, that technology is in some way the enemy of job formation; and yet we need only look at our nation's actual experience to see that this is not so." He noted that when he was younger, "high technology" was found in Charles Lindbergh's flight across the Atlantic, a time when 44 million Americans were employed. "Yet between 1930 and 1980, a time when our nation made steady and remarkable technological progress, the American economy employed on average some 11 million more workers every decade. And to take still more recent evidence, during the economic expansion of the past 52 months, a time of technological breakthrough after breakthrough, our nation actually created over 13 million more jobs," Reagan said. He declared, "No, technology is not the enemy of job creation but its parent, the very source of our economic dynamism and creativity."[86]

Acknowledging his position as one of the nation's oldest presidents ever, Reagan, in his grandfatherly way, turned to the students to remind them that the ideas on how technology will build better lives for all of mankind will come, "But those answers will have to come from generations other than my own. As you work out your own destiny, those answers will have to come from you." Recalling his college days and one of his best jobs ever, working as a dishwasher in a girls' dormitory, Reagan said, "I had to work my way through college . . . those were days when announcements telling people not to leave home looking for work, because there was none, were made on the radio. Well, when I got my diploma, unemployment was around 25 percent. Yet here we are just half a century later, and we Americans are enjoying a standard of living undreamed of when I was your age."[87] He continued:

> Across the Nation, Americans are living longer, healthier lives. I've already lived some two decades longer than my life expectancy when I was born, and that's a source of annoyance to a number of people. Look at the technological marvels that we take for granted that didn't even exist back then: computers, space flights, high technology classrooms and laboratories like the ones I saw today. But I guess what I'm trying to say is this: If our nation has made all these tremendous advances during my lifetime . . . the only limits for your own generation will be the limits of your own imaginations. So, have faith. Place your trust in the enduring values, in the beliefs that have sustained Americans through two centuries and raised our nation to greatness: God, the family, and freedom. And know that in your own minds and

hearts, in your own capacity for wonder and imagination, therein lies the true economy. In this land of freedom, my friends, you only have to dream great dreams, then do your best to make them come true.[88]

Reagan returned to Indiana in July 1987 for two stops to promote his "Economic Bill of Rights" at both Danville in Hendricks County and Indianapolis. Speaking first in Danville from the Hendricks County Courthouse, Reagan's political advisers clearly understood his popularity remained higher in Indiana than elsewhere, and it was friendly territory to address the nation's latest recession. Prior to his speech, Reagan met inside the courthouse with Governor Orr and other state and local officials. Outside, the president opened his remarks by noting:

> driving into Danville today felt like coming home, so much does Hendricks County feel— or remind me of growing up in Illinois. There are the beautiful homes so well cared for, the American flag on display everywhere, and of course this wonderful county courthouse. I was especially struck when, on the way in, someone mentioned that Hendricks County was also the home of the famous Van Buren Elm, a magnificent tree named for President [Martin] Van Buren when he visited nearby Plainfield. I thought that naming a tree in honor of a President was a fine thing to do, and I even daydreamed for a moment about having a tree named after myself. And then I found out a little more about the Van Buren Elm. It turns out that Van Buren was riding in a carriage when the driver took a sharp turn around the elm, throwing Van Buren out of the carriage and into the mud. And in case you're wondering, the answer is, yes, I've warned the Secret Service to be on the lookout for elms.[89]

Reagan reminded the overflow downtown audience that he had visited nearby Mooresville just two years earlier, pushing for major reforms to the nation's tax system, reforms that were now the law of the land. "This time I'm stumping for something I believe even more important, even more historic than tax reform," he said. "It's an Economic Bill of Rights. I first announced this campaign on the steps of the Jefferson Memorial during the Fourth of July weekend, outlining four essential guarantees for all Americans: The freedom to work—and that means eliminating government barriers to opportunity; the freedom to enjoy the fruits of your own labor—and that means bringing to an end, once and for all, excessive government borrowing, spending, and taxation; and the freedom to own and control your own property, including intellectual property like technological innovations; the freedom to participate in a free market, and that means government must work to foster, not hinder, economic growth."[90]

Leaving Danville for the Indiana Convention Center in downtown Indianapolis, Reagan addressed a large confab of 4,000 members of the National Association of Counties meeting there. In a speech essentially matching what he said in Danville, but in more detail, Reagan asserted that his Economic Bill of Rights was "a bill that will restore to us the freedoms that our Founding Fathers believed we should always have, a bill of rights that will protect us and future generations from the needless and wrongful encroachment of government upon our lives. For make no mistake, the danger is grave. And many in Congress are intent upon returning to the days of unrestrained and irresponsible government."[91]

Smarting from weeks of questions raised in Washington about whether members of the Reagan administration had violated American policy—and law—by trading arms for hostages in the Iran/Contra Affair, Reagan sounded a defensive note: "Now, I have been accused in recent days of campaigning for our Economic Bill of Rights in order to distract attention from other events in Washington. Well, it so happens that I've been campaigning for economic rights for more than three decades, and I intend to go on doing so for years to come. But more important, the truth is just the other way around. There are those who would like to distract attention from the real business of government: putting an end to unrestrained spending. And I'm convinced that the great majority of Americans believe simply this: Stop the spending, and no more taxes." He added, "And while I am getting a few things off my chest, something else has been bothering me lately. Critics have claimed that in opposing our administration on the issues, they're at some kind of an unfair disadvantage, that this Presidency is somehow based more on personality than on policy. Well, the truth is, no President can remain popular unless he retains the fundamental support of the American people on the issues. So, I invite my critics—I welcome my critics—to go after me on the issues just as hard as they please. We'll let the people decide who's right and who's wrong."[92]

Reagan's final visit ever to Indiana came on March 9, 1988, as he visited Notre Dame for the unveiling of the new twenty-two-cent Rockne commemorative stamp issued by the U.S. Postal Service. It was a fun visit, not particularly political in nature, but a good way for Reagan to connect once again to one of his most famous film roles as George "The Gipper" Gipp in the 1940 Warner Brothers film, *Knute Rockne: All American*. Reagan said he was pleased to be back at Notre Dame, recalling "the first time I ever saw Notre Dame was when I came here as a sports announcer, two years out of college, to broadcast a football game. You won, or I wouldn't have mentioned it. And then, of course, I was here with

Pat O'Brien and a whole host of Hollywood stars for the world premiere of *Knute Rockne*."[93] As an actor, Reagan said he had longed for the role of Gipp, although the character dies in some of the earliest scenes in the movie. He noted:

> I know that to many of you today Rockne is a revered name, a symbol of greatness and, yes, a face now on a postage stamp. But to my generation, well, we actually knew the legend as it happened. We saw it unfold, and we felt it was saying something important about us as a people and a nation. And there was little room for skepticism or cynicism; we knew the legend was based on fact. . . . It is difficult to stand before you and make you understand how great that legend was at that time. It isn't just a memory here and of those who knew him, but throughout this nation he was a living legend. Millions of Americans just automatically rooted for him on Saturday afternoon and rooted, therefore, for Notre Dame. Now, of course, the Rockne legend stood for fair play and honor, but you know, it was thoroughly American in another way. It was practical. It placed a value on devastating quickness and agility and on confounding the opposition with good old American cleverness. But most of all, the Rockne legend meant this—when you think about it, it's what's been taught here at Notre Dame since her founding: that on or off the field, it is faith that makes the difference, it is faith that makes great things happen.[94]

Reagan recalled for the audience that he had to convince the big shots at Warner Brothers that he was right for the role. After having cast O'Brien, Reagan said the studio wanted a "big name" for the part of the Gipp. Reagan said it was a dream of his to play the role, and he lobbied producers and directors until they finally agreed to cast him in the role. The president said his old Eureka College football coach had summed up his football prowess by describing the young Reagan "as eager, aggressive, better on defense, overall an average football player, but an outstanding talker." Interspersed between Reagan's memories of making the Rockne movie and the Rockne legend itself, the president made a strong pitch for the achievements of his administration— and without saying it directly—for continuing on the same path by promoting Vice President George H. W. Bush to the presidency. He ended his lengthy remarks by quoting Rockne, "'Some time when the team is up against it and the breaks are beating the boys, tell them to go out there with all they've got and win just one for the Gipper. I don't know where I'll be then, but I'll know about it, and I'll be happy.' Good luck in the years ahead and God bless you all."[95]

Once he left office, Reagan dedicated his presidential library and museum in November 1991 in Simi Valley, California. He delivered one of his last political speeches at the 1992 Republican National Convention, and his last major public appearance came at the funeral of former president Richard Nixon in April 1994. On November 5, 1994, Reagan released a handwritten letter in which he disclosed he was suffering from the onset of Alzheimer's disease. Reagan wrote:

> I have recently been told that I am one of the millions of Americans who will be afflicted with Alzheimer's disease. Upon learning this news, Nancy and I had to decide whether as private citizens we would keep this a private matter or whether we would make this news known in a public way. . . . So now we feel it is important to share it with you. In opening our hearts, we hope this might promote greater awareness of this condition. Perhaps it will encourage a clear understanding of the individuals and families who are affected by it. At the moment, I feel just fine. I intend to live the remainder of the years God gives me on this earth doing the things I have always done. I will continue to share life's journey with my beloved Nancy and my family. I plan to enjoy the great outdoors and stay in touch

with my friends and supporters. . . . In closing, let me thank you, the American people, for giving me the great honor of allowing me to serve as your president. When the Lord calls me home, whenever that may be, I will leave with the greatest love for this country of ours and eternal optimism for its future. I now begin the journey that will lead me into the sunset of my life. I know that for America there will always be a bright dawn ahead.[96]

Reagan lived another ten years as his disease progressed, and he made no public appearances during that period. He died of a combination of pneumonia and complications of Alzheimer's disease at his home in Bel Air, California, on June 5, 2004. He was ninety-three years old.

Walter Mondale

As the vice president for one term between 1977 and 1981, Mondale did what all number two members of major party tickets do—he went where prospects were low and time and resources allowed. For 1980 that meant Mondale was dispatched to Indiana for a quick two-day swing before the Democratic primary. (Carter made no preprimary campaign visits to Indiana in 1980.)

As part of his visit, Mondale met privately with leaders of the state's major labor unions, including Communications Workers of America and the Indiana State Teachers Association, both of whom were backing Carter's re-election. The powerful United Auto Workers and AFL-CIO had remained neutral in Indiana between Carter and Kennedy. Later, Mondale met with sparse crowds on a Saturday stop at the City Market in downtown Indianapolis. Mondale told reporters he was confident that the president would do well in the Indiana primary: "I hope the citizens of Indiana will re-nominate President Carter," he said. "We are now well on the way to nomination, but

this primary is an important one. The nation will be looking at Indiana. We are asking the people of Indiana to please give us the support we need to carry on the work of this blessed nation."[97] Before his Indianapolis appearances, Mondale made a quick one-day stop in Fort Wayne.

Defeated along with Carter in November 1980, Mondale quickly became the front-runner for the 1984 Democratic nomination after Kennedy opted not to try and revive his unsuccessful 1980 chase for the nomination. Without an incumbent president, and a field of other contenders who failed to elicit much excitement, Mondale quickly lined up party leaders across the nation, although not without first having to dispatch both former Senator Gary Hart of Colorado and Reverend Jesse Jackson of Illinois. A series of other Democratic hopefuls quickly withdrew, including Senator John Glenn of Ohio, former senator George McGovern of South Dakota, Senator Alan Cranston of California, Senator Ernest "Fritz" Hollings of South Carolina, and former Florida governor Reubin Askew.

Mondale's campaign got off to a rocky start, finding Hart a difficult challenger to shake. Leading into the May 8 Indiana primary, Mondale had won eleven contests, Hart had won eight, and Jackson took the Washington, D.C. primary. In the Midwest, Mondale had run well in Michigan, Illinois, Wisconsin, and Pennsylvania, but Indiana was proving to be more competitive. As the primaries wore on into the spring, both the Mondale and Hart campaigns were becoming cash-strapped, and as the *New York Times* reported, Mondale was counting heavily on the support of organized labor unions in Indiana. "Organized labor, one of the driving forces of Walter Mondale's campaign for the Democratic Presidential nomination, has barely begun to crank up its engines here in the industrialized heart of Indiana, with the May 8 primary less than three weeks away."[98] Labor leaders explained the late start as an arti-fact of the fact no one had expected the Indiana primary to be a factor, or to even be competitive, assuming Mondale would have had the nomina-tion sewn up by May.

Beyond the fact that Hart's campaign was still lurking, Jackson planned a major effort in Indiana and expected to do well among large segments of the state's African American popula-tions in the urban centers of Indianapolis, Fort Wayne, South Bend, and northwest Indiana. Re-gardless of these challenges, Mondale made only two preprimary appearances in Indiana, includ-ing one at a Chrysler plant in Indianapolis, where he reminded workers of his senatorial support of a 1979 federal loan guarantee that kept Chrysler open. Mondale described Hart's charge that the Chrysler deal had not saved any jobs as "pure bunk" and said, "It's time for Gary Hart to admit that he made a mistake when he opposed helping the Chrysler Corporation."[99]

In Gary Mondale told steelworkers that "it may be an old idea, but it's an American idea, that when you're out of work, we ought to have a President who hurts when you hurt and does something to put people back to work. I think we ought to respect and honor working men and women in this country again." Mondale drew a hearty laugh when he referred to former Sena-tor Bayh, one of his biggest supporters in the state, by saying, "The thing about Birch Bayh, he always reminds you, you don't have to be a jerk in public office."[100]

During an Indianapolis news conference, Mondale charged that Reagan's policies "have contributed to a more dangerous world," and discussing Reagan's address on relations with the Soviets added, "A speech is no substitute for ac-tive, direct presidential involvement."[101]

Mondale screened no television advertising in Indiana, although Hart's campaign expended more than $80,000 for television ads. Mondale was also betting on a good finish in Ohio, Mary-land, and North Carolina, all also holding their primaries on the same day as Indiana.[102] At Fort Wayne, Mondale began testing a message that he was "chomping at the bit" to take to Reagan and "wanted to be done" with his fight with Hart.[103] Mondale's campaign aides said he planned a Har-ry S Truman approach, trying to mount a come-from-behind race and restoring the Democratic Party. "Everybody counted Harry Truman out," Mondale said. "Then Harry Truman . . . traveled all over America and he talked about people . . . and about how they needed a friend in the White House to defend them. I'm a people's Democrat, and I'm going to win the same way."[104]

Mondale, looking past Hart and Jackson, focused his words on Reagan: "We've got a some-one who'll go to China for a week . . . but he won't go to Youngstown [Ohio] to see that community and that valley where people are suffering. He'll go to Dallas and talk to big-shot homebuilders, but he won't go down to the Rio Grande Val-ley, where 25 percent of the people are unem-ployed. . . . In short, we've got a government that doesn't seem to understand or care about the problems of the average American, and that has got to stop, and that will stop next fall."[105]

Mondale's approach in Indiana may have cost him. Hart eked out a narrow win of less than 2 percent, along with a better than 2 percent margin of victory in next-door Ohio. The former vice president seemed to understand his ap-proach in Indiana had not worked, telling report-ers after his loss, "I had hoped to do better, but I also knew it was going to be very close. I did not make my case. The contrasts were not as clearly drawn. . . . I don't think we joined the issues as well as we could in a regular debate. . . . I will continue to draw contests with Mr. Hart and Mr. Jackson where indicated."[106] Mondale took the Maryland and North Carolina contests solidly, but Hart's finishes in Indiana and Ohio assured that his campaign would continue. The delegate victory went to Mondale for the four primaries. He captured 186 delegates to Hart's 139, with 42 going to Jackson.[107]

The momentum toward Mondale continued, as did the money to keep his campaign floating above the rest, and he won the Democratic nomination in San Francisco in July 1984. Everyone except Mondale seemed to make news at the convention. Jackson wowed the audience inside the George Moscone Center in San Francisco, along with a national television audience, with a stirring speech built around the call, "our time has come." Jackson asked delegates for their votes on the first ballot as a symbolic gesture, but pledged his support for Mondale. He noted, "We are gathered here this week to nominate a candidate and adopt a platform which will expand, unify, direct, and inspire our party and the nation to fulfill its mission. My constituency is the desperate, the damned, the disinherited, the disrespected, and the despised. They are restless and seek relief. They have voted in record numbers. They have invested the faith, hope and trust that they have in us. The Democratic Party must send them a signal that we care. I pledge my best not to let them down."[108] His pledge of support notwithstanding, the battle between Mondale and his two primary rivals, Jackson and Hart, had taken some nasty turns and healing would take time.

George H. W. Bush

During a September 1984 campaign swing through Indianapolis, a safe and secure state on the Reagan-Bush list, Vice President Bush took advantage of the questions that continued to swirl around the personal finances and taxes of the Democratic vice presidential nominee, Congresswoman Geraldine Ferraro, by declaring that he planned to release three years' worth of his previous tax returns. His move, upping the ante on Ferraro, put further pressure on her to be forthcoming with her tax returns and those of her husband and took his own taxes off the table as an issue. Reagan and Mondale were already releasing such information, and Bush initially had hesitated because of a blind trust he had created while he served in public office for his rather large personal portfolio.

Prior to appearing before an audience of more than 2,000 at the Indiana Convention Center for the State Republican Dinner, Bush gave reporters in Indianapolis a statement that said, "In keeping with my long-standing personal practice of full financial disclosure which goes beyond the spirit and letter of any law, I will release the essential information of my 1981, 1982 and 1983 tax returns."[109] During his remarks to the party faithful, a fund-raiser expected to pull in about $300,000 to the Indiana GOP and the Reagan-Bush campaign, the vice president said that he and President Reagan had provided "leadership that trusts the people, that's why Indiana's so strong today, that's why Indiana is back. . . . More people found jobs in the last 20 months than in almost any 20-month period in the history of the U.S., and more people have held jobs this year than at any other time in the history of our country."[110] Bush declared that "because of our strength, our firmness, our decisiveness, America is safer today and our peace more secure than at any time in the nuclear age. Peace through strength is the answer, not peace through vacillation."[111]

Perhaps trying to remind his audience of the painful memories of the Iranian hostage crisis that had badly damaged the Carter administration, Bush addressed the 1983 U.S. invasion of Grenada, a small island nation in the Caribbean that had undergone a military coup: "When Americans were in grave danger in Grenada, President Reagan didn't wait until 1,000 students were taken hostage, he acted before a crisis became a humiliation."[112]

The economy, however, was front and center on Bush's Indiana agenda, telling reporters earlier in the day that "what's going to determine the election is the economy, and it's always been that way."[113] Addressing concerns raised by Mondale and Ferraro about rising federal deficits, Bush said, "We send a budget up there [to Congress] every year and the President will be doing that in the next budget cycle. Our proposal is to keep the growth going in the economy. The biggest deficit reducer there is is economic growth."[114] Bush defended Reagan administration policies to eliminate protectionist policies on American steel. He later added for good measure, "We are going to carry this state and carry it big."[115] Bush's prediction would prove accurate, with the Reagan-Bush ticket rolling to a victory in Indiana with 62 percent of the 1984 vote.

During his tenure as vice president, Bush was a frequent and happy visitor to Indiana always with a clear agenda: impenetrable support for the Reagan agenda and tireless effort to raise money for Republican candidates on all levels. Along the way, of course, Bush ingratiated himself to party faithful near and far in preparation for the 1988 election. In both 1983 and 1986, the Indiana Republican Party said Bush's participation in its annual state dinner helped raise a total of nearly a million dollars for the state party coffers. Indiana Republican Party chair Gordon Durnil told a re-

porter, "There's really no one on the national level who has been better to the Indiana Republican Party [than Bush]."[116] Bush's 1986 visit included stops in Gary and Indianapolis and a strong pitch for a second term for the state's young junior U.S. senator, Quayle, with Bush cautioning party members to avoid becoming too complacent that a second Quayle term was inevitable. Referring to Quayle and others, Bush said, "Strong leaders like these . . . and the strong organization here makes me believe that this November, Indiana is going to do its part in making 1986 nothing more and nothing less than the best off-year election for the Republican Party in the history of the United States."[117]

In Gary the vice president attended the dedication of a $300 million addition to the eighty-year-old U.S. Steel plant. "Today I saw once again what American industry and American workers are made of," Bush said. "Many industries, like steel, have been through rough times. A lot of people have been hurt. A lot of people have been put out of their jobs. But I believe they have the stuff to fight back."[118]

In September 1987 Bush was back in Indiana for a quick three-hour visit to raise money—this time for his expected 1988 campaign, including one event priced at $1,000 per person to attend. Upon his arrival at the Indianapolis International Airport, reporters quizzed him about how he planned to step out of the shadow of the popular Reagan. "Yes, you have to have your own identity," Bush explained, "your own convictions, your own beliefs, your own things that you want to do and I will do that. I have stood with this President. I believe in what he has done to benefit this country. The people of Indiana are much better off than they were six and a half years ago when he came into office." Bush said his coming campaign was about "talking about what we've done,

Vice President George H. W. Bush waves to the crowd during a visit to Indianapolis with President Reagan.

IHS, BASS PHOTO COMPANY COLLECTION, P 130

saying here's what we've accomplished, and now here's what George Bush will do, and here's how I will go about doing it." The two top priorities remained the same, he said, jobs and peace.[119]

As 1988 opened, Bush was the odds-on favorite for the Republican nomination, although the assumed endorsement he carried from Reagan did not stop several others from entering the fray. Bush faced primary challenges from U.S. Senator Bob Dole of Kansas, Congressman Jack Kemp of New York, Governor Pierre S. "Pete" du Pont of Delaware, former Secretary of State Alexander Haig, and television evangelist Pat Robertson. Bush's challegers were all to the right of his own record as a centrist, progressive Republican, but the Reagan backing helped secure necessary fund-raising, along with a pile of political chits collected in eight years as vice president.

Bush's campaign had a rocky start in 1988, however, as he finished third in the first-in-the-nation Iowa caucus and trailed Dole for the New Hampshire primary before the Bush campaign unleashed a bare-knuckled attack on the Kansan (along with the stiff support of New Hampshire governor John Sununu). Dole followed with a series of victories in Minnesota, South Dakota, and Wyoming, before Bush opened up an insurmountable lead by sweeping sixteen of the seventeen Super Tuesday primaries on March 8, 1988 (narrowly finishing third in Washington behind Robertson and Dole). By the time the Indiana primary rolled around on May 3, Bush was unstoppable and rolled up 80 percent of Republican ballots over a decimated field that still included Dole, Robertson, Kemp, and du Pont.

Even with the field cleared for the May primary, Bush made stops in the state, not only to benefit his own campaign, but also to help raise money for Indiana Republicans. His first visit came in late April before an audience of more

than 3,000 at the University of Southern Indiana in Evansville. In his remarks the vice president heaped ample praise on Orr for his efforts to reduce class sizes in Indiana classrooms. "The answer to solving the problems of education or the homeless or daycare or whatever it is, is not to turn back to the formulations of the past that failed us," Bush said. "It's to do what Bob Orr was talking about, keep this recovery going, this opportunity economy moving so those men and women who don't have jobs will get jobs in the private sector." Bush said educational success in the states was not reliant upon the federal government "doing it all. The last thing we need is for the curriculum to be chosen, the teachers to be selected in some federal program."[120]

In an interesting preview of what was to come, Indiana reporters quizzed Bush about his "short list" of potential running mates. "I will be looking for the man or woman best able to take over for the President," Bush said. Asked specifically whether Senator Richard G. Lugar of Indiana was a candidate under consideration, Bush said he had "high regard for him as a national political figure."[121]

Days later, during a stop in Fort Wayne to tour a Magnavox plant just before the primary, Bush's remarks reflected he had shed the GOP field and was focused instead on the presumptive Democratic nominee, Massachusetts governor Michael Dukakis. Bush said Dukakis was more concerned about "pink slips and plant closings" than creating new jobs—his response to Dukakis's stated support of legislation that would require employers to provide advance notice of pending mass layoffs. "All that does is guarantee misery," Bush said about Dukakis's idea. "I'm for plant openings. [Dukakis] is talking about pink slips and plant closings. We're not talking about closing factories, we're about opening factories until every man and woman who wants a job has a job. I want to talk about the fact that . . . there are more Americans at work now than at any time in the history of the country."[122]

Speaking before a Republican fund-raising breakfast in Fort Wayne, Bush turned his remarks to efforts to curb illicit drugs in the nation. "There's some big drug problems in this country," Bush said. "I hear a lot of campaign rhetoric. I hear both Jackson and Dukakis assailing the administration on this and thus denigrating those men and women in the DEA [Drug Enforcement Administration] . . . trying to stem the flow of drugs coming in and catching the criminals. But I haven't heard them talk about how tough they want to be in changing the laws . . . [to] put some muscle in. I strongly favor the death penalty for the narco-traffickers, those kingpins that are pushing the poison on our kids."[123]

Bush also took a swipe at Dukakis's "waffling" position on retaliation against Iran for a mine attack on a U.S. Navy frigate. "The President's different than anything else," Bush said. "You can't wait around, hold your finger in the wind and see what the polls show. You can't do that when you're President. You can't wait around to see which way the wind blows."[124] Bush told the party insiders gathered that former president Carter "hangs over the Democrats like a shadow, an unwanted reminder of the failure of their policies the last time they were in power. Now Mike Dukakis and Jesse Jackson are trying to sell that same old Democratic bill of goods. More taxes. More spending. More government control over your lives. I'm not running against Jimmy Carter, but you've got to put into perspective where the policies of the liberal Democrats got us before the Republican administration. You know and I know when Carter blamed us for a malaise in the spirit of the people that the blame belonged where the

voters put it—on the Carter Administration and on that liberal Democratic philosophy."[125]

Later during a stop in Indianapolis, Bush responded strongly to reporters who questioned whether Reagan's attorney general, Edwin Meese III, still held the moral and ethical authority to lead after a variety of questions had been raised about his conduct. Bush warned that he was ready to combat any "sleaze factor" the Democrats may engage in attacking Meese or other members of the Reagan team. "I think the Democrats are fair," Bush said. "I know the Democrats. I hear them talking about it. But there is plenty of evidence to kind of go into a guilt-by-association mode where we can find in Massachusetts politics or campaign staff or things of that nature. I hope we don't have to do it."[126] Smirking, the vice president said, "We will have some fun, too, trying to look into what is going on in Illinois or Massachusetts, depending upon which one wins the Democratic nomination. You know we've got some cannon fodder, if you want to get into that."[127] Appearing before a friendly Republican rally, Bush declared to Dukakis and Jackson, "Let me throw this challenge down. I favor the death penalty for narcotics kingpins. Now will the Democrats join us on that or not?"[128]

A few days later Bush made a quick stop at the AM General Plant in Mishawaka which had produced more than 48,000 vehicles for the military between 1983 and 1988 and had existing contracts for 20,000 more. The plant and its 500 workers produced the Hummer, the modern replacement of the venerable Jeep. Questions lingered about whether AM General would keep its contract going forward, which made Bush's visit to the plant a curious choice, but he pledged he would "try" to keep the production line open. The stop did give Bush a chance to criticize congressional Democrats' efforts to cut military spending requests from the Reagan administration, and to try and highlight his own foreign policy experience.[129]

"Inexperience in foreign policy could hurt not only our national security, but also our economic health," Bush said in discussing whether his likely Democratic opponent was qualified to lead the nation. "The country wants to move ahead, not go back to the misery we inherited through the very policies Jackson and Dukakis are talking about. You listen to what Dukakis and Jackson are saying, and their policies will set this country back, and we must not let that happen."[130] Bush also addressed what he said was "a substantial imbalance" in conventional forces between the United States and the Soviet Union and that Democratic military cuts did not help. He said the Soviets had twice as many tanks and artillery pieces as the North Atlantic Treaty Organization alliance. "As we seek to reduce our reliance on nuclear weapons, it's critical that we maintain, strengthen and modernize our conventional deterrent in Europe," Bush said. "The Hummer is an integral part of that. We took a $31 billion cut in defense because of the opposition in Congress, a lot of it affecting what happens on this very production line in the future. . . . I think it's shortsighted to fool around with the defense muscle of the United States of America."[131]

Bush also addressed rising concerns about long-term American support of the corrupt regime of President Manuel Noriega in Nicaragua. Bush said Dukakis would have to come up with more than just "some macho statements" and said, "I can't wait for Mr. Dukakis to discuss the Noriega matter. One of the beautiful things about being a new candidate is that you can make dramatic statements without necessarily having the proof," adding that Dukakis needed

to be more circumspect regarding the Noriega issue. Bush said he would ask Dukakis, "What would you do about it? It's fine sitting out there. You see, you can make a lot of unfounded criticism. But what's his suggestion? What's he going to do, and do it in a way that handles the delicate Central American relationships that we're building?"[132]

Bush defended the Reagan administration reaction to allegations that Noriega had engaged in illicit drug activities: "When it became demonstrably clear that Noriega was involved in drugs, we moved against him."[133] He added, "We're moving towards democracy. Ninety percent are living under democracy in this hemisphere. We don't want to set that back by some kind of macho statement out of Harvard" (a swipe at Dukakis's law degree from Harvard, the rival to Bush's alma mater, Yale University).[134]

As the GOP convention in New Orleans approached in August, the only open question was who Bush intended to designate as his vice president. The list of potential running mates included a stellar list of Republican stars, including former U.S. Senator Howard Baker of Tennessee, Congressman Dick Cheney of Wyoming, California governor George Deukmejian, Dole, and Kemp. Back in Indiana, there was no reason to believe or even suggest that Indiana would play any role whatsoever in the 1988 presidential race. The state was widely expected to be safe Republican territory as normal, and besides, the attention of Indiana political figures was focused on a surprisingly competitive gubernatorial contest shaping up between Lieutenant Governor John Mutz (the GOP nominee) and Secretary of State Evan Bayh (the Democratic nominee), the young thirty-three-year-old son of former Senator Birch Bayh.

Nobody from Indiana appeared poised to play a major role in the Bush campaign, with the possible exception of the state's senior senator, Lugar, a well-respected member of the Congress and a national leader on issues of foreign affairs. Even Lugar, however, had failed to make any floated "short lists" for Bush running mates (despite having made a similar list for Reagan in 1980). What only a handful of deep insiders in the Republican Party knew was that Bush had his eye on another Hoosier, one who even the most-informed politicos could not name: James Danforth Quayle, at age forty-one, the junior senator from Indiana. Swept into office in the Reagan Revolution in 1980, Quayle was an attractive candidate and had established a record as a tough campaigner, but had a relatively undistinguished Senate record in only his second term. Quayle had joined the Senate at an interesting time of renewed strength for Republicans, but was hardly viewed as a rising star among the Old Guard GOP Senate still dominated by the likes of Dole, Barry Goldwater, Baker, Pete Domenici, Paul Laxalt, William Roth, John Danforth, Orrin Hatch, Arlen Spector, and Bob Packwood.

One of Bush's top confidants and advisers, James A. Baker, said the idea of tapping Quayle had been on the minds of the Bush insiders for months, particularly Bush himself. The Bush team seemed to acknowledge that it was living in the long and deep shadow of Reagan, noting that beyond Reagan's speech and Bush's acceptance speech at the 1988 GOP convention in New Orleans, their convention lacked any drama or interest. As Baker put it, "If we didn't gin up more excitement, George would be presented to the nation through the jaundiced filter of journalistic boredom. The one big mystery we had left, of course, was the selection of a vice presidential running nominee. If we played it right, that would add some drama, or so we thought."

But Baker admitted, "We didn't play it right, but we got drama anyway."[135] Quayle's selection quickly raised more questions than support.

On August 19, 1988, Bush and Quayle flew from New Orleans to Fort Wayne and then traveled via motorcade to nearby Huntington for a massive rally on the lawn of the Huntington County Courthouse. An approving crowd of more than 10,000 was on hand to welcome Quayle home and to greet Bush and his wife, Barbara. "I am going to win with the help and support of one of Indiana's finest products, your man and mine, Dan Quayle," Bush told the cheering throng. "Dan Quayle represents the two great issues of this campaign, jobs and peace. That is what this election is about and he and I are right on both those issues."[136] Bush said his candidacy was about completing a mission started in 1980 by the Reagan-Bush team and pledged his best to fight inflation and unemployment. "We're going to make 30 million new jobs in eight years," Bush promised. "I'm not going to raise your taxes, I think you pay enough."[137] His latter remark mirrored his "read my lips" remark from his convention acceptance speech—a pledge that would come to haunt Bush in subsequent years when federal taxes were, in fact, raised.

Bush's speech was successful and set up the campaign's coming three-day tour of the battleground states of Ohio and Illinois, but what Bush said seemed secondary to Quayle's performance, which remained under heavy scrutiny by the national media. Bush stood by Quayle—for both 1988 and 1992—having selected a running mate from the same generation (and with the same lacking Vietnam pedigree) as his oldest son and part-time campaign adviser, George W. Bush.

During his presidency, noteworthy as Bush became the first sitting vice president since Martin Van Buren to be elevated to the presidency by the voters, Indiana visits remained highly steeped in Republican Party fund-raising efforts and little else. For the little-celebrated Arbor Day and Earth Day holidays in April 1990, Bush flew aboard Air Force One to Indianapolis to plant a tree in a just-completed downtown "park" (little more than a traffic island constructed near the intersection of Alabama and Washington Streets). Officially, it was part of Bush's pledge to plant a tree in each of the nation's fifty states and part of his push to pass the first major reform of the Clean Air Act in more than a decade. His trip, however, drew criticism from Democrats because his "official" duties seemed rather light, even though the trip was financed by the federal government. His main purpose for being in Indianapolis seemed to be to boost the senatorial campaign of Congressman Dan Coats. Coats was running in the 1990 special election, having been appointed to replace Quayle in the Senate after Bush-Quayle won the 1988 election. (Coats served two full terms and retired, only to be elected again to a six-year term in 2010 following the retirement of Senator Evan Bayh, his predecessor.)

During his remarks before about 5,000 people at the corner of Washington and Alabama Streets in Indianapolis, Bush asked that the tree he planted that day "be Ryan's tree," referring to Ryan White who lay near death at a nearby hospital. "[Ryan White] has created a special legacy of his own and he is in our prayers today," the president said. "He's been fighting a courageous battle against a deadly disease, but also against ignorance and fear. Ryan has helped us to understand the truth about AIDS and he's shown all of us the strength and bravery of the human heart. So today, as we together plant this beautiful American elm, the symbol of new life, let it be Ryan's tree."[138]

As usual, Bush praised the support and work of "a great Hoosier and an even greater Vice President," Quayle, and said he was sorry that volatile IU men's basketball coach Knight was not present. "It wouldn't hurt him to be around a kinder, gentler event like planting trees, but nevertheless, please give him my very best."[139] The bulk of the president's remarks, however, were a lobbying effort for his Clean Air Act proposal and for funding the National Tree Trust Act of 1990 (a part of Bush's treasured "Thousand Points of Light" program), which would provide $175 million for the planting of one billion trees across the nation. "Trees, of course, can help ensure clean air," Bush said. "Consider, one recent study showed that trees, much more than water, consume the carbon dioxide that is building up in our atmosphere. Research also shows that trees can lower peak energy demand in urban areas by 20 to 40 percent. . . . The record's clear; we need trees economically and environmentally. And we also need them to lift our minds and our hearts. Trees are something all can plant—for while they can be fragile or sturdy, they are always precious."[140]

At the conclusion of his public remarks, Bush and his entourage made a short trek to the Murat Shrine just north on Alabama Street for a private fund-raising luncheon benefiting Coats's campaign (organized in part by Indianapolis Colts owner Robert Irsay). Bush opened his remarks with some awkward jokes offered in his sometimes broken manner of speaking, acknowledging that he had arrived too late to eat lunch with the assembled group. "On the way over I was notified that the Secret Service had found my food taster face down in the salad. Somebody had washed my lettuce with Perrier! It could have been worse—broccoli—could have been worse!"[141]

As he did often in his public life, Bush railed against "the scourge of drugs in American life" and said, "Nothing ravishes the American family more than drug abuse. Our national drug strategy . . . deals with all sides of the issue, from education and prevention to expanded treatment, to stronger penalties and stepped up enforcement. It's a tough approach, but it is a sensible approach. No part of American life is safe from the scourge of drugs. This is not simply an inner city problem or a border problem. . . . We've got to get PCP and crack [cocaine] off every street and out of every school in America, and it's time we got more federal resources into the hands of those in the thick of the fight, those on the front lines. If we are to build a better future for this country, America first must be drug free."[142]

Dan Quayle

Quayle's debut on the national stage in 1988 was greeted with widespread belief that his presence on the Republican ticket represented a misstep by George H. W. Bush in his first big choice in the post-Reagan era. Quayle's lack of service in Vietnam (instead given a stateside assignment to write news releases for the Indiana National Guard) and his inability to untwist his own tongue sent massive doubts across the nation.

Democrats were quick to point out doubts about Quayle from the moment he was announced until the moment Quayle was later leveled in a vice presidential debate on October 5, 1988, by the Democrats' choice, Senator Lloyd Bentsen of Texas. The selection of Quayle put Indiana on the presidential map—at least for one day—as Bush-Quayle stumbled out of New Orleans for their first stop in Huntington, Quayle's adoptive hometown. There a crowd of Hoosiers filled the Huntington County Courthouse square to greet the GOP standard-bearers (along with

singer Pia Zadora who warmed up the masses). Bush praised Quayle as "a man of character" and delivered remarks focused on his campaign, emphasizing economic opportunity and peace, essentially the elements of a "third" Reagan term if the sitting president was not term limited. Bush told Huntington residents, "No more fitting place could be found than this, Huntington, right in the heart of the United States," to begin his campaign.[143] Quayle's remarks and subsequent exchange with reporters from the dais constructed outside the courthouse stole the headlines for the day, however.

"It is a genuine, deep honor for me to be back home in Huntington," Quayle said. "I am deeply honored by the confidence that George Bush has placed in me." He drew applause as he praised the small-town values found in the people of Huntington as representative of "the things we love, our family, our churches, our neighborhood, and yes, we love the National Guard."[144]

Once he completed his remarks and Bush left the stage, Quayle stayed on to take shouted questions from reporters from the side of the stage for about twenty-five minutes. As reporters asked their questions, a throng of Republican faithful booed and heckled them for asking continued questions about Quayle's military record. The senator denied that in 1969 he had pulled any special privilege as the son of a powerful Indiana newspaper publishing family to get a National Guard assignment as opposed to active military combat service in Vietnam. "I asked no one to break any rules, and as far as I know, no rules were broken at all," Quayle said. "I am very proud of my service in the Indiana National Guard. . . . I could have been called up to Vietnam, as other Indiana units were, and if I had been called, I would have gone."[145]

Quayle, referring to himself in the third person, said, "The implication is somehow Dan

Quayle, by voluntarily signing up for the Indiana National Guard, was not patriotic, and I resent that. Like any 22-year-old college senior, when you think about the major decisions in your life and how you're going to serve your country, you call home. I talked to my mother and father and said I'm interested in joining the National Guard." He said that decision supported his future plans to go to law school, while still allowing him to support America's efforts to promote democracy in Southeast Asia.[146]

Questions continued to swirl about Quayle's military service and Bush's selection of him to be one heartbeat away from the presidency, eventually relegating Quayle to a lesser role in the campaign. In mid-October the Associated Press moved a national story under the headline of "Quayle out of the spotlight" and emphasized the twisted-tongue rhetoric he sometimes employed,

IHS, DAN QUAYLE CENTER AND MUSEUM GIFT

Dan Quayle was the ninth Hoosier to be nominated for the vice presidency and the fifth to be elected to office.

including saying that the Nazi Holocaust of the Jews in Germany was "an obscene period in our nation's history" and then awkwardly adding, "I didn't live in this century."[147] He continued to face questions about whether his presence on the ticket was hurting Bush's chances offering a circular form of logic: "Obviously, there's going to be continued interest in me and the reason for that is there's been so much interest in me up to now. But it will be very much of a background issue because the American people are trying to make up their minds on the top of the ticket."[148]

The Bush-Quayle express never again stepped on Indiana soil for the 1988 campaign, although Quayle did appear in the state on solo appearances meant to give him favorable, friendly audiences. For an October visit to Indianapolis, reporters were once again booed and heckled by Quayle supporters when they attempted to ask him questions. The crowd shouted down reporters with "Just say no!" at one point. Quayle was sharpening his skills, however, and showing signs of the bare-knuckled fighter Hoosiers had witnessed in 1980 when he upset Bayh. Quayle delivered some strong punches to the Dukakis campaign—as was his expected role as the vice presidential nominee, including raising the issue of a controversial prison furlough program in Massachusetts that the Bush-Quayle campaign said had resulted in the release of a murderous inmate and another sixty-two criminals listed as missing or escaped from the state's prison system. Quayle told his Indiana supporters, "We plan on taking some heat, but staying in the kitchen. But in the end, we'll get the job done. We have just begun to fight."[149]

Elected to the vice presidency, Quayle served as a mostly effective lieutenant to Bush, though a few spoken missteps continued to occur. In Indiana, his stock remained high, and Quayle headlined a state Republican fund-raiser in 1989 that brought in $200,000 toward a reported half-million-dollar deficit the party had incurred in losing the governorship for the first time in twenty years in 1988. The Indianapolis fund-raising event was set up to celebrate the one year anniversary of Quayle's election and included a basket for shooting hoops. Reporters quickly noted that Quayle went one-for-six in his attempts at the line, while his wife, Marilyn, hit half of her free throws. Quayle's words to the Indiana GOP seemed designed to lift their spirits after the gubernatorial debacle, noting that "we're a family that during tough times pulls together, a family that sticks together. When the going gets tough, you can always count on the family. Over the years, this political family has won far more battles than we've lost. This family that's gathered here understands the importance of sticking together."[150]

In August 1990 Quayle was the headline speaker for the annual national convention of the American Legion being conducted in Indianapolis, the legion's national headquarters. His remarks came at a critical period for the Bush administration, with American actions in Operation Desert Storm having just started in Kuwait. Quayle welcomed an audience of more than 3,000 to Indiana and praised the Legion's work. Quayle noted that the world had changed dramatically since Bush had addressed them two years earlier. "In Eastern Europe, tyrants toppled and a wall in Berlin came tumbling down," said Quayle. "In the Soviet Union we have witnessed a remarkable transformation toward greater openness and an increased cooperation with the West. And right here in our own hemisphere, we have seen democracy take some giant strides forward."[151] Quayle said recent developments promised "a new era of mankind" and "a new hope for

IHS, *INDIANAPOLIS RECORDER COLLECTION*, P. 303

Senator Quayle poses with Harriet M. Thompson of Indianapolis, the executive director of Operation Late Start Inc.

this era that negotiation and peace will replace intimidation and violence. This is the great dream that has inspired mankind throughout the ages. Today, thanks in large part to American leadership this dream is closer than ever to realization. But this new international order hasn't come into being yet. Around the world there are those who would destroy this dream if they could. There are still brutal dictators who prefer the rule of the jungle to the rule of the law."[152]

One of those dictators, Quayle said, was Iraqi leader Saddam Hussein, "a man who rules through terror and slaughter; who has used poison gas against his own countrymen; who invaded Iran in a war that cost the lives of over a half a million people; who plunders tiny Kuwait and threatens Saudi Arabia; who aspires to gain control of oil resources on which the entire world depends for its economic well-being; who threatens his neighbors with weapons of mass destruction and who poses a growing threat to the peace and stability of the region."[153] Quayle repeated Bush's statement that Hussein's aggression could not continue and that the president knew the mission would not be easy, "make no mistake about it. What is at stake in the Persian Gulf is nothing less than the shape of tomorrow. This is the first international crisis in the post-Cold War era. If Saddam Hussein's aggression remains unchecked, new and more terrible aggressions will surely follow. That is why President Bush has drawn the line in the sand against Saddam Hussein's aggression. Here then is the first lesson of the current crisis: We need to act decisively today to preserve world order for tomorrow."[154]

Geraldine Ferraro

Former vice president Mondale took a giant step toward invigorating his 1984 campaign and gave party progressives something to cheer about with his selection of Congresswoman Ferraro of New York as his running mate. As the first female selected by either major party to be a nominee for president or vice president, Ferraro made history in 1984 and gave Mondale a needed lift in the polls against a popular incumbent, Reagan. Ferraro's presence on the ticket, however, stirred controversy, especially given scandals and made-up controversies constructed by Reagan campaign operative Karl Rove, who worried about Ferraro's ability to get voters to notice Mondale's sagging campaign.

Questions about Ferraro's past campaign fund-raising activities, the personal finances of both her and her husband, John Zaccaro, and her positions on abortion rights (a Catholic, this put her in conflict with the positions of the Roman Catholic Church) quickly dominated her campaign. While on a campaign swing through Indiana in early September 1984, Ferraro was forced to address the abortion issue and her Catholicism directly. The Archbishop of New York, John J. O'Connor, had taken public issue with Ferraro's claim that the church's position on abortion was open to personal interpretation and that she was misrepresenting the Church to others. While in Indianapolis on September 11, Ferraro said she opposed abortion as a Catholic, but supported the rights of women to decide for themselves whether to have one. She denied having ever made a statement that misrepresented the Church's position and that she had personally telephoned the archbishop from Indianapolis to discuss the matter. Ferraro said she "pointed out to the Archbishop that I have never made a public statement describing or misrepresenting the teachings of my church" and that "I explained to the Archbishop that I support the right of everyone to speak out on important issues of the day. When bishops speak out they are doing their duty as church officials. I also said that when I speak out I am doing my duty as a public official and my foremost duty as a public official is to uphold the United States Constitution, which guarantees freedom of religion. I cannot fulfill that duty if I seek to impose my own religion on other American citizens. And I am determined to do my duty as a public official."[155]

While in Indianapolis, Ferraro attended two fund-raisers at the Merchants Plaza Hotel with tickets costing $50 for one event and $500 for the other. She was introduced at the events by Ann DeLaney, the Democratic nominee for lieutenant governor of Indiana, who along with Ferraro shared the distinction of being the first woman so nominated. Ferraro said she and DeLaney had a lot in common: "We're both prosecutors. We both have three children. And we're both going to have a new job in January."[156]

Ferraro told her audience of about three hundred people who paid the $50 ticket price that Reagan had failed to deliver a workable plan to reduce the nation's growing debt. "We are facing $180 billion deficits this year and those deficits are going to continue unless we do something about it," she said. "What we are saying to President Reagan is put your plan on the table."[157] She added, "Quite frankly, Fritz Mondale has put up his deficit reduction package. What we're doing is saying to President Reagan, 'Put yours on the table. Put it on the table before the November election so that at least the people of America would know what you're talking about and what they can anticipate over the next couple of years.'"[158]

While her comments were well received among Democratic Party faithful, outside the hotel about two dozen protesters gathered with signs, carrying phrases such as "Ferraro equals abortion" and "Baby killers and queers vote for Ferraro."[159]

Having given up her seat in the House to run for vice president, Ferraro left Congress in 1985. She made two subsequent attempts (in 1992 and 1998) to be elected to the Senate from New York, losing both times. She succumbed to cancer on March 26, 2011, at the age of seventy-five, while undergoing treatment at a hospital in Boston, Massachusetts.

Michael Dukakis

Massachusetts governor Dukakis and Reverend Jackson were the only two Democrats standing as the 1988 Indiana primary approached, and both showed for the annual Jefferson-Jackson Day Dinner in Indianapolis just four days before the May vote. The two rivals shook hands politely on the stage at the Indiana Convention Center, and Jackson listened to Dukakis speak for about

sixteen minutes (although Dukakis left and did not stay in the room for Jackson's thirty-five-minute speech that followed). Dukakis countered blasts from Jackson that the nation needed more than just a competent manager, by acknowledging that he was "no razzle-dazzle artist," but quickly added, "That is not what this country needs. After seven years of razzle-dazzle in the White House, this country needs some competence in a leader. Maybe that's why I'm ahead."[160]

Dukakis continued, "When it comes to leadership, I'm very proud of the fact I'm governor of a state that's generally viewed to be way out front on jobs, economic development, on education, on training, on welfare reform. You don't get those kinds of things done unless you're a leader." Without referring directly to Jackson, whose barbs had continued to grow more pointed, the governor described himself as a "dyed-in-the-wool, true-blue Democrat" and said the challenge for Democrats was to have a debate that "stayed positive and constructive."[161]

As part of his visit to Indianapolis, Dukakis and his wife, Kitty, attended a fund-raising dinner and made a quick stop at the Greenwood High School prom under way at the Indiana Roof Ballroom in downtown Indianapolis. There, Dukakis delivered a few brief remarks, urging the students to avoid drinking and driving and danced not only with a student, but also with Greenwood mayor Jeanette Surina, a fellow Democrat, who was attending the prom.

Beyond May, the Dukakis-Bentsen ticket, derisively referred to as the "Boston-Austin" connection among liberal Democrats, made no real campaign effort in Indiana. The presence of Indiana's junior senator on the GOP national ticket and the record-setting gubernatorial campaign under way in the state in 1988 meant the Democratic national ticket had its focus elsewhere. In the end, it made sense. Bush rolled to an easy victory in Indiana over Dukakis (piling up nearly 1.3 million votes), mirroring the GOP landslide nationally as Bush won forty states to Dukakis's ten.

Gary Hart

By 1984 the Reagan Revolution was in full swing and Democrats stood little chance in upsetting the "great communicator," Reagan. Optimistic Democrats, however, were not giving up, including Hart. Undeterred by conventional wisdom that predicted former vice president Mondale was next in line for the Democratic nomination, Hart took his upstart campaign across the nation in the early months of 1984, including Indiana. Hart's message to Indiana Democrats was clear: He was their best chance to defeat Reagan.

"This is not just a contest between Democrats and Republicans," Hart told an Evansville audience in the final days before the May 1984 primary. "It is a contest between our nation's future and its past." Repeating his oft-mentioned theme of representing "the politics of the future" and hoping to round up Democratic votes from those weary of Mondale's connection to the failed Carter administration, Hart told a small gathering of less than five hundred supporters that he needed a strong showing in Indiana (and other upcoming primaries) to remain competitive against the growing Mondale tide. "I think we've come to the point in this contest where if [Mondale] wants to claim the experience of the [vice presidency], he's going to have to take responsibilities for the failures as well," Hart said.[162]

While in Evansville, Hart took the unusual step of riding a paddleboat on the Ohio River, stopping at a nearby retirement community, but finding an audience of only thirty people,

media reports indicated. Undeterred, Hart told the seniors that he had fought to save Medicare and Medicaid from cuts proposed by Reagan and would continue to fight for their interests. Perhaps inspired by the Ohio River, Hart added, "There is no reason why the roads and bridges of Indiana should deteriorate while thousands of people in this state go without work."[163] Ending a less-than-spectacular two-hour visit to Indiana, Hart's campaign bypassed about two dozen supporters who waited for him and boarded a plane for richer pastures in Baltimore and Dallas.

Three days later, Hart made a stop in South Bend and met with union and industrial workers and chastised Mondale for proposing welfare programs of the past that would further drive up the debt. "President Reagan seems to think deficits are the workers' salvation," Hart said. "The truth is they are the workers' devastation. Put bluntly, the deficits are Ronald Reagan's economic Vietnam." He said federal deficits estimated to top $200 billion in 1984 were "stealing from our future. Mr. Reagan's modest and temporary election-year recovery is being paid for entirely out of the pockets of coming generations, to whom Mr. Reagan will bequeath a few films of dubious quality, a smiling countenance, and a $2 trillion national debt."[164]

In the final forty-eight hours before the Indiana primary vote, Hart was back in the state and acting more confident. After touring a printing plant and greeting workers in Indianapolis, Hart was asked when he planned to pull the plug on his Mondale challenge and begin helping unify Democrats for the fall campaign. "Unity works in all directions," Hart replied. "There is more patching up to be done from Mr. Mondale's side than from my side. I think if a hand has to be reached out, it must come from Mr. Mondale to me given the negative campaign he has run."[165]

Hart's campaign was open about the importance of the Indiana primary, declaring it "winnable" and as crucial to him as Indiana was for Robert F. Kennedy in 1968. Political pundits offered that Hart turned to Indiana because his other options were drying up quickly and because of Mondale's strength in big-state primaries in the Midwest and elsewhere, including New York, Tennessee, and Alabama. Hart's campaign told reporters they were willing to let Mondale and Jackson fight it out for urban and labor votes among Democrats, while their man focused on a "south of U.S. 40" strategy in southern Indiana.

Though he won a narrow victory in both Indiana and Ohio in the May primary, Hart still struggled to catch Mondale in the delegate count for the upcoming Democratic National Convention in San Francisco. His delegate shortage was made no better by a postprimary partnership formed between the Mondale and Jackson campaigns that formed a majority among the eighty-eight Indiana delegates when combined. Jackson's supporters went for the deal with the Mondale forces after realizing their chances at gaining the nomination were slipping away and in exchange for powerful positions on the party's rules committee. Jackson's supporters in Indiana, led by State Senator Julia Carson and State Representative William Crawford, both of Indianapolis, made it clear that the Mondale-Jackson deal did not necessarily mean the Jackson delegates would support Mondale on a first ballot at the convention.[166]

Jesse Jackson

Jackson of Illinois was not the first black candidate for the Democratic presidential nomination. Shirley Chisholm had earned that title in 1972, but his was the first campaign to make an actual impact on the determination of the party's nomination. Jackson had participated in the nation's first National Black Political Convention that drew more than 5,000 black leaders to Gary in July 1972, an event Chisholm skipped in allegiance to the Democratic Party. Jackson's appearance there, as head of the fledgling Rainbow Coalition in Chicago, impressed many. He declared, "In the names of Chaka, Cettiwayo, Nat Turner, Sojourner Truth, Mary McLeod Bethune, Marcus Garvey, Malcolm X, and Martin Luther King, Jr., let us build a nation for all black families to enjoy as long as the earth has air and the sky has sun."[167] He urged the convention attendees to "form a black political party" and added that "without the option of a black political party, we are doomed to remain in the hip pocket of the Democratic Party and the rumble seat of the Republican Party. . . . There is a balm in Gilead that assures me that all of us here do care, that we can save a world from despair, that this world is not destined to die, that we can save the children and holler love across the nation."[168]

By 1984 Jackson had returned to the Democratic fold and staged a serious challenge for the party's presidential nomination in several key states, including Indiana, hanging tough against better-financed and better-known foes, Mondale and Hart. In April 1984 Jackson worked throughout the Easter weekend in black churches and elsewhere, hoping to draw attention for his cash-strapped campaign and to get votes. In Indianapolis he told supporters that he supported a surtax on annual incomes of $25,000 or more to generate more federal resources for social programs. "This could generate in the neighborhood of $50 billion for social programs," he said. He also proposed cutting military spending for certain weapons systems.[169] Jackson said his proposal would be "a temporary surtax aimed at cutting into or reducing the budget deficit. We simply have an emergency on our hands, and those making $25,000 or more, and corporations, must share the burden."[170]

"All this must be done because the urban crisis, now at least three decades old, has never been solved," Jackson said. "We have in the White House an administration which is running away from its basic responsibility to solve it."[171] He also took aim at social services cuts initiated by the Reagan administration, saying, "In some sense social cuts are not only immoral, they have also been cost inefficient."[172]

Reporters, focused on the horse-race aspect of the contest between Mondale, Hart and Jackson, asked Jackson whether he would pursue an independent candidacy for the presidency if he were to fail to become the Democratic nominee. "At this point, we must strengthen our party," he said in Indianapolis. "We must expand our party; and we must heal our party. . . . It's clear none of us can win without each other. I'm quite optimistic about our leadership coming together."[173]

Jackson's candidacy in 1984, although not gaining him the party's nomination, however, served an important function by activating a large block of African American voters who became increasingly important to the Democrats. One study found that the percentage of black voter turnout eventually grew to exceed white voter turnout among Democrats in seven states, including Indiana. Jackson had also successfully drawn a respectable percentage of nonblack voters in Indiana, almost 30,000 votes out of the 98,223 votes he pulled in the May 1984 primary—28.3 percent of his total vote.[174]

Four years later, Jackson's 1988 campaign demonstrated he had learned a lot from his previous run, and he proved a worthy opponent to front-runner Dukakis. During preprimary ap-

pearances in Indiana in April 1988, Jackson was asked about continued questions being raised about his candidacy by a large block of Jewish voters in New York, including doubts raised by New York City mayor Ed Koch. Jackson assessed his chances among Jewish voters by saying, "You'll never get all of any one group. All you can do is reach out. I've reached out and I'm glad to see people are responding."[175] Jewish voters remained skittish about Jackson's support for a separate Palestinian state—doubts further fueled by a widely circulated photo of Jackson in the company of Yasser Arafat, leader of the Palestine Liberation Organization.

By the time the Indiana primary arrived in early May 1988, only Dukakis and Jackson remained active candidates, and the two shared the stage for the annual Jefferson-Jackson Day Dinner sponsored by the Indiana Democratic Party. During his remarks, Jackson told Hoosier Democrats that "I will not just manage, I will lead. People don't want a manager when they can have a leader. Why settle for margarine when you can have butter? I will lead our ticket to higher heights. Don't manage it, change it. Leaders lead and leaders build constituencies."[176]

In the weeks that followed, as Dukakis wrapped up the nomination (including a solid win in the Indiana primary), news reports emerged indicating Jackson's feelings were bruised considerably when he was passed over as Dukakis's running mate for Bentsen. In one sharply worded statement, Jackson had compared Dukakis's failure to consult him about his running mate choice as symbolic of a relationship between a plantation owner and a slave. As a preconvention Jackson bus caravan made its way from Chicago to Atlanta, a stop in Indianapolis was included. There, Jackson toned down some of the rhetoric, but only slightly: "It is too much to expect that I will go out in the field and be the champion vote picker and bale them up and bring them back to the big house and get a reward of thanks, while people who do not pick nearly as much voters, who don't carry the same amount of weight among the people, sit in the big house and make the decisions."[177]

In the days before the still-fractured Democratic convention was scheduled to open in Atlanta, Jackson spoke at an Indianapolis news conference about how Chicago (code word: Jackson) had been ignored by the Dukakis campaign. He said he viewed the upcoming convention as "open," but told reporters at Indianapolis, "We hope in the next three or four days that matters will be resolved."[178] Jackson noted that "one way to address this impasse would be to spend some time with President Carter. He has an acute sensitivity," in response to a proposal that the former president serve as a mediator between the Dukakis and Jackson camps.

In further Indianapolis remarks, Jackson made it clear that he was not just seeking an apology for not being selected the vice presidential running mate, or even being informed of the final choice. "The issue for my constituency is not about the time of a call. It is not about a recommendation of a running mate," he noted. "It is about an equation upon which a relationship must be built, based on shared responsibility. At this point, my constituency has no place on the team. I do not seek a personal apology. The progressive wing of the Democratic Party needs inclusion. The 'Boston-Austin connection' [Dukakis and Bentsen] leaves Chicago out of the equation. . . . We are shareholders in and board members of the party. We have a substantial investment. We do not intend to pull our investment out. We have too much at stake. We simply want a fair return on our investment."[179]

Later, when standing before a partisan audience of black Democrats at an Indianapolis church, Jackson sounded more conciliatory themes saying, "We have every reason to seek a bridge" and that "we're getting ready to send George Bush back into private life. We're picking up registration all the way down the line."[180]

New York Times writer Michael Oreskes noted that Jackson's bus tour through Indiana had meaning: "The bus ride dramatically demonstrated one of Mr. Jackson's greatest skills—and one of Mr. Dukakis's greatest irritations right now. For someone who holds no office, Mr. Jackson has an ability, probably unequaled in American politics, to gain attention. And he is doing it just when Mr. Dukakis and Mr. Bentsen would like turning maximum attention on them to get a head start on the Republicans."[181]

After 1988 Jackson never again engaged in a serious campaign for the presidency and instead focused his skills on coalition building, civil rights, and promoting peace among Americans more aligned with his background as a minister. In April 1990 then, it was not surprising to find Jackson alongside Jeanne White and her daughter, Andrea, for a bedside vigil at James Whitcomb Riley Hospital for Children in Indianapolis for an ailing Ryan White. Ryan, the Howard County boy who made national headlines in 1985 and 1986 after being barred from attending school after it was learned he carried the HIV virus that causes AIDS, was eighteen years old and in the final days of his life. White died on April 8, 1990, and Jackson remained in Indianapolis with the White family through the funeral services conducted for him at Second Presbyterian Church in Indianapolis. First Lady Barbara Bush was among 1,500 who attended the funeral, along with talk-show host Phil Donahue and entertainers Michael Jackson and Elton John.[182]

In December 1992 DePauw University in Greencastle welcomed Jackson as a campus lecturer. In his talk he emphasized the continued need to create "a politics of inclusion" that reached out to more than ten million Americans unemployed, more than seventeen million underemployed, and more than forty million Americans living without health insurance. "Most poor people are not black," Jackson told the Greencastle gathering. "They are white, female and young. . . . Most poor people aren't on welfare. They work every day. They flip hamburgers, clean the lavatories, sweep out the streets. . . . They work every day. No job is beneath them. But when they get sick, they have no health insurance."[183] Repeating themes that he used during several appearances in Indianapolis in the early 1990s in response to bubbling civil rights struggles focused on police-community relations, Jackson stated,: "We must not swap pain for pain or hate for hate if we are to get better. An eye for an eye and a tooth for a tooth will make us all blind and disfigured. I submit this to you: At some point forgiveness and redemption must be circuit breakers in the cycle of pain."[184]

Gerald R. Ford

Former president Ford appeared in Evansville in September 1980 on behalf of Orr's campaign for governor of Indiana, but he did not spare President Carter criticism. Ford said Carter's foreign policy approaches had reached such a level of failure that "we are no longer treated by our allies or respected by our adversaries."[185] Ford also hammered away at worsening economic conditions in the nation. "Jimmy Carter was given an economic situation in this country on a silver platter," Ford said, referring to the economy when he left office. "Things were getting better. He blew it, and the American people ought to hold him accountable."[186]

Ford said he felt he had no choice other than to participate in the 1980 campaign by advocating for the election of Reagan in order to ensure Carter was a one-term president. "After looking at the dismal record of Jimmy Carter, Betty and I decided we could not sit out this election," Ford said, noting he was visiting thirty states on behalf of the campaign of his former GOP rival, Reagan. Ford said Reagan was "honest, forthright and responsible," apparently forgetting the hard-edged rhetoric shared between the two men four years earlier.[187] Ford moved on to Fort Wayne the same day to support a fund-raiser for a little-known but up-and-coming congressman, Quayle. Ford told Quayle's supporters that they owed it to the nation to do all they could to elect him to the Senate. "If you do any less, your conscience will bother you for the rest of your life," Ford said.[188]

As a former president, Ford remained a loyal party man, offering to help the Republican Party wherever his help could make a difference. On the "lecture circuit" and enjoying his retirement, Ford accepted more than six hundred speaking engagements across the nation, including a March 28, 1985, speech for Ball State University students at Emens Auditorium in Muncie. Ford seemed to understand his growing role in American life—both as a former president but also as the husband of Betty Ford, namesake of the Betty Ford Clinic at Eisenhower Center in California, which would eventually help thousands of people kick their addiction to drugs and alcohol (as Mrs. Ford had done herself).

"Most of you would agree, my wife Betty has always been far, far more popular than I," Ford told the Muncie audience. "Her ratings, her poll numbers have always exceeded mine. There are many who believe Betty could have been elected in 1976." Adding that his youngest son, Steve, was a regular cast member on the CBS daytime drama *The Young and the Restless,* Ford said he was always glad when he was introduced as something other than "Betty Ford's husband, or Steve Ford's dad."[189]

Ford continued in a light mood, talking about his golf course friendship with comedian Bob Hope. "Bob is one of the truly great Americans in our country, and I say that with all seriousness," Ford said. "Bob is a good golfer, he is a tough competitor, and he hates to lose. And confidentially, Bob Hope hates to pay once he loses." He added that he had heard what Hope would say about him around the country, "commercializing off my golfing inadequacy." Ford said, "He tells these huge, huge audiences that I've made golf a combat sport. He says that I'm the only person who can play four golf courses simultaneously. He calls me the 'Hitman for the PGA' . . . then he feels badly, because of our friendship, so he tries to make up to me and usually concludes his bit by saying the president played better the other day, saying he hit an eagle, a birdie, a moose, elk, and a Mason!"[190]

Turning to serious political matters, Ford said he wanted to address the presidential nomination process, which he said "takes much, much too much time and costs much too much money. . . . In my judgment this process is not in the best interest of our country. The long nomination process bores the voting public, and as a result, there is less and less interest in the public in participating in the final vote in November."[191] He elaborated that when "the public has listened to campaign oratory for two years or more, there is a tendency to be uninterested on the vital day (in November) when the president is actually selected. In addition, this grueling experience takes a toll on the candidates and they become mentally and physically worn out. In addition,

because they are always asked how do you stand on this issue, or what is your stand on that issue, and they participate in a good many debates, inevitably the candidate will take a stand on an issue in order to get the nomination, which, if he should be nominated, and subsequently elected president, he wishes he had never made that commitment. When he gets to the Oval Office, it is a lot different making a decision in the Oval Office when you have the reality of the situation then when you're out on the campaign trail trying to scurry around for votes."[192]

Ford said he supported Reagan's approach to foreign policy, declaring it "the right track," including developing superior defense systems and extending a hand for arms negotiation to the Soviets. Wanting to set the record straight, Ford recalled that he met with former Soviet Premier Leonid Brezhnev for about three days. "I sat opposite, across the bargaining table from him, and had some hard headed negotiations with him," Ford declared. "When I returned from those there was some criticism. People said President Ford agreed with Marxism by negotiating with Mr. Brezhnev. I say hogwash! Hogwash! It is ridiculous for anyone to make that accusation. I have no sympathy whatsoever with the political and economic ideology of the Soviet system. However, an American president has the responsibility to make an honest effort to help reduce the nuclear threat not only for our country but for all mankind as a whole. I happen to believe that we are on the right path and it is my judgment that over the period of time our negotiators will be able to negotiate an agreement which would only be consummated, of course, with a final summit meeting between Mr. Reagan and Mr. Gorbachev."[193]

Counting on the growing affection the Hoosiers and Americans held for Ford and the role he and his family had played in history, he encouraged Democrats and Republicans to "learn to disagree without being disagreeable." He concluded:

> We have had some tough political campaigns in recent years. And differences will inevitably become sharper, but let us all remember that as we go through this process that it is OK to singe, but we should never burn. Remember that all of us Democrats, Independents, and Republicans are striving in our own way to create a more perfect union of liberty, equality and justice for all. I respectfully suggest that we should remember our unwritten compact: Respect for the conviction of others, and of faith in the decency of others which gives us in America the luxury of a vibrant political and economic system. May I conclude with this observation, let's all work to banish war from our shrinking world and hate from our expanding heart. Let us make this whole planet one full of friendship, as much friendship as we find in this hall this wonderful evening.[194]

All of Ford's visits to Indiana, however, were not on purpose or were even ones that made much news. Ford's last "public" visits to Indiana came unexpectedly and were far from the fanfare that had accompanied his earlier visits. In the summer of 1986, a thunderstorm forced a private jet carrying the former president to land temporarily at Baer Field in Fort Wayne. Television reporter Ken Owen engaged the former president for a few moments at the airport. A year later, Valparaiso's cable access television star, Michael Essany, scored an interview with Ford for his low-budget E! cable network talk show taped in the basement of his parents' home.

Ford remained a popular figure in American life, respected for his calm and thoughtful leadership in the shortest presidency in American history (not ended by the death of a president in office). Physically active and highly supportive of

his wife Betty's groundbreaking efforts to address drug and alcohol addiction, Ford died on December 26, 2006, at his home in Rancho Mirage, California, of cerebrovascular disease. At the time of his death he was ninety-three years and 165 days old, making him the longest lived U.S. president.

Richard M. Nixon

Nixon, mostly a political pariah throughout the 1980s, found a welcome audience in La Porte County in 1983 as the guest of the county's Republican Party. Four hundred party loyalists paid $50 each to hear Nixon speak and answer questions from the audience. Admitting he had come to Indiana for a rare campaign appearance for "sentimental reasons" because Indiana was the birth state of his mother, he answered a question about any remaining political desires by saying, "I don't itch anymore. I do appreciate the welcome. Indiana has always been pretty good to me."[195]

The nation's thirty-seventh president predicted that the fortieth and current president, Reagan, would easily win re-election. "The best thing that President Reagan has going for him is the Democratic candidates," Nixon said. "There is not one of them who has the charisma. I don't see any one of them meeting Ronald Reagan in a close election and beating him."[196] As always, Nixon addressed foreign affairs, expressing grave concerns about the suicide bombing of the U.S. embassy in Beirut, Lebanon, that killed sixty Americans, including Marines stationed there. "The tragedy there must not deter us from playing a role for peace," Nixon said. "We're going to leave a vacuum there if we leave and there's somebody waiting to take our place—the Soviet Union. We want peace. They want the Mideast."[197]

Nixon's public life in subsequent years was limited to speeches around the world, but was mostly lived through nine best-selling and well-received books. In 1981 he accepted Reagan's request to lead a delegation of himself and two other former presidents, Ford and Carter, at the state funeral for assassinated Egyptian president Anwar Sadat. Nixon died on April 22, 1994, four days after suffering a massive stroke in New York City. His funeral five days later at his museum and library at Yorba Linda, California, drew all of the living presidents who succeeded him, including Ford, Carter, Reagan, G. H. W. Bush, and Clinton. President Clinton, who had hosted Nixon at the White House as a personal adviser just a year earlier, eulogized that the "entire country owes him a debt of gratitude for his service." He went on to say:

> Oh yes, he knew great controversy amid defeat as well as victory. He made mistakes, and they, like his accomplishments, are part of his life and record. But the enduring lesson of Richard Nixon is that he never gave up being part of the action and passion of his times. He said many times that unless a person has a goal, a new mountain to climb, his spirit will die. Well, based on our last phone conversation and the letter he wrote me just a month ago, I can say that his spirit was very much alive to the very end. . . . Today is a day for his family, his friends, and his nation to remember President Nixon's life in totality. To them, let us say, may the day of judging President Nixon on anything less than his entire life and career come to a close. May we heed his call to maintain the will and the wisdom to build on America's greatest gift, its freedom, to lead a world full of difficulty to the just and lasting peace he dreamed of. . . . And so, on behalf of all four former presidents who are here, President Ford, President Carter, President Reagan, President Bush, and on behalf of a grateful nation, we bid farewell to Richard Milhous Nixon.[198]

12

The New Millennium, 1992–2008

George H. W. Bush

Polls during portions of Bush's first term indicated he had become so popular among the American people, especially during the Gulf War that became known as "Operation Desert Storm" following the Iraqi invasion of Kuwait, that many Democratic candidates sized up 1992 and decided to take a pass. They had reason to be concerned. At the end of 1991, with Kuwait's liberation by American and allied forces, Bush's approval rating soared to above 80 percent, though climbing unemployment rates throughout 1991–92 indicated support for Bush may be soft. A little-known Arkansas governor, Bill Clinton, seemed to understand that better than anyone, including Bush himself.

The patrician Bush, who represented establishment money and power in American politics and the Republican Party, could sometimes seem awkward and out of touch with most Americans in spite of his stellar military record as a navy flyer during World War II. His fascination with a grocery store scanner during a trip outside of Washington, D.C., for example, seemed to galvanize what some Americans saw in Bush—a nice, old man who was painfully out of touch with ordinary people dealing with a struggling economy. A portion of Bush's political problems came from within his own party.[1] Forever viewed as

suspect by GOP conservatives, Bush further cast doubt on his rightist bona fides when he showed a willingness to compromise with congressional Democrats (including signing off on a federal tax increase, breaking his "read my lips, no new taxes" pledge from the 1988 campaign).

Among those willing to publicly challenge Bush from within his own party was GOP gadfly and former Richard Nixon speechwriter Patrick J. Buchanan of Virginia. Bush eventually dispatched Buchanan, but not before his campaign rolled up more than a third of the Republican vote in the New Hampshire primary—a strong showing against an incumbent president—and polled nearly three million primary votes, assuring him a role at the 1992 Republican National Convention. Once there, Buchanan hurt, rather than helped, Bush's fall campaign, by delivering a vitriolic "culture wars" speech that turned off independent voters.

With a tougher-than-expected fight for the nomination behind him, Bush accepted the invitation of the University of Notre Dame to be its commencement speaker at South Bend on May 17, 1992. Bush described his remarks to the graduates as nonpolitical, but they clearly set up the coming "family values" theme Bush and the Republicans had planned for their campaign.

While the audience was mostly supportive, media reports emerged that a small number of the 2,353 graduates wore white armbands to protest the university's choice of inviting an active presidential candidate to speak. "One red-robed graduate student stood in front of Mr. Bush, his back turned to the President, throughout the speech," the *New York Times* reported.[2]

"I'm not here in the mode of politics. I'm here to tell you the values that I strongly believe in," Bush said. "Those values can be summarized by the three major legacies that I certainly want to leave behind for my grandchildren, hopefully, for yours: jobs, both for today's workers who are actively seeking work and for graduates entering the work force; strong families, to sustain us as individuals, to nurture and encourage our children, and to preserve our Nation's character and culture; and peace, peace around the world, on our streets, and in our schools as well."[3]

While making reference to freedom that has "swept the world," Bush noted that "our children and our grandchildren now sleep in a world less threatened by nuclear war. That is dramatic change, and it's something good that we can take great pride in. Now we must concentrate on change here in America, in ways no less dramatic or important. We're taking a fresh look at government and how we solve national problems. In Lincoln's words, we must think anew, act anew."[4] While the president's remarks demonstrated his growing awareness (and that of his campaign) of the traction the Democrats were making with messages of "time for a change," Bush's take on the change America needed came from someone who had stood at the center of power for a dozen years, and lacked the personalized, "I feel your pain" style seemingly perfected by Bush's coming challenger, Clinton.

Bush also talked about family values—additional recognition that he had work to do to get conservatives excited about his candidacy after having been tempted away by Buchanan's insurgency. "At the heart of the problems facing our country stands an institution under siege," Bush said. "That institution is the American family. Whatever form our most pressing problems may take, ultimately, all are related to the disintegration of the family. Let us look objectively at a few brief and sad facts. In comparison with other countries, the Census Bureau found that the United States has the highest divorce rate, the highest number of children involved in divorce, the highest teenage pregnancy rates, the highest abortion rates, the highest percentage of children living in a single-parent household, and the highest percentage of violent deaths among our precious young. These are not the kind of records that we want to have as a great country. . . . If America is to solve her social problems, we must, first of all, restore our families."[5]

Bush said instilling a faith in God was critical to building character among the nation's youth. "When we instill faith in our youth, faith in themselves, faith in God, we give them a solid foundation on which to build their future." Quoting Pope John XXIII, Bush said "'the family is the first essential cell of human society.' The family is the primary and most critical institution in America's communities."[6] In comments that reflected more finesse than those attempted by Vice President Dan Quayle two days later in California, Bush turned to the graduating class and said:

> All of us realize that merely knowing what's right is not enough. We must then do what's right. Today I'm asking you to carefully consider the personal decisions that you'll make about marriage and about how you will raise your children. Ultimately, your decisions about right and wrong, about loyalty

and integrity, and yes, even self-sacrifice, will determine the quality of all the other decisions that you'll make. And as you think about these decisions, remember: It is in families that children learn the keys to personal economic success and self-discipline and personal responsibility. It is in families that children learn that moral restraint gives us true freedom. It is from their families that they learn honesty and self-respect and compassion and self-confidence. You would do well to consider the simple but profound words of Notre Dame's own Father [Theodore] Hesburgh when he said, 'The most important thing a father can do for his children is to love their mother." Think how this vitally important commitment from fathers to mothers would radically transform for the better both the lives of thousands of our nation's hurting children and their struggling mothers as well.[7]

Three months later to the day, Bush came to Indianapolis to speak to a key voter constituency, the Veterans of Foreign Wars National Convention. Bush's stop in Indianapolis came as he was en route to the Republican National Convention opening in Houston, Texas. Bush joked that his friends in the VFW wanted "to hear form a leader with charisma and popularity, whose words are revered from coast to coast. Unfortunately, Barbara wanted *me* [emphasis added] to speak, but I'm delighted she's here with me." He drew more hearty laughs when he said he would, despite the heated nature of the campaign, try to avoid making a highly partisan political speech. "You don't need to hear a political speech," he said. "You've already sacrificed enough for your country."[8]

Declaring that the Cold War was over he encouraged the veterans, "If anyone tells you that imperial communism fell on its own, you tell them that you helped punch it in the gut and sent it tumbling back down the back stairs of history. Each of you who served, each of you,

won the battle for humanity's heart and soul. . . . Hermann Goering thought the American fighting forces were a pushover. We showed him. Kim Il-sung in Korea thought he could take us. Wrong again. And Saddam Hussein miscalculated. He thought we'd grown soft over the years. He didn't think we'd commit our Armed Forces. He misread the will of the American people, and he didn't believe we would do what it would take to win. But our men and women showed him. To put it real simple: We kicked a little Baghdad bully."[9]

As had become customary in the years following the close of the Vietnam War, Bush made a special mention of that era's veterans, many of whom made up a growing number of VFW members. Saying that the Vietnam War was "controversial" in his rapid-fire, incomplete-sentence manner of speaking, Bush added, "Many refused to serve. The Government didn't go all out to win. You were fighting with one hand tied behind your back, and still, you fought with courage and with valor. But your nation, when that war ended, never appropriately said thanks. Then 20 years later, America was called to fight again, and this time we did what was needed to win. We fought quickly; we fought with purpose. And when the Desert Storm troops came home, a wondrous thing happened. America saluted, unanimously saluted, not just those heroes but our forgotten heroes, the men and women who served in Vietnam. The tribute was genuine. It was heartfelt, and it came from every corner of this nation. And so, let me say this: It was long overdue. God bless those of you who served in that troubled war."[10]

After making broad pledges to improve health-care services for veterans, and plans to fight Congress to cut military spending, Bush turned briefly to economic issues and family values. On family values, he said, "Some ridicule me. Some ridicule us when we talk about family values. But it's the family that teaches us right from wrong, teaches us discipline, respect for the law. As every vet knows, it [is the] family that wipe the tears away when we cry. Strengthening the family is not something we ought to do; it is something we have to do."[11]

Bush never again returned to Indiana as a candidate, although polls showed the race could be close with Ross Perot's third-party candidacy cutting into Bush's expected strong vote. Bush ended up with 43 percent of the Indiana vote to Clinton's 37 percent (while Perot polled just under 20 percent). The Indiana results mirrored the mixed bag Bush experienced nationally, as Clinton won a plurality of the vote, but not a popular majority, in denying Bush a second term.

Bush remained an active figure in Republican politics and participated in postpresidential projects, including relief efforts for earthquake and tsunami victims in combined efforts with the man who defeated him, Clinton. Bush and Clinton both attended the May 2003 running of the Indianapolis 500, though their appearances did not include any formal public events. Bush returned to Indianapolis in March 2006, some of his physical challenges beginning to show as he walked with a cane, for a speech at Butler University to help commemorate the university's 150th anniversary (Clinton also spoke at Butler as part of the observances in November 2005).

Dan Quayle

Despite an improved performance on the stump and in his official duties as vice president, efforts to dump Quayle from the 1992 ticket remained. Quayle had become a favorite target for comedians of all sorts and he damaged his image with serious political analysts with a May 1992 speech before the Commonwealth Club of California, where he took aim at what he viewed

were the decaying moral values of America, particularly those related to the family. Quayle said television and other elements of popular culture were undermining the family: "It doesn't help matters when primetime TV has Murphy Brown—a character who supposedly epitomizes today's intelligent, highly paid, professional woman—mocking the importance of fathers, by bearing a child alone, and calling it just another 'lifestyle choice.'"[12] Some social conservatives applauded Quayle's remarks, but others did not, joining liberals at poking fun at the idea that Quayle had decided to use a fictional television character as the centerpiece to make his point about family values. Still others became incensed, believing that Quayle's remarks were a putdown of single mothers. Incidentally, Quayle's remarks were not altogether different than those Bush emphasized in his family-values speeches, but it was Quayle who absorbed most of the criticism.

Inside the Bush campaign, the effort to "dump Quayle" was real. As one of Bush's top aides James Baker later wrote, "There was one obvious way for George [Bush] to demonstrate he was a change agent [in 1992]: by replacing his running mate. Dan Quayle was not a problem in 1988. . . . By 1992, however, Dan had become a liability in George's uphill fight for reelection."[13] Bush, however, was in no mood to kick Quayle off the ticket, Baker said, despite ample evidence from pollsters that the vice president was a drag on the ticket. Hopes that Quayle would go quietly into the night on his own also did not come to pass, as Quayle had no intentions of leaving the national stage. Baker contends Bush would have accepted a Quayle resignation from the ticket in 1992, but loyalty forbade him from asking for one.

With the GOP ticket set for the 1992 election, Bush and Quayle struggled despite a virtually clear Republican field. Texas oilman and Bush-tormentor Perot jumped into the race as a third-party nominee of the Reform Party, and effectively siphoned off enough votes to retire Bush-Quayle once and for all. Clinton and his running mate, Senator Al Gore of Tennessee, won the 1992 race with less than 50 percent of the vote, but enough to end the last of the Ronald Reagan era. Quayle's place in national politics came essentially to an end that year—he rebuffed efforts to recruit him to run for Indiana governor in 1996, and abandoned a later attempt for the Republican presidential nomination following poor showings among early straw-polls of party faithful.

Quayle was seemingly on his own for the 1992 election, going where he wanted to, and relegated to another second-tier role. He fared better and redeemed himself in his vice presidential debate against Gore in 1992, easily matching Gore in making Perot's running mate, retired navy vice admiral James Stockdale, look painfully out of his league. The end of Quayle's efforts came in Indiana, as he undertook his normal Election Day ritual of having his teeth cleaned. As the expected election returns rolled in on November 3, showing Bush-Quayle were not going to win a second term, the vice president, joined by his wife, Marilyn, and his children, addressed supporters in Indianapolis, far from the president's concession party in Texas. Quayle encouraged the GOP faithful: "We have made a difference and we will continue to make a difference. I have always stood up for what I believe in and I will continue to stand up and to speak for what I believe in." Outside of the earshot of the crowd, he told reporters, "You could feel this thing slipping away in the last days of the campaign," and that lingering questions from the Iran-Contra scandal of the Reagan administration continued

to be a drag on the Bush record, ignoring what most analysts attributed as the driving force of the 1992 vote, a sagging economy. In an attempt to reassure disappointed Republicans, Quayle said if Clinton ran the country as well as he ran his campaign, the nation would be OK. He predicted that Clinton "may be calling on Republican help from time to time. He did not run as a traditional Democrat. He ran as a new type of Democrat, a more conservative Democrat. And some of his ideas may be more compatible with ideas of mine than some of the liberal Democrats in Congress."[14] Later that night, on a flight from Indianapolis back to Washington, Quayle engaged reporters about whether his continued presence on the ticket had hurt Bush's re-election chances. "Just the opposite," Quayle said. "I felt I had a good campaign. I'm part of the ticket. The Bush-Quayle team lost last night."[15]

Bill Clinton

As the May 1992 Democratic primary approached, *New York Times* political writer R.W. Apple Jr. analyzed the myriad advantages Arkansas governor Clinton held in sweeping Indiana and, for his benefit, finally finishing off former California governor Jerry Brown, the lone challenger remaining in the fray. The other serious contender, former senator Paul Tsongas of Massachusetts, had already abandoned his run (although his name remained on the Indiana ballot). "Mr. Clinton has made only one appearance here so far, has offices in four cities in the state . . . and comes into the Indiana campaign with all of the advantages of solid victories in New York and Pennsylvania," wrote Apple. "And to top it all off, Indiana is Mr. Clinton's kind of state. Hoosiers are a culturally cautious lot, more turned off than voters in many other states by the former California Governor's interest in Buddhism and his unconventional dress. A visitor hears the mocking nickname 'Governor Moonbeam' everywhere. What's more, the southern half of the state behaves politically like a southern state, giving Indiana as a whole a decidedly conservative cast."[16]

Brown, who qualified for the ballot with the backing of the steelworkers union, told an audience in Gary that "Clinton is getting very close [to locking up the nomination], but he's not there yet. We're here because in a democratic society there's got to be a debate. Issues have got to be raised and fought over."[17] Brown's campaign seemed to gain its most traction in the smaller, progressive pockets of the state, such as northwest Indiana, Indianapolis, Fort Wayne, and Bloomington. In Indianapolis Brown stood before an abandoned house and talked about the troubling race riots that had erupted in Los Angeles. "I'm telling you that what happened in Los Angeles is going to happen again because you can't cage people up, deprive them of jobs, treat them like second-class citizens and expect to escape the consequences," he warned.[18] In Fort Wayne Brown described Clinton as a "weak candidate" who was being bought by major party donors jumping on his bandwagon. "There's a cancer eating away at democracy and the party I belong to," Brown said. "I want to fight to restore the party. The whole game now in politics is sell and buy." Brown repeated his previous concerns about racial relations in the nation, declaring, "The country is being divided, black and white, Latino and Anglo. The average person's wages are going down. What we have today is a collection of international corporations that are able to buy and sell and influence our country in a way that takes no proper regard for the communities."[19]

Before the primary, Clinton made a stop in Indiana in late March to pick up the endorsement of Governor Evan Bayh and all of the Democratic members of the state's congressional delegation. He also attended two private fund-raisers during his visit.

Upon winning the 1992 nomination, Clinton and his running mate, Gore, decided on a unique way to emphasize their hope to directly connect with voters. Instead of relying on flying into and out of major media markets, they set out on an eight-state bus tour of the nation that brought them to several counties across southern Indiana along Interstate 64. On July 20, 1992, the bus tour crossed the Ohio River from Louisville, Kentucky, for a variety of scheduled and unscheduled stops (causing the tour to run about three hours behind schedule all day). "Al Gore and I are devoted to building a better future for you and your kids," Clinton told one of the unscheduled impromptu crowds at New Albany. "If you give us a chance, we'll work with you and bring this country back."[20] For his part, Gore said, "We're not saying that Bush and Quayle are bad people, we're saying their approach to governing has failed badly."[21]

The bus tour eventually made its way to Evansville, where Bayh led Clinton and Gore on a tour of the Ivy Tech Community College and job training programs. Reporters in Evansville asked Clinton if he intended to continue his campaign by bus tour and the Arkansas governor smiled widely and said, "It's been effective beyond my wildest dreams. These crowds, they show me that people are hungry for change." He did add, "We're going to take it off the road for a little while, take time to regroup and organize, but we'll probably do it again."[22]

As 1992 rolled along, polling continuing to offer surprising reports that the Clinton campaign was doing better than most Democrats could expect in Indiana (partially helped by strong support for Perot, who was cutting into Bush's base in the state). As a result, the Clinton-Gore campaign continued to focus attention on Hoosier voters. Clinton's campaign style, seemingly tireless and showing up everywhere, included an important speech on September 11, 1992, at Notre Dame's Stephen Center. While Clinton's remarks reflected his Baptist faith and the connections he said it had with Catholicism, he still faced a few hecklers in the audience, who vehemently disagreed with Clinton's prochoice views on abortion rights. The antiabortion protestors present were relentless, jeering and booing throughout Clinton's speech and following him outside to heckle him as he shook hands with spectators on the way to his car. Clinton attempted to define his position on abortion rights and preservation of the family during his talk by noting, "If we truly believe—as almost everyone says no matter what they believe on certain issues—that children are God's most precious creation, then surely we owe every child born in the U.S.A. the chance to make the most of his or her God-given potential. I want an America that offers every child a healthy start in life, decent schooling and the chance to go on to college or to job training worthy of the name, not only because that's essential for our economic success but because providing opportunities is how we fulfill obligations to each other and the moral principles we honor."[23]

"I want an America that values the freedom and dignity of the individual," Clinton continued. "All of us must respect the reflection of God's image in every man and woman. And so we must value their freedom, not just their political freedom, but their freedom of conscience in matters of philosophy and family and faith."[24]

Taking on the strong family values message that emanated from the just-completed Republican convention, Clinton referred (but not by name) to the poorly received speech there by Buchanan. At the GOP confab in Houston, Buchanan took the party's aim far right when he declared, "There is a religious war going on in this country for the soul of America. It is a cultural war as critical to the kind of nation we shall be as the Cold War itself, for this war is for the soul of America. And in that struggle for the soul of America, Clinton is on the other side, and George Bush is on our side."[25]

Clinton told his South Bend audience, "Like so many Americans, I've been appalled to hear the voices of intolerance that have been raised in recent weeks, voices that proclaim that some families aren't real families, some Americans aren't real Americans, and what this country needs is a religious war. America doesn't need a religious war. America needs a reaffirmation of the values that for most of us are rooted in our religious faith."[26]

While Clinton had, until arriving in South Bend, enjoyed enthusiastic and supportive crowds in Indiana and elsewhere, his supporters were pressed into duty at Notre Dame to help shout and cheer down not only antiabortion protestors in the room, but also a large number of Bush supporters, the *New York Times* reported. Clinton noticed the growing clamor by saying when the heckling grew louder, "We know that in this room at least, our supporters can win the cheer contest. I would hope that in this great university, we would also prevail in the civility contest. I hope if my opponents or his running mates show up at this great university during this campaign, I hope you will go there and quietly express your support for me, but I hope you will let him speak."[27]

Summarizing his views, Clinton said, "I want an America that does more than talk about family values. I want an America that values families," noting that the role of public service and government support for families (in terms of family leave legislation, job creation, and living wage antipoverty programs) were a key aspect of achieving such value. "We all have the right to wear our religion on our sleeves, but we should also hold it in our hearts and live it in our lives," he said. "And, if we are truly to practice what we preach, then Americans of every faith and viewpoint should come together to promote the common good."[28]

Clinton-Gore won the 1992 election and officially brought to a close a twelve-year Republican hold on the White House. As president, Clinton's first official visit to Indiana came on May 14, 1994, for a special day for members of two famous American families, the Kennedys and the Kings. A cold, windy rainstorm failed to spoil the day as Clinton led a dedication ceremony for a new memorial to commemorate Robert F. Kennedy's Indianapolis remarks on April 4, 1968, the day Martin Luther King Jr. was assassinated. The memorial, located at the center of a neighborhood park near Seventeenth and Broadway Streets, has Kennedy and King reaching across a sidewalk, their images cut from metal created from the melting of guns. Given that it was guns that cut down the life of these two notable Americans, the statute is a strong and permanent signal about the need to end violence. Present for the event were Kennedy's widow, Ethel, and his brother, Senator Edward M. "Ted" Kennedy of Massachusetts, and Martin and Dexter, two of King's children.

Clinton began his remarks by encouraging the faithful thousands who showed up in spite of the weather. "We're all being tested by a little rain," he said. "Those of us who grew up in farming areas know that rain is a gift from God. It's

going to help all of us grow a little."[29] Clinton, a son of the South who grew up amongst the challenges to Jim Crow in Arkansas, said the speech and events commemorated in Indianapolis were ones that served to inspire him to run for president: "I was inspired . . . when I was a young man, and I believed we could do better. I believed that we could build a country where we would go forward instead of backward, and where we would go forward together, where people would deal with one another across the bounds of race and religion and income, and even different political parties and philosophies, with respect and honor."[30] Comparing recent events in South Africa that finally toppled the racist apartheid regime there, Clinton said "everywhere in the world people have looked to us for an example. And I ask you today, have we created that miracle here at home? What you saw in Robert Kennedy's speech was a miracle that night."[31]

Later that same day, Clinton spoke to an even larger audience at the annual Jefferson-Jackson Day luncheon sponsored by the Indiana Democratic Party and the Democratic Governors Association. His speech was "classic Clinton," as his Democratic admirers would note. Lengthy and dense, the president's remarks were sprinkled with humorous and warm reflections that were the hallmark of a Clinton speech. The president started out by recalling that when he was elected governor of Arkansas, he had been the nation's youngest governor—that is until Bayh came along. "When I met Evan Bayh, I really resented him," Clinton joked. "I mean, he was so young and handsome, and I realized I'd never be that young again, I'd never look that good again. Come to think of it, I still sort of resent him for that. When we play golf, he hits the ball longer than I do. When we come in, he graciously fabricates the truth and tells people that I won when I didn't."[32]

Along with Bayh, a cadre of Indiana Demo-crats was on the dais with the president, includ-ing Lieutenant Governor Frank O'Bannon, At-torney General Pamela Carter, Secretary of State Joe Hogsett, and current and former Democratic members of the Indiana congressional delega-tion, including Lee Hamilton, Phil Sharp, Frank McCloskey, Andy Jacobs Jr., and Jim Jontz. Staying with his emphasis on state government, Clinton said "I owe a lot to the years I spent as Governor. Basically, I ran for president because I was tired of what I thought was the stale rhetoric in Washington, the incredible partisan gridlock, and the politics of division and diversion, and often personal destruction. . . . And the people of this country were being lost in the whole process, and we were at risk of losing the American dream as we moved toward the twenty-first century."[33]

Clinton's remarks at Indianapolis this day would come five years before he faced the ulti-mate result of "the politics of personal destruc-tion," as he was impeached by the House of Rep-resentatives in 1999, but acquitted by members of the Senate. Clinton said he still believed in "opportunity for all Americans, responsibility from all Americans, and a belief that we are one community, that we really believe in our national motto, E Pluribus Unum, that we are one from many, and that we are all in this together and that ultimately we will go up or down together."[34] He cited lengthy congressional debates about the Brady Bill that would control handgun sales in America, and the nation's new family medical leave law. The process, stalled amidst a growing Washington gridlock, "is too long for Americans to wait while partisan differences get resolved and people's lives hang in the balance."[35]

Clinton did not return to Indiana until its geographic location proved valuable on August 28, 1996. Clinton and Gore were making their way to the Democratic National Convention in Chicago to accept nomination to run for a second term. Although engaged in a whistle-stop style campaign through battleground states such as Ohio and Michigan, once in Indiana at Michigan City, Clinton and Gore disembarked from their train and made their way to the Old Lighthouse inside Washington Park to greet a huge, sun-baked crowd estimated at 40,000. Bayh, who had delivered the keynote speech at the Democratic convention the night before, introduced the president. While political critics were tough on Bayh and his speech, he won rave reviews from the president, with Clinton noting, "I wouldn't be surprised at all if someday Evan Bayh were to come back here to Michigan City as the President of the United States!"[36]

As part of his introductory remarks, Clinton addressed an earlier accident when a large, el-evated speaker stand toppled over, injuring thir-teen people. "I know there was an accident here earlier," he said, "and I want you to keep those folks in your prayers. As far as we know, they're okay, but we haven't gotten a final report."[37] Clin-ton was concerned about the heat and humidity, more than once urging audience members to get some free water being distributed. "If you need water, take it. I don't want anybody passing out here. I want you to be just hot enough to be ex-cited, but not anymore," the president said.[38]

Clinton made a strong pitch for the massive welfare reform program he had enacted during his first term and noted that for it to be success-ful, state governments had to follow through in order "to give people who have been trapped on welfare the same kind of life we want for all American families. We want people to succeed as parents and succeed as workers."[39] Repeatedly interrupted by chants of "Four more years! Four more years!" from the partisan audience, the president noted that "this will be the last race I ever make and I wanted to make this trip through the heartland to look into the faces, the eyes, the hearts of the people that I ran for president to help, the people I have worked for and fought for for four years. And I have loved every mile of the track, all the people I have seen."[40]

The president's remarks emphasized increases in employment and home ownership, reductions in the nation's debt, drops in crime rates, and investments in education and safe schools, as well as public health and the environment. "We have done all this in a way that brings the American people together," he said. "We have faced a lot of tough challenges around the world, and I've had to do some things that were, frankly, unpopular with a majority of you."[41] Specifically, Clinton noted the commitment of American troops to bring peace to Bosnia after troubling reports of ethnic cleansing sweeping the European nation.

In a second term, Clinton promised to keep focused on employment for all Americans who needed a job, protections against losing one's job because of sickness or injury, help for small businesses, and tax deductions for parents who wanted to send their children to college. "I want you to support that, not just four more years of Bill Clinton and Al Gore," he said. "I want you to support four more years of opportunity, more responsibility, and more community. I want you to support the idea that when the year 2000 comes around we will be going into the 21st century as the greatest nation in the world, with our best days before us!"[42]

It would be four more years before Clinton returned to Indiana for a public appearance. Although wildly popular among Democrats, Indiana voters disapproved of Clinton by a wide margin, especially as details emerged in 1998 of an alleged extramarital affair the president engaged in with a White House intern Monica Lewinsky. Impeachment proceedings against Clinton did nothing to add to his previously stellar political record, and by 2000, another election year, Clinton's political help was sought sparingly by most Democrats. In Indiana, Democratic candidates remained heavily cautious about appearing with Clinton publicly for fear of backlash from conservative Hoosier voters. Two Indiana politicians, O'Bannon and Congresswoman Julia Carson, however, were among incumbent Democrats willing to enlist Clinton's help for their campaigns. Clinton headlined a March 28, 2000, reception and fund-raiser for O'Bannon's bid for a second term as governor. Interestingly, the event was held far from Indiana at the Hyatt Regency Hotel on Capitol Hill in Washington, D.C., and received limited media coverage in Indiana.

Few members of Congress embraced Clinton publicly as much as Carson. She scheduled him to appear on her behalf at an October 7 fund-raiser in the Indianapolis home of Jeff Smulyan. The president, citing night-and-day negotiations to win a new peace accord in the Mideast, said he could not leave Washington, but phoned the event from his personal residence inside the White House. He told the Indiana Democrats listening on a conference call, "I've been up for virtually two days now trying to stop the violence in the Middle East and get the peace process back on track. It's a difficult situation. We're down to all the hard issues now, and it's just something I couldn't leave. I can't get away from the phone because of what's going on there and in the U.N. and in other countries. I have to be available here 100 percent of the time."[43]

Clinton made up for missing the Carson fund-raiser, as he returned to Indianapolis to speak to an overflow crowd of 5,000 happy supporters at the Indiana State Fairgrounds a few weeks later on October 21. To start his remarks, Clinton joked with his arm wrapped around Carson's shoulder, "I'll tell you why I came here: Because Julia Carson asked me, and I *always* do whatever she asks me to do—because I learned very early I could do it the right away or I could just wait and let her grind on me until I finally broke down and said yes. So I just say yes right away to Julia now, and it solves a lot of my problems."[44] Still in a happy mood, Clinton said, "I get tickled—you know, when our Republican friends were in, they took credit for everything that happened in America. They took credit when the Sun came up. One of their campaigns was, 'It's morning in America. The Sun came up in the morning. Give it to us. We did it.'"[45] Speaking more slowly and brandishing his well-known style of looking his audience in the eye, the president said, "thank you for helping me have a chance to serve the country for the last eight years. I'm grateful to you." He then added, "I've been reading what I could about what the experts are saying about this election. And they say it's tight as a tick, and they say that there are a lot of undecided voters, and they say that there are a lot of voters who aren't sure what the differences are and what the consequences are to them, so maybe it doesn't matter for whom they vote or whether they vote. Now, let me tell you something. I've done everything I could do for eight years to turn this country around, pull this country together, and move the country forward—everything I could do. But in America, our public life is always about tomorrow."[46]

Before arriving at the fairgrounds, Clinton made a quick stop at the home of Mel and Bren Simon in Indianapolis for a private reception used to raise funds from Hoosier donors for his wife, Hillary Rodham Clinton, and her ongoing Senate campaign in New York. Clinton's appearances for Carson would be his last in the state as president, but as history would show, they would hardly be his last overall. Fast forward eight years to 2008 and Hillary's latest political effort, seeking the Democratic nomination for president, and Bill would become a regular feature among Hoosier voters.

Al Gore

Beyond the Clinton-Gore bus tour that stretched across southern Indiana for a few days after the Democratic National Convention in the summer of 1992, the Democrats gave little attention to Indiana, although Gore appeared at an Indianapolis rally at the Indiana State Fairgrounds on October 15, 1992. *Indianapolis Star* political reporter Jon Schwantes wrote, "It used to be that Hoosier Democrats running for state, local or congressional office would keep the party's national ticket at arm's length. This year, they're embracing it. The transformation was apparent Thursday night when Tennessee Sen. Al Gore brought his message of change to a rally at the State Fairgrounds. Amid more than 5,000 sign-waving Gore supporters were scores of Democratic candidates, all scrambling to be seen with the vice presidential hopeful . . . before Gore delivered his standard stump speech, a 30-minute litany of President Bush's failures."[47]

In his remarks before enthusiastic Democrats, buoyed by polling that showed Clinton-Gore was within striking distance of Bush-Quayle in Indiana, Gore said, "When I published my schedule several days ago, and Indiana showed up on the schedule, some of the people around the country who get copies of the schedule called in and said: 'What is going on here? Why are you going to Indiana? That is simply a safe state for Bush and Quayle?'" Gore suggested that Indiana could be turned to the Democratic column on Election Day, and reminded voters that "everything that should be down is up, and everything that should be up is down," when citing statistics regarding unemployment, trade deficits, national debt, workers' income, consumer confidence, and housing starts.[48]

During the Clinton administration, Gore proved a loyal and hardworking lieutenant, standing by the president through thick and thin, including a painful and sometimes embarrassing impeachment process that dominated major portions of the second Clinton-Gore term. During the first term, however, Gore's role as vice president was quite traditional. In July 1993 Clinton dispatched Gore to Indianapolis to address the annual meeting of the National Association for the Advancement of Colored People during a period of unusually strained relations between the administration and a key constituency—black voters. Gore's visit came in the wake of a controversial decision by Clinton to withdraw the name of Harvard University law professor Lani Gunier as his nominee for Assistant U.S. Attorney General for Civil Rights. Gunier had been the subject of a widespread campaign by congressional conservatives to highlight more controversial aspects of her academic and legal views on a variety of issues, including civil rights.

On the Gunier issue, Gore made only brief remarks about the matter, stating generally, "We intend to have a great attorney general for civil rights—one that you and we and our country can be proud of, I promise you that." News reports indicated Gore's remarks were "politely" received. On other issues, Gore said the administration was committed to a strong effort to combat "environmental justice" and said, "It's time we stopped automatically putting waste dumps and other forms of pollution in neighborhoods that

have the least political and economic power."[49]

Gore praised NAACP leaders for their efforts to advance civil rights in the era of Reagan and Bush—years he said that required "fighting a rear-guard action"—that had included attempts to challenge school desegregation efforts, housing, and voting rights advances. "The fact is, most of what we call progress was in place more than a decade ago," Gore said. "The radical right, the purveyors of the politics of hate and division, have had their successes." He made a pitch for the continued support of black leaders, saying, "We'll need the help of every person in this room if we are to win, especially on the anti-poverty initiatives."[50]

In the closing years of the Clinton administration and as it became more and more apparent Gore would seek the Democratic presidential nomination in 2000, the vice president accepted the invitation of Senator Bayh to visit Arlington High School in Indianapolis to promote fatherhood issues. At Arlington, Gore and Bayh met with a group of "Security Dads" who helped patrol the school and interacted with students. Gore told the group, "The new jobs in the 21st century deal with computers and access to knowledge. Learning is the key skill. In order to deal with information, you have to get an education" and that education cannot happen in schools that are not secure. "You can't improve education if our schools aren't safe," he said. "Parents need the peace of mind that their children will be safe when they go to school."[51]

Part of the response of the Clinton-Gore administration, he said, included increased law enforcement resources and services directly for students. "We're emphasizing job training and mentoring programs to keep young people from getting involved in gangs and drugs," Gore said. "We need to provide incentives for after-school programs. We've already made massive investments in wonderful facilities, but schools sit idle for most of the day."[52] Gore emphasized that after-school programs offered between 3:00 p.m. and 6:00 p.m. each day could make a big impact and required local groups, such as those at Arlington High School, to get involved.

While the fatherhood and education themes were not new fare among modern politicos, Gore was desperate to create space between himself and the growing Lewinsky scandal engulfing Clinton. On the same day Gore was visiting Indianapolis, Clinton was being issued a subpoena to provide a blood sample for DNA testing by Special Prosecutor Ken Starr, and days later testified before a federal grand jury that he had engaged in "inappropriate intimate contact" with Lewinsky.[53]

Bob Dole

A modern tradition in the Republican Party has been to give special consideration to its candidates for the presidential nomination based off past activity in the party. Unlike the Democratic Party, which as recently as 1992 had opened its arms to a complete newcomer—a little-known southern governor from Arkansas—the Republican Party was known for going with establishment candidates. As a result, there was little question that Senator Bob Dole of Kansas, the longtime Senate Republican leader, the party's 1976 vice presidential nominee, and who had staged a respectable run for the nomination in both 1980 and 1988 may have arrived at his chance for the big prize in 1996. Further helping Dole's position was the decision by the former chair of the Joint Chiefs of Staff Colin Powell, and several other prominent Republicans, to skip the 1996 race.

In the lead-up to 1996, Dole did all of the things a potential nominee did, including appear-

ing before friendly audiences, such as the national convention of the American Legion meeting in Indianapolis in September 1995. As a second lieutenant in the U.S. Army's Tenth Mountain Division, Dole entered combat in World War II in the Apennine Mountains in Italy, where he was critically injured in his right arm and back by German machine-gun fire. He faced years of physical recovery to try and regain his life after the war and was decorated with two Purple Hearts and a Bronze Star with a combat "V" for valor. Indianapolis had held a special place in Dole's life story; in 1986 he was reunited with Bill Roberts, a retired Indianapolis firefighter, who was credited with saving Dole's life after Dole was wounded on April 14, 1945. Roberts organized German prisoners of war to carry Dole on a makeshift gurney for more than ten hours until they reached an aid station.[54]

Dole's military record to the nation well-known, the American Legion audience warmly welcomed Dole, who once quieting the audience told them he was reminded of the first speech he had ever made outside of Kansas, which was at an American Legion Hall in Indiana. "I was a freshman Congressman, and the local dinner committee knew they needed to find a way to encourage people to come to the dinner," Dole said. "When I arrived, I was whisked off to the local radio station, where the announcer was supposed to interview me to boost attendance. He began with a less than accurate rendition of my résumé." Dole noted the radio broadcaster seemed more interested in promoting the fact that a drawing to win a free television set was going to occur at the dinner. The announcer told his listeners that Dole had fought and was wounded in Italy during World War II and noted, drawing laughter, that "he had suffered a serious head injury. Then he went into politics."[55]

Offering the requisite praise to his fellow veterans and pledging he would do all he could to ensure that the Department of Veterans Affairs remained adequately funded, Dole said that the purpose of his speech was his desire to keep America strong. His remarks staked out a clearly right-wing position as he prepared for the upcoming primary season. This was probably to forestall an attack he knew likely was coming from "outside Washington" conservatives in the Republican Party who believed Dole to be too willing to compromise with congressional Democrats. His Indianapolis speech came just days after an earlier speech in Hollywood in which he lambasted the film, television, and music industry for what he viewed was an assault on traditional American values.

Dole told the veterans, "Because of you, and those who came before you, we Americans are the freest people on earth. And you know as well as I do how we stay that way: we must remain the strongest country on earth. That's what I want to talk with you about today. Keeping America strong—in her might and in her heart, in the face of external enemies and in the presence of threats from within. America is still the land of the free and the home of the brave, and a great century of hope and opportunity is about to unfold before us. But to claim that future, America needs your help. For some in America believe our might is no longer needed, and some think our definition of what it means to be an American is out of date. Of course, neither is true."[56]

He declared that although the Cold War had been won by the West, threats of totalitarianism and oppression remained, including the threat of chemical and nuclear weapons falling into dangerous hands in Russia, Iran, and North Korea. Dole characterized the North Atlantic Treaty Organization as "impotent" in reacting to such challenges and said, "Washington seems filled with people who want to dismantle our defenses." He said defense budget cuts undertaken during Clinton's first term had gone too far. "In fact, this administration had set us on a path that would have ended with America spending about as much of our gross national product on defense as we were when Pearl Harbor was attacked," said Dole. "But the good news is that this year this Congress refused to go along. We rejected the policies that would lead us back to a hollow military. We kept the faith. We increased spending on defense, for the demands of freedom require us to modernize our forces, to maintain our technological edge, and to ensure that America remains the world's one and only superpower. We will never apologize for that. Our goal is not just to be strong enough to turn back a threat. We must be so strong no one ever again is even tempted to threaten us, at all."[57]

Dole said it was more than defense cuts that posed a threat to America's greatness. He said:

> We must return as a people to the original concept of what it means to be American. This means tackling subjects the arbiters of political correctness don't even want discussed: For example, English must be recognized as America's official language. Western tradition and American greatness must be taught in our schools. And the Federal government must end its war on traditional American values. America has always been more than just a place on a map, it has held a claim on our hearts. We are a nation dedicated to a proposition: that all men and women are created equal, endowed by our Creator with certain, inalienable rights. Our forefathers rejected race and religion as the forces to form a nation, choosing instead the ideals of freedom and democracy. It was a radical gamble, and ever since we have held it to be an article of faith that those who would be Americans must first abandon lesser allegiances. . . . Succeeding waves of

immigrants have been drawn to America by this idea. Lacking the centuries-old, primal bonds of other nations, we have used our language, our history and our code of values to make the American experiment work. We have used them to forge millions of diverse individuals into one people with a common purpose. Language, history and values: these are the strings that bind our hearts to America. These are the forces that have held us together—allowing us to be diverse and yet united, to absorb untold millions of immigrants while coming the closest any country ever has to the classless, upwardly mobile society of our ideals.[58]

Dole expressed concern about "government and intellectual elites who seem embarrassed by America. What we see as opportunity, they see as oppression. What we see as a proud past, they see as shame. What we hold as moral truth, they call intolerance. They have false theories, long dissertations and endless studies to back them up. But they know so much they have somehow missed the fact that the United States of America is the greatest force for good the world has ever known." Dole said a variety of challenges remained in America but that he refused to surrender to the "embarrassed-to-be-American crowd" and said their support of certain federal programs, such as affirmative action, was "untying the strings of citizenship."[59]

Drawing heavy applause, Dole said he favored making English the official language of the United States, as well as backing state and federal legislation that required schools to teach English to all students. "We must stop the practice of multi-lingual education as a means of instilling ethnic pride, or as a therapy for low self-esteem out of an elitist guilt over a culture built on the traditions of the West," he said. "With all the divisive forces tearing at our country, we need the glue of language to help hold us together."[60]

Further, he lambasted revised history curriculums that failed to place enough emphasis on American patriotism, and said he supported a Constitutional amendment to make burning the U.S. flag illegal.

Eventually a crowded and conservative field of candidates emerged to challenge Dole for the nomination, including Buchanan, businessman Steve Forbes, former Tennessee governor Lamar Alexander, and Senators Phil Gramm of Texas and Richard G. Lugar of Indiana. Only Buchanan and Forbes made any headway, with Dole winning forty-four state primary and caucus contests, while Buchanan took four and Forbes two. For the May 7 Indiana Republican Primary, Dole rolled to an easy victory, gathering 71 percent of the vote (with the endorsement of Lugar), while Buchanan polled 19 percent, and Forbes 10 percent. Bruised by Buchanan's sometimes sharp-edged campaign, Dole quickly passed over any consideration of him as a running mate and settled on former Congressman Jack Kemp of New York. To further boost his campaign, Dole took the unusual step of giving up his Senate seat, telling reporters that he had "nowhere to go but to the White House or home" after thirty-five years in Congress. He told the American people that when his resignation became effective on June 11, "I will then stand before you without office or authority, a private citizen, a Kansan, an American, just a man."[61]

Dole's fall campaign was behind from the start, despite earlier indications that Clinton would be vulnerable fueled in part by the 1994 Republican Revolution in which the GOP had recaptured control of the House for the first time in forty years. However, by 1996 Clinton had used his policy of "triangulation" of working with Senate Democrats and House Republicans to aplomb. The result was the political landscape had changed dramatically by the time the fall campaign rolled around. Even third-party hopeful Perot was unable to gain any traction against what appeared to be a solid Clinton re-election campaign.

In a last-ditch effort to try and revive his waning chances, Dole took a thirty-six-hour, around-the-clock campaign trek to twelve states on November 1 and 2, including Indiana, as Election Day loomed. Speaking before about 2,500 Republicans on November 2 at an airplane hangar at the Indianapolis International Airport, Dole declared, "We're going to go around the clock, around the clock and around the clock to win this race. We are going to take the checkered flag and take the victory lap—it's going to happen!"[62] Dole quickly moved to his key messages: reducing federal taxes by 15 percent across the board, providing a new $500 per child tax credit for every child under the age of eighteen, and cutting the capital gains tax that he said was hurting American businesses.

Dole also touched on his belief that military spending should be increased, the need for a Constitutional amendment to ban flag burning, prayer in public schools, and turning more control for the nation's schools back to state and local officials. Hoping to shore up support and excitement among conservative voters, Dole said that as president if a bill arrived on his desk that banned partial-birth abortions, he would sign it. "Whether we're pro-life or pro-choice . . . there is never any need for this terrible, terrible procedure. It should not happen. And I will sign to ban that procedure forever in the United States of America," he said.[63]

Turning to Clinton, Dole's comments became less structured and more off-the cuff, as he accused the president of being absent without leave in the war on drugs for the last four years,

saying that statistics showed that drug use had doubled for teens between the ages of twelve and seventeen since 1992. Dole also attacked ethical challenges in the administration, saying "This White House has set a bad example from day one. . . . And I would say as a Republican we had our problems too a few years back, but they're having their problems now and I'm willing to say, right now, if [Clinton] is re-elected, he's going to spend half his time next year with investigations," said Dole. "Who knows what will happen in the next 24 months, or 36 months?" Dole pledged that as president he would restore duty, honor, country, decency, and integrity to the presidency.[64]

Cautioning against Clinton's proposals for universal health coverage for all Americans, he called such a proposal "the takeover of the greatest health-care delivery system in the world" that the Democrats "would rather put [health care] in the hands of the federal government. Seventeen new taxes [to fund it], price controls, you couldn't choose your own doctor. And then he says he's not a liberal! Give me a break!"[65]

While Dole was easily dispatched by Clinton on Election Day, Indiana voters were good to the Kansas native, with Dole capturing 47 percent of the vote to Clinton's 42 percent, and Perot's 10 percent, making Indiana the only upper midwestern state carried by Dole.

In May 1998 Dole returned to Indiana for a special dedication ceremony for the state's new World War II memorial, the latest addition to the American Legion Mall in downtown Indianapolis. Although a steady rainfall dampened the proceedings, about 1,000 residents turned out to hear Dole not only dedicate the Indiana memorial, but make a strong pitch for the need for a long overdue national World War II memorial in Washington, D.C. To his Indianapolis audience seeking shelter under umbrellas in a steady rain,

Dole said like many young men called up to service in World War II, he did not see the "big picture" or the purpose of the war—one that would take him outside the twenty-mile radius around Russell, Kansas—the only "world" he had known to that point in his young life. "We saw the small struggles," Dole said. "We did not hear the call of history. We heard the voices of friends that still haunt and comfort the memory of the war veterans. Like all veterans of those times, I can still hear their voices as if it were yesterday, frozen in time by the intensity of the experience."[66]

Dole noted that "some say war never settles anything, but World War II settled a great deal," including ensuring freedom and tolerance in the world.[67] He added, "World War II has been called 'the good war,' but there are no good wars. They are only good causes."[68]

As national chairman of the campaign to raise $100 million for the new World War II memorial on the National Mall, Dole said 6.7 million World War II veterans were still living in America, "but we lose about 1,000 every day." The war itself, he noted, claimed about 500,000 American lives, including 12,000 Indiana men and women. "There is still no national memorial to the veterans of World War II," Dole reminded the audience. "We owe them a debt."[69]

H. Ross Perot

Texas billionaire Perot served as an interesting, and mostly disruptive, force in both the 1992 and 1996 presidential election cycles. Unhappy with the direction of the nation under his longtime rival and fellow Texan, George H. W. Bush, in 1992 Perot launched an unlikely independent bid for the White House. Cantankerous and often impatient with reporters on all levels, Perot's plain-spoken, lecturing style seemed to draw in voters looking for a straight answer

to the nation's problems. At the center of the Perot agenda, beyond a sprinkling of libertarian ideas on most domestic issues, was the need to eliminate the federal deficit. Everything about Perot's was unconventional, launching his 1992 effort during an appearance on the CNN program *Larry King Live* and successfully capturing most of the media's attention after Bush and Clinton wrapped up their party's nominations early in the primary season. At one point polls showed Perot in the lead over the two major party candidates, but his demanding control style—well suited for high finance and business from where he had earned his stripes—ran thin among political figures. His campaign, pushed along by an army of dedicated volunteers, even managed to insult many of them after demanding they sign "loyalty oaths" to the Perot effort. By July Perot was crabbier than ever and again on the King show. This time he announced he was withdrawing from the race. Alternating between saying he did not want to see the presidential election thrown into the House of Representatives and accusations that Republican operatives planned to spoil his daughter's upcoming wedding and despoil her name, Perot said he was out.

Weeks later, however, Perot had a change of heart and reentered the race. By September what was left of the Perot campaign announced that he had qualified for the ballot in all fifty states, including Indiana. Campaign volunteers, however, had been shed during the bizarre summer days in which Perot seemed to abandon his army of supporters over reasons that sounded increasingly paranoid when he tried to explain them. For the 1992 race, Perot had an organized campaign in Indiana, although he did not campaign in the state. In the November vote, he polled an impressive figure, almost half a million votes or just under 20 percent of the total, almost all of it drawn off votes that likely would have gone to Bush. Perot's Indiana totals roughly matched what he did nationally, just enough to deny Bush a victory, but not enough to give him a real chance of winning.

Four years later, Perot seemed ready to try again, this time accepting the nomination of the newly minted Reform Party (one he started and financed in 1995). His second effort, however, failed to gain the same traction as 1992, including being shut out of the presidential debates between Clinton and Dole. Dole's camp was unwilling to proceed if Perot was included, refusing to repeat a mistake they believed Bush had made by including the vociferous Perot in the proceedings.

Perot did make an appearance in Indiana on April 29, 1996, at the invitation of DePauw University at Greencastle. His remarks, however, came before he had formally announced his second run for the White House. At DePauw he hit on familiar themes, including his belief that number one growth industry in America was the size of the federal government. "And they don't sell a product," Perot said. "They tax."[70]

Taking seriously the fact that his presentation was a lecture, Perot broke into his familiar style of presentation saying:

> Business is conducted on a rational basis and has generally accepted standards of ethics and conduct. Politics is not conducted on a rational basis. There are no rules of conduct or ethical standards. War has rules. Mud wrestling has rules. Politics has no rules. If you question that, go back and analyze the recent Republican primary where they just chewed on one another mercilessly. You and I have got to just turn 'em off when they start the personal attacks say, 'Tell me how you're going to solve our country's problems and stop chewin' on the guy next to you." That's what it's all about.[71]

Emphasizing his background in business, Perot said the American political system had become "a blend of magic acts and illusion," contrasting it with business, "where you get promoted based on your performance . . . and this may be the most important thing I say to you tonight: In politics, you get elected based on your acting ability."[72]

Perot said he, unlike Washington politicians Clinton and Dole, was qualified to address the nation's debt and other problems. "If someone as blessed as I am is not willing to clean out the barn, who will? . . . The next generation to be born will pay 82 percent tax rates. Is there anyone in this room who wants to leave their children and grandchildren a country where they only keep 18 cents out of every dollar of their paycheck? I don't think so, and we won't. . . . There's too much debt. We've got work to do, and bluntly put, if we don't, we will destroy the American dream."[73]

Perot's 1996 effort in Indiana failed to reach even half of his previous effort, drawing just under 225,000 votes or only 10 percent, reflecting the nonfactor he had become politically.

George W. Bush

Bush proved a popular figure in Indiana for both his presidential campaigns, rolling up impressive numbers among Hoosier voters—capturing 57 percent in 2000 and 60 percent in 2004. The general election efforts in Indiana, however, came only after the young Texas governor dispatched an initially crowded field of GOP hopefuls that sought to turn around the party's fortunes following two losses to Clinton. The most serious challenger to Bush, however, was Senator John McCain of Arizona, who believed he was next in line for the nomination. Bush, son of George H. W., was little known outside Texas and cast a vastly different figure than his father but enjoyed access to the same organizational and fund-raising apparatus. By the time the May 2 Indiana Republican primary arrived, Bush had successfully put McCain's campaign on the ropes and, with McCain having suspended active campaigning, Bush captured 81 percent of the primary vote.

In July 2000, just before the opening of the Republican National Convention in Philadelphia, Bush visited Indianapolis at the invitation of Mayor Stephen Goldsmith to bolster his oft-visited themes of "compassionate conservatism" and to outline his plans for a faith- and community-based initiative to meet social concerns in American cities. Bush said the federal government had an important role to play to "rally the armies of compassion in our communities" and could do so with favorable tax incentives for churches and neighborhood groups. "Government can spend money," Bush said, "but it cannot put hope in our hearts or a sense of purpose in our lives. That is done in churches and synagogues and mosques and charities that warm the cold of life."[74] His Indianapolis speech, referred to by the national media as his first major policy address, and the first time he had fleshed out in detail what his term "compassionate conservatism" meant. Bush proposed committing $8 billion in federal money for the effort "to encourage an outpouring of giving in America. In every instance when my administration sees a responsibility to help people, we will look first to faith-based institutions, to charities and to community groups that have shown their ability to save and change lives."[75]

Reporters in Indianapolis questioned Bush about whether his proposals would violate constitutional requirements for separation of church and state, but Bush said he was confident they would not. "I'm told by the legal experts that my initiative will pass constitutional muster. We will send money to fund services, but the money does not go to fund the religious programs of the institution," he said.[76] Bush added that the more important question to be answered was not who was implementing programs that helped people, but whether those programs worked. Goldsmith, who had undertaken his own faith- and community-based initiative in the city under the title of "the Front Porch Alliance," gave Bush a platform to emphasize the role community organizations could play in fighting crime and reducing poverty.

Bush said the nation needed to "change the laws and regulation that hamper the cooperation of government and private institutions" and "allow private and religious groups to compete to provide services in every federal, state and local social program." Bush said his message was directed to the government as well as members of his own party declaring: "We must apply our conservative and free-market ideas to the job of helping real human beings, because any ideology, no matter how right in theory, is sterile and empty without that goal." Departing from the volunteering emphasis that his father had championed under the "Thousand Points of Light" program, the younger Bush said, "It is not enough to call for volunteerism . . . without more support and resources—both public and private—we are asking them to make bricks without straw."[77]

By autumn, the battle for the White House between Bush and Gore was fully engaged and reflected in Bush's demeanor during a stop in Indianapolis on September 6, 2000. National reporters noted that Bush used his remarks in Indiana to accuse Gore of making so many promises to so many groups of Americans that a Gore presidency would eat up the nation's $4.6 trillion federal surplus in less than a decade. Combined with his remarks, the Bush campaign rolled out endorsements of 300 Nobel laureates and other economists who praised his proposed approaches to fiscal policy.

"I want America to add up all the promises my opponent has made," Bush said. Highlighting local blue-collar workers for the Indiana rally (as well as for ones in Pennsylvania and Wisconsin), Bush told his audiences that "we trust you with your money. We trust you to make decisions with your lives. We don't trust bureaucrats in Washington, D.C. We don't believe in planners and deciders making decisions on behalf of America."[78]

The nation was headed for a historically close presidential election, with Bush carrying twenty-nine states on Election Day, Gore twenty, and the state of Florida in question for days. With Florida's twenty-five electoral votes hanging in the balance, a circus-like recount got under way in four Florida counties (as requested by Gore) to determine the winner. Eventually, state election officials in Florida declared Bush the winner of the state by an incredibly slim margin of 537 votes. Gore contested that result and a Florida Supreme Court ruling affirmed his appeal, ordering the state to recount more than 70,000 ballots previously excluded for a variety of technicalities.

On December 9, 2000, thirty-two days after the election, the Supreme Court offered a concurring ruling in a case captioned as *Bush v. Gore* and ordered the recount ended and the final results certified. On December 13 Gore conceded the election, Florida was declared for Bush, and the Texas governor was elected the nation's forty-third president. In the end, while Bush won the Electoral College by a vote of 271 to 266, Gore had won the national popular vote by a margin of 543,895 votes out of more than 100 million cast.

Bush made his first appearance in Indiana just five months into his first term, invited to be the graduation speaker at Notre Dame in May

2001, a honor his father had received less than a decade earlier. His father was on his mind as Bush prefaced his remarks by reminding the audience that he had spoken once before on the campus, back in 1980 in support of his father's vice presidential campaign. He drew laughter when he predicted he was sure all six of the people present for his remarks back in 1980 had remembered them. On this occasion Bush emphasized his familiar campaign themes that called for a new era of conservative compassion for the nation's poor. "Notre Dame, as a Catholic university, carries forward a great tradition of social teaching," the president said. "It calls on all of us, Catholic and non-Catholic, to honor family, to protect life in all its stages, to serve and uplift the poor. This university is more than a community of scholars; it is a community of conscience and an ideal place to report on our nation's commitment to the poor and how we're keeping it."[79]

Bush recalled that in 1964, the year he entered college, President Lyndon Johnson delivered a famous graduation speech in which he declared the nation's "War on Poverty." Bush said that Johnson's proposal "had noble intentions and some enduring successes" but added, "yet, there were also some consequences that no one wanted or intended. The welfare entitlement became an enemy of personal effort and responsibility, turning many recipients into dependents. The War on Poverty also turned too many citizens into bystanders, convinced that compassion had become the work of government alone."[80] Bush lauded the 1996 welfare reform efforts that placed caps on benefits and required workplace training for some recipients—"a tribute to the Republicans and Democrats who agreed on reform. . . . Our nation has confronted welfare dependency. But our work is only half done. Now we must confront the second problem, to revive the spirit of citizenship, to marshal the compassion of our people to meet the continuing needs of our nation. This is a challenge to any administration and to each one of you. We must meet that challenge because it is right and because it is urgent."[81]

Bush acknowledged that "welfare as we knew it has ended, but poverty has not" with more than 12 million American children living below the federal poverty limit, and millions of welfare recipients bumping against the reform enacted five-year limit on benefits. Bush noted that the easiest cases to help move up and off welfare have already passed, but "the hardest problems remain, people with far fewer skills, and greater barriers to work, people with complex human problems like illiteracy and addiction, abuse and mental illness. We do not yet know what will happen to these men and women or their children, but we cannot sit and watch, leaving them to their own struggles and their own fate." He added, "Our task is clear, and it's difficult. We must build our country's unity by extending our country's blessings."[82]

Invoking the name of Mother Teresa and her work across the world, and Lou Nanni, former director of the Center for the Homeless in South Bend, Bush said:

> Much of today's poverty has more to do with troubled lives than a troubled economy. And often when a life is broken, it can only be restored by another caring, concerned human being. The answer for an abandoned child is not a job requirement; it is the loving presence of a mentor. The answer to addictions is not a demand for self-sufficiency; it is a personal support on the hard road to recovery. The hope we seek is found in safe havens for battered women and children, in homeless shelters, in crisis pregnancy centers, in programs that tutor and conduct job training and help young people who may happen to be

on parole. All of these efforts provide not just a benefit but attention and kindness, a touch of courtesy, a dose of grace.[83]

Bush used his remarks as a lead up for promotion of his White House Office on Faith-Based and Community Initiatives to bring together church and community groups in helping answer the needs of their fellow citizens. "And we're in the process of implementing and expanding charitable choice, the principle already established in federal law that faith-based organizations should not suffer discrimination when they compete for contracts to provide social services." Bush said. "Government should never fund the teaching of faith, but it should support the good works of the faithful."[84] To add to his efforts, Bush said he was submitting a new budget to Congress that included additional funding for community-based housing programs, such as Habitat for Humanity, and $1.6 billion in new funds to close the so-called treatment gap that he said trapped five million Americans needing drug treatment from the two million currently receiving help.

For the 2002 midterm congressional elections, Bush showed extraordinary interest in two races in Indiana, considered to be battleground districts for Republicans hoping to maintain control of the House of Representatives. Bush actively campaigned for Congressmen Chris Chocola in northern Indiana, while Vice President Dick Cheney stumped for Republican challenger Mike Sodrel in southern Indiana. In September 2002 Bush made his way to the Century Center in South Bend for a fund-raising dinner for the Chocola campaign, who was seeking to recapture the seat he lost in the 2000 election to Democrat Timothy Roemer. In his lengthy remarks boosting Chocola's candidacy, Bush said he was particularly pleased to learn from Chocola's wife, Sarah, that she grew tired of him watching the Sunday morning news shows and complaining about things in Washington, and instead urged him to run for office. "Chis Chocola is a man of faith and family," Bush said. "He's got good, solid Indiana values. He married above himself—as so did I. . . . I appreciate a good wife who stands by her husband who is willing to work to see the best interests of this district are represented in Washington, D.C. I also love the fact that they place high priority on their children. There's nothing more important than having people in Washington, D.C., who understand that their most important job is to be a good mom and a good dad."[85]

Bush said he needed men like Chocola in Congress because they shared his values on how to move the nation forward and up out of the lingering post–9/11 recession. He said Chocola understood that "the role of government is not to create wealth. The role of government is to create an environment in which the entrepreneur can flourish, in which small businesses can grow to be big businesses, in which America's producers can flourish. And that starts with creating a tax environment that is hospitable to growth and jobs." The president defended his record tax cuts for some of the nation's highest wage earners—tax cuts he said were critical to stimulating economic growth and job development. "The textbook we read from says if you let a person keep more of their own money, you will enhance the demand for goods and services," Bush said. "And if somebody demands an additional good or a service, somebody is going to produce that good or a service. And when somebody produces that good or a service, somebody is more likely to find work. What we're interested in is stimulating the entrepreneurial spirit of America, stimulating small-business growth, so people in America can find work."[86]

Making a strong pitch for his No Child Left Behind educational initiative, Bush devoted the remainder of his remarks to how he felt Chocola would help him stand strong against terrorists who opposed America:

> Our biggest challenge is to make sure that the enemy doesn't hit us again. And they're out there. That's the reality of the world in which we live. The battlefields of the past have shifted. The battlefield can now be here in America, as we learned tragically. And there's still a group of people out there, nothing but a bunch of cold-blooded killers, by the way, that hate America. And they hate us because we love freedom. I want you to tell your kids that the reason there is an enemy that wants to strike America is because this great country, this great land, loves freedom. We love the fact that people can worship freely in America. We love the fact that people can speak their mind. We love a free press. We love everything that freedom offers, and we're willing to defend it at all costs. The more we love freedom, the more the enemy hates us, and that's why we've got to protect the homeland.[87]

Earlier in the day, Bush had visited the ATA Terminal at South Bend Regional Airport, the official or nonpolitical portion of his trip to Indiana, complete with Air Force One in the background. Bush made permanent enactment of his tax cuts the centerpiece of his remarks, but also argued strongly for a new energy bill "which will encourage conservation, that will help unleash the technology necessary for us to conserve more, the technologies and the research necessary for us to do a better job with renewable sources of energy." He said decreasing America's dependency on foreign sources of oil was important to preserving national security, but also required flexibility at home on how crude oil can be captured. Finally, he argued for his plan to provide a "terrorism insurance policy" for developers seeking to start new projects, but who are hindered by the inability to get insurance in place that protects projects even in the midst of terrorist attacks.[88]

Bush told his audience that he was optimistic about the nation's future. "I know the resiliency of our country, I know the strengths of our country," he said. "And while some hurt now because of the economic slowdown, I'm optimistic about our future. I really am. I feel strong—I feel strongly that there are better days ahead for people who can't find work. The foundation is there, and we'll keep working. My biggest job, however, is to protect you, the American people. That's my biggest job now, is to secure the homeland, to make sure that we're safe, to make sure our American families our protected. That job still exists, and it's important today because there's still an enemy out there that hates us."[89]

Promoting the value of the newly minted Department of Homeland Security, Bush said it was "important for all of us to communicate the right message to our children when we talk with these harsh words. But you need to tell your kids that these killers hate America because of what we love," and noted "that's not the way the enemy thinks. See, they've hijacked a great religion and they don't care about life. They've got their desires, their dark, dark ambitions and if people are in the way of them, that's just too bad, as far as they're concerned. But the problem—what they've got is, they've got a mighty nation that stands between them and their ambitions."[90]

The president's South Bend visit came between his major push in Congress to harness American and allied strength to focus on Iraq and the removal of Saddam Hussein, as well as his address to the United Nations Security Council in which he argued for enforcement of UN sanctions against Iraq. In October, with bipartisan support from Democrats and Republicans, the U.S. Senate voted 77–28 to authorize Bush to use military force against Iraq.

With Chocola locked in a tight race for the congressional seat, Bush made another airport stop in South Bend on October 31, 2002, just before Election Day. Getting quickly to the point, Bush advocated for Chocola's election by telling northern Indiana voters, "You can make a difference in the campaign, you can actually determine the outcome. So when you go to your houses of worship or your coffee shops or your community centers, put out the word. And remember there are some discerning Democrats who live up here, people who know the difference between a shrill voice and a solid voice. There are good independents up here, people who want somebody to represent them who will bring honor and dignity to the office. There are people who understand it makes sense to have somebody who has been an entrepreneur serving in the United States Congress, somebody who has actually met a payroll, somebody who knows what it means to put people to work and to take risks." He added, "And if it helps, you tell them the President wants him standing by his side in Washington, D.C., too. I need somebody from this district whose vote I can count on. I don't need to be worrying about somebody who's running a focus group or a poll. I need a solid United States Congressman up there, who will support me in making America a stronger and safer and better place for every citizen."[91]

Bush's speech crystalized the Republican approach for 2002—a strong emphasis on maintaining their tax-cut plans and emphasizing their efforts in responding to terrorist threats from abroad. "And we're making progress," Bush said. "Sometimes it's hard to tell we're making progress. Some of the old vets will tell you, in the old days, you could measure progress by the number of tanks you destroyed or the number of enemy aircraft that were shot down out of the sky. This bunch we're fighting, they don't have tanks. They're the kind that hide in caves, kind of move around the dark corners of some of the cities of the world, and then send youngsters to their suicidal deaths. That's the kind of people they are."[92] The president's efforts paid off; not only did Chocola win the first of two terms in the House, but Republicans maintained control of the House and retook control of the Senate.

On May 13, 2003, Bush returned to Indianapolis for another pitch in support of his tax-relief plans. His visit included a private meeting with a small group of Hoosiers and a speech at the Indiana State Fairgrounds that came just hours after a deadly car-bomb terrorist attack on the Riyadh military compound in Saudi Arabia that killed thirty-nine people (including nine Americans) and injured 160 others. The attack was quickly linked to cells of the Al-Qaeda terrorist network and affirmed U.S. State Department warnings that travel in the region was particularly dangerous for westerners at that time. Bush used the attack as a reminder that Americans "have a challenge to protect our fellow citizens from terrorism. Today's attacks in Saudi Arabia, the ruthless murder of American citizens and other citizens, remind us that the war on terror continues. My thoughts and prayers and those of our fellow citizens are with the families of the victims of yesterday's murder in Saudi Arabia. We pray for them. We mourn the loss of life. These despicable acts were committed by killers whose only faith is hate. And the United States will find the killers, and they will learn the meaning of American justice."[93]

Bush continued in remarks interrupted by heavy applause, "The nation has been tested—for 20 months we have waged a relentless campaign against global terror. You see, the enemy hit us, and they didn't realize the nature of this country. They probably thought we would just fold our tents and go home. They don't understand America. They don't understand how much we love freedom. They don't understand how much we cherish it. They probably thought we would forget, but anytime anybody attacks our homeland, anybody, anytime anybody attacks our fellow citizens, we'll be on the hunt, and we'll find them, and they will be brought to justice. Just ask the Taliban."[94]

Defending American efforts in Afghanistan and Iraq, Bush said that in Iraq "we removed the dictator, but we've got work to do. First, we're going to help rebuild the country, make sure the people have got food on the table, make sure the children can go to school, make sure those who need medical supply can find medical supply. We're going to turn the lights on all around the country so that life can return back to normal. And then we'll work with the Iraqi people to have a government of, by, and for Iraqi citizens. We'll work to make sure that democracy takes hold, because we believe people everywhere love freedom. And then we're coming home."[95] The president's remarks reflected a growing sentiment among many Americans that the war effort in Iraq and Afghanistan was taking too long and costing too high a toll in American casualties.

Bush affirmed, however, that "a free Iraq will make the world more peaceful, because you see, when people are free, they're less likely to promote terrorism. When people are free, they're more likely to work to realize their aspirations in a positive way. Freedom around the world will bring peace, and that's why America stands so strong for free people everywhere across this globe."[96]

The bulk of Bush's remarks, however, attempted to portray everything he was doing to address the growing recession, unemployment, and rising fuel costs. The combination of national security and tax cuts mantra that had worked well for Bush in the 2002 election cycle was more of a challenge, as both the war and the recession dragged on with no clear resolution for either struggle in sight. The president again expressed confidence in a coming economic recovery, but his comments came in the shadow of a damaging report from the Joint Congressional Committee on Intelligence that outlined multiple failures of U.S. security agencies in detecting and/or preventing the terrorist attacks of September 11, 2001.

By September 2003 Bush's approval rating continued to drop, while his disapproval rating rose (both of them at about 50 percent at the time in Gallup Polls), and he did what Richard Nixon and Ronald Reagan had done before: He went to the supportive Republican territory of Indiana to find a friendly audience. His visit focused on the fifty-five employees of the Langham Logistics Company in Indianapolis at the invitation of the company's owners. "There are a lot of Americans looking for work, and we need to do something about that in Washington, D.C.," said Bush. "We've taken steps to get our economy growing again, and there are some very hopeful signs that progress is being made. . . . Yet today's unemployment report shows we've got more to do, and I'm not going to be satisfied until every American who's looking for a job can find a job." Bush said he had "laid out a comprehensive plan for job creation all across America" and urged Congress to act on it. Langham Logistics Company provided Bush a valuable platform from which to emphasize his efforts to support small business owners with favorable tax laws. "The tax relief plan we passed will let you keep more

of your own money and came at the right time," Bush said. He added, "Tax relief helped small businesses all across America, small businesses just like this, and that's important because small business create most of the new jobs in America. If your small-business sector is vibrant and healthy, somebody is likely to find a job."[97]

The president singled out his hosts by noting, "When the Langham's spend money, not only does it help their own employees, not only will it help the five folks that they're fixing to hire, but it helps the people providing products for this company. Tax relief is stimulating growth, and tax relief is stimulating job creation all across the country."[98]

As had become his practice, Bush finished off his visit to Indiana with a political event, this one a fund-raiser at the Murat Centre in downtown Indianapolis in support of the upcoming Bush-Cheney 2004 re-election campaign, and the expected gubernatorial campaign of his former aide, Mitch Daniels. "What we're doing is laying the groundwork for a strong foundation for what will become a great victory in November of 2004," Bush told the GOP faithful. "The political season is coming pretty soon, and I'm loosening up. I'm getting ready, but right now I've got a job to do. And my job is to work on behalf of the people of America. I'm going to continue to work hard to earn the confidence of every American, keeping this nation secure and strong and prosperous and free."[99]

Articulating themes that would be the cornerstone of his 2004 campaign, Bush said:

In the last 2½ years, our nation has acted decisively to confront great challenges. I came to this office to solve problems, not to pass them on to future Presidents and future generations. I came to seize opportunities instead of letting them slip away. I believe this administration is meeting the tests of our time. Terrorists declared war on the United States of America, and war is what they got. We've captured or killed many leaders of the Al Qaida network, and the rest of them know we're on their trail. In Afghanistan, in Iraq, we gave ultimatums to terror regimes. Those regimes chose defiance, and those regimes are no more. Fifty million people—50 million people in those two countries once lived under tyranny, and now they live in freedom. . . . Our strong and prosperous Nation must also be a compassionate nation. I will continue to advance our agenda of compassionate conservatism. We will apply the best and most innovative ideas to the task of helping our fellow citizens in need.[100]

In May 2004 Bush made his only appearance during the presidential election cycle, a quick stop at South Bend Regional Airport in support of Daniels's campaign for governor. "I am proud to be standing by the side of my friend Mitch Daniels," Bush said. "Mitch is going to be the governor of the state of Indiana, and I know for certain the people of this state will love this guy as their governor. See, I've seen him firsthand. I know what it's like to work with Mitch. He's smart, he's capable, he's well organized. He's got a fabulous sense of humor. I gave him a lot of tough jobs, and he did each of them with great professionalism and class."[101] While Cheney made campaign stops in Indiana for 2004, Bush focused his attentions elsewhere in a surprisingly close contest with Senator John Kerry of Massachusetts, the Democratic nominee. The Bush campaign tipped the campaign in their favor by picking up razor-thin wins in both Ohio and Florida, reflecting Bush's overall re-election total of just over 50 percent of the popular vote (compared to Kerry's 48 percent). In Indiana the Bush-Cheney calculation that the state was not in play proved accurate as they rolled up one of their strongest finishes, grabbing 60 percent of Hoosier ballots.

For his second-term priority, Bush chose Notre Dame for a March 4, 2005, panel discussion on reforming the Social Security system, then struggling to keep pace with the large mass of baby boomers entering retirement. Acknowledging that Social Security had widely become known as the deadly "third rail" of politics that could fatally injure anyone who dared talk about reforming it, the president said, "Let me start off my saying something really important, and we'll talk about this as this discussion goes on. If you're relying upon Social Security, nothing will change. I don't care what the [television] ads say, what the politicians say, you're going to get your check. That's just the way it is. That is a fact."[102]

The problem however, Bush said, "is not for those who now depend upon it. Listen, Social Security has been a great safety net. It's been a vital part of our country. But we're getting some holes in the safety net, particularly for younger generations of Americans." Bush said despite the political risks, he wanted to talk about Society Security "because I see a problem, and I believe I have a duty as the President of the United States to bring problems forward for public discussion. So I'm traveling our country, which I like to do, by the way, talking about the problem and reassuring seniors that you don't have anything to worry about—unless you're worried about your grandkids, like most seniors are."[103]

Bush said that beginning in 2008, millions of Americans would turn sixty-two years of age (including himself), creating a "bulge of retirees" looking to access their benefits. Adding to the struggle, Bush said, was that the lifespan of Americans was longer than ever "and the government has promised us benefits that are much greater than the previous generations. So you're beginning to get a sense for the math: A lot of people living longer, being promised greater benefits. And the problem is . . . that the number of workers paying into the system is shrinking dramatically."[104] The resulting "pay-as-you-go-system" cannot be sustained, Bush said, because it is building up a large pile of IOUs that must be paid and by 2018 more money would go out than would be coming into the Social Security system. He predicted that by 2027 the federal government would have to raise $200 billion in new payroll taxes "to make good on our promises." He said by 2042 the Social Security system would be "flat broke."[105]

While emphasizing he was open to ideas to save the system from either Democrats or Republicans, he strongly advocated for his own plan that would allow younger Americans to opt out of the entitlement program. "Younger workers ought to be allowed to take some of their own money—and remember, when you pay in payroll taxes, it's your money, not the government's money—you ought to be allowed to take some of your own money and set it aside in a personal savings account that you call your own." Doing so, he said, would promote a "compounding rate of interest" that could provide greater benefits for future retirees than they might realize under the Social Security system alone.[106]

After his opening remarks, Bush acted as moderator for a series of speakers, including Doctor Jeffrey R. Brown, an economics and finance professor from the University of Illinois and a Bush adviser; retirees Mark and Betty Batterbee of nearby Edwardsburg, Michigan, parents of eleven children and grandparents of thirty-five; Francisco Martinez, a steel purchasing manager from South Bend; Deborah Johnson, a business development manager for a Mishawaka credit union; and John Paul Surma, a small business owner from Rolling Prairie. Each of them offered their personal perspectives on the Social Security system, although none expressed any disagreement or challenge to Bush's proposals.

Just over a year later, Bush came to Indianapolis to speak before the July 14, 2005, corporate luncheon of the Indiana Black Expo. The Indianapolis appearance was a compromise of sorts; Bush had never appeared before the National Association for the Advancement of Colored People, the first modern-day president to skip interaction with that group. Speaking in broad terms before the polite, but hardly enthusiastic audience on the floor of the RCA Dome, Bush said:

> It's an honor to be here with so many charitable and civic leaders. You see, we share a belief in the founding promises of this nation, a sense of optimism about our future, the future for all citizens, including African Americans. We believe in the power of the human spirit to lift communities and to change lives. Together, we're working to achieve a great national goal, making our country a place where opportunity and prosperity are within reach for all Americans. I see an America where all our children are taught the basic skills they need to live up to their God-given potential. I see an America where every citizen owns a stake in the future of our country and where a growing economy creates jobs and opportunity for everyone. I see an America where most troubled neighborhoods become safe places of kinship and community. I see an America where every person of every race has the opportunity to strive for a better future and to take part of the promise of America. That's what I see. And I believe the government has a role to play in helping people gain the tools they need to build lives of dignity and purpose. That's at the heart of what I call compassionate conservatism.[107]

The remainder of Bush's remarks focused on his education policies that he said benefited America's most needy families and communities, and his support of Small Business Administration programs that benefited small businesses, many of them African American owned. He also argued for more help for working families to become homeowners and increased support for local law enforcement to address street crime in the nation's cities (highlighting that violent crime was at its lowest point in thirty years).

In February 2006 Bush made another stop on behalf of Chocola, this time locked in a tough re-election campaign for a third term. Speaking to an overflow crowd at Bethel College in Mishawaka, Bush said he was there because he believed Chocola "is an honest, decent, down-to-earth, practical man who deserves to be re-elected to the United States Congress. Chris is a rising star in the House of Representatives, and when you find a rising star, it makes a lot of sense to keep him serving you."[108] In comments that would be repeated months later, Bush set up the prospect that the ongoing war on terror in Iraq and Afghanistan was likely to continue. "We're living in historic times," he said. "I wish I could report to you that the war on terror was over, but it's not. These are serious times that require serious thought and serious purpose in order to do our most important duty, which is to protect the American people." He reiterated his idea that the war in Afghanistan was key to eliminating any "safe haven" for terrorists to hide. "By the way, I wish I wasn't talking about war. No President ever says, 'Gosh, I hope there's war.' For those of you who are young here, I want you to know what I'm leading to is how to keep the peace and do my job that you expect me to do, which is to prevent the enemy from attacking again."[109]

In other remarks that would later be mocked by comedians, Bush said he enjoyed being president. He said the job description was easy: "I make a lot of decisions. I'm a decision maker."[110]

On March 26, 2006, Bush was back in Indiana for a fund-raising reception for Sodrel's campaign to win a second term in the House. As he did in his earlier remarks for the Chocola campaign, Bush said, "It's important to have members of the United States Congress who understand the stakes and understand the nature of the enemy. They cannot exist without safe haven. And so one of the doctrines and one of the lessons learned after September the 11th is that we must hold people to account for harboring terrorists. If you harbor a terrorist, if you feed a terrorist, if you house a terrorist, you're equally guilty as the terrorists. Michael Sodrel understands that. He also understands that when the President speaks, he better mean what he says. And I meant what I said when I said that, and that's why I told the Taliban—I said, 'Get rid of Al Qaida.' They refused. We sent a liberation force into Afghanistan to uphold doctrine, to protect ourselves and, in so doing, liberated 25 million people from the clutches of a barbaric regime."[111]

Speaking of his decision-making processes, Bush said:

> I'm going to tell you something about me. I'm not going to make up my mind about Iraq based upon polls and focus groups. I will make up my mind about troops based upon the recommendations of the United States military, not politicians in Washington, D.C. . . . As I make decisions as to how to protect you, I want you to know I'm guided by this principle: I believe there's an Almighty, and I believe the Almighty's great gift to every man and woman, every man and woman, on the face of the Earth is freedom. Freedom is universal. It is non-negotiable. And as freedom takes hold, the world becomes more peaceful. Democracies don't war. So as you explain what we're trying to do in Iraq, and will do in Iraq, to your friends and neighbors, remind them about the history of Europe. America lost hundreds of thousands of soldiers on the continent of Europe in two world wars. And yet today, Europe is whole, free, and at peace, and the reason why is, democracies don't war.[112]

As 2006 wore on, and Bush's poll numbers continued to sag, so did the fortunes of many Republican congressional candidates, including Sodrel and Chocola. As a result, Bush was back in Indiana on October 28, 2006, in one last push to try and get Sodrel a second term in Congress in a rubber match with former congressman Baron Hill, a Democrat. In highly partisan remarks at Sellersburg, Bush said, "The stakes are high in this election. Your vote will have an impact not only on your lives here, but an impact that will help determine the course of this nation. I want to thank you for supporting this good man. The election of Mike Sodrel is important for the United States of America." Bush told the Republican faithful to ignore the polls and pundits that predicted the 2006 elections would favor the Democrats, and said "we will win this election because we got a record to run on."[113]

Drawing heckles and boos when he mentioned Democratic House leader Nancy Pelosi of California, Bush said many Democrats in Congress had still not learned the lessons of September 11:

> I'm not saying these people are unpatriotic; I'm saying they're wrong. You cannot win a war if you're unwilling to fight the war. Retreat before the job was done would embolden the enemy. It would provide new safe haven. It would enable the enemy to recruit. It would dash the hope of millions who want to simply live in peace. It would dishonor the sacrifice of the men and women who have worn the uniform of the United States of America. This is a different kind of war, and it's important for Republicans and Democrats and independents to understand this fact: If we were to leave before the job was done, the enemy would follow us to the United States. And that is why victory is our goal, and that is why we will achieve victory. A victory will be a blow to the terrorists. A victory will say to those in the Middle East—

"Do you believe in freedom?"—that we do. A victory will make Iraq an ally on the war on terror. A victory in Iraq will make generations of young Americans more secure. And that is why we will stay, we will fight, and we will win.[114]

The wishes of Bush and his audience notwithstanding, Pelosi did become Speaker of the House, the first woman ever elevated to the post, as the Democrats reclaimed control of the lower chamber in the November 2006 election. Both Chocola and Sodrel failed to win new terms as their seats were claimed by Democrats.

Although widely viewed as a lame-duck president with approval ratings sagging well below 50 percent, Bush again returned to the friendly confines of Indiana for a pitch for his educational reform plans at Silver Street Elementary School in New Albany. The March 2, 2007, appearance, along with Daniels, focused mostly on Bush's desire to reauthorize his No Child Left Behind education program, "one of the most substantial pieces of legislation I will have had the honor to sign," Bush said.[115] The president explained that he "first became directly involved with public schools from a public policy perspective as the Governor of Texas, and I was deeply concerned about systems that quit early on a child and just moved them through. In other words, I was concerned about a system where people would walk in the classroom and say, 'These children are hard to educate; therefore, let's just move them through the system.' It may not have happened in Indiana, but it happened in Texas. And it was unacceptable, because guess who generally got shuffled through the system? The poor, the newly arrived, the minority student. And I knew that unless we confronted a system which gave up on children early, that my State would not be a hopeful place."[116]

He added, "So I decided to do something about it, and I took that spirit to Washington, D.C. Now, look, I fully understand some are nervous when they hear a President talking about federal education. You start thinking to yourself, the government is going to tell you what to do here at the local level. Quite the contrary, in this piece of legislation, I strongly believe in local control of schools. I believe it's essential to align authority and responsibility. And by insisting upon local control of schools, you put the power where it should be—closest to the people . . . the No Child Left Behind program says, if you spend money, you should insist upon results. Now, I recognize the federal government only spends about 7 percent of the total education budgets around the country, and frankly, that's the way I think it should be. In other words, if local people are responsible or the State is responsible, that's where the primary funding ought to come. But I also strongly subscribe to the idea of the federal government providing extra money for what's called Title I students, for example, students who go to this school—money that I think bolsters education for students in the community."[117] Congress did not reauthorize Bush's plan, but pieces of it remained in educational waiver programs initiated by President Barack Obama in 2011.

In April 2007 Bush welcomed members of the Super Bowl champion Indianapolis Colts to the White House for the traditional presidential honor, and interestingly, just months later he was back in southern Indiana, in New Albany. He paid a quick stop at a luncheon meeting with business leaders at Sam's Tavern that included among its guests PGA and Masters Tournament champion Frank "Fuzzy" Zoeller. Later Bush offered lengthier remarks in a speech about his proposed new budget at the Grand Convention

Center—remarks he said reflected that "I had something on my mind" and "I thank you for giving me a chance to come and share it with you."[118] As he spoke, Bush was proposing a budget that some in Washington, D.C., predicted was dead on arrival. Unable to seek a third term, and with Republican prospects looking dim for the 2008 presidential election, Bush again chose Indiana to make his budget pitch. Bush's visit, coming months before a recession hit in 2008–09, allowed the president to tout a variety of positive economic factors (at least from his perspective), including fifty continuous months of job growth, the longest period of uninterrupted job growth on record, more than 8.3 million new jobs created since 2003, and a national unemployment rate of 4.7 percent (4.5 percent in Indiana). In the months ahead, economic conditions would dramatically decline fueled by a collapse among many of the nation's creditors.

In his remarks Bush said:

One of the keys to meeting economic challenges is wise policy from your federal government. Wise policy helps keep us resilient; lousy policy will hurt the ability for this economy to grow. The decisions we make in Washington have a direct impact on the people in our country, obviously. And as we debate the decisions, you got to understand there are two very different philosophies being played out. My philosophy is that the American people know how to spend their money better than the government can. That's the core of my philosophy, that I'd rather you have more of your own money to spend, save, and invest as you see fit. Every time the government collects a dollar in taxes, it means you have a dollar less to invest in your business or to spend on your family or to put aside for the future. Government has certain responsibilities, such as protecting our citizens—and we're going to meet those responsibilities. But we must always remember that your paycheck belongs to you and that the economy thrives the more money you have in your pocket. That philosophy has been the center piece of my economic policy since I've been honored to be your President. Since I took office, we've cut taxes for every American who pays income taxes. We've worked to restrain spending, while ensuring that we have the resources necessary to protect the homeland and to make sure our military has what it needs to do the job. We set a goal to balance the budget by 2012, and we're on pace to meet that goal.[119]

Bush returned to familiar Republican rhetoric used two decades earlier to great effect by President Reagan, accusing Congressional Democrats of engaging a never-ended tax-and-spend policy with the nation's resources. Among the problems, Bush said, was the Democrat's proposal to take away tax cuts enacted during Bush's first term. He declared, "We need to make sure the message is heard in the nation's Capital, and I've come to New Albany, Indiana, to let you know I'm going to do my part. Under the Constitution, the President has the power to veto bills he thinks are unwise. And with all the other pressures on our economy, raising taxes is one of the most unwise things Congress could possibly do. I hope the leaders in Congress will cooperate and send me reasonable spending bills that I can sign. But if they insist on trying to raise taxes on the American people, I will not hesitate to use my veto pen to stop them."[120] He also addressed rising gasoline prices, something most Hoosiers and Americans could relate to, with oil prices to nearly $100 a barrel. "America clearly needs legislation that expands the use of ethanol and biodiesel, promotes energy conservation, invests in advanced technologies like clean coal and nuclear power," said Bush. "Listen, breaking our reliance on oil and gas is not going to happen overnight. Congress should also authorize

environmentally responsible oil exploration offshore and in the Arctic National Wildlife Refuge. American consumers and businesses are looking to Washington for action on this issue. And Congress needs to pass a bill that encourages the development of more energy that makes us less dependent on foreign sources of oil, and they need to do it now."[121]

Al Gore/Joe Lieberman

For the 2000 election, Vice President Al Gore took a familiar path for Democrats in Indiana—he skipped the state. For the primary, Gore dispatched his wife, Tipper, to Indianapolis, where she visited a luncheon honoring Indiana high school basketball championship teams. "Al and I have found the best examples of community-building are right here in Indiana and right here in this room," she told the students. Later she headlined a fund-raising event for her husband at the Skyline Club atop the AUL Building in downtown Indianapolis, an event hosted by Senator Bayh and Governor O'Bannon.[122]

As the general election campaign shaped up to be incredibly close, and with polls continually showing Bush far ahead in Indiana, Gore remained outside the state. His running mate, Senator Joseph Lieberman of Connecticut, did accept an invitation to address faith-related issues at an October 24, 2000, forum at the Notre Dame. His remarks, however, were more focused on his personal religious views than making any sort of pitch for the Gore-Lieberman campaign in the state.

Lieberman, the first Jewish person nominated for one of the nation's highest offices by either party, addressed what he viewed as a "vacuum of values" in the nation and encouraged Americans to embrace religious faith "in this moment of moral uncertainty."[123] Lieberman's comments were widely viewed as a further effort by the Gore campaign to separate itself from the troubling revelations coming from the extra-marital sex scandal involving Clinton and a White House intern. Part of Lieberman's appeal for Gore as a running mate had been his open and well-articulated criticism of Clinton during the impeachment process. While he did not mention Clinton in his speech, Lieberman declared that "moral ambivalence" in the nation made it more and more difficult to answer day-to-day questions of right and wrong, such as, "Why is it wrong to lie or cheat or steal? Why is it wrong to be unfaithful to one's spouse?" Lieberman drew applause by noting that God had provided, via Moses, Ten Commandments, "not ten suggestions." He added, "More and more people feel free, I fear, to pick and choose among them" and said "Vice President Gore and I share this belief in a higher purpose. We can exert leadership from our public pulpits."[124]

Although Lieberman's remarks seemed to play well before the mostly Catholic audience of 600, one student stood up and interrupted Lieberman as he spoke, saying that his support of abortion rights was "cultivating a culture of death." The senator responded by saying, "You made your point. I respect it. I ask only that you respect my right to speak, as I have come here to do," drawing applause from the audience.[125] Lieberman continued, "At this moment, which I take to be a moment of moral uncertainty, I believe our best hope for rekindling the American spirit and renewing our common values is to have faith again" and said he felt emboldened by discussions of separation of church and state, and that critics of religious faith "to have forgotten that the Constitution promises freedom *of* religion, not freedom *from* religion."[126]

Dick Cheney

Although not much of a political force nationally with public opinion polls showing the stern-faced Cheney as among the most unpopular public figures in Washington, D.C., Cheney's role remained mostly as a campaign fund-raiser for Republican hopefuls around the nation. In Indiana he found numerous audiences though none of his appearances drew any sort of national attention or interest. Cheney's typical political activities in Indiana could be found in both March and April 2004, the former being a fund-raising dinner for congressional candidate Sodrel in Jeffersonville, as well as a speech before a Young Republicans meeting, and the latter an Indianapolis fund-raiser for Daniels as he attempted to become the first Republican elected governor of Indiana since 1984.

For the Sodrel dinner, Cheney recalled his decade of service in the House of Representatives as the only representative from thinly populated Wyoming, noting that the state's one-man House delegation was "a quality one," and that he "loved my time in the House of Representatives." Cheney also said, "President Bush and I are behind [Sodrel] all the way, and we're asking the people of Indiana to send Mike Sodrel to the United States Congress. President Bush and I have now begun the fourth year of our administration, a period defined by serious challenges, hard choices, and the need for decisive action. As Mike knows, there are many tasks that those of us in public service must take on, but none is more important than working to ensure the citizens of this great country are safe and secure."[127]

Cheney reminded the audience that the nation and the world was much changed over the last four years. He noted:

The attacks of September 11, 2001, signaled the arrival of an entirely new era. We suffered massive civilian casualties on our own soil. We awakened to dangers even more lethal— the possibility that terrorists could gain chemical, biological or even nuclear weapons from outlaw regimes and turn those weapons against the United States. Remembering what we saw on the morning of 9/11, and knowing the nature of these enemies, we have as clear a responsibility as could ever fall to government, we must do everything in our power to protect our people from terrorist attack, and to keep terrorists from ever acquiring weapons of mass destruction. This great and urgent responsibility has required a shift in our national security policy. For many years prior to 9/11, terror attacks against Americans were treated as isolated incidents and answered, if at all, on an ad hoc basis—and rarely in a systematic way. Even after the attack inside our own country, the 1993 bombing at the World Trade Center in New York, there was a tendency to treat terrorist attacks as individual criminal acts to be handled primarily through law enforcement. The man who perpetrated that 1993 attack in New York, was tracked down, arrested, convicted, and sent off to serve a life sentence. Yet behind that one man was a growing network with operatives inside and outside the United States waging war against our country.[128]

In remarks that properly reflected his hawkish reputation and ones that drew heavy applause, Cheney added, "Our strategy has several key elements. We have strengthened our defenses here at home, organizing the government to better protect the homeland. But a good defense is not enough. The terrorist enemy holds no territory, defends no population, is unconstrained by rules of warfare, and respects no law of morality. Such an enemy cannot be deterred, contained, appeased or negotiated with—it can only be destroyed, and that, ladies and gentlemen, is the business at hand."[129]

Although Cheney's remarks came weeks before Kerry had secured the Democratic nomination. Kerry's front-runner status among Democratic hopefuls still drew the vice president's ire. Cheney ridiculed Kerry's claims that his views regarding the war on terror had gained the support of unnamed international leaders, and Kerry's twisted quote noting that he had voted for the military buildup to fight the war, before he was against it. "Senator Kerry also had a few things to say about our support for our troops now on the ground in Iraq. Among other criticisms, he asserted that those troops were not receiving the material support they need," said Cheney. "May I remind the Senator that last November, at the President's request, Congress passed legislation providing funding for vital supplies—for body armor and other important equipment, hazard pay, health benefits, ammunition, fuel and spare parts for our military. The legislation passed overwhelmingly with a vote in the Senate of 87 to 12. Senator Kerry voted no. As a way to clarify the matter and explain his vote, Senator Kerry said, and I quote: 'I actually did vote for the $87 billion before I voted against it.' End quote. When it comes to Iraq, at least this much is clear, had the decision belonged to Senator Kerry, Saddam Hussein would still be in power today in Iraq. In fact, because Senator Kerry voted against the Persian Gulf War in 1991, Saddam Hussein would almost certainly still be in control, as well."[130]

Less than a month later, Cheney returned to Indiana for a fund-raiser for Daniels' gubernatorial campaign at the Union Station Grand Hall in Indianapolis. Cheney said he was happy to be in Indiana, particularly given that "in this political year, I spend a lot of time appearing with other candidates for office. It's a lot easier to do when you actually know the guy. And in the case of Mitch Daniels, it's even better: Not only do I know the man, but I consider Mitch one of the finest public servants I've ever worked with." Cheney recalled that during the first two years of the Bush Administration, Daniels had served admirably as the director of the Office of Management and Budget, declaring that "Mitch is a natural-born executive. He's a person with an instinct for common sense and fairness, a guardian of the taxpayer dollars. We didn't call him 'The Blade' for nothing."[131]

Making the case for Bush's re-election, Cheney delivered nearly identical remarks to those he made weeks earlier in Jeffersonville. He concluded by noting, "On issue after issue, from national security, to economic growth, to improving our schools, President Bush has led the way in making progress for the nation. The President has a clear vision of the future for the nation: Abroad, he will use America's great power to serve great purposes, to turn back the forces of terror, and to spread hope and freedom throughout the world. Here at home, we will continue building prosperity that reaches every corner of the land so that every child who grows up in the United States will have a chance to learn, to succeed, and to rise in the world. President Bush and I are both honored by your confidence in us and by your commitment to the cause we all share. We're grateful to our many friends in Indianapolis and across this great state."[132]

Cheney's help seemed to do the trick in 2004—both Sodrel and Daniels won their campaigns in a strong year for Republicans in Indiana. Two years later, with the war on terror continuing to be ramped up, Cheney came to Camp Atterbury near Edinburgh in Johnson County to address a rally for the Indiana Air and Army National Guard. The vice president said, "This is a superb military installation. Not long

after the attacks of 9/11, Camp Atterbury was activated as a joint theater immersion site for training Americans to serve abroad. It's one of only a handful of such facilities in the United States, and more than 30,000 soldiers, sailors, and airmen have passed through this camp in the last five years. Thanks to you, they've gone into the fight well prepared, and they've achieved great results for the United States. I want you to be proud of the work you're doing here every day. The excellence and the commitment shown at Camp Atterbury is one of the reasons we're going to win the war on terror."[133]

Cheney recalled that he had enjoyed a strong working relationship with the National Guard both as vice president and during his time as secretary of defense. "The citizen soldier is absolutely vital to protecting this nation and to preserving our freedom," he declared. "We know this from history, and we know it from current events. In this time of war we have turned to National Guard personnel for missions that are difficult and dangerous. You've never let us down. I want all of you to know that we respect the sacrifices you make, and we admire your skill and your devotion to duty. I'm honored to be in your presence, and I bring you gratitude and good wishes from the President of the United States, George W. Bush."[134]

Cheney's speech laid out the complexities of the war being fought in both Afghanistan and Iraq, a war which he said began with the terrorist attacks on the United States on September 11, 2001. "From that day to this," said Cheney, "America's objectives have been clear: First, we understand that to win this war, we have to go on the offensive, and stay on the offensive, until the killers are brought to justice and the danger is removed. Second, we must defeat the terrorists' ideology of hatred and resentment by offering a hopeful vision of freedom, justice, and human rights."[135]

Cheney added:

This nation harbors no illusions about the nature of our enemies, or the beliefs they hold. . . . They hate us, they hate our country, they hate the liberties for which we stand. They want to destroy our way of life, so that freedom no longer has a home and a defender in this world. That leaves us only one option: to rise to America's defense, to take the fight directly to the enemy, and to accept no outcome but victory for the cause of freedom.[136]

During his remarks, Cheney singled out Staff Sergeant Richard Blakley of Avon, Indiana, who was struck by sniper fire earlier in 2006 in battle in Iraq and returned to active duty the same day. Blakley, presented a Purple Heart for his heroism, returned to active duty and was wounded a second time—this time fatally—ending a seventeen-year career in the Indiana National Guard. Cheney noted remarks that Blakley had nothing left to prove from military service, but "gave his life for his country. Americans will remember Richard Blakley, as we remember all of the fallen, and we will honor their names forever."[137]

On November 1, 2007, as the Bush administration was drawing to a close and polling showed the American people widely dissatisfied with political events in Washington, D.C., Cheney accepted a friendly invitation to address a meeting of the American Legion at the Indiana War Memorial in Indianapolis. The bulk of the vice president's remarks concerned the ongoing war in Iraq that continued to wage on with rising American casualties, and no end in sight. Cheney seemed to understand the growing impatience of the nation, noting, "We have no illusions about the road ahead in Iraq. It won't become a perfect democracy overnight, but success will have an enormously positive impact on the future of the

Middle East, and will have a direct effect on our own security, as well. The only illusion to guard against is the notion that we don't have to care about what happens in that part of the world, or to think that when we took down Saddam Hussein, our job was done. America has no intention of abandoning our friends, of permitting the overthrow of a democracy, and allowing a country of 170,000 square miles to become a staging area for further attacks against us. Tyranny in Iraq was worth defeating. Democracy in Iraq is worth defending."[138]

John Kerry

The 2004 Indiana Democratic Primary took on a familiar tone. Although five candidate's names appeared on the ballot, only one of them remained in contention by the time of the May 4 vote—Kerry. Kerry had weeks earlier sewed up the nomination against a once-crowded field with his chief challengers being former senator John Edwards of North Carolina, retired General Wesley Clark of Arkansas, former Vermont governor Howard Dean, and Congressman Dennis Kucinich of Ohio.

Although Kerry made no preprimary appearances in Indiana, he rolled up 72 percent of the Democratic vote and momentarily considered Bayh as a possible running mate. Kerry named his vice president pick, Edwards, on July 6, 2004, in time for a trip to Indianapolis. "John Kerry placed the call Monday evening he'd chosen John Edwards as his running mate," Associated Press political writer Liz Sidoti noted. "But that first call went to an employee of the company that would add Edwards' name to the side of his campaign plane. To meet a deadline for the job, Kerry had to make up his mind by 6 p.m. Monday if he wanted to fly from Pittsburgh to Indianapolis sporting his running mate's name on the fuselage."[139] Kerry did not telephone Edwards until early Tuesday morning to let him know he was his choice for vice president.

Once in Indianapolis with his newly minted plane in place, Kerry made his way quickly to the Indiana Convention Center to address 10,000 members of the African Methodist Episcopal Church, a powerful black church with heavy membership in the South and Midwest. Kerry said he wanted to bring the delegates up to date on his just-completed announcement in Pittsburgh. "As I hope you know by now, I was proud to announce my Vice Presidential running mate," he said. "I have chosen a man who understands and defends the values of America, a man who has shown courage and conviction as a champion for middle class Americans and those struggling to reach the middle class—a man who has shown guts, determination and political skill in his own race for the Presidency—a man whose life has prepared him for leadership and whose character brings him to exercise it. And if by some chance you haven't heard it, I am pleased to announce that the next Vice President of the United States will be Senator John Edwards of North Carolina."[140] Kerry's remarks would ring painfully ironic years later when a distasteful personal scandal forever soured Edwards' name among Democrats.

Kerry said he was eager to speak to the church leaders. "Your lives speak volumes: While America is a land of tolerance for every belief, it can never be a place of indifference to faith," he said. "We should never separate our highest beliefs and values from our treatment of one another and our conduct of the people's business. That is what I want to talk with you about today. America needs a new era of responsibility. And those of us in leadership would do well to follow your lead."[141] In his remarks, Kerry also emphasized the need for job creation, a stable housing environment, proper education for children, an end to urban violence, and health care and compassions for Americans "of color from diseases like cancer and AIDS and diabetes."[142]

Turning quickly to the incumbent Bush administration (and perhaps recognizing polls that still showed him trailing), Kerry brought the audience to its feet with a powerful rift on his view of the current state of the nation. He noted: "Today, we have an administration in Washington that looks at the challenges we face here at home and around the world and says this is the best we can do. They say this is the best economy of our lifetimes. They have even called us pessimists for speaking truth to power. Well, I say the most pessimistic thing you can say is that America can't do better."[143]

Kerry's voice rose as he said:

Don't tell us disenfranchising a million African Americans and stealing their votes is the best we can do. This time, in 2004, not only will every vote count—we're going to make sure that every vote is counted. Don't tell us 1.8 million lost jobs is the best we can do, when we can create millions of new jobs. We can do better . . . and we will. Don't tell us unemployment is not a problem anymore, when we see that African American unemployment is now above 10 percent—double the rate for whites. We can do better . . . and we will. Don't tell us overcrowded schools and underpaid teachers are the best we can do. We have the means to give all our children a first-rate education. We can do better . . . and we will. Don't tell us $2 a gallon at the pump is the best we can do. We have the technology to make America energy independent of Mideast oil. We can do better . . . and we will. Don't tell us in the richest country in the world, that we can't do better than 44 million people uninsured. We can do better . . . and we will. Don't tell us that it takes four years of rhetoric about AIDS in Africa and African development to get something done. As president, I will fully fund the fight against

AIDS in Africa and make sustainable development on the continent a priority.[144]

Focusing additional comments on the importance of fatherhood and reminding his audience of his distinguished service in Vietnam, Kerry said he had been complimented recently in a speech given by Clinton. Mentioning Clinton was undoubtedly a strategic move—the former president was measurably more popular among black voters than any other Democrat in 2004. "President Clinton paid me the compliment of telling that audience whenever there was a call to service in war or in peace, I have always answered that call," Kerry said.

> Today I say, when we look at the problems of this present age, we must all answer, "Send me." With one clear voice, we must all say: Send me to fight for good-paying jobs that let American families actually get ahead—an America where the middle class is doing better, not being squeezed. Send me to make it clear that health care is a right, not a privilege in America, reserved only for the wealthy or the elected or the connected. Send me to fight for a good education for all our children with funding that truly leaves no child behind. Send me to alleviate poverty and hopelessness wherever they exist in America. Send me to make this nation energy independent so that no young American in uniform is ever held hostage to our dependence on Mideast oil. Send me to build a strong military, and lead strong alliances, so young Americans are never put in harm's way because we needlessly insisted on going it alone. My friends, we can create an America stronger at home and respected in the world if we put aside our divisions and come together in common purpose. If we all answer the call by saying, "Send me." If we remember the words of your founder, Richard Allen, who said, "Skin may differ but ability dwells in black and white the same."[145]

His speech completed—and his visit to Indiana only coincidental to the fact that the AME church was conducting its quadrennial convention in Indianapolis—Kerry never returned to the state for his campaign. Polling showing Indiana firmly in the Bush column, the Kerry-Edwards campaign had to focus its money and time elsewhere. Indiana voters gave Bush a rousing endorsement for a second term—60 percent of the vote—to a lower than expected performance by Kerry (at 40 percent). Independent Ralph Nader was a nonfactor in Indiana, polling less than 1 percent of the vote and badly trailing even the Libertarian Party nominee. Nationally, Kerry did much better, gaining 48 percent of the popular vote, but losing several key battleground states to Bush, including Colorado, Florida, Missouri, Nevada, Ohio, and Virginia.

Barack Obama

As was the case forty years earlier in 1968, the life and death of Doctor Martin Luther King Jr. played a role in the Indiana primary campaign of 2008. While Senators Hillary Clinton and McCain went to Memphis, Tennessee, to join in observances of King's assassination on April 4, 1968, Obama stayed in Indiana and addressed students and community members during an event at Wayne High School in Fort Wayne.

"You know, Dr. King once said that the arc of the moral universe is long, but it bends toward justice," Obama told his audience. "But here's the thing—it does not bend on its own. It bends because each of us in our own ways put our hand on that arc and we bend it in the direction of justice. So on this day of all days, let us each do our part to bend that arc. Let's bend it toward justice. Let's bend it toward opportunity. Let's bend that arc toward prosperity for all."[146]

Obama's remarks came about a month after he launched his campaign in Indiana. His first major appearance in the state came in March 2008, at Plainfield High School in Hendricks County. There Obama spoke before about 3,500 supporters packed into the school's gym for twenty minutes and answered questions from the audience for another forty-five minutes. "We are going to be campaigning actively in Indiana," he said. "This is your campaign. This is your chance to make your mark on history. Right now. Right here." The focus of Obama's remarks remained similar to what he raised in other states—a responsible withdrawal of American forces from Iraq, health care reforms that included universal coverage for all Americans, and an energy plan to reduce reliance upon foreign sources. "If we don't take care of those three things, we won't be able to afford any of the other initiatives that we're talking about because we will be broke," he warned.[147]

Amidst growing chants of Obama's campaign theme—"Yes we can!"—the junior senator from Illinois directly addressed continued questions about his preparation to become the nation's leader. Only forty-six years old and a member of the Senate for only four years, Obama said he understood why some thought he should yield to Clinton and wait to run for the White House. But added, "I remind them of what Dr. King called the fierce urgency of now, because I believe there is such a thing as being too late, and that hour is almost upon us. I believe that if we can come together that there is no challenge we can't face now. There is no destiny we cannot fulfill. After having run now for 13 months . . . I am here to report that the people are ready for change."[148]

Senator Barack Obama makes a campaign stop at Plainfield High School, March 15, 2008, during his Indiana Democratic primary against Hillary Clinton.

In the days before Obama's Plainfield appearance, videos surfaced of Reverend Jeremiah Wright, pastor of Obama's home church, Trinity United Church of Christ of Chicago, delivering controversial remarks following the terrorist attacks of September 11, 2001. Obama said, "The forces of division have started to raise their ugly heads again," referring to Wright as his "former pastor," who he said had used 'incendiary words" that divided people, rather than united them.[149]

Speaking at Roosevelt High School in Gary on April 10, Obama focused his remarks on the nation's sagging economy and attempted to turn his campaign focus on the likely Republican nominee, McCain. "Under George Bush, we've seen tax cuts for the wealthiest Americans who don't need them and didn't ask for them," Obama said. "We've been giving tax breaks to companies that ship jobs overseas when we should be giving them to companies that create good jobs here at home. We've been extending a hand to Wall Street, but not lifting a finger for Main Street. And we wonder why polls show folks are more downbeat about their futures than they've been in nearly 50 years."[150]

Obama said while he respected McCain as "a worthy opponent," he reminded his audience that "he's been a staunch supporter of Washington's failed policies, and in this election he will offer more of the same policies that have set back working people. I admired Senator McCain when he stood up and said that the Bush tax cuts for the wealthiest Americans offended his 'conscience.' But he got over that, and now he's all for them, and for continuing to do the same things that have taken us toward recession. Just look at the speech he's giving today about our economy. Senator McCain is making some proposals about how to deal with our housing crisis. And I'm glad he's finally decided to offer a plan. Better late

Obama speaks at a Change We Need rally at the Indiana State Fairgrounds October 8, 2008.

than never. But don't expect any real answers. Don't expect it to actually help struggling families. Because Senator McCain's solution to the housing crisis seems a lot like the George Bush solution of sitting by and hoping it passes while families face foreclosure and watch the value of their homes erode."[151]

Obama advocated a three-point plan, extending unemployment benefits for those who had lost their jobs in recent months, immediate creation of a $10 billion "Foreclosure Prevention Fund" to help struggling homeowners, and $10 billion in relief for state and local governments hit by the housing and economic crisis. "But understand, if we're serious about strengthening our economy, we've got to invest in long-term job growth as well," Obama said. "Now, back in the 1950's, Americans were put to work building the Interstate Highway system and that helped expand the middle class in this country. We need to show the same kind of leadership today. That's why I've called for a National Infrastructure Reinvestment Bank that will invest $60 billion over 10 years and generate nearly two million new jobs—many of them in the construction industry that's suffered during this housing crisis. . . . This is the kind of help Americans need. And this is the kind of help Washington has to provide. It's time to end the Bush-McCain approach that tells the American people—'you're on your own'—because we know we're all in this together as Americans. That's what brought you here today. And that's the idea we'll restore in the White House when I'm President of the United States."[152]

The controversy surrounding Wright's remarks were not the only issues dogging Obama as he entered Indiana. In the days leading up to the Indiana campaign, Obama headlined a private fund-raiser in San Francisco in which one of the attendees audio recorded him assessing the voters he had met in Pennsylvania and other northern industrial states. "It's not surprising then they get bitter, they cling to guns or religion or antipathy to people who aren't like them or anti-immigrant sentiment or anti-trade sentiment as a way to explain their frustrations," he told his donors. His choice of words and the reaction in Indiana and elsewhere tended to underscore a concern some Democrats already had about the young Illinois senator—that he could be elitist and out of touch.[153]

During a visit to Ball State University in Muncie a few days later, Obama attempted to explain his comments to voters during a town hall meeting amidst growing national criticism—and criticism directly from Clinton. Saying he had used the wrong words to describe growing frustration among small-town citizens in Indiana and elsewhere, he explained, "I said something that everybody knows is true, which is that there are a whole bunch of folks in small towns in Pennsylvania, in towns right here in Indiana, in my hometown in Illinois, who are bitter. So I said, well, you know, when you're bitter you turn

to what you can count on. So people, they vote about guns, or they take comfort from their faith and their family and their community. Now, I didn't say it as well as I should have."[154]

Later, Obama told reporters that "the underlying truth of what I said remains, which is simply that people who have seen their way of life upended because of economic distress are frustrated and rightfully so. If I worded things in a way that made people offended, I deeply regret that."[155]

At Terre Haute, Obama explained that "people don't vote on economic issues because they don't expect anybody is going to help them. So people end up voting on issues like guns and are they are going to have the right to bear arms. They vote on issues like gay marriage. They take refuge in their faith and their community, and their family, and the things they can count on. But they don't believe they can count on Washington."[156]

Sharp jabs emerged during the Indiana portion of the campaign, mostly from the Clinton camp in the form of television ads that questioned Obama's commitment to working families and economic relief. In a town hall meeting in Anderson, Obama said, "I was convinced that the American people were tired of the politics that's all about tearing each other down. The American people were tired of spin and PR, they wanted straight talk and honesty from their elected officials. If you watched the last few weeks of the campaign [in Indiana], you'd think all politics is about negative ads and bickering and arguing, gaffes and sideline issues. There is no serious discussion about how to bring jobs back to Anderson."[157]

Obama also kept his focus on energy independence for the nation amidst skyrocketing gasoline prices that shocked most Americans,

INDIANAPOLIS STAR

Obama shakes hands with Anthony Hurt (left), Indianapolis, as he visits with booth mates John Hubler, Greenwood (white shirt), and Kelsey Bail, Indianapolis, during a breakfast stop at Four Seasons Family Restaurant in Greenwood, Indiana, on May 6, 2008.

including Hoosiers in all quarters. Speaking at an Indianapolis gas station, he said, "Everywhere I go in Indiana, and across this country, I'm talking to folks who are working harder and harder just to get by. At a time when our economy is in turmoil and wages are stagnant, hardworking families are struggling to pay rising costs, and few costs are rising more than the one folks pay at the pump. For the well-off in this country, high gas prices are mostly an annoyance, but to most Americans, they're a huge problem, bordering on a crisis. Here in Indiana, gas costs about $3.60 a gallon—and across the country, gas costs more than at any time in almost 30 years. Over the last year alone, the price of oil has shot up more than 80 percent, reaching a record high of more than $110 a barrel—all of which helps explain why the top oil companies made $123 billion last year."[158]

Obama chided decades of inaction on energy independence for the nation, calling the system in Washington "broken," where lobbyists for oil companies carried more clout than any voter. "We need a President who's looking out for families in Indiana, not just doing what's good for multinational corporations, and that's the kind of President I'll be," Obama said. He drew a contrast between himself and Clinton and McCain—whom he referred to as "the candidates with Washington experience—my opponents—[who] are good people. They mean well, but they've been in Washington a long time, and even with all that experience they talk about, nothing has happened."[159]

Obama brushed aside opportunities to take swings at Clinton, instead saying he was interested in ending the interparty battle in favor of a campaign focused on drawing contrasts with the Republicans. "I've been trying to resist [negative campaigning] in this campaign," Obama said, "and I will continue to resist it when I'm Presi-

dent of the United States. I have my differences with Senator Clinton and she has her differences with me. We will be united in November and beat John McCain and the Republicans. John McCain said he's different, but when you look at his policies he's got no agenda for you, how to make you a little more successful."[160]

At Evansville, Obama sounded a similar theme noting that "after 14 long months, it's easy to forget what this campaign's about from time to time. It's easy to get caught up in the distractions and the silliness and the tit-for-tat that consumes our politics, the bickering that none of us are entirely immune to, and it trivializes the profound issues: two wars, an economy in recession, a planet in peril, issues that confront our nation. That kind of politics is not why we are here tonight. It's not why I'm here and it's not why you're here."[161]

Later, during a town hall meeting with more than 2,000 supporters in economically ravaged Marion, Obama attempted to reach out to independent and progressive Republican voters, stressing his working relationship with Indiana's popular Republican senator, Richard G. Lugar. "Dick Lugar and I have worked together closely," Obama said, "I consider him a friend and I think he is one of the finest senators that we have." He added, "I want Republicans involved in this movement for change. I want to bring together Republicans and Democrats. I just don't like a certain kind of Republicanism that George Bush and Karl Rove, have been peddling over the last seven and a half years."[162]

Obama's campaign included several retail and direct contact events, including attending morning worship services at Saint Luke's United Methodist Church in Indianapolis on April 27, 2008, as well as stopping off for lunch at the Country Kitchen Soul Food Place at Nineteenth Street and College Avenue in Indianapolis, just a block away from the site of Robert F. Kennedy's historic April 1968 speech.

Campaigns being what they are, a few days later in northwest Indiana, Obama could not resist Clinton's jabs entirely and during a spirited speech before workers at the Munster Steel Corporation in Lake County, he had some fun at Clinton's expense and her proposal to temporarily suspend the federal tax on gasoline. He went so far as to compare her to the Bush administration and its noted strong-arm approaches to winning support for its agenda, saying, "She even borrowed one of Bush's favorite phrases. She said every member of Congress should have to tell us whether they are with us or against us."[163] Further, Obama launched his own television ads in response to the Clinton ads running in Indiana labeling her plan as "a bogus gas tax gimmick," but Obama acknowledged before an Elkhart audience that, "Look, people do need serious relief.

They are getting hammered. I mean—people who can't go on job searches because they can't fill up their gas tank. And so, what I've said is, let's accelerate the second half of a tax stimulus proposal that I have put forward that would put, immediately, hundreds of dollars into people's pockets to get through the summer."[164]

On the last Sunday of the campaign, Obama taped an interview for the NBC News program *Meet the Press* from the studios of WTHR in Indianapolis in which most of the questions posed to him concerned his relationship with his former pastor, Wright. A videotape of Wright had been widely distributed in the weeks prior depicting a sermon the pastor delivered in the days following the terrorist attacks on September 11, 2001, in which he said it was not a time for God to bless America, but a time for God to damn America. "It's important for people to understand that when I joined Trinity United Church

Democratic presidential candidate Obama speaks at the Hamilton County Family Picnic next to a shelter at Forest Park in Noblesville on May 3, 2008.

INDIANAPOLIS STAR

of Christ, I was committing not to Pastor Wright. I was committing to a church, and I was committing to Christ." In the same interview, Obama took a swipe at Clinton's previous claims that she would support a full-scale American attack to "obliterate" Iran if they were to ever attack Israel. "It's not the language we need right now," Obama said of Clinton's remarks. "I think it's reflective of George W. Bush."[165]

Later that same day, Obama and Clinton both appeared (though not simultaneously) at the Jefferson-Jackson Day Dinner sponsored by the Indiana Democratic Party and attended by more than 2,000 excited Hoosier Democrats. Preceded by remarks from Howard Dean, chairman of the Democratic National Committee calling for unity, Obama said he would confront the political bickering that had deadlocked Washington in recent years. He also emphasized his own tax relief plans as "real relief for middle-class families, seniors and homeowners; lower premiums for those who have health care and coverage for everyone who wants it; five million green jobs right here in America; a world-class education that will allow every American to reach their God-given potential and compete in this global economy. All of this is possible, but it's just a list of policies until you decide that it's time to make Washington work." Obama noted that Indiana Democrats were in a unique position to help form the party's direction for many years to come. "If you want to take another chance on the same kind of politics we've come to know in Washington, there are other candidates to choose from," Obama said. "But I still believe we need to fundamentally change Washington if we want change in America. I believe that this election is bigger than me or John McCain or Hillary Clinton. It's bigger than the Democrats versus Republicans. It's about who we are as Americans."[166]

As Obama and Clinton crisscrossed the state in search of votes, both staged final "big name" rallies in Indianapolis that drew impressive crowds. An estimated 20,000 supporters showed up for Obama's Get Out the Vote Rally at the American Legion Mall in downtown Indianapolis. Although a light rain fell on the night before the primary vote, recording artist Stevie Wonder had the crowd fired up by the time Obama arrived at about 9:30 p.m. following a lengthy nineteen-hour day of campaigning across Indiana (and North Carolina where Obama spent five hours of his day before returning to Indianapolis). As he wrapped up the downtown rally around midnight, Obama went to the factory gates at Automotive Components Holding to shake hands with third-shift workers.[167]

During his well-received remarks downtown, Obama said, "We've got to remember what unites us. I am tired of the politics of division. . . . I have told people that I understand this time, this moment to be one that would not allow us to wait. I understand what Dr. King meant when he said there are times when we are called to act because we feel the fierce urgency of now. The

Obama greets Andrea Raes (in black), who is holding her daughter, Sophia Raes, during a stop outside of the polls at Hinkle Fieldhouse on Butler University's campus, May 6, 2008.

fierce urgency of now—times when you can't afford to wait. Fifteen months ago I said this is one of those times. Our nation is involved in two wars, one we have to win against Al Qaeda terrorists and those who viciously murdered 3,000 Americans, and a second war in Iraq that I believe should never have been authorized and should never have been waged."[168]

He added:

But it wasn't just the challenges we face overseas, there is something happening in America that tells me we cannot afford to wait. Despite the fact that we had gone through an economic expansion, the average income of families in America has actually declined by $1,000. People are worse off than they were seven and a half years ago. Jobs were being shipped overseas all across America. Millions of Americans didn't have health insurance, and if you did have health insurance coverage, you were seeing your premiums and co-pays going up and up and up. It was harder to save and harder to retire, and most of all, the American people have lost faith that our government can do anything about it. . . . What we don't see is a Washington that understands the everyday struggles that people are going through. . . . I am convinced that the American people are tired of a politics that was all about tearing people down and they wanted a politics that was about lifting people up. I am convinced that the American people want honesty and truthfulness from their leaders, and they are tired of spin and PR. And most of all I am convinced that if the American people are unified, there is nothing that can stop us. Despite years of divided politics, years of blue states and red states and all the things that keep us from coming together, there is a core decency among the American people. . . . There is no reason why we cannot come together, black and white and Hispanic and Asian, young and old, rich and poor, gay and straight, if all of us can remember we are Americans first, there is nothing we cannot do, no problem we cannot solve.[169]

In the closing days of the primary, the final night rally notwithstanding, the Obama campaign mostly abandoned the large-scale rallies that drew thousands of cheering supporters in lieu of smaller, low-key events, including visits to picnics, parks, and roller-skating rinks. In addition, Obama appeared on the campaign trail not only with his wife, Michelle, but also with the couple's two young daughters, Malia and Sasha—the first time the two Obama daughters had appeared publicly as part of the campaign since the Iowa Caucuses in January. As the *Washington Post* noted, "Obama was not reaching his usual crowds of thousands in small-scale events, but campaign advisers were betting that the images would resonate more effectively with Indiana voters by showing Obama as down-to-earth and in touch with ordinary Hoosier life."[170]

Part of the retail approach Obama employed included a stop at the Four Seasons Family Restaurant in Greenwood on Primary Day. One patron of the restaurant, thirty-nine-year-old Steve Czajkowski, jokingly said Obama could seal the deal if he would pick up the check for his breakfast and the rest of his table. Senator Obama took the bait and insisted on paying the bill out of his own pocket, about $25. Czajkowski told reporters he liked Obama, but despite his kind gesture he had not won his vote. Czajkowski was a Canadian citizen and could not vote in Indiana or any other U.S. state.[171]

Obama's best effort in Indiana, however, came up just short as Clinton edged out a narrow victory among Hoosier Democrats. It was a split decision, however, as the same day Obama won a decisive victory among North Carolina Democrats. In the end he won the nomination of the Democratic Party to be its standard-bearer in 2008.

In the months that followed, as Clinton's campaign eventually folded, Obama and Clinton

Democratic presidential nominee Obama speaks at Concord High School in Elkhart, Indiana, August 6, 2008.

took leadership positions in bringing the highly divided Democratic Party back together as a united front to take back the White House. In the summer months prior to the August 2008 Democratic National Convention in Denver, speculation grew about a potential running mate for Obama—a list that included Clinton and several others, including Bayh (although he had been a primary supporter of Clinton instead of Obama). Further fueling the speculation that Bayh was under consideration was a July 16, 2008, joint appearance between the two men (along with former U.S. senator Sam Nunn of Georgia) at Purdue University in West Lafayette to discuss national security issues.

Making frequent references to the congressional review commission that examined (and exposed) national security threats existing prior to the terrorist attacks of September 11, 2001, Obama said, "It's time to update our national security strategy to stay one step ahead of the terrorists—to see clearly the emerging threats of our young century, and to take action to make the American people more safe and secure." He continued, "It's time to look ahead—at the dangers of today and tomorrow rather than those of yesterday. America cannot afford another president who doesn't understand the threats that confront us now and in the future. Today, we will focus on nuclear, biological, and cyber threats—three twenty-first century threats that have been neglected for the last eight years. It's time to break out of Washington's conventional thinking that has failed to keep pace with unconventional threats. In doing so, we'll better ensure the safety of the American people, while building our capacity to deal with other challenges—from public health to privacy."[172]

Outlining his proposals for continued nuclear nonproliferation efforts with Russia, comprehensive efforts to tackle bioterrorism, and creation of a national "cyber adviser" to help protect the nation's technological infrastructure, he said, "To protect our national security, I'll bring together government, industry, and academia to determine the best ways to guard the infrastructure that supports our power." He added:

> Fortunately, right here at Purdue we have one of the country's leading cyber programs. We need to prevent terrorists or spies from hacking into our national security networks. We need to build the capacity to identify, isolate, and respond to any cyber-attack. And we need to develop new standards for the cyber security that protects our most important infrastructure—from electrical grids to sewage systems; from air traffic control to our markets. All of this will demand the greatest resource that America has—our people. In the Cold War, we didn't defeat the Soviets just because of the strength of our arms—we also did it because at the dawn of the atomic age and the onset of the space race, the smartest scientists and most innovative workforce was here in America.[173]

While political observers wrote off Obama's appearance at Purdue University in the weeks before the Democratic convention as more of an effort to "vet" Bayh and to emphasize foreign policy issues, Obama was back in Indiana on August 6 to host a town hall meeting at Concord High School in economically ravaged Elkhart County. Obama was clear in stating what he thought was at stake:

> We meet at a moment when this country is facing a set of challenges unlike any we've ever known. Right now, our brave men and women in uniform are fighting two differ-

ent wars while terrorists plot their next attack. Our changing climate is putting our planet in peril and our security at risk. And our economy is in turmoil, with more and more of our families struggling with rising costs, falling incomes, and lost jobs. So we know that this election could be the most important of our lifetime. We know that the choices we make in November and over the next few years will shape the next decade, if not the century. And central to each of these challenges is the question of what we will do about our addiction to foreign oil. Without a doubt, this addiction is one of the most urgent threats we've ever faced—from the gas prices that are wiping out your paychecks and straining businesses, to the jobs that are disappearing from this state; from the instability and terror bred in the Middle East, to the rising oceans, record drought, and spreading famine that could engulf our planet.[174]

Obama's Elkhart speech captured well his fall strategy, offering not only a laser-like focus on the nation's economic woes, but also a reminder that electing McCain was in most respects the equivalent of a third term for the nation's unpopular incumbent president, Bush. Reflecting the weariness and confusion many Hoosiers felt as the "recovery" from the latest recession limped along, Obama gave voice to the feelings: "How, exactly, did we get to this point? Well, you won't hear me say this too often, but I couldn't agree more with the explanation that Senator McCain offered a few weeks ago. He said, 'Our dangerous dependence on foreign oil has been 30 years in the making, and was caused by the failure of politicians in Washington to think long-term about the future of the country.' What Senator McCain neglected to mention was that during those thirty years, he was in Washington for 26 of them! Now, yesterday, Senator McCain started running a TV ad saying that Washington is broken. No kidding! It only took Senator McCain those 26 years in Washington to figure that out."[175]

Turning more serious, Obama said, "But here's the thing, Elkhart. I'm having a little trouble squaring that statement with Senator McCain's declaration a few months ago that we've made 'great progress economically' over the past eight years. Or his boast that he's voted with President Bush over 90 percent of the time. Or his assertion that overall, the American people are better off now than they were when George W. Bush came into office. You know from your own lives that we're not better off than we were eight years ago."[176]

Citing statistics that eight years ago a gallon of gasoline cost about $1.80 and was costing closer to $4 a gallon in 2008, he also lamented rising electric and heating oil costs faced by Indiana residents. "This didn't happen by accident," Obama said. "It happened because for too long, we haven't had a real energy plan in this country. We've had an oil company plan. We've had a gas company plan. But we haven't had a plan that made sense for the American people. So if Senator McCain wants to talk about why Washington is broken, that's a debate I'm happy to have. Because Senator McCain's energy plan reads like an early Christmas list for oil and gas lobbyists. And it's no wonder—because many of

Obama shakes hands with the crowds after his speech at Concord High School.

his top advisers are former oil and gas lobbyists. Instead of offering a plan with significant investments in alternative energy, he's offering a gas tax gimmick that will pad oil company profits and save you—at most—a quarter and a nickel a day over the course of an entire summer. That's why Washington is broken."[177]

By October, the hoped-for return of Indiana voters to the Republican fold was not occurring. Statewide polls showed that Obama continued to be at least tied, if not leading, McCain among all Hoosier voters. Few believed Obama had a real shot at winning the state—something only Franklin D. Roosevelt and Lyndon B. Johnson had ever done in nearly a century of trying by Democratic hopefuls. Undeterred, Obama was back in October for a rally at the Indiana State Fairgrounds during the same week the McCain and GOP campaigns took the rare step of airing television ads in Indiana (resources normally saved for other battleground states).

Obama's October 8 rally drew more than 10,000 supporters to the grandstand at the Indiana State Fairgrounds—a site Roosevelt had spoken from in 1932—a day after a televised debate with McCain. Obama told his audience that "we meet today at a moment of great uncertainty for America." He added, "In last night's debate, John McCain and I each had the chance to make the case for change—to talk about what we would do differently from the last eight years when it comes to lifting our middle-class, growing our economy, and restoring our prosperity. But all we heard from Senator McCain was more of the same Bush economics that led us to this point."[178]

Obama noted the continued drop in the stock market as news of the financial crisis involving home mortgage lenders continued to grow and action by the Federal Reserve "to stem what is now a full-blown global financial crisis. I support that action, as I've said before that this is a global problem and it needs to be solved through a global effort. I hope this global response continues as leaders of major financial institutions and representatives from nations around the world gather in Washington soon."[179]

Obama continued:

We are facing a very serious challenge, and all of us—all of us—have a stake in its solution. Because the credit markets are frozen right now, there's a ripple effect throughout our economy. Businesses large and small are finding it impossible to get loans, which means they can't buy new equipment or make payroll. Auto plants that have been around for decades are closing their doors and laying off workers who've never known another job in their entire life. And we have already lost three-quarters of a million jobs just this year. Here in Indianapolis and all across America, you're seeing your hours get cut or realizing that you can't pay every bill that's sitting on the kitchen counter. It's harder to make the mortgage or fill up your gas tank and some people don't even know whether they'll be able to keep the electricity on at the end of the month. The money you've been putting away for your retirement or your kids' college education is disappearing faster than you can count. The dream that so many generations have fought for feels like it's slowly slipping away.[180]

But as was his normal approach, after setting up in stark detail the woes facing the nation, Obama struck a chord of hope. "I am here today to tell you that there are better days ahead," he said. "I know these are tough times. I know that many of you are anxious about the future. But this isn't a time for fear or panic. This is a time for resolve and leadership. I know that we can steer ourselves out of this crisis. Because that's who we are. Because this is the United States of America. This is a nation that has faced down

war and depression; great challenges and great threats. And at each and every moment, we have risen to meet these challenges—not as Democrats, not as Republicans, but as Americans. With resolve. With confidence. With that fundamental belief that here in America, our destiny is not written for us, but by us. That's who we are, and that's the country we need to be right now."[181]

On October 23 Obama returned to American Legion Mall in downtown Indianapolis for another massive rally just days before Election Day. In his opening remarks, the Illinois senator noted the significance of the date and the location: "It is fitting that we meet today on the mall of the American Legion, surrounded by monuments to our nation's heroes. Because on this day, 25 years ago, the Marine barracks in Beirut were bombed; 241 Americans laid down their lives for this country and for the peace they were there to protect. We revere their service. We honor their sacrifice. And we keep their families in our prayers. We will never forget them."[182]

Turning quickly to the issue at hand, Obama reminded Hoosiers that in just twelve short days the change many of them had hoped for was at hand, "but we know that change never comes without a fight. In the final days of campaigns, anything, do-anything politics often takes over. We've seen it before, and we're going to see it again, the ugly phone calls, the misleading mail and TV ads, the careless and outrageous comments, all aimed at keeping us from working together, all aimed at stopping change. Well, what we need now is not misleading charges and divisive attacks. What we need is honest leadership and real change, and that's why I'm running for President of the United States."[183]

Obama took pains to remind voters that McCain had voted with Bush's agenda 90 percent of the time and defended Bush's "lavish tax cuts" for corporations and America's top earners. "It's true that I want to roll back the Bush tax cuts on the wealthiest Americans and go back to the rate they paid under Bill Clinton," Obama said. "John McCain calls that socialism. What he forgets is that just a few years ago, he himself said those Bush tax cuts were irresponsible. He said he couldn't 'in good conscience' support a tax cut where the benefits went to the wealthy at the expense of 'middle class Americans who most need tax relief.' Well, he was right then, and I am right now. Let me be crystal clear: If you make less than a quarter of a million dollars a year—which includes 98 percent of small business owners—you won't see your taxes increase one single dime. Not your payroll taxes, not your income taxes, not your capital gains taxes—nothing. That is my commitment to you. For the last eight years, we've given more and more to those with the most and hoped that prosperity would trickle down to everyone else. And guess what? It didn't. So it's time to try something new. It's time to grow this economy from the bottom-up. It's time to invest in the middle-class again."[184]

Convinced an Indiana victory was within reach, after voting along with Michelle in his Hyde Park neighborhood in Chicago, Obama took a quick flight to Indianapolis for one last pitch for votes. While there he stopped in at UAW Local 550 operating a get-out-the-vote phone bank on the city's southwest side. Obama helped make a few calls, having to convince at least one woman that yes, it was Barack Obama personally calling her and asking for her vote. To reporters, Obama said, "It's going to be tight as a tick here in Indiana. I think we can win Indiana, otherwise I wouldn't be in Indiana."[185]

Obama's assessment was spot on—in the final tally he won an incredibly close race in the Hoosier State, polling 49.95 percent of the vote to 48.91 percent for McCain. In becoming only the third Democrat to win an Indiana contest in a century of trying, his Indiana win was the third closest in the nation along with North Carolina (where he also won).

Hillary Clinton

The students of Mishawaka High School found themselves in a lucky position on March 28, 2008, after South Bend school district officials nixed a request by Clinton's presidential campaign to hold an open rally at one of their high schools. Viewing the request as too political, South Bend officials said no, but Mishawaka said yes. Clinton's speech at the Mishawaka High School gymnasium was a strong signal that Indiana's normally uneventful May primary was set to be an actual contest—and one that Clinton needed to win. In addition to Mishawaka, Clinton scheduled stops at Hammond, Fort Wayne, Muncie, Indianapolis, and New Albany during a two-day swing meant to boost her chances against the surging campaign of Senator Obama, who had already opened the door in Indiana with a mid-March appearance at Plainfield in Hendricks County.

Clinton had entered 2008 as the odds-on favorite among Democrats for the party's nomination, and, as she had elsewhere, had lined up significant support among key Democrats in Indiana, led by Senator Bayh. Several of the state's "super delegates" were also pledged Clinton's way. But as Obama continued to make headway, that would change. Former governor Joe Kernan, a popular figure among Saint Joseph County voters, introduced Clinton to her Mishawaka audience by noting that "this is the first time in 40 years that Indiana has had a say in determining our presidential nominee. We have to take that responsibility very seriously." Clinton took it seri-

INDIANAPOLIS STAR

On March 20, 2008, Democratic presidential candidate Hillary Clinton, joined by Senator Evan Bayh, visited downtown Terre Haute, Indiana, for a "Solutions for America" event.

ously—her campaign made more than seventy-five separate appearances across the state, splitting up the duties between herself, her husband, and the former first daughter, Chelsea.

The theme of Clinton's opening Mishawaka rally was "Solutions for the American Economy," in which she emphasized that her campaign was "about the middle class and what kind of changes we're going to provide so people can make the most of your God-given potential and your ability and your willingness to work hard." Her speech recognized the diverse nature of the state's economy, its emphasis on manufacturing and its long-standing position as an agricultural leader. Praising Hoosiers for being among "the hardest workers in the world," she said Indiana "factories and farms really keep this nation going and help prepare for our national defense." She said, "I don't see a rust belt. I see the potential to build a 21st century manufacturing belt, an innovation belt, an opportunity belt that will encircle our country. Let's close the tax loophole for companies that outsource jobs out of Indiana to another country."[186]

Repeating themes she made during her Hammond appearance, Clinton said tax loopholes allowed certain companies to avoid paying $15 billion in corporate taxes and encouraged outsourcing jobs. "If we had a manufacturing agenda," she said, "we could also create and keep more jobs in Indiana's steel industry. Indiana's steel is not only critical for your jobs and the economy of this state, but for America's economy and for our national security. We cannot be dependent on other countries for the steel we need to produce the Humvees and other kinds of defense materials."[187] Clinton's reference to the Humvee, the military's replacement for the venerable Jeep, was no accident. AM General in Mishawaka held large federal contracts to produce the vehicle.

For an April 12, 2008, campaign speech before an enthusiastic audience at Allison Transmission in Indianapolis, Clinton reminded her audience of her midwestern roots—born and raised in next-door Illinois—and her "unshaken faith in America and its promise." She took special aim at comments attributed to Obama about the alleged bitterness of Americans in small towns across the midwestern rust belt. "Like some of you may have been," she said, "I was taken aback by the demeaning remarks Senator Obama made about people in small town America. Senator Obama's remarks are elitist and they are out of touch. They are not reflective of the values and beliefs of Americans, certainly not the Americans I know—not the Americans I grew up with, not the Americans I lived with in Arkansas, or represent in New York."[188]

Knowing that polling showed many Indiana voters viewed Obama as an elitist and a foe to gun rights, and spotting an opening to draw in southern Indiana and more conservative Democrats, Clinton also addressed her belief in the Second Amendment "as a matter of Constitutional rights" and "Americans who believe in God believe it is a matter of personal faith. Americans who believe in protecting good American jobs believe it is a matter of the American dream. When my dad grew up, it was in a working class family in Scranton. I grew up in a church-going family, a family that believed in the importance of living and expressing our faith." She said, "People don't need a President who looks down on them; they need a President who stands up for them."[189]

Driving home her point, Clinton added, "The people of faith I know don't 'cling to' religion because they're bitter. People embrace faith not because they are materially poor, but because they are spiritually rich. Our faith is the faith of

INDIANAPOLIS STAR

Clinton speaks at a town hall event at the Wigwam in Anderson, Indiana, on March 20, 2008, as part of a three-community swing through the state that also saw her visit Terre Haute and Evansville.

our parents and our grandparents. It is a fundamental expression of who we are and what we believe. I also disagree with Senator Obama's assertion that people in this country 'cling to guns' and have certain attitudes about immigration or trade simply out of frustration." She said Hoosiers were "fair-minded and good-hearted people" who face their challenges and problems with faith and added, "Americans out across our country have borne the brunt of the Bush administration's assault on the middle class. Contrary to what Senator Obama says, most Americans did much better during the Clinton years than they have done during the Bush years."[190]

During the same weekend in which she championed gun rights and took on the "elitist" nature of Obama's remarks about "bitter Americans," Clinton joined Hammond Mayor Thomas McDermott in throwing back a shot of whiskey and hoisting a mug of beer—a true "Boilermaker"—during a meet-and-greet event at

Bronko's Restaurant in Crown Point. Obama was having none of it, in a rare off-the-cuff moment, telling reporters that "she's running around talking about [how his comments were] an insult to sportsmen, how she values the Second Amendment, she's talking like she's Annie Oakley! Hillary Clinton's out there like she's on the duck blind every Sunday, she's packin' a six shooter! C'mon! She knows better. That's some politics being played by Hillary Clinton. I want to see that picture of her out there in the duck blinds. Shame on her, she knows better."[191]

During an appearance at Terre Haute, Obama drew heavy applause when he denied he was out of touch and elitist. "I know exactly what's going on in Pennsylvania, I know what's going on in Indiana. I know what's going on in Illinois. People are fed up, they're angry, they're frustrated, they're bitter and they want to see a chance in Washington. That's why I'm running for President of the United States of America."[192]

Later in April, as polling continued to show Clinton and Obama neck-and-neck with Indiana voters and Clinton's campaign in desperate need of a victory, a new debate proposal was offered by Clinton. During an appearance at Stanley Coveleski Baseball Stadium in South Bend, Clinton said she favored a new series of Abraham Lincoln/Stephen Douglas style debates between herself and Obama: "Just the two of us, going for 90 minutes, asking and answering questions, we'll set whatever rules seem fair."[193] It was an offer Obama's campaign was not interested in, his spokesman noting that Clinton and Obama had already appeared together twenty-one times during the 2008 primary season. In Jeffersonville, Clinton added the extra note that perhaps she and Obama should meet atop a flatbed truck in front of Hoosiers and debate openly for the votes to be cast.

A *New York Times* political reporter followed Clinton as she raced across Indiana—more than seventy separate appearances in 2008—from Portage near the shores of Lake Michigan to Jef-fersonville along the banks of the Ohio River and noted that "she is waving her fists across Indiana, signing autographs on boxing gloves" and declaring that "we need a President who is a fighter again," a president "who understands what it is like to get knocked down and get back up; that's the story of America."[194] While noting Clinton's fighting spirit and some inside criticism that her campaign had grown "ruthless" in its desire to catch Obama, the *Times* noted a certain emerging edge in the Clinton rhetoric as key Indiana endorsements for Clinton slipped away. Representative Baron Hill and former Democratic National Committee Chair Joe Andrew—two Hoosier "Super Delegates"—defected from Clinton to Obama in the late going in Indiana. "While Mrs. Clinton is casting herself as a warrior for ordinary Americans who need jobs, health care and cheaper gasoline, she is also establishing a contrast with her opponent," the *Times* analyzed, "suggesting he is an untested lightweight. She mocks Mr. Obama's rhetoric as naïve and challenges him to debate her on the back of a flat-bed truck."[195]

INDIANAPOLIS STAR

Former Indiana lieutenant governor Kathy Davis (right) applauds Clinton on the stage set up on the Ben Davis High School gymnasium floor in Indianapolis on March 29, 2008, for Clinton's "Solutions for the American Economy" town hall.

Clinton told reporters she was aware that the grit and determination she was demonstrating could be mistaken for ruthlessness and that her aggressive style was intended to contrast with the "cooler" approach Obama employed. She said Obama's campaign "has been about creating an atmosphere" and added, "I've never understood that, because it's not easy. I've been in a lot of these fights."[196]

In the waning days of the campaign, Clinton kept Bayh close at her side and hammered away on themes of reviving the nation's industrial economy. "We can do that again," she said, "but we need, as Senator Bayh said, a president who doesn't just talk about it but who actually rolls up her sleeves and gets to work."[197] Accompanying Clinton's speech rhetoric were a barrage of new TV ads broadcast across the state that drew stark contrasts between her positions and those of Obama and asked, "What has happened to Barack Obama?" and that "Hillary wants the oil companies to pay for the gas tax this summer—so you don't have to. Barack Obama wants you to keep paying, $8 billion in all. Hillary is the one who gets it."[198]

Appearing at a fire station in Merrillville, Clinton told a small crowd that "I do see you, I do hear you" and repeated her call for a gas tax holiday. "There is a big difference between us," Clinton said hours later in Fort Wayne, "and the question is: Who understands what you're going through and who do you count on being on your side? I believe I have what it takes to stand up and fight for you when you need a President on your side."[199]

During an appearance on the ABC News program *This Week with George Stephanopoulos*, originating from the Conrad Hotel in Indianapolis (an appearance Obama's campaign skipped), Clinton defended her gas tax proposal against claims by Obama that it was a gimmick. "I'm not going

Clinton shakes hands with Brent Miller of Indianapolis as she enters the gymnasium at Ben Davis High School for her town hall event on March 29, 2008.

to put my lot in with economists," Clinton said. "When the federal government, through the Fed and the Treasury, gave $30 billion in a bailout to Bear Stearns, I didn't hear anybody jump in and say, 'That's not going according to the market, that's rewarding irresponsible behavior.'"[200] She added, "We have to get out of the mind-set where, somehow, elite opinion is always on the side of doing things that really disadvantage the vast majority of Americans."[201]

Hours later at the annual Jefferson-Jackson Day Dinner at the Marriott Hotel in Indianapolis, Clinton told Hoosier Democrats that "there's one thing you know about me. I am no shrinking violet. I may get knocked down. But I will always get right back up, and I will never quit until the job is finished. All we need is a president who will seize this moment, lift this nation and lead this world, a president who will go into the Oval Office on January 20, 2009, and roll up her sleeves and get to work."[202]

The Clinton campaign, in short, was all-encompassing expending as much energy and effort before a crowd of about 1,000 at the Gibson County Courthouse in Princeton (the county's first presidential campaign visit in almost fifty years), as in a star-studded concert event at White River State Park in Indianapolis featuring John Mellencamp, Academy Award-winning actor Susan Sarandon, Emmy-Award winning actor Ted Danson, *Rudy* star Sean Astin, and actor/director Rob Reiner. At Princeton, Clinton found surprising support for her call to "bring home" the funds being used to support two wars in Iraq and Afghanistan. "We have to end the war in Iraq, and win the war in Afghanistan," she said, "and as we end these wars and bring our troops home, we have to take care of them. We are not taking care of our veterans. They're not getting the health care and the compensation and the services they deserve."[203]

Upon claiming a narrow and late-reported victory over Obama on May 6, 2008, Clinton took to the stage at the Murat Centre in Indianapolis before a roaring group of supporters and a national television audience to declare "Thank you, Indiana! Thank you! Not too long ago, my opponent made a prediction. He said I would probably win Pennsylvania. He would win North Carolina, and Indiana would be the tie-breaker. Well, tonight we've come from behind, we've broken the tie, and thanks to you, it's full speed on to the White House."[204]

Clinton said campaigning across Indiana has been "an extraordinary experience" and praised meeting thousands of Hoosiers seeking change. She said her campaign had been directed at "everyone who holds your breath at the gas pump, afraid to see how much it will cost today, and for everyone working day and night because you want the world for your kids. For every young person with big dreams who deserves a world of opportunity, and for all those who aren't in the headlines but have always written America's story, tonight is your victory, right here."[205]

Taking a moment to acknowledge Obama's victory in the day's other primary—in North Carolina and the historic nature of a campaign coming down to a choice between a female candidate and an African American candidate—she said, "We are, in many ways, on the same journey. It's a journey begun before we were born. It is a journey of men and women who have been on a mission to perfect our union, who marched and protested, who risked everything they had to build an America that embraces us all."[206]

Invoking the memory of her father who served in World War II and built his own business in suburban Park Ridge, Illinois, and her mother who never had a chance to attend college, Clinton said she had met many Hoosiers who felt invisible to the political leaders of America:

> You feel invisible when the money you took to the grocery store no longer meets your needs for the next week. You feel invisible when your health insurance disappears and college is out of reach. And you can't believe how invisible you feel when your loved one who served our country in war is ill-served back at home. I know these stories and I see you and I hear you. And I know how hard you're working, working for yourselves and your families. And I will never stop fighting for you, so that you can have the future you deserve. Tonight, Hoosiers have said that you want a president who stands strong for you, a President who is ready on day one to take charge as Commander-in-Chief and keeps our families safe, a President who knows how to make this economy work for hardworking middle-class families.[207]

While Clinton's Indiana victory was significant, it ultimately served only to resuscitate her campaign for a few more weeks. Obama gathered enough delegates to claim the Democratic nomination following the South Dakota and Montana primaries on June 3, 2008. Four days later, Clinton stood before a standing-room-only audience in Washington, D.C. and officially ended her campaign and conceded the nomination to Obama. She said:

> Well, this isn't exactly the party I'd planned, but I sure like the company. I want to start today by saying how grateful I am to all of you—to everyone who poured your hearts and your hopes into this campaign, who drove for miles and lined the streets waving homemade signs, who scrimped and saved to raise money, who knocked on doors and made calls, who talked and sometimes argued with your friends and neighbors, who emailed and contributed online, who invested so much in our common enterprise, to the moms and dads who came to our events, who lifted their little girls and little boys on their shoulders and whispered in their ears, "See, you can be anything you want to be."[208]

She added, "To all those who voted for me, and to whom I pledged my utmost, my commitment to you and to the progress we seek is unyielding. You have inspired and touched me with the stories of the joys and sorrows that make up the fabric of our lives and you have humbled me with your commitment to our country—eighteen million of you from all walks of life—women and men, young and old, Latino and Asian, African American and Caucasian, rich, poor and middle class, gay and straight—you have stood strong with me. And I will continue to stand strong with you, every time, every place, and every way that I can. The dreams we share are worth fighting for."[209]

In gracious endorsement remarks for her opponent, Clinton praised Senator Obama and

INDIANAPOLIS STAR

Questioned at a town hall event at the Wigwam in Anderson about being Clinton's vice presidential running mate, Bayh quipped that it had been the first time he had been linked to "vice."

directed her supporters that "the way to continue our fight now—to accomplish the goals for which we stand—is to take our energy, our passion, our strength and do all we can to help elect Barack Obama the next President of the United States." She added:

> Today, as I suspend my campaign, I congratulate him on the victory he has won and the extraordinary race he has run. I endorse him, and throw my full support behind him. And I ask all of you to join me in working as hard for Barack Obama as you have for me. I have served in the Senate with him for four years. I have been in this campaign with him for 16 months. I have stood on the stage and gone toe-to-toe with him in 22 debates. I have had a front row seat to his candidacy, and I have seen his strength and determination, his grace and his grit. In his own life, Barack Obama has lived the American Dream. As a community organizer, in the state senate, as a United States Senator—he has dedicated himself to ensuring the dream is realized. And in this campaign, he has inspired so many to become involved in the democratic progress and invested in our common future. . . . I understand that we all know this has been a tough fight. The Democratic Party is a family, and it's now time to restore the ties that bind us together and to come together around the ideals we share, the values we cherish, and the country we love.[210]

The line best remembered and repeated from Clinton's gracious remarks concluded, "Although we weren't able to shatter that highest, hardest glass ceiling this time, thanks to you, it's got about 18 million cracks in it. And the light is shining through like never before, filling us all with the hope and the sure knowledge that the path will be a little easier next time. That has always been the history of progress in America."[211]

In the weeks that followed, Clinton and Obama met privately to discuss the way forward and in late June appeared together in the tiny

Clinton meets with workers at Allison Transmission in Indianapolis, April 12, 2008.

village of Unity, New Hampshire, where both of the candidates had received 107 votes in the early primary there. Emphasizing the unity that it would take for the Democrats to retake the White House, Clinton endured additional weeks of questions about whether she would accept nomination as Obama's running mate, but ultimately was not named to the ticket, but remained true to her commitment, and she and her husband, former president Bill Clinton, campaigned hard for Obama's fall effort.

Bill Clinton/Chelsea Clinton

Former president Clinton's role in his wife's primary campaign in 2008 found him on the back roads and in the smaller towns of Indiana, something that did not go unnoticed by reporters.

For an early April swing a full month before the state's Democratic Primary, Clinton made his third trek through the state with visits to Columbus and Seymour. His schedule reflected the Clinton strategy of emphasizing pitches among southern Indiana Democrats, and those in the working-class manufacturing centers of the state. On March 23, 2008 at Logansport, the ex-president spoke before a surprisingly small audience of only 500 listeners. "You need to vote for somebody that's not going to forget what you look like tonight," he said. "You need to remember that the only thing you are, for a brief moment in time, is the most fortunate public servant on the face of the earth. If you forget that, the consequences can be devastating. All you need to do is look at [President George W.] Bush's second term."[212]

Speaking directly of why he thought his wife would make a good president, he said, "I've never met anybody as good as she is at looking at a problem and making it better for other people. She has certainly been tested. If you ever doubted she has the courage and grit to be president, you know it now. She's been in the public spotlight for 15 years, and taken all the criticism. They don't have anything else to say to her." Before he arrived at Logansport, Clinton made earlier stops in South Bend, Rochester, and Lafayette. He was doing so, he said, because "in a very real sense, Indiana may hold the fate of this country in its hands."[213] Clinton said his wife "has her heart in the right place" and that when they discussed together the idea of her running for president, he said he asked her "How will you know you did a good job if you're president?' She said, 'I think I will have done a good job if the American people are better off when I quit than when I started, and the nation is coming together instead of being torn apart.'"[214]

Focusing on his wife's proposal to declare a moratorium on mortgage foreclosures faced by as many as two million homeowners, the former president alleged that mortgage lenders engaged in practices that were more regulated—and even prohibited—by regular banks. Failing subprime mortgage markets found these same lenders ruthlessly raising the payments on variable interest rates. "All people think about when they take out a mortgage is simple: Can I make the month-

ly payment?" Clinton said. "Nobody told them they would have their mortgage basically put on a roulette wheel. You need somebody who understands this. The foreclosure rate is the highest its been in 40 years. And if housing prices drop another 15 percent, a third of all Americans have more in their houses than they're worth. This is a serious problem."[215]

Clinton said, "We all know why: Incomes are flat and costs are exploding. What caused this was the trickle-down economy, a failed economic theory . . . the reason we study history is that we don't want to make the same mistake twice. Well, in this case, we've already made the same mistake twice, so we don't want to make it a third time. . . . You cannot increase incomes unless we create jobs and tighten the labor market, and the best way to grow jobs is to make a serious commitment to energy independence."[216] Concluding his remarks with a strong appeal for Indiana Democrats to support his wife's candidacy, Clinton said, "I believe if she's elected president, and she can implement her plans on energy, jobs, health care, rebuilding the military and bringing our soldiers home, this country will have more prosperity, more broadly shared, than when I was President. Say yes to her, and say yes to your future."[217]

In early April Clinton brought along Chelsea for a series of appearances in South Bend and Mishawaka for the annual Dyngus Day celebrations. Also on hand was Kathleen Kennedy Townsend, daughter of slain Robert F. Kennedy. Downing a few beers and Polish sausages at the West Side Democratic Club in South Bend, Clinton urged Democrats to embrace his wife's candidacy for the future.[218]

Clinton's 2008 effort on behalf of his wife proved once again he was a tireless and effective campaigner and also opened up dozens of

Indiana communities to a rare treat—access to a former president of the United States. Among the communities he visited were Angola, Avon, Bedford, Beech Grove, Bloomington, Boonville, Clinton, Columbia City, Columbus, Corydon, Decatur, Greencastle, Greenfield, Hartford City, Indianapolis, Jasper, Kendallville, La Porte, Lawrenceburg, Lebanon, Logansport, Marion, Martinsville, New Castle, Plymouth, Richmond, Rochester, Seymour, Shelbyville, South Bend, Vincennes, Warsaw, and West Lafayette.

Chelsea's efforts were equally impressive and sent her to even smaller Indiana communities and college campuses, some of them, such as Goshen, deep in traditionally Republican territory. At Goshen College, an interesting exchange unfolded as a local Amish man stood and asked Chelsea questions about family values, as did Spanish-speaking members of the community's growing Latino community who spoke through a Clinton campaign volunteer serving as a translator. Chelsea said, "I believe my mother is the strongest candidate on every issue that is important to me." The former First Daughter, who was twenty-eight years old in 2008 and already a graduate of both Stanford University and the University of Oxford, was remembered by most Americans as a little girl during her father's tenure in the White House who had been shielded from any significant media coverage. In 2008 it was clear she was all grown up and an effective campaigner for her mother, addressing issues of energy, corporate tax breaks for oil companies, universal health care, child care costs, and unemployment. She also was questioned about deportation policies that affected the nation's burgeoning Latino population. "My mom supports comprehensive immigration reform," Chelsea said, emphasizing that her mother supported clamping down on employers who exploit undoc-

umented laborers and stronger border control to eliminate illegal entry into the nation.[219]

While Chelsea's Goshen College appearance provided an interesting contrast between the varied cultures of Indiana, her appearance at Butler University made national headlines. Surprisingly, perhaps, she had been active on the campaign trail but had yet to be asked any personal questions regarding the extramarital affair that rocked her father's administration and prompted an unsuccessful effort to impeach him. Evan Strange, a student reporter for the *Butler Collegian*, asked Chelsea her opinion "on the criticism of her mother how she handled the [Monica] Lewinsky scandal" and that "it might be a sign of weakness and she might not be a strong enough candidate to be President."[220]

Reporters described Chelsea's response as a "stinging rebuke" and quoted her as addressing Strange: "Wow, you're the first person actually that's ever asked me that question in the, I don't know, maybe 70 college campuses I've now been to, and I do not think that is any of your business." Strange later defended his question and told national reporters, who quickly jumped on the controversy, that he was a supporter of Hillary Clinton and that Chelsea had missed an opportunity to highlight her mother's personal strength.[221]

John McCain

As the 2008 race for the Republican presidential nomination approached and with George W. Bush ineligible to run for a third term, Vice President Cheney's personal health continuing to be in question, and Secretary of State Condoleezza Rice ruling out a run, the GOP field quickly filled with hopefuls. The leader among moderates was Senator McCain of Arizona, who had staged a challenge to Bush for the nomination in 2000, and among many party leaders, was the next in line for the nomination. McCain's moderate views on certain issues (as expressed during his lengthy Senate career), including immigration, meant there was considerable room for more conservative Republicans to see paths to the nomination. The field quickly filled up with former Arkansas governor Mike Huckabee, former Massachusetts governor Mitt Romney, Congressman Ron Paul of Texas, former senator Fred Thompson of Tennessee, former ambassador Alan Keyes, and former New York City mayor Rudolph Giuliani.

The nomination calendar for 2008 favored well-financed and well-organized candidates such as McCain, with eight caucus and primary contests getting under way in January, the first on January 3 in Iowa (won by Huckabee with Romney a close second). McCain focused his effort on New Hampshire, South Carolina, and Florida and won all three contests, the latter of which essentially ended Giuliani's effort as he staked his hopes on stopping McCain in Florida. Twenty-one contests were held on Super Tuesday on February 5, with McCain carrying nine contests (including the big prize of California), while Romney won seven contests and Huckabee five. By March 4 McCain had the nomination sewed up and the party began closing in behind his now eventual nomination. Regardless of McCain's strong showing, however, the Republican primaries were quickly overshadowed by the historic and ongoing battle among Democrats to name their nominee—a race that included for the first time in history a woman and an African American as the prime two contenders.

For his primary effort in Indiana, McCain had to expend little effort. By the time of the Indiana vote on May 6, the contest was decided and the Arizona senator ran up 78 percent of the vote. On February 22 McCain led a town hall meeting inside the corporate headquarters of the Emmis Communications Corporation at Monument Circle in Indianapolis. Only two hundred people were admitted to the town hall (another hundred were turned away), and McCain's event seemed aimed at convincing doubting Republicans of his conservative credentials. McCain fielded questions on his positions regarding health care, immigration, the war in Iraq, abortion rights, and veterans' affairs. One local Coast Guard veteran drew applause from the assembled when he said he was "infuriated" by attacks on McCain and his distinguished military career. During the event McCain took pains to identify himself as "a conservative Republican" and affirmed Bush's appointment of John Roberts, an Indiana native, to be chief justice of the Supreme Court. Acknowledging "difficult times" in the U.S. economy, McCain said, "We need to have tax cuts so that people will be able to keep and invest more of their money."[222]

McCain's Indianapolis event mostly gained attention because as he arrived in the city he was asked to defend his use of Washington lobbyists as campaign advisers. McCain had come under fire for the use of lobbyists because of his long-standing record as a "reform" candidate who sought to reduce the influence of special interests in politics. Further, reports by the *Washington Post* and the *New York Times* suggested that McCain's senior campaign team was made up of lobbyists, including one female lobbyist who may have worked to advance the interests of her clients via her access to the senator. Asked how he squared such realities with his reputation, he said, "I square it one way, the right to represent interests or groups of Americans is a constitutional right. There are people that represent firemen, civil servants, retirees, and those people are legitimate representatives of a variety of interests in America."[223]

"These people have honorable records, and they're honorable people, and I'm proud to have them as part of my team," McCain said when questioned by reporters as he left his Indianapolis event.[224] Turning his focus to the Democrats, McCain attempted to change the subject by questioning a statement by Obama during a Democratic debate in which he said he would meet with Cuba's new president, Raul Castro, the brother of Cuba's Communist revolutionary leader, Fidel Castro. "Meet, talk and hope may be a sound approach in a state legislature," McCain said, "but it is dangerously naïve in international diplomacy where the oppressed look to America for hope and adversaries wish us ill."[225] McCain's remark was well crafted to remind voters that Obama had limited national experience.

McCain returned to Indianapolis on July 1 at the invitation of the National Sheriffs' Association conducting its annual conference at the Indiana Convention Center. It was a friendly audience of 2,000 law enforcement leaders who tended to support Republican candidates anyway. McCain saluted the sheriffs and deputy sheriffs, noting that "some functions of government take place far from public view, and success and failure can be hard to measure. But that is never true in your calling. In law enforcement, the standard is always 100 percent success, and there is no such thing as 'close enough' for government work. Protecting innocent citizens from those who would do them harm is the most elementary responsibility of government. Law enforcement work is often hard, sometimes heroic, and always necessary. We are all in your debt, and I thank you for your service."[226]

McCain recalled his audience had heard from Reagan twenty-four years earlier in which

he announced a new approach to law enforcement that focused on vigorous enforcement of existing laws and tougher sentencing outlines. "Criminal justice is a part of the Reagan revolution that is often forgotten today," McCain said. "But over time, America became a better, and more just country because of those reforms."[227] McCain also touted his own efforts in Congress to enhance support for law enforcement, including increased penalties for repeat offenders of violent crimes involving a firearm, enhanced background checks for persons with criminal histories seeking to purchase a firearm, and a growing Federal Crime Victims Fund to reimburse victims and to bar offenders from profiting from their crimes.

"We also expanded public registry requirements for convicted sex offenders," McCain said, "because to prevent and punish the exploitation of children, the surest policy is zero-tolerance. When anyone is convicted of sexual assault on a child, they should stay in prison for a long time, and their names should stay forever on the National Sex Offender Public Registry. . . . And, under a bill I have authored as a senator, and intend to sign into law as President, we're going to get serious against Internet predators: Anyone who uses the Internet in the commission of a crime of child exploitation is going offline and into prison for an additional 10 years."[228]

Using a days-old Supreme Court decision that knocked out a Louisiana state law that would classify child molest as a capital offense, McCain lamented that "five justices decided the people's judgment didn't take into account 'evolving standards of decency,' and so they substituted their judgment for that of the people of Louisiana, their legislators, their governor, the trial judge, the jury, the appellate judge, and the other four justices of the Supreme Court."[229]

McCain accused Obama of having changed his position on the issue, noting that Obama now opposed the court's move to strike down the Louisiana law all the while saying he supported "these same justices he usually holds out as the model for future nominations" and noted that the ruling "was exactly the kind of opinion we could expect from an Obama court."[230]

McCain further stated that if he was elected president the American people could expect him to appoint "accomplished men and women with a proven record of excellence in the law, and a proven commitment to judicial restraint." He said that the criminal justice system must "put the interests of law-abiding citizens first—and above all the rights of victims. When we formulate criminal justice policy, words of praise for the good work of law enforcement are not enough. We must give active support to officers of the peace across America, by providing the tools you need to meet new dangers."[231]

Briefly addressing the enhanced role of law enforcement in the fight against domestic terrorism, McCain quickly turned to the "tens of thousands of felons—in custody and at large—[who] entered our country illegally." He asked, "Why has it fallen to sheriffs and other local officials to protect their citizens from these foreign-born felons? Because our federal government failed to protect our borders from their entry, and this serious dereliction of duty must end."[232]

Known for having addressed compromise immigration policies in the past in the Congress—ones that drew support from both Democrats and Republicans—McCain spoke from a position of authority as his home state of Arizona remained a central point for illegal entries into the country. In 2008, however, McCain had staked out a considerably more conservative position on immigration, which focused less on integration of the millions of undocumented aliens already in the nation and more on crackdown on current or future undocumented people. "Our compassion for laborers who entered this country unlawfully, our understanding of their struggles, even as we act to secure the border, speaks well of America," McCain said. "But this respect does not extend to criminals who came here to break our laws and do harm to people. . . . Too often, however, states are left to deal with the high costs and excessive regulation involved in deportation proceedings, and many local officers are left waiting for immigration agents to show up on site. So, as president, I will expand the Criminal Alien Program. We will require that the federal government assume more of the costs to deport and detain criminal aliens—because this is a problem of the federal government's own making."[233]

Following his Indianapolis speech, McCain set off on an unusual three-day visit to Colombia and Mexico to examine the effects of the North American Free Trade Agreement between the United States, Mexico, and Canada that McCain supported. As McCain departed, his presumptive Democratic opponent, Obama, vowed to renegotiate the NAFTA agreement. McCain said he had work to do to convince workers in states such as Indiana and others that NAFTA would eventually benefit them and their employment prospects and again pledged his support for new programs for displaced workers. "I have to convince them the consequences of protectionism and isolationism could be damaging to their future," McCain said. "I understand, it's very tough. But for me to give up my advocacy of free trade would be a betrayal of trust. And the most precious commodity I have with the American people is that they trust me."[234]

On the very last day of campaigning for the 2008 campaign, McCain found himself again in

Indianapolis and facing the prospect of being the first Republican to lose Indiana in a general election since 1964. Polls showed Obama was slightly ahead among Indiana voters, a result that few Republicans were willing to admit was anything but an error in calculation, but regardless, McCain put Indianapolis on the list for a final swing through seven "battleground" states.

McCain's appearance, a quick in-and-out inside an empty airport hangar at the Indianapolis International Airport, was all he could afford to give. He declared that despite polling showing that Obama was en route to winning the election, McCain said, "I'm an American and I choose to fight!"[235] Fighting was what he was doing, campaigning for eighteen straight hours trying to turn the tide.

"When I'm President," McCain said, "we're going to win in Afghanistan, win in Iraq, and our troops will come home with victory and honor." The audience responded in unison with cries of "John McCain! John McCain!" and "USA! USA!" Reporters noted that McCain's voice "had grown noticeably hoarse" by the time he reached Indianapolis, "but if McCain harbored concerns about the uphill battle he faced, he showed little sign of it as he took the stage at campaign rallies with his wife, Cindy, daughter, Meghan, and a host of friends from his long career in Washington," the Associated Press reported.[236]

Sarah Palin

Though Alaska governor Palin proved a controversial choice as the Republican nominee for vice president in 2008, in Indiana she remained a popular draw among Hoosiers. For three campaign appearances in the state, on October 17, 25, and 29 in Noblesville, Fort Wayne, and Jeffersonville, respectively, her "Road to Victory" rallies drew loud, enthusiastic crowds.

At the Verizon Music Center near Noblesville in Hamilton County, Palin drew an audience of 20,000 that waited several hours for her arrival. Embracing the traditional role for a vice presidential nominee to lead the attack on the presidential nominee of the opposing party, Palin focused most of her remarks on concerns she said Obama presented. She noted his campaign's association with the Association of Community Organizations for Reform raised serious questions of voter fraud in as many as a dozen states. She noted, "It is not mean-spirited, and it is not negative campaigning when we talk about someone's record. ACORN endorsed [Obama] this year, and they're working pretty hard on their behalf. All of this would be a lot of baggage to drag into the Oval Office. Americans are entitled to answers before Election Day. We need a little straight talk. These associations are important and they go to the heart of someone's judgment and truthfulness. On Election Day, you are going to be asked to choose between a candidate who will not disavow a group committing voter fraud and a leader who will not tolerate it."[237]

Attempting to draw contrasts between Obama and McCain, Palin emphasized what she saw as Obama's lack of experience, while not mentioning she had only served two years as a governor of a sparsely populated state. She said, "Senator Obama said he wants to spread the wealth. He wants the government to take more of your money and decide for government's self how best to redistribute that. Joe 'The Plumber' said to him it sounded kind of like socialism. For a campaign that says it's all about the future, we noticed our opponents' sure want to talk a lot about the past. It's going to be the choice between a politician who puts his faith in government and a leader who puts his faith in all of you."[238]

Palin also questioned Obama's commitment to American forces overseas in Iraq and Afghanistan, asserting that "John is the only man in this race who talks about the wars that America is fighting, and he isn't afraid to use the word 'victory.' Our opponent gives speech after speech about the wars that America is fighting, and it sure would be nice if for once he would say that he wants America to win." She added, "I thank God that we have a man who is ready and worthy; someone who inspires us with worthy and trustworthy deeds and not just words."[239]

Concluding her remarks, Palin reminded her audience, "Indiana, this election is going to come down to the wire. I hear in the home of the Indianapolis 500, you all know something about close races. You know how to sprint right down to the finish line and the victory lap, and that's why I'm asking for your vote."[240]

Eight days later Palin and country and western singer Hank Williams Jr. drew a large crowd to the venerable Memorial Coliseum in Fort Wayne, where she made frequent contrasts between the economic plans of the Republican and Democratic nominees. Referring to Obama as "Barack the wealth-spreader," she said his plans for America would hurt the middle class and small businesses across Indiana. "He says he's for a tax credit," Palin said, "which is when the government takes more of your money to give it away to someone else according to that politician's priorities. John McCain and I, we are for a real tax cut, which is when the government takes less of your earnings in the first place."[241]

She urged voters to "really listen to our opponent's words" and said to "hear what he is saying and even the nuances there in his answers because he's hiding his real agenda of redistributing your hard-earned money."[242]

Four days later, Palin spoke again in Indiana before an overflow crowd packed into the River Ridge Commerce Center in Jeffersonville. Her remarks—strikingly similar to her two previous speeches in Indiana—reflected the highly managed nature of her campaign. Republican operatives, concerned about Palin's less-than-stellar performance before members of the national media and in a one-on-one comparison with Senator Joe Biden, Obama's running mate, provided Palin with scripted speeches and she rarely veered off from her prepared remarks.

Appearing again with Williams, Palin introduced her husband, Todd, and briefly gloated about his work as a commercial fisherman and his championships in snow machine races in Alaska. "So good to be here," she said, "and it is not a wonder that they call Indiana the Crossroads of America, so many good, hard-working, patriotic people in this state and I knew walking out here tonight, I saw so many of you with your veterans' hats on . . . we want to thank you. We do thank you for your service and your sacrifice."[243] Her remarks served as a basis for her contention that as a senator, Obama had voted to "cut off funding for our troops in Iraq and Afghanistan" and to remind the audience that "John McCain, himself having served in uniform for 22 years, five and a half of those as a POW, he understands how great the challenges are to overcome. . . . He is exactly the kind of man I want as our Commander in Chief. On national security issues, there is no question who has the experience and the courage and the leadership, and that is John McCain."[244]

Turning to continued troubling reports from Wall Street and Washington about the vulnerability of the American economy, Palin said, "Our country is facing some tough times right now, some tough economic times, and now more than ever we need someone tough as President. We need a leader with the experience and the courage and the good judgment and the truthfulness who has a bold and fair and free plan to get this economy back on the right track. We need John McCain!" She said the McCain-Palin ticket offered Americans help "to keep their homes and we are going to clean up the corruption and greed on Wall Street that brought us the housing crisis to begin with. We are going to help our retirees keep their pensions and their savings, the retirees, our esteemed elders who have built our country and our families. They have entrusted others to manage their dollars and their savings for the future. It is because of that greed and corruption that we read so much about now that they are forced to worry about their security. That's not right, that's not fair, and we are going to help secure them. And we are going to help all of our college students to be able to afford to pay for college. And we are going to help families to afford good health care. Our pro-growth, pro-private sector growth will get this economy back on the right track."[245]

Remarks mirroring almost word-for-word what she offered in Fort Wayne days earlier, Palin told her Jeffersonville audience that Obama "has an ideological commitment to bigger government and higher taxes" and that it was not negative campaigning to "call someone out on their plans and their record and their associations—and we're going to do it. Calling someone out on their plans based on their record is only in fairness to you, the voters, the working people."[246]

Palin also briefly addressed the coal industry of southern Indiana, while emphasizing energy independence by tapping more domestic sources of fossil fuels. She added, "There are a couple of assignments that I cannot wait to get started on for you as your Vice President . . . a mission that is especially close to my heart and that is to help our families with children with special needs. It is time. Too often children with special needs have been too often set apart and made to feel there is no place for them in our country. This attitude is a grave disservice to these children, to our families, and to America, and I am going to work to change that. John McCain and I have a vision of America where every innocent life counts."[247]

Joe Biden

With the fall campaign fully engaged in Indiana as a result of positive polling showing the Obama-Biden team within reach of winning the state, Senator Biden of Delaware made two key appearances, on September 24, 2008, for a speech at Warder Park in Jeffersonville, and again just before Election Day on November 1, 2008, outside the Vanderburgh County Courthouse in downtown Evansville.

At Jeffersonville, Biden focused his remarks on the troubled housing market across the nation, including failing mortgages for many families. "Eight to 10,000 people per day are going into foreclosure," Biden said. "These foreclosures are more than an economic crisis for these people, they are an emotional crisis. It means turning to your son or daughter and saying, 'you've got to empty the bedroom, honey.' It means you can't come back to the neighborhood. You can't play in the same club. The middle class is under siege and we will end that siege."[248]

Biden said Republican nominee McCain was "flat out of touch" with the needs of the American middle class and told 2,300 loud supporters that a vote for McCain and Palin was a vote for a third term for Bush and a continuation of his policies. "Eight years ago the Republican nominee claimed he wasn't a typical Republican, claimed he was a reformer," Biden charged. "He said he'd bring honor back to the White House. Now, eight years later, we have another man telling us he's different. We've seen this movie before, and the sequel is always worse than the original."[249]

Obama's campaign was focused on how the nation could return to a time when families could afford to send their children to college, buy a new car when needed, and a nation that demanded the world's respect. "I have no doubt in my mind that Barack Obama will be that bridge between what we can imagine and what we can achieve," Biden said. "We have a culture in Washington where the very few--the wealthy, the powerful— have a seat at the table, and the rest of us are on the menu. Ladies and gentlemen, that must change."[250]

For his late campaign speech in Evansville, Biden spoke before about 2,000 Democratic Party faithful charged with getting out the vote in southwest Indiana. His remarks made news because of their conflict with comments he had offered just hours before. Earlier Biden told national reporters that he had high hopes that Senator McCain would end his campaign on a positive note, a particular "strength" Biden said his fellow senator possessed. However, in Evansville he let loose on a different type of commentary on McCain, noting that "in my view, over the last few weeks, John McCain's campaign has gone way over the top. They are trying to take the low road to the highest office in the land. It's not only George Bush's economic policies that John McCain has bought hook, line and sinker. He's also bought (Republican strategist) Karl Rove's brand of political tactics. It's disappointing."[251]

He added, "I never thought I'd see this from a McCain campaign. They're calling Barack Obama every name in the book. They are going out in a way that I don't recall it being more personally vicious."[252] Biden said, "I have known John a long time" and that he was "genuinely disappointed that we continue to play this game" and that "we have had enough of this stuff. It does not have to be this way, it does not have to be this way."[253] He told his friendly audience that "we have to unite this country, we have to move past the political attacks that we have seen in the last few weeks of this campaign."[254]

At the same time, Biden flashed signs of his common-man approach, searching the crowd to see if he could see a local nun who had reminded him earlier that he still needed to attend mass for All Saints Day. "Sister Jean-Michelle, I made 9 o'clock, I made the 9 o'clock mass. I just want to thank you," Biden said. "I'll call my mom sometime during the day and the first thing she will ask me, 'Joey, did you go to mass today?' So you saved me sister, you saved me."[255]

Notes

Introduction

1. Alyn Brodsky, *Grover Cleveland: A Study in Character* (New York: Macmillan, 2000).

2. *Valparaiso Vidette-Messenger*, Sept. 12, 1936.

Chapter1

1. Paul F. Boller, Jr., *Presidential Campaigns: From George Washington to George W. Bush* (New York: Oxford University Press, 2004).

2. Thomas W. Howard, "Indiana Newspapers and the Presidential Election of 1824," *Indiana Magazine of History* 63 (September 1967): 178.

3. Ibid.

4. Resident Population Data. U.S. Census Bureau.

5. Paul Tincher Smith, "Indiana's Last October Campaign," *Indiana Magazine of History* 19 (December 1923): 332.

6. *Centerville-Wayne County Record*, October 5, 1842.

7. Ibid.

8. Charles W. Osborn, "Henry Clay at Richmond: The Abolition Petition," *Indiana Magazine of History* 4 (September 1908): 121.

9. Ibid., 119.

10. *Centerville-Wayne County Record*, October 5, 1842.

11. Ibid.

12. Calvin Colton, ed., *The Life, Correspondence, and Speeches of Henry Clay*, 6 vols. (New York: A. S. Barnes and Company, 1857), 6:385.

13. Ibid., 385, 386.

14. Ibid., 386.

15. Ibid.

16. Ibid.

17. Ibid., 387.

18. Ibid., 387–88.

19. Ibid., 388–89.

20. Ibid., 389.

21. Ibid., 390.

22. *Centerville-Wayne County Record*, October 5, 1842.

23. *Indianapolis Journal*, October 7, 1842.

24. Ibid.

25. *Indiana State Sentinel*, June 14, 1842.

26. Ibid.

27. Ibid.

28. Ibid.

29. Ibid.

30. *Indianapolis Journal*, June 14, 1842.

31. *Washington (DC) Globe*, June 21, 1842.

32. *Indiana Statesman*, June 17, 1842.

33. *Indianapolis Journal*, June 14, 1842.

34. Ibid.

35. *Washington (DC) Globe*, June 21, 1842.

36. *Indianapolis Journal*, June 14, 1842.

37. Ibid.

38. *Indiana State Sentinel*, June 24, 1842.

39. Ibid.

40. Kenneth R. Stevens, "The Triumph of Old Tip: William Henry Harrison and the Election of 1840," *Traces of Indiana and Midwestern History* 2, no. 4 (Fall 1990): 14–21.

41. Charles S. Todd and Benjamin Drake, *Sketches of the Civil and Military Services of William Henry Harrison* (Cincinnati: J. A. and U. P. James, 1847), 137.

42. Ibid., 137.

43. Ibid.

44. Ibid., 138–39.

45. Ibid., 139.

46. Adam A. Leonard, "Personal Politics in Indiana 1816–1840," *Indiana Magazine of History* 19 (June 1923): 164.

47. Ibid., 150.

48. Robert G. Gunderson, "Thurlow Weed's Network: Whig Party Organization in 1840," *Indiana Magazine of History* 48 (June 1952): 116.

49. Reginald Horsman, "William Henry Harrison: Virginia Gentleman in the Old Northwest," *Indiana Magazine of History* 96 (June 2000): 125–49.

50. Ibid., 147.

51. Ibid., 148.

52. Betty Carolyn Congleton, "The Whig Campaign of 1840: The Editorial Policy of George D. Prentice," *Indiana Magazine of History* 63 (September 1967): 244.

53. Horsman, "William Henry Harrison," 148.

54. Robert V. Friedenberg, *Notable Speeches in Contemporary Presidential Campaigns* (Westport, CT: Praeger, 2002), 26.

55. *Indianapolis State Sentinel*, April 13, 1841.

56. Ibid.

57. Ibid.

58. Ibid.

59. Ibid.

60. U.S. Constitution, Article II, Section 1.

61. Bert Joseph Griswold, *The Pictorial History of Fort Wayne, Indiana: A Review of Two Centuries of Occupation of the Region about the Head of the Maumee River*, 2 vols. (Chicago: Robert O. Law Company, 1917), 1:363

62. Ibid.

63. Ibid., 363–64.

64. George H. Hickman and Richard Rush, *The Life of General Lewis Cass: With His Letters and Speeches on Various Subjects* (Baltimore: N. Hickman, 1848), 30.

Chapter 2

1. David Vanderstel, "Lincoln in Indiana," *American Outlook* 13 (Summer 2013).

2. Ibid.

3. Roy P. Basler, *The Collected Works of Abraham Lincoln*, 8 vols. (New Brunswick, NJ: Rutgers University Press, 1953–55).

4. *Williamsport-Warren Republican*, September 22, 1859.

5. Basler, *Collected Works of Abraham Lincoln*, 3:463.

6. Ibid., 463–64.

7. Ibid., 464.

8. Ibid., 465.

9. Ibid., 466.

10. Ibid., 466, 469, 470.

11. David M. Potter, *The Impending Crisis: America before the Civil War, 1848–1861* (New York: Harper and Row Publishers, 1976).

12. George S. Cottman, "Lincoln in Indianapolis," *Indiana Magazine of History* 24 (March 1928): 3.

13. *Lafayette Daily Courier*, February 11, 1861.

14. Ibid.

15. *Indianapolis Daily Sentinel*, February 12, 1861.

16. Cottman, "Lincoln in Indianapolis," 4.

17. L. E. Chittenden, ed., *Abraham Lincoln's Speeches* (New York: Dodd, Mead and Company, 1895), 224

18. Cottman, "Lincoln in Indianapolis," 6.

19. Chittenden, ed., *Abraham Lincoln's Speeches*, 225.

20. Ibid., 226.

21. Ibid., 227.

22. Ibid.

23. Cottman, "Lincoln in Indianapolis," 10–11.

24. *Cincinnati Daily Commercial*, February 13, 1861.

25. Cottman, "Lincoln in Indianapolis," 11–12.

26. Ibid., 12.

27. Ibid., 13.

28. Ibid.

29. Ibid., 14.

30. Geoff Elliott, "An Unscheduled Funeral for Lincoln," The Abraham Lincoln Blog, http://abrahamlincolnblog .blogspot.com/2010/05/unscheduled-funeral-for-lincoln .html.

31. Martin H. Quitt, *Stephen A. Douglas and Antebellum Democracy* (Cambridge, MA: Cambridge University Press, 2012).

32. Ibid.

33. *New Albany Daily Ledger*, October 1, 1860.

34. Ibid.

35. Ibid.

36. Ibid.

37. Ibid.

38. Ibid.

39. Ibid.

40. *Lafayette Journal*, October 2, 1860.

41. Ibid.

42. Ibid.

43. Ibid.

44. Ibid.

45. Ibid.

46. Ibid.

46. *Williamsport-Warren Republican*, October 4, 1860.

48. Ibid.

49. *Logansport Democratic Pharos*, October 3, 1860.

50. Hans L. Trefousse, *Andrew Johnson: A Biography* (New York: W. W. Norton and Company, 1989), 131.

51. *Indianapolis Journal*, October 4, 1864.

52. Ibid.

53. Ibid.

54. Ibid.

55. *New York Times*, September 11, 1866.

56. Ibid.

57. Ibid.

58. *Indianapolis Gazette*, September 11, 1866.

59. *New York Times*, September 11, 1866.

60. Ibid.

61. Ibid.

62. Ibid.

63. *Indianapolis Gazette*, September 11, 1866.

64. Ibid.

65. *New York Times*, September 12, 1866.

66. Ibid.

67. Ibid.

68. Ibid.

69. Ibid.

70. Ibid.

71. Ibid.

72. Ibid.

73. *Indianapolis Gazette*, September 11, 1866.

74. *New York Times*, September 12, 1866; *Indianapolis Gazette*, September 12, 1866.

75. Associated Press, November 8, 1868.

76. *New York Times*, April 24, 1871.

77. Ibid.

78. *Indianapolis People*, October 1, 1871.

79. *New Castle Courier*, September 29, 1871.

80. *Brownstown Banner*, August 29, 1872.

81. *Fort Wayne Daily Sentinel*, September 27, 1871.

82. Ibid.

83. *New York Times*, September 3, 1872.

84. Ibid.

85. Ibid.

86. *Logansport Journal*, December 10, 1879.

87. *New York Times*, December 9, 1879.

88. Ibid.

89. Ibid., October 30, 1868.

90. *Indianapolis Sun*, October 27, 1868.

91. Ibid.

92. Ibid.

93. *New York Times*, August 1, 1868.

94. Ibid.

95. Ibid., August 3, 1868.

96. Ibid., August 1, 1868.

97. Ibid.

98. Ibid., October 9, 1868.

99. Ibid.

100. *Indianapolis Journal*, October 7, 1868.

101. Ibid.

102. Ibid.

103. *New Albany Daily Commercial*, October 29, 1868.

104. Ibid.

105. Ibid.

106. Ibid.

107. *New York Times*, July 10, 1992.

108. Ibid., July 7, 1871.

109. Ibid., June 26, 1872.

110. Ibid.

111. Ibid., August 7, 1872.

112. Ibid., September 24, 1872.

113. Ibid.

114. Ibid.

115. Ibid.

116. *Chicago Tribune*, September 25, 1872.

117. *New York Times*, September 24, 1872.

118. Ibid.

119. Robert C. Williams, *Horace Greeley: Champion of American Freedom* (New York: New York University Press, 2006).

120. Horace Greeley, *The Autobiography of Horace Greeley; or, Recollections of a Busy Life* (New York: E. B. Treat, 1872).

121. Jodie Steelman Wilson, Emily Griffin Winfrey, and Rebecca McDole, *The Hidden History of Montgomery County, Indiana* (Charleston, SC: History Press, 2012), 38.

122. *New York Times*, September 14, 1877.

123. *Cincinnati Enquirer*, September 14, 1877.

124. *Madison Weekly Herald*, September 19, 1877.

125. *Jeffersonville National Democrat*, September 20, 1877.

126. President Rutherford B. Hayes remarks, September 18, 1877, Jeffersonville, Indiana. Rutherford B. Hayes Presidential Center, Fremont, OH.

127. *Jeffersonville National Democrat*, September 20, 1877.

128. *New York Times*, October 3, 1879.

129. *Indianapolis Journal*, October 3, 1879.

130. *New York Times*, December 2, 1885.

131. Former President Rutherford B. Hayes speech, August 15, 1888, Fort Wayne, Indiana. Hayes Presidential Center.

132. *Fort Wayne Sentinel*, August 15, 1888.

133. Fred D. Cavinder, *The Indiana Book of Records, Firsts, and Fascinating Facts* (Bloomington: Indiana University Press, 1985), 148.

134. Theodore P. Cook, *The Life and Public Services of Honorable Samuel J. Tilden: Democratic Nominee for President of the United States* (New York: D. Appleton and Company, 1876), 434.

135. *Fort Wayne Weekly Sentinel*, September 27, 1876.

136. Ibid.

137. Ibid.

138. Ibid.

139. Thomas A. Hendricks speech, Indianapolis, Indiana, July 12, 1884, in John Walker Holcombe and Hubert Marshall Skinner, eds., *Life and Public Services of Thomas A. Hendricks: With Selected Speeches and Writings* (Indianapolis: Carlon and Hollenbeck, 1886), 603.

140. Ibid.

141. Ibid., 605.

142. Vice President Thomas A. Hendricks speech, Masonic Hall, Indianapolis, Indiana, September 8, 1885, in Holcombe and Skinner, eds., *Life and Public Services of Thomas A. Hendricks*, 633-34.

143. Ibid., 635.

144. Associated Press, December 1, 1885.

145. Ibid.

146. Ibid., December 2, 1885.

147. *New York Times*, November 26, 1885.

148. Ibid.

149. Associated Press, November 30, 1885.

150. Ibid.

151. *New York Times*, December 2, 1885.

152. Ibid.

Chapter 3

1. *New York Herald*, June 10, 1880.

2. *Goshen Times*, June 10, 1880.

3. *New York Tribune*, June 10, 1880.

4. *New York Times*, Oct. 3, 1880.

5. *Indianapolis Journal*, Oct. 12, 1880.

6. *New York, Times*, Oct. 10, 1880.

7. *Indianapolis Journal*, Oct. 10, 1880.

8. Ibid, Oct. 12, 1880.

9. *Shelbyville Daily Evening Democrat*, Dec. 29, 1883.

10. *Indianapolis Journal*, Oct. 12, 1880.

11. *Boonville Weekly Enquirer*, Oct. 9, 1880.

12. Ibid.

13. *New York Times*, July 11, 1880.

14. Larry J. Sabato and Howard R. Ernst, *Encyclopedia of American Political Parties and Elections* (New York: Infobase Publishing, 2014), 327.

15. *New York Times*, Oct. 6, 1880.

16. Frederick E. Goodrich, *The Life and Public Services of Winfield Scott Hancock, Major General, U.S.A.* (Boston: Lee and Shepard, 1880), 347.

17. Ibid., 367.

18. Ibid., 372.

19. Ibid., 372–73, 375.

20. *New York Times,* September 28, 1880; Kenneth D. Ackerman, *Dark Horse: The Surprise Election and Political Murder of President James A. Garfield* (New York: Carroll and Graf Publishers, 2003).

21. Ackerman, *Dark Horse*.

22. David M. Jordan, *William Scott Hancock: A Soldier's Life* (Bloomington: Indiana University Press, 1988).

23. *New Albany Daily Ledger*, August 2, 1883.

24. Ibid.

25. Ibid.

26. Ibid., August 3, 1883.

27. Ibid.

28. Ibid.

29. *Lafayette Daily Courier*, August 2, 1883.

30. Ibid.

31. Ibid.

32. Ibid.

33. *New Albany Daily Ledger*, August 3, 1883.

34. *Lafayette Daily Courier*, August 3, 1883.

35. *New Albany Daily Ledger*, August 3, 1883.

36. Associated Press, October 6, 1887.

37. Ibid.

38. *Warsaw Daily Times*, October 3, 1887.

39. Associated Press, October 6, 1887.

40. Ibid.

41. Ibid.

42. Ibid.

43. Ibid.

44. *Warsaw Daily Times*, October 3, 1887.

45. Ibid.

46. *The Presidential Campaign and Election of 1892* (Stanford, CA: Stanford University Press, 1970).

47. Associated Press, October 18, 1884.

48. *New York Times*, October 22, 1884.

49. *Ligonier Leader*, October 23, 1884.

50. Ibid.

51. Ibid.

52. *Fort Wayne Weekly Gazette*, October 23, 1884.

53. *Brazil Register*, October 23, 1884

54. Ibid.

55. *Fort Wayne Weekly Gazette*, October 23, 1884.

56. Associated Press, October 22, 1884.

57. Ibid.

58. Ibid.

59. Ibid.

60. Ibid.

61. *New York Times*, October 12, 1888.

62. Ibid.

63. Ibid., October 13, 1888.

64. Paul F. Boller, *Presidential Anecdotes* (New York: Oxford University Press, 1996).

65. Benjamin Harrison remarks, June 30, 1888, 674 N. Delaware Street, Indianapolis, Ind., in Charles Hedges, comp., *Speeches of Benjamin Harrison, Twenty-Third President of the United States: A Complete Collection of His Public Addresses from February 1888 to February 1892* (New York: United States Book Company, 1892), 33.

66. Ibid.

67. Ibid., 34, 35.

68. Ibid., 34.

69. Ibid.

70. Ibid.. 35.

71. Harrison remarks, July 4, 1888, 674 N. Delaware Street, Indianapolis, Ind., Hedges, comp., *Speeches of Benjamin Harrison*, 36–37.

72. Ibid., 37.

73. Harrison remarks, September 4, 1888, Fort Wayne, Ind., Hedges, comp., *Speeches of Benjamin Harrison*, 99.

74. Ibid.

75. Ibid., 100–101.

76. Harrison remarks, September 4, 1888, Huntington, Ind., Hedges, comp., *Speeches of Benjamin Harrison*, 101.

77. Harrison remarks, September 4, 1888, Peru, Ind., ibid., 102.

78. Harrison remarks, September 4, 1888, Kokomo, Ind., ibid., 103.

79. Ibid.

80. Harrison remarks, September 4, 1888, Tipton, Ind., Hedges, comp., *Speeches of Benjamin Harrison*, 104.

81. Harrison remarks, September 4, 1888, Noblesville, Ind., ibid., 104.

82. Harrison remarks, September 4, 1888, Union Station, Indianapolis, Ind., ibid., 105.

83. Harrison remarks, September 8, 1888, 674 N. Delaware Street, Indianapolis, Ind., ibid., 107.

84. Ibid.

85. Ibid.

86. Harrison remarks, September 13, 1888, Clayton, Ind., Hedges, comp., *Speeches of Benjamin Harrison*, 116.

87. Ibid., 116–17.

88. Ibid., 117.

89. Ibid., 117, 118.

90. Harrison remarks, October 6, 1888, Tomlinson Hall, Indianapolis, Ind., Hedges, comp., *Speeches of Benjamin Harrison*, 169.

91. Harrison remarks, October 25, 1888, Tomlinson Hall, Indianapolis, Ind., ibid., 183.

92. Ibid.

93. Ibid., 184.

94. Harrison remarks, November 6, 1888, 674 North Delaware Street, Indianapolis, Ind., Hedges, comp., *Speeches of Benjamin Harrison*, 188–89.

95. President-elect Benjamin Harrison remarks, January 1, 1889, George H. Thomas GAR Post No. 17, Indianapolis, Ind., ibid., 189–90.

96. President-elect Harrison remarks, February 25, 1889, Union Station, Indianapolis, Ind., in ibid., 191.

97. President-elect Harrison remarks, February 25, 1889, Knightstown, Ind., ibid., 192.

98. President-elect Harrison remarks, February 25, 1889, Richmond, Ind., ibid., 192.

99. President Benjamin Harrison remarks, August 21, 1889, College Corner, Ind., ibid., 212.

100. President Benjamin Harrison remarks, August 21, 1889, Union Station, Indianapolis, Ind., ibid., 212

101. Ibid., 214.

102. Harrison remarks, August 22, 1889, Monument Circle, Indianapolis, Ind., Hedges, comp., *Speeches of Benjamin Harrison*, 214.

103. Ibid.

104. Harrison remarks, August 22, 1889, Tomlinson Hall, Indianapolis, Ind., Hedges, comp., *Speeches of Benjamin Harrison*, 216.

105. Harrison remarks, October 7, 1890, Lawrenceburg, Ind., ibid., 236.

106. Harrison remarks, October 7, 1890, North Vernon, Ind., ibid., 237.

107. Harrison remarks, October 7, 1890, Seymour, Ind., ibid.

108. Harrison remarks, October 7, 1890, Terre Haute, Ind., ibid., 239.

109. Ibid., 239–40.

110. Harrison remarks, October 13, 1890, Anderson, Ind., Hedges, comp., *Speeches of Benjamin Harrison*, 271.

111. Harrison remarks, October 13, 1890, Muncie, Ind., ibid., 272.

112. Harrison remarks, May 14, 1891, Montezuma, Ind., ibid., 480.

113. Harrison remarks, May 14, 1891, Union Station, Indianapolis, Ind., ibid., 482.

114. Ibid., 482–83.

115. Harrison remarks, May 14, 1891, Richmond, Ind., Hedges, comp., *Speeches of Benjamin Harrison*, 484.

116. *Indianapolis Journal*, October 25, 1892.

117. Ibid.

118. Associated Press, October 31, 1892.

119. Ibid., March 7, 1893.

120. Ibid.

121. Ibid.

122. Ibid.

123. Ibid., April 25, 1894.

124. *Goshen Daily News*, October 31, 1896.

125. Ibid.

126. Associated Press, September 2, 1892.

127. *Rochester Daily Republican*, September 8, 1892.

128. *Logansport Daily Pharos-Tribune*, September 8, 1892.

129. Ibid.

130. Ibid., September 9, 1892.

131. Ibid.

132. *Goshen Daily News*, October 28, 1896.

133. Ibid.

134. *Columbus Daily Herald*, October 28, 1892.

135. *Logansport Daily Pharos*, October 25, 1892.

136. Ibid.

137. Ibid.

138. *Logansport Journal*, October 25, 1892.

139. Ibid

140. *Logansport Daily Pharos*, October 25, 1892.

141. *New York Times*, October 28, 1892.

142. International Circus Hall of Fame, Peru, Ind., http://www.circushalloffame.com/; *New York Times*, October 27, 1892.

143. *Logansport Journal*, October 29, 1892.

144. *Warsaw Daily Times*, September 14, 1892.

145. Ibid.

146. Ibid.

147. Ibid.

148. Charles Morris, *The Authentic Life of William McKinley* (Ann Arbor: University of Michigan Press, 1901).

149. Associated Press, September 27, 1894.

150. President William McKinley remarks, Terre Haute, Ind., October 15, 1898, in William McKinley, *Speeches and Addresses of William McKinley: From March 1, 1897 to May 30, 1900* (New York: Doubleday and McClure Company, 1900), 122–23.

151. Ibid., 123.

152. McKinley remarks, Logansport, Ind., Oct. 21, 1898, McKinley, *Speeches and Addresses of William McKinley*, 139.

153. Ibid.

154. McKinley remarks, Kokomo, Ind., October 21, 1898, McKinley, *Speeches and Addresses of William McKinley*, 140.

155. Ibid., 141.

156. Associated Press, November 1, 1898.

157. McKinley remarks, Tipton, Ind., October 21, 1898, McKinley, *Speeches and Addresses of William McKinley*, 142.

158. Ibid.

159. McKinley remarks, Atlanta, Ind., October 21, 1898,. McKinley, *Speeches and Addresses of William McKinley*, 143.

160. McKinley remarks, Noblesville, Ind., October 21, 1898, ibid.

161. Ibid.

162. McKinley remarks, Indianapolis, Ind., October 21, 1898, McKinley, *Speeches and Addresses of William McKinley*, 145.

163. Ibid.

164. McKinley remarks, Rushville, Ind., October 21, 1898, McKinley, *Speeches and Addresses of William McKinley*, 146.

165. McKinley remarks, College Corner, Ind., October 21, 1898, ibid., 148

166. McKinley remarks, Evansville, Ind., October 11, 1899, ibid., 253–54.

167. McKinley remarks, Vincennes, Ind., October 11, 1899, ibid., 256.

168. McKinley remarks, Terre Haute, Ind., October 11, 1899, ibid.

169. McKinley remarks, Michigan City, Ind., October 17, 1899, ibid., 332.

Chapter 4

1. *New York Times*. September 9, 1900.

2. Ibid.

3. *New York Times*, October 10, 1900.

4.Ibid.

5. Ibid.

6. Ibid.

7. Ibid.

8. Associated Press, October 11, 1900.

9. *New York Times*, October 10, 1900.

10. Ibid.

11. Wayne County Historical Society, Richmond, Ind.

12. Associated Press, October 11, 1900.

13. Ibid.

14. Ibid., September 23, 1902.

15. President Theodore Roosevelt speech, Logansport, Ind., September 23, 1902, in *Addresses and Presidential Messages of Theodore Roosevelt, 1902–1904* (New York: G.P. Putnam's Sons, 1904), 74.

16. Ibid., 75.

17. Ibid., 76–77

18. Ibid., 80, 81

19. *Logansport Morning Journal*, September 24, 1902.

20. Ibid.

21. Ibid.

22. Ibid.

23. Theodore Roosevelt speech, Columbia Club, Indianapolis, Ind., September 23, 1902, in *A Compilation of the Messages and Speeches of Theodore Roosevelt, 1901–1905* ([New York]: Bureau of National Literature and Art, 1906), 169.

24. Ibid., 169, 170–71.

25. Associated Press. September 23, 1902.

26. Roosevelt speech, Columbia Club, Indianapolis, Ind., September 23, 1902, *Compilation of the Messages and Speeches of Theodore Roosevelt*, 168, 169.

27. Associated Press, September 24, 1902.

28. *Indianapolis Sentinel*, September 24, 1902.

29. Ibid.

30. Ibid.

31. Associated Press, September 24, 1902.

32. *New York Times*, November 26, 1904.

33. Ibid.

34. *Washington Post*, April 5, 1905.

35. Ibid.

36. Ibid.

37. *New York Times*, May 31, 1907.

38. Ibid.

39. Ibid.

40. Ibid., November 1, 1904.

41. *Elkhart Daily Review*, November 1, 1904.

42. Ibid.

43. Ibid.

44. Ibid.
45. *New Albany Evening Tribune*, November 4, 1904.
46. Ibid.
47. Ibid.
48. *New York Times*, November 6, 1904.
49. Ibid., March 11, 1907.
50. Associated Press, October 22, 1896.
51. Ibid.
52. Ibid.
53. Ibid.
54. Ibid.
55. *New York Times*, January 8, 1899.
56. *Boston Evening Transcript*, July 27, 1899.
57. *New York Times*, August 8, 1900.
58. Ibid.
59. Ibid.
60. William Jennings Bryan speech, Military Park, Indianapolis, Ind., August 8, 1900, Voices of Democracy: The U.S. Oratory Project, voicesofdemocracy.umd.edu/.
61. Ibid.
62. Ibid.
63. Ibid.
64. Ibid.
65. Ibid.
66. Ibid.
67. Ibid.
68. Ibid.
69. *Boston Evening Transcript*, October 6, 1900.
70. Ibid.
71. Ibid.
72. Ibid.
73. Ibid.
74. *New York Times*, October 6, 1900.
75. Ibid., November 2, 1900.
76. Ibid.
77. *Crawfordsville Weekly News Review*, February 13, 1903.
78. Ibid.
79. *Indianapolis Star*, October 13, 1904.
80. Ibid.
81. Associated Press, October 18, 1904.
82. Ibid.
83. *New York Times*, October 6, 1904.
84. *Petersburg-Pike County Democrat*, November 10, 1910.
85. Ibid.
86. Ibid.
87. Jodie Steelman Wilson, Emily Griffin Winfrey, and Rebecca McDole, *The Hidden History of Montgomery County, Indiana* (Charleston, SC: History Press, 2012), 41.
88. Edgar A. Horning, "Campaign Issues in the Presidential Election of 1908," *Indiana Magazine of History* 54 (September 1958): 249.
89. Howard F. McMains, "The Road to George Ade's Farm: Origins of Taft's First Campaign Rally, September, 1908," *Indiana Magazine of History* 67 (December 1971): 317.
90. *Indianapolis News*, September 23, 1908.
91. McMains, "Road to George Ade's Farm," 330.
92. Ibid., 331.
93. Ibid., 332.
94. *Philadelphia Record*, October 22, 1908.
95. Ibid.
96. *Elkhart Daily Review*, October 23, 1908.
97. Ibid.
98. Associated Press, October 24, 1908.
99. *New York Times*, October 24, 1908.
100. Associated Press, October 24, 1908.
101. Ibid.
102. *Elkhart Daily Review*, October 23, 1908.
103. *New York Times*, October 24, 1908.
104. Ibid.
105. Ibid.
106. *Indianapolis Star*, October 23, 1908.
107. Ibid., October 24, 1908.
108. *Elkhart Daily Review*, October 23, 1908.
109. *New Albany Tribune*, October 26, 1908.
110. *Goshen Daily Democrat*, October 27, 1908.
111. Ibid.
112. Ibid.
113. *Elkhart Daily Review*, October 23, 1908.
114. *Boston Evening Transcript*, April 6, 1910.
115. *Marion Chronicle-Tribune*, July 4, 1911.
116. Associated Press, July 4, 1911.
117. Ibid.
118. Ibid.
119. Ibid.
120. Ibid., July 5, 1911.
121. Ibid.
122. Ibid.
123. Ibid.
124. Ibid.
125. Ibid.
126. Ibid.
127. Ibid.
128. *New York Times*, October 14, 1910.
129. Ibid.
130. Ibid.
131. Ibid.
132. Ibid.
133. Associated Press, October 15, 1910.

134. *New York Times*, October 14, 1910.

135. Ibid.

136. Ibid.

137. Ibid.

138. *Petersburg-Pike County Democrat*, November 10, 1910.

Chapter 5

1. *New York Times*, October 4, 1912.

2. *Boston Evening Transcript*, October 4, 1912.

3. *New York Times*, October 4, 1912.

4. Ibid.

5. Ibid.

6. Ibid.

7. *Indianapolis Star*, October 4, 1912.

8. Ibid.

9. Ibid.

10. *Boston Evening Transcript*, October 5, 1912.

11. Ibid.

12. *Indianapolis Star*, October 5, 1912.

13. Ibid.

14. J. W. Schulte Nordholt, *Woodrow Wilson: A Life for World Peace* (Berkeley: University of California Press, 1991), 145; *New York Times*, January 8, 1915.

15. Associated Press, January 9, 1915.

16. Ibid.

17. *Indianapolis News*, January 9, 1915.

18. Associated Press, January 9, 1915.

19. *Indianapolis News*, January 9, 1915.

20. Ibid.

21. Ibid.

22. Ibid.

23. Associated Press, October 11, 1916.

24. *Richmond Evening Item*, October 11, 1916.

25. Associated Press, October 12, 1916.

26. Ibid.

27. *Indianapolis Star*, September 5, 1919.

28. *New York Times*, September 5, 1919.

29. Ibid.

30. *Indianapolis Star*, September 5, 1919.

31. *New York Times*, September 5, 1919.

32. President Woodrow Wilson speech, Indiana State Fairgrounds, Indianapolis, Ind., September 4, 1919, *Addresses of President Wilson* (Washington, DC: Government Printing Office, 1919), 19.

33. Ibid., 20.

34. Ibid.

35. Ibid., 21.

36. Ibid., 21–22.

37. Ibid., 23

38. Ibid., 25

39. J. M. Hogan, *Woodrow Wilson's Western Tour: Rhetoric, Public Opinion, and the League of Nations* (College Station: Texas A&M University Press, 2006), 81.

40. Wilson speech, Indiana State Fairgrounds, Indianapolis, Ind., September 4, 1919, *Addresses of President Wilson's Western Tour*, 27–28.

41. Ibid., 28

42. *Indianapolis Star*, September 5, 1919.

43. Associated Press, September 12, 1919.

44. Ibid.

45. Ibid.

46. Ibid.

47. Ibid.

48. *New York Times*, September 5, 1919.

49. *Indianapolis Star*, September 8, 1912.

50. Jodie Steelman Wilson, Emily Griffin Winfrey, and Rebecca McDole, *The Hidden History of Montgomery County, Indiana* (Charleston, SC: The History Press, 2012).

51. *Fort Wayne Journal-Gazette*, April 7, 1918.

52. *New Harmony Times*, March 7, 1919.

53. Associated Press, March 2, 1912.

54. Ibid.

55. *Indianapolis News*, June 14, 1912.

56. Associated Press, April 9, 1912.

57. Ibid.

58. *Indianapolis Star*, April 9, 1912.

59. Ibid.

60. Ibid.

61. Ibid.

62. *Indianapolis News*, June 14, 1912.

63. James R. Parker, "Beveridge and the Election of 1912: Progressive Idealist or Political Realist," *Indiana Magazine of History* 63 (June 1967):103–13.

64. *Indianapolis Star*, October 13, 1912.

65. Milwaukee Sentinel, October 14, 1912.

66. Ibid.

67. *New York Times*, June 12, 1918.

68. Ibid., June 13, 1918.

69. Ibid.

70. Ibid.

71. Ibid.

72. Ibid.

73. Ibid.

74. Ibid.

75. Chip Bishop, *The Lion and the Journalist: The Unlikely Friendship of Theodore Roosevelt and Joseph Bucklin Bishop* (Guilford, CT: Lyons Press, 2012), x.

76. *Indianapolis World*, June 20, 1903, retrieved from the collection of Eugene V. Debs Papers Project, Indiana State University, Terre Haute, IN (hereafter cites as Debs Papers Project).

77. Ibid.

78. Ibid.

79. Eugene V. Debs speech, Masonic Hall, Indianapolis, Ind., Sept. 1, 1904, Debs Papers Project.

80. Ibid.

81. Ibid.

82. Ibid.

83. Ibid.

84. Ibid.

85. *Boston Evening Transcript*, August 26, 1912.

86. S. J. Hammond, K. R. Hardwick, and H. L. Lubert, *Classics of American Political and Constitutional Thought*, vol. 2, *Reconstruction to the Present* Indianapolis: Hackett Company, 2007), 373.

87. *Terre Haute Tribune*, December 28, 1921.

88. *Milwaukee New Day*, May 20, 1922.

89. Associated Press, September 29, 1908.

90. *Boston Evening Transcript*, October 2, 1908.

91. *Goshen Daily Democrat*, September 22, 1916.

92. Ibid., September 23, 1916.

93. *Goshen Weekly News-Times*, September 29, 1916.

94. *Goshen Daily Democrat*, September 23, 1916.

95. Associated Press, September 22, 1916.

96. *Fort Wayne Journal-Gazette*, September 23, 1916.

97. Ibid.

98. Ibid.

99. Ibid.

100. *New York Times*, September 23, 1916.

101. Ibid.

102. Ibid.

103. *Pittsburgh Gazette-Times*, September 24, 1916.

104. *New York Times*, September 24, 1916.

105. Ibid.

106. Ibid.

107. Ibid.

108. Associated Press, November 1, 1916.

109. Ibid., September 2, 1916.

110. *New York Times*, September 16, 1916.

111. Associated Press, September 24, 1916.

112. Ibid., October 16, 1916.

113. *New York Times*, October 31, 1916.

114. Ibid., November 24, 1916.

115. Associated Press, August 20, 1912.

116. *New York Times*, August 21, 1912.

117. Ibid.

118. Ibid.

119. *Fort Wayne News-Sentinel*, August 21, 1912.

120. *Washington Post*, September 1, 1916.

121. Associated Press, May 20, 1920.

122. Ibid.

123. *Oak Leaves*, Manchester College, North Manchester, Ind., May 23, 1925.

124. Ibid.

125. Ibid.

126. Ibid.

127. Ibid.

128. Ibid.

129. *Warsaw Times-Union*, April 12, 1912.

130. Michael Kazin, *A Godly Hero: The Life of William Jennings Bryan* (New York: Random House Digital, 2007), 136.

131. Wayne County Historical Society, Richmond, Ind.

132. *New York Times*, August 9, 1916.

133. J. Frank Hanly, *Fallacies Exposed* (Indianapolis: Hanly & Stewart, 1915).

134. J. Frank Hanly, *Messages and Documents of J. Frank Hanly: Governor of Indiana, January 9, 1905-January 11, 1909* (Indianapolis: William B. Burford, 1909), 102.

135. *New York Times*, August 9, 1916.

136. Ibid.

137. Associated Press, October 18, 1916.

138. *Indianapolis Star*, November 5, 1916.

139. Raymond H. Scheele, "J. Frank Hanly," in Linda C. Gugin and James E. St. Clair, eds., *The Governors of Indiana* (Indianapolis: Indiana Historical Society Press, 2006), 224-31.

140. *New York Times*, March 27, 1920.

141. *Kokomo Tribune*, March 27, 1920.

142. *New York Times*, March 27, 1920.

143. Ibid.

144. *Kokomo Tribune*, March 27, 1920.

145. *Rushville Republican*, April 21, 1920.

146. *Connersville News-Examiner*, April 14, 1920.

147. *Logansport Pharos-Tribune*, April 19, 1920.

148. Ibid.

149. Ibid.

150. Ibid.

151. John Wesley Dean, *Warren G. Harding* (New York: Macmillan, 2004), 56.

152. Ibid., 72

153. Associated Press, September 10, 1920.

154. Ibid., October 17, 1920.

155. Ibid., October 19, 1920.

156. Ibid., October 18, 1920.

157. Ibid., October 19, 1920.

158. Ibid., October 16, 1920.

159. Ibid.

160. Francis Russell, *The Four Mysteries of Warren Harding* (New York: American Heritage Publishing Company, 1963).

161. R. H. Ferrell, *The Strange Deaths of President Harding* (Columbia: University of Missouri Press, 1998).

162. *New York Times*, October 10, 1920.

163. Ibid.

164. Ibid.

165. Ibid.

166. *Logansport Pharos-Tribune*, October 9, 1920.

167. Ibid.

168. *Sullivan Daily Tribune*, October 14, 1920.

169. Ibid.

170. Ibid.

171. Ibid.

172. Ibid.

173. Ibid.

174. Ibid.

175. Ibid.

176. Ibid.

177. *Lafayette Times*, October 15, 1920.

178. Ibid.

179. Associated Press, October 13, 1920.

180. *New York Times*, October 14, 1920.

181. Ibid.

182. *Fort Wayne Journal-Gazette*, October 14, 1920.

183. *New York Times*, October 14, 1920.

184. Associated Press, October 13, 1920.

185. *Fort Wayne Journal-Gazette*, October 14, 1920.

186. Ibid.

187. Ibid.

188. *New York Times*, October 14, 1920.

189. Ibid.

190. Associated Press, October 14, 1920.

191. *New York Times*, October 16, 1920.

192. Ibid., October 16, 1920.

193. Ibid., October 22, 1920.

194. Ibid.

195. Associated Press, January 28, 1922.

196. Ibid.

197. Ibid.

198. *New York Times*, November 11, 1926.

199. Ibid.

200. Ibid.

201. Calvin Coolidge, *The Autobiography of Calvin Coolidge* (New York: Cosmopolitan Book Corporation, 1929), 129.

202. President Calvin Coolidge speech, Wicker Memorial Park, Hammond, Ind., June 14, 1927, The American Presidency Project, http://www.presidency.uscb.edu/.

203. Ibid.

204. Ibid.

205. Ibid.

206. Ibid.

207. *New York Times*, June 15, 1927.

208. *Logansport Morning Press*, September 21, 1924.

209. Associated Press, September 20, 1924.

210. Ibid.

211. Ibid.

212. Ibid.

213. *New York Times*, September 20, 1924.

214. United Press, September 21, 1924.

215. Associated Press, September 20, 1924.

216. United Press, September 21, 1924.

217. Associated Press, September 20, 1924.

218. *New York Times*, October 12, 1924.

219. Ibid.

220. Ibid.

221. Ibid., October 14, 1924.

222. Ibid.

223. Ibid.

224. Ibid., October 23, 1924.

225. Ibid., October 14, 1924.

226. Associated Press, October 22, 1924.

227. Robert M. LaFollette, *LaFollette's Autobiography: A Personal Narrative of Political Experiences*, Matthew Rothschild, ed. (Madison: University of Wisconsin Press, 2013), 244.

228. *Indianapolis Star*, January 7, 1912.

229. Ibid.

230. Ibid.

231. United Press, October 9, 1920.

232. Ibid.

233. Ibid.

234. *Lewiston (ME) Daily Sun* , April 28, 1928.

235. Associated Press, March 8-9, 1928.

236. United Press, May 6, 1928.

237. Scripps-Howard News Service, March 29, 1928.

238. United Press, May 6, 1928.

239. *New Republic*, May 9, 1928.

240. Associated Press, May 10, 1928.

241. *New York Times*, July 16, 1928.

242. *Madison Daily Herald*, October 22, 1929.

243. Ibid.

244. Ibid.

245. Ibid.

246. Ibid., October 23, 1929.

247. Ibid.

248. Ibid.

249. Ibid.

250. Ibid.

251. President Herbert Hoover sympathy telegram to Mr. and Mrs. Strothers B. Earls, Madison, Ind., October 24, 1929, The American Presidency Project, http://www.presidency.uscb.edu/.

252. Hoover sympathy telegram to Mayor Marcus R. Sulzer, Madison, Ind., October 24, 1929, ibid.

253. Hoover remarks, train platform, Greensburg, Ind., June 15, 1931, ibid.

254. Hoover speech, Indiana State Fairgrounds, Indianapolis, Ind., June 15, 1931, ibid.

255. Ibid.

256. Ibid.

257. Ibid.

258. Ibid.

259. Ibid.

260. Ibid.

261. Ibid.

262. *New York Times*, October 22, 1928.

263. Ibid.

264. Ibid.

265. Associated Press, October 21, 1928.

266. *Indianapolis News*, October 22, 1928.

267. Ibid.

268. *New York Times*, October 22, 1928.

269. Ibid.

270. *Indianapolis Star*, October 22, 1928.

271. *Indianapolis Times*, October 22, 1928.

272. Associated Press, October 23, 1928.

273. *Indianapolis Star*, October 22, 1928.

274. United Press, October 21, 1928.

Chapter 6

1. Jodie Steelman Wilson, Emily Griffin Winfrey, and Rebecca McDole, *Hidden History of Montgomery County, Indiana* (Charleston, SC: History Press, 2012).

2. United Press, June 2, 1931.

3. Associated Press, October 21, 1932.

4. Franklin D. Roosevelt speech, Monument Circle, Indianapolis, Ind., October 20, 1932, Franklin D. Roosevelt Presidential Library and Museum, Hyde Park, NY (hereafter cited as Roosevelt Library).

5. Ibid.

6. Ibid.

7. Associated Press, October 21, 1932.

8. Ibid.

9. Ibid., October 22, 1932.

10. Ibid., October 21, 1932.

11. Ibid., December 10, 1935.

12. Ibid.

13. United Press, December 10, 1935.

14. Ibid.

15. Roosevelt speech, George Rogers Clark Memorial, Vincennes, Ind., June 14, 1936, Roosevelt Library.

16. Ibid.

17. Ibid.

18. Ibid.

19. James Philip Fadely, "Editors, Whistle Stops and Elephants: The Presidential Campaign of 1936 in Indiana," *Indiana Magazine of History* 85 (June 1989):111–12.

20. *New York Times*, August 27, 1936.

21. Ibid.

22. Roosevelt remarks, rear train platform, Gary, Ind., Aug. 26, 1936, Roosevelt Library.

23. Ibid.

24. Ibid.

25. Ibid.

26. Fadely, "Editors, Whistle Stops and Elephants," 115–16.

27. *Independent News Service*, September 5, 1936.

28. Roosevelt speech, Indianapolis Athletic Club, Indianapolis, Ind., September 5, 1936, Roosevelt Library.

29. Ibid.

30. Ibid.

31. *New York Times*, April 30, 1943.

32. United Press, April 29, 1943.

33. Associated Press, April 29, 1943.

34. Ibid.

35. Darrel E. Bigham, *Evansville: The World War II Years* (Charleston, SC: Arcadia Publishing, 2005), 17.

36. *Fort Wayne Journal-Gazette*, October 25, 1944.

37. Franklin D. Roosevelt remarks, Union Station, Fort Wayne, Ind., October 28, 1944, The American Presidency Project, http://ww.presidency.uscb.edu/ (hereafter cited as American Presidency Project).

38. Ibid.

39. Ibid.

40. Ibid.

41. Ibid.

42. Ibid.

43. United Press, June 16, 1931.

44. Herbert Hoover remarks, rear train platform, Fort Wayne, Ind., October 5, 1932, American Presidency Project.

45. Hoover remarks, rear train platform, Connersville, Ind., October 6, 1932, ibid.

46. Hoover remarks, rear train platform, Rushville, Ind., October 6, 1932, ibid.

47. Associated Press, October 29, 1932.

48. Ibid.

49. Ibid.

50. Ibid.

51. Ibid.

52. Ibid.

53. Ibid.

54. Hoover speech, Butler University Fieldhouse, Indianapolis, Ind., October 28, 1932, American Presidency Project.

55. Ibid.

56. Ibid.

57. Ibid.

58. *Elkhart Truth*, November 4, 1932.

59. Hoover remarks, rear train platform, Nappanee, Ind., November 4, 1932, American Presidency Project.

60. *Elkhart Truth*, November 4, 1932; *Goshen News-Times*, November 4, 1932.

61. *Elkhart Truth*, November 4, 1932.

62. Hoover remarks, rear train platform, Wellsboro, Ind., November 4, 1932, American Presidency Project.

63. *Gary Post-Tribune*, November 4, 1932.

64. Ibid.

65. Hoover remarks, Gateway Park, Gary, Ind., November 4, 1932, American Presidency Project.

66. *Gary Post-Tribune*, November 4, 1932.

67. Hoover remarks, Gateway Park, Gary, Ind., November 4, 1932, American Presidency Project.

68. Ibid.

69. *Gary Post-Tribune*, November 4, 1932.

70. Herbert Hoover remarks, Gateway Park, Gary, Ind., November 4, 1932, American Presidency Project.

71. Associated Press, April 4, 1936.

72. Ibid.

73. Ibid.

74. Ibid.

75. Ibid.

76. Ibid.

77. Ibid.

78. United Press International, April 6, 1959.

79. Ibid.

80. Fadely, "Editors, Whistle Stops, and Elephants," 101.

81. *Valparaiso Vidette-Messenger*, September 12, 1936.

82. Fadely, "Editors, Whistle Stops and Elephants," 120–21.

83. *Valparaiso Vidette-Messenger*, September 12, 1936.

84. Ibid.

85. Ibid.

86. Fadely, " Editors, Whistle Stops, and Elephants," 122.

87. Associated Press, September 12, 1936.

88. Ibid.

89. United Press International, October 15, 1936.

90. Associated Press, October 15, 1936.

91. United Press International, October 15, 1936.

92. *Indianapolis News*, October 15, 1936.

93. Fadely, "Editors, Whistle Stops, and Elephants," 132.

94. Ibid.

95. Ibid., 133; Associated Press, October 24, 1936.

96. *Greensburg Daily News*, October 27, 1936.

97. United Press, October 24, 1936.

98. Ibid.

99. Ibid.

100. Ross Gregory, "Politics in an Age of Crisis: America, and Indiana, in the Election of 1940," *Indiana Magazine of History* 86 (September 1990):256.

101. Ibid., 257.

102. Ibid.

103. *Elwood Call-Leader*, August 8, 1940.

104. *Indianapolis Star*, August 18, 1940.

105. Ibid.

106. Wendell L. Willkie speech, Callaway Park, Elwood, Ind., August 17, 1940, American Presidency Project.

107. Ibid.

108. Ibid.

109. Ibid.

110. Ibid.

111. Ibid.

112. Ibid.

113. Ibid.

114. Ibid.

115. Ibid.

116. Ibid.

117. Ibid.

118. Ibid.

119. *Elwood Call-Leader*, August 19, 1940.

120. Ibid.

121. Ibid.

122. United Press, August 19, 1940.

123. Associated Press. August 19, 1940.

124. Ibid.

125. United Press, August 20, 1940.

126. Ibid., September 7, 1940.

127. Associated Press, October 29, 1940.

128. Gregory, "Politics in an Age of Crisis," 279–80.

129. Associated Press, February 25, 1941.

130. *Baltimore Afro-American*, March 6, 1943.

131. Associated Press, October 9, 1944.

132. United Press, October 17, 1944.

133. *Christian Science Monitor*, April 16, 1940.

134. *New York Times*, April 16, 1940.

135. *Christian Science Monitor*, April 16, 1940.

136. Ibid.

137. United Press, May 21, 1940.

138. Ibid.

Chapter 7

1. President Harry S Truman remarks, rear train platform , Fort Wayne, Ind., June 4, 1948, The American Presidency Project, http://www.presidency.ucsb.edu/ (hereafter cited as American Presidency Project).

2. Ibid.

3. Ibid.

4. Truman remarks, rear train platform, Gary, Ind., June 4, 1948, American Presidency Project.

5. Ibid.

6. Ibid.

7. Ibid.

8. Truman remarks, rear train platform, Terre Haute, Ind., June 17, 1948, American Presidency Project.

9. Ibid.

10. Ibid.

11. Truman remarks, rear train platform, Richmond, Ind., June 17, 1948, American Presidency Project.

12. Truman remarks, rear train platform, Mount Vernon, Ind., September 30, 1948, ibid.

13. Truman remarks, rear train platform, Evansville, Ind., September 30, 1948, ibid.

14. Ibid.

15. Ibid.

16. Ibid.

17. Truman remarks, rear train platform, Richmond, Ind., October 12, 1948, American Presidency Project.

18. Ibid.

19. Zachary Karabell, *The Last Campaign: How Harry Truman Won the 1948 Election* (New York: Random House Digital, Inc., 2007), 247.

20. Truman remarks, rear train platform, Greenfield, Ind., Oct. 12, 1948, American Presidency Project.

21. Ibid.

22. Ibid.

23. Truman remarks, rear train platform, Crawfordsville, Ind., October 12, 1948, American Presidency Project.

24. Ibid.

25. Ibid.

26. Truman remarks, rear train platform, Hammond, Ind., October 15, 1948, American Presidency Project.

27. Ibid.

28. Ibid.

29. Truman remarks, rear train platform, North Judson, Ind., October 15, 1948, American Presidency Project.

30. Truman remarks, rear train platform, Logansport, Ind., October 15, 1948, ibid.

31. Ibid.

32. Truman remarks, rear train platform, Kokomo, Ind., October 15, 1948, American Presidency Project.

33. Ibid.

34. Ibid.

35. William J. Bray oral history interview, Recollections of the 1948 Campaign, recorded August 1964, Harry S. Truman Library and Museum, Independence, MO (hereafter cited as Truman Library).

36. Ibid.

37. Truman remarks, rear train platform, Tipton, Ind., October 15, 1948, American Presidency Project.

38. Truman remarks, rear train platform, Noblesville, Ind., October 15, 1948, ibid.

39. William J. Bray oral history interview.

40. Truman speech, Indianapolis Athletic Club, Indianapolis, Ind., October 15, 1948, American Presidency Project.

41. Ibid.

42. Ibid.

43. Ibid.

44. Ibid.

45. Ibid.

46. Ibid.

47. Ibid.

48. Ibid.

49. William J. Bray oral history interview.

50. Ibid.

51. Truman remarks, rear train platform, Garrett, Ind., October 25, 1948, American Presidency Project.

52. Ibid.

53. Truman speech, Memorial Auditorium, Gary, Ind., October 25, 1948, American Presidency Project.

54. Ibid.

55. Ibid.

56. Truman remarks, rear train platform, South Bend, Ind., October 26, 1948, American Presidency Project.

57. Truman remarks, rear train platform, Elkhart, Ind., October 26, 1948, ibid.

58. Truman remarks, rear train platform, Terre Haute, Ind., October 30, 1948, ibid.

59. *Christian Science Monitor*, October 10, 1948.

60. Ibid.

61. Truman remarks, rear train platform, Vincennes, Ind., November 4, 1948, American Presidency Project.

62. Ibid.

63. U.S. Constitution, Twenty-second Amendment.

64. Truman remarks, Union Station, Indianapolis, Ind., October 9, 1952, American Presidency Project.

65. Ibid.

66. Truman remarks, rear train platform, Anderson, Ind., October 9, 1952, American Presidency Project.

67. Ibid.

68. Truman remarks, rear train platform, Muncie, Ind., October 9, 1952, American Presidency Project.

69. Ibid..

70. Ibid.

71. Truman speech, Memorial Auditorium, Gary, Ind., October 27, 1952, American Presidency Project.

72. *Milwaukee Sentinel*, October 28, 1952.

73. Associated Press, November 1, 1952.

74. Ibid.

75. Ibid., June 21, 1953.

76. Matthew Algeo, *Harry Truman's Excellent Adventure: The True Story of a Great American Road Trip* (Chicago: Chicago Review Press, Inc., 2009).

77. Ibid.

78. Associated Press, July 9, 1953.

79. Ibid.

80. Ibid.

81. Ibid.

82. United Press, August 27, 1955.

83. *New York Times*, August 28, 1955.

84. Ibid.

85. Ibid.

86. *Milwaukee Sentinel*, August 29, 1955.

87. Associated Press. September 12, 1958.

88. Ibid.

89. Truman speech, Memorial Auditorium, Gary, Ind., October 18, 1956, Post-Presidential Papers, Truman Library.

90. Ibid.

91. Ibid.

92. Ibid.

93. Ibid.

94. Ibid.

95. Ibid.

96. Ibid.

97. United Press, March 12, 1944.

98. Ibid.

99. Robert A. Taft, "Usurpation of Power by the Executive Branch," *Congressional Record*, 90(8) (March 13, 1944).

100. United Press, March 12, 1944.

101. Taft, "Usurpation of Power by the Executive Branch."

102. Ibid.

103. *New York Times*, June 24, 1951.

104. Ibid.

105. Ibid.

106. Ibid., June 8, 1952.

107. Ibid., June 7, 1952.

108. Ibid., October 10, 1952.

109. Associated Press, October 12, 1952.

110. United Press International, October 10, 1952.

111. *New York Times*, October 11, 1952.

112. United Press International, October 11, 1952.

113. *Elkhart Truth*, October 11, 1952.

114. *Kokomo Tribune*, October 11, 1952.

115. President Dwight D. Eisenhower statement, July 31, 1953.

116. William J. Bray oral history interview.

117. *Time* magazine, October 25, 1948.

118. *New York Times*, October 16, 1948.

119. Ibid.

120. *Valparaiso Vidette-Messenger*, October 14, 1948.

121. *Rensselaer Republican*, October 16, 1948.

122. *Valparaiso Vidette-Messenger*, October 18, 1948.

123. *Rensselaer Republican*, October 16, 1948.

124. Ibid.

125. Ibid.

126. *Valparaiso Vidette-Messenger*, October 18, 1948.

127. G. A. Donaldson, *Truman Defeats Dewey* (Lexington: University Press of Kentucky, 2000).

128. Associated Press, April 3, 1948.

129. *Chicago Tribune*, January 9, 1948.

130. United Press, March 22, 1948.

131. Associated Press, April 7, 1948.

132. Ibid., April 7, 1948.

133. Henry A. Wallace speech, Memorial Coliseum, Evansville, Ind., April 6, 1948, collection of University of Iowa Libraries, Iowa City, IA (hereafter cited as University of Iowa Libraries).

134. Ibid.

135. Ibid.

136. Ibid.

137. Ibid.

138. Ibid.

139. Ibid.

140. Ibid.

141. *Baltimore Sun*, April 8, 1948.

142. Associated Press, April 8, 1948.

143. Henry A. Wallace speech, Indiana National Guard Armory, Indianapolis, Ind., April 7, 1948, f University of Iowa Libraries.

144. Ibid.

145. United Press, April 12, 1948.

146. Wallace speech, April 7, 1948.

147. Ibid.

148. Wallace speech, Gary, Ind., April 8, 1948, University of Iowa Libraries.

149. Ibid.

150. Ibid.

151. *New York Times*, April 20, 1948.

152. United Press, September 27, 1948.

153. Ibid.

154. Wallace speech, September 24, 1940, Cadle Tabernacle, Indianapolis, Ind., University of Iowa Libraries.

155. Ibid.

156. Ibid.

157. Ibid.

158. Ibid.

159. Ibid.

160. Ibid.

161. Ibid.

162. Ibid..

163. Ibid.

164. Ibid.

165. Ibid.

166. Morrison-Reeves Library, Richmond, IN, www .mrlinfo.org/famous-visitors/Eisenhower.htm.

167. *New York Times*, September 10, 1952

168. Ibid.

169. Ibid.

170. Ibid.

171. Ibid., September 16, 1952.

172. Ibid., September 15, 1952.

173. Ibid.

174. Ibid..

175. Ibid., September 16, 1952.

176. Ibid., September 15, 1952.

177. Ibid., September 16, 1952.

178. Ibid.

179. Ibid., September 15, 1952.

180. Associated Press, September 16, 1952.

181. *New York Times*, September 16, 1952.

182. Ibid., September 15, 1952.

183. Ibid., September 16, 1952.

184. Ibid.

185. Ibid.

186. Associated Press, September 16, 1952.

187. *New York Times*, September 16, 1952.

188. Associated Press, October 16, 1954.

189. President Dwight D. Eisenhower speech, Butler Fieldhouse, Butler University, Indianapolis, Ind., October 15, 1954, American Presidency Project.

190. Ibid.

191. Associated Press, October 16, 1954.

192. Eisenhower speech, Columbia Club, Indianapolis, Ind., October 15, 1954, American Presidency Project.

193. Ibid.

194. Ibid.

195. Ibid.

196. Jean H. Baker, *The Stevensons: A Biography of an American Family* (New York: W. W. Norton and Co., 1996), ix.

197. *New York Times*, September 26, 1952.

198. Ibid.

199. Ibid.

200. Ibid.

201. Ibid.

202. Ibid.

203. Ibid.

204. Ibid

205. Ibid.

206. Associated Press, October 23, 1952.

207. *Elkhart Truth*, December 23, 1955; *Goshen News*, December 23, 1952.

208. *Saint Petersburg (FL) Times*, March 29, 1956.

209. Associated Press, September 28, 1956.

210. United Press, September 28, 1956.

211. Ibid.

212. Ibid, October 22, 1956.

213. Ibid.

214. Ibid.

215. Ibid.

216. Ibid.

217. *Richmond Palladium-Item*, May 15, 1949.

218. Ibid.

219. Ibid.

220. Ibid.

221. Ibid.

222. *New York Times*, October 16, 1952.

223. Ibid.

224. Ibid., October 25, 1952.

225. Ibid.

226. Ibid., September 24, 1954.

227. *Warsaw Times-Union*, September 19, 1955.

228. Ibid.

229. Associated Press, September 18, 1955.

230. Ibid.

231. Ibid.

232. Ibid.

233. Ibid.

234. Ibid.

235. *New York Times*, October 23, 1956.

236. Ibid.

237. *Indianapolis Star*, May 12, 1957.

238. *Rochester News-Sentinel*, October 5, 1959.

239. Associated Press, October 6, 1959.

240. William Bridges, "An Almost Great Man (1956)," Green Market Press Blog: the Books and Writings of William Bridges, https://greenmarketpress.wordpress.com/2009/08/22/journalism-i/.

241. Ibid.

242. *New York Times*, May 6, 1956.

243. Associated Press, May 6, 1956.

244. *New York Times*, August 25, 1951.

245. Ibid.

246. Ibid.

247. Ibid.

248. Ibid.

249. John F. Kennedy speech, Executive Committee-American Legion, Indianapolis, Ind., October 16, 1953, http://www.jfklibrary.org/Research/Research-Aids/JFK-Speeches/Indianapolis-IN_19531016.aspx.

250. Ibid.

251. Ibid.

252. John F. Kennedy speech, United Negro College Fund Convocation, Indianapolis, Ind., April 12, 1959, http://www.jfklibrary.org/Research/Research-Aids/JFK-Speeches/Indianapolis-IN_19590412.aspx.

253. Ibid.

254. Ibid.

255. Ibid.

256. United Press International, April 15, 1959.

257. Associated Press, April 14, 1959.

258. United Press International, October 4, 1959.

259. Ibid., October 3, 1959.

260. Ibid.

261. Ibid., October 5, 1959.

262. *Jasper Herald*, October 5, 1959.

263. Ibid.

Chapter 8

1. Christopher Matthews, *Kennedy and Nixon: The Rivalry That Shaped Postwar America*. (New York: Simon and Schuster, 1996), 15.

2. Ibid.

3. *Indianapolis Star*, September 12, 1960.

4. Vice President Richard M. Nixon speech, Monument Circle, Indianapolis, Ind., September 12, 1960, Gerhard Peters and John T. Woolley, The American Presidency Project, http://www.presidency.ucsb.edu/ (hereafter cited as American Presidency Project).

5. Ibid.

6. Ibid.

7. Ibid.

8. Ibid.

9. Ibid.

10. Ibid.

11. Ibid.

12. *Indianapolis Star*, September 13, 1960.

13. United Press International, September 21, 1960.

14. *Warsaw Times-Union* , September 22, 1960.

15. Nixon speech, Allen County Courthouse, Fort Wayne, Ind., September 21, 1960, American Presidency Project.

16. Ibid.

17. Ibid.

18. Ibid.

19. Ibid.

20. Ibid.

21. Ibid.

22. Ibid.

23. Ibid.

24. Nixon speech, Roberts Municipal Auditorium, Evansville, Ind., October 1, 1960, American Presidency Project.

25. Ibid.

26. Ibid.

27. Associated Press, October 2, 1960.

28. Alonzo L. Hamby, "1948 Democratic Convention," *Smithsonian Magazine* (August 2008).

29. Associated Press, February 9, 1960.

30. Ibid.

31. John F. Kennedy news conference, Weir Cook Airport, Indianapolis, Ind., February 4, 1960, John F. Kennedy Presidential Library, http://www.jfklibrary.org/Research/Research-Aids/JFK-Speeches/Indianapolis-IN_19600204.aspx/.

32. Ibid.

33. Ibid.

34. *Chicago Sun-Times*, February 8, 1960.

35. Ibid.

36. Ibid.

37. Associated Press, February 4, 1960.

38. Ibid.

39. Ibid.

40. Ibid.

41. John F. Kennedy speech, Lake County Democratic Women's Club, Gary, Ind., February 5, 1960, http://www.jfklibrary.org/Research/Research-Aids/JFK-Speeches/Gary-IN_19600205.aspx/.

42. Ibid.

43. Ibid.

44. John F. Kennedy speech, Lake County Democratic Luncheon, East Chicago, Ind., February 5, 1960, http://www.jfklibrary.org/Research/Research-Aids/JFK-Speeches/East-Chicago-IN_19600205.aspx/.

45. Ibid.

46. Ibid.

47. John F. Kennedy speech, Wabash Valley Lecture Series, Terre Haute, Ind., February 5, 1960, http://www.jfklibrary.org/Research/Research-Aids/JFK-Speeches/Terre-Haute-IN_19600206.aspx/.

48. *Chicago Sun-Times*, February 8, 1960.

49. *New York Times*, March 21, 1960.

50. Associated Press, March 21, 1960.

51. Ibid.

52. *New York Times*, March 21, 1960.

53. John F. Kennedy speech, Farm Forum, Alexandria, Ind., April 7, 1960, http://www.jfklibrary.org/Research/Research-Aids/JFK-Speeches/Alexandria-IN_19600407.aspx/.

54. Ibid.

55. Ibid.

56. John F Kennedy speech, Tippecanoe County Jefferson-Jackson Day Dinner, April 7, 1960, http://www.jfklibrary.org/Research/Research-Aids/JFK-Speeches/Lafayette-IN_19600407.aspx/.

57. *South Bend Tribune*, April 9, 1960.

58. Ibid.

59. Ibid.

60. Ibid., April 7, 1960.

61. John F. Kennedy speech, Earlham College, Richmond, Ind., April 29, 1960, http://www.jfklibrary.org/Asset-Viewer/9wR9mbJ6GUS_8eNMAAW1qg.aspx/.

62. Ibid.

63. Ibid.

64. Ibid.

65. John F. Kennedy speech, Wayne County Jefferson-Jackson Day event, Richmond, Ind., April 29, 1960, http://www.jfklibrary.org/Research/Research-Aids/JFK-Speeches/Richmond-IN_19600429.aspx/.

66. Ibid.

67. John F. Kennedy speech, Howard County Courthouse, Kokomo, Ind., April 29, 1960, http://www.jfklibrary.org/Research/Research-Aids/JFK-Speeches/Howard-County-IN_19600429.aspx/.

68. Ibid.

69. John F. Kennedy speech, Vigo County Courthouse, Terre Haute, Ind., October. 5, 1960, http://www.jfklibrary.org/Research/Research-Aids/JFK-Speeches/Terre-Haute-IN_19601005.aspx/.

70. Ibid.

71. Ibid.

72. *Indianapolis Star*, October 5, 1960.

73. Ibid.

74. Ibid.

75. Franklin D. Roosevelt speech, Philadelphia, Pa., June 27, 1936, American Presidency Project.

76. John F. Kennedy speech, State Fairgrounds Coliseum, Indianapolis, Ind., October 4, 1960, American Presidency Project.

77. Ibid.

78. Ibid.

79. Ibid.

80. John F. Kennedy speech, train platform, Anderson, Ind., October 5, 1960, http://www.jfklibrary.org/Research/Research-Aids/JFK-Speeches/Anderson-IN_19601005.aspx/.

81. Ibid.

82. John F. Kennedy speech, train platform, Pendleton, Ind., October 5, 1960, http://www.jfklibrary.org/Research/Research-Aids/JFK-Speeches/Pendleton-IN_19601005.asp/.

83. John F. Kennedy speech, train platform, Muncie, October 5, 1960, http://www.jfklibrary.org/Research/Research-Aids/JFK-Speeches/Muncie-IN_19601005.aspx.

84. Ibid.

85. Ibid.

86. John F. Kennedy remarks, Muncie Gear Works Factory, Muncie, Ind., October 5, 1960, http://www.jfklibrary.org/Research/Research-Aids/JFK-Speeches/Muncie-IN_19601005-Gear-Works.aspx/.

87. John F. Kennedy speech, Vanderburgh County Courthouse, Evansville, Ind., October 4, 1960, http://www.jfklibrary.org/Research/Research-Aids/JFK-Speeches/Evansville-IN_19601004.aspx/.

88. Ibid.

89. Ibid.

90. *Indianapolis Star*, October 4, 1960.

91. John F. Kennedy speech, White House, Washington, D.C., October 22, 1962, American Presidency Project.

92. John F. Kennedy speech, Weir Cook Airport, Indianapolis, Ind., October 13, 1962, ibid.

93. Ibid.

94. Ibid.

95. Ibid.

96. Ibid.

97. Ibid.

98. United Press International, September 29, 1960.

99. Ibid.

100. Ibid.

101. Ibid.

102. Ibid.

103. Associated Press, September 29, 1960.

104. United Press International, October 7, 1963.

105. Associated Press, October 8, 1963.

106. Ibid.

107. United Press International, October 7, 1963.

108. Associated Press, October 8, 1963.

109. Ibid.

110. Ibid., September 23, 1960.

111. *Benton Harbor (MI) News-Palladium*, September 23, 1960.

112. Ibid.

113. Associated Press, September 23, 1960.

114. Ibid.

115. Ibid.

116. Ibid.

117. Ibid.

118. Ibid.

119. Senator Hubert H. Humphrey speech, Claypool Hotel, Indianapolis, January 30, 1960, collection of the Minnesota Historical Society.

120. Ibid.

121. Ibid.

122. Humphrey news release dated September 8, 1958, Minnesota Historical Society.

123. Ibid.

124. University of Notre Dame *Scholastic* magazine, December 9, 1955.

125. Senator Hubert H. Humphrey news release dated January 29, 1951, collection of the Minnesota Historical Society.

126. Ibid.

127. Ibid.

128. University of Notre Dame *Scholastic* magazine, October 16, 1964.

129. Ibid.

130. Associated Press, December 13, 1959.

131. Theodore H. White, *The Making of the President 1960* (New York: Harper Collins, 1961), 74.

132. University of Notre Dame *Scholastic* magazine, May 20, 1960.

133. Associated Press, June 6, 1960.

134. Ibid.

135. Ibid.

136. Dwight D. Eisenhower speech, Jasper County Courthouse, Rensselaer, Ind., September 13, 1962, Eisenhower Presidential Library, Abilene, KS.

137. Ibid.

138. Ibid.

139. Ibid.

140. Ibid.

141. Ibid.

142. *Rensselaer Republican*, September. 14, 1962.

143. United Press, September 13, 1962.

144. *Rensselaer Republican*, September 14, 1962.

145. Recording of White House meeting with President John F. Kennedy and former president Dwight D. Eisenhower, White House Meeting Recordings, September 10, 1962, Tape 21, Miller Center Collection, University of Virginia, Charlottesville, VA.

146. Associated Press, September 6, 1960.

147. Ibid.

148. Notes on the 1960 Presidential Campaign, Harry S. Truman Presidential Library and Museum, Independence, MO.

149. Associated Press, October 7, 1962.

150. United Press International, October 8, 1962.

151. Associated Press, October 8, 1962.

152. Ibid., October 7, 1962.

153. *New York Times*, March 31, 1964.

154. Civil Rights Act of 1964, Public Law 88-352, enacted July 2, 1964.

155. R. D. Johnson and K. B. Germany, eds., *The Presidential Recordings of President Lyndon B. Johnson*, volume 46 (Charlottesville, VA: Miller Center of Public Affairs, 2007).

156. White House Press Secretary news release, April 24, 1964.

157. President Lyndon B. Johnson remarks, Lulu V. Cline School, South Bend, Ind., April 24, 1964, American Presidency Project.

158. Ibid.

159. Ibid.

160. Associated Press, October 8, 1964.

161. Johnson speech, Washington High School, East

Chicago, Ind., October 8, 1964, American Presidency Project.

162. Ibid.

163. Ibid.

164. Ibid.

165. Ibid.

166. Ibid.

167. Associated Press, October. 8, 1964.

168. Ibid.

169. Johnson speech, Monument Circle, Indianapolis, Ind., October 8, 1964, American Presidency Project.

170. Ibid.

171. Ibid.

172. Ibid.

173. Scripps-Howard News Service, October 8, 1964.

174. Johnson remarks, Evansville Memorial Airport, Evansville, Ind., October 27, 1964, American Presidency Project.

175. Ibid.

176. Johnson remarks, South Bend Municipal Airport, South Bend, Ind., April 14, 1965, American Presidency Project.

177. Johnson speech, Monument Circle, Indianapolis, Ind., July 23, 1966, ibid.

178. William Stewart Logan, *Hanoi: Biography of a City* (Sydney, Australia: University of New South Wales Press, Ltd., 2000).

179. Johnson speech, July 23, 1966.

180. Ibid.

181. Ibid.

182. Ibid.

183. Ibid.

184. Ibid.

185. *New York Times*, July 24, 1966.

186. Johnson remarks, George Rogers Clark National Historic Park, Vincennes, Ind., July 23, 1966, American Presidency Project.

187. Ibid.

188. Ibid.

189. Ibid.

190. Ibid.

191. Ibid.

192. Ibid.

193. Johnson speech, U.S. Post Office, Jeffersonville, Ind., July 23, 1966, American Presidency Project.

194. Ibid.

195. Ibid.

196. Inaugural Address of Governor George C. Wallace, Alabama State Capitol, Montgomery, Ala., January 14, 1963, Alabama Department of Archives and History, Montgomery, AL.

197. *Time* magazine, April 15, 1964.

198. *New York Times*, April 1, 1964.

199. Ibid.

200. *The Nation*, May 4, 1964.

201. *New York Times*, April 30, 1964.

202. Ibid.

203. Ibid., May 1, 1964.

204. Ibid.

205. *Charleston (SC) News & Courier*, May 2, 1964.

206. Ibid.

207. Ibid.

208. Associated Press, April 24, 1964.

209. Ibid.

210. Ibid.

211. Ibid.

212. Jodie Steelman Wilson, Emily Griffin, and Rebecca McDole, *The Hidden History of Montgomery County, Indiana* (Charleston, SC: History Press, 2012).

213. A. King, "George Corley Wallace--Four-Term Governor of Alabama," in Bernard K. Duffy and Richard W. Leeman, eds, *American Voices: An Encyclopedia of Contemporary Orators* (Westport, CT: Greenwood Press, 2005).

214. Associated Press, April 22, 1964.

215. *New York Times*, April 17, 1964.

216. Associated Press, April 16, 1964.

217. *The Nation*, May 4, 1964.

218. *New York Times*, April 17, 1964.

219. *Charleston (SC) News & Courier*, May 5, 1964.

220. Ibid.

221. Ibid.

222. Ibid.

223. Ibid.

224. *Time* magazine, April 24, 1964.

225. *Charleston (SC) News & Courier*, May 5, 1964.

226. *New York Times*, April 26, 1964

227. Ibid.

228. Rick Perlstein, *Before the Storm: Barry Goldwater and the Unmaking of the American Consensus* (New York: Nation Books, 2009).

229. Associated Press, April 22, 1964.

230. Perlstein, *Before the Storm.*

231. Matthew E. Welsh, "Civil Rights and the Primary Election of 1964 in Indiana: The Wallace Challenge," *Indiana Magazine of History* 75 (March 1979): 2.

232. Perlstein, *Before the Storm*.

233. *New York Times*, October 8, 1964.

234. *South Bend Tribune*, May 30, 1998.

235. Ibid.

236. Ibid.

237. John William Middendorf, *A Glorious Disaster: Barry Goldwater's Presidential Campaign and the Origins of the Conservative Movement* (New York: Basic Books, 2006).

238. *New York Times*, October 2, 1964.

239. Associated Press, October 2, 1964.

240. Ibid.

241. Ibid.

242. Ibid.

243. Ibid.

244. Ibid.

245. *Toledo (OH) Blade*, October 2, 1964.

246. Associated Press, October 2, 1964.

247. *Toledo (OH) Blade*, October 2, 1964.

248. Associated Press, October 2, 1964.

249. *Logansport Pharos-Tribune*, October 2, 1964.

250. *New York Times*, October 11, 1964.

251. Ibid.

252. *South Bend Tribune*, April 24, 1994.

Chapter 9

1. Lyndon B. Johnson Speech, March 31, 1968, http://www.lbjlib.utexas.edu/johnson/archives.hom/speeches.hom/680331.asp.

2. Edward M. Kennedy, *True Compass* (New York: Hachette Book Group, 2009).

3. *Time* magazine, May 3, 1968.

4. Ibid., May 17, 1968.

5. *Oakland (CA) Tribune*, May 6, 1968.

6. Ibid.

7. John B. Straw, "RFK in Middletown: Robert Kennedy's Speech at Ball State University, April 4, 1968," Archives and Special Collections, Ball State University Library, http://libx.bsu.edu/cdm/ref/collection/RFKen/id/23.

8. Ibid.

9. Robert F. Kennedy speech, Seventeenth Street and Broadway Avenue, Indianapolis, Ind., April 4, 1968, http://www.jfklibrary.org/Research/Research-Aids/Ready-Reference/RFK-Speeches/Statement-on-the-Assassination-of-Martin-Luther-King.aspx/.

10. Ibid.

11. Ibid.

12. James Kilpatrick national column, *Tuscaloosa (AL) News*, April 28, 1968.

13. Associated Press, May 5, 1968.

14. James Kilpatrick national column, *Tuscaloosa (AL) News*, April 28, 1968.

15. *Youngstown (OH) Vindicator*, April 29, 1968.

16. Ray E. Boomhower, *Robert F. Kennedy and the 1968 Indiana Primary* (Indianapolis: Indiana Historical Society Press, 2008), 110.

17. *New York Times*, May 5, 1968.

18. Ibid.

19. Associated Press, May 3, 1968.

20. *New York Times*, May 5, 1968.

21. Boomhower, *Robert F. Kennedy and the 1968 Indiana Primary*, 11.

22. *Time* magazine, May 17, 1968.

23. Ibid.

24. Ibid.

25. Ibid.

26. Senator Edward M. "Teddy" Kennedy, eulogy of his brother Robert F. Kennedy, St. Patrick's Cathedral, New York City, June 8, 1968, AmericanRhetoric.com/.

27. *New York Times*, April 28, 1968.

28. Ray E. Boomhower, "Roger D. Branigin," in *The Governors of Indiana,* edited by Linda C. Gugin and James E. St. Clair (Indianapolis: Indiana Historical Society Press), 349–50.

29. Ibid., 346, 350.

30. *New York Times*, May 5, 1968.

31. *Time* magazine, May 3, 1968 .

32. United Press International, April 28, 1968.

33. Ibid., May 2, 1968.

34. Associated Press, May 6, 1968.

35. *Newsweek* magazine, May 20, 1968.

36. *Oakland (CA) Tribune*, May 6, 1968.

37. *South Bend Tribune*, September 28, 1968.

38. *New York Times*, April 22, 1968.

39. Ibid.

40. Jodie Steelman Wilson, Emily Griffin, and Rebecca McDole, *The Hidden History of Montgomery County, Indiana* (Charleston, SC: History Press, 2012).

41. *Oakland (CA) Tribune*, May 6, 1968.

42. *Time* magazine, May 3, 1968.

43. Dominic Sanbrook,. *Eugene McCarthy: The Rise and Fall of Postwar American Liberalism* (New York: Random House Digital, Inc., 2004), 191.

44. *Toledo (OH) Blade*, April 25, 1968.

44. Ibid.

46. *Newsweek* magazine, May 20, 1968, p. 40.

47. Sanbrook, *Eugene McCarthy*, 188.

48. Associated Press, May 6, 1968.

49. Sanbrook, *Eugene McCarthy*, 199.
50. *New York Times*, May 5, 1968.
51. Ibid.
52. Ibid.
53. Associated Press, April 26, 1968.
54. Darcy G. Richardson, *A Nation Divided: The 1968 Presidential Campaign* (Bloomington, IN: iUniverse, 2002), 90.
55. *New York Times*, August 17, 1968.
56. Ibid., September 16, 1968.
57. Ibid., August 17, 1968.
58. Ibid.
59. Ibid.
60. Ibid.
61. Ibid.
62. Ibid., September 16, 1968.
63. *Miami (FL) News*, August 20, 1968.
64. United Press International, October 4, 1968.
65. Associated Press, October 10, 1968.
66. United Press International, October 4, 1968.
67. Associated Press, October 4, 1968.
68. Ibid.
69. Ibid.
70. Ibid., October 10, 1968.
71. United Press International, October 10, 1968.
72. Associated Press, October 10, 1968.
73. United Press International, October 27, 1968.
74. Carl Solberg, *Hubert Humphrey: A Biography* (Minneapolis: Minnesota Historical Society, 2003), 332.
75. Ibid., 333.
76. Ibid.
77. *Washington Post*, May 19, 1968.
78. United Press International, October 15, 1968.
79. Associated Press, October 15, 1968.
80. United Press International, October 15, 1968.
81. Associated Press, October 15, 1968.
82. United Press International, October 15, 1968.
83. Associated Press, October 15, 1968.
84. Ibid.
85. United Press International, October 15, 1968.
86. Ibid.
87. Edmund S. Muskie speech, University of Notre Dame, South Bend, Ind., September 11, 1968, Collection of the Edmund S. Muskie Archives, Bates College, Lewistown ME (hereafter cited as Muskie Archives).
88. Ibid.
89. Muskie speech, West Side Democratic Club, South Bend, Ind., September 11, 1968, Muskie Archives.
90. Ibid.
91. Muskie speech, Lawrence Central High School, Indianapolis, Ind., September 11, 1968, Muskie Archives.
92. Ibid.
93. Ibid.
94. Ibid.
95. Ibid.
96. Muskie speech, Hammond, Ind., October 18, 1968, Muskie Archives.
97. John Chamberlain column, May 20, 1968, King Features Syndicate.
98. United Press International, May 4, 1968.
99. Associated Press, May 4, 1968.
100. *Valparaiso Vidette-Messenger*, May 3, 1968.
101. Ibid.
102. Ibid.
103. Ibid.
104. Associated Press, May 4, 1968.
105. Ibid.
106. United Press International, September 13, 1968.
107. Ibid.
108. Richard M. Nixon remarks, Weir-Cook Municipal Airport, Indianapolis, Ind., February 5, 1970, Gerhard Peters and John T. Woolley, The American Presidency Project, http://www.presidency.ucsb.edu/ (hereafter cited as American Presidency Project).
109. Ibid.
110. Nixon speech, City-County Building, Indianapolis, Ind., February 5, 1970, American Presidency Project.
111. *South Bend Tribune*, April 24, 1994.
112. Nixon speech, February 5, 1970.
113. Ibid.
114. Sears, John, as quoted in Jules Witcover, *Very Strange Bedfellows: The Short and Unhappy Marriage of Richard Nixon and Spiro Agnew* (New York: Public Affairs--Perseus Book Group, 2007).
115. Nixon speech, February 5, 1970.
116. Nixon speech, Memorial Coliseum, Fort Wayne, Ind., October 20, 1970, American Presidency Project.
117. Ibid.
118. Ibid.
119. Ibid.
120. Ibid.
121. Ibid.
122. Ibid.
123. Ibid.
124. Nixon farewell remarks to White House Staff, August 9, 1974, Washington, D.C, American Presidency Project.

125. *Washington Post*, June 25, 1971.

126. Associated Press, June 25, 1971.

127. Nixon remarks at the dedication of a plaque commemorating birthplace of his mother, Jennings County Courthouse, Vernon, Ind., June 24, 1971, American Presidency Project.

128. Ibid.

129. Ibid.

130. Ibid.

131. *Washington Post*, June 25, 1971.

132. Nixon remarks, June 24, 1971.

133. United Press International, June 24, 1971.

134. Ibid., October 16, 1968.

135. Ibid.

136. Associated Press, October 16, 1968.

137. Ibid.

138. United Press International, October 16, 1968.

139. Ibid.

140. Ibid.

141. Ibid.

142. Ibid.

143. Associated Press, October 20, 1970.

144. *Chicago Tribune*, June 14, 1968.

145. Ibid.

146. Ibid.

147. *Anderson Herald-Bulletin*, June 16, 1968.

148. United Press International, June 14, 1968.

149. *Chicago Tribune*, June 14, 1968.

150. *New York Times*, July 16, 1968.

151. United Press International, September 30, 1968.

152. Ibid.

153. Ibid.

Chapter 10

1. Associated Press, October 5, 1972.

2. Ibid.

3. *San Francisco Chronicle*, February 19, 1974.

4. Richard M. Nixon televised remarks, White House, Washington, D.C., August 8, 1974, http://millercenter.org/president/speeches/speech-3871.

5. Associated Press, July 25, 1974.

6. President Gerald R. Ford speech, White House, Washington, D.C., August 9, 1974, Gehard Peters and John T. Woolley, The American Presidency Project, http://www.presidency.ucsb.edu/ (hereafter cited as American Presidency Project).

7. Ibid.

8. Ford speech, Indiana Convention Center, Indianapolis, Ind., October 16, 1974, American Presidency Project.

9. Ibid.

10. Ibid.

11. Ibid.

12. Ford speech, University of Notre Dame Athletic & Convocation Center, South Bend, Ind., March 17, 1975, American Presidency Project.

13. Ibid.

14. Ibid.

15. Ibid.

16. Ibid.

17. Gerald R. Ford, *A Time to Heal: The Autobiography of Gerald R. Ford* (New York: Harper and Row, 1979), 322.

18. Ibid.

19. Ford remarks at White House, December 6, 1973, American Presidency Project.

20. Ford, *Time to Heal*, 322.

21. Ibid., 369.

22. Ford remarks, Weir-Cook Municipal Airport, Indianapolis, Ind., April 22, 1976, American Presidency Project.

23. *Indianapolis Star*, April 23, 1976.

24. Ford remarks, Baer Field Airport, Fort Wayne, Ind., May 2, 1976, American Presidency Project.

25. Ford remarks, Three Rivers Room, Marriott Hotel, Fort Wayne, Ind., May 2, 1976, ibid.

26. *Indianapolis Star*, April 30, 1976.

27. Ibid.

28. Ford speech, Murat Shrine Temple, Indianapolis, Ind., May 3, 1976, American Presidency Project.

29. Ford, *Time to Heal*, 369.

30. Ford speech, May 3, 1976.

31. Ibid

32. *Indianapolis Star*, May 4, 1976.

33. Ibid.

34. Ford speech, May 3, 1976.

35. Ibid.

36. Ford remarks, Fort Wayne, Ind., May 2, 1976.

37. Ford speech, Allen County Memorial Coliseum, Fort Wayne, Ind., May 2, 1976, American Presidency Project.

38. Ibid.

39. President Gerald R. Ford's Schedule for May 2, 1976, Collection of the Gerald R. Ford Library and Museum, Grand Rapids, MI.

40. Ford remarks, Three Rivers Room, Marriott Hotel, Fort Wayne, Ind., May 2, 1976.

41. Ibid.

42. *Newsweek*, May 17, 1976.

43. *Indianapolis Star*, April 23, 1976.

44. Ford speech, Hinkle Fieldhouse, Butler University, Indianapolis, Ind., April 22, 1976, American Presidency Project.

45. Ibid.

46. Ibid.

47. Ibid.

48. Ibid.

49. Ibid.

50. Associated Press, April 23, 1976.

51. Ford remarks, Dress Regional Airport, Evansville, Ind., April 23, 1976, American Presidency Project.

52. Ford speech, Vanderburgh County Auditorium & Convention Center, Evansville, Ind., April 23, 1976, ibid.

53 Ibid.

54. Ibid.

55. Ford remarks, Florida Room, Executive Inn Hotel, Evansville, Ind., April 23, 1976, American Presidency Project.

56. Ford remarks, Fort Wayne, Ind., May 2, 1976.

57. Ibid.

58. Ford speech, Indiana Convention Center, Indianapolis, Ind., June 22, 1976, American Presidency Project.

59. Ibid.

60. Ibid.

61. *Newsweek*, Oct. 11, 1976.

62. Ibid.

63. *U.S. News & World Report*, October 18, 1976.

64. Ford speech, Scottish Rite Cathedral, Indianapolis, Ind., October 28, 1976, American Presidency Project.

65. Ibid.

66. Ibid.

67. Ibid.

68. *Goshen News*, December 8, 1977.

69. Ibid.

70. *Indianapolis Star*, April 24, 1976.

71. Ibid., April 17, 1976.

72. Associated Press, May 2, 1976.

73. *U.S. News & World Report*, April 5, 1976.

74. Ibid.

75. *New York Times*, May 3, 1976.

76. United Press International, April 28, 1976.

77. Ibid.

78. Ibid.

79. *Anderson Herald-Bulletin*, April 28, 1976.

80. United Press International, April 28, 1976.

81. Ibid.

82. *New York Times*, April 24, 1976.

83. Associated Press, April 23, 1976.

84. Ibid.

85. *Newsweek*, May 3, 1976.

86. *Time* magazine, May 17, 1976.

87. Ibid.

88. Ibid.

89. *Indianapolis Star*, April 24, 1976.

90. Ibid.

91. *Time* magazine, May 17, 1976.

92. *Indianapolis Star*, April 24, 1976.

93. Ibid.

94. Ibid.

95. *New York Times*, May 2, 1976.

96. Ibid.

97. Ibid.

98. Ford remarks, Weir-Cook Municipal Airport, Indianapolis, Ind., April 22, 1976, American Presidency Project.

99. *The Economist*, May 8, 1976.

100. Ibid.

101. *Time* magazine, May 17, 1976.

102. *The Economist*, May 8, 1976.

103. *New York Times*, May 5, 1976.

104. Ibid.

105. United Press International, October 25, 1976.

106. Associated Press, September 10, 1976.

107. *New York Times*, October 4, 1972.

108. Ibid.

109. Ibid.

110. Ibid.

111. Ibid.

112. Ibid.

113. Associated Press, April 27, 1972.

114. NBC News, *Meet the Press,* July 25, 2007.

115 United Press International, November 4, 1972.

116. Associated Press, November 4, 1972.

117. Ibid.

118. Ibid.

119. Ibid.

120. Ibid.

121. Theodore H. White, *The Making of the President: 1972* (New York: Harper Collins, 2010), 197.

122. Ibid.

123. Notre Dame *Scholastic,* October 23, 1970.

124. Ibid.

125. Ibid.

126. Ibid.

127. Ibid., November 16, 1973.

128. Ibid.

129. Ibid.

130. Ibid.

131. Ibid.

132. Senator George McGovern speech, Indiana University Southeast, New Albany, Ind., September 9, 1979, Reference Library, IU–Southeast, New Albany, IN.

133. Ibid.

134. Ibid.

135. Ibid.

136. Ibid.

137. White, *Making of the President: 1972.*

138. *New York Times*, April 18, 20, 1972.

139. United Press International, April 14, 1972.

140. Ibid.

141. Ibid., April 29, 1972.

142. Ibid.

143. Associated Press, April 30, 1972.

144. United Press International, April 29, 1972.

145. Ibid.

146. Ibid., April 30, 1972.

147. Ibid., April 6, 1972.

148. Ibid., April 29, 1972.

149. Ibid.

150. Ibid.

151. *Time* magazine, May 15, 1972.

152. Associated Press, March 20, 1972.

153. United Press International, April 27, 1972.

154. Ibid.

155. *New York Times*, April 30, 1972.

156. Associated Press, April 19, 1972.

157. *Milwaukee (WI) Journal*, April 26, 1972.

158. United Press International, April 30, 1972.

159. *Milwaukee (WI) Journal*, April 26, 1972.

160. *Time* magazine, May 15, 1972.

161. *Terre Haute Tribune-*Star, April 25, 1972.

162. Ibid.

163. Ibid.

164. Ibid.

165. *Anderson Herald-Bulletin*, April 30, 1972.

166. *Anderson Herald-Bulletin*, April 30, 1972.

167. United Press International, April 27, 1972.

168. *New York Times*, May 3 and 4, 1972.

169. Ibid., May 8, 1972.

170. *USA Today*, August 5, 2012.

171. *New York Times*, January 11, 1976.

172. Ibid.

173. Associated Press, March 6, 1976.

174. *Indianapolis Star*, April 17, 1976.

175. Ibid., April 23, 1976.

176. Ibid.

177. Ibid.

178. Ibid.

179. Ibid., May 4, 1976.

180. Ibid.

181. Ibid.

182. *New York Times*, July 8, 1976.

183. Ibid., April 28, 1976.

184. Edmund S. Muskie speech, Knights of Columbus Hall, East Chicago, Ind., March 16, 1972, Edmund S. Muskie Archives, Bates College, Lewiston, ME (hereafter cited as Muskie Archives); Associated Press, March 17, 1972.

185. Muskie speech, East Chicago, Ind., March 16, 1972.

186. United Press International, March 17, 1972.

187. Muskie speech, Knights of Columbus Hall, East Chicago, Ind., March 16, 1972.

188. Associated Press, April 7, 1972.

189. *New York Times*, March 10, 1972.

190. Ibid., March 16, 1972.

191. David Frum, *How We Got Here: The '70s* (New York: Basic Books, 2000).

192. Muskie speech, Indiana State Fairgrounds, Indianapolis, Ind., April 23, 1971, Muskie Archives.

193. Ibid.

194. Ibid.

195. Ibid.

196. Ibid.

197. Associated Press, April 24, 1972.

198. Ibid.

199. Ibid., October 6, 1972.

200. Ibid.

201. Ibid.

202. United Press International, October 7, 1972.

203. Ibid.

204. Ibid.

205. *New York Times*, October 11, 1972.

206. Ibid.

207. Associated Press, October 12, 1972.

208. Ibid.

209. Ibid., December 11, 1974.

210. Ibid., October 24, 1975.

211. Ibid.

212. Ibid., November 4, 1975.

213. Ibid., April 2, 1976.

214. Ibid.

215. Facts on File: World News Digest, April 17, 1976.

216. Associated Press, April 9, 1976.

217. Facts on File: World News Digest, April 17, 1976.

218. Associated Press, April 9, 1976.

219. *Sarasota (FL) Herald-Tribune*, April 12, 1976.

220. *New York Times*, May 1, 1976.

221. Ibid., April 28, 1976.

222. Facts on File: World News Digest, May 8, 1976; *Newsweek*, May 17, 1976.

223. *Indianapolis Star*, April 29, 1976.

224. Ibid.

225. *Sarasota (FL) Herald-Tribune*, April 12, 1976.

226. *The Disciple* magazine, March 7, 1976.

227. Jimmy Carter speech, June 19, 1976, Purdue University, West Lafayette, Ind., Archival collection of Wheaton College, Wheaton, IL (hereafter cited as Wheaton College Collection).

228. Ibid.

229. Ibid.

230. Ibid.

231. Ibid.

232. Ibid.

233. Ibid.

234. Associated Press, September 22, 1976.

235. United Press International, September 17, 1976.

236. Associated Press, September 29, 1976.

237. Ibid.

238. Ibid.

239. Facts on File: World News Digest, October 16, 1976.

240. United Press International, October 11, 1976.

241. Associated Press, October 10, 1976.

242. United Press International, October 11, 1976.

243. Associated Press, October 11, 1976.

244. Ibid.

245. Carter speech, University of Notre Dame, South Bend, Ind., May 22, 1977, Wheaton College Collection.

246. *Notre Dame* magazine, summer 2001.

247. Carter speech, May 22, 1977.

248. Ibid.

249. *Glasgow (Scotland) Herald*, May 23, 1977.

250. Carter remarks, Tehran, Iran, Dec. 31, 1977, Archival collection of Wheaton College of Illinois.

251. Carter speech, Indiana Convention Center, Indianapolis, Ind., June 2, 1979, ibid.

252. Ibid.

253. Ibid.

254. Ibid.

255. Ibid.

256. Ibid.

257. Associated Press, September 11, 1976.

258. Ibid.

259. Ibid.

260. Ibid., October 28, 1976.

261. Ibid.

262. Ibid.

263. *Toledo (OH) Blade*, October 28, 1976.

264. Ibid.

265. Ibid.

266. Associated Press, October 28, 1976..

Chapter 11

1. Associated Press, April 30, 1980.

2. Ibid.

3. United Press International, June 2, 1980.

4. *Washington Post*, June 2, 1980.

5. *The New Yorker*, February 24, 1997.

6. Associated Press, July 14, 1980.

7. Norwegian Nobel Committee, October 11, 2002.

8. Jimmy Carter speech, Conseco Fieldhouse, Indianapolis, Ind., September 15, 2001, Carter Center Archive, Atlanta, GA.

9. Ibid.

10. Ibid.

11. Ibid.

12. Ibid.

13. *Boston Globe*, November 8, 1979.

14. *Washington Post*, May 7, 1980.

15. ABC News archive.

16. United Press International, May 1, 1980.

17. Ibid.

18. Ibid.

19. Associated Press, May 1, 1980.

20. *Washington Post*, May 7, 1980.

21. Ibid.

22. Associated Press, April 22, 1980.

23. Ibid.

24. Ibid.

25. Ibid., April 16, 1980.

26. Ibid., April 22, 1980.

27. Ibid., September 9, 1980.

28. Ibid.

29. United Press International, September 8, 1980.

30. *Toledo (OH) Blade*, September 8, 1980.

31. *Kokomo Tribune*, September 9, 1980.

32. Ibid.

33. *New York Times*, May 20, 1981.

34. Ibid.

35. *Notre Dame* magazine, Summer 2001.

36. Ronald Reagan speech, Athletic & Convocation Center, University of Notre Dame, South Bend, Ind., May 17, 1981, Gehard Peters and John T. Woolley, The American Presidency Project, http://www.presidency.ucsb.edu/ (hereafter cited as American Presidency Project).

37. Ibid.

38. Ibid.

39. Ibid.

40. Ibid.

41. Ibid.

42. Reagan speech, Indiana State House, Indianapolis, Ind., February 9, 1982, American Presidency Project.

43. Ibid.

44. Ibid.

45. Ibid.

46. Ibid.

47. Ibid.

48. Ibid.

49. Ibid.

50. Ibid.

51. *Milwaukee (WI) Sentinel*, March 17, 1982.

52. Ibid.

53. Ibid.

54. Ibid.

55. Ibid.

56. Reagan speech, Indiana Convention Center, Indianapolis, Ind., December 8, 1983, American Presidency Project.

57. Ibid.

58. Ibid.

59. Ibid.

60. Ibid.

61. Ibid.

62. Ibid.

63. Ibid.

64. Ibid.

65. Reagan speech, Mac's Family Restaurant, Mooresville, Ind., June 19, 1985, American Presidency Project.

66. Ibid.

67. Ibid.

68. Ibid.

69. Ibid.

70. Ibid.

71. Reagan speech, Indiana Convention Center, Indianapolis, Ind., June 19, 1985, American Presidency Project.

72. Ibid.

73. Ibid.

74. Ibid.

75. Reagan speech, Roberts Memorial Stadium, Evansville, Ind., October 29, 1986, American Presidency Project.

76. Ibid.

77. Ibid.

78. Ibid.

79. Ibid.

80. Ibid.

81. Ibid.

82. Reagan remarks, Purdue University Airport, West Lafayette, Ind., April 9, 1987, American Presidency Project.

83. Reagan speech, Mackey Arena, Purdue University, West Lafayette, Ind., April 9, 1987, ibid.

84. Ibid.

85. Ibid.

86. Ibid.

87. Ibid.

88. Ibid.

89. Reagan speech, Hendricks County Courthouse, Danville, Ind., July 13, 1987, American Presidency Project.

90. Ibid.

91. Reagan speech, Indiana Convention Center, Indianapolis, Ind., July 13, 1987, American Presidency Project.

92. Ibid.

93. Reagan speech, Joyce Athletic & Convocation Center, University of Notre Dame, South Bend, Ind., March 9, 1988, American Presidency Project.

94. Ibid.

95. Ibid.

96. *New York Times*, November 6, 1994.

97. Associated Press, May 3, 1980.

98. *New York Times*, April 21, 1984.

99. Associated Press, April 25, 1984.

100. Jack Germond and Jules Witcover, "Politics Today," *Baltimore Sun*, May 5, 1984.

101. Associated Press, January 18, 1984.

102. United Press International, May 2, 1984.

103. *Washington Post*, May 7, 1984.

104. Ibid.

105. Ibid.

106. Associated Press, May 9, 1984.

107. Ibid.

108. Rev. Jesse Jackson speech, George Moscone Center, San Francisco, Calif., July 18, 1984, http://www .americanrhetoric.com/speeches/jessejackson1984dnc.htm.

109. *New York Times*, September 26, 1984.

110. United Press International, September 27, 1984.

111. *Anderson Herald-Bulletin*, September 27, 1984.

112. Ibid.

113. Associated Press, September 27, 1984.

114. *Anderson Herald-Bulletin*, September 27, 1984.

115. Associated Press, September 27, 1984.

116. Ibid., June 5, 1986.

117. Ibid.

118. Ibid.

119. Ibid., September 18, 1987.

120. Ibid., April 27, 1988.

121. United Press International, April 27, 1988.

122. Associated Press, April 29, 1988.

123. Ibid.

124. Ibid.

125. *New York Times*, May 1, 1988.

126. Associated Press, April 29, 1988.

127. Ibid., April 30, 1988.

128. Ibid.

129. Ibid., May 3, 1988.

130. Ibid.

131. Ibid.

132. Ibid.

133. Ibid.

134. Ibid.

135. James A. Baker III and Steve Fiffer, *Work Hard, Study—And Stay out of Politics! Adventures and Lessons from an Unexpected Public Life* (New York: G. P. Putnam's Sons, 2006), 245.

136. *Kokomo Tribune*, August 20, 1988.

137. Ibid.

138. George H. W. Bush speech, Alabama and Washington Streets, Indianapolis, Ind., April 3, 1990, American Presidency Project.

139. Ibid.

140. Ibid.

141. George H. W. Bush speech, Murat Shrine Auditorium, Indianapolis, Ind., April 3, 1990, American Presidency Project.

142. Ibid.

143. Ibid.

144. Associated Press, August 21, 1988

145. Ibid.

146. Ibid.

147. *Kokomo Tribune*, August 20, 1988.

148. Associated Press, October 15, 1988.

149. Ibid.

150. Ibid., October 12, 1988.

151. Ibid., November 9, 1989.

152. Dan Quayle speech, Indiana Convention Center, Indianapolis, Ind., August 29, 1990, Collection of the American Legion, "Proceedings of the 72nd National Convention of the American Legion, Indianapolis, Indiana, August 28–30, 1990."

153. Ibid.

154. Ibid.

155. Ibid.

156. *New York Times*, September 12, 1984.

157. Associated Press, September 11, 1984.

158. United Press International, September 11, 1984.

159. Associated Press, September 11, 1984.

160. United Press International, September 11, 1984.

161. *New York Times*, May 3, 1988.

162. Associated Press, May 1, 1988.

163. Ibid., May 2, 1984.

164. Ibid.

165. Ibid., May 5, 1984.

166. United Press International, May 8, 1984.

167. Ibid., May 26, 1984.

168. *New York Times*, July 9, 1972.

169. Ibid.

170. United Press International, April 20, 1984.

171. Associated Press, April 21, 1984.

172. United Press International, April 20, 1984.

173. Associated Press, April 21, 1984.

174. Ibid.

175. Lucious J. Barker and Ronald W. Walters, *Jesse Jackson's 1984 Presidential Campaign: Challenge and Change in American Politics* (Urbana: University of Illinois Press, 1989).

176. Associated Press, April 7, 1988.

177. *New York Times*, May 3, 1988.

178. Ibid., July 15, 1988.

179. Associated Press, July 15, 1988.

180. *New York Times*, July 15, 1988.

181. *Milwaukee (WI) Journal*, July 15, 1988.

182. *New York Times*, July 15, 1988.

183. Associated Press, April 9, 1990.

184. Rev. Jesse Jackson speech, DePauw University, Greencastle, Ind., December 3, 1992, http://www.depauw.edu/news/index.asp?id=13995.

185. Ibid.

186. Associated Press, September 30, 1980.

187. Ibid.

188. Ibid.

189. Ibid.

190. Gerald R. Ford speech, Emens Auditorium, Ball State University, Muncie, Ind., March 28, 1985, collection of Ball State University Historic Audio Recordings, Muncie, IN.

191. Ibid.

192. Ibid.

193. Ibid.

194. Ibid.

195. Ibid.

196. Associated Press, April 20, 1983.

197. Ibid.

198. Ibid.

199. Bill Clinton remarks, Richard Nixon Funeral, Yorba Linda, Calif., April 27, 1994, American Presidency Project.

Chapter 12

1. *New York Times*, February 5, 1992.

2. Ibid., May 18, 1992.

3. George H. W. Bush speech, University of Notre Dame, South Bend, Ind., May 17, 1992, Gerhard Peters and John T. Woolley, The American Presidency Project, http://www.presidency.ucsb.edu/ (hereafter cited a American Presidency Project).

4. Ibid.

5. Ibid.

6. Ibid.

7. Ibid.

8. George H. W. Bush speech, Indiana Convention Center, Indianapolis, Ind., August 17, 1992, American Presidency Project.

9. Ibid.

10. Ibid.

11. Ibid.

12. *San Francisco (CA) Chronicle*, May 20, 1992.

13. James A. Baker III and Steve Fifer, *Work Hard, Study—And Stay out of Politics! Adventures and Lessons from an Unexpected Public Life* (New York: G. P. Putnam's Sons, 2006), 217.

14. Associated Press, November 4, 1992.

15. Ibid., November 5, 1992.

16. *New York Times*, May 1, 1992.

17. Ibid.

18. Ibid., May 4, 1992.

19. Associated Press, April 29, 1992.

20. *Indianapolis Star*, July 21, 1992.

21. Ibid.

22. Associated Press, July 22, 1992.

23. *New York Times*, September 12, 1992.

24. Ibid.

25. Ibid.

26. Ibid.

27. Ibid.

28. Ibid.

29. Bill Clinton speech, Kennedy-King Park, Indianapolis, Ind., May 14, 1994, American Presidency Project.

30. Ibid.

31. Ibid.

32. Bill Clinton speech, Indiana Convention Center, Indianapolis, Ind., May 14, 1994, American Presidency Project.

33. Ibid.

34. Ibid.

35. Ibid.

36. Bill Clinton speech, Washington Park, Michigan City, Ind., August 28, 1996, American Presidency Project.

37. Ibid.

38. Ibid.

39. Ibid.

40. Ibid.

41. Ibid.

42. Ibid.

43. Bill Clinton remarks, Julia Carson for Congress Fundraiser, via telephone from the White House, October 7, 2000, American Presidency Project.

44. Bill Clinton speech, Indiana State Fairgrounds, Indianapolis, Ind., October 21, 2000, ibid.

45. Ibid.

46. Ibid.

47. *Indianapolis Star*, October 16, 1992.

48. Ibid.

49. *New York Times*, July 13, 1993.

50. Associated Press, July 13, 1993.

51. *Anderson Herald-Bulletin*, August 4, 1998.

52. Ibid.

53. *Washington Post*, August 17, 1998.

54. Associated Press, October 26, 1984 and January 8, 1986.

55. Robert Dole speech, Indiana Convention Center, Indianapolis, Ind., September 4, 1995, American Presidency Project.

56. Ibid.

57. Ibid.

58. Ibid.

59. Ibid.

60. Ibid.

61. *New York Times*, May 11, 1996.

62. Associated Press, November 3, 1996.

63. Dole speech, Indianapolis International Airport, Indianapolis, Ind., November 3, 1996, American Presidency Project.

64. Ibid.

65. Ibid.

66. *Indianapolis Star*, May 23, 1998.

67. Ibid.

68. Associated Press, May 22, 1998.

69. Ibid.

70. H. Ross Perot speech, DePauw University, Greencastle, Ind., April 29, 1996, http://www.depauw.edu/news/index.asp?id=13934

71. Ibid.

72. Ibid.

73. Ibid.

74. *New York Times*, July 23, 2000.

75. Ibid.

76. Ibid.

77. Ibid.

78. Ibid., September 7, 2000.

79. George W. Bush speech, University of Notre Dame, South Bend, Ind., May 20, 2001, American Presidency Project.

80. Ibid.

81. Ibid.

82. Ibid.

83. Ibid.

84. Ibid.

85. George W. Bush speech, Century Center, South Bend, Ind., September. 5, 2002, American Presidency Project.

86. Ibid.

87. Ibid.

88. George W. Bush speech, South Bend Regional Airport, South Bend, Ind., September 5, 2002, American Presidency Project.

89. Ibid.

90. Ibid.

91. George W. Bush speech, South Bend Regional Airport, South Bend, Ind., October 31, 2002, American Presidency Project.

92. Ibid.

93. George W. Bush speech, Indiana State Fairgrounds, Indianapolis, Ind., May 13, 2003, American Presidency Project

94. Ibid.

95. Ibid.

96. Ibid.

97. George W. Bush speech, Langham Company, Indianapolis, Ind., September 5, 2003,. American Presidency Project

98. Ibid.

99. George W. Bush speech, Murat Center, Indianapolis, Ind., September 5, 2003, American Presidency Project.

100. Ibid.

101. George W. Bush remarks, South Bend Regional Airport, South Bend, Ind., May 3, 2004, American Presidency Project.

102. George W. Bush remarks, University of Notre Dame, South Bend, Ind., March 4, 2005, ibid.

103. Ibid.

104. Ibid.

105. Ibid.

106. Ibid.

107. George W. Bush speech, RCA Dome, Indianapolis, Ind., July 14, 2005, American Presidency Project.

108. George W. Bush speech, Bethel College, Mishawaka, Ind., February 23, 2006, ibid.

109. Ibid.

110. Ibid.

111. George W. Bush speech, Murat Center, Indianapolis, Ind., March 24, 2006, American Presidency Project.

121. Ibid.

113. George W. Bush speech, Sellersburg, Ind., October 28, 2006, American Presidency Project.

114. Ibid.

115. George W. Bush speech, New Albany, Ind., March 2, 2007, American Presidency Project.

116. Ibid.

117. Ibid.

118. George W. Bush speech, New Albany, Ind., November 13, 2007, American Presidency Project.

119. Ibid.

120.. Ibid.

121. Ibid.

122. Associated Press, March 25, 2000.

123. Ibid., October 25, 2000.

124. Ibid.

125. Ibid.

126. Ibid.

127. Dick Cheney speech, Jeffersonville, Ind., March 26, 2004, American Presidency Project.

128. Ibid.

129. Ibid.

130. Ibid.

131. Cheney speech, Union Station Grand Hall, Indianapolis, Ind., April 23, 2004, http://georgewbush-whitehouse.archives.gov/news/releases/2004/04/text/20040426-1.html.

132. Ibid.

133. Cheney speech, Camp Atterbury, Edinburgh, Ind., October 20, 2006, http://georgewbush-whitehouse.archives.gov/news/releases/2006/10/text/20061020-3.html.

134. Ibid.

135. Ibid.

136. Ibid.

137. Ibid.

138. Cheney speech, Indiana War Memorial, Indianapolis, Ind., November 1, 2007, .https://georgewbush-whitehouse.archives.gov/news/releases/2007/11/20071101-2.html.

139. Ibid.

140. John Kerry speech, Indiana Convention Center, Indianapolis, Ind., July 6, 2004, American Presidency Project.

141. Ibid.

142. Ibid.

143. Ibid.

144. Ibid.

145. Ibid.

146. Associated Press, April 5, 2008.

147. *Indianapolis Star*, March 18, 2008.

148. Ibid.

149. Ibid.

150. Barak Obama speech, Roosevelt High School, Gary, Ind., April 10, 2008, American Presidency Project.

151. Ibid.

152. Ibid.

153. Reuters News Service, April 13, 2008.

154. Ibid.

155. Ibid.

156. Associated Press, April 12, 2008.

157. Ibid., April 27, 2008.

158. Obama remarks, Indianapolis, Ind., April 25, 2008, American Presidency Project.

159. Ibid.

160. Associated Press, April 27, 2008.

161. Ibid., April 23, 2008.

162. Ibid., April 27, 2008.

163. Ibid., May 3, 2008.

164. *Washington Post*, May 5, 2008.

165. *Indianapolis Star*, May 5, 2008.

166. Ibid.

167. *New York Times*, May 6, 2008.

168. Obama speech, American Legion Mall, Indianapolis, Ind., May 5, 2008, American Presidency Project.

169. Ibid.

170. *Washington Post*, May 5, 2008.

171. Associated Press, May 6, 2008.

172. Obama remarks, Purdue University, West Lafayette, Ind., July 16, 2008, American Presidency Project.

173. Ibid.

174. Obama speech, Concord High School, Elkhart, Ind., August 6, 2008, American Presidency Project.

175. Ibid.

176. Ibid.

177. Ibid.

178. Obama speech, Indiana State Fairgrounds, Indianapolis, Ind., October 8, 2008, American Presidency Project.

179. Ibid.

180. Ibid.

181. Ibid.

182. Obama speech, American Legion Mall, Indianapolis, Ind., October 23, 2008, American Presidency Project.

183. Ibid.

184. Ibid.

185. Associated Press, November 4, 2008.

186. *South Bend Tribune*, March 29, 2008.

187. Ibid.

188. Hillary Clinton speech, Allison Transmission plant, Indianapolis, Ind., April 12, 2008, American Presidency Project.

189. Ibid.

190. Ibid.

191. Associated Press, April 13, 2008.

192. *New York Times*, April 12, 2008.

193. Associated Press, April 27, 2008.

194. *New York Times*, May 5, 2008.

195. Ibid.

196. Ibid.

197. Associated Press, April 27, 2008.

198. *New York Times*, May 5, 2008.

199. *Washington Post*, May 5, 2008.

200. Ibid.

201. *Indianapolis Star*, May 5, 2008.

202. Ibid.

203. *Mount Carmel (IL) Republican Register*, April 30, 2008.

204. Hillary Clinton speech, Murat Centre, Indianapolis, Ind., May 6, 2008, American Presidency Project.

205. Ibid.

206. Ibid.

207. Ibid.

208. Hillary Clinton speech, Washington, D.C., June 7, 2008, American Presidency Project.

209. Ibid.

210. Ibid.

211. Ibid.

212. *Kokomo Tribune*, March 24, 2008.

213. Ibid.

214. Ibid.

215. Ibid.

216. Ibid.

217. Ibid.

218. Notre Dame *Scholastic*, April 3, 2008.

219. *Goshen News*, May 6, 2008.

220. Associated Press, March 26, 2008.

221. Ibid.

222. Ibid., February 22, 2008.

223. Ibid.

224. Ibid.

225. Ibid.

226. John McCain speech, Indiana Convention Center, Indianapolis, Ind., July 1, 2008, American Presidency Project.

227. Ibid.

228. Ibid.

229. Ibid.

230. Ibid.

231. Ibid.

232. Ibid.

233. Ibid.

234. Associated Press, July 2, 2008.

235. Ibid., November 3, 2008.

236. Ibid.

237. *Indiana Daily Student*, October 20, 2008; *Fort Wayne Journal-Gazette*, October 17, 2008.

238. *Indiana Daily Student*, October 20, 2008.

239. Ibid.

240. Ibid.

241. Ibid., October 26, 2008.

242. Ibid.

243. Sarah Palin speech, River Ridge Commerce Center, Jeffersonville, Ind., October 29, 2008, www.cpan.org/.

244. Ibid.

245. Ibid.

246. Ibid.

247. Ibid.

248. *Indiana University Southeast Horizon*, October 4, 2008.

249. Ibid.

250. *Indiana Daily Student*, November 25, 2008.

251. CNN, November 1, 2008.

252. Ibid.

253. Reuters News Service, November 1, 2008.

254. Associated Press, November 1, 2008.

255. CNN, November 1, 2008.

Index